India's Partition: Process, Strategy and Mobilization

OXFORD IN INDIA READINGS

Themes in Indian History

GENERAL EDITORS

- Basudev Chatterji
- Neeladri Bhattacharya
- C. A. Bayly
- Romila Thapar
- Muzaffar Alam

INDIA'S PARTITION
Process, Strategy and Mobilization

Edited by
MUSHIRUL HASAN

OXFORD
UNIVERSITY PRESS

OXFORD
UNIVERSITY PRESS

YMCA Library Building, Jai Singh Road, New Delhi 110 001

Oxford University Press is a department of the University of Oxford. It furthers the University's objective of excellence in research, scholarship, and education by publishing worldwide in

Oxford New York

Auckland Bangkok Buenos Aires Cape Town Chennai
Dar es Salaam Delhi Hong Kong Istanbul Karachi Kolkata
Kuala Lumpur Madrid Melbourne Mexico City Mumbai Nairobi
São Paulo Shanghai Singapore Taipei Tokyo Toronto

Published in India
By Oxford University Press, New Delhi

First published 1993
Oxford India Paperbacks 1994
Seventh impression 2002

ISBN 019 5635043

Printed in India at Rajkamal Electric Press, New Delhi 110033
Published by Manzar Khan, Oxford University Press
YMCA Library Building, Jai Singh Road, New Delhi 110 001

Contents

General Editors' Preface

This series focuses on important themes in Indian history, on those which have long been the subject of interest and debate, or which have acquired importance more recently.

Each volume in the series consists of, first, a detailed Introduction; second, a careful choice of the essays and book-extracts vital to a proper understanding of the theme; and, finally, an Annotated Bibliography.

Using this consistent format, each volume seeks as a whole to critically assess the state of the art on its theme, chart the historiographical shifts that have occurred since the theme emerged, rethink old problems, open up questions which were considered closed, locate the theme within wider historiographical debates, and pose new issues of inquiry by which further work may be made possible.

This volume seeks to understand the tragic story of the Partition of India. The history of Partition is often associated with a series of apparent paradoxes: the Muslim League, which had no social support till the early 1940s, spearheaded a movement which fractured India; Jinnah, known as a secular nationalist till the early 1930s, became the spokesman of the Pakistan demand; the Congress, which had fought for national unity for decades, accepted the Partition plan with unseemly ease. How and why did all this happen? The essays in this volume try to make sense of these paradoxes.

The two-nation theory saw Partition as the logical and inevitable outcome of the irreconcilable opposition between Hindus and Muslims. For the nationalists, the Partition had no natural basis, the two nations were politically separated through the manoeuvres of communal forces and imperial design. The nationalists identified the 1940 Lahore resolution of the League as the turning point: the idea of sovereign and independent Muslim states was, for the first time, proposed in this resolution, and from then on the League and Jinnah resolutely pressed for Partition.

In recent discussions, at one level, the focus has shifted from the national level to the provinces, a shift which also reflects an interest in new issues. There is a deeper concern with questions of identity formation and social mobilization, with the specific relationship between the developments of the 1940s and the long history of communal politics in different provinces. At another level, the high politics of Partition has also been reconsidered. The revisionist school focuses on the compulsions and contradictions of Muslim League and Congress politics, in order to understand the failure to work out a system of confederation of Indian States as implied by the Lahore resolution and the subsequent developments leading to the Partition of India.

In the introduction to the volume, Mushirul Hasan critically surveys the vast literature on Partition. He brings out the regional patterns of development, analyses the parallel histories of communal conflict and cross-cultural exchanges, and attempts to recover the experiences of those who lived through those times, their fears and sense of loss, their anguish and suffering.

Acknowledgements

We thank the following for permission to reproduce the material included in this volume:

The Publications Division, Navajivan Trust, Ahmedabad, for the extracts from *The Collected Works of Mahatma Gandhi*. The Signet Press, Calcutta, for the extracts from their edition of *The Discovery of India*, pp. 469–72. *Modern Asian Studies* for: Farzana Shaikh, 'Muslims and Political Representation in Colonial India', *MAS*, 20, 3 (1986), pp. 539–58; Asim Roy, 'The High Politics of India's Partition: The Revisionist Perspective', *MAS*, 24, 2 (1990), pp. 385–415; R.J. Moore, 'Jinnah and the Pakistan Demand', *MAS*, 17, 4 (1983), pp. 529–61; David Gilmartin, 'Religious Leadership and the Pakistan Movement in the Punjab', *MAS*, 13, 3 (1979), pp. 485–517; Lance Brennan, 'The Illusion of Security: The Background to Muslim Separatism in the United Provinces', *MAS*, 18, 2 (1984), pp. 237–72; Ian Copland, 'Communalism in Princely India: The Case of Hyderabad, 1930–40', *MAS*, 22, 4 (1988), pp. 783–814. *The Journal of Commonwealth and Comparative Politics* for: Partha Chatterjee, 'Bengal Politics and the Muslim Masses', *JCCP*, 13, 1 (March 1982); Ian A. Talbot, 'The Growth of the Muslim League in the Punjab, 1937–46', *JCCP*, 13, 1 (March 1982); Leonard A. Gordon, 'Divided Bengal: Problems of Nationalism and Identity in the 1947 Partition, *JCCP*, 16, 2 (July 1978). Verso Publishers for Saadat Hasan Manto's short story in *Kingdom's End and Other Short Stories* (1987). George Allen and Unwin Ltd., London, for: Mohammad Mujeeb, 'The Partition of India in Retrospect', in Philips and Wainwright (eds), *The Partition of India: Policies and Perspectives* (1970), pp. 406–14, and Raja of Mahmudabad, 'Some Memories', in the same volume.

Introduction*

India's independence in August 1947 was the culmination of a prolonged and sustained movement. The birth of neighbouring Pakistan, on the other hand, would seem to be an aberration, a historical accident caused by a configuration of forces at a particular historical juncture. Even at its most euphoric stage, the campaign for a 'Muslim' nation was hardly embedded in the 'historical logic' of the two-nation theory. In fact the theory on its own hardly reflected the consciousness of a community, for it was conceived by a small group, in a specific context, as an ideological counterweight to secular nationalism.[1]

Some of the themes relating to the genesis and growth of the Pakistan 'movement' were elaborated by contributors to a volume edited by C.H. Philips and M.D. Wainwright in 1970.[2] Today, 'specialists' and 'non-specialists' alike grapple with much the same issues that were once a historian's delight but are now a nightmare. A case in point was the lively debate sparked off by the release of Maulana Abul Kalam Azad's 'thirty pages' in 1989. Newspapers splashed stories on the inept handling of the 'communal' tangle by the country's premier organization, the Indian National Congress, on Jinnah's 'motives' and his use of 'Pakistan' as a bargaining counter to extract concessions from an obdurate Congress leadership. Cryptic

* I am most grateful to Aijaz Ahmad, Chris Bayly, David Taylor, Neeladri Bhattacharya, Robi Chatterji and Mukul Kesavan for their critical comments and invaluable suggestions.

1 The use of the expression secular nationalism in the context of India's nationalist struggle may be contested on the grounds that nationalism and its secular dimension was associated with an amalgam which ranged all the way from Gandhi to Savarkar. I have consciously used the expression because, in theory at least, the Congress and its allies in the left parties and groups subscribed to secular values and were committed to the building of a secular society—a legacy bequeathed to the makers of India's constitution. It is of course arguable that Jinnah tried to fashion a particular variant of secular nationalism for the Indian Muslims, in the perspective of 'modern' ideas of ethno-territorial nationhood and self-determination. I am inclined not to agree with this view for reasons made clear in this Introduction.

2 *The Partition of India: Policies and Perspectives, 1935–1937* (London, 1970).

comments were offered on the machinations of the colonial government, specially its last representative, Earl Mountbatten, who hastened India's partition into two sovereign nations. The baldly stated conclusions in much of the literature that has appeared since the publication of the 'Complete Version' of *India Wins Freedom* are that Partition could have been averted if the Gandhi–Nehru leadership in the Congress had been magnanimous towards the Muslim League demands, if Mountbatten's predecessors—Linlithgow and Wavell—had shown greater enterprise in devising political initiatives, and if Jinnah had been less intransigent during his dialogues with the representatives of the Crown and the Congress high command.

This debate, often conducted in a polemical and acrimonious spirit, goes on ceaselessly as more and more information comes to light and as individual and collective memories are revived time and time again through the medium of the vast Indian television network and its screening of popular 'serials' like *Buniyad* and *Tamas*. These are memories of broken homes and families, the wounds inflicted by Partition generally, the 'unequalled mistrust, acerbity and frenzied warfare',[3] and the 'general sense of gloom and despondency that pervaded the subcontinent'.[4]

It is tempting, even four decades after Independence and Partition, to reflect on the agony so many experienced, review part of the literature afresh, and explore themes for future research. The story told in the following pages is just a tentative reappraisal of an agonizing process. Many vital areas remain uncovered, not because their importance is not recognized, but because they are perceptively explored elsewhere. The colonial government's policies, so central to the evolution of 'separatist' politics, is more than adequately analysed and documented.[5] Similarly, a number of studies have dealt with

[3] G.D. Khosla, *Stern Reckoning: A survey of the events leading up to and following the partition of India* (Delhi, 1989), p. vii.

[4] K.A. Abbas, *I Am Not an Island: An Experiment in Autobiography* (Delhi, 1987); A.K. Gupta (ed.), *Myth and Reality: The Struggle for Freedom in India, 1945–7* (Delhi, 1987), especially the contributions of Alok Rai, Tapati Chakravarty and S.S. Hans.

[5] Francis Robinson, *Separatism Among Indian Muslims: The Politics of the United Provinces Muslims, 1880–1923* (Cambridge, 1974); Bipan Chandra, *Communalism in Modern India* (Delhi, 1984); Gyanendra Pandey, *The Construction of Communalism in Colonial North India* (Delhi, 1990); Sandria Freitag, *Collective Action and Community: Public Arenas and the Emergence of Communalism in North India* (California, 1989).

ideological and social forces which aided 'separatist' politics and reinforced communitarian identities around shared values and symbols.[6] These are discussed in section IV below, to illustrate the different frameworks for the general study of communalism.

This Introduction neither purports to detail the history of Hindu–Muslim strife,[7] though some aspects of inter-community relations are analysed,[8] nor the tortuous course of Congress–League–British negotiations leading to Independence and Partition. The Simla Conference, the Cripps Mission, the Cabinet Mission and the Mountbatten Plan do not figure in the discussion. The emphasis is on the years 1937–40, which are only partially explored in much of the secondary literature. These years are seen as crucial to the legitimization of the Muslim League as a powerful political force and as the spokesman of an aggrieved and beleaguered 'community' which gradually distanced itself from secular nationalism—the rallying cry of the Congress—to create a separate Muslim/Islamic nation-state. Fears and apprehensions generated during these critical years offered Jinnah and the League a constituency which they had not managed to secure for so long. In the months following the resignation of the Congress Ministries they were able to press home the political advantage thus secured.

I

The decade preceding Partition frequently escapes historical scrutiny. Part of the reason is that the genesis of Pakistan is traced, quite mistakenly, to the activities of Syed Ahmad Khan and his comrades at the M.A.O. College in Aligarh. They are identified as the only vocal group which raised the spectre of Hindu domination, the first to introduce the language and vocabulary of minorityism. They were

[6] Peter Hardy, *The Muslims of British India* (Cambridge, 1971); Robinson; Freitag; S. Gopal (ed.), *Anatomy of a Confrontation: The Babri Masjid-Ramjanambhumi Issue* (Delhi, 1991); K.N. Panikkar (ed.), *Communalism in India: History, Politics and Culture* (Delhi, 1991).

[7] For example, Suranjan Das, *Communal Riots in Bengal, 1905–1947* (Delhi, 1991), and Gyanendra Pandey, 'In Defence of the Fragment: Writing about Hindu–Muslim Riots in India Today', *Economic and Political Weekly*, annual Number, 1991.

[8] I have discussed this aspect in detail in 'Competing Symbols and Shared Codes: Inter-Community Relations in Modern India', in S. Gopal (ed.), *Anatomy of a Confrontation*.

backed by the Muslim 'elites' of Upper India who turned to 'separatist' politics to safeguard their 'interests', which were under threat from British educational policies, bureaucratic reforms and powerful Hindu revivalist campaigns. Muslim government servants and landowners, in particular, whose power was most obviously reduced by the pressure of change in the late nineteenth century, organized the Simla Deputation and founded the Muslim League.[9] Their insistence on separate electorates and reservations, coupled with the concern to defend deeply-cherished religio-cultural symbols, which were being gradually drawn into the public arena and contested by Arya Samajists and Hindu Mahasabhites, was designed to create the space for a distinct Muslim identity in politics. Colonial policies, which began to tilt in favour of the Muslims from the days of Mayo and Dufferin, legitimized such initiatives through an accommodation of sectional interests in the power structures created by legislative enactments in 1909 and thereafter.[10]

This is in some ways a familiar story told in several different ways—the story of the pressure placed on the 'Islamic gentry' by the rise of monied men and the resurgence of Hindu landholding communities;[11] the dreaded fear of elective, representative government and majority rule, vividly described by Syed Ahmad Khan in his 1883 speech of a local self-government bill for the Central provinces;[12] and the grave apprehensions caused by Hindu revivalism and its stridently anti-Muslim posture.[13] These factors, together with the theories and institutions for 'separatism' developed by the religious and political

[9] Robinson, *Separatism among Indian Muslims.*

[10] Mushirul Hasan, *Nationalism and Communal Politics in India, 1885–1930* (Delhi, 1991).

[11] C.A. Bayly, *Rulers, Townsmen and Bazaars: North Indian Society in the Age of British Expansion, 1770–1870* (Cambridge, 1983), pp. 456–7.

[12] For an extract of the speech, C.H. Philips (ed.), *The Evolution of India and Pakistan 1858–1947* (London, 1962), p. 185.

[13] A substantial monograph on Hindu revivalist movements is still awaited, though some of the aspects are adequately covered in: J.R. McLane, *Indian Nationalism and the Early Congress* (Princeton, 1987) (for an excellent account of the cow-protection movement); Kenneth W. Jones, *Arya Dharm: Hindu Consciousness in 19th-Century Punjab* (California, 1976) and J.T.F. Jordens, *Dayananda Sarasvati: His Life and Ideas* (Delhi, 1978), for the Arya Samaj movement; Robinson, pp. 66–82, for Hindu nationalism, in D.A. Low (ed.), *The Indian National Congress: Centenary Hindsights* (Delhi, 1985). And recently, Gyanendra Pandey, 'Hindus and Others: the Militant Hindu Construction', *Economic and Political Weekly*, 28 December 1991.

leadership in the last decade of the nineteenth century, point to the heightening of communitarian consciousness. But the process until the Muslim League burst on the political scene in the 1940s was a slow and tardy one. It was impeded by the differentiated structure of the 'community', its regional and local diversities, and by deep-rooted sectarian and doctrinal disputes. It was by no means easy to remove these constraints, without which there was no hope of even nursing the vision of a closely-knit and unified community of Islam. No amount of pious exhortation could bridge the wide gulf separating, say, a Muslim peasant in Mymensingh from a Muslim *taluqdar* in Awadh. Nor could religious leaders from Deoband or Nadwat al-ulama, who began to play an important role in public affairs from the early decade of the twentieth century, settle their theological differences with other 'schools'. The Barelwis and the Deobandis had little in common. The Ahmadiyas and the Ahl-i Hadith had a running battle over this or that doctrinal matter. And the Shias and the Sunnis were estranged, especially in Lucknow, with separate mosques, religious endowments and educational establishments.[14]

Inter-community relations too were not greatly strained until the post-Khilafat and Non-Cooperation days. If anything, the lines of cleavage in north India were more sharply drawn between the Sunnis and the Shias than between Hindus and Muslims.[15]

Thus the initiative towards the creation of a separate Muslim homeland, though spurred by political rumblings from the days of Syed Ahmad Khan, had its own contextual and ideological specificity. It was the outcome of a particular scenario on the eve of and during the Second World War which altered the tenor of political discourse in India and created, much to Jinnah's relief, the space for his manoeuvrings. A beleaguered war-time government, which had in the past refused to deal with Jinnah, now turned to him for political and moral support and, in the process, legitimized his critique of the Congress claim to represent all the communities of India. The inglorious breakdown of cross-community alliances and the accompanying, though expected, collapse of the coalition governments in Punjab and Bengal, which were the last bastions of resistance to the Muslim League,

[14] Mushirul Hasan, 'Sectarianism in Indian Islam: The Shia-Sunni Divide in the United Provinces', *The Indian Economic and Social History Review*, 27, 2, 1990.

[15] The argument is elaborated in my *Nationalism and Communal Politics*, ch. 2.

helped turn Jinnah's dream into a reality.[16] That this would happen on the midnight of 14 August 1947 was unthinkable a decade before that date.

There was, after all, no blueprint of a future Pakistan in the 1930s, no Islamic flag, no visible symbol, no common platform, no shared goals and objectives. Rehmat Ali's scheme, nurtured in Cambridge, was an illustration of obscurantist political eccentricity. It caused much political embarrassment back home and was dismissed as 'chimerical' and 'impracticable.'[17] Mohammad Iqbal's blueprint, outlined three years earlier, did not envisage a *separate* Muslim state. He merely made out a case for provincial autonomy in Punjab, the North-West Frontier Province, Sind and Baluchistan *within the body-politic of India* (emphasis added) for much the same reason that prompted the Motilal Nehru Committee of August 1928 to recommend the separation of Sind from the Bombay Presidency and to constitute the North-West Frontier Province into an 'independent' administrative unit.[18] In the same speech, Iqbal, whose vibrant patriotic poems continued to be sung in schools and colleges all over India, referred to autonomous states being formed, obviously not all-Muslim, based on the unity of

[16] It is a comment on fluctuating loyalties that Fazlul Haq, who was so virulent in denouncing the Congress ministries, had this to say after his fallout with Jinnah. He wrote that the Muslim League had roused Muslim passions against the Congress and the Hindus through ceaseless propaganda and 'clever distortion of facts'. Muslims were 'naturally drawn towards the Muslim League as the only organized political body among the Muslims and their only heaven (*sic*) of refuge against Hindu oppression'. British imperialist policy favoured such a development as it 'expected to be able to set off the Muslim League against the political ascendancy of the Congress'. The result 'is that the Muslim League has now got a foothold in the land which is not justified by the extent to which it can truly claim to be representative of Muslim interests'. A.K. Fazlul Haq, *Bengal Today* (Calcutta, Dec. 1944), p. 46.

It is equally significant that Fazlul Haq, the champion of 'Muslim interests', was quite prepared to forego this role and fill the vacancy in the Viceroy's Council created by the death of Sir Akbar Hydari. He wanted the Viceroy to give him a chance 'to serve my king and my country in a position of much greater responsibility than that I have yet occupied in my activities in the provincial sphere'. To Linlithgow, 12 January 1942, Linlithgow Papers (125/124), India Office Library and Records (IOLR), London.

[17] Aziz Ahmad, *Islamic Modernism in India and Pakistan, 1857–1964* (London, 1967), p. 169.

[18] *All Parties Conference, 1928: Report of the Committee Appointed by the Conference to Determine the Principles of the Constitution for India* (Allahabad, 1928).

languages, race, history, religion and identity of common interests. He did so in the context of '*India where we are destined to live*' (emphasis added).[19] This was surely not the swan-song of the Pakistan movement.

If Pakistan was still a pipe-dream, the Muslim League was little more than a paper organization.[20] Having been in the wilderness during the agitation over the Khilafat, its membership had plummeted to 1,330 in 1927. The branch in Bombay, the homeground of Jinnah, could only boast of 71 members.[21] The 1929 session was adjourned for lack of quorum. When Iqbal presented his address in Allahabad

[19] S. Pirzada, (ed.), *Foundations of Pakistan: All-India Muslim League Documents 1906–1947* (Karachi, 1970), vol. 2, p. 159.

[20] A comprehensive history of the Muslim League is yet to be written. For the early history of the organization, see the highly readable works of S.R. Wasti, *Lord Minto and the Indian Nationalist Movement 1905 to 1910* (Cambridge, 1964); Matiur Rahman, *From Consultation to Confrontation: A Study of the Muslim League in British Indian Politics 1906–1912* (London, 1970); and M. Yusuf Abbasi, *London Muslim League (1908–1928): An Historical Study* (Islamabad, 1988). The works of Mohammad Noman (1942) and Lal Bahadur (1954) were superficially written and are of no intrinsic value to a historian. The post-1937 phase of the Muslim League, following its political eclipse during the Khilafat movement, is covered in a lucid way by K.B. Sayeed, *Pakistan: The Formative Phase* (London, 2nd edn, 1948), and by Z.H. Zaidi, 'Aspects of the Development of Muslim League Policy 1937–47', in Philips and Wainwright (ed.), *The Partition of India,* pp. 245–75. Stanley Wolpert's *Jinnah of Pakistan* (New York, 1984) has a wealth of information on the League. So also Ayesha Jalal, *The Sole Spokesman: Jinnah, the Muslim League and the Demand for Pakistan* (Cambridge, 1985). The post-1937 history of the Muslim League in Punjab is explored by Ian Talbot in his monographs and numerous articles. See, *Provincial Politics and the Pakistan Movement: The Growth of the Muslim League in North-West and North-East India 1937–1947* (Delhi, 1988).

[21] The membership was 1093 in 1922, 1097 in 1923 and 1184 in 1924. *Annual Report of the All India Muslim League* (Lucknow, n.d.). Choudhry Khaliquzzaman recalled how the League merely lived on paper during the Khilafat days and how afterwards a 'new set of Nawabs' wrested control of the body. They merely attended the annual sessions and received praise from their equally honourable hosts for having undertaken the journey in a first-class compartment at great inconvenience to themselves, and their staying as guests in good, well-decorated buildings with the most delicious dishes to devour and plenty of pans (betels) and cigarettes to chew and smoke'. The proceedings, after the session, were duly sent to the Press, though long before the British officials received from their own inner sources news of every word spoken at the meeting. 'The end of the session was the end of the organization for the year and no one took notice of what had been said except in the critical record of the Government of India'. *Pathway to Partition* (Lahore, 1961), pp. 137–8.

in 1930, the meeting failed to muster the required quorum of 75 members.[22] It was a pathetic sight for an organization that made such tall claims on behalf of the Muslims. The organizers of the 1933 session in Delhi had a busy time filling up the hall with students of the Anglo-Arabic College. The League's income that year was Rs 1,318, with 92 out of the 300 Council members under notice to pay their arrears of membership.[23] A visiting Turkish author commented, in 1935, that no one talked of the League as an arbiter of Muslim destiny.[24]

The League leadership was fragmented, battered and bruised by frequent splits caused by factional feuds. Nawabzada Liaquat Ali Khan, credited with having persuaded Jinnah to return to India in 1934, set his eyes on securing the High Commissionership in London.[25] Khaliquzzaman was placed uneasily because of his loyalty to the Nehru household in Allahabad and his ambition to carve out his own sphere of influence in UP politics.[26] Nawab Mohammad Yusuf Khan solicited Malcolm Hailey's help in securing a knighthood or a place in the Viceroy's Executive Council. His credentials, in his own words, were: 'I have neither spared money nor energy in creating a mentality among the landholders, the Muslims and other stable elements that their only salvation did lay in throwing their lot with the Government.'[27] The Aga Khan, mellowed after his hectic lobbying at the Round Table Conferences in London, was busy promoting the idea of a Vatican city in the territory of a protected ruler either in India or in the Persian Gulf.[28] And Jinnah, crestfallen after the rebuff he received at the National Convention in December 1928, nursed his

[22] An eyewitness account of the session is cited in Mushirul Hasan, 'Congress Muslims and Indian Nationalism, Dilemma and Decline 1928–34', Jim Masselos (ed.), *Struggling and Empire: Indian National Congress 1885–1985* (Delhi, 1987), p. 117, f.n. 22.

[23] Sayeed, *Pakistan: The Formative Phase,* p. 176.

[24] Halide Edib, *Inside India* (London, 1937), p. 348.

[25] Liaquat Ali Khan to Willingdon, 14 September 1934, Samuel Hoare Papers (4), IOLR.

[26] Harry Haig took special note of the factional struggles in the UP Muslim League and keenly followed the moves of Khaliquzzaman, 'an extremely astute and ambitious man'. Haig to Linlithgow, 2 December 1936, Harry Haig Papers, microfilm, Nehru Memorial Museum & Library (NMML).

[27] Malcolm Hailey to Melville, 14 April 1934, Hailey Papers (E 220/27B), IOLR.

[28] Hoare to Willingdon, 8 March 1935, Samuel Hoare Papers (4).

political wounds at his Hampstead home.[29] In 1934, the year of his return to India, Hailey commented that Muslims had 'too many third-class leaders. There was no solidarity in the community, more so after the Communal Award which removed the sense of danger and prevents reunion under a strong leadership'.[30]

There were some signs of revival following Jinnah's return to Bombay, some endeavours to refurbish the League's image and rescue it from the political wilderness. Yet, there was no evidence to suggest that the League was beginning to emerge as a political adversary or a force counterpoised against the Congress. When the Raja of Mahmudabad, a close friend of Sarojini Naidu, Tej Bahadur Sapru and the Nehrus, joined the Muslim League in 1936, he believed that the Congress and the League 'were like two parts of the same army fighting a common enemy on two fronts'.[31]

The Raja's belief was grounded in hard facts. The Congress and the League had berated the Act of 1935. Both shared, despite the *perceived* clash of ideologies, a perspective on political and agrarian issues. The League manifesto, minus its rhetoric designed to create a Muslim constituency, reflected a fair measure of agreement with Congress policies: the manifesto showed as much awareness of the people's needs as that of the Congress. In UP the League and the Congress even came to an arrangement in the matter of putting up Muslim candidates for the elections. Jinnah hoped that the Congress and the League, together in partnership, could give new life and inspiration to their followers by demonstrating that even the most intractable problem could be solved through dialogue and understanding.[32] So, when the Congress accepted office in March, 1937, Jinnah talked of a 'united front'. 'There is no difference', he proclaimed on 18 September 1937, 'between the ideals of the Muslim League and of the Congress'.[33]

[29] Jinnah's stay in London from 1930 to 1934 is covered in Wolpert, *Jinnah of Pakistan*, pp. 119–33.

[30] To the Nawab of Chattari, 15 February 1934, Hailey Papers (27-A), and Haig to Linlithgow, 29 October and 2 December 1936, January 1937, Haig Papers.

[31] Raja of Mahmudabad, 'Some Memories', in Philips and Wainwright (ed.), *The Partition of India,* p. 387.

[32] For details, see Sharif al-Mujahid, 'Jinnah and the Congress Party', in Low (ed.), *The Indian National Congress: Centenary Hindsights.*

[33] Quoted in Mujahid, pp. 230–1 and Zaidi, 'Aspects of Muslim League Policy', pp. 290–1. Some writers do not, however, share such a view. Notice the observation that in 1936–7 a clash between Congress and the Muslim League, spear-

Jinnah's own political conduct was above reproach. He was liberal, eclectic and secular to the core in private and public life. As a legislator, a role suited to his style and temperament, he generally acted in unison with the Congress. As leader of the League, which was still gasping for breath, he initiated and backed proposals to break the communal impasse. 'If out of 80 million Muslims', he observed on 20 October 1936, 'I can produce a patriotic and liberal-minded nationalist block, who will be able to march hand in hand with the progressive elements in other communities, I will have rendered great service to my community'.[34] What India required, he stated a year later, was a united front. 'And then by whatever name you call your government is a matter of no consequence so long as it is a government of the people, by the people, for the people'.[35] This was not the language of a religious bigot but a reaffirmation of Congress' political creed. That should explain why the Viceroy thought of Jinnah as 'more Congress than the Congress' and why others regarded him as an 'arch enemy' of colonialism and a rallying symbol of secular forces.[36] Nobody expected him to create fissures in the liberation movement or foist the flag of Islam on an area supposedly defined by Iqbal and Rehmat Ali. India's unity was an ideal he still cherished.

In the face of such evidence, it is hard to make sense of Jinnah's subsequent crusade against the Congress and his repudiation of the principles he himself espoused with much eloquence and tenacity for nearly three decades. It is much less easy to explain why, in the mid-1930s, the League was seen in some quarters as a political adversary out on a mission to destroy India's liberation struggle. It was right to expose, as Nehru did, the League's predominantly feudal character, its links with government and with obscurantist and reactionary social classes. But it was equally important to marry this

---

headed by Nehru and Jinnah, lay in the logic of history'. Bimal Prasad, 'Congress versus the Muslim League 1935–1937', in Richard Sisson and Stanley Wolpert (eds.). *Congress and Indian Nationalism: The Pre-Independence Phase* (California, 1988), p. 309.

34 *Civil and Military Gazette, March 1936*, quoted in Zaidi, p. 230.

35 Pirzada (ed.), *Foundations of Pakistan,* vol. 2, p. 267.

36 See Raja of Mahmudabad, 'Some Memories' in Philips and Wainwright (ed.), *Partition of India,* p. 384, and the impressions of some prominent individuals associated with Jinnah. For example, M.R.A. Baig, *In Different Saddles* (Bombay, 1967) and M.C. Chagla, *Roses in December: An Autobiography* (Bombay, 1977); Kanji Dwarkadas, *India's Fight for Freedom, 1913–1937* (Bombay, 1966) and his *Ten Years to Freedom* (Bombay, 1968).

perspective with the fact that not everybody in the League was cast in the same mould. People like Liaquat Ali Khan, the Raja of Mahmudabad and Khaliquzzaman, for whom Nehru had a 'warm corner' in his heart,[37] were constantly 'torn between two loyalties'[38] but not necessarily imbued with an anti-Congress spirit or swayed by the League's communal claptrap.[39]

Was it not possible to draw such estranged comrades back into the Congress fold and assuage their feelings? Nehru would have said 'no' at the time. Rajendra Prasad, on the other hand, thought otherwise. Referring to the large number of 'Congress sympathizers' among the successful Muslim candidates in the 1937 elections who were willing to arrive at some settlement with Abul Kalam Azad, he argued that 'if the proposed agreement between the Independent Muslims and the Congress had materialized, the communal animosity which the Muslim League whipped up later might never have been brought about'.[40]

Rajendra Prasad was reflecting on such events a decade after Independence and Partition. Jinnah was not. He had pleaded with Nehru and with Rajendra Prasad, even at the risk of being rebuffed yet again, that there was no serious difference between the Congress and the League, except that the latter stood for the safeguard of 'Muslim rights'. Nehru concurred. He told Nawab Mohammad Ismail Khan of Meerut in November 1937: 'I do not quite know what our

[37] Nehru hoped that Khaliq would some day break from 'the reactionaries who surround him'. To Abdul Wali, 30 March 1837, All India Congress Committee (AICC) Papers (G-5, K.W. i, 1937), NMML.

[38] Khaliquzzaman to Nehru, 29 June 1937, AICC Papers (G-61, 1937).

[39] In 1936, Haig was of the view that the 'great majority of UP Muslims' had serious reservations about the Muslim League and were opposed to the policy of 'running a communal party'. That is why they were keen to wrest control of the provincial League, 'so as to render the All India Muslim League nugatory'. To Linlithgow, 21 May 1936, Linlithgow Papers (11/B). Three years later, Haig commented, despite the crucial changes in the political scenario during the intervening years, that, except for the Muslim landlords in UP, all others in the Muslim League were 'in general outlook much nearer the Congress'. 'For these reasons', he pointed out, 'if the right wing in the Congress found it necessary to strengthen themselves in this Province, they might do so by a coalition with the Muslim League rather than with landlords as such'. To Linlithgow, 10 June 1939, Haig Papers. Read in the proper sequence of events, these observations reflect on a powerful strand in UP 'Muslim politics'—a strand overlooked by other political commentators. It has also not figured in the recent historical discourse on partition and 'communalism'.

[40] Rajendra Prasad, *Autobiography* (Delhi, 1957), p. 446.

differences are in politics. I had imagined that they were not great'.[41] If this was so it was an error of judgement to treat the League as a counter-force and an adversary. Instead of making clear its own terms of secular and composite nationhood,[42] the Congress leaders, including the secular-minded amongst them, settled for a soft option—one that Jinnah was implicitly hinting at in his March 1940 speech at Lahore.

The Congress truculence over a coalition ministry with the League was, in its historical sequence, a political miscalculation. This is an oft-repeated argument, perhaps a bit worn out. Yet, its validity is yet to be questioned with any degree of conviction. Hence its mention is not out of place in tracing the broad sequence of events.

To carry the story forward, it needs to be stressed that as champion of national unity and as a mediator between rival groups and warring factions, a role performed by the Congress with such adroitness since its inception in 1885, its leaders had two clear-cut options. These were to reach out to the Muslim masses who, in Nehru's reckoning, had rallied round the Congress flag in large numbers, and weaning away that section of the League which was both desperate and dispirited after the party's poor showing in the elections. But nothing of this kind happened. The Muslim Mass Contact Campaign, launched amid much fanfare, petered out thanks to the opposition of the Congress right-wing, which feared an influx of Muslim activists and their critical and unacceptable influence on party policy.[43] The prospect of a Congress–League coalition was, on the other hand, dimmed for reasons which had very little to do with principles, more so because the Congress had not just concluded pacts and agreements with the Muslim League, as in December 1916, but also with other sectional groups such as the Akalis in Punjab.

Both Jawaharlal Nehru and Rajendra Prasad explained the 'breach

[41] Cited in Zaidi, 'Aspects of Muslim League Policy', p. 256.

[42] The 'terms' were, of course, never made explicitly clear, for they ranged from Gandhi's 'Ram–Rahim' approach to the Malaviya-Lajpat Rai vision of 'Hindu India'. 'Indian' nationalism was so often seen as a manifestation of a more 'genuine' expression—'Hindu' nationalism'. In 1939, K.M. Ashraf, who headed the Muslim Mass Contact Campaign, lamented that 'the Congress position regarding communal organisations and the communal activities of the Congress members has been dangerously vague until now'. To Mohanlal Saxena, 5 September 1939, AICC Papers (Miscellaneous: 30, 1937).

[43] See Mushirul Hasan, 'The Muslim Mass Contacts Campaign: Analysis of a Strategy of Political Mobilization', in Sisson and Wolpert (eds), *Congress and Indian Nationalism*.

of faith' in terms of the unexpectedly large Congress majority secured in the elections, which made all talk of a coalition indefensible. In addition, Nehru referred to the feeling in Congress circles that without the League they would be freer to quarrel with Harry Haig, UP's governor, and break with him on their own terms.[44]

Nehru should have added that the Congress strategy was moulded by two conflicting forces, though each aimed to achieve a common goal—jettisoning all hopes of a Congress-League entente. There was, first of all, the stranglehold of the Hindu Mahasabha and other Hindu militant bodies who were consistent, from the days of the Lucknow Pact, in opposing a Congress–League rapprochement. They acted purposefully and effectively. Still, their effectiveness was, in large measure, due to their Congress patrons who were themselves firmly anchored in the Hindu revivalist traditions and were deeply suspicious of the coming together of the Congress and the League. According to B.S. Moonje, the architect of the Hindu Mahasabha, Vallabhbhai Patel and other right-wing Congressmen constantly urged him to 'stand firm on a variety of points in the interest of Hinduism'.[45] The message, given out in specific context, was loud and clear.

The Congress strategy was guided by the perceptions of Congress Muslims as well. Wary of losing their secure and privileged position in the Congress hierarchy, they opposed, despite Azad's assertion to the contrary,[46] the idea of a coalition government in UP. Their instinct of political survival may have prompted them to do so. K.M. Ashraf, a relatively new arrival on the political stage, disapproved of 'the old methods of coalition, of pacts with Jinnah and others'.[47] The more experienced politician-journalist, Syed Abdullah Brelvi, felt Congressmen should 'wash our hands' of pacts, alliances and negotiations.[48] Noble thought, yes, but quite out of tune with the realities of power politics. More importantly, not quite consistent with Congress' own track record. While it was fair to berate elite forms of com-

44 Linlithgow to Zetland, 29 March 1940, L/PJ/8/50-B, IOLR; Rajendra Prasad put forth the same reasons in his *Autobiography*, pp. 446–7.

45 B.S. Moonje, quoted in Linlithgow to Zetland, 17 Sept. 1940, L/PJ/8/507.

46 A.K. Azad, *India Wins Freedom: The Complete Version* (Delhi, 1988), p. 170. For a different version, S. Gopal, *Jawaharlal Nehru: A Biography, Volume One*: *1889–1947* (Delhi, 1975), p. 222.

47 To Syed Abdullah Brelvi, 5 May 1937, AICC Papers (G-67/1937).

48 To K.M. Ashraf, 5 May 1937, ibid. Also, Abdul Wali (of Barabanki in UP) to Nehru, 28 March 1937, AICC Papers (G-5, K.W. i, 1937).

promise-hatching, it was hard to justify Nehru's unwarranted rhetoric against the League which overwhelmed people like Ashraf. Besides, how could Congress Muslims advocate a 'principled' posture only in relation to the League when so many of their party stalwarts were unabashedly loyal to the Mahasabha and the RSS creed? This thought weighed heavily on their secular-nationalist conscience. Yet they were unable to articulate it in the way M.A. Ansari had done in his indignant note of protest against Gandhi's decision to launch civil disobedience in 1930.[49] Without bothering to make their own independent assessment, they accepted Nehru's verdict on the Muslim League. They offered no sober judgement, no balanced appraisal.

The ill-advised Congress decision in the summer of 1937 created the space for the revival of the Muslim League and offered Jinnah the chance to establish his hold in UP, a province where his initial overtures were repeatedly spurned. With Khaliquzzaman and Nawab Ismail Khan losing face and the National Agriculturist Party in a state of disarray, Jinnah had his first taste of victory in Lucknow. It was his finest hour. Appearing belligerent and impatient with his numerous detractors in the North-West Frontier Province, Punjab, Sind and Bengal, he lost no time in imposing his terms on the recalcitrant elements. A mass contact campaign, launched under the aegis of the League, was his antidote to the Congress-sponsored programme. The person who consistently opposed the mixing of religion with politics and, for that reason, remained on the fringes of Indian politics during the massive pan-Islamic upsurge in the early 1920s, was now prepared to press the *ulama* into service, cultivate two of Deoband's renowned theologians—Shabbir Ahmad Usmani and Ashraf Ali Thanwi—and create fissures in the ranks of the *ulama*. His prized trophy was no doubt the university at Aligarh. What was once a politically benign campus turned into the 'arsenal of Muslim India'. An atmosphere of 'mystic frenzy' prevailed as students and teachers[50] 'poured their idealistic zeal into the emotionalism of Pakistan'. An American student at the university recalled how his fellow students in 1939–40 perceived Pakistan 'as a bright dream, a passionate goal, the vision of

[49] See Mushirul Hasan, *A Nationalist Conscience: M.A. Ansari, the Congress and the Raj* (Delhi, 1989).,

[50] Mushirul Hasan, 'Nationalist and Separatist Trends in Aligarh, 1915–1947', in A.K. Gupta (ed.), *Myth and Reality,* pp. 123–6; W.C. Smith, *Modern Islam in India* (Lahore, 1943), pp. 181–2.

a Muslim paradise on earth'. A great many—though not all—shared their fancy.[51]

Unwittingly, the Congress bolstered Jinnah's claim to be Muslim India's sole spokesman and improved the League's image as a beleaguered organization, a victim of Congress machinations. Rajendra Prasad's view has been referred to earlier. Equally revealing is the observation of UP's governor. Writing to the viceroy on 3 June 1939, he commented that 'Muslim solidarity would soon have been undermined' had the Congress agreed to a coalition with the League. He added:

> There are bound to be differences between Muslims on the main agrarian and economic issues. The Muslims in office would have to make themselves responsible for definite policies in regard to these matters; they would have received the support of some Muslims and aroused the opposition of others. Nothing seems to be so effective in disintegrating a party as the taking of office.[52]

Harry Haig was implicitly stating an old axiom of British policy in India, which lay at the heart of the principle of dyarchy detailed in the Montagu-Chelmsford Reforms of 1919. The reckless course adopted by the Congress would have been averted had the party learnt from its own experiences with dyarchy. Bringing the League into government may well have given rise to inter-party feuds. At the same time, rejecting its representatives had the effect of creating a far broader unity among the League factions and greatly hardening their stance thereafter.

II

The coalition issue cast an ugly shadow over the Congress ministry in UP and elsewhere. There was talk of overt manifestations of aggressive Hindu nationalism, of the tyranny of a Hindu brute 'majority' over the Muslim 'minority' and a reiteration of the fear—expressed

51 Phillips Talbot, 'I am a Pakistani', 28 November 1956, Ian Stephens Papers, Centre for South Asian Studies, Cambridge. Talbot went to India in 1939 and studied at the Aligarh Muslim University before joining the US Naval Liaison Office at Bombay in 1941. He joined the American Universities Field Staff in 1951.

52 Draft letter in enclosure: Haig to Linlithgow, 3 June 1939, Haig Papers.

by Syed Ahmad Khan in the 1880s, by the Simla Deputationists of 1906 and by Mohamed Ali at the Round Table Conference in 1930—that a non-Muslim majority would use its powers under democratic institutions to undermine 'Muslim interests' and offend cultural sensitivities and religious susceptibilities.

Complaints ranged from the general to the specific. There were pointed references to Hindu Mahasabhites 'in the garb of Congressites' and to 'Hindu Congress Cabinets' which paid only lip service to nationalism and religious impartiality: 'The elephant tusks are only for display but it uses its real teeth for chewing its food'.[53] Reports from certain districts spoke of the 'arrogance and oppression of Hindu officials' and the coming of 'Hindu raj'.[54] In UP Haig noticed an unduly large number of cases against Muslim police officers being sent to the Anti-Corruption department. He intervened to 'protect Muslim officials from unjust treatment'.[55] In Bombay Roger Lumley was impatient with the arrogance of the Congress leadership in general and with the rank and file in the districts. What, in his view, angered the Muslim leadership were the tales of woe that came up to them from Muslims in villages and towns 'where the local Congress boss has made it apparent that in his eyes Congress Rule meant that he now wielded local power and that he had every intention of making things uncomfortable for the Muslim minority'.[56] Finally, the scale of Hindu–Muslim rioting led Muslim publicists to conclude: 'Never before in India's history did riots take a heavier toll of life and property within such a short space of time than during the two and a half years of Congress administration in some of the Provinces of India'.[57]

[53] *Haqiqat* (Lucknow), *Hamdam* (Lucknow), United Provinces Native Newspaper Reports (UPNNR), week ending 4 September 1939.

[54] *Hamdam,* UPNNR, week ending 18 December 1937.

[55] Haig to Linlithgow, 6 December 1939, L/PJ/8/645.

[56] F.V. Wylie to Linlithgow, 14 December 1939, L/PJ/8/645.

[57] There was a marked deterioration in communal relations, affecting large parts of the north and centre of India. There was rioting in CP on the occasion of Dussehra (October 1937) and at Jabalpur on Holi (March 1938). This was followed by a whole series of riots spreading from the south-west corner of Berar, right across the Jabalpur district in the extreme north-east of CP. In UP there were riots at the Dadri fair in Ballia (20 November 1937), Banaras (15 March 1938), Tanda (25 August 1939), Allahabad (17 March 1938) and at Kanpur (7–15 February 1939). The casualties in the Banaras and Kanpur riots were high. See *It Shall Never Happen Again* (Department of Publicity & Information, All-India Muslim League, Delhi, 1946). This is a collection of articles published in *Dawn,*

There were added grievances, most of which were either localized or specific to a region—for example, the anti-Muslim bias of a welfare officer in the Delhi Cloth Mills or the declining strength of Muslim wholesale foodgrain dealers in Delhi.[58] On the other hand, contentious issues of a general nature, such as the form of electorates, representation in services and professions, and the future of Urdu, did not bother Muslims everywhere. What irked them in Meerut was the ill-advised policy of the Food Control authorities which caused hardship to Muslim traders in rice,[59] the punitive police tax in Budaun,[60] and the Congress alliance with textile-owners and the Mazdoor Sabha in Kanpur, an alliance forged to weaken the large Muslim working force.[61] Again, in Kanpur, their prime concern was with the working of the municipal board which fanned the fires of Hindu–Muslim violence and, to add insult to injury, doled out services, contracts and scholarships to its Hindu benefactors.[62] Here and elsewhere Muslims were clearly aggrieved at being left out of the patronage network. Finally, ill-will was sometimes engendered by happenings which could have taken place anywhere and in any other period of history—from offering prayers within the school compound, or Muslim boarders at the Etah Government High School being prevented from cooking beef and being told to participate in games during the holy month of fasting and prayer.[63]

In Bihar and the Central Provinces, the Wardha and Vidya Mandir schemes of education, the singing of the Bande Mataram song and the hoisting of the Congress flag were serious issues of communal

---

with a foreword by Qazi Mohammad Isa, President of the Baluchistan Muslim League. Riots in UP and Bihar are described in Ashiq Husain Butalwi, *Hamari Qaumi Jaddo-Jahed (Our National Struggle): January 1939 se December 1939 Tak* (Lahore, 1968); Maulana Basituqqal Ghori, *Meri Sarguzasht ya Congress ka Raaz* (Unnao, 1938). Publications like *Uriyaan-e Muraqqa* (Budaun, 1939) described the riots in Bareilly and Budaun districts.

58 All-India Muslim League Papers (hereafter AIML Papers) (12), History of the Freedom Movement Archives, University of Karachi.

59 The lead in the matter was taken by the district Muslim League in Saharanpur, one of the largest centres of rice industry in UP. Ibid.

60 L/P&J/8/86.

61 *Al-Bashir* (Etawah), UPNNR, week ending 4 December 1939.

62 *Hamari Awaaz,* UPNNR, week ending 20 November 1937; *Sarguzasht* and *Asia,* UPNNR, week ending 4 December 1937; *Haq,* UPNNR, week ending 11 December 1937.

63 *Hamdam,* UPNNR, week ending 18 December 1939.

mobilization. Added to these were local grievances: inadequate Muslim representation in certain branches of administration,[64] dissatisfaction with the housing schemes of the Improvement Trust,[65] discrimination in disbursing loans and educational grants, and minor but incredibly trivial issues such as withdrawal of the Jabalpur riot cases of 1938, the arrest of 15 Muslims in the Chandur–Biswa murder case, and the release of a convicted Hindu in the Hoshangabad *paan* (betel) poisoning case.[66] Such incidents, even when unrelated to the policies or actions of the Congress governments, were cited to highlight their 'tyranny'.

The Bombay ministry was held responsible for the discharge of Muslim employees in some Ahmedabad mills. But the fact of the case was that the millowners, some of whom were decidedly not free of communal prejudices and hostility towards the Muslim working force, dismissed 7,000 to 10,000 Muslim workers so as to avoid the risk of having communal trouble inside the mills.[67] They did so despite loud protests from the ministry. Likewise, the UP administration was placed in the dock for fomenting Hindu–Muslim riots in, say, Kanpur or Marehra, a small town in Etah district. As for Kanpur, aggressive action by a rowdy Muslim crowd started the chain of events leading to a bloody feud. In Marehra, as listed in Dr Ziauddin's memorandum against the Congress administration, ill-feeling was caused through a Congress flagpole having been bent by a *tazia* procession, perhaps accidentally. This led to brick throwing on the *tazia* procession. And then all hell broke loose. An enraged mob went on the rampage. Several Hindus were killed, their shops looted, and a temple desecrated. Whatever the provocation, the Muslims were undoubtedly the aggressors.[68]

This is not all. So many of the grievances catalogued in the Pirpur and Shareef Reports and in Ziauddin's tale of woes were of a longstanding nature and were by no means specific to the years of Congress rule. For example, riots occurred from 1893 onwards, though their frequency and intensity increased only in the aftermath of the Khilafat movement. Nor was there any novelty in issues connected with the

[64] F.V. Wylie to Linlithgow, 24 December 1939, L/P&J/8/645; Syed Iftikhar Ali, *Working of the C.P. Congress Ministry* (Nagpur, n.d).

[65] Hallet to Brabourne, 6 September 1938, Linlithgow Papers (126/1010).

[66] Wylie to Linlithgow, 2 December 1939, L/P&J/8/645.

[67] Roger Lumley to Linlithgow, 23 Jan. 1940, L/P&J/8/686.

[68] Haig to Linlithgow, 10 May 1939, Haig Papers.

representation and form of electorates. These were advanced time and time again in Punjab, UP and Bengal, and were contested with equal vehemence. Notice the hue and cry following the Lucknow Pact, or the indictment of the Swarajist party in Bengal, the relentless crusade against Fazl-i Husain's ministry in Punjab, and the denunciation of the Nehru Committee Report by the Ali Brothers and their newly-found allies in the so-called 'All-India' Muslim Conference.[69]

In the mid-1930s, however, many of the old fears gained an altogether new kind of intensity because of a significant, though less visible, shift in the structural situation. What lent a sharp edge to the debate then was how power and authority, which flowed directly out of the Act of 1935, was going to heighten competition and enlarge arenas of conflict, and how social classes and communities, whose interests were delicately safeguarded by the colonial authority in the constitutional arrangement embodied in the Act of 1935, were pitted against each other in an uneasy and sometimes antagonistic relationship. Increasingly, local bodies were embroiled in this unlovely struggle. In areas like UP, where the number of municipalities had increased steadily along with the representation of non-official Indians, there were unmistakable signs of a bitter contest to command resources in order to reinforce patronage networks. Thus a report on municipal administration for the year 1937–8 noted:

> The year's working was disfigured by the same unhealthy party action and intrigue, the same interminable wrangles about motions of no confidence, the same jobbery and injustice in connexion with appointments, the same reckless irresponsibility in the financial sphere.[70]

The same report pointed to how 'communal dissensions in many places exerted a sinister influence on account of appointments, transfers and postings'. A year later the administration of over 30 municipalities was tarnished by communal dissensions, party strife, and intrigue. Boards of Farrukhabad, Fatehpur, Soron, Mainpuri, Mussoorie, Barant, Chandausi and Moradabad were the worst offenders.[71]

At the same time, such dissensions were not always between Hindus and Muslims *per se.* Haig commented on how the 'general political criticisms are the stock in trade of opposition, voiced by

[69] See Hasan, *Nationalism and Communal Politics,* ch. 5.

[70] *Report on the Municipal Administration and Finances in the UP of the Year 1937–38* (Allahabad, 1940), p. 9.

[71] Ibid., 1938–9, p. 9.

non-Congress Hindus just as much as by Muslims'. Thus vocal Muslim groups of his province indicted the G.B. Pant cabinet only for the reason that they did not have the same degree of pull and influence enjoyed by the supporters of the ministry. In essence, therefore, their grievance was not a religious one, though it assumed an intensely communal form.[72]

The conduct of some Muslim zamindars illustrates how class issues could so easily degenerate into religious squabbles, how particularistic concerns were so conveniently drawn into the public arena and identified with the fortunes of an entire 'community'. Both the taluqdars of Awadh and the zamindars of eastern and western UP raised the bogey of Islam to denounce the Congress agrarian programme, including the UP Tenancy Bill, even though they knew full well that the party in power was committed to land reforms well before the ministry was formed, and that the Bill, piloted by Rafi Ahmad Kidwai, was directed against an exploiting class and not specially against the Muslim zamindars. Muslim landlords were a target of attack not *qua* Muslims but *qua* opponents of the Congress and its land reforms.[73]

Similarly, when the Bombay ministry levied property tax to pay for prohibition on *all* urban property owners in the city, it was held by Muslims to be designed as an anti-Islamic measure on the grounds that they invested savings in property rather than in stocks and shares and that they possessed a large number of religious endowments. In reality, however, the main grouse was against Brabourne, Governor of Bombay, who had not insisted on a Muslim League minister being included in the cabinet. From that moment, the League publicists put the worst possible construction on everything the ministry did.[74]

What about the perception of those Muslims who regarded the ministry, say in UP, as a 'Hindu' administration, the ministers as 'renegades' and the Congress as a 'Hindu' party? It is true that the Congress record was not without blemish. The Wardha and Vidya Mandir schemes of education were ill-conceived.[75] The neglect of Urdu in UP and Bihar, notwithstanding the pro-Urdu sentiments of

72 To Linlithgow, 10 May 1939, Haig Papers.

73 Ibid.

74 Lumley to Linlithgow, 14 December 1939, Linlithgow Papers (107).

75 Ashraf to Syed Mahmud, 14 June 1938 and Ashraf to Abul Kalam Azad, 3 September 1938, AICC Papers (Misc: 30/1937).

Gandhi and Nehru, was deliberate.[76] So was the systematic exclusion of Muslims from district and provincial Congress committees. The presence of Hindu militants in the ranks of the Congress was not unusual, but their overbearing attitude was a major irritant, a source of considerable discord. Ramgopal Gupta, secretary of the district Congress committee in Mahoba, Hamipur, reported:

The other day the Education Committee of the District Board elected a Hindu Chairman as a result of coalition among the Hindu members on the cry of danger to Hinduism. The defeat of the Muslim candidate through Hindu communalism has angered the Muslim public who cannot distinguish between a Mahasabhite Hindu and a Congressite Hindu.[77]

There were other irritants as well. Ashraf highlighted some of them in his correspondence with Congress office-bearers. In July 1938 he pointed out how the Congress had ignored 'the Muslim sentiment in matters of detail and permitted a number of things to happen which gave the [Congress] annual session a distinctly Hindu appearance'. The Muslim League papers emphasized that there were no Urdu posters or Urdu signposts to guide the delegates, no gates and arches named after Muslim leaders, and finally, that propaganda for cow-protection and Hindi was carried on in the Congress Nagar. Ashraf

[76] Aftab Ahmad (from Calcutta) to Abul Kalam Azad, n.d, ibid.

[77] Ramgopal Gupta to Ashraf, 3 July 1937, AICC Papers (38/1938). Such unholy alliances were quite common. This meant that it was becoming increasingly difficult for Muslim Congressmen to secure a position in the Congress hierarchy at the provincial and district levels. Cases from Nagpur, the stronghold of the RSS and the Hindu Mahasabha, were reported by Manzar Rizvi to the Secretary, Nagpur PCC, 24 June 1938, ibid. K.M. Ashraf was greatly upset with the outcome of a by-election in a Muslim constituency in Amritsar. The Congress candidate was defeated owing to an alliance between the party bosses and the Hindu Mahasabha. 'I could go on multiplying instances', wrote Ashraf, 'to prove that the Congress machinery is fast disintegrating and our provincial and district Congress committees are more or less confident that no direction will come from the Centre and in any case they will be left free to do what they please in a given situation'. To Narsinh, 4 June 1938, ibid. Fida Husain Sherwani, cousin of the Congress stalwart, T.A.K. Sherwani, commenting on the lack of preparedness on the eve of the election, shared his anguish with Nehru: 'I have all the time been feeling that my enthusiasm for the Congress is second to none including yourself and Mahatma Gandhi but this heartless neglect of us by the so-called socialist party in power has made me believe for the last three days that a Mussalman has no place in the Congress and that a good and true Mussalman like myself has no alternative but to commit suicide'. To Nehru, 30 June 1937, AICC Papers (G-61/1937).

regarded these as 'trifles' but grudgingly conceded the need to allay such apprehensions and to make the right gestures. 'Considering its psychological effect on the Muslim visitors', he observed, 'and particularly in view of the fact that a number of Muslim papers have made it a point to exaggerate to a willing audience, we must take every precaution that the Congress session in Mahakoshal meets all possible susceptibilities.'[78]

In the light of the League's charges, it is an awesome task to prepare a balance sheet of the ministries' performance. Yet it is worth the effort so as to place the League's Congress-baiting in perspective and uncover the motives behind such a well-orchestrated campaign.

It is an undeniable fact, often ignored in secondary literature, that the Congress and its allied partners embarked upon an ambitious programme of legislation especially to protect the interests of the cultivating class.[79] In the North-West Frontier Province, *naubat chaukidari* was done away with. The Agricultural Debtors' Relief Act limited the rate of interest realized by moneylenders and cancelled interest due to creditors on 1 October 1937.[80] In UP, the Tenancy Bill was a significant piece of legislation and a forerunner of the abolition of zamindari in 1952. In CP and Berar, the Relief of Indebtedness Act, the CP Revision of Land Revenue of Estates Act, and the CP Tenancy (Amendment) Act were examples of radical legislation. The governor of the Province admitted that 'there was much of value in

[78] Ashraf to the Secretary, Reception Committee, Mahakoshal session, Jabalpur, 25 July 1938, AICC Papers (Misc: 30/1937).

[79] This is not to deny the inadequacy of some legislative enactments or implementation. Many of the Congress supporters were, in general, quite dissatisfied with the performance of the ministries in certain spheres and there was widespread criticism from public platforms and in newspaper articles. There are many reasons why this was so. But at least in the case of one UP minister, Sampurnanand, the predicament was succinctly expressed. 'We have to work', he wrote in *Congress Socialist*, 'within the four walls of the Government of India Act, against which we revolt with every fibre of our being. It is not easy. We feel like kicking over the traces. Believe me, not one of the ministers I know does not, immersed in his files, pine for the old days. We live in an atmosphere of unreality. There are many of us who would like to get out of it. But there we are. To my knowledge, there is no historical parallel to the circumstances in which we accepted office. A people struggling for national Independence, meaning to continue to fight for it, stop half-way to accept administrative responsibility! This is a contradiction in our position which creates difficulties'. Quoted in J.C. Donaldson to Puckle, 16 September 1938, Linlithgow Papers (101).

[80] George Cunningham to Linlithgow, 19 November 1941, ibid. (109).

the Congress programme and undoubtedly the Congress as a body was striving towards the objective of a better India'.[81] In Orissa serious efforts were made to place the tenant in a position of independence, free him from his contract with the landlord, and provide credit and relief from debt.[82] And finally, in Bombay the governor recognized the importance of the Agricultural Debtor's Relief Act—the 'most important legacy left by the legislatures'. His general impression was that the ministry was 'inspired by a real ideal of service to the public' and that its performance 'was certainly not bad. And when one takes into account the strange circumstance of . . . the fact that the Ministers, and most legislators, had practically no previous experience of their tasks . . . it was remarkably good and held out promise for the future'.[83]

UP's governor believed—and there is little reason to doubt his opinion—that the provincial ministry had performed admirably in communal matters and that some of its policies, such as the Rural Development Scheme, benefited the Muslims.[84] They fared well in public services, occupying 39.6 per cent of the posts in the Provincial Executive Service, 25 per cent in the Judicial Service and 24.4 per cent of Class I positions in the UP Agricultural Service (Table 1). Not surprisingly, there was hardly a case where the governor used his special powers to protect the 'beleaguered' Muslims. The story was no different in CP, Bihar and Bombay. The CP Muslims 'have hitherto suffered little, if any, serious injustice at the hands of the Congress Ministry'. The governors of Bihar and Bombay sent out similar reports.[85] They took note of the fact that ministers here and elsewhere were susceptible to criticisms and were usually anxious to err on the

[81] Henry Twynam to Linlithgow, 10 March 1941, ibid.

[82] Hawthorne to Linlithgow, 6 January 1942, ibid.

[83] Roger Lumley to Linlithgow, 11 April 1942, ibid. See Rani Dhavan Shankardass, *The First Congress Raj* (Delhi, 1982), for an assessment of the Bombay ministry.

[84] In Sitapur, for example, the Rural Development movement was of help to Muslim weavers as well as the Hindu cultivators. Besides, out of the 789 rural development organizers 20 per cent were Muslims recruited from rural areas. This was by no means a low percentage considering that the Muslim population in UP was largely concentrated in the towns. Haig to Linlithgow, 10 May 1939, Harry Haig Papers; Hallet to Linlithgow, 1 January 1940, Linlithgow Papers (125/103).

[85] Wylie to Linlithgow, 18 April 1939, Hallet to Linlithgow, 8 May 1939, L/P&J/8/686. See also *The Central Provinces and Berar Government at Work* (Nagpur, 1939).

side of generosity wherever 'Muslim interests' were affected. The Bombay Ministry withdrew the textbooks prescribed by the Jamia Millia Islamia and its Vice-Chancellor Zakir Husain. It also refused to ban cow-slaughter. The CP government allowed Muslim donors to finance Urdu schools for Muslim boys on lines similar to those of Vidya Mandirs and agreed to extend official support to such schools (*Bait al-Islam*).[86]

TABLE 1

HINDU AND MUSLIM REPRESENTATION IN UP PUBLIC SERVICES

Services	*Hindus*		*Muslims*	
	Number	*Percentage*	*Number*	*Percentage*
Civil				
Executive Service	175	52.5	132	39.6
Tahsildars	106	54.99	84	43.6
Naib Tahsildars	117	55.9	87	44.1
Agricultural Service				
Class I	9	64.2	3	24.4
Class II	32	76.0	5	12.0
Subordinate	401	73.3	137	25.0
Police				
DSP	28	56.0	14	28.0
Inspectors	105	46.4	68	30.0
Sub-Inspectors	1029	54.2	832	43.8
Head Constables	898	35.2	1638	64.4
Naiks	884	51.5	883	47.9
Constables	14,063	53.00	12,289	46.4
Educational Service				
Class I	11	73.3	4	26.7
Class II	78	73.6	14	13.2
Subordinate Service:				
Teaching branch	1062	69.0	372	24.2

[86] Wylie to Linlithgow, 24 December 1939, L/P&J/8/645.

Services	Hindus		Muslims	
	Number	Percentage	Number	Percentage
Inspecting branch	169	64.0	85	32.2
Judicial Service	159	72.0	55	25.0
Medical Service				
Civil Surgeons	25	83.3	4	13.3
Medical Officers	78	75.0	21	20.1
Assistants	271	80.4	61	18.1
Service of Engineers				
Class I	3	60.00	1	20.0
Class II	21	72.4	3	10.4
Subordinate	104	91.0	8	7.0
Income Tax Department				
Class I and II	24	61.5	12	30.7
Forest Service	12	57.0	4	19.0
Rangers	87	80.5	20	18.5
Deputy-Rangers	175	74.4	59	25.1
Co-operative Societies				
Gazetted Officers	5	62.5	3	37.5
Subordinate	120	77.0	36	22.9

NOTE: Grants made to Muslim institutions by the Education Department (excluding grants made by local boards) for 1938–9 amounted t Rs 3,83,201. This included a special grant Rs 48,396 made out to the Arabic *madrasas*

SOURCE: Address by G.B. Pant to members of the UP Press Consultative Committee, 11 January 1939, L/P&J/8/686, India Office Library & Records (ILOR)

In the end, however, we have to reckon with the fact that Muslim grievances existed, and that it was exceedingly difficult to dissipate these by any process of reasoning. After two and a half years of Congress rule, Muslims were profoundly embittered by instances (very difficult for the most part to prove, but nevertheless symptomatic of the atmosphere that prevailed) of the continued oppression of Muslim minorities in the Congress provinces. Side by side was the growing realization of the importance, from their point of view, of the Congress claim to be the sole mouthpiece of Indian opinion and the sole party to negotiate with the Raj, and an anxiety to secure their own position before their bargaining capacity with Pax Britannica deteriorated further. The result was, of course, seen in the consolidation of the Muslim League, the crystallization of Muslim demands, and the pitching of those demands on a very much higher level. The demands were that future constitutional arrangements should be made not on the basis of population but on the basis of communities, that the Muslims be treated on complete equality with the Hindus, and that no constitutional change be made without the consent and approval of the two communities. In basing demands on communities rather than parties, the Muslim League hoped to take advantage of the fact that the Hindu Mahasabha contested the Congress claims, while the Scheduled Castes still demanded to be treated separately. This was the first tangible step towards delineating the contours of the Pakistan demand. It was very much the outcome of the Congress ministries. The League's success was in making this perception look *real*.

III

Jinnah raised the war cry at Lahore, the city with a glorious history of cultural synthesis and integration. The mild, moderate statesman, tutored in the liberal traditions of Dadabhai Naoroji, spoke angrily and defiantly, sending out alarm signals all around. Much to the consternation of the Congress Muslims, including Abul Kalam Azad who had only just set out the political agenda for his co-religionists at Ramgarh, Jinnah talked of 'two nations', of Muslims having 'their homelands, their territory and their state'. Refuting the theory of a plural, composite nationhood, which was advocated with such tenacity by Ajmal Khan, Ansari and Azad, Jinnah argued that it was a 'dream' for Hindus and Muslims to evolve a common nationality. They belonged to 'two different civilizations which are based on conflicting ideas and competition'. To yoke together two such 'nations' under a single State 'would lead to growing discontent, and the final destruction of any fabric that may be so built up for the government of such a State'.

These were ominous remarks; yet they did not lower the final curtain on the prospect for a united India. The crusade against 'Hindu

India' had been launched amid cries of 'Allah-o-Akbar', but the syntax and import of the phrases used in the 'Pakistan Resolution' were obscure. The silver lining was that Jinnah had, albeit consciously, refused to define his 'nation' and had thereby left his 'scheme' open to diverse interpretations. The viceroy regarded it as 'very largely in the nature of a bargaining. . . . 'Half the strength of his [Jinnah's] position is that he has refused to define it and I am quite certain that he would refuse to define it now if asked to. . . .'[87] E. J. Benthall, president of the Bengal Chamber of Commerce and an astute political observer, commented in March 1940 that Jinnah did not want to be dragged into the details of the Pakistan 'scheme' in order to avoid being tangled up in interminable discussions, possibly to the disadvantage of his own case. After an hour-long conversation, Jinnah consistently refused to be pinned down to future constitutional proposals. 'His main interest was to keep Congress out while he builds up power and influence'.[88] Resignation of the Congress ministries, combined with the domestic and global compulsions of the British government during the World War, enabled the future Quaid to play his 'Pakistan' card to outmanoeuvre his opponents and detractors. Having been rebuffed and rejected by the Congress leadership for well over a decade, he had at long last earned, so to speak, his moral right and established his political claim to be heard as the chief, if not the sole, spokesman of 'Muslim India'.

Yet, initial reactions to the 'Pakistan Resolution' may not have brought much comfort to the League diehards. Sikander Hyat Khan, averse to Jinnah's intrusion into his political territory, was 'disturbed' as the resolution drafted by him at Lahore provided for definite links with the Centre so as to preserve India's national unity.[89] Muslim

[87] Linlithgow to Amery, 2 May 1943, L/P7J/8/512 (part 2).

[88] E.J. Benthall Papers, file nos. 12 & 19, Centre for South Asian Studies, Cambridge.

[89] Malcolm Darling to Linlithgow, 25 April 1940, L/P&J/8/506 (part B). Also, the anguish of Khizar Hyat Khan who felt that Pakistan, deeply tinged as it was with religious prejudice, was getting at a point at which it could not be resisted. He wanted the British government to define 'Pakistan' and to reject the idea if found unreasonable. But Linlithgow did not agree. The government's response, in his view, would convey to the Muslim League and the Hindu Mahasabha the mistaken impression of its bias in favour of either position. He told the secretary of state for India: 'I fear Khizar and his friends will have trouble with the Muslim League, and Khizar may be . . . much less qualified to deal with it than Sikander'. Linlithgow to Amery, 2/4 May 1943, L/P&J/8/512 (part 2).

leaders elsewhere were dismayed. In Bombay, they saw little in Jinnah's scheme to bolster their self-confidence: 'the best that any Muslim has said . . . is that Jinnah is using it [Pakistan] as a bargaining weapon',[90] an impression not easy to dispel in other quarters as well. As late as the spring of 1946 when Mirza Ismail, the knighted Dewan of Mysore, was asked if Jinnah was serious about Pakistan, he said: 'no, it was a move in the political game'.[91] In UP, too, the Pakistan idea was long held to be a bargaining move, 'a counter demand to that of the Congress'.[92] People like the Nawab of Chattari, architect of the UP National Agriculturist Party, were unsure how the Lahore resolution would protect Muslims in 'Hindu-majority provinces'.[93] Muslims in such areas were decidedly 'unhappy' at the prospect of Partition.[94] Their fears were confirmed in August 1947 when Jinnah's Pakistan simply provided a homeland for those living in majority areas but not elsewhere.[95]

There were still others—the socialists, the Congress Muslims of Azad's generation, the *ulama* in the Jamiyat al-ulama, the Ahrars, the Shias, the Khudai Khidmatgars and the Momins—who repudiated, though not always for the same reasons, the two-nation theory and

[90] Governor of Bombay to Linlithgow, 30 March 1940, ibid.

[91] 'Punjab Memories 1910–1941' (typescript, 1971), James Penney Papers, Centre for South Asian Studies, Cambridge.

[92] Enclosure 2 in: Governor of UP to Governor-General (Telegram), 31 March 1940, Linlithgow Papers (125/108). The Viceroy referred to the 'uncertainty of the Muslims and the leaders as to where they stand and what policy they are to pursue'. Linlithgow to Haig, 17 April 1939, Linlithgow Papers (125/102).

[93] To Jinnah, n.d. (probably written in early January 1940), L/P&J/8/507. The role of the Nawab of Chattari illustrates how personal or class interests rather than ideology dictated political preferences. In August 1934 he was averse to the Muslim League and suggested the revival of the defunct All-India Muslim Conference. In April 1936 he broke away from the Muslim League Parlia-mentary Board to revive a 'mixed Party in preference to a Muslim communal organisation'. But his subsequent experiences compelled him to re-think his position *vis-a-vis* the National Agriculturist Party and the Muslim League. Chhatari to Linlithgow, 4 August 1936, Linlithgow Papers (125/11B); Chattari to Hailey, 28 Oct. 1936, Hailey Papers (220/28C).

[94] Linlithgow to Amery, 6 April 1940, L/P&J/B/506 (B).

[95] In an anonymous letter to *Dawn* dated 19 January 1948, a correspondent who styled himself 'A Musulman' enquired from the newspaper's readers whether or not refugees from India such as himself had been cleverly duped by the creation of Pakistan: the country was surely meant not for them but rather for the people of Punjab, Sind, Baluchistan and Bengal alone. Quoted in Sarah Ansari, *Modern Asian Studies*, 24, 4, 1990, p. 819.

doggedly adhered to their vision of a united India.[96] The All-India Ahrar Conferences, held in 1943 and 1945 and attended by Maulana Ataullah Shah Bukhari and Mazhar Ali Azhar, denounced Jinnah's plan to divide the country. The Momin Conference, convened in September 1945 by its charismatic leader, Abdul Qayyum Ansari, took a similar stand. The slogan of Pakistan, stated Ansari, was 'invented' by well-to-do Muslims to grind down their impoverished co-religionists. The nationalist concerns of the Jamiyat al-ulama, which had already declared complete independence as its goal in 1939,[97] was reflected in the activities of learned and distinguished men like Maulanas Husain Ahmad Madani, Ahmad Said, and Kifayatullah. While remaining true to their faith, they made large sacrifices for India's independence and unity. They were insulted, rebuffed and violently attacked,[98] but refused to capitulate to the forces of political reaction and religious fanaticism. Their role must not be written off or relegated to a historian's footnote. In the evolution of a composite, nationalist ideology, which no doubt suffered a jolt during the dark days of 1947–8, the turbaned men with flowing gowns had as much role to play as their counterparts among the western-educated intelligentsia.

Finally, some of Jinnah's own close associates, who were unable to tear themselves apart from their social milieu and cultural moor-

[96] The Haripura session of the Congress in February 1938 took special note of the growth in anti-imperialist feelings among the Muslims. In November 1939, Nehru listed a large number of Muslim organizations which had rallied round the Congress. 'So you will see', he informed Krishna Menon, 'that it is quite absurd to talk of the Congress facing the Muslims. I am quite sure that as matters develop, large numbers of Muslims will be with us'. Report of the Indian National Congress, Haripura, February 1938, p. 7; Nehru to Krishna Menon, 8 Nov. 1939, S. Gopal (ed.), *Selected Letters of Jawaharlal Nehru* (Delhi, 1977), vol. 10, pp. 230–2.

[97] Statement of the Working Committee of the Jamiyat al-ulama. Home Deptt. (Political), file no. 37/1939, National Archives of India (NAI).

[98] The Muslim League rowdies insulted and, in some cases, physically assaulted leaders of the Jamiyat al-ulama and the Central Muslim Parliamentary Board. Abul Kalam Azad was ill-treated in Delhi and Aligarh. His friend, Abdur Razzaq Malihabadi, editor of *Hind*, was attacked in Calcutta. Maulanas Mohammad Quddus and Mohammad Ismail escaped a murderous assault in Gaya. And in Saidpur (Bengal), the police and a handful of volunteers prevented Husain Ahmad Madani, president of the Jamiyat, from being lynched by an angry mob. See, *Shaikh al-Islam Hazrat Maulana Syed Husain Madani par Leagueoon ka Sharmnaak Hamla* (Bijnor, 1945).

ings, quibbled and hesitated. That is why Ismail Khan and the Nawab of Chhatari, friends of the Nehrus, decided to stay put in India. People like Khaliquzzaman and the Raja of Mahmudabad, brought up in the liberal and composite ethos of Lucknow and Allahabad, were caught in a dilemma. For long they dithered. But when the reality, so to speak, dawned on them, they journeyed to Pakistan with a sense of unease and remorse. Like so many in their generation, they were pained to bid adieu to the symbols of their faith—the great Imambaras of Lucknow and Matiya Burj, the sacred shrines at Ajmer and Delhi, and the *dargahs* at Bansa, Rudauli, Kakori and Dewa Sharif in Awadh. They were no less agonized to snap their ties with Lucknow and Delhi, the cities of Mir Anis and Ghalib, or the *qasbahs* in Awadh which served as centres of cultural and intellectual life. Perhaps, on their arrival in the land designated 'Pakistan', they echoed the sentiment of the nineteenth-century Urdu poet, Mir Taqi Mir:

> Why do you mock at me and ask yourselves
> Where in the world I come from, easterners?
> There was a city, famed throughout the world,
> Where dwelt the chosen spirits of the age:
> Delhi its name, fairest among the fair.
> Fate looted it and laid it desolate,
> And to that ravaged city I belong.[99]

There were memories on both sides of the fence, memories of living side by side for generations with a shared heritage, memories of friends and of long-standing associations. The birth of Pakistan severed cultural ties and fragmented an intellectual tradition which was neither 'Hindu' nor 'Muslim' but, in its essence, Hindustani. Qurat-ul-ayan Hyder's Urdu novel *Mere Bhi Sanamkhane* ('My Temples Too'), published in 1947, was able to capture the anguish of a group in Lucknow whose dream of a united India was shattered by the grim and tragic happenings in 1946–7. What was there for them to celebrate at the fateful midnight hour or at the dawn of independence. In the words of Faiz Ahmad Faiz:

> This is not that long-looked-for break of day
> Not that clear dawn in quest of which those comrades
> Set out, believing that in heaven's wide void
> Somewhere must be the star's last halting place,

[99] Ralph Russell and Khurshidul Islam, *Three Mughal Poets: Mir, Sauda, Mir Hasan* (London, 1969), p. 260.

Somewhere the verge of night's slow-washing tide,
Somewhere an anchorage for the ship of heartache.[100]

Which country did an author like Saadat Hasan Manto belong to? India or Pakistan? When he sat down to write he tried in vain to 'separate India from Pakistan and Pakistan from India'. He would repeatedly ask himself: 'to whom will now belong what had been written in undivided India? Will that be partitioned too'?[101] Other Urdu writers and poets, including Josh Malihabadi, Krishen Chander, Khadeeja Mastoor, Khalilur Rahman Azmi, Rajinder Singh Bedi and Ram Lal shared and described their agony and experiences in their own inimitable styles. Khwaja Ahmad Abbas, a key figure in the Progressive Writer's movement, bemoaned the 'death' of one's country. 'Who killed India?' he asked indignantly: '. . . that an imperialist power planned the dismemberment of our country is not surprising. The wonder and the tragedy is that India should have been killed by the children of India'.[102]

IV

So, why did a 'Pakistan' come about which served the interests of most Muslims so poorly? Why did the ill-defined and vague concept of 'Pakistan' sway the masses in such large numbers? What enabled Jinnah to create and popularize the symbol of a separate Muslim nation? Why did the Congress, having championed national unity with such gusto, capitulate without offering much resistance to the two-nation theory? Was it a case of 'betrayal', as Azad pointed out retrospectively, or an implied recognition of the failure of secular nationalism? Or should we search for clues in two of Nehru's statements?—one made in April 1940 when he told Malcolm Darling that he would accept Pakistan rather than not have freedom,[103] and the other in 1960 when he confessed to Leonard Mosley: 'The truth is that we were tired men and we were getting on in years . . . the plan for partition offered a way out and we took it. . .'.[104] Or, perhaps, in a highly

[100] V.G. Kiernan (ed.), *Poems by Faiz* (London, 1971), p. 123.
[101] Khalid Husain, *Scoreboard* (Lahore, 1984), p. 37.
[102] Abbas, *I Am Not an Island*, p. 280.
[103] Darling to Linlithgow, 25 April 1940, L/P&J/8506 (B).
[104] Leonard Mosley, *The Last Days of the British Raj* (London, 1961), p. 77.

suggestive post-facto justification of Congress acquiescence to the country's vivisection: in an appeal to the Indian electorate on the eve of the first general election in 1952 it was stated:

The price of freedom was Partition. The Congress and its leaders resisted the idea of Partition till the last moment and they yielded only when they realized that the alternative was indefinite perpetuation of foreign rule or civil war or both. The short experiment of coalition government with the Muslim League in 1946–7 demonstrated that no real co-operation was possible between the secular nationalism of the Congress and the narrow communalism and the two-nation theory of the Muslim League. *A strong and stable Central Government could be established by peaceful means only through Partition. . . . It should not be for-gotten that without Partition there might have been no transfer of power at all, or the whole of India might have been involved in a civil war the consequences of which would have been infinitely more tragic than the sad events of the latter half of 1947.*[105] (emphasis added)

Some of the questions listed above, as indeed the clues offered by the election appeal of 1953, have been tackled from a wide range of perspectives. There are, first, the proponents of the two-nation theory, who see 'Muslim nationalism' as linked with the demand of a 'nationality' apprehensive of its future in a 'Hindu-dominated' federal structure, and who regard 'secular nationalism' as out of place in a society where the 'divisive forces have proved much more dynamic than the cohesive ones'.[106] Hindu-Muslim antagonism was thus 'embedded in the historical logic of India'.[107] Farzana Shaikh has pitched the debate at a more sophisticated level by arguing that the evolution of 'Muslim politics', and ultimately the call to Partition, were driven by a long history of ideas that saw the Muslims as an exclusive political entity separate from others, an 'awareness of the ideal of Muslim

105 *Vote Congress—Congress and the Welfare State* (Published by the Central Publicity Board, New Delhi, n.d.).

106 Aziz Ahmed, *Islamic Culture in the Indian Environment* (Oxford, 1964), p. 74.

107 This view is consistently reflected in the works of Ishtiaq Husain Qureshi who, after his *hijrat* from the University of Delhi to Karachi, turned into the chief ideologue of the two-nation theory. He is still remembered by his alma mater, where his former students have instituted a memorial lecture at St. Stephen's College. Qureshi's work, in general, has influenced the tenor of historiography in Pakistan. There are, of course, some more sophisticated versions, most notably by scholars based in western academic institutions. Prominent amongst them are Aziz Ahmad, Khalid bin Sayeed and Hafeez Malik. The late Aziz Ahmad was an outstanding scholar who did pioneering work in the history of Islam in India.

brotherhood, a belief in the superiority of Muslim culture, and a recognition of the belief that Muslims ought to live under Muslim governments'.[108]

Such refined interpretations, coupled with crude expositions of the two-nation idea, are grounded first of all in the mistaken belief that the ideologues of 'Muslim nationalism' had shared paradigms or a common 'Islamic' framework as a starting point for determining the place and status of Islam and of Muslims in the subcontinent. Did Mohamed Ali and Ansari share the same worldview? Did Muzaffar Ahmad and Fazlul Haq have a common discourse? Was there any compatibility between Azad's secular vision and Jinnah's adherence to the two-nation idea? Was there no difference in the perspectives of the *ulama* of Deoband, Nadwat al-ulama, and Firangi Mahal? Moreover, even if one were to recognize, for the sake of argument, a common theme across the political spectrum, what place does one assign to the Ahrars, the Khaksars, the Khudai Khidmatgars and the followers of the Momin Conference, the Shia Political Conference and the Jamiyat al-ulama?[109] The presence of such groups communicates forcefully the message that Indian Muslims had a strong secular and nationalist tradition as well which ought not to be forgotten, and that their perspective should not be submerged beneath the rationalizations of the 'victors', the founders of Pakistan.[110]

Furthermore, the two-nation theory is grounded in the mistaken belief that Hindus and Muslims constitute exclusive, autonomous entities, with no common points of contact and association, and that religious loyalty takes precedence over ties and bonds of relationship based on tangible inter-social connections, cross-cultural exchanges and shared material interests. A corrective to this approach, which asserts the primacy of religion, is required so that the movement towards Partition is understood in its specific context and not viewed as a 'logical' sequel to developments dating back to the pre-colonial era.

[108] Farzana Shaikh, *Community and Consensus in Islam: Muslim Representation in Colonial India, 1860–1947* (Cambridge, 1989), p. 230.

[109] For an elucidation of the role of some of these groups, see my *A Nationalist Conscience: M.A. Ansari, the Congress and the Raj,* and my introduction to Mushirul Hasan (ed.), *Islam and Indian Nationalism: Reflections on Abul Kalam Azad* (Delhi, 1992).

[110] See the reviews of *A Nationalist Conscience* by Francis Robinson in *Modern Asian Studies*, 1989, pp. 609–19, and by P.G. Robb in the *Bulletin of the School of Oriental and African Studies*, 1, 1991, pp. 104–25.

It needs to be reiterated that 'communalism' or 'separatism', both in their latent and overt forms, did not always embrace large segments of society: they only touched limited groups in certain areas. Their impact was transient as groups embroiled in inter-religious feuds at a given moment could be seen living harmoniously at other times. The governor of Bengal, where Hindu–Muslim conflicts were almost endemic, commented on how the rank and file of the two communities co-existed peacefully, and that it was 'only at rare intervals, when religious feelings became inflamed, that they treat each other as enemies and clashes occur'.[111] Recent studies reveal the fusion of Hindu and Muslim 'folk' worship, with the practices and teachings of the high or 'orthodox' Islamic tradition and the participation, as in the case of the Muslim weavers of Banaras, in public ceremonials relating to particular Hindu figures.[112] There are also instances—such as the one from Bahraich in eastern UP, where the outbreak of cholera in 1930 prompted Muslims to join in great force to worship the goddess Bhawani to induce her to remove the pestilence—which illustrate the extent to which religious barriers could be transcended and strict codes of behaviour transgressed.[113] Or the way Islamic ceremonies relating to birth, marriage and death were observed in many areas, though the 'outer labels' were sometimes discarded as a concession to the reformist movements to make the rituals and practices look 'Islamic'.[114] 'The rigidity of intolerance on view', remarked the author of the 1921 Census report, 'which is a marked feature of the religion of Islam in its purer form, does not extend to the masses, who are quite willing to recognize and assist the efforts of their neighbours to keep on peaceful terms with unknown powers'.[115]

Much work needs to be done on the historical development of Islam and of Muslim communities in various regions of the Indian

[111] Earl of Lytton, *Pundit and Elephants: Being the Experiences of Five Years as Governor of an Indian Province* (London, 1942).

[112] Judy F. Pugh, 'Divination and Ideology in the Banaras Muslim Community', in K.P. Ewing (ed.), *Shariat and Ambiquity in South Asian Islam* (Delhi, 1988); contributions to Sandria Freitag (ed.), *Culture and Power in Banaras: Community, Performance and Environment 1800–1980* (Delhi, 1989), and her *Collective Action and Community.*

[113] *Census of India*, 1931, p. 515.

[114] Rafiuddin Ahmad, 'Conflicts, and Contradictions in Bengali Islam', in Ewing (ed.), *Shariat and Ambiguity*, p. 134, and the excellent study of Asim Roy, *The Islamic Syncretistic Tradition in Bengal* (Princeton, 1983).

[115] *Census of India*, 1921, p. 115.

subcontinent. On the basis of existing studies, we can safely trace the strength of composite and syncretistic tendencies, though their growth and progress were neither unilinear nor unimpeded. Islam in Kashmir developed a resilient tradition of its own, incorporating many social and cultural practices of pre-Islamic origin.[116] Islam in Punjab provided a repertoire of concepts and styles of authority which served to encompass potentially competing values, including the values of tribal kinship, within a common Islamic idiom.[117] The religion of Mohammed took many forms in Bengal and assimilated values and symbols not always in conformity with Quranic ideals and precepts. The cultural idioms, rooted in the Quran and the *hadith* (traditions), underwent a rapid transformation, giving birth to a set of popular beliefs and practices which, in essence, represented the popular culture of rural Bengal rooted in the pre-Islamic past.[118] Finally, Islam in South India evolved a tradition of worship which was marked by a striking capacity to accommodate itself to indigenous patterns of faith and worship. Islam gained a foothold because of its capacity to forge links with the religions and peoples of the wider society, to offer a form of access to the divine which could be grasped and built upon through means already present within these societies. This interpenetration was neither 'degenerate' nor a product of superficial accretions from Hinduism. The sharing of belief and practice was, in fact, built up into a dynamic and expansive religious system.[119]

Nationalist writers in the 1940s and thereafter were wedded to the concept of composite nationality, a quintessential feature of India's liberation struggle, and laid stress on cultural assimilation and social intermingling between Hindus and Muslims. Perhaps there was a tendency to portray, so we are told, an idyllic picture, to disregard elements of discord and disharmony. Still, the essential thrust of their

116 M. Ishaq Khan, 'Islam in Kashmir: Historical Analysis of its Distinctive Features', in C.W. Troll (ed.), *Islam in India: Studies and Commentaries* (Delhi, 1985), and his 'The Significance of the Dargah of Hazratbal in the Socio-religious and Political life of Kashmiri Muslims', in C.W. Troll (ed.), *Muslim Shrines in India: Their Character and Significance* (Delhi, 1989).

117 David Gilmartin, 'Customary Law and Shariat in Punjab', in Ewing (ed.), *Shariat and Ambiguity*, p. 44.

118 Rafiuddin Ahmad, 'Conflicts and Contradictions in Bengal Islam', in ibid., p. 115.

119 Susan Bayly, *Saints, Goddesses and Kings: Muslims and Christians in South Indian Society 1700–1900* (Cambridge, 1990), pp. 13–14.

argument—that the followers of different religious creeds had co-existed peacefully even in turbulent times—was profoundly valid. Nehru's reflections in Ahmednagar jail and Azad's introspection at Ramgarh, though lacking in scholarly rigour for present-day 'specialists', are as relevant today as they were in the 1940s. India's Partition did not make their perspective any less relevant.

In his book published in 1971, Anil Seal, the doyen of the 'Cambridge School', questioned the common assumption, which marred historical narratives of previous decades, that the Indian Muslim 'community' formed a bloc of peoples whose conditions were generally equal, whose interests were generally the same and whose solidarity was generally firm. Unevenness of socio-economic development, he argued, produced disparities between Muslims in different provinces and between Muslims in the same province, just as it was doing between Hindus. In 'so shapeless, so jumbled a bundle of societies, there were not two nations, there was not one nation, there was no nation at all, what was India?—a graveyard of nationalities and the mother of new nationalisms struggling to be born'.[120]

Following the same framework, Paul Brass argued, with greater conviction, that the ideology of Muslim separateness did not flow out of the objective differences between Hindus and Muslims but out of the use made of those differences through a conscious process of symbol selection. Nor was it the consequence of the objective circumstances of Muslims in UP, who were better placed than Hindus in urbanization, literacy, English education, social communications and government employment.[121] Francis Robinson arrived at similar conclusions; the threat of becoming backward, rather than backwardness itself, encouraged UP Muslims to organize themselves separately. Their influence in the province helped them to do so with much effect.[122] More recently though, Robinson has sought to establish a 'fundamental' connection between Islamic traditions and 'political separatism'. In a lively debate with Paul Brass, he rejects the 'instrumentalist' view to assert, in much the same way as Farzana occasions, a motivating role to play amongst the elites of UP.[123]

[120] Anil Seal, *The Emergence of Indian Nationalism: Competition and Collaboration in the Later Nineteenth Century* (Cambridge, 1968), p. 339.

[121] Paul Brass, *Language, Religion and Politics in North India* (Cambridge, 1974), p. 178 and ff.

[122] Robinson, *Separatism*, ch. 1.

[123] Francis Robinson, 'Nation Formation: The Brass Thesis and Muslim

In much of the writings until the 1980s—the works of Seal, Brass, Robinson, Chris Bayly, Harold Gould, Gyanendra Pandey and Zoya Hasan included—UP was seen as the heartland of Hindu and Muslim revitalization movements, the chief arena where competing elites devised and followed their political trajectory within communitarian frameworks. Historians have since turned to regions outside the Indo-Gangetic belt to traverse the terrain of elite politics within formal imperial structures. Thus the works of David Page, Kenneth Jones, Imran Ali, Ian Talbot, Prem Choudhry and David Gilmartin on Punjab, and of Rafiuddin Ahmad, Asim Roy, Kenneth Mcpherson, Rajat Ray, Shila Sen and Suranjan Das on Bengal, have individually and collectively shifted the focus from UP to the 'Muslim-majority' provinces of British India.

David Page detailed the profoundly divisive effects of the Montagu-Chelmsford Reforms in Bengal and Punjab. His story is about how Hindu–Muslim antagonism became a permanent feature of provincial politics, how 'communal' interests were consolidated around 'communal' issues, how 'Muslim attitudes' were formed towards the emergence of provincial autonomy and towards the eventual withdrawal of imperial control.[124] Talbot and Gilmartin carry the story further to trace the roots of Partition in Punjab. In Talbot's analysis, the 'decisive shift' took place as late in the day as the 1946 provincial elections, when landholders tilted the balance in favour of the League.[125] Gilmartin, on the other hand, examines the evolution of support for the Pakistan movement in terms of a search for ideological identity amid the severe contradictions established by colonial rule. The Pakistan movement remains essentially a paradox to Gilmartin: millennarian tendencies and Islamic revivalism on the one hand; political objectives shaped by the structures of the colonial state on the other. Yet many of the political pressures that produced Pakistan—and led to Punjab's Partition—originated outside the province. The events of 1947 in Punjab owed much to the broader currents that brought the decline of the British empire, the rise of the Congress and the rapid progress of the Muslim League in other parts of India. Indeed, Jinnah's

Separatism', and reply by Paul Brass, *Journal of Commonwealth and Comparative Politics*, 15, 3, pp. 215–34.

124 David Page, *Prelude to Partition: The Indian Muslims and the Imperial State System of Control 1920–1932* (Delhi, 1982).

125 Ian Talbot, *Punjab and the Raj* and *Provincial Politics and the Pakistan Movement, 1849–1947* (Delhi, 1988).

political ascendancy, which in its beginnings owed little to Punjab, ultimately shaped events there deeply. But in the end the Punjabi Muslims decided their own future, for after the elections of 1946 the creation of Pakistan could not be denied.[126]

Studies of this nature have enriched the debate on India's 'Great Divide', for they lay bare the main contours of political 'separatism' in the critical regions of British India, establish the linkages between provincial and national leaders, and trace the strength of social/cultural interconnections as instruments of mobilization. The appeal of ideology—nationalist or otherwise—is best mirrored in the specific context of a region. So also its use by the political and religious leadership.

Regional studies on 'communalism' and the Pakistan movement do not, in any way, diminish the value of other works which explore the national scene, concentrate on all-India leaders and organizations, and try to unfold the happenings at the apex. For example, Anita Inder Singh is able to fill in some of the gaps in our knowledge of the interplay of British, Congress and Muslim League strategies. She assesses, with much sensitivity, the attitudes and tactics of the three parties in the negotiations for the transfer of power and the factors that induced the Congress and the British to accept the idea of Pakistan.[127] It is not very often that the story of such negotiations is told with such clarity and objectivity.

R.J. Moore provides useful insights into the official mind in Delhi and Whitehall. *The Crisis of Indian Unity* deals with the problems of wresting freedom from the British and keeping the country united in the wake of the Pakistan demand. *Churchill, Cripps and India* and *Escape from Empire* trace the evolution of the Labour Party's policies to solve the many-sided Indian problem.[128] Read together with the earlier versions and interpretations of Leonard Mosley, Penderel Moon, V.P. Menon, H.V. Hodson and P.S. Gupta,[129] Moore's impres-

[126] David Gilmartin, *Empire and Islam: Punjab and the Making of Pakistan* (London, 1988) and its review by Sarah Ansari, *Modern Asian Studies,* 24, 4, 1990.

[127] *The Origins of the Partition of India 1936–1947* (Delhi, 1987).

[128] *The Crisis of Indian Unity 1917–1947* (Oxford, 1974); *Churchill, Cripps and India 1939–1945* (Oxford, 1979), *Escape from Empire: The Attlee Government and the Indian Problem* (Oxford, 1989).

[129] For a useful bibliographical survey, see A.K. Majumdar, 'Writings on the Transfer of Power', in B.R. Nanda (ed.), *Essays in Modern Indian History* (Delhi, 1980).

sive researches cover important aspects of British policy and strategy towards Independence and Partition.

Many of the themes delineated in the writings of Talbot, Gilmartin, Anita Inder Singh and Moore figure in a work of outstanding merit —Ayesha Jalal's *The Sole Spokesman: Jinnah, the Muslim League and the Demand for Pakistan.* It is by far the most refined, though by no means authoritative, statement on a cataclysmic and violent event in the subcontinent. Jalal has raised the standard of debate on Partition. More than any other historian, she underlines the importance of Jinnah's cleverly disguised manoeuvres and the significance of keeping the terms of the Lahore Resolution vague and amorphous. The critical importance of her work, according to Asim Roy, lies in presenting the Resolution as a tactical manoeuvre and in her success in elevating this interpretation basically from the realm of doubts and speculations and giving it academic authenticity and credibility.[130] Equally important is the way in which the provincial world of Bengal and Punjab is thrown wide open and the argument that behind the simple cry of Pakistan lay a host of complex and conflicting interests, some of which had very little to do with the shape Pakistan was coming to assume in Jinnah's guarded exposition at Lahore in March 1940 or thereafter. Finally, Jalal's summation of Mountbatten's role is a powerful indictment of a man who made such tall claims for so modest a 'feat'—conducted an administrative operation which left hundreds of thousands dead and rendered millions homeless. His 'great operation' was an ignominious scuttle enabling the British to extricate themselves from the awkward responsibility of presiding over India's 'communal madness'.

There are, however, notable gaps in an otherwise interesting exposition. Part of the reason why this is so is because Jalal's perspective is based on high politics and diplomacy. Jinnah occupies centrestage in her narrative, with provincial leaders rather than interest groups extracting their price for supporting the Quaid. That is why we get no sense of a growing movement drawing its constituents from different regions and social classes at various stages of its progress and development. Also missing is a perspective on the ideological content of the movement, an aspect Farzana Shaikh covers with finesse, on the social base of the Muslim League, its mobilization techniques after the

[130] Asim Roy, 'The High Politics of India's Partition: The Revisionist Perspective', p. 116 below.

adoption of the Lahore Resolution, and its ability to use Islam as a rallying symbol with such great effect. Other writers, who have used the Muslim League records at Karachi University with much profit, have been able to highlight these aspects. Both Talbot and Gilmartin have argued, on the strength of Muslim League documents, how the linking of Islamic appeals to social and economic grievances and their transmission through the all-important rural idiom of *biradari* and Sufi networks succeeded in transmitting the League's message from its strongholds in the towns to the countryside, where the bulk of the voters was to be found.

Jalal's version of the Congress' part in the making of Pakistan is unmistakably one-sided, because her book is almost solely based on official sources, on Muslim League records and on Jinnah's private collection. Several questions relating to the Congress role remain unanswered in her book, in particular, and in other works generally. While it is possible to argue, as Asim Roy does, that the Congress steadily and deliberately worked itself up to a position where Jinnah was forced to take his 'Pakistan' and leave the scene for good,[131] the nature of its political intervention awaits careful historical scrutiny. Perhaps Jalal will return to India to examine the vast collection of private papers and newspapers in Indian libraries and archives. Perhaps the exercise will change her perspective, or perhaps not.

While Jalal marshalls an array of facts to establish Jinnah's popularity and the League's acceptability, she fails to underline the fact that, even after the resistance in Bengal and Punjab had crumbled Pakistan was not everybody's dream and Jinnah not everybody's Quaid. It is a lesser known fact that in terms of the actual number of votes secured and against the background of the tremendous build up to Pakistan, 'nationalist Muslim' groups did not fare too poorly in the 1946 elections (Table 2). Their performance in some UP constituencies, such as Bahraich (south), Meerut (east), Gorakhpur (east) and Pilibhit was, in fact, comforting. Though Congress stalwarts like Rafi Ahmad Kidwai lost in Rae Bareli, success came to Nisar Ahmad Khan Sherwani in Mainpuri and Etah, Bashir Ahmad in Bijnor south-east, and Hafiz Mohammad Ibrahim in Garhwal and Bijnor north-west. Some additional gains were possible had the Congress put up Muslim candidates in the general urban and rural constituencies, and if its nominees in the Muslim urban constituencies were chosen with care

[131] Ibid., p. 123.

TABLE 2

VOTES POLLED IN THE MUSLIM CONSTITUENCIES

Parties	*Seats contested*	*Votes polled*	*Percentage*
Muslim League	64	515,229	64.7
Congress	29	107,877	13.54
Nationalist Muslims	32	114,686	14.39
Ahrars	2	10,154	1.27
Sunni Board	1	11,188	1.40
Shia Conference	2	5,847	0.73
Khaksars	3	176	0.02
Independents	30	31,491	3.95

SOURCES: L/PJ/8/478 and L/PJ/8/483, IOLR, London.

and not arbitrarily. It was a mistake, for example, to pit Abdul Aleem of the Aligarh Muslim University against Haji Mohammad Shakoor in the Jaunpur-Gorakhpur constituency. Similarly, Aftab Ali was too weak a candidate to be pitted against Jamshed Ali Khan, the Nawab of Baghpat and a recent convert to the Muslim League creed. A more formidable rival could have performed better at the hustings.

In any case, asking people to sit on judgement on the Partition plan, which had already been thrashed out during the prolonged confabulations at the viceregal lodge, was an act of deception, a monumental fraud. The die was cast, more so after the 1946 elections which were held under a restricted franchise but were treated as the final verdict of the people. The predictable collapse of the interim government and the fire of violence in Bihar and Bengal, which nobody tried to extinguish,[132] offered to every party an opportunity and an excuse

[132] Commenting on the massacre of August 1946 in Calcutta, Leonard Mosley remarked: 'A few weeks later, however, you would have found it difficult to believe that anyone (with the possible exception of Mahatma Gandhi) had taken any notice of them at all. Not the Hindus. Not the Muslims. Not the British'. Mosley, *The Last Days of the British Raj*, p. 40.

I believe one should attach some weight to Maulana Abul Kalam Azad's judgement that 'the people of India had not accepted Partition. In fact their heart and soul rebelled against the very idea. I have said that the Muslim League enjoyed

to hammer out the modalities of transferring power to two separate nations. Never before in South Asian history did so few decide the fate of so many. And rarely did so few ignore the sentiments of so many in the subcontinent. A distraught eye witness to the trauma of 1946–7 recalled on the eve of her departure from Rajshahi:

> Tears began to flow, I realized for the first time that the part of Bengal which had been my home was no longer my home. It was a foreign land. . . . The underlying feeling was that we were being driven from our own country. . . . We were angry with both Nehru and Jinnah for not handling the situation properly.[133]

Such impressions need to be reflected in our historical discourse. Only then will it become clear that, in the ultimate analysis, it does not matter whether, in the penultimate phase of the League crusade, Jinnah bargained for a separate nation or not. What mattered was his articulation of the two-nation idea and his successful mobilization of the community. The whims and personal idiosyncrasies of individuals do not give birth to new nations. The conjunction of forces and circumstances do. For many of us in the subcontinent, still confronted with and troubled by the bitter legacy of Pakistan, the critical and unresolved issue is how Jinnah and the League were able to secure the support of so many Muslims in so short a time.

Does the explanation lie in UP society and polity? In the evolution of ideas, reinforced by colonial policies, from the days of Syed Ahmad

---

the support of many Indian Muslims but there was a large section in the community which had always opposed the League. They were naturally deeply cut by the decision to divide the country. As for the Hindus and Sikhs, they were to a man opposed to partition. . . .' *India Wins Freedom*, p. 224. At the same time, it must be said that the Maulana, like everybody else, readily agreed to the Partition Plan. In the crucial meeting of the Congress Working Committee held on 2 June 1947, the Maulana, according to Ram Manohar Lohia, a special invitee to the meeting, 'sat in a chair throughout the two days of the meeting in a corner of the very small room which packed us all, puffed away at his endless cigarettes and spoke not a word'. According to Lohia, barring four persons—himself, Jayaprakash Narayan, Ghaffar Khan and Gandhi—'none spoke a word in opposition of Partition'. And though the Mahatma 'turned to Mr Nehru and Sardar Patel in mild complaint that they had not informed him of the scheme of Partition before committing themselves to it', he stopped well short of obstructing 'a leadership united for acceptance'. Quoted in Rajmohan Gandhi, *Patel: A Life* (Ahmedabad, 1992), p. 402.

133 H. Ghoshal, 'The Memsahib I could never be', Centre for South Asian Studies, Cambridge, p. 8.

Khan? In the unequal contest between Hindu and Muslim revitalization movements? In the conflict between the symbols of Kaaba and Kashi? In the self-perception of a minority community placed in a disadvantageous position in relation to the power structures? In the manipulation of religious and cultural symbols by competing elites? Jalal does not address herself to these possibilities. In any event, she does not think, though it is nowhere explicitly stated in her book, that in making Jinnah the 'sole spokesman' of 'Muslim India' the part played by the UP Muslims was of any consequence. She is inclined not to attach much importance to the role of Muslim landlords, the students and teachers of the university at Aligarh, described by Jinnah as the 'arsenal of Muslim India', a section of the Deobandi *ulama* and leading priests of the Barelwi school who had much following amongst the weavers, artisans, and other entrepreneurial groups in the qasbahs. Did Jinnah not have such groups in mind when he spoke of those . . .

> Who spread the light when there was darkness in the majority provinces. It is they who . . . suffered for you in the majority provinces, for your sake, for your benefit and for your advantage.[134]

These were comforting remarks, though one cannot help concluding with a not-so-comforting thought—never before in South Asian history did so few divide so many, so needlessly.

Today, the people and governments of India and Pakistan, tormented by the legacy of Partition, are confronted with the daunting challenge of neutralizing the effects of that division. The ability of all concerned to do so may serve the cause of peace and progress in the subcontinent.

> The fire of the liver, the tumult of the eye, burning of the heart,
> There is no effect on any of them of (this) cure for separation.
> Whence came that darling of a morning breeze, whither has it gone?
> The lamp beside the road has still no knowledge of it;
> In the heaviness of night there has still come no lessening.
> The hour of the deliverance of eye and heart has not arrived.
> Come, come on, for that goal has still not arrived.[135]

It is worth striving to achieve that elusive 'goal' defined by Faiz Ahmad Faiz and a generation of creative writers, poets and painters.

[134] Pirzada (ed.), *Foundations of Pakistan*, p. 224.
[135] Kiernan (ed.), *Poems by Faiz*, vol. 2, p. 127.

Chapter One

An Extract from the Presidential Address of M.A. Jinnah—Lahore, March 1940*

You remember that one of the tasks, which was imposed on us and which is far from completed yet, was to organize Muslim Leagues all over India. We have made enormous progress during the last 15 months in this direction. I am glad to inform you that we have established Provincial Leagues in every Province. The next point is that in every by-election to the Legislative Assemblies we had to fight with powerful opponents. I congratulate the Musalmans for having shown enormous grit and spirit throughout our trials. There was not a single by-election in which our opponents won against Muslim League candidates. In the last election to the U.P. Council, that is the Upper Chamber, the Muslim League's success was cent per cent. I do not want to weary you with details of what we have been able to do in the way of forging ahead in the direction of organizing the Muslim League. But I may tell you that it is going up by leaps and bounds.

Next, you may remember that we appointed a committee of ladies at the Patna Session. It is of very great importance to us, because I believe that it is absolutely essential for us to give every opportunity to our women to participate in our struggle of life and death. Women can do a great deal within their homes even under *purdah*. We appointed this committee with a view to enable them to participate in the work of the League. The objects of this central committee were (1) to organize provincial and district Muslim Leagues; (2) to enlist a larger number of women to the membership of the Muslim League; (3) to carry on an intensive propaganda amongst Muslim women throughout India in order to create in them a sense of a greater political

* S. Pirzada (ed.), *Foundations of Pakistan*, vol. 2.

consciousness—because if political consciousness is awakened amongst our women, remember, your children will not have much to worry about; (4) to advise and guide them in all such matters as mainly rest on them for the uplift of Muslim society. This Central Committee, I am glad to say, started its work seriously and earnestly. It has done a great deal of useful work. I have no doubt that when we come to deal with their report of work done, we shall really feel grateful to them for all the services that they have rendered to the Muslim League.

We had many difficulties to face from January 1939 right up to the declaration of war. We had to face the Vidya Mandir in Nagpur. We had to face the Wardha Scheme all over India. We had to face ill-treatment and oppression of Muslims in the Congress-governed provinces. We had to face the treatment meted out to Muslims in some of the Indian States, such as Jaipur and Bhavnagar. We had to face a vital issue that arose in that little State of Rajkot. Rajkot was the acid test made by the Congress, which would have affected one-third of India. Thus the Muslim League had all along to face various issues from January 1939 up to the time of the declaration of war. Before the war was declared, the greatest danger to the Muslims of India was the possible inauguration of a federal scheme in the Central Government. We know what machinations were going on. But the Muslim League was stoutly resisting them in every direction. We felt that we could never accept the dangerous scheme of the Central Federal Government embodied in the Government of India Act, 1935. I am sure that we have made no small contribution towards persuading the British Government to abandon the scheme of the Central Federal Government. In creating that mind in the British Government, the Muslim League, I have no doubt, played no small part. You know that the British people are a very obdurate people. They are also very conservative; and although they are very clear, they are slow in understanding. After the war was declared, the Viceroy naturally wanted help from the Muslim League. It was only then that he realized that the Muslim League was a power. For it will be remembered that up to the time of the declaration of war, the Viceroy never thought of me, but of Gandhi and Gandhi alone. I have been the leader of an important party in the Legislature for a considerable time, larger than the one I have the honour to lead at present, the Muslim League Party in the Central Legislature. Yet, the Viceroy never thought of me before. Therefore, when I got this invitation from the Viceroy along with Mr Gandhi, I wondered within myself why I was so suddenly promoted, and then I concluded that the answer was the 'All-India Muslim League', whose President I happen to be. I believe that was the worst shock that the Congress High Command received, because it challenged their sole authority to speak on behalf of India. And it is quite clear from the attitude of Mr Gandhi and the High Command that they have not yet recovered from that shock. My point is that I want you to realize the value, the importance, the significance of organizing ourselves, I will not say anything more on the subject.

But a great deal yet remains to be done. I am sure from what I can see and hear that Muslim India is now conscious, is now awake, and the Muslim League has by now grown into such a strong institution that it cannot be destroyed by anybody, whoever he may happen to be. Men may come and men may go, but the League will live for ever.

Now, coming to the period after the declaration of war, our position was that we were between the devil and the deep sea. But I do not think that the devil or the deep sea is going to get away with it. Anyhow our position is this: We stand unequivocally for the freedom of India. But it must be the freedom of all India, and not the freedom of one section or, worse still, of the Congress caucus, and slavery for Musalmans and other minorities.

BUILDING UP SELF-RELIANCE

Situated in India as we are, we naturally have our past experiences, and particularly from the experiences of the past two and a half years of Provincial Constitution in the Congress-governed provinces, we have learnt many lessons. We are now, therefore, very apprehensive and can trust nobody. I think it is a wise rule for everyone not to trust anybody too much. Sometimes we are led to trust people; but when we find in actual experience that our trust has been betrayed, surely that ought to be sufficient lesson for any man not to continue his trust in those who have betrayed him.

Ladies and gentlemen, we never thought that the Congress High Command would have acted in the manner in which they actually did in the Congress-governed provinces. I never dreamt that they would ever come down so low as that. I never could believe that there would be a gentlemen's agreement between the Congress and the Government to such an extent that, although we cried ourselves hoarse, week in and out, the Governors would be supine and the Governor-General helpless. We reminded them of their special responsibilities to us and to other minorities, and the solemn pledges they had given to us. But all that had become a dead letter. Fortunately, Providence came to our help, and that gentlemen's agreement was broken to pieces, and the Congress, thank Heaven, went out of office. I think they are regretting their resignations very much. Their bluff was called. So far so good.

I, therefore, appeal to you, in all the seriousness that I can command, to organize yourselves in such a way that you may depend upon none except your own inherent strength. That is your only safeguard and the best safeguard. Depend upon yourselves. This does not mean that we should have ill-will or malice towards others. In order to safeguard your rights and interests, you must create that strength in yourselves with which you may be able to defend yourselves. That is all that I want to urge.

Issues for the Future Constitution

Now, what is our position with regard to the future Constitution? It is that, as soon as circumstances permit, or immediately after the war at the latest, the whole problem of India's future Constitution must be examined *de novo*, and the Act of 1935 must go once for all. We do not believe in asking the British Government to make declarations. These declarations are really of no use. You cannot possibly succeed in getting the British Government out of this country by asking them to make declarations. However, the Congress asked the Viceroy to make a declaration. The Viceroy said, 'I have made the declaration.' The Congress said, 'No no, we want another kind of declaration. You must declare, now and at once, that India is free and independent, with the right to frame its own Constitution, through a Constituent Assembly to be elected on the basis of adult franchise, or as low a franchise as possible. This Assembly will of course satisfy the minorities' legitimate interests.' Mr Gandhi says that if the minorities are not satisfied, then he is willing that some tribunal of the highest character, and most impartial, should decide the dispute. Now apart from the impracticable character of this proposal, and quite apart from the fact that it is historically and constitutionally absurd to ask the ruling power to abdicate in favour of a Constituent Assembly—apart from all that, suppose we do not agree as to the franchise according to which the Central Assembly is to be elected, or suppose we, the solid body of

Muslim representatives, do not agree with the non-Muslim majority in the Constituent Assembly, what will happen? It is said that we have no right to disagree with regard to anything that this Assembly may do in framing a National Constitution of this huge Subcontinent, except in those matters which may be germane to the safeguards of the minorities. So we are given the privilege to disagree only with regard to what may strictly be called safeguards of the rights and interests of minorities. We are also given the privilege to send our own representatives by separate electorates. Now, this proposal is based on the assumption that as soon as the Constitution comes into operation the British hand will disappear. Otherwise there will be no meaning in it. Of course, Mr Gandhi says that the Constitution will decide whether the British will disappear, and if so to what extent. In other words, his proposal comes to this: first give me the declaration that we are a free and independent nation, then I will decide what I should give you back.

Does Mr Gandhi really want the complete independence of India when he talks like this? But whether the British disappear or not, it follows that extensive powers must be transferred to the people. In the event of there being a disagreement between the majority of the Constituent Assembly and the Musalmans, in the first instance, who will appoint the tribunal? And suppose an agreed tribunal is possible, and the award is made and the decision given, who will, may I know, be there to see that this award is implemented or carried out in accordance with the terms of that award? And who will see that it is honoured in practice, because, we are told, the British will have parted with their power, mainly or completely? Then what will be the sanction behind the award which will enforce it? We come back to the same answer; the Hindu majority would do it—and will it be with the help of the British bayonet or Mr Gandhi's 'Ahimsa'? Can we trust them any more? Besides, ladies and gentlemen, can you imagine that a question of this character, of a social contract upon which the future Constitution of India would be based, affecting 90 millions of Musalmans, can be decided by means of a judicial tribunal? Still, that is the proposal of the Congress.

Before I deal with what Mr Gandhi said a few days ago, I shall deal with the pronouncements of some of the other Congress leaders—each one speaking with a different voice. Mr Rajagopalachari, the ex-Prime Minister of Madras, says that the only panacea for Hindu-Muslim unity is the joint electorate. That is his prescription, as one of the great doctors of the Congress Organization. Babu Rajendra Prasad, on the other hand, only a few days ago said, 'Oh, what more do the Musalmans want?' I will read you his words. Referring to the minority question, he says:

'If Britain would concede our right of self-determination surely all these differences would disappear.'

How will our differences disappear? He does not explain or enlighten us about it.

'But so long as Britain remains and holds power, the differences would continue to exist. The Congress has made it clear that the future Constitution would be framed not by the Congress alone, but also by representatives of all political parties and religious groups. The Congress has gone further and declared that the minorities can have their representatives elected for this purpose by separate electorates, though the Congress regards separate electorates as an evil. It will be representative of all the peoples of this country, irrespective of their religion and political affiliations, who will be deciding the future Constitution of India, and not this or that party. What better guarantees can the minorities have?' So, according to Babu Rajendra Prasad, the moment we enter the Assembly we shall shed all our political affiliations, and religions and everything else. This is what Babu Rajendra Prasad said as late as the 18th of March, 1940.

And this now is what Mr Gandhi said on the 20th of March, 1940. He says:

'To me, Hindus, Muslims, Parsis, Harijans are all alike. I cannot be frivolous—'but I think he is frivolous'—I cannot be frivolous when I talk of Quaid-i-Azam Jinnah. He is my brother.'

The only difference is this, that brother Gandhi has three votes and I have only one vote!

'I would be happy indeed if he could keep me in his pocket.'

I do not know really what to say to this latest offer of his.

'There was a time when I could say that there was no Muslim whose confidence I did not enjoy. It is my misfortune that it is not so to-day.'

Why has he lost the confidence of the Muslim to-day? May I ask, ladies and gentlemen?

'I do not read all that appears in the Urdu Press, but perhaps I get a lot of abuse there, I am not sorry for it. I still believe that without a Hindu-Muslim settlement there can be no *Swaraj*.'

Mr Gandhi has been saying this now for the last 20 years.

'You will perhaps ask in that case why do I talk of a fight. I do so because it is to be a fight for a Constituent Assembly.'

He is fighting the British. But may I point out to Mr Gandhi and the Congress that they are fighting for a Constituent Assembly which the Muslims say they cannot accept—which, the Muslims say, means three to one, about which the Musalmans say that they will never be able, in that way, by the counting of heads, to come to any agreement which will be a real agreement from the heart, which will enable all to work as friends; and, therefore, this idea of a Constituent Assembly is objectionable, apart from other objections. But he is fighting for the Constituent Assembly, not fighting the Musalmans at all.

He says, 'I do so because it is to be a fight for a Constituent Assembly. If Muslims who come to the Constituent Assembly', mark the words, 'who come to the Constituent Assembly through Muslims votes'—he is first forcing us to come to that Assembly, and then say—"declare that there is nothing common between Hindus and Muslims, then alone would I give up all hope; but even then I would agree with them because they read the Quran and I have also studied something of that holy book.'

So he wants the Constituent Assembly for the purpose of ascertaining the views of the Musalmans; and if they do not agree, then he will give up all hopes, but even then he will agree with us. Well, I ask you, ladies and gentlemen, is this the way to show any real, genuine desire—if there existed any—to come to a settlement with the Musalmans? Why does not Mr Gandhi agree—and I have suggested this to him more than once, and I repeat it again from this platform—why does not Mr Gandhi honestly now acknowledge that the Congress is a Hindu Congress, that he does not represent anybody except the solid body of a Hindu people? Why should not Mr Gandhi be proud to say, 'I am a Hindu, the Congress has solid Hindu backing'? I am not ashamed of saying that I am a Musalman. I am right I hope, and I think even a blind man must have been convinced by now, that the Muslim League has the solid backing of the Musalmans of India. Why then all this camouflage? Why all these machinations? Why all these methods to coerce the British to overthrow the Musalmans? Why this declaration of non-co-operation? Why this threat of civil disobedience? And why fight for a Constituent Assembly for the sake of ascertaining whether the Musalmans agree or they do not agree? Why not come as a Hindu leader proudly representing your people and let me meet you proudly representing the Musalmans. This is all that I have to say so far as the Congress is concerned.

NEGOTIATIONS WITH THE BRITISH

So far as the British Government is concerned, our negotiations are not concluded yet, as you know. We had asked for assurances on several points. At any rate, we have made some advance with regard to one point, and that is this. You remember, our demand was that the entire problem of the future Constitution of India should be examined *de novo*, apart from the Government of India Act of 1935. To that, the Viceroy's reply, with the authority of His Majesty's Government, was—I had better quote that, I will not put it in my own words. This is the reply that was sent to us on the 23rd of December:

'My answer to your first question is that the declaration I made with the approval of His Majesty's Government on October the 13th last does not exclude—'Mark the words'—does not exclude examination of any part either of the Act of 1935 or of the policy and plans on which it is based.'

As regards other matters, we are still negotiating and the most important are: that no declaration should be made by His Majesty's Government with regard to the future Constitution of India without our approval and consent, and that no settlement of any question should be made with any party behind our back, unless our approval and consent is given to it. Well, ladies and gentlemen, whether the British Government in their wisdom agree to give us that assurance or not, I trust that they will still see that it is a fair and just demand, when we say that we cannot leave the future fate and the destiny of 90 millions of people in the hands of any other judge. We and we alone wish to be the final arbiter. Surely that is a just demand. We do not want that the British Government should thrust upon the Musalmans a Constitution which they do not approve of, and to which they do not agree. Therefore, the British Government will be well advised to give that assurance, and give the Musalmans complete peace and confidence in this matter, and win their friendship. But whether they do that or not—after all, as I told you before, we must depend on our own inherent strength—I make it plain from this platform that if any declaration is made, if any interim settlement is made without our approval and without our consent, the Musalmans of India will resist it. And no mistake should be made on that score.

Then the next point was with regard to Palestine. We are told that endeavours, earnest endeavours, are being made to meet the reasonable, national demands of the Arabs. Well, we cannot be satisfied by earnest endeavours, sincere endeavours, best endeavours. We want that the British Government should in fact and actually meet the demands of the Arabs in Palestine.

Then the point was with regard to sending troops outside. Here there is some misunderstanding. But anyhow we have made our position clear, that we never intended, and, in fact, the language does not justify it, if there is any misapprehension or apprehension that Indian troops should not be used to the fullest in the defence of our own country. What we wanted the British Government to give us assurance of was that Indian troops should not be sent against any Muslim country or any Muslim Power. Let us hope that we may yet be able to get the British Government to clarify the position further.

This, then, is the position with regard to the British Government. The last meeting of the Working Committee had asked the Viceroy to reconsider his letter of the 23rd of December, having regard to what has been explained to him in pursuance of the resolution of the Working Committee, dated the 3rd of February, and we are informed that the matter is receiving his careful consideration.

THE HINDU–MUSLIM SITUATION

Ladies and gentlemen, that is where we stand after the war and up to the 3rd of February. As far as our internal position is concerned, we have also been examining it; and, you know, there are several schemes which have been sent by various well-informed constitutionalists and others who take interest in the problem of India's future Constitution, and we have also appointed a subcommittee to examine the details of the schemes that have come in so far. But one thing is quite clear. It has always been taken for granted mistakenly that the Musalmans are a minority, and of course we have got used to it for such a long time that these settled notions sometimes are very difficult to remove. The Musalmans are not a minority. The Musalmans are a nation by any definition.

The British and particularly the Congress proceed on the basis.

'Well, you are a minority after all, what do you want? What else do the minorities want? Just as Babu Rajendra Prasad said. But surely the Musalmans are not a minority.' We find that even according to the British map of India, we occupy large parts of this country where the Musalmans are in a majority—such as Bengal, Punjab, NWFP, Sind and Baluchistan.

Now the question is, what is the best solution of this problem between the Hindus and the Musalmans? We have been considering—and as I have already said, a committee has been appointed to consider the various proposals. But whatever the final scheme for a Constitution, I will present to you my views and I will just read to you, in confirmation of what I am going to put before you, a letter from Lala Lajpat Rai to Mr C.R. Das. It was written I believe, about 12 or 15 years ago, and the letter has been produced in a book by one Indra Prakash, recently published, and that is how this letter has come to light. This is what Lala Lajpat Rai, a very astute politician and a staunch Hindu Mahasabhite said—but before I read his letter, it is plain that you cannot get away from being a Hindu if you are Hindu. The word 'Nationalist' has now become the play of conjurers in politics. This is what he says:

There is one point more which has been troubling me very much of late and one which I want you to think (about) carefully, and that is the question of Hindu–Mohammedan unity. I have devoted most of my time during the last six months to the study of Muslim history and Muslim law, and I am inclined to think it is neither possible nor practicable. Assuming and admitting the sincerity of Mohammedan leaders in the non-co-operation movement, I think their religion provides an effective bar to anything of the kind.

You remember the conversation I reported to you in Calcutta which I had with Hakim Ajmal Khan and Dr. Kitchlew. There is no finer Mohammedan in Hindustan than Hakim Ajmal Khan, but can any Muslim leader override the Quran? I can only hope that my reading of Islamic law is incorrect.

I think his reading is quite incorrect.

And nothing would relieve me more than to be convinced that it is so. But if it is right, then it comes to this, that although we can unite against the British, we cannot do so to rule Hindustan on British lines. We cannot do so to rule Hindustan on democratic lines.

Ladies and gentlemen, when Lala Lajpat Rai said that we cannot rule this country on democratic lines it was all right, but when I had the temerity to speak the same truth about 18 months ago, there was a shower of attacks and criticism. But Lala Lajpat Rai said 15 years ago that we cannot do so, *viz.* rule Hindustan on democratic lines. What is the remedy? The remedy according to the Congress is to keep us in the minority and under the majority rule. Lala Lajpat Rai proceeds further:

What is then the remedy? I am not afraid of the seven crores of Musalmans. But I think the seven crores in Hindustan plus the armed hosts of Afghanistan, Central Asia, Arabia, Mesopotamia and Turkey will be irresistible.

I do honestly and sincerely believe in the necessity or desirability of Hindu–Muslim unity. I am also fully prepared to trust the Muslim leaders. But what about the injunctions of the Quran and the Hadis? The leaders cannot override them. Are we then doomed? I hope that your learned mind and wise head will find some way out of this difficulty.

Now, ladies and gentlemen, that is merely a letter written by one great Hindu leader to another great Hindu leader 15 years ago. Now, I should like to put before you my views on the subject, as it strikes me, taking everything into consideration at the present moment. The British Government and Parliament, and more so the British nation, have been, for many decades past, brought up and nurtured with settled notions about India's future, based on developments in their own country which have built up the British constitution, functioning now through the Houses of Parliament and the Cabinet system. Their concept of party-government, functioning on political planes, has become the ideal with them as the best form of government for every country; and the one-sided and powerful propaganda which naturally appeals to the British has led them into a serious blunder, in producing a constitution envisaged in the Government of India Act of 1935. We find that the leading statesmen of Great Britain, saturated with these notions, have in their pronouncements seriously asserted and expressed a hope that the passage of time will harmonize the inconsistent elements in India.

A leading journal like the London *Times*, commenting on the Government of India Act of 1935, wrote:

Undoubtedly the difference between the Hindus and Muslims is not of religion in the strict sense of the word, but also of law and culture, that they may be said indeed to represent two entirely distinct and separate civilizations. However, in the course of time the superstitions will die out, and India will be moulded into a single nation.

So, according to the London *Times*, the only difficulties are superstitions. These fundamental and deep-rooted differences, spiritual, economic, cultural, social and political, have been euphemized as mere 'superstitions'. But surely, it is a flagrant disregard of the past history of the subcontinent of India, as well as the fundamental Islamic conception of society, *vis-a-vis* that of Hinduism, to characterize them as mere 'superstitions'. Notwithstanding a thousand years of close contact, nationalities which are as divergent today as ever cannot at any time be expected to transform themselves into a one nation merely by means of subjecting them to a democratic constitution and holding them forcibly together by unnatural and artificial methods of British Parliamentary Statutes. What the unitary Government of India for 150 years had failed to achieve cannot be realized by the imposition of a central federal government. It is inconceivable that the fiat or the writ of a government so constituted can ever command a willing and loyal obedience throughout the Subcontinent from various nationalities except by means of armed force behind it.

Autonomous National States

The problem in India is not of an intercommunal but manifestly of an international character, and it must be treated as such. So long as this basic and fundamental truth is not realized, any constitution that may be built will result in disaster and will prove destructive and harmful not only to the Musalmans, but also to the British and Hindus. If the British Government are really in earnest and sincere to secure the peace and happiness of the people of this Subcontinent, the only course open to us all is to allow the major nations separate homelands, by dividing India into 'autonomous national States'. There is no reason why these States should be antagonistic to each other. On the other hand, the rivalry and the natural desire and efforts on the part of the one (community) to dominate the social order and establish political supremacy over the other in the government of the country will disappear. It will lead more towards natural goodwill by international pacts between them (the states) and they can live in complete harmony with their neighbours. This will lead further to a friendly settlement all the more easily with regard to minorities by reciprocal arrangements and adjustments between the Muslim India and the Hindu India, which will far more adequately and effectively safeguard the rights and interests of Muslims and various other minorities.

It is extremely difficult to appreciate why our Hindu friends fail to understand the real nature of Islam and Hinduism. They are not religions in the strict sense of the word, but are, in fact, different and distinct social orders. It is a dream that the Hindus and Muslims can ever evolve a common nationality, and this misconception of one Indian nation has gone far beyond the limits, and is the cause of most of our troubles, and will lead India to destruction, if we fail to revise our notions in time. The Hindus and the Muslims belong to two different religious philosophies, social customs, and literature. They neither intermarry, nor interdine together, and indeed they belong to two different civilizations which are based mainly on conflicting ideas and conceptions. Their aspects on life and of life are different. It is quite clear that Hindus and Musalmans derive their inspiration from different sources of history. They have different epics, their heroes are different, and they have different episodes. Very often the hero of one is a foe of the other, and likewise, their victories and defeats overlap. To yoke together two such nations under a single State, one as a numerical minority and the other as a majority, must lead to growing discontent and the final destruction of any fabric that may be so built up for the government of such a State.

History has presented to us many examples, such as the Union of Great Britain and Ireland, of Czechoslovakia and Poland. History has also shown to us many geographical tracts, much smaller than the Subcontinent of India, which otherwise might have been called one country, but which have been divided into as many states as there are nations inhabiting them. The Balkan Peninsula comprises as many as seven or eight sovereign States. Likewise, the Portuguese and the Spanish stand divided in the Iberian Peninsula. Whereas under the plea of the unity of India and one nation, which does not exist, it is sought to pursue here the line of one Central Government, when we know that the history of the last 12 hundred years has failed to achieve unity and has witnessed, during the ages, India always divided into Hindu India and Muslim India. The present artificial unity of India dates back only to the British conquest and is maintained by the British bayonet; but the termination of the British regime, which is implicit in the recent declaration of His Majesty's Government, will be the herald of an entire break up, with worse disaster than has ever taken place during the last one thousand years under the Muslims. Surely that is not the legacy which Britain would bequeath to India after 150 years of her rule, nor would the Hindu and Muslim India risk such a sure catastrophe.

Muslim India cannot accept any Constitution which must necessarily result in a Hindu majority Government. Hindus and Muslims brought together under a democratic system forced upon the minorities can only mean Hindu Raj. Democracy of the kind with which the Congress High Command is enamoured would mean the complete destruction of what is most precious in Islam. We have had ample experience of the working of the provincial Constitutions during the last two and a half years; and any repetition of such a Government must lead to civil war and raising private armies, as recommended by Mr Gandhi to Hindus of Sukkur, when he said that they must defend themselves violently or non-violently, blow for blow; and if they could not, they must emigrate.

Musalmans are not a minority, as it is commonly known and understood. One has only got to look round. Even today, according to the British map of India, 4 out of 11 provinces, where the Muslims dominate more or less, are functioning notwithstanding the decision of the Hindu Congress High Command to non-co-operate and prepare for civil disobedience. Musalmans are a nation according to any definition of a nation, and they must have their homelands, their territory and their State. We wish to live in peace and harmony with our neighbours as a free and independent people. We wish our people to develop to the fullest our spiritual, cultural, economic, social and political life in a way that we think best, and in consonance with our own ideals and according to the genius of our people. Honesty demands—and the vital interests of millions of our people impose a sacred duty upon us to find—an honourable and peaceful solution which would be just and fair to all. But at the same time, we cannot be moved or diverted from our purpose and objective by threats or intimidations. We must be prepared to face all difficulties and consequences, make all the sacrifices that may be required of us to achieve the goal we have set in front of us.

CONCLUSION

Ladies and gentlemen, that is the task before us. I fear I have gone beyond my time limit. There are many things that I should like to tell you; but I have already published a little pamphlet containing most of the things that I have been saying, and I think you can easily get that publication, both in English and in Urdu, from the League Office. It might give you a clearer idea of our aims. It contains very important resolutions of the Muslim League and various other statements.

Anyhow, I have placed before you the task that lies ahead of us. Do you realize how big and stupendous it is? Do you realize that you cannot get freedom or independence by mere arguments? I should appeal to the intelligentsia. The intelligentsia in all countries in the world have been the pioneers of any movements for freedom. What does the Muslim intelligentsia propose to do? I may tell you that unless you get this into your blood, unless you are prepared to take off your coats and are willing to sacrifice all that you can, and work selflessly, earnestly and sincerely for your people, you will never realize your aim. Friends, I therefore want you to make up your minds definitely, and then think of devices, and organize your people, strengthen your organization and consolidate the Musalmans all over India. I think that the masses are wide awake. They only want your guidance and lead. Come forward as servants of Islam, organize the people economically, socially, educationally and politically, and I am sure that you will be a power that will be accepted by everybody.[1]

[1] *India's Problem of her Future Constitution*, with Preface by M.A. Jinnah, pp. 1–15.

Chapter Two

An Extract from Presidential Address of Abul Kalam Azad—Ramgarh, December 1940*

THE MINORITIES AND THE POLITICAL FUTURE OF INDIA

I have briefly placed before you the real question of the day. That is the vital question for us, all else are subsidiary to it. It was in relation to that question that the Congress put forward its invitation to the British Government in September last, and made a clear and simple demand, to which no community or group could possibly object. It was not in our remotest thoughts that the communal question could be raised in this connection. We realize that there are some groups in the country which cannot keep step with the Congress in the political struggle or go as far as the Congress is prepared to go; we know that some do not agree with the method of direct action which the great majority of political India has adopted. But so far as the right of the Indian people to independence is concerned and the full admission of India's birthright to freedom, an awakened and impatient India has passed far beyond the early stages, and none dare oppose our demand. Even those classes who cling to their special interests and fear change lest this might affect them adversely, are rendered helpless by the spirit of the times. They have to admit and to agree to the goal we have set before us.

A time of crisis is a testing time for all of us, and so the great problem of the day has tested us and exposed many an aspect of our present-day politics. It has laid bare also the reality that lies behind the communal problem. Repeated attempts were made, in England and India, to mix up the communal question with the vital political

* A.M. Zaidi & S.G. Zaidi (eds.), *The Encyclopedia of the Indian National Congress*, vol. 12, pp. 355–6.

question of the day, and thus to confuse the real issue. Again and again, it was sought to convince the world that the problem of the minorities barred the way to a proper solution of India's political problem.

For a hundred and fifty years British imperialism has pursued the policy of divide and rule, and by emphasising internal differences, sought to use various groups for the consolidation of its own power. That was the inevitable result of India's political subjection, and it is folly for us to complain and grow bitter. A foreign government can never encourage internal unity in the subject country, for disunity is the surest guarantee for the continuance of its own domination. But when we were told, and the world was asked to believe, that British imperialism had ended, and the long chapter of Indian history dominated by it had closed, was it unreasonable for us to expect that British statesman would at last give up this evil inheritance and not exploit the communal situation for political ends? But the time for this is yet distant; we may not cling to such vain hopes. So the last five months with their succession of events have established. Imperialism, in spite of all assurances to the contrary, still flourishes; it has yet to be ended.

But whatever the roots of our problems might be, it is obvious that India, like other countries, has her internal problems. Of these, the communal problem is an important one. We do not and cannot expect the British Government to deny its existence. The communal problem is undoubtedly with us, and if we want to go ahead, we must need take it into account. Every step that we take by ignoring it will be a wrong step. The problem is there; to admit its existence, however, does not mean that it should be used as a weapon against India's national freedom. British Imperialism has always exploited it to this end. If Britain desires to end her imperialistic methods in India and close that dismal chapter of history, then the first signs of this change must naturally appear in her treatment of the communal problem.

What is the Congress position in regard to this problem? It has been the claim of the Congress, from its earliest beginnings, that it considers India as a nation and takes every step in the interest of the nation as a whole. This entitles the world to examine this claim strictly and the Congress must establish the truth of its assertion. I wish to examine afresh this question from this point of view.

There can be only three aspects of the communal problem: its existence, its importance, and the method of its solution.

The entire history of the Congress demonstrates that it has always acknowledged the existence of the problem. It has never tried to minimise its importance. In dealing with this problem, it followed a policy which was the most suitable under the circumstances. It is difficult to conceive of a different or better course of action. If, however, a better course could be suggested, the Congress was always, and is today, eager to welcome it.

We could attach no greater importance to it, than to make it the first condition for the attainment of our national goal. The Congress has always held this belief; no one can challenge this fact. It has always held to two basic principles in this connection, and every step was taken deliberately with these in view.

(i) Whatever constitution is adopted for India, there must be the fullest guarantee in it for the rights and interests of minorities.

(ii) The minorities should judge for themselves what safeguards are necessary for the protection of their rights and interests. The majority should not decide this. Therefore the decision in this respect must depend upon the consent of the minorities and not on a majority vote.

The question of the minorities is not a special Indian problem. It has existed in other parts of the world. I venture to address the world from this platform, and to enquire whether any juster and more equitable course of action can be adopted in this connection, than the one suggested above? If so, what is it? Is there any thing lacking in this approach, which necessitates that the Congress be reminded of its duty? The Congress has always been ready to consider any failure in the discharge of its duty. It is so prepared today. I have been in the Congress for the last nineteen years. During the whole of this period there is not a single important decision of the Congress in the shaping of which I have not had the honour to participate. I assert that during these last nineteen years, not for a single day did the Congress think of solving this problem in any way other than the way I have stated above. This was not a mere assertion of the Congress, but its determined and decided course of action. Many a time during the last fifteen years, this policy was subjected to the severest tests, but it stood firm as a rock.

The manner in which the Congress has dealt with this problem today in connection with the Constituent Assembly, throws a flood of light on these two principles and clarifies them. The recognised minorities have a right, if they so please, to choose their representatives by their votes. Their representatives will not have to rely upon the votes of any other community except their own. So far as the question of the rights and the interests of the minorities is concerned, the decision will not depend upon the majority of the votes in the Constituent Assembly. It will be subject to the consent of the minority. If unanimity is not achieved on any question, then an impartial tribunal, to which the minorities have also consented, will decide the matter. This last proviso is merely in the nature of a provision for a possible contingency, and is most unlikely to be required. If a more practical proposal is made, there can be no objection to it.

When these principles are accepted and acted upon by the Congress, what is it that obliges British statesmen to remind us so often of the problem of the minorities, and to make the world believe that this stands in the way of Indian freedom? If it is really so, why does not the British Government recognize clearly India's freedom and gives us an opportunity to solve this problem for ever by mutual agreement amongst ourselves?

Dissensions were sown and encouraged amongst us, and yet we are taunted because of them. We are told to put an end to our communal conflicts, but opportunity to do so is denied us. Such is the position deliberately created to thwart us; such are the chains that bind. But no difficulties or constraints can deter us from taking the right steps with courage and fortitude. Our path is full of obstacles but we are determined to overcome them.

We have considered the problems of the minorities of India. But are the Muslims such a minority as to have the least doubt or fear about their future? A small minority may legitimately have fears and apprehensions, but can the Muslims allow themselves to be disturbed by them? I do not know how many of you are familiar with my writings, twenty-eight years ago, in the 'Al Hilal'. If there are any such here, I would request them to refresh their memories. Even then I gave expression to my conviction, and I repeat this today, that in the texture of Indian politics, nothing is further removed from the truth than to say that Indian Muslims occupy the position of a political minority. It is equally absurd for them to be apprehensive about their rights and interests in a democratic India. This fundamental mistake has opened the door to countless misunderstandings. False arguments were built up on wrong premises. This error, on the one hand, brought confusion into the minds of Musalmans about their own true position, and, on the other hand, it involved the world in misunderstandings, so that the picture of India could not be seen in right perspective.

If time had permitted, I would have told you in detail, how, during the last sixty years, this artificial and untrue picture of India was made, and whose hands traced it. In effect, this was the result of the same policy of divide and rule which took particular shape in the minds of British officialdom in India after the Congress launched the national movement. The object of this was to prepare the Musalmans for use against the new political awakening. In this plan, prominence was given to two points. First: that India was inhabited by two different communities, the Hindus and the Musalmans, and for this reason no demand could be made in the name of a united nation. Second: that numerically the Musalmans were far less than the Hindus, and because of this, the necessary consequence of the establishment of democratic institutions in India would be to establish the rule of the Hindu majority and to jeopardize the existence of the Muslims. I shall not go into any greater detail now. Should you, however, wish to know the early history of this matter, I would refer you to the time of Lord Dufferin, a former Viceroy of India, and Sir Auckland Colvin, a former Lieutenant Governor of the NWP, now the United Provinces.

Thus were sown the seeds of disunity by British Imperialism on Indian soil. The plant grew and was nurtured and spread its nettles, and even though fifty years have passed since then, the roots are still there.

Politically speaking, the word minority does not mean just a group that is numerically smaller and therefore entitled to special protection. It means a group that is so small in number and so lacking in other qualities that give strength, that it has no confidence in its own capacity to protect itself from the much larger group that surrounds it. It is not enough that the group should be relatively the smaller, but that it should be absolutely so small as to be incapable of protecting its interests. Thus this is not merely a question of numbers; other factors count also. If a country has two major groups numbering a million and two millions respectively, it does not necessarily follow that because one is half the other, therefore it must call itself politically a minority and consider itself weak.

If this is the right test, let us apply it to the position of the Muslims in India. You will see at a glance a vast concourse, spreading out all over the country; they stand erect, and to imagine that they exist helplessly as a 'minority' is to delude oneself.

The Muslim in India number between eighty and ninety millions. The same type of social or racial divisions, which affect other communities, do not divide them. The powerful bonds of Islamic brotherhood and equality have protected them to a large extent from the weakness that flows from social divisions. It is true that they number only one-fourth of the total population; but the question is not one of population ratio, but of the large numbers and the strength behind them. Can such a vast mass of humanity have any legitimate reason for apprehension that in a free and democratic India, it might be unable to protect its rights and interests?

These numbers are not confined to any particular area but spread out unevenly over different parts of the country. In four provinces out of eleven in India there is a Muslim majority, the other religious groups being minorities. If British Baluchistan is added, there are five provinces with Muslim majorities. Even if we are compelled at present to consider this question on a basis of religious groupings, the position of the Muslims is not that of a minority only. If they are in a minority in seven provinces, they are in a majority in five. This being so, there is absolutely no reason why they should be oppressed by the feeling of being a minority.

Whatever may be the details of the future constitution of India, we know that it will be an all-India federation which is, in the fullest sense, democratic, and every unit of which will have autonomy in regard to internal affairs. The federal centre will be concerned only with all-India matters of common concern, such as foreign relations, defence, customs, etc. Under these circumstances, can any one who has any conception of the actual working of a democratic constitution, allow himself to be led astray by this false issue of majority and minority. I cannot believe for an instant that there can be any room whatever for these misgivings in the picture of India's future. These apprehensions are arising because, in the words of a British statesman regarding Ireland, we are yet standing on the banks of the river and, though wishing to swim, are unwilling to enter the water. There is only one remedy; we should take the plunge fearlessly. No sooner is this done, we shall realize that all our apprehensions were without foundation.

A Basic Question for Indian Musalmans

It is now nearly thirty years since I first attempted to examine this question as an Indian Musalman. The majority of the Muslims then were keeping completely apart from the political struggle and they were influenced by the same mentality of aloofness and antagonism, which prevailed amongst them previously in 1888. This depressing atmosphere did not prevent me from giving my anxious thought to this matter, and I reached quickly a final conclusion, which influenced my belief and action. I saw India, with all her many burdens, marching ahead to her future destiny. We were fellow-passengers in this boat and we could not ignore its swift passage through the waters; and so it became necessary for us to come to a clear and final decision about our plan of action. How were we to do so? Not merely by skimming the surface of the problem but by going down to its roots, and then to consider our position. I did so and I realized that the solution of the whole problem depended on the answer to one question: Do we, Indian Musalmans, view the free India of the future with suspicion and distrust or with courage and confidence? If we view it with fear and suspicion, then undoubtedly we have to follow a different path. No present declaration, no promise for the future, no constitutional safeguards, can be a remedy for our doubts and fears. We are then forced to tolerate the existence of a third power.

This third power is already entrenched here and has no intention of withdrawing and, if we follow this path of fear, we must need look forward to its continuance. But if we are convinced that for us fear and doubt have no place, and that we must view the future with courage and confidence in ourselves, then our course of action becomes absolutely clear. We find ourselves in a new world, which is free from the dark shadows of doubt, vacillation, inaction and apathy, and where the light of faith and determination, action and enthusiasm never fails. The confusions of the times, the ups and downs that come our way, the difficulties that beset our thorny path, cannot change the direction of our steps. It becomes our bounden duty then to march with assured steps to India's national goal.

I arrived at this definite conclusion without the least hesitation, and every fibre of my being revolted against the former alternative. I could not bear the thought of it. I could not conceive it possible for a Musalman to tolerate this, unless he has rooted out the spirit of Islam from every corner of his being.

I started the 'Al Hilal' in 1912 and put this conclusion of mine before the Muslims of India. I need not remind you that my cries were not without effect. The period from 1912 to 1918 marked a new phase in the political awakening of the Muslims. Towards the end of 1920, on my release after four years of internment, I found that the political ideology of the Musalmans had broken through its old mould and was taking another shape. Twenty years have gone by and much has happened since then. The tide of events has ever risen higher, and fresh waves of thought have enveloped us. But this fact still remains unchanged, that the general opinion amongst the Muslims is opposed to going back.

That is certain; they are not prepared to retrace their steps. But again they are full of doubts about their future path. I am not going into the reasons for this; I shall only try to understand the effects. I would remind my co-religionists that today I stand exactly where I stood in 1912 when I addressed them on this issue. I have given thought to all those innumerable occurrences which have happened since then; my eyes have watched them, my mind has pondered over them. These events did not merely pass me by; I was in the midst of them, a participant, and I examined every circumstance with care. I cannot be false to what I have myself seen and observed; I cannot quarrel with my own convictions; I cannot stifle the voice of my conscience. I repeat today what I have said throughout this entire period, that the ninety millions of Muslims of India have no other right course of action than the one of which I invited them in 1912.

Some of my co-religionists, who paid heed to my call in 1912, are in disagreement with me today. I do not wish to find fault with them, but I would make appeal to their sincerity and sense of responsibility. We are dealing with the destinies of peoples and nations. We cannot come to right conclusions if we are swept away by the passions of the moment. We must base our judgements on the solid realities of life. It is true that the sky is overcast today and the outlook is dark. The Muslims have to come into the light of reality. Let them examine every aspect of the matter again today, and they will find no other course of action open to them.

The Musalmans and a United Nation

I am a Musalman and am proud of that fact. Islam's splendid traditions of thirteen hundred years are my inheritance. I am unwilling to lose even the smallest part of this inheritance. The teaching and history of Islam, its arts and letters and civilization are my wealth and my fortune. It is my duty to protect them.

As a Musalman I have a special interest in Islamic religion and culture and I cannot tolerate any interference with them. But in addition to these sentiments, I have others also which the realities and conditions of my life have forced upon me. The spirit of Islam does not come in the way of these sentiments; it guides and helps me forward. I am proud of being an Indian. I am a part of the indivisible unity that is Indian nationality. I am indispensable to this noble edifice and without me this splendid structure of India is incomplete. I am an essential element which has gone to build India. I can never surrender this claim.

It was India's historic destiny that many human races and cultures and religions should flow to her, finding a home in her hospitable soil, and that many a caravan should find rest here. Even before the dawn of history, these caravans trekked into India and wave after wave of new-comers followed. The vast and fertile land gave welcome to all and took them to her bosom. One of the last of these caravans, following the footsteps of its predecessors, was that of the followers of Islam. This came here and settled here for good. This led to a meeting of the culture-currents of two different races. Like Ganga and Jumna, they flowed for a while through separate courses, but nature's immutable law brought them together and joined them in a *sangam*. This fusion was a notable event in history. Since then, destiny, in her own hidden way, began to fashion a new India in place of the old. We brought our treasures with us, and India too was full of the riches of her own precious heritage. We gave our wealth to her and she unlocked the doors of her own treasures to us. We gave her, what she needed most, the most precious of gifts from Islam's treasury, the message of democracy and human equality.

Full eleven centuries have passed by since then. Islam has now as great a claim on the soil of India as Hinduism. If Hinduism has been the religion of the people here for several thousands of years, Islam also has been their religion for a thousand years. Just as a Hindu can say with pride that he is an Indian and follows Hinduism, so also we can say with equal pride that we are Indians and follow Islam. I shall enlarge this orbit still further. The Indian Christian is equally entitled to say with pride that he is an Indian and is following a religion of India, namely Christianity.

Eleven hundred years of common history have enriched India with our common achievements. Our languages, our poetry, our literature, our culture, our art, our dress, our manners and customs, the innumerable happenings of our daily life, everything bears the stamp of our joint endeavour. There is indeed no aspect of our life which has escaped this stamp. Our languages were different, but we grew to use a common language; our manners and customs were dissimilar, but they acted and reacted on each other and thus produced a new synthesis. Our old dress may be seen only in ancient pictures of bygone days; no one wears it today. This joint wealth is the heritage of our common nationality and we do not want to leave it and go back to the times when this joint life had not begun. If there are any Hindus amongst us who desire to bring back the Hindu life of a thousand years ago and more, they dream, and such dreams are vain fantasies. So also if there are any Muslims who wish to revive their past civilization and culture, which they brought a thousand years ago from Iran and Central Asia, they dream also and the sooner they wake up the better. These are unnatural fancies which cannot take root in the soil of reality. I am one of those who believe that revival may be a necessity in a religion but in social matters it is a denial of progress.

These thousand years of our joint life has moulded us into a common nationality. This cannot be done artificially. Nature does her fashioning through her hidden processes in the course of centuries. The cast has now been moulded and destiny has set her seal upon it. Whether we like it or not, we have now become an Indian nation, united and indivisible. No fantasy or artificial scheming to separate and divide can break this unity. We must accept the logic of fact and history and engage ourselves in the fashioning of our future destiny.

Conclusion

I shall not take any more of your time. My address must end now. But before I do so, permit me to remind you that our success depends upon three factors: unity, discipline and full confidence in Mahatma Gandhi's leadership. The glorious past record of our movement was due to his great leadership, and it is only under his leadership that we can look forward to a future of successful achievement.

The time of our trial is upon us. We have already focused the world's attention. Let us endeavour to prove ourselves worthy.

Chapter Three

Extracts from *The Collected Works of Mahatma Gandhi*

A Baffling Situation*

A question has been put to me:

Do you intend to start general civil disobedience although Quaid-e-Azam Jinnah has declared war against Hindus and has got the Muslim League to pass a resolution[1] favouring vivisection of India into two? If you do, what becomes of your formula that there is no swaraj without communal unity.

I admit that the step taken by the Muslim League at Lahore creates a baffling situation. But I do not regard it so baffling as to make civil disobedience an impossibility. Supposing that the Congress is reduced to a hopeless minority, it will still be open to it, indeed it may be its duty, to resort to civil disobedience. The struggle will not be against the majority, it will be against the foreign ruler. If the struggle succeeds, the fruits thereof will be reaped as well by the Congress as by the opposing majority. Let me, however, say in parenthesis that, until the conditions I have mentioned for starting civil disobedience are fulfilled, civil disobedience cannot be started in any case. In the present instance there is nothing to prevent the imperial rulers from declaring their will in unequivocal terms that henceforth India will govern herself according to her own will, not that of the rulers as has happened hitherto. Neither the Muslim League nor any other party can oppose such a declaration. For the Muslims will be entitled to dictate their own terms. Unless the rest of India wishes to engage in internal fratricide, the others will have to submit to Muslim dictation if the Muslims will resort to it. I know no non-violent method of compelling the obedience of eight crores of Muslims to the will of the rest of

* *The Collected Works of Mahatma Gandhi* (hereafter, *CWMG*). vol. 71.
[1] At its Lahore session in March.

India, however powerful a majority the rest may represent. The Muslims must have the same right of self-determination that the rest of India has. We are at present a joint family. Any member may claim a division.

Thus, so far as I am concerned, my proposition that there is no swaraj without communal unity holds as good today as when I first enunciated it in 1919.

But civil disobedience stands on a different footing. It is open even to one single person to offer it, if he feels the call. It will not be offered for the Congress alone or for any particular group. Whatever benefit accrues from it will belong to the whole of India. The injury, if there is any, will belong only to the civil disobedience party.

But I do not believe that Muslims, when it comes to a matter of actual decision, will ever want vivisection. Their good sense will prevent them. Their self-interest will deter them. Their religion will forbid the obvious suicide which the partition would mean. The 'two nations' theory is an untruth. The vast majority of Muslims of India are converts to Islam or are descendants of converts. They did not become a separate nation as soon as they became converts. A Bengali Muslim speaks the same tongue that a Bengali Hindu does, eats the same food, has the same amusements as his Hindu neighbour. They dress alike. I have often found it difficult to distinguish by outward sign between a Bengali Hindu and a Bengali Muslim. The same phenomenon is observable more or less in the South among the poor who constitute the masses of India. When I first met the late Sir Ali Imam I did not know that he was not a Hindu. His speech, his dress, his manners, his food were the same as of the majority of the Hindus in whose midst I found him. His name alone betrayed him. Not even that with Quaid-e-Azam Jinnah. For his name could be that of any Hindu. When I first met him, I did not know that he was a Muslim. I came to know his religion when I had his full name given to me. His nationality was written in his face and manner. The reader will be surprised to know that for days, if not months, I used to think of the late Vithalbhai Patel as a Muslim as he used to sport a beard and a Turkish cap. The Hindu law of inheritance governs many Muslim groups. Sir Mahommed Iqbal used to speak with pride of his Brahmanical descent. Iqbal and Kitchlew are names common to Hindus and Muslims. Hindus and Muslims of India are not two nations. Those whom God has made one, man will never be able to divide.

And is Islam such an exclusive religion as Quaid-e-Azam would have it? Is there nothing in common between Islam and Hinduism or any other religion? Or is Islam merely an enemy of Hinduism? Were the Ali Brothers and their associates wrong when they hugged Hindus as blood brothers and saw so much in common between the two? I am not now thinking of individual Hindus who may have disillusioned the Muslim friends. Quaid-e-Azam has, however, raised a fundamental issue. This is his thesis.[2]

It is extremely difficult to appreciate why our Hindu friends fail to understand the real nature of Islam and Hinduism. They are not religions in the strict sense of the word, but are, in fact, different and distinct social orders, and it is a dream that the Hindus and Muslims can ever evolve a common nationality. This misconception of one Indian nation has gone far beyond the limits and is the cause of most of our troubles and will lead India to destruction if we fail to revise our notions in time.

The Hindus and Muslims have two different religious philosophies, social customs, literatures. They neither intermarry, nor dine together, and indeed, they belong to two different civilizations which are based mainly on conflicting ideas and conceptions. Their aspects on life and of life are different. It is quite clear that Hindus and Mussalmans derive their inspiration from different sources of history. They have different epics, their heroes are different, and they have different episodes. Very often the hero of one is a foe of the other and, likewise, their victories and defeats overlap. To yoke together two such nations under a single State, one as a numerical minority and the other as majority, must lead to growing discontent and final destruction of any fabric that may be so built up for the government of such a State.

He does not say some Hindus are bad; he says Hindus as such have nothing in common with Muslims. I make bold to say that he and those who think like him are rendering no service to Islam; they are misinterpreting the message inherent in the very word Islam. I say this because I feel deeply hurt over what is now going on in the name of the Muslim League. I should be failing in my duty, if I did not warn the Muslims of India against the untruth that is being propagated amongst them. This warning is a duty because I have faithfully served them in their hour of need and because Hindu-Muslim unity has been and is my life's mission.

Sevagram, April 1, 1940
Harijan, 6–4–1940

[2] As expounded in his Presidential address at Lahore.

HINDU–MUSLIM TANGLE*

The partition proposal[3] has altered the face of the Hindu–Muslim problem. I have called it an untruth. There can be no compromise with it. At the same time I have said that, if the eight crores of Muslims desire it no power on earth can prevent it, notwithstanding opposition, violent or non-violent. It cannot come by honourable agreement.

That is the political aspect of it. But what about the religious and the moral which are greater than the political? For at the bottom of the cry for partition is the belief that Islam is an exclusive brotherhood, and anti-Hindu. Whether it is against other religions it is not stated. The newspaper cuttings in which partition is preached describe Hindus as practically untouchables. Nothing good can come out of Hindus or Hinduism. To live under Hindu rule is a sin. Even joint Hindu-Muslim rule is not to be thought of. The cuttings show that Hindus and Muslims are already at war with one another and that they must prepare for the final tussle.

Time was when Hindus thought that Muslims were the natural enemies of Hindus. But as is the case with Hinduism, ultimately it comes to terms with the enemy and makes friends with him. The process had not been completed. As if nemesis had overtaken Hinduism, the Muslim League started the same game and taught that there could be no blending of the two cultures. In this connection I have just read a booklet by Shri Atulanand Chakrabarti which shows that ever since the contact of Islam with Hinduism there has been an attempt on the part of the best minds of both to see the good points of each other, and to emphasize inherent similarities rather than seeming dissimilarities. The author has shown Islamic history in India in a favourable light. If he has stated the truth and nothing but the truth, it is a revealing booklet which all Hindus and Muslims may read with profit. He has secured a very favourable and reasoned preface from Sir Shafaat Ahmed Khan and several other Muslim testimonials. If the evidence collected there reflects the true evolution of Islam in India, then the partition propaganda is anti-Islamic.

* *CWMG*, vol. 72

[3] The All-India Muslim League meeting at Lahore passed a resolution on March 23, recording the view that no constitutional plan would be workable unless it was based on territorial readjustment and the creation of independent Muslim States.

Religion binds man to God and man to man. Does Islam bind Muslim only to Muslim and antagonize the Hindu? Was the message of the Prophet peace only for and between Muslims and war against Hindus or non-Muslims? Are eight crores of Muslims to be fed with this which I can only describe as poison? Those who are instilling this poison into the Muslim mind are rendering the greatest disservice to Islam. I know that it is not Islam. I have lived with and among Muslims not for one day but closely and almost uninterruptedly for twenty years. Not one Muslim taught me that Islam was an anti-Hindu religion.

Sevagram, April 29, 1940
Harijan, 4–5–1940

Chapter Four

An Extract from *The Discovery of India*

JAWAHARLAL NEHRU

Any division of India on a religious basis as between Hindus and Moslems, as envisaged by the Moslem League today, cannot separate the followers of these two principal religions of India, for they are spread out all over the country. Even if the areas in which each group is in a majority are separated, huge minorities belonging to the other group remain in each area. Thus instead of solving the minority problem, we create several in place of one. Other religious groups, like the Sikhs, are split up unfairly against their will and placed in two different States. In giving freedom to separate to one group, other groups, though in a minority, are denied that freedom and compelled to isolate themselves from the rest of India against their emphatic and deeply-felt wishes. If it is said that the majority (religious) must prevail in each area, so far as the question of separation is concerned, there is no particular reason why the majority view should not decide the question for the whole of India. Or that each tiny area should not decide its independent status for itself and thus create a vast number of small States—an incredible and fantastic development. Even so it cannot be done with any logic, for religious groups are intermingled and overlap in the population all over the country.

It is difficult enough to solve such problems by separation where nationalities are concerned. But where the test becomes a religious one it becomes impossible of solution on any logical basis. It is a reversion to some medieval conception which cannot be fitted into the modern world.

If the economic aspects of separation are considered it is clear that India as a whole is a strong and more-or-less self-sufficient economic unit. Any division will naturally weaken her and one part will have to depend on the other. If the division is made so as to separate the predominantly Hindu and Moslem areas, the former will comprise far the greater part of the mineral resources and industrial areas. The Hindu areas will not be so hard hit from this point of view. The Moslem areas, on the other hand, will be the economically backward, and often deficit, areas, which cannot exist without a great deal of outside assistance. Thus the odd fact emerges that those who today demand separation will be the greatest sufferers from it. Because of a partial realization of this fact, it is now stated on their behalf that separation should take place in such a way as to give them an economically balanced region. Whether this is possible under any circumstances I do not know, but I rather doubt it. In any event, any such attempt means forcibly attaching other large areas with a predominantly Hindu and Sikh population to the separated area. That would be a curious way of giving effect to the principle of self-determination. I am reminded of the story of the man who killed his father and mother and then threw himself on the mercy of the Court as an orphan.

Another very curious contradiction emerges. While the principle of self-determination is invoked, the idea of a plebiscite to decide this is not accepted, or at most, it is said that the plebiscite should be limited to Moslems only in the area. Thus in Bengal and the Punjab and Moslem population is about 54 per cent or less. It is suggested that if there is to be voting only this 54 per cent should vote and decide the fate of the remaining 46 per cent or more, who will have no say in the matter. This might result in 28 per cent deciding the fate of the remaining 72 per cent.

It is difficult to understand how any reasonable person can advance these propositions or expect them to be agreed to. I do not know, and nobody can know till an actual vote takes place on this issue, how many Moslems in the areas concerned would vote for partition. I imagine that a large number of them, possibly even a majority, would vote against it. Many Moslem organizations are opposed to it. Every non-Moslem, whether he is a Hindu or Sikh or Christian or Parsi, is opposed to it. Essentially this sentiment in favour of partition has grown in the areas where Moslems are in a small minority, areas which, in any event, would remain undetached from the rest of India. Moslems in provinces where they are in a majority have been less influenced by it; naturally, for they can stand on their own feet and have no reason to fear other groups. It is least in evidence in the North-West Frontier Province (95 per cent Moslem) where the Pathans are brave and self-reliant and have no fear complex. Thus, oddly enough, the Moslem League's proposal to partition India finds far less response in the Moslem areas sought to be partitioned than in the Moslem minority areas which are unaffected by it. Yet the fact remains that considerable numbers of Moslems have become sentimentally attached to this idea of separation without giving thought to its consequences. Indeed the proposition has so far only been vaguely stated and no attempt has been made to define it, in spite of repeated requests.

I think this sentiment has been artificially created and has no roots in the Moslem mind. But even a temporary sentiment may be strong enough to influence events and create a new situation. Normally, adjustments would take place from time to time, but in the peculiar position in which India is situated today, with power concentrated in foreign hands, anything may happen. It is clear that any real settlement must be based on the good-will of the constituent elements and on the desire of all parties to it to co-operate together for a common objective. In order to gain that any sacrifice in reason is worthwhile. Every group must not only be theoretically and actually free and have equal opportunities of growth, but should have the sensation of freedom and equality. It is not difficult if passions and unreasoning emotions are set aside, to devise such freedom with the largest autonomy for provinces and States and yet a strong central bond. There could even be autonomous units within the larger provinces or States, as in Soviet Russia. In addition to this, every conceivable protection and safeguard for minority rights could be inserted into the constitution.

All this can be done, and yet I do not know how the future will take shape under the influence of various indeterminate factors and forces, the chief of these being British policy. It may be that some division of India is enforced, with some tenuous bond joining the divided parts. Even if this happens, I am convinced that the basic feeling of unity and world developments will later bring the divided parts nearer to each other and result in a real unity.

That unity is geographical, historical and cultural and all that. But the most powerful factor in its favour is the trend of world events. Many of us are of opinion that India is essentially a nation; Mr Jinnah has advanced a two-nation theory and has lately added to it and to political phraseology by describing some religious groups as sub-nations, whatever these might be. His thought identifies a nation with religion. That is not the usual approach today. But whether India is properly to be described as one nation or two or more really does not matter, for the modern idea of nationality has been almost divorced from Statehood. The national State is too small a unit today and small States can have no independent existence. It is doubtful if even many of the larger national States can have any real independence. The national State is thus giving place to the multinational State or to large federations. The Soviet Union is typical of this development. The United States of America, though bound together by strong national ties, constitute essentially a multinational State. Behind Hitler's march across Europe there was something more than the Nazi lust for conquest. New forces were working towards the liquidation of the small States system in Europe. Hitler's armies are now rapidly rolling back or are being destroyed, but the conception of large federations remains.

Mr H.G. Wells has been telling the world, with all the fire of an old prophet, that humanity is at the end of an age—an age of fragmentation in the management of its affairs, fragmentation politically among separate sovereign States and economically among unrestricted business organizations competing for profit. He tells us that it is the system of nationalist individualism and uncoordinated enterprise that is the world's disease. We shall have to put an end to the national State and devise a collectivism which neither degrades nor enslaves. The prophets are ignored and sometimes even stoned by their generation. And so Mr Wells's warnings, and those of many others, are voices in the wilderness so far as those in authority are concerned. Nevertheless they point to inevitable trends. These trends can be hastened or delayed or, if those who have power are so blind, may even have to await another and greater disaster before they take actual shape.

In India, as elsewhere, we are too much under the bondage of slogans and set phrases deriving from past events and ideologies which have little relevance today, and their chief function is to prevent reasoned thought and a dispassionate consideration of the situation as it exists. There is also the tendency towards abstractions and vague ideals, which arouse emotional responses and are often good in their way, but which also lead to a woolliness of the mind and unreality. In recent years a great deal has been written and said on the future of India and especially on the partition or unity of India. And yet the astonishing fact remains that those who propose 'Pakistan' or partition have consistently refused to define what they mean or to consider the implications of such a division. They move on the emotional plane only, as also many of those who oppose them, a plane of imagination and vague desire, behind which lie imagined interests. Inevitably, between these two emotional and imaginative approaches there is no meeting ground. And so 'Pakistan' and 'Akhand Hindustan' (undivided India) are bandied about and hurled at each other. It is clear that group emotions and conscious or subconscious urges count and must be attended to. It is at least equally clear that facts and realities do not vanish by our ignoring them or covering them up by a film of emotion; they have a way of emerging at awkward moments and in unexpected ways. Any decisions taken primarily on the basis of emotions, or when emotions are the dominating consideration, are likely to be wrong and to lead to dangerous developments.

It is obvious that whatever may be the future of India, and even if there is a regular partition, the different parts of India will have to co-operate with each other in a hundred ways. Even independent nations have to co-operate with each other, much more so must Indian provinces or such parts as emerge from a partition, for these stand in an intimate relationship to each other and must hang together or deteriorate, disintegrate, and lose their freedom. Thus the very first practical question is: what are the essential common bonds which must bind and cement various parts of India if she is to progress and remain free, and which are equally necessary even for the autonomy and cultural growth of those parts. Defence is an obvious and outstanding consideration, and behind that defence lie the industries feeding it, transport and communications, and some measure at least of economic planning. Customs, currency and exchange also and the maintenance of the whole of India as an internally free-trade area, for any internal tariff barriers would be fatal barriers to growth. And so on; there are many other matters which would inevitably, both from the point of view of the whole and the parts, have to be jointly and centrally directed. There is no getting away from it whether we are in favour of Pakistan or not, unless we are blind to everything except a momentary passion. The vast growth of air services today has led to the demand for their internationalization, or to some form of international control. Whether various countries are wise enough to accept this is doubtful. But it is quite certain that air developments can only take place in India on an all-India basis; it is inconceivable for a partitioned India to make progress in regard to them in each part separately. This applies also to many other activities which already tend to outgrow even national boundaries. India is big enough as a whole to give them scope for development, but not so partitioned India.

Thus we arrive at the inevitable and ineluctable conclusion that, whether Pakistan comes or not, a number of important and basic functions of the State must be exercised on an all-India basis if India is to survive as a free State and progress. The alternative is stagnation, decay and disintegration, leading to loss of political and economic freedom, both for India as a whole and its various separated parts. As has been said by an eminent authority: 'The inexorable logic of the age presents the country with radically different alternatives: union plus independence or disunion plus dependence.' What form the union is to take, and whether it is called union or by some other name, is not so important, though names have their own significance and psychological value. The essential fact is that a number of varied activities can only be conducted effectively on a joint all-India basis. Probably many of these activities will soon be under the control of international bodies. The world shrinks and its problems overlap. It takes less than three days now to go right across the world by air, from any one place to another, and tomorrow, with the development of stratosphere navigation, it may take even less time. India must become a great world centre of air travel. India will also be linked by rail to western Asia and Europe on the one side, and to Burma and China on the other. Not far from India, across the Himalayas in the north, lies in Soviet Asia one of the highly developed industrial areas, with an enormous future potential. India will be affected by this and will react in many ways.

The way of approach, therefore, to the problem of unity or Pakistan is not in the abstract and on the emotional level, but practically and with our eyes on the present-day world. That approach leads us to certain obvious conclusions: that a binding cement in regard to certain important functions and matters is essential for the whole of India. Apart from them there may be and should be the fullest freedom to constituent units, and an intermediate sphere where there is both joint and separate functioning. There may be differences of opinion as to where one sphere ends and the other begins, but such differences, when considered on a practical basis, are generally fairly easy of adjustment.

But all this must necessarily be based on a spirit of willing co-operation, on an absence of a feeling of compulsion, and on the sensation of freedom in each unit and individual. Old vested interests have to go; it is equally important that no new ones are created. Certain proposals, based on metaphysical conceptions of groups and forgetting the individuals who comprise them, make one individual politically equal to two or three others and thus create new vested interests. Any such arrangement can only lead to grave dissatisfaction and instability.

The right of any well-constituted area to secede from the Indian Federation or Union has often been put forward, and the argument of the U.S.S.R. advanced in support of it. That argument has little application for conditions there are wholly different and the right has little practical value. In the emotional atmosphere in India today it may be desirable to agree to this for the future in order to give that sense of freedom from compulsion which is so necessary. The Congress has in effect agreed to it. But even the exercise of that right involves a pre-consideration of all those common problems to which reference has been made. Also there is grave danger in a possibility of partition and division to begin with, for such an attempt might well scotch the very beginnings of freedom and the formation of a free national State. Insuperable problems will rise and confuse all the real issues. Disintegration will be in the air and all manner of groups, who are otherwise agreeable to a joint and unified existence, will claim separate States for themselves, or special privileges which are encroachments on others. The problem of the Indian States will become far more difficult of solution, and the States system, as it is today, will get a new lease of life. The social and economic problems will be far harder to tackle. Indeed, it is difficult to conceive of any free State emerging from such a turmoil, and if something does emerge, it will be a pitiful caricature full of contradictions and insoluble problems.

Before any such right of secession is exercised there must be a properly constituted, functioning, free India. It may be possible then, when external influences have been removed and real problems face the country, to consider such questions objectively and in a spirit of relative detachment, far removed from the emotionalism of today, which can only lead to unfortunate consequences which we may all have to regret later. Thus it may be desirable to fix a period, say ten years after the establishment of the free Indian States, at the end of which the right to secede may be exercised through proper constitutional process and in accordance with the clearly expressed will of the inhabitants of the area concerned.

Chapter Five

Muslims and Political Representation in Colonial India: The Making of Pakistan*

FARZANA SHAIKH

One of the principal difficulties in arriving at a constitutional settlement in India during the 1940s stemmed from the inherent conflict between Congress's emphasis upon the principle of majority rule and fluid political alignments and the Muslim League's commitment to the Islamic conviction that numerical configurations were irrelevant to politics and that what mattered was the rigid ideological divide between Muslims and non-Muslims.

Any real understanding of this problem in these terms depends, however, upon some discussion of the chief differences that characterize Islamic and liberal-democratic approaches to representation. More specifically, some attempt must be made to pay closer attention to Islam's antipathy to that aspect of liberal representation that upholds the central importance of a procedural consensus based on the notion of majority rule and shifting political loyalties.

The attempt to establish the ideological basis of Muslim representative politics in India has necessarily implied the assumption that ideology may, in some instances, constitute an independent variable in politics. The task of defining its proper limits has been made more urgent not only by the inherent limitations of existing historical approaches to

* *Modern Asian Studies*, 20, 3, 1986, pp. 539–57.

the study of Indian Muslim separatism, but also by recent events in the Islamic world.

The inadequacy of contemporary historical scholarship stems from the sharp division between those who maintain that the role of Islamic ideology in the conduct of Indian Muslim politics was either illusory or wholly instrumental, and those who argue that Islam was the only explanatory factor behind partition and Pakistan.[1] At the same time, the emergence of Muslim fundamentalism in parts of the Middle East and Southeast Asia has clearly demanded that we reassess and redefine the role of Islam in terms of its potential not only to legitimize, but also to impel political action and behaviour. The specificity of historical studies which have until now tended to view Indian Muslims as a case apart must therefore, it seems, be complemented by a broader approach which regards them as part of a wider ideological tradition which has assumed a characteristic and clearly identifiable political expression in radically different contexts.

The study of Indian Muslim attitudes to representation provides an opportunity to gauge the influence of ideology in the definition of political issues and the formulation of political demands. It is neither insignificant nor coincidental that the manner in which Indian Muslims expressed their opposition to western representation conformed closely to the basic political norms of Islam. Nor can the mere fact that these ideological tenets were sometimes congruent with political interests either disprove the primacy or deny the directive nature of ideology.

The impact of western representation upon Indian Muslims in

[1] For a classic exposition of the instrumental role of Islam see Paul Brass, *Language, Religion and Politics in North India* (London, New York: Cambridge University Press, 1974). For arguments that categorically dismiss the explanatory power of ideology see, John Gallagher *et al.* (eds), *Locality, Province and Nation: Essays on Indian Politics, 1870–1947* (Cambridge: Cambridge University Press, 1973) and Anil Seal and A. Jalal, 'Alternative to Partition: Muslim Politics between the Wars', *Modern Asian Studies*, vol. 15, no. 3, 1981, pp. 415–54. The paramount importance of Islam as the principal catalyst of Muslim political action in colonial India is emphasized, amongst others, in Hafeez Malik, *Moslem Nationalism in India and Pakistan* (Washington: Public Affairs Press, 1963); I.H. Qureshi, *The Struggle for Pakistan* (Karachi: University of Karachi Publications, 1965) and Riazul Islam, 'The Religious Factor in the Pakistan Movement: A Study in Motivation', *Proceedings of the First Congress on the History and Culture of Pakistan*, vol. 3 (Islamabad: National Commission on Historical and Cultural Research, 1976).

colonial India points sharply to the conclusion that such representation was seen to consist not just of a threat to deprive the Indian Muslim minority of a share in political power. On the contrary, there is evidence to support the view that western liberal representation posed a radical challenge to key Islamic notions espoused by Indian Muslims, believers or not, concerning the relationship between the individual and his communal group; the nature of political consensus and the organization of power in society.

In order to assess the significance of the ideological dichotomies between Islam and western liberalism and their bearing upon the problem of representation in the creation and subsequent history of independent Pakistan, it is necessary to look more closely at some of the differences that characterize their approaches to representation. Broadly speaking, these differences relate to:

1. the unit of representation,
2. the basis of representative status, and
3. the organization of representative bodies.

Modern liberal representation has, on the whole, tended to assume that the unit of representation consists primarily of the individual and his interests. This quintessentially European view which emerged early in the nineteenth century was vitally related to the principle of individual equality. The idea acquired particular significance at a time when the rights of individuals were being upheld against the established orders of Church, State and landed aristocracy.[2]

In Islam, on the other hand, the preoccupation with communal identity has necessarily entailed a focus upon communal claims and the communal group as the basic unit of representation and focus of loyalty. The abiding Islamic concern with communal solidarity has meant that Muslims tend, more often than not, to evaluate their situation in primarily communal terms. The absence of any theory of individual rights as such, except within the framework of the Islamic *umma*, has implied that the liberal notion of individual political auto-

[2] Samuel Beer, 'The Representation of Interests in British Government: Historical Background', *American Political Science Review*, vol. 51, no. 3, September 1957, p. 630. For a more provocative discussion of the question of individual autonomy and representation in the context of western liberalism see John Dunn, *Western Political Theory in the Face of the Future* (Cambridge: Cambridge University Press, 1979).

nomy is often seen to be wholly alien to the normative contextual framework of Islam.[3]

The demand for Muslim communal representation in India in October 1906 reflected this preoccupation with the integrity of the Muslim community.[4] The introduction of individual representation was seen not just as a threat to the position of a Muslim minority but as a danger to their cohesion as Muslims, as well as their claim to be an exclusive community with exclusive interests.[5]

The second difference between Islamic and liberal approaches to representation lies in their contrasting views as to what constitutes representativeness or representative status. Liberal representation has traditionally been concerned with what might be termed a strictly 'electoral theory of representation' wherein political legitimacy is seen to depend primarily upon elected status.[6] The basis of political legitimacy and representative status in Islam, on the other hand, has tended to rely much more upon visibly shared social and communal affiliations between the representative and his communal group than upon his elected status *per se*. Indeed, it would not be inappropriate to contend that within the context of Islamic political values, it is more important to Muslims to be represented by Muslims than by elected, politically accountable, non-Muslims. It is, then, primarily the incidence of similarity, essentially communal in nature, between the candidate and his constituency that constitutes the foremost condition of representativeness in Islam.[7] But the contention that those who are

[3] Louis Gardet, *La Cité Musulmane: vie sociale et politique* (Paris: Librairie Philosophique J. Vrin, 1961), p. 57. See also, G.E. von Grunebaum, *Modern Islam: The Search for Cultural Identity* (New York: Vintage Books, 1964), pp. 246–7.

[4] The question of the centrality of the communal group in Islam has been extensively discussed in Fazlur Rahman, *Islam* (London: Weidenfeld and Nicolson, 1966); Montgomery Watt, *Islamic Political Thought: The Basic Concepts* (Edinburgh, The University Press, 1968) and Louis Gardet, *L'Islam: religion et communauté* (Paris, Bibliotheque française de philosophie, 1967).

[5] Farzana Shaikh, *Islam: Ideology or Instrument? Muslims and Political Representation in British India*, 1860–1946 (Cambridge: Cambridge University Press. forthcoming).

[6] Giovanni Sartori, 'Representation: Representational Systems' in *International Encyclopaedia of the Social Sciences* (London: Macmillan, 1968), p. 468. See also, A.H. Birch, 'The Theory and Practice of Representation', 7th World Congress of the International Political Science Association (Brussels, 1967).

[7] This is, of course, not unique to Islamic societies but may occur in any sharply divided society where politics is conducted on communal and ethnic lines, see

of the group are preeminently qualified to be *for* the group, is wholly at odds with the liberal view which distinguishes sharply between a representative's political commitments on the one hand and his religious and communal affiliations on the other.

An approach to representation founded on ascriptive criteria is likely to pose major difficulties in the way of consolidating a liberal democracy in Muslim societies. Firstly, the emphasis upon representativeness as a function of belonging and being similar to the group may tend to devalue the intrinsic importance of the elective principle.[8] At the same time, it may in some instances enable representative claims to be made without the endorsement of a popular electoral mandate so long as ascriptive affiliations between claimant and constituency are established. This was most dramatically illustrated in the summer of 1937 when the All India Muslim League, despite its dismal electoral performance, proclaimed itself the authentic representative of Indian Muslims on the grounds that it was an exclusively *Muslim* party.[9] Secondly, the emphasis on ascriptive criteria could question the legitimacy of mixed political constituencies that are familiar to liberal democracies. The centrality of the communal group in Islam, its exclusive orientations and its total claim upon the individual's political loyalties inevitably makes it the sole constituency for potential Muslim representatives. Representative claims not sanctioned by the communal group could therefore be considered invalid. Thus, Muslims elected by predominantly Hindu constituencies in British India were systematically dismissed as not being 'truly' representative of their community.

The final area which distinguishes liberal from Islamic notions of

---

Robert Kearney, ***Communalism and Language in the Politics of Ceylon*** (Durham, North Carolina: Duke University Press, 1967) and Alvin Rabushka and Kenneth Shepsle, ***Politics in Plural Societies: A Theory of Democratic Instability*** (Columbus, Ohio: Charles L. Merrill Publishing Company, 1972). What is unique to Islamic societies is the manner in which the organization of politics on communal lines is actively pursued in the name of a Divine Law which is seen to endorse it.

[8] Sartori maintains 'If representation is defined merely as an *idem sentire*, as the fact of 'coincidence in opinion with', any method of selection or even no method at all might do. What matters is not the procedure . . . but the existence of such coincidence'. Giovanni Sartori, 'Representation', p. 467.

[9] See, B.C. Parekh, 'India: A Case Study in the Ideology of Representation', 7th World Congress of the International Political Science Association (Brussels, 1967) for an excellent interpretation of the way in which the League asserted its claim to be the sole authentic representative of the Muslim community in India.

representation relates to their respective approaches to the organization of representative bodies. Modern liberal democracy has tended to regard representative institutions as the repositories of a national consensus which is periodically renewed by elected political majorities.[10] Muslims, on the other hand, view political institutions as reflections of the essentially communal make-up of society. As such, they are seen to consist not of fluid political majorities and minorities, but of conglomerations of rigidly-defined, mutually exclusive communal groups, divided principally along religious lines.[11]

These differing perspectives are intimately linked to radically different images of society. Whereas modern liberalism conceives of society as capable of generating fluid political alignments based on the premise that 'the political assembly no longer represents estates, classes, or orders as such, but free and equal heads—abstract political persons', Muslims tend to view society as a mosaic of fixed communal groups which aspire to representation within an evenly balanced political assembly.[12]

The liberal conception of representative institutions was, in part, dictated by the need to evolve effective political bodies that could resolve diverging interests and generate a system of common civil law. For Muslims, committed to the view that society is irrevocably divided between Muslims and non-Muslims, the idea of communally mixed political majorities implementing common programmes, is wholly unacceptable.

The extent to which these perspectives actually impinged upon the question of liberal representation amongst Indian Muslims was eminently clear in the course of the constitutional crisis of the 1940s when Muslim opposition to representative institutions based on flexible political alignments proceeded on the assumption that society was divided into immovable political blocs consisting of Muslims and

[10] The traditional justification for liberal majority rule was precisely that it avoided any permanent minorities. See, J. Lively, *Democracy* (Oxford: Basil Blackwell, 1973) and Robert Dahl, *Polyarchy* (New Haven: Yale University Press, 1971).

[11] See, *The Encyclopaedia of Islam*, vol. I (Leiden: E.J. Brill, 1913), pp. 958–9; Kenneth Cragg, *The House of Islam*, 2nd edn (Encino, Calif.: Dickinson Publishing Company, 1975), pp. 82–4, and R.B. Sarjeant, 'The "Constitution of Medina" ', *Islamic Quarterly*, vol. 8, no. I, 1964, pp. 3–16.

[12] C. Beard and J.D. Lewis, 'Representative Government in Evolution', *American Political Science Review*, vol. 26, no. 2, April 1932, p. 235.

non-Muslims. The League's opposition to a representative federal centre which would eventually have been responsible for the implementation of a common civil law, stemmed in part from the characteristic Muslim rejection of the idea of a common law equally applicable to Muslims and non-Muslims. Indeed, it could be argued that the League's demand for parity and exclusive representation signified not only the means to check the power of a non-Muslim majority, but constitutionally to restrict its access to a Muslim electorate without which the legitimacy of a common law could not be fully established.

And it is really to this problem, that is to say the conflict between liberal majority rule and the notion of parity founded on the assumption of a substantive Islamic consensus, that I now wish to turn. Its salience was clearly evident in the decade immediately preceding the creation of Pakistan. But it also assumed enormous significance in the context of post-independence Pakistan where the claims of liberal-democratic representation were repeatedly countered by the need to consolidate a state committed primarily to the expression of a substantive, if often assumed, Islamic consensus.

Here let me focus on the meaning of this conflict in the debate on representation which led eventually to the partition of India and the creation of a separate Muslim state. The characteristic position of the League in the 1940s was one that rejected Congress's claim to be the majority party and therefore the principal wielder of political power in independent India. Instead, the League postulated its demand for representative parity, independent of numerical proportions, on the inherent dichotomy between Muslims and non-Muslims. Bi-polar parity would consist therefore of the League as the sole representative of a unanimous Muslim political consensus and Congress as the principal spokesman of non-Muslim interests. The League's claim to exclusive representation owed its ideological authenticity to the Islamic conviction that Muslims were, or ought to be, bound by a substantive consensus and that such a consensus demanded a single Muslim medium.

It is not being argued that Indian Muslim politics or for that matter, the politics of the League, was dictated at every moment by a set of Islamic normative concerns. Indeed, as we shall see, there were also specific historical and political factors that determined the nature of the League's demands. Nevertheless, in order to appreciate the

League's own understanding of parity as indispensable to the integrity and cohesion of the Muslim community, it is necessary to grasp its relation to the vision of societal organization propounded by Islam and espoused by Muslims.

The historical context within which the question of parity versus majority rule was framed was dominated by three principal events: the outbreak of the Second World War in September 1939; the consequences of Congress rule in the provinces from 1937 to 1939 and the growing interest among various Muslim groups in schemes for territorial redistribution designed to guarantee Indian Muslims complete control over their own affairs in areas where they constituted a majority. I shall look briefly at each of these factors in order to assess their significance in the formulation of the League's stance on parity.

The outbreak of the war signalled a final Muslim onslaught upon liberal political institutions which was decisively to undermine the possibility, and indeed the legitimacy, of western democracy in a united India. The British government's determination to co-opt social and political groups willing to support the war effort enabled Indian Muslims to seize the opportunity of obtaining recognition as a distinct 'nation'—a status hitherto overridden by the claims of a supra-communal Indian nationalism.

The consequences for liberal democracy were to be profound. For the first time, India's representative politics came to be wholly dominated by two rigidly defined corporate groupings whose political importance appeared to bear little or no relation to their numerical proportions and whose relative standing was assumed to be equal. So it was that the entire framework of liberal representation in India was jeopardized by the equation of minority and majority and the assertion of multiple nations entitled to equal representation and parity.

The idea that Muslims were more than a mere political minority and were, in fact, a distinct political entity, had, of course, emerged long before the war and had even influenced colonial policy on representation. But the importance assumed by the idea of a Muslim 'nation' was undoubtedly favoured by existing political circumstances which radically transformed the status of the Muslim League and enabled it to demand outright parity with Congress on the grounds that it was a national and *not* a communal organization. The resignation of Congress ministries and their refusal to co-operate with the war effort, along with the government's growing need for allies, led the League to define its position and dictate the terms of its support quite early on in the war. Essentially, it demanded that Indian Muslims be recognized as a 'constituent factor' in all further constitutional negotiations; that they be allowed to play 'an equal part' with the majority community and that it be deemed the only organization to speak on behalf of 'Muslim India'.[13]

The government's own position wavered dangerously between its commitment to give full weight to minority views and interests and its determination not to allow a minority, whatever its size, to interrupt the course of reforms towards full responsible government.[14] The tenor of official discussions suggests that although the value of Muslim support was not lost upon officials, they refused to be drawn into a precise definition of the constitutional status of Indian Muslims such as would empower them with a political veto. At the same time, the government's appreciation of the League's claim to parity was clearly linked to the official tendency to invoke the traditional view of Indian society as consisting of mutually exclusive social categories which effectively precluded a broad consensus of Indian opinion. This, in turn, lent credence to official policy which recognized the inherent legitimacy of separate interests as if they were on a par, thereby entitling them to separate representation and a potentially decisive constitutional role.[15]

One of the most important consequences of Congress rule in the provinces was its impact upon the League's campaign to redefine the constitutional position of Indian Muslims. The League argued that Muslim self-determination was vitally related to, and a result of, the system of permanent Hindu domination instituted by Congress ministries.[16]

[13] Resolution of the Working Committee of the All India Muslim League on the War Crisis, 17–18 September 1939 in M. Gwyer and A. Appadorai (eds), *Speeches and Documents on the Indian Constitution*, 1921–47, vol. II (London: Oxford University Press, 1957), pp. 488–9.

[14] For evidence of these contradictory positions see Marquess of Linlithgow, *Speeches and Statements*, 1936–43 (Simla: Government of India Press, 1945), p. 209 and Zetland (Secretary of State for India) to the Viceroy Lord Linlithgow, 4 February 1940, Zetland Collection, MSS EUR E 609, India Office Library, no. 11.

[15] See Linlithgow's Statement on 'War Aims' and 'War Effort', 18 October 1939, in Marquess of Linlithgow, *Speeches and Statements*, p. 210.

[16] The League's position was coherently argued by Jinnah in his article entitled 'On the Communal Question', 1 March 1938, reprinted in Gwyer and Appadorai (eds), *Speeches*, vol. I, pp. 407–10. See also, S.S. Pirzada (ed.), *Quaid-e-Azam*

The idea that political alignments are essentially communal in nature and therefore permanently defined was actively espoused by the League. In a Report commissioned by its Working Committee in 1938 to investigate grievances under Congress rule, the League reaffirmed its opposition to the theory and practice of liberal democracy by asserting that 'the existence of permanent religious groupings' necessarily 'defined the complexion of political parties'.[17] It was precisely its assumption that Muslims were a permanently defined, distinct social category that enabled the League to claim parity of status and representation for Indian Muslims. Whereas prior to 1939 the League had tended to emphasize these communal configurations as the indisputable facts of Indian reality, they now appeared to constitute desirable norms which made possible the institution of more equitable modes of representation than those professed by western political liberalism.

Congress was of course aware of the League's assumptions concerning the nature of political alignments and their implications for the organization of representative bodies in India. In March 1937, Nehru told a meeting of Congress legislators that his party viewed with alarm the prevailing tendency to regard India's communal groups as politically rigid, mutually exclusive entities without a sense of shared common interests.[18] Later, in the Spring of 1938, Congress rejected the League's proposals for coalition ministries in some provinces on the grounds that their failure to incorporate the principle of flexible alignments and majority rule would inevitably result in 'disjointed' and 'ineffective' bodies.[19] Clearly, Congress's fears were founded on the very real possibility that an acceptance of the League's terms would mean the end of any common political programme as well as the institutionalization of Congress and League as exclusive communal parties.

Jinnah's Correspondence (Karachi: Guild Publishing House, 1966, 2nd edn), pp. 443–9.

[17] See, The Report of the Inquiry Committee appointed by the Council of the All India Muslim League to inquire into Muslim grievances in Congress Provinces, 15 November 1938 (Pirpur Report) in Gwyer and Appadorai (eds), *Speeches*, vol. I, pp. 411, 412.

[18] J. Nehru's presidential address to the All India National Convention of Congress Legislators, *The Indian Annual Register* (1937), vol. I, pp. 207–8.

[19] *Nehru-Jinnah Correspondence* (Allahabad: All India Congress Committee, n.d.), pp. 61–73.

And indeed, the League appeared to have little time to entertain liberal political preferences. Throughout the 1940s, Jinnah repeatedly and categorically dismissed the suitability of applying the principles of arithmetic to the problem of representation. The issue at hand, he asserted, was not how to manage the demands of shifting political patterns, but how constitutionally to recognize the claims of political 'nations'.

The third and final factor which contributed significantly to the League's demand for parity was the growing preoccupation amongst groups of Indian Muslims with constitutional schemes aimed at securing the boundaries of a 'Muslim India'.[20] Their implications were to be profoundly disturbing for the institution of liberal representation for at least two reasons. Firstly, because they all postulated a statutory balance between the existing four Muslim provinces (excluding Baluchistan) and the seven Hindu provinces;[21] and secondly, because they asserted that Indian Muslims were not a minority but a majority, albeit in certain areas, and therefore entitled, as were all majorities, to 'real power'.[22] The thrust of this second, and more important claim, lay in the view elaborated by Jinnah that, if the majority status of Hindus entitled them to represent an Indian 'nation', there was no reason why the Muslim community which constituted an absolute majority in clearly defined areas could not make similar claims for itself.

Contemporary schemes for Muslim autonomy did not, however, restrict themselves to these issues alone. Equally important was the view that the conduct and practice of Islam required relatively independent areas where its adherents could abide by the tenets of their faith. For Muhammad Iqbal, 'the life of Islam as a cultural force' and 'the development of the Shariat' clearly depended upon the creation of 'one or more Muslim states with absolute majorities'.[23] For

[20] Although the phrase itself was first used by Maulana Hasrat Mohani in the early 1920s, its notoriety clearly derives from Mohammad Iqbal's presidential address to the 21st session of the Muslim League in December 1930. See, S.S. Pirzada (ed.), *Foundations of Pakistan: All India Muslim League Documents 1906–47*, vol. II (Karachi: National Publishing House, n.d.), p. 159.

[21] S.R. Mehrotra, 'The Congress and the Partition of India' in C.H. Philips and M.D. Wainwright (eds), *The Partition of India: Policies and Perspectives 1935–1947* (London: George Allen and Unwin, 1970), p. 202.

[22] Jinnah's speech to the Muslim University Union, Aligarh, 6 March 1940 in Jamil-ud-din Ahmed (ed.), *Speeches and Writings of Mr Jinnah*, vol. I (Lahore: Shaikh Muhammad Ashraf, 1960), p. 138.

[23] See Muhammad Iqbal's presidential address to the 21st session of the Muslim

Chaudhri Rahmat Ali, a separate Muslim federation 'on par with the federation of India' was essential to the preservation of an Islamic way of life.[24]

The twin themes of a Muslim majority-nation and the urgency of securing a Muslim way of life were to appear repeatedly in other contemporary schemes regardless of whether or not they actually envisaged partition and independent Muslim states.[25] It was within the context of these prevailing schemes which all drew attention away from the minority status of Muslims in India as a whole and towards their composition as a territorially defined majority with a distinct code of conduct and system of laws that the League was to formulate its own official scheme in March 1940.

Otherwise known as the Pakistan Resolution, the scheme emphatically rejected the minority status of Indian Muslims. It argued that Indian Muslims constituted a majority-nation in the north-west and east of India and, as such, ought to be treated on a par with the Hindu majority in all further constitutional arrangements.[26] In short, by concentrating entirely upon the provincial status of Indian Muslims, the League was able to be seen as doing no more than advocating the legitimate claim of a majority to absolute power.

The League's decision in April 1946, to alter the wording of the Pakistan Resolution to read the creation of a 'sovereign, independent Muslim state' instead of *two* Muslim states, did not result merely from the need to accommodate its strategy to the Cabinet Mission's plan for a federal rather than a partitioned India (although this was important).[27] Equally important was the growing realization that bi-partisan

---

League in December 1930 in S.S. Pirzada (ed.), *Foundations of Pakistan*, vol. II, p. 159 and Iqbal to Jinnah, 28 May 1937 in Pirzada (ed.), *Quaid-e-Azam Jinnah's Correspondence*, pp. 159, 160.

[24] Chaudhri Rahmat Ali, *Pakistan: The Fatherland of the Pak Nation*, (Cambridge, Pakasia Literature, 3rd edition, 1947), pp. 213, 216. See also, Chaudhri Rahmat Ali to unidentified person, 8 July 1935 enclosed in M.R. Jayakar Papers and cited in Uma Kaura, *Muslims and Indian Nationalism: The Emergence of the Demand for the Partition of India, 1920–1940* (New Delhi: South Asia Books, 1977), p. 154.

[25] For details of these schemes see, Gwyer and Appadorai (eds), *Speeches*, vol. II, pp. 443–65.

[26] See Resolution I adopted by the 27th session of the Muslim League on 23 March 1940 in Pirzada (ed.), *Foundations of Pakistan*, vol. II, p. 337.

[27] See the 'Delhi Resolution' passed by the Convention of League Legislators on 9 April 1946, ibid., vol. II, pp. 512–13.

parity between the League and Congress in an all-India federation could be secured only through the consolidation of a single Muslim constitutional entity. After all, the League's demand for bi-partisan parity ultimately rested on the claim that it represented a cohesive entity known as the Muslim 'nation'. The constitutional division of this supposedly unified electorate into two groups of Muslim provinces clearly threatened to undermine the idea of Muslim solidarity and with it, the basis of the League's political ideology.

Although a discussion of the broad historical context is important for an understanding of the circumstances in which the notion of parity arose, it can tell us little about its actual ideological bases. These were to emerge much more vividly in the course of constitutional negotiations which revealed that the claim for parity developed steadily from simple *political parity* between League and Congress to *communal parity* between Muslims and Hindus and culminated finally in the demand for *ideological parity* between Muslims and non-Muslims. Indeed, it was this final insistence by the League that Indian Muslims be granted statutory parity *vis-à-vis* the *totality* of non-Muslim Indian groups, that was to undermine the chances of liberal democracy in a united India. I wish to examine, very briefly, four constitutional issues which illustrated the progression of the League's claim to parity. They are: the government's August Offer to 1940; the Cripps proposals of 1942; the Viceroy, Lord Wavell's proposals for an Interim Government in 1945 and the Cabinet Mission's plan for an Interim Government and a confederation of India in 1946.

THE AUGUST OFFER

Widespread criticism of the government's decision to engage India in the war without prior consultation with elected Indian representatives led to the announcement in October 1939 that the government was prepared to expand the Governor-General's Executive Council with the intention of making it more representative and possibly more acceptable to Indian critics.[28]

In July 1940, Jinnah declared that the League's participation in the proposed Executive Council could proceed only on the basis of

[28] Linlithgow's Statement on 'War Aims' and the 'War Effort', 18 October 1939 in Gwyer and Appadorai (eds), *Speeches*, vol. II, pp. 490–3.

parity between Congress and League. However, he implied that such parity must also consist of a communal balance between Hindus and Muslims founded principally on the basis of the League's exclusive claim to nominate Indian Muslims.[29]

The Viceroy's Offer of August 1940 suggested that although the government was willing to reaffirm its commitment to the League's position on majority rule, it could not do so on the League's terms, namely constitutional parity between Congress and League as strictly communal organizations.[30] In short, however attractive the League's offer of co-operation, the government was clearly unwilling constitutionally to endorse the principle of political and communal parity based on the logic of exclusive representation.

Not surprisingly, the League eventually rejected the government's August Offer on the grounds that it did not provide any assurance that the League's position on the Council would not be prejudiced by the nomination of Muslim members by Congress, or of such members of remaining minorities as were likely to side with Congress in the event of a vote.[31]

As for Congress, it rejected the Offer by pointing to the unwarranted degree of control that had been granted to minorities while denying full responsibility to India's elected majority. There was, of course, no question of accepting statutory parity between Congress and League, let alone any proposal to concentrate the nomination of Muslim members in the hands of the League.[32]

THE CRIPPS PROPOSALS

In March 1942, there was once again talk of new proposals aimed at resolving the constitutional impasse in India. But Churchill signalled

[29] See Jinnah's tentative proposals for co-operation with the government, 1 July 1940, ibid., vol. II, pp. 502–3.

[30] See Linlithgow's statement on the expansion of the Governor General's Executive Council and the establishment of a War Advisory Council, 8 August 1940, ibid., vol. II, pp. 504–5.

[31] See, 'Notes of a Conversation between Linlithgow and Jinnah, 14 and 24 August 1940, *Linlithgow Collection*, MSS EUR F 125, India Office Library and the Resolution of the Working Committee of the Muslim League, 28 September 1940 in *Indian Annual Register*, 1940, vol. II, p. 251.

[32] Resolution of the All India Congress Committee, 15–16 September 1940 in Gwyer and Appadorai (eds), *Speeches*, vol. II, pp. 505–6.

a fresh approach when he announced that while Britain intended to continue protecting minority interests, she would no longer allow a minority to impose an indefinite veto upon the wishes of the majority.[33]

But the Cripps Mission which arrived in India later that year evaded rather than confronted the issue of parity. The thrust of its Draft Declaration did not so much recognize a minority's right to a constitutional veto as its right to opt out of any future constitutional arrangement and evolve a wholly new constitution.[34] The League's reaction was swift and predictable. Jinnah emphasized that the Mission had seriously overlooked the question of the integrity of the Muslim community and had failed to recognize that India's problem was primarily 'international in character'.[35] The issue, according to the League, was not whether this or that province wished to accede to the Union, but whether in fact a nation could assert its right to self-determination and equality with another nation.[36]

For its part, Congress rejected any notion of self-determination for minorities. It reiterated its commitment to responsible government based on majority rule and warned the Mission that it would not accept any settlement based on a priori minority participation, let alone on an equal basis.[37] Nevertheless, the League's claim to parity was to receive a substantial boost in the Summer of 1945 when renewed efforts were made to create a representative Interim Government.

Proposals for an Interim Government

Towards this end, plans were announced for a reconstruction of the Viceroy's Executive Council on the basis of a balanced representation of the main Indian communities and 'an equal proportion of Muslims and Caste Hindus'.[38] By doing so, the government hoped to appease

[33] Sir Winston Churchill's speech to the House of Commons, 11 March 1942, *Hansard's Parliamentary Debates*, 1942, vol. 378, col. 1069.

[34] Draft Declaration for discussion with Indian leaders, *Times of India*, 30 March 1942.

[35] See Jinnah's presidential address to the Muslim League on 3 April 1942 in Pirzada (ed.), *Foundations of Pakistan*, vol. II, p. 388.

[36] Resolution of the Working Committee of the Muslim League passed on 2 April 1942. *Statesman*, 11 April 1942.

[37] Resolution of the Working Committee of the All India National Congress, 2 April 1942, ibid.

[38] Statement by L.S. Amery to the House of Commons, 14 June 1945 in Gwyer

the League by conceding a form of communal parity while preserving an overall Hindu majority by providing for the separate representation of Scheduled Caste Hindus.

But the government's understanding of communal parity was to prove unsatisfactory to the League. Jinnah denied that parity between Muslims and Caste Hindus could ever be meaningful, and explained that in the event of a coalition between Caste Hindus and members of smaller parties, Indian Muslims would immediately be reduced to a third on the proposed Council, thereby destroying any semblance of parity.[39]

The thrust of Jinnah's claim lay in the conviction that all Indian minorities, with the exception of Indian Muslims, shared Congress's commitment to a united India founded on the principle of liberal democracy. This led, by implication, to the novel contention that neither political parity between League and Congress nor communal parity between Hindus and Muslims could really accommodate the notion of parity. The issue was really about a form of ideological parity between Muslims and non-Muslims as undifferentiated political categories; between those who advocated parity and those who stood for majority rule; between the proponents of partition and the defenders of a united India.

Congress's initial position *vis-à-vis* the proposals revealed that it was wholly averse to the idea of communal parity between Muslims and Caste Hindus as well as to the suggestion that it would have no say in the selection of Scheduled Caste Hindu and Muslim representatives.[40] Consequently, despite its distinctly more conciliatory posture at the conference convened to discuss the proposals, Congress remained adamantly opposed to the idea of any party's exclusive right to nominate members of a specific community or to any provisions aimed at restricting any party's claim to a communally diverse electorate.[41] Clearly, whatever compromises Congress was willing to make,

---

and Appadorai (eds), *Speeches*, vol. II, p. 559.

[39] Jinnah's statement on the new proposals made at a press conference in Simla on 29 June 1945 in Jamil-ud-din Ahmed (ed.), *Jinnah*. vol. II pp. 175–80.

[40] See Gandhi to Wavell, 17 June 1945. *Indian Annual Register*, 1945, vol. I, p. 245. See also, Archibold Percival Wavell, *Wavell: The Viceroy's Journal*, edited by Penderel Moon (London: Oxford University Press, 1973), p. 145.

[41] See, Instructions issued by the Working Committee of the Indian National Congress to its representatives attending the Simla Conference, 21–2 June 1945. *Indian Annual Register*, 1945, vol. I, p. 224.

it would not countenance the erosion of a free Indian electorate nor jeopardize its own identity as a supra-communal political organization.

The government's own response indicates that it was, for its own part, wholly reluctant to concede the League's demands for ideological parity or accept its proposals for the exclusive nomination of Hindus and Muslims by Congress and League respectively.[42] And yet the debate on ideological parity and exclusive representation was to resurface once again and for the last time, in the course of new proposals for a confederal India and an Interim Government under the Cabinet Mission Plan of 1946.

THE CABINET MISSION PLAN

The League's impressive electoral victory at the provincial and central levels in 1946, hardened its resolve to push 'once for all' for a recognition of parity between Muslims and non-Muslims based on the League's exclusive claim to represent Indian Muslims.[43] A convention of League legislators resolved to press for the equal recognition of 'two separate constitution making bodies . . . of Pakistan and Hindustan' representing the interests of Muslims and non-Muslims respectively.[44] It was precisely on the basis of the distinction between Muslims and non-Muslims and the relative equality of Pakistan and Hindustan that the League was to wage its final battle against liberal democracy in India.

The Mission's preliminary proposals provided for two groups of provinces, one predominantly Muslim and the other predominantly Hindu in composition. Their parity was implied by the provision that the Executive and the Legislature of the proposed Indian Union would consist of 'equal proportions from the Muslim and Hindu majority provinces'.[45] At the Tripartite Conference which opened in May 1946

[42] See Wavell's lengthy accounts of his interviews with Jinnah on 24 and 27 June in *The Viceroy's Journal*, pp. 146–7, 148–50. See also Wavell's letter to Jinnah on 9 July 1945 in the *Indian Annual Register*, 1945, vol. I, p. 140.

[43] See Jinnah's speech to the Convention of League Legislators on 7 April 1946 in Pirzada (ed.), *Foundations of Pakistan*, vol. II, p. 510.

[44] See the 'Delhi Resolution' passed by the Convention of the League's Legislators on 9 April 1946, ibid., vol. II, pp. 512–13.

[45] See Lord Pethick-Lawrence to Maulana Abul Kalam Azad and M.A. Jinnah, 27 April 1946 in Gwyer and Appadorai (eds), *Speeches*, vol. II, p. 572 and

it became evident that the principal sticking point between Congress and League was the question of parity.[46] Congress strongly resisted the idea of a constitutional organization of permanent groups of provinces and firmly opposed the parity of representation between groups of provinces. Nehru emphasized that his party would not negotiate any settlement based on the League's notion of ideological parity between Indian Muslims and the totality of all other Indian groups, nor would it allow the extension of such status to the mutual relations between groups of provinces designated as Hindustan and Pakistan.

In an effort to resolve the new deadlock, the Mission then proposed on 16 May an alternative confederal structure consisting of *two* predominantly Muslim sets of provinces in the northwest and east of India and *one* predominantly Hindu group of provinces.[47] But by doing so, the Mission had effectively undermined the constitutional and ideological dichotomy between Hindustan and Pakistan which had formed the crux of the League's claim to parity.

The implications of the Mission's new plan were swiftly exposed by Jinnah. He claimed that by dividing the Pakistan group into two, the Mission had struck at the heart of Muslim solidarity as well as destroyed the ideological balance between Muslims and non-Muslims. The Mission's new proposals, he concluded, were clearly designed to deny his community's legitimate right to parity and self-determination.[48]

Despite these protests of dismay, however, the League accepted the Mission's plan on 6 June.[49] Its acceptance was based primarily on the assurance provided by the Viceroy that the proposed Interim Government intended to ensure parity by allocating 5 portfolios to the

---

Suggested Points of Agreement between the Congress and the League put forward by the Cabinet Mission Plan, 8 May 1946 in *Papers Relating to the Cabinet Mission to India 1946* (Delhi: Manager of Publications), p. 15.

[46] See, Terms offered by the Muslim League as a Basis of Agreement, 12 May 1946 in Gwyer and Appadorai (eds), *Speeches*, vol. II, pp. 20–1 and Terms offered by Congress as a Basis of Agreement, 12 May 1946, ibid., pp. 22–3.

[47] See statement by the Cabinet Mission to India and the Viceroy, 16 May 1946, ibid., vol. II, pp. 577–84.

[48] See Jinnah's statement on the Cabinet Mission's Plan on 23 May 1946, in Jamil-ud-din Ahmed (ed.), *Jinnah*, vol. II, pp. 291–5.

[49] Resolution of the Muslim League Council on the Cabinet Mission's Plan on 6 June 1946 in L.A. Sherwani (ed.), *Pakistan Resolution to Pakistan: 1940–1947: A Selection of Documents presenting the Case for Pakistan* (Karachi: National Publishing House, 1969).

League; 5 to Congress and 2 to remaining minorities (possibly Sikhs and Christians).[50] The League could not have been unaware that although there was no provision for exclusive communal representation, its introduction would be fairly certain. For if Congress wished to prevent the Hindu majority from being reduced to a minority, it could not afford to nominate a Muslim member on its quota whatever the dictates of its political ideology. For the first time institutional patterns of representation promised to uphold the League's traditional claim that Congress was, in fact, a representative of Hindu interests and the League, the authoritative voice of 'Muslim India'.

But no sooner had negotiations begun on the character and composition of the Interim Government, than the Viceroy denied that there was any firm commitment on the 5:5:2 ratio.[51] In fact, the government had little option in the face of Congress's continuing opposition to any form of parity that would result in Congress and League functioning as exclusively communal organizations.

On 16 June the Mission announced its intention to expand the Interim Government to a total of 14 members of which 6 members (5 Caste and 1 Scheduled Caste Hindu) would be nominated by Congress; 5 members all Muslims, nominated by the League, and 3 members nominated by the Sikh, Christian and Parsi communities.[52] The new proposals revealed the government's intention simultaneously to conciliate Congress by providing for a Hindu majority and appease the League by granting it the exclusive right to nominate Muslims.[53] Thus, even as parity was abandoned, the consolidation of Congress and League as primarily communal representatives seemed assured.

The failure of these proposals which signalled the end of all further efforts to ensure liberal democracy in a united India stemmed from the clash of two wholly irreconcilable sets of political norms. The League was clearly unwilling to compromise on the view that Muslims

[50] Wavell to Jinnah, 4 June 1946 in Pirzada (ed.), *Quaid-e-Azam Jinnah's Correspondence*, p. 320 and Jinnah to Wavell, 8 June 1946, ibid., p. 321.

[51] Wavell to Jinnah, 12 June 1946, ibid., p. 323.

[52] See Statement by the Cabinet Delegation and the Viceroy on the formation of an Interim Government, 16 June 1946, *Papers Relating to the Cabinet Mission to India 1946*, pp. 43–4.

[53] The insinuation was, however, hotly resisted by Cripps in his statement to the House of Commons in July 1946. See his speech in the House of Commons on 18 July 1946. *Hansard's Parliamentary Debates*, 1946, vol. 425, cols 1394–416.

and non-Muslims were rigid, monolithic political entities whereas Congress would accept no arrangement that threatened to undermine the legitimacy of freely arrived, political alignment.[54] In order to appreciate the League's demand for parity it is necessary to understand its relation to Muslim perceptions of society as fundamentally heterogeneous and immune to a system of common legislation for Muslims and non-Muslims. Indeed, the organization of political society is seen by Muslims to consist primarily in a system of parallel laws which enables each communal group to pursue the dictates of its own religious code. It was the absence of any real commitment to a system of common legislation that ultimately precluded the League's espousal of a liberal democracy founded on a common law reflecting a broad area of intercommunal consensus.

Certainly, some Indian Muslims, including Chaudhri Rahmat Ali and Mohammed Iqbal, had expressed their objections to Indian nationalism and liberal democracy in precisely these terms.[55] Both regarded the idea of a common Indian federation and common Indian legislation as not only unattainable but essentially undesirable insofar as it worked against 'the development of each group according to its own cultural traditions'.[56] Both affirmed the positive aspects of political exclusivism by their commitment to communalism which they regarded as the highest expression of culture. More importantly, their position was consistent with Islamic values insofar as these are seen, theologically, to uphold such exclusivism on the grounds that the inclusion of non-Muslims into an Islamic community would endanger its essential solidarity characterized by a singular loyalty to the final revelation of God's word.

Ultimately it mattered little whether Indian Muslims were in fact an indivisible community: what was important for the League and its Muslim adherents was that all politics should be conducted as if they were. It was not enough therefore that Congress did not actually

[54] See Jinnah to Wavell, 19 June 1946 in Pirzada (ed.), *Quaid-e-Azam Jinnah's Correspondence*, p. 328 and Maulana Abul Kalam Azad to Wavell, 25 June 1946 in Gwyer and Appadorai (eds), *Speeches*, vol. II, p. 606.

[55] See, Chaudhri Rahmat Ali, *Pakistan*, as well as his, *What Does the Pakistan National Movement Stand for*? (Cambridge: W. Heffer & Sons, 1st edn, 1933) and Iqbal's presidential address to the 21st session of the Muslim League in December 1930 in Pirzada (ed.), *Foundations of Pakistan*, vol. II, pp. 157–63.

[56] Iqbal's presidential address to the Muslim League in December 1930 in Pirzada (ed.), *Foundations of Pakistan*, vol. II, p. 161.

represent the vast majority of Indian Muslims, for what was really at stake was the institutionalization of politics on the basis that Congress *could not* represent Indian Muslims.

Chapter Six

The High Politics of India's Partition: The Revisionist Perspective*

ASIM ROY

A real need for revaluation of the high politics of India's partition has been boldly underscored by some recent developments. One of these is the most valuable revisionist contribution of Ayesha Jalal of the University of Cambridge.[1] Whether or not the centenary years for the Indian National Congress (henceforth the Congress) witnessed any significant publications on the Congress politics, two major studies in the politics of the All-India Muslim League (henceforth the League), its 'Great Leader' (*Quaid-i Azam*), Muhammad Ali Jinnah, and the partition have come down to us in quick succession: 1984 saw the publication of Stanley Wolpert's Jinnah of Pakistan,[2] and the following year receive Ayesha Jalal's, as mentioned above. The importance of these studies does not merely consist in the wide polarity of their approaches and views. Much greater significance is attached to the fact that their sharp difference underlines a strong and long-felt need for questioning some of the great old assumptions and myths enshrined in the orthodox historiography of British India's partition, as discussed below.

February 1988 saw the beginning of a series of developments, focusing on the politics of partition, which stemmed from the much expected disclosure of the thirty pages of Maulana Abul Kalam Azad's

* Review Article, *Modern Asian Studies*, 24, 2, 1990, pp. 385–415.

[1] A. Jalal, *The Sole Spokesman. Jinnah, the Muslim League and the Demand for Pakistan* (Cambridge: Cambridge University Press, South Asian Studies, no. 31, 1985) [henceforth *Jinnah*].

[2] S. Wolpert, *Jinnah of Pakistan* (New York: Oxford University Press, 1984).

book[3] left sealed for thirty years, and due to be released at the time. The delayed public disclosure of the material in early November 1988, due to some legal tangle, fuelled public curiosity and speculations about the politics of partition.[4] The contents of the excised portion, though it appeared disappointing to some for not making startling revelations,[5] deviates vitally from the book at least in one major respect. In this section, the release of which almost coincides with the birth centenary of Jawaharlal Nehru, Azad points his finger in a much more determined manner at the former's responsibility for the partition. He claims to have initiated the move for Nehru's succession as the Congress president in 1946, and regrets his decision as a 'blunder' of 'himalayan' proportion. He writes:

> I can never forgive myself when I think that if I had not committed these mistakes the history of the last 10 years would have been different . . . I warned Jawaharlal that history would never forgive us if we agreed to Partition. The verdict would be that India was not divided by the Muslim League but by the Congress.[6]

These are indeed strong words, and may even seem bizarre to the multitude who have been brought up with the traditional assumptions about the partition. This brings us to what recent historical research clearly reveals as long-cherished myths of India's partition.

The polarity between the historical theses of Wolpert and Jalal as well as Azad's contentions touch respectively on the twin partition myths locked in a symbiotic relationship: 'The League for partition' and 'the Congress for unity'. The traditional understanding of the political process leading to partition has remained strongly rooted in these two 'unquestionable' popular assumptions, reinforced by a long and powerful tradition of academic sanctification. It would be most surprising not to find a great majority of people, having a basic familiarity with the major developments preceding the Indian partition, identifying the Lahore Resolution of the League (March 1940) with the demand for Pakistan and partition, and regarding 14 August

[3] M.A.K. Azad, *India Wins Freedom* (Calcutta: Orient Longmans, 1957).
[4] *The Statesman Weekly* (Calcutta & New Delhi), 29 October 1988, pp. 3, 7.
[5] Ibid., 'The Maulana's Lament', Editorials; 12 November 1988, p. 9.
[6] Ibid., 5 November 1988, p. 6. For a further discussion, see below.

1947 as its logical culmination.[7] Likewise, the Indian nationalist component of this historiographical orthodoxy has been content to project partition as the tragic finale of a heroic struggle of the Indian patriots against the sinister Machiavellian forces out to destroy the sacred Indian unity. Like all myths one may find a modicum of truth to defend more moderate versions of such perceptions. But, with greater accession to our knowledge in recent times and accentuation of clarity to our perceptions on modern politics in India, such positions have become totally indefensible.[8] The traditional perspective seems desperately remiss in not conveying not merely the true nature of the high drama but also its nuances, subtleties and intricacies. This flat and linear perspective is astonishingly indifferent to or ignorant of the undercurrents as much in the League as in Congress high politics during the critical decade before partition. As early as December 1938, while moving the tenth resolution at the twenty-sixth League session in Patna, repudiating the federal scheme under the Government of India Act of 1935 and investing Jinnah with the supreme authority 'to adopt such a course as may be necessary with a view to exploring the possibility of a suitable alternative which would safeguard the interests of the Mussalmans', Maulana Zafar Ali Khan spoke about the League's 'antagonism' not 'towards the Hindus generally, but against the Congress High Command', foreshadowed the ensuing struggle

[7] '. . . there is universal agreement that Mahomed Ali Jinnah was central to the Muslim League's emergence after 1937 as the voice of a Muslim nation; to its articulation in March 1940 of the Pakistan Demand for separate statehood for the Muslim majority provinces of north-western and eastern India; and to its achievement in August 1947. . . .' R.J. Moore, 'Jinnah and the Pakistan Demand', *Modern Asian Studies*, XVII, 4 (1983), p. 529. cf also: 'In August 1947, the Muslim League was the only party to achieve what it wanted.' A.I. Singh, *The Origins of the Partition of India* (Delhi: Oxford University Press, 1987), p. 252. See also A. Roy, 'Review' of Jalal's *Jinnah* in *South Asia*, X, 1 (June 1987), p. 101.

[8] The most valuable recent edition of the documentary sources on the transfer of power in India is undoubtedly N. Mansergh (ed. -in-chief), E.W.R. Lumby and P. Moon (eds.), *Constitutional Relations Between Britain and India: The Transfer of Power 1942–1947*, [henceforth *TP Documents*], 12 vols. (London, 1970–83). In addition, the *Quaid-i Azam* Papers, All-India Muslim League Papers, and the 'Partition Papers'—all rendered accessible in the National Archives of Pakistan, Islamabad, together with a variety of private papers and other documentary material made available in the Indian National Archives and the Nehru Memorial Museum and Library, New Delhi, form a substantive corpus of new material on the politics of partition.

between the two parties as a gigantic 'battle of wits', and expressed his concern to see 'who emerged victorious from the contest'.[9] The revisionist perspective offers a much clearer and more logical and convincing interpretation of this 'battle between Jinnah and the Congress in which both openly stood for what they did not want, said what they did not mean, and what they truly wanted was not stated publicly but only betrayed in their vital and purposive political decisions and actions. The long persistence of orthodox beliefs in these matters has clearly been in accord with the most commonly perceived interconnections among Muslim 'nationalism', 'separatism', the Muslim League, the Lahore Resolution and partition. But 'the conspiracy of silence' resorted to both by Jinnah and the Congress in regard to the real motives underlying their respective political strategies and tactics must also be seen as largely contributing to the perpetuation of these traditional myths. The acceptance of the emerging historical truth makes a huge demand on everyone grown up with the old verity in as much as the new is totally opposed to what has so far been largely given to the world, namely, that it was not the League but the Congress who chose, at the end of the day, to run a knife across Mother India's body.

Jalal has initiated the much needed task of historical reconstruction by taking upon herself the challenge of demolishing the first of the twin myths which concerns Jinnah and the League's actual role in the making of Pakistan. It seems a remarkable coincidence that Wolpert's precedes Jalal's and provides a perfect foil, in its orthodoxy, to set off the critical significance of Jalal's valuable revisionist contribution which deserves a very special place in the corpus of the modern South Asian historiography on the partition of India. The academic popularity of this orthodox historiography is clearly attested by the fact that Wolpert is both preceded and followed, within the short span of a decade, by some powerful advocates of the conventional position, such as U. Kaura (1977),[10] R.J. Moore (1983),[11] and A.I. Singh

[9] S.S. Pirzada (ed.), *Foundations of Pakistan. All-India Muslim League Documents: 1906–1947*, II (Karachi/Dacca: National Publishing House, 1970), p. 321.

[10] U. Kaura, *Muslims and Indian Nationalism. The Emergence of the Demand for India's Partition 1928–1940* (New Delhi: South Asia Books, 1977).

[11] R.J. Moore, 'Jinnah and Pakistan', pp. 529–61.

(1987),[12] leaving aside a host of scholars supportive of this position but whose involvements with this issue are peripheral.

Where does one draw the line between the conventional and the revisionist positions on the issue of Pakistan and partition in relation to Jinnah and the League? On both chronological and thematic grounds the Lahore Resolution of 1940 clearly emerges as the divide between the two distinct interpretative approaches. Until then no sharp differences and disagreements seem to figure very prominently in the orthodox and revisionist analyses of Muslim politics between the two world wars. In the orthodox view, the resolution adopted at the Annual Session of the League at Lahore on 24 March 1949 was the first official pronouncement of the 'Pakistan' or 'partition' demand by the party. Though the term 'Pakistan' is nowhere to be found in the resolution, it is, nonetheless, seen to have provided for the separation of the Muslim majority areas in the north-western and eastern zones of India as 'sovereign' and 'independent states', and thereby formed the basis of the 'Pakistan demand'. Along with this perceived reformulation of the League's political objectives, there is also, intrinsic to this view, an equally significant assumption of a major turn and break in Jinnah's political development: the Islamization of the 'nationalist' and 'secular' Jinnah—'the ambassador of Hindu–Muslim unity' emerging as the most potent and dynamic influence in partitioning British India on religious ground. Both these assumptions are challenged in the revisionist analyses: the Lahore Resolution was not meant to be the 'Pakistan demand' but a 'tactical move' and a 'bargaining counter', and hence, it implied no ideological or religious metamorphosis of Jinnah, no basic changes in his political aims but a significant shift in his strategies and tactics.

In the period between Jinnah's declining influence in the Congress that led to his resignation from the party in 1920, with the corresponding rise of Gandhi and his populist politics, and the adoption of the Lahore Resolution, Jinnah and the League's political aims and objectives are commonly perceived by both orthodox and revisionist writers as seeking to ensure a secure and legitimate place for Muslims in the changing world of India as well as build up the League's position and power as central to the interests of all Muslims in India. In achieving these goals the central league leadership were internally confronted with a serious challenge of working out a delicate balance of interests

[12] A.I. Singh, *Origins of the Partition.*

and power with the growing authority and influence of the provincial Muslim political bosses in the Muslim majority areas, especially Bengal and the Punjab, reinforced by the enlarged political opportunities under the 'Montford' Reforms of 1919. Externally, their attempts, as a 'weighted minority' to secure a 'substantial' representation at the centre, were subjected to the competing claims, machinations, and much greater strength of the Indian majority represented by the Congress. Both the traditionalist and revisionist opinions find concurrence in stressing the League and Jinnah's political efforts throughout this period, towards a resolution of the Muslim problem within the constitutional framework of a united India. The detailed political analyses of the major developments of the period are aimed at revealing how, as a moderate constitutionalist and nationalist, seeking adequate safeguards for the minority interests of Indian Muslims, Jinnah's political aims were as much frustrated as was his political position undermined, in stages, during this period. The steady demise of constitutionalism and moderatism in Indian politics since 1917; Jinnah's relegation from the centre of nationalist politics consequent upon the simultaneous rise of the Pan-Islamists and Gandhi in Indian politics since 1919–20; the aggravation of communalist tendencies in politics both by the introduction of representative institutions under the 1919 Reforms, and the bitterness, frustrations and confusions resulting from the collapse of the Non-cooperation–Khilafat Movement (1922) as well as abolition of the Khilafat (1924); the steep and significant rise in the position and influence of the provincial Muslim political bosses in the Muslim majority areas in the northwestern and eastern regions in the interwar period; the reluctance or inability of the Congress to strengthen the hands of the 'left' faction of the League under Jinnah in the course of negotiations among the Indian political parties in the years 1926–8; the unilateral declaration by the Congress of its political goal of total independence (*purna swaraj*)—all find, in varying degrees of importance, common historiographical recognition as indicative of the predicaments of both League and Jinnah, forcing the latter to withdraw temporarily from Indian politics and move to London. The growing impotence and irrelevance of the League in the world of Muslim *real-politik*, *vis-a-vis* the growing authority of the Muslim provinces and provincial leaders, as revealed in the subsequent developments in the Round Table Conference and the Communal Award in the early 1930s, prepared the ground for Jinnah's return, on the supplication of the League leaders of the Muslim minority areas, to resurrect the central role of the organization and liberate it from the suffocating embraces of the provincial leaders. An essential continuity in Jinnah's aims and policies, on his return, finds general acceptance among most writers. The continuity is to be found in the common Congress and League objectives of promoting their respective national or central dominance at the expense of the provincial bases of power. Likewise, the League was not uninterested in the Congress efforts to make the British concede power at the centre which they continued to monopolize under the provisions of the Government of India Act of 1935, the ultimate League objective being a negotiated pattern of sharing power with the Congress on the basis of a substantial League representation at the centre.

The agreements between the orthodox and revisionist views are also extended to a recognition of the supreme importance of the provincial elections of 1937 held in eleven British provinces under the Act of 1935. It is, however, in regard to the nature and meanings of this significance that their divergences begin. There is no room for disputations about the crippling discomfiture of the League candidates in the election as against the overwhelming success of the Congress in the non-Muslim constituencies. Of the eleven provinces of British India, the Congress emerged with a clear majority in six and as the largest single party in three others. The revelation of the utter weakness of the League and Jinnah positively diminished their importance to the Congress, as soon experienced by the League in the growing intransigence of the Congress revealed in their post-election attitudes and dealings. For Jinnah, who had striven for Muslim political unity at the national level, the political reality of the post-1937 British India that while Hindus would dominate in all the Hindu majority provinces, Muslims seemed unable to dominate even the two largest Muslim majority provinces of the Punjab and Bengal, looked menacing. It seemed more so in view of a clear prospect of the Congress dominance at the centre as well, should the British even decide to implement the federal provisions of the 1935 Act which offered Muslims not more than one-third of the central representation. More than ever he now clearly saw the lack of any political choice other than turning the League into the 'third' focus of power in India and the 'sole spokesman' for Muslims. 'An honourable settlement', he came to realize, 'can only be achieved between equals' and 'politics means power and not relying only on cries of justice or fair play or goodwill'.[13]

[13] Pirzada, *Muslim League Documents*, II, p. 269; also J. Ahmad (ed.), *Speeches*

The conflicting perceptions of Jinnah's realization are quite significant. The orthodox perception is one of a complete transformation of the mores of Jinnah's personality, ideology and policy. His old secularist idea of a Muslim minority problem to be resolved through substantial representation at the centre and provincial autonomy stood totally discomfited, and came, therefore, to be discarded in favour of the radically new demand for 'parity' at the centre based on the recognition of the Muslim claim of being a separate religious 'nation'—the much-publicized 'two-nation theory' of Jinnah. The use of religious slogans and symbols proved immeasurably useful not just in rousing sentiments against the Congress ministries in the provinces. It also helped the League in reaching the Muslim masses over the head of the provincial leaders. Jinnah's task was facilitated further by the political exigencies arising from the outbreak of the Second World War. The Congress 'intransigence' drew the government closer to the League and made them realize the obvious importance of promoting Jinnah as the spokesman for Indian Muslims. Reassured by the government suspension of efforts at federation and armed with a practical veto upon any further constitutional advance offered by the government, Jinnah found the British ready to concede his demands. On 24 March 1940 Jinnah told the world what he wanted. In Jinnah's minds, so a major protagonist orthodox school tells us, 'partition . . . was the only long-term solution to India's foremost problem' and, having arrived at and taken this decision, he 'lowered the final curtain on any prospects for a single united independent India'.[14] From that moment Jinnah was 'set on his seven year campaign to realize the sovereign state of Pakistan'.[15] *Quaid-i Azam* had indeed forged the 'League into a political weapon powerful enough to tear the subcontinent apart'.[16] The academic judgement thus lends its weight to both the popular 'hagiology' and 'demonology' of Jinnah, the former representing the teeming millions of adoring believers whom Jinnah led to 'the promised land', while, to even greater numbers of the latter persuasion, his memory is perpetuated as a diabolical and sinister influence behind 'the vivisection of Mother India'.

---

and Writings of Mr Jinnah, I (Lahore: S.M. Ashraf, 7th edn., 1968), p. 32.

[14] Wolpert, *Jinnah*, p.182.

[15] F. Robinson, 'Review' of Jalal's *Jinnah*, in *Modern Asian Studies*, XX, 3 July 1986, p. 613.

[16] S. Wolpert, *A New History of India* (New York: Oxford University Press, 1982), p. 325.

The revisionist view, in contrast, envisages no real change in Jinnah's political goals but in his political strategies and tactics. His aims still continued to be to secure Muslim interests 'within' and not in total separation from India. No doubt he came to realize the grave limitations and political danger of Muslims trying to operate on the basis of the formula of a majority-minority differentiation. With the abandonment of the minority status was also discarded the notion of a simple unmodified federation which, as the 1937 election at the provincial level had clearly shown, was likely only to condemn Muslims to a virtual and perpetual dominance by the Congress. The political answer to the problem of all Indian Muslims, scattered unevenly over the subcontinent, could not have been in a total separation of the Muslim majority areas. As Muslims living in areas where they formed the majority had different needs from co-religionists in Hindu areas, Jinnah had to balance the demand for a separate Muslim state against safeguards for Muslim minorities. Viewed from this position, the Lahore Resolution, though couched in terms of separation of Muslim majority areas, did not reflect Jinnah's 'real political aims'.[17] It is simplistic, in this view, to take it as a final commitment to partition or Pakistan, if the latter term is used in its conventional sense of partition and not in Jinnah's special sense of being a strategically important embodiment of the recognition of the Muslim right and claim of being a nation—a recognition that could then be used to overcome the obvious political disadvantage of a minority status in a federal constitution. The thrust of Jinnah's political strategy underpinning the resolution was initially to secure the recognition of the Indian Muslim nationhood on the basis of acceptance of the 'Pakistan' demand by the British and Congress, and thereby gain an equal say for Muslims in any arrangement about India's political future at the centre. Once the principle of the Muslim right to self-determination, as embodied in the Lahore Resolution, was conceded, the resultant Muslim state or states could either 'enter into a confederation with non-Muslim provinces on the basis of parity at the centre' or make, as a sovereign state, 'treaty arrangement with the rest of India about matters of common concern'.[18] The resolution, in this sense, was,

[17] Jalal, *Jinnah*, p. 4; Roy, 'Review' of Jalal's *Jinnah*.

[18] Ibid., p. 241. Jinnah's vision perhaps anticipated the contemporary Canadian situation in relation to Quebec. French Quebec decided against separation in 1980. In accordance with the arrangements of the new Accord signed between the Canadian Federal Government and the Provinces, Quebec's power in the Centre

therefore, nothing more than a 'tactical move' and a 'bargaining counter'.[19]

How do these bear comparison on logic and evidence? The conventional view, on a close analysis, reveals serious inadequacies, and fails to accommodate certain pieces of the jigsaw.

The Lahore Resolution has given rise to three main issues, of which we have already mentioned two: the first concerns its relation to the Pakistan demand, and the second has reference to Jinnah's political aims and strategies in the most critical years between the resolution and the actual partition. There is a third question which caused some political dissent between the League and the provincial Muslim leaders, especially of Bengal, having resurfaced much later during the political conflict between West and East Pakistan. This relates to the doubts concerning the federal or unitary character of the separated Muslim majority areas as envisaged in the resolution.

Of all these three issues the last is the least ambiguous. Adopted at a time when the League's authority over the Muslim majority provinces was far from established, the resolution found it expedient to make unequivocal reference to 'independent states' rather than a single state. Only in 1946, as Jinnah needed to present a collective Muslim front to the Cabinet Mission, and also as the League and Jinnah had indeed emerged as the 'sole spokesman' for Indian Muslims, Jinnah felt himself strong enough to change the wording of the resolution from the plural to the singular 'state', providing a rather amusing justification, though no Leaguer seemed to have had the courage to ask for one at the time, that the plural was a 'misprint'. The decision was carried through the meeting of the Muslim League Council in Delhi. The provincial Muslim leaders, like Fazlul Huq, who tried unsuccessfully to resist Jinnah's centralizing arm, subsequently felt bitter about this change. Huq, the mover of the resolution in Lahore, later accused Jinnah of 'betrayal' of its letter and spirit. Significantly enough, the United Front, led by Huq, H. Suhrawardy and Maulana Bhasani, which decimated the Muslim League in the general election of 1954 in East Pakistan, justified its claims for the

---

has been substantially reinforced without compromising its right to contract out of Federal Programmes.

[19] Ibid., p. 57.

provincial autonomy, contained in its 'Twenty-one Demands', in terms of the Lahore Resolution.

The traditional understanding of and explanations for the other two seminal issues are patently uncritical and inadequate. A whole range of doubts concerning a facile equation between the resolution and the Pakistan demand as well as Jinnah's political calculations are either ignored or glossed over.

To begin with, the very omission of the word 'Pakistan' from the so-called Pakistan Resolution cannot but raise doubts in this context. Much greater significance is added to such doubts when Jinnah's initial displeasure at this equation is considered. Why did he find 'fault' with Hindus for 'foisting' and 'fathering' the word 'Pakistan' on Muslims? In his Presidential speech at the thirteenth Delhi session of the League in April 1943 Jinnah spoke his mind quite strongly:

> I think you will bear me out that when we passed the Lahore Resolution, we had not used the word 'Pakistan'. Who gave us this word? [Cries of 'Hindus'] Let me tell you it is their fault. They started damning the resolution on the ground that it was Pakistan. . . . They fathered this word upon us. Give the dog a bad name and then hang him. . . . You know perfectly well that Pakistan is a word which is really foisted upon us and fathered on us by some section of the Hindu press and also by the British press.[20]

Jinnah was quite right about the beginning of this identification: the adoption of the resolution was widely reported in the Hindu and British press as the acceptance of the 'Pakistan demand'.

The second major source of doubt about the logic of Jinnah demanding partition, in 1940, stems from a consideration of the obvious and callous disregard or 'sacrifice' (*qurbani*) of less than two score million Muslim, unfortunate enough to be born and/or live on the wrong side of the 'holy land' namely, the Muslim minority areas. If anything, partition was likely to increase their vulnerability and render their position more precarious. Much of the rationale underlying Jinnah's long political career is inseparable from his anxiety to ensure a secure and rightful place for all Muslims of British India in transition. One could scarcely afford to forget that it was the Muslim minority-area leaders who made Jinnah's return from the political wilderness in London possible, and he would have been unlikely to turn his back on them, that is, as long as he could help it. He was, of

20 Pirzada, *Muslim League Documents*, II. p. 425.

course, eventually unable to help it, and the paradox of the resultant Pakistan is 'how it failed to satisfy the interests of the very Muslims who are supposed to have demanded its creation'.[21]

Thirdly, not even the interests of the Muslim majority areas were either expected to be or actually served by the partition. There is as much sense as pathos in Ayesha Jalal's most critical and searching question about the most publicized creation of the largest contemporaneous Muslim state in the world (about sixty million Muslims, leaving another thirty-five million out of it in India where it became the largest number of Muslims in a non-Muslim state): 'how did a Pakistan come about which fitted the interests of most Muslims so poorly?'[22] The situational and circumstantial differences as well as the disjunction of interests between the Muslim majority and minority areas were significant determinants of Muslim politics. The Muslim political bosses of the majority areas, who benefited most from the expanded political opportunities in the interwar period, were both dependent on and adept in intercommunal politics increasingly dominated by Muslims. Their political future was assured in a federal structure with provisions for strong provincial governments. The Lahore Resolution based on the principle of a separate Muslim nationhood communalized politics and destroyed the rationale and basis of intercommunal politics. Logically and surely, the two largest Muslim provinces—Bengal and Punjab—were later partitioned with all its economic, political and psychological consequences. As for the Muslims of Sind, NWFP and Baluchistan, the creation of Pakistan 'bundled them willy-nilly into a state dominated by their more numerous co-religionists from western Punjab and placed them under the tight central control . . . [of] Pakistan', and the depth of their fervour for Pakistan h'can be gauged by their efforts since independence to throw off the yoke of the Punjab'.[23]

Fourthly, barring some zealots of the likes of the 'Cambridge student group', the viability of a partitioned Pakistan had been a crucial question in the minds not only of the British and non-Muslim Indian contemporaries but also of most thinking Muslims, including the *Quaid-i Azam*. Serious doubts had been expressed from time to time on the economic and defence implications of the partition, given

[21] Jalal, *Jinnah*, p. 2.
[22] Ibid., p. 4.
[23] Ibid., p. 3.

particularly the geographic absurdity of its two major western and eastern components being separated by nearly a thousand miles of Hindu-dominated territory. Jinnah's desperate appeal for a small corridor interlinking eastern and western wings of Pakistan in the final stages of the partition-talks is a pointer to his own sharing of such doubts.

Fifthly, one of the major weaknesses of the conventional interpretation is that it offers no convincing explanations for the strange dichotomy between the rhetoric and reality of Jinnah's politics since the adoption of the resolution. His responses, in particular to the Cripps Offer (1942) and the Cabinet Mission Plan (1946), remain the weakest links in traditional arguments. His rejection of the former as well as the acceptance (until the Congress attitudes and response forced its rejection) of the latter clearly run counter to the popular view that Jinnah craved for partition. The principle of 'secession' embodied in the Cripps Offer, whereby an unwilling province could 'opt out' of the Union, was a direct British response to the Lahore demand, providing Jinnah and the League with the surest means of fully realizing the stated goals of the Lahore Resolution namely, independent and sovereign Muslim 'states'. Yet the proposals were rejected by the League, ostensibly and curiously on the ground that 'Pakistan' was not explicitly named. Most writers remain content with this tenuous explanation, regardless of the fact that Jinnah himself did not care much for the magic word and deliberately excluded it from the Lahore Resolution, as noted above. Not totally unaware of the problem, perhaps, some others have sought explanations elsewhere. Wolpert believes that the 'Muslim League were prepared to accept the offer, since it essentially embodied their Pakistan demand, but the Congress rejection left them no political option but to do likewise in order to compete most effectively for mass support'.[24] Masselos emphasizes 'the political disadvantages' of the League 'being the only open supporter of the scheme in the current climate of opinion. . . .'[25] Attribution of such political concerns to the Muslim League, in the period following the election of 1937, and more so, after the Lahore Resolution, may seem more than dubious. Leaving aside the resolution itself which was a total rejection of the Congress platform and the wishes of the large

[24] Wolpert, *New History*, p. 335.

[25] J. Masselos, *Indian Nationalism: An History* (New Delhi: Sterling Publishers, 1985), p. 206.

majority of Indians, the League's political strategy, throughout this period, was geared to the object of reinforcing its political identity and position as the sole spokesman by exploiting every opportunity of opposing as well as discrediting the Congress. When all is said and done, the simple fact about the Cripps Offer remains that Jinnah and the League could, had they so desired, take the Muslim majority provinces out of the Indian Union. The Cabinet Mission Plan, on the other hand, categorically rejected partition—nor was Pakistan mentioned anywhere in the document—yet on 6 June 1946 the League accepted the Mission's Plan, long before the Congress indicated its 'conditional' acceptance. These two responses put together raise unqualified doubts about Jinnah's attitudes to the partition demand, the intent of the Lahore Resolution, and also the uncritical assumptions of the orthodox historiography.

Finally, the most serious objection to the conventional viewpoints relates to their inability to identify the continuity in Jinnah's political career, as already mentioned. This view is both misleading and unfair to Jinnah in presenting him as a paradox: one who had been a firm believer in Indian nationalism and also in essentially secular political values chose, in 1940, to throw away all he had striven for at a time when partition was by no means a certainty. Undoubtedly, Jinnah's politics since his shattering discomfiture in the 1937 election entered into a new phase, but the change, properly understood, is not so much one of political goal as one of tactics, as noted above. Additionally, the paradoxical view of Jinnah seems to contradict Wolpert's own psychoanalytical approach to Jinnah's politics. If Jinnah possessed those traits underlined by Wolpert—vanity, ambition, and a 'need to play the starring role'—he was even more likely to be seeking a dominant role in the much larger political arena of India, comprising about four-hundred million of which ninety-five million in the whole of India and eighty million in British India were Muslim, than his 'moth-eaten Pakistan' with its total population of about sixty million.

Serious misgivings and inadequacies of this nature in the orthodox views created demands for revisionist historical research and studies in this area. Ayesha Jalal has precisely filled this disturbing historical gap, and thereby laid South Asian historiography under an enormous debt to herself. Irrespective of the enormous significance of her study, the question of the originality of Jalal's thesis needs, however, to be set in clear perspective. In his otherwise excellent review of this particular Cambridge publication in the Cambridge Journal of *Modern Asian Studies*, Francis Robinson calls Jalal's 'a novel thesis'.[26] No discerning student of the history of Indian partition should find this claim totally acceptable. Like all major works of historical revisionism Jalal's edifice is reared on an existing foundation. The centre piece both of Jinnah's political strategy in the last crucial decade before the partition and of Jalal's thesis on Jinnah has been, as already observed, the Lahore Resolution with its intriguingly 'vague' and 'amorphous' wordings. The mainspring of this thesis has clearly been a marginal, unorthodox and lesser known minority view that has long questioned the purpose of the resolution and found Jinnah's political strategy more 'a tactical move' or 'a bargaining counter' than an outright demand for partition or Pakistan.

The 'ambiguity' of the resolution drew contemporary attention. Dr B.R. Ambedkar, whose thoughts on the idea of Pakistan or partition met with Jinnah's approval, noted in 1940:

> . . . the Resolution is rather ambiguous, if not self-contradictory. It speaks of grouping the zones into 'independent States in which the constituent units shall be autonomous and sovereign.' The use of the terms 'constituent units' indicates that what is contemplated is a Federation. If that is so, then, the use of the word 'Sovereign' as an attribute of the units is out of place. Federation of units and sovereignty of units are contradictions. It may be that what is contemplated is a confederation. It is, however, not very material for the moment whether these independent states are to form into a federation or confederation. What is important is the basic demand, namely, that these areas are to be separated from India and formed into independent states.[27]

Reginald Coupland, who met Jinnah in the early 1940s, expressed similar doubts:

> It was not clear exactly what this paragraph of the resolution meant. It could scarcely mean that the constituent units of the independent States were really to be 'sovereign', but that it did mean that the States were to be really 'independent' was shown by a subsequent paragraph.[28]

The notion of some ambiguities built into the resolution was jux-

[26] Robinson, 'Review' of Jalal's *Jinnah*, p. 617.

[27] B.R. Ambedkar, *Pakistan or the Partition of India* (Bombay: Thacker, 3rd edn. 1946), pp. 4–5.

[28] R. Coupland, *Indian Politics 1936–1942, Report on the Constitutional Problem of India* (London: Oxford University Press, 1944), p. 206

taposed to a less publicized but responsible view, both contemporaneous and later, that it was not intended as a specific demand for partition but as a 'bargaining point'. Penderel Moon, an observant contemporary British official, wrote later in 1961: 'Privately Jinnah told one or two people in Lahore that this Resolution was a "tactical move"; and the fact that six years later he was ready to accept something less than absolute partition suggests that in 1940 he was not really irrevocably committed to it.'[29] Hugh Tinker wrote, in 1967, that many British politicians and administrators considered the resolution as a 'deliberate overbid'.[30] Jalal herself cites several important contemporary sources casting doubts on the notion of a total separation as integral to the resolution. H.V. Hodson, as the Reform Commissioner in 1941, reported that the Muslim Leaguers 'interpreted Pakistan as consistent with a confederation'. Hodson found it the least surprising, as 'Pakistan' offered nothing to Muslims in the minority areas.[31] I.I. Chundrigar, a Leaguer who later became a Prime Minister of independent Pakistan, saw the object of the resolution as not to create 'Ulsters', but to get 'two nations . . . . welded into united India on the basis of equality'. He believed that the resolution looked for an 'alternative to majority rule, not seeking to destroy the unity of India'.[32] Jinnah himself blamed Hindus, in 1943, as mentioned above, for having 'foisted and fathered' the word Pakistan on the Muslim League.[33]

All this should dispel the illusion of any claim of 'novelty' at least in regard to the core of Jalal's thesis that the resolution of 1940 had been a 'bargaining counter'. The critical importance of Jalal's work lies, therefore, not so much in presenting the resolution as a tactical manoeuvre as in her success in elevating this interpretation basically from the realm of doubts and speculations and giving it an academic authenticity, coherence and credibility. Her success in this regard is facilitated as much by her own ability as the availability of a large

[29] P. Moon, *Divide and Quit* (London: Chatto & Windus, 1961), p. 21.

[30] H. Tinker, *Experiment with Freedom: India and Pakistan 1947* (London: Oxford University Press, 1967), p. 24; also P. Hardy, *The Muslims of British India* (Cambridge: Cambridge University Press, South Asian Studies, no. 13, 1972), p. 232.

[31] H.V. Hodson, *The Great Divide: Britain, India, Pakistan* (London: Hutchinson, 1969), p. 69.

[32] Quoted, Jalal, *Jinnah*, p. 70.

[33] See p. 112.

corpus of new documents, as mentioned above.[34] Admittedly, many of the building blocks in Jalal's edifice have been drawn from the steadily expanding store-house of historical knowledge and interpretations derived from prior research and investigations. These are, for example, the dichotomy of interests between the Muslim majority and minority areas; the vested and entrenched positions of the provincial Muslim leaders; Jinnah's aim and strategy to acquire for the League and for himself the position and the right to speak for all Indian Muslims; his determined and sustained efforts at securing theoretical and/or practical recognition of that right and position by the recalcitrant Muslim provincial bosses, the Congress and the British government; the political expediency of the transition of the League politics conducted from the vantage point of a religious and political minority to that of a nation; refurbishing the religious contents of the Pakistan idea to facilitate the League's cause; Jinnah's political calculations behind the rejection of the Cripps Offer and the eagerness to accept the Cabinet Mission Plan, and so on. But Jalal has put them all together for us into one whole coherent piece—authentically as well as creatively refined, modified and enlarged—a piece of historical study that for its thoroughness and excellence is most likely to remain for quite some time the paradigm of a revisionist thesis on Jinnah's politics in the decade before partition.[35]

The revisionist critique is logical and persuasive. Its seminal contribution consists in demystifying the politics of the League, Jinnah and Pakistan in that critical decade, as presented in the conventional historigraphy which is riddled with confusing paradoxes and inconsistencies, as discussed above. The essential integrity and continuity in Jinnah's long political life, subject to a significant shift in his strategy, broadly since 1937, for achieving his political aims, the overt and covert meanings of the Lahore Resolution, with the very specific contents of 'Pakistan' in Jinnah's mind, his rejection of the Cripps Offer and the intriguing wheelings and dealings with the British, his determined and persistent political manoeuvres to pull all provincial Muslim leaders into line, his eager acceptance of the Cabinet Mission Plan until the Congress forced him to reject it, and his 'continuing attempts to preserve his strategy in his many shifts and ploys' even in those closing months of the undoing of his strategy 'down to his

[34] See above, fn.8.
[35] Roy, 'Review' of Jalal's *Jinnah*, p. 101.

May 1947 demand for a corridor through Hindustan to connect the two halves of Pakistan, and his June 1947 proposal that the constituent assemblies of the two new states should both meet in Delhi'[36]—are some of the major disconcerting puzzles in the orthodox versions which the revisionist historical reconstructions help to resolve so convincingly.

Jinnah's tasks, in the revisionist perspective, emerge infinitely more complex and daunting than what the traditionalists would have us believe. For Jinnah, it was far easier to aim at rousing the primordial instincts of Indian Muslims, with a view to mobilizing them to achieve a division of the land, as we have so far been told, and as it eventually happened. This now seems a rather simplistic as well as distorting perception of the more mature, intricate and delicate political position of Jinnah, adept in playing a 'long, slow game'. While he undoubtedly needed the Islamic fervour to rally the Muslim masses to achieve his political aims, he could scarcely afford to push it too far to jeopardize his constant and vital objective of securing the interests of all Indian Muslims which could only have been possible within a framework of Indian unity. This was not all. Jinnah was no less interested in a strong centre than the Congress in the interests of securing and maintaining the dominant national position of the League against the provincial Muslim bases of power. But here again, Jinnah and the League, unlike the Congress, had to curb their natural instincts for a strong centre in a federal structure which would have provided a strong leverage for the Congress dominance. Thus, confronting Jinnah was a political challenge that seemed almost a 'political sphinx' and almost impossible to achieve: a Muslim nation with its 'right' to be independent, but not actually willing to break away from India, forfeiting, thereby, the control over thirty-five million Muslims to be left in a partitioned India; a strong centre essential for keeping the League in a dominant position and the Muslim provinces in line, but not without some constitutional and structural device to prevent the total Congress dominance by virtue of its brute majority. Jinnah's ideal solution lay in two federations—one Muslim- and the League-dominated, the other Hindu- and the Congress-dominated—making it in every way possible to bring the two into a system of political unity on a confederal basis or a similar structure based on treaty arrangements between them.

This view goes a long way in explaining many of those per-

[36] Robinson, 'Review' of Jalal's *Jinnah*, p. 617.

plexities mentioned before. We understand better why the Lahore Resolution seems rather interested in the 'right' of the Muslim majority areas to be independent, and leaves every other vital concern shrouded in ambiguity. We can also see why Jinnah would not originally intend or even like the use of the word Pakistan in the resolution, though later accepted it as a 'convenient synonym' for 'this long phrase'.[37] We get the feeling that the word, which gradually came to symbolize Muslim nationhood, would recommend itself to Jinnah. Again, Jinnah's rejection of the Cripps Offer, which has been one of the weakest points in the orthodox case, provides a strong justification for the revisionist arguments.

Jinnah's strategy centring round the Lahore Resolution was almost immediately welcomed by the British Government through its 1946 'August Offer'. The Cripps Offer carried it even further by conceding, through its 'opt out' provision, the effective demands of the resolution. The League's rejection, though intriguing, is better explained from the revisionist position. Cripps's proposal contained two serious problems for Jinnah. If Jinnah was rather more interested, as noted above, in the matter of recognition of the Muslim right for self-determination than the actual severance of the Muslim states, he was denied explicit recognition of that right—a denial given as the official justification for the League's rejection of the offer. More importantly, Jinnah, in the early 1940s, unable to assert his full authority over the Muslim majority provinces, maintained a calculated silence—quite apparent in the Lahore Resolution—on the issue of the centre, its nature and its relationship with the Muslim provinces. A weak centre was integral to the demand of the Muslim provinces for provincial autonomy, while the League's entire political strategy, as representatives of all Indian Muslims, demanded a strong centre. Before such time as Jinnah could indeed become the sole spokesman for all Muslims and impose his will on the provinces he chose not to raise the awkward question until the Cripps Offer resulted in 'flushing Jinnah out into the open and forcing him to show where he stood on the question of the centre'. The Congress rejection of the offer made it easier for Jinnah also to reject it and avert what seemed 'the gravest threat to his entire strategy'.[38]

37 Pirzada, *Muslim League Documents*, II, p. 426. 'We wanted a word and it was foisted on us, and we found it convenient to use it as a synonym for the Lahore Resolution.' (ibid.)

38 Jalal, *Jinnah*, p. 76.

The Cabinet Mission came to recompense Jinnah for much of what was denied to him by Cripps. The compulsory grouping of Muslim provinces—leaving Bengal and Assam in a separate grouping for ten years—offered him the effective contents of the Muslim federation on a platter, and brought the Muslim provinces under the control of the League at the centre. It denied the principle of secession and preserved India's integrity. It stipulated for a weak centre, thwarting the prospects for a total Congress dominance. The Mission Plan came so close to so much of what Jinnah's political vision embraced. The offer, certainly, was not his ideal: the prospects for the 'parity' he would have wished at the centre were very doubtful coming from the Congress; the centre itself would not have been as strong as he would have liked to ensure his authority over the Muslim provinces. But the communal provisions held out the promise of a powerbroking role at the centre. *Quaid-i Azam* had indeed come the closest to realizing his political dream.

Jinnah could not, however, have shown total indifference to the likely impact of the denial of a 'sovereign' Pakistan on his followers. The League acceptance of the Plan on 6 June 1946 was justified on the ground that the 'basis of Pakistan' was 'inherent' in the plan.[39] He also had to give them an undertaking that he would join no interim government without parity for the League.[40] In the League's statement of acceptance there was further mention of the League's co-operation with the constitution-making apparatus in the 'hope' that their efforts would ultimately be rewarded with the 'establishment of a completely sovereign Pakistan'.[41] This is an extraordinary response if one adheres to the view that Jinnah really wanted a sovereign Pakistan. How could this man, who as recently as 7 April had claimed: 'we cannot accept any proposal which would be, in any way, derogatory to the full sovereignty of Pakistan',[42] forsake the zeal that had consumed his career since 1940 for 'hope'? Rhetoric aside, Jinnah was clearly prepared on 6 June to accept something less than what almost every one else knew as Pakistan.

Just as Jinnah thought himself on the verge of reaping the harvest of a long, chequered and an almost stoically determined political

[39] Mansergh, *TP Documents*, VII, doc. no. 469, Enclosure, L/P & J/5/337: PP 418–20, p. 837.

[40] Jalal, *Jinnah*, p. 202.

[41] Mansergh, *TP Documents*, VII, doc. no. 469, Enclosure, p. 838.

[42] Pirzada, *Muslim League Documents*, II, p. 509.

career, a variety of political factors and circumstances combined to snatch the cup of victory from his lips. The Congress, apparently, began the undoing of his strategy, and the 'last thirteen months of British rule', in Jalal's words, 'saw the tragic collapse of Jinnah's strategy'.[43] On 25 June 1946 the Congress Working Committee gave qualified assent to the plan; the All-India Congress Committee, under Maulana Azad's presidency, voted its approval along the same lines, on 6 July, exactly a month later than the League's acceptance of the plan. Delighted with the prospects for success, the Mission left India on 29 June. Within days Nehru took over as President and declared that the Congress was 'uncommitted' to the plan. He cast grave doubts over the grouping procedures and stressed that the central government would require some overall power to intervene in grave crisis or breakdown, warning that such central power 'inevitably grows'. He also rejected parity for the League in the Interim Executive Council. The Congress did indeed seem to be trying to make it impossible for Jinnah to use the Cabinet Mission Plan as an answer to India's political impasse. It seemed hell bent on scuttling the plan. But why?

The answer to this question raises the concomitant issue of the revisionist thesis: if Jinnah and the League sought to avoid partition how did it come about? It also brings us to the second myth of partition, based on a hoary assumption about 'the Congress for unity', as mentioned at the outset. If Jalal has been able to mount a successful challenge at the conventional assumptions about Jinnah and the League's politics of partition, we already have equally strong reasons and ample, though scattered, evidence to throw a challenge at the other 'verity' of the orthodox historiography, that is, the commitment of the Congress to Indian unity.

The Congress commitment to freedom with unity, which has been integral to the Congress ideology and politics ever since its inception, began to lose its fervour in the wake of the ineffectual and frustrating all-parties negotiations in the late 1920s, culminating in the unilateral declaration by the Congress, on 26 January 1930, of its goal of 'total independence' (*purna swaraj*). The Congress sublimated its frustrations and its own share of responsibilities for the failure in resolving the Muslim Question by taking a convenient line that freedom should

[43] Jalal, *Jinnah*, p. 208.

precede and not follow the resolution of the communal problem. It began to speak of this as a basically 'economic' problem which was incapable of being resolved in a country which was in chains. This shift of emphasis on 'freedom first' had considerable bearings on the issue of 'unity', as evident in subsequent developments where unity was sacrificed on the altar of freedom. Further, the changed League strategy, in the post-1937 political exigencies, sharpened the focus on what appears, in retrospect, the most vital, critical and determining factor in the partition namely, the nature of the central government. Provincial autonomy logically based on a weak centre had been an unchanging component of the perception of a secure future in free India among Muslims of all political shades, including the Congress Muslims. The demand for a combination of a weak centre and substantial Muslim negotiations in the pre-1937 phase. In the subsequent phase the concept of Muslim nationhood and its complementary notion of parity at the centre prompted the League to exert strong pressures on the government to revoke the federal part of the Government of India Act, 1935, which provided for a strong centre. Linlithgow obliged Jinnah by giving him a veto on India's political future.

Confronted with a choice between 'unity' and a 'strong centre', the Congress had been steadily coming to realize what might very well have to become the price for freedom namely, division. The unqualified commitment of the Congress to a strong centre stemmed from its vision of a strong, united and modernized India. Congressmen like Nehru, with socialist streaks in them, found the concept of a strong centre inseparable from the need and demand for India's economic reconstruction based on centralized planning. The bitter communal experiences of the provincial Congress ministries after 1937 as well as that in the interim government in the nineteen-forties reinforced the Congress reluctance to seek political accommodation with the League. Finally, the Congress could hardly have been expected to overlook the supreme importance of a strong centre to ensure its own dominance in India after independence, as has been the case with what is often characterized as India's 'one-party dominance system'.[44] V.P. Menon could not have better stated the Congress case for the strong centre.

[44] S.A. Kochanck, *The Congress Party of India. The Dynamics of One-Party Democracy* (Princeton, New Jersey: Princeton University Press, 1968); *Studies*, Occasional Papers of the Centre for Developing Societies, no. 1 (Bombay: Allied Publishers, 1967), pp. 1–18; also G. Krishna, 'One Party Dominance—Developments and Trends' in ibid., pp. 19–98.

Partition, he said, would 'enable Congress to have at one and the same time a strong central government able to withstand the centrifugal tendencies all too apparent at the moment, and to frame a truly democratic constitution unhampered by any communal considerations'.[45]

It is difficult to trace closely the process of the major Congress leaders in not merely coming to terms with but actually favouring the idea of partition. V.P. Menon recalled that by May 1947 Nehru was no longer averse to a proposed partition.[46] Maulana Azad's contrasting positions, as revealed in the book and the excised portion, have been mentioned above.[47] In the book he places the responsibility squarely on Lord Mountbatten, or rather, the Mountbattens:

> Within a month of Lord Mountbatten's arrival in India, Jawaharlal, the firm opponent of partition, had become, if not a supporter, at least acquiescent to the idea. I have often wondered how Jawaharlal was won over by Lord Mountbatten . . . Jawaharlal was greatly impressed by Lord Mountbatten but perhaps even greater was the influence of Lady Mountbatten . . .[48]

Leonard Mosley held very similar views. There was, he believed, 'no doubt in any one's mind in India that the viceroy, in persuading Nehru, had performed the confidence trick of the century'.[49]

Such observations on either Nehru's or many other Congress leaders' attitudes toward the partition alternative derive credence and sustenance from an unquestioning faith in the Congress dedication to unity until the very last stage. With the arrival of the Mountbattens the patriots, in this romanticized view, seemed to gear up for the last-ditch battle, but found themselves emasculated and disarmed by the former's viceregal charisma and charm. The historical truth seemed to lie elsewhere. There are strong reasons and evidence to suggest that long before the arrival of the Mountbattens on the scene, the upper echelon of the non-Muslim Congress leaders had been calmly calculating the distinct and pragmatic values of the partition formula. While making this assumption that it was Mountbatten who swung Nehru round to partition, Azad and others obviously ignored the

45 V.P. Menon, *The Transfer of Power in India* (Princeton, New Jersey: Princeton University Press, 1957), p. 358.

46 Ibid., p. 360.

47 See p. 102.

48 Azad, *India Wins Freedom*, p. 165.

49 L. Mosley, *Last Days of the British Raj* (London: Weidenfeld & Nicholson, 1961), p. 97.

possibility that the reverse might be true, and the Englishman was converted by the Indian. In a mirror-image of the dichotomy between Jinnah's professions and intentions, the Congress continued to present the facade of the ideal of unity, while it steadily and deliberately worked itself up to a position where Jinnah was forced to take his 'Pakistan' and leave the scene for good. The Lahore Resolution opened up the way for the Congress, groping since the Purna Swaraj Resolution of 1930 for an answer to the Muslim Question that made no demand on its 'sacred cow', that is, the strong centre.

Almost as early as the Lahore Resolution became public knowledge, most senior Congress leaders, like Gandhi and Nehru, had made known their feelings which seemed remarkably cool and pragmatic. Not many days after the Lahore session Gandhi observed:

> Unless the rest of India wishes to engage in internal fratricide, the others will have to submit to the Muslim dictation, if the Muslims will resort to it. . . . The Muslims must have the same right of self-determination that the rest of India has. We are at present a joint family. Any member may claim a division.[50]

Further,

> As a man of non-violence, I cannot forcibly resist the proposed partition if the Muslims of India really upon it . . . it means the undoing of centuries of work done by numberless Hindus and Muslims to live together as one nation. . . . My whole soul rebels against the idea that Hinduism and Islam represent two antagonistic cultures and doctrines. . . . But that is my belief. I cannot thrust it down the throats of the Muslims who think that they are a different nation.[51]

On 15 April 1940, questioned about the resolution, Nehru was reportedly

> pleased, not because he liked it—on the contrary he considered it to be tne most insane suggestion—but because it very much simplified the problem. They were now able to get rid of the demands about proportionate representation in legislatures, services, cabinets, etc. . . . [He] asserted that if people wanted such things as suggested by the Muslim League at Lahore, then one thing was clear, they and people like him could not live together in

[50] D.G. Tendulkar, *Mahatma* (Bombay: Jhaveri & Tendulkar, 1952), v. pp. 333–4.

[51] Ibid., pp. 336–7.

India. He would be prepared to face all consequences of it but he would not be prepared to live with such people.[52]

The very next day he rejoined:

Many knots of the Hindu–Muslim problem had been merged into one knot, which could not be unravelled by ordinary methods, but would need an operation . . . he would say one thing very frankly that he had begun to consider them [the Muslim Leagues] and people like himself, as separate nations.[53]

In the confines of the Ahemedabad jail, in the early 1940s, he wrote: 'Wrong steps have to be taken sometimes lest some worse peril befall us. . . . Unity is always better than disunity, but an enforced unity is a sham and a dangerous affair, full of explosive possibilities.'[54] Nehru's thoughts and attitudes to the unity proposals, as in the Cabinet Mission Plan, were clearly revealed several months before the occurrence of the plan. In January 1946, during his 'four-hour discussion' with Woodrow L. Wyatt, Personal Assistant to Cripps on the Cabinet Mission, Nehru was reported to have 'conceded that the British Government might have to declare for Pakistan . . . granted however (a) a plebiscite, and (b) territorial readjustments so that solid blocks of Hindu territory were not included, he accepted Pakistan'.[55] In a letter of the same month to Cripps, we have even positive indications that he had already seen through Jinnah's game: 'It seems clear that he [Jinnah] is not after nothing at all except to stop all change and progress.'[56] Realization of this nature did very little for his respect of Jinnah. Duckworth, a British official covering Nehru's trip to Malaya during 18–26 March 1946, reported in April 1946, that Nehru was

scornful of Jinnah and doubted very much whether he had either the intention or the power to start a revolt in India if he did not secure Pakistan. . . . 'Jinnah', he said, 'rather reminds me of the man who was charged with the

[52] *Leader*, 15 April 1940, quoted S.R. Mehrotra, 'The Congress and the Partition of India', in C.H. Philips & M.D. Wainwright (eds), The Partition of India. Policies and Perspectives 1935–1947 (London: Allen & Unwin, 1970), p. 210.

[53] Ibid., 16 April 1940, quoted in ibid.

[54] J. Nehru, *The Discovery of India* (Bombay: Asia Publishing House, reprint, 1969), p. 526.

[55] Wavell to Pethick-Lawrence, 15 January 1946; Mansergh, *TP Documents*, VI, doc. no. 357, L/P/O/10/23, p. 796.

[56] Nehru to Cripps, 27 January 1946; ibid., doc. no. 384, L/P & J/10/59: ff. 42–4, pp. 855–6.

murder of his mother and father and begged the clemency of the court on the ground that he was an orphan'.[57]

Later in his life Nehru indicated how both age and patience might have had their share in making the minds of the Congress veterans even more receptive to the partition formula. 'The truth', Nehru told Mosley in 1960, 'is that we were tired men and we were getting on in years. . . . The plan for partition offered a way out and we took it. . . .'[58] There might also have been a lingering hope in the back of their minds that they had not perhaps been committing themselves to a final and irrevocable judgement, as Nehru also admitted to Mosley, 'we expected that a partition would be temporary, that Pakistan was bound to come back to us.[59] Elsewhere he remarked: 'The united India that we have laboured for was not one of compulsion and coercion but a free and willing association of free people. It may be that in this way we shall reach that united India sooner than otherwise and then she will have a stronger and more secure foundation'.[60]

Such sentiments were also expressed by Azad: 'The division is only on the map of the country and not in the hearts of the people, and I am sure it is going to be a short lived partition.'[61] Other front-ranking Congress leaders also are on record to lend their support to the Pakistan demand, and some of them at an earlier stage than later. On 23 April 1942 the Madras Legislature passed a resolution, at the insistence of C. Rajagopalachari, the Congressman with a reputation of being politically cunning, recommending a policy based on the acceptance of the Lahore Resolution. The resolution, though rejected by the All India Congress Committee, drew a significant early response from the Congress Working Committee which emphatically declared that it 'cannot think in terms of compelling the people in any territorial unit to remain in an Indian Union against their declared and established will'.[62] In early 1946 Sardar Patel, the 'strong man' of the Congress, emphatically asserted that the time had come to 'cut the

[57] Note by Duckworth, 4 April 1946; ibid., VII, doc. no. 54, L/P & J/8/636: ff. 3–6, p. 136.

[58] Mosley, *British Raj*, p. 248.

[59] Ibid.

[60] M. Gwyer and A. Appadorai (eds.), *Speeches and Documents on the Indian Constitution 1921–1947* (London: Oxford University Press, 1957), II, p. 682.

[61] *Leader*, 16 June 1947, quoted Mehrotra, 'Congress and Partition', p. 220.

[62] Quoted in Menon, *Transfer of Power*, p. 132.

diseased limb' and be done with the Muslim League.[63] V.P. Menon's claim that he converted Patel to the idea of Pakistan in early 1947 is, again, as in Nehru's case, misleading. The Sardar, in an interview with the Associated Press of America on 9 May 1947, maintained: 'Congress would like to have a strong centre . . . it was absolutely essential that there should be a strong army, and for a defence a strong central govt . . . if the Muslim League insists it wants separation, the Congress will not compel them to remain by force.'[64] G.D. Birla, the capitalist devotee of the *Mahatma*, was also known to have favoured Partition.[65]

The Congress played the game in a masterly fashion. Jinnah's whole strategy *vis-a-vis* the Congress was to use the 'spectre' of the Pakistan demand which was clearly based on the assumption that the Congress would be forced, at the end of the day, to stretch itself fully to accommodate Jinnah's 'real' demands and prevent the calamity of Mother India's dismemberment. But, as Jinnah's game became apparent to the Congress, the latter chose to 'cut off the head' to get rid of the 'headache'. When all the chips were down, after Jinnah's acceptance of the Cabinet Mission Plan, the Congress called Jinnah's bluff and shattered his political strategy and ambition. Jinnah was caught in a bind because he had already presented his acceptance of the Mission Plan as a great 'sacrifice' and a proof of his 'goodwill'. By accepting something less than Pakistan, he had lost the bargaining counter which the demand for the fully sovereign Pakistan gave him.

There were the added dimensions of subtleties and dexterities involved in the Congress strategy in this regard. For the Congress High Command openly to push for partition would have been politically disastrous, and would have been viewed as an acceptance of the League's communalist view of Indian society. There was the added implication of betraying the Congress Muslims, especially when Azad remained the President between 1940 and July 1946. Azad, in his book, greets the initial acceptance of the Cabinet Mission Plan as 'a glorious event in the history of the freedom movement in India', and attributes its ultimate failure to the intransigence of the League. Nehru's press statements contributing to its destruction are glossed over as 'unfortunate events which changed the course of history'.[66]

63 D.V. Tahmankar, *Sardar Patel* (London: Allen & Unwin, 1970), p. 191.
64 Mansergh, *TP Documents*, X, doc. no. 375, L/P & J/10/79: f. 248, p. 717.
65 Tahmankar, *Patel*, p. 272.
66 Azad, *India Wins Freedom*, pp. 135, 138.

To Mountbatten he spoke of the Congress's responsibility in much more positive terms. The 'blame' for the breakdown of the Cabinet Mission Plan, he said, 'in the first place must be laid on Congress . . .'.[67] And, in the excised portion of his book, the finger he points at Nehru is unmistakable.[68]

Despite the Congress being 'on to Jinnah's game', it is conceivable that he could have gone on with his game for some more time at least had it not been for the totally unforeseen, abrupt and rapid change involving the British presence and policies in India in the aftermath of the Second World War. The British refusal to impose a settlement on India and willingness to stay on until the Indians reached an agreement formed a major condition for the success of Jinnah's policy.[69] The return of a Labour Government to power, with its serious commitment to post-war reconstruction at home and demobilization and decolonization abroad, changed the Indian political scene rather dramatically. It was not merely the unilateral British decision to withdraw from India within a short specified period that constituted the sole threat to Jinnah. Equally importantly, or perhaps even more so, Britain appeared particularly concerned now about leaving behind a strong and centralized government in India capable of defending the British economic and political interests in the regions of the Indian Ocean. The Congress seemed keen, and looked both confident and able to take over that role. It did not take very long, in the altered conditions of time, for the British and the Congress to discover their common interests in an India with a strong centre, and the quickest way of achieving the purpose was to aim at Jinnah's 'Achilles' heel'—his Pakistan demand—to oust him by conceding his professed and not real objective.

The passion roused by the partition demand gave it a momentum too strong for Jinnah's sophisticated politics. The Pakistan idea, how-

[67] Mansergh, *TP Documents, Mountbatten Papers, Viceroy's Interview No. 14*, 27 March 1947, X, doc. no. 27, p. 34.

[68] *The Statesman Weekly*, 5 November 1988, p. 6; also above, notes 3–6. It was reported that Rabindranath Roy, who was additional private secretary to Humayun Kabir, the co-author of the book, and who also typed out the manuscript, affirmed that the sealed pages contained 'no adverse comments on Jawaharlal Nehru or members of his family'. This statement was immediately contradicted by the publishers of the book, Orient Longmans, saying that the excised pages 'do make critical references to Jawaharlal Nehru . . .', ibid., 29 October 1988, pp. 3, 7.

[69] Jalal, *Jinnah*, pp. 243 ff.

ever vague and undefined, could not but touch a very tender point in the Muslim mind, continually nourished by dreams and hopes of an Islamic State. Jinnah's unspecified political designs, mystifying political actions, and desultory tactics left many of his followers increasingly confused and bewildered. The growing restiveness and discontent among them, especially after the fiasco and bitterness of the Cabinet Mission Plan, were bound to force his hand. Likewise, the logic and the inevitable political consequence of the Muslim 'nation' theory, with its right of self-determination, generated fear and agitation among non-Muslim minorities in the Muslim majority areas in the Punjab and Bengal, resulting in the partition of these two provinces and the further shrinkage of Jinnah's 'moth-eaten' and 'truncated' Pakistan which was destined to split even further in 1971.

The revisionist perspectives on the highly complex and complicated partition politics of the League and the Congress in the nineteen-forties diverge so substantially and significantly from the standard orthodox positions as to raise concern about some fundamentals of this history. There are strong grounds to challenge a few major dominant assumptions on the politics of partition, and to demand a reconstruction of the historical verities. Robinson expressed the desirability and likelihood of Jalal's work becoming 'the orthodox academic interpretation' of 'the role of Jinnah in the making of Pakistan'.[70] With greater accession to historical knowledge and, more importantly, given our willingness to forsake the comfort and complacency of the traditional and a blinkered view of the history of partition, one would like to think that the revisionist versions of both League and Congress politics of partition cannot but gain recognition as orthodox history.

Undeniably, not all doubts can be answered at the present stage of our knowledge, and again, not all the answers given are, in themselves, unquestionable. Jalal's verdict on the Lahore Resolution and Jinnah's political astuteness, for example, seem to leave some lingering doubts. The 'vagueness' and 'ambiguity' of the wording of the resolution have been universally admitted. There is also a generally agreed suggestion of its being 'deliberately vague'. Jalal moves further than this position and stresses it as Jinnah's 'strength' and political sagacity. Both the assumptions of the alleged vagueness and Jinnah's astuteness seem a little dubious. Perhaps the resolution did initially appear vague, as we have discussed above. But we have also noted

70 Robinson, 'Review' of Jalal's *Jinnah*, p. 617.

that the press and public soon identified it with the Pakistan demand. Jinnah did nothing to dispel this view so that ultimately, to all concerned—the Congress, the British, and indeed to most League members and supporters, except perhaps Jinnah and a small coterie of his confidants—it clearly implied a separate Muslim homeland. The words 'autonomous', 'independent' and 'sovereign' in the resolution could not have been interpreted any differently. Without a clear acceptance of such an identification—and Jinnah himself accepted and even welcomed this identification[71]—it is absurd to think that the Congress and the British Raj could have eventually found it possible to impose Pakistan on Jinnah and the League.

This, in its turn, casts serious doubts on the soundness and strength of Jinnah's political strategy. Given his ultimate political goal of maximization of Muslim interests within a framework of confederal or federal (under the Cabinet Mission Plan he was quite prepared to accept a federal scheme, as already noted) unity of India, comprising, ideally, a Hindu and a Muslim unit, as opposed to the idea of total separation, one has to question the rationale of his entire political strategy, centering round the resolution. No final judgement on Jinnah's politics could be offered unless we are in a position to determine the precise place of the partition formula among his political options. Was he totally opposed to the notion of partition? Or did he leave this option open, despite his preference for a solution short of partition? Answers to such questions alone can provide the true measure of his failure. Granted, however, the thrust of his policy to seek a solution other than partition, which we indeed believe to have been the case, it seems a rather dubious and self-defeating tactic for Jinnah to continue, since the Lahore Resolution, to play the way he did with the 'spectre' of partition. It seems very likely, as discussed above, that the resolution sought to gain recognition of Muslim nationhood through its demand for the right of Muslim majority areas to secede. Whatever vagueness one may talk about, the resolution does not appear vague about the right of Muslim majority areas to break away and form 'independent states'. The obvious political capital to be derived from a recognition of this right induced Jinnah not to contradict the almost universal assumption about the League's association and commitment to Pakistan in the sense of partition. Were partition an unwelcome prospect, these tactics risked its achievement. It was

[71] See above p.116 also fn. 32.

less than political good sense and foresight not to have secured the interests of Muslims in the minority areas precisely against the strong possibility of the Congress seeking the easiest and hence the most tempting answer to this highly complex problem by trying to cut the Muslim League and Muslims out of India. The 'hostage theory' was nothing more than an after-thought—a later rationalization calculated to offer some psychological comfort to the minorities concerned. The Lahore Resolution could afford, so it may seem, greater political tact, maturity and vision in attempting to integrate, openly and clearly, the demands of Muslims of the minority areas with those of their co-believers in the majority areas. Alongside the demand for the right of the majority areas to secede, could the resolution not have indicated its preference, in the interests of all Indian Muslims, for a solution avoiding partition? There is a tacit admission of failure of this strategy as well as an obvious touch of sadness when Jinnah expressed his regrets to Lord Mountbatten, in April 1947, for 'his inability to reconsider the Cabinet Mission Plan', and added: '... it was clear that in no circumstances did Congress intend to work the plan either in accordance with the spirit or the letter.'[72]

One wonders about the ultimate logic of Jinnah choosing to adopt his secretive approach—not wanting partition and yet using the partition threat to hang, like the sword of Damocles, over the country until it was too late to be discarded. What if he tried to confront the Congress with his 'real' demands to secure the interests of all Muslims in India, openly rejecting the partition option, and continue to play his usual 'long, slow game'? If partition was never an option for the League and Jinnah, would the Congress and the British, even in the changed circumstances in the latter half of the 1940s, have found it as easy as they did to force it on eighty million Muslims of British India? Instead of this precarious and dangerous gamble intrinsic to 'poker', would Jinnah have done better to match the strength and skill of the Congress in an open game of 'chess'? Then, perhaps, we have hindsight on our side.

Issues of this nature will engage us in debate and discourse, as revisionist efforts are elevated to the status of orthodoxy. Meanwhile, revisionism on Jinnah's role in the creation of Pakistan questions the very legitimacy of the state brought into existence by the *Quaid-i Azam* as the universally acknowledged 'Father of Pakistan'.

[72] Mansergh, *TP Documents, Viceroys Personal Report No. 3*, 17 April 1947, x, doc. no. 165, L/PO/6/123: ff. 42–9, p. 301.

Chapter Seven

The Muslim Mass Contacts Campaign: Analysis of a Strategy of Political Mobilization*

MUSHIRUL HASAN

From the days of the 1916 Lucknow Pact, the leadership of the Indian National Congress expressed eagerness to negotiate with a handful of Muslim politicians in order to arrive at a consensus on major political and constitutional issues. The logic of such negotiations stemmed from the belief that Indian Muslims were entitled to certain concessions and safeguards because of their distinct political identity and because their interests were different from those of other groups in Indian society. The political language within which such accommodation was expressed and the energy that derived from a recognition of this conception of society necessarily implied that the very terms of reference precluded any lasting solution to the communal tangle. At the same time, by negotiating with Muslim politicians whose organizational base and political stature were by no means assured, Congress perpetuated their legitimacy as spokespersons of the whole community—a recognition that flowed largely from the organizational and political structures within which the Congress leadership was itself elaborated. Rather than forcing these so-called leaders into a situation where they had, as it were, to demonstrate their implied support, Congress consistently refused to draw out the conditions for such a confrontation, from an apparent desire not to weaken the integral and unified nature of the national movement and also from fear that the

* From Richard Sisson and Stanley Wolpert (eds), *Congress and Indian Nationalism: The Pre-Independence Phase*, pp. 198–222.

consequences of such a confrontation would reveal a divide too profound to remedy. Since national integrity was Congress' cardinal political assumption, such a confrontation had to be avoided.

The dramatic collapse of the Congress–Khilafat alliance in 1922–3, the revival of communal bodies, and the recrudescence of widespread Hindu–Muslim riots in the aftermath of the Khilafat and Non-Cooperation movements exposed the limitations of Congress' approach in dealing with what came to be regarded as the communal question. Some contemporary commentators believed that the Hindu–Muslim alliance was artificially cemented on the 'unreliable foundations of religious sentimentalism'. 'The present debacle', noted the Communist Party of India manifesto, 'was a foregone conclusion of such ill-started movement'. 'The Congress programme', observed another manifesto, 'has to be denuded of all sentimental trimmings. . . . The object for which the Indian people will fight should not be looked for somewhere in the unknown region of Mesopotamia or Arabia or Constantinople, it should be found in their immediate surroundings—in their huts, on the land, in the factory. Hungry mortals cannot be expected to fight indefinitely for an abstract ideal'.[1]

Later attempts to revive the spirit of the Khilafat days through widely publicized unity conferences and hastily concluded pacts failed to resolve the communal deadlock; such was the fate of the so-called Indian National Pact (1923), the C.R. Das Pact (1923), and the Nehru Committee Report (1928).[2] Likewise, the 'Ram-Rahim' approach of Gandhi and his initiatives in the form of fasts, such as the one undertaken during the bloody Kohat riots of 1924, did not improve deteriorating communal relations.[3]

The problem of attracting Muslim support became an issue within Congress as well. Writing to M.A. Ansari, whose own efforts to bring about communal rapprochement were noteworthy, Gandhi conceded in early 1930 that the Hindu–Muslim problem was to be approached 'in a different manner from the one we have hitherto adopted—not, as at present, by adjustment of the political power but by one or the

[1] G. Adhikari (ed.), *Documents of the History of the Communist Party of India*, vol. 1: *1917–1922* (New Delhi, n.p., 1971), p. 345; vol. 2: *1923–1925* (New Delhi, n.p., 1974), p. 210.

[2] For details, see Mushirul Hasan, *A Nationalist Conscience: M. A. Ansari, The Congress, and the Raj* (New Delhi: Manohar, 1987).

[3] Mushirul Hasan, *Nationalism and Communal Politics in India, 1916–1928* (New Delhi: Manohar, 1979).

other acting on the square under all circumstances'.[4] In a more candid recognition of Congress' failure, Motilal Nehru observed that 'no amount of formulae based upon mutual concessions . . . will bring us any nearer Hindu–Muslim unity than we are at present'. 'It is my firm conviction', he continued, 'that Hindu–Muslim unity cannot be achieved by preaching it. We have to bring it about in a manner which will accomplish it without either Hindus or Muslims realizing that they are working for unity. *This can only be done on an economic basis and in the course of the fight for freedom from the* usurper'.[5] (Emphasis added)

Motilal's formulation was close to that of his son, Jawaharlal, but did not reflect the thinking of most Congress leaders, who persisted with the belief that the surest and perhaps the easiest way of coming to terms with the Muslim community was to settle the controversy over the issue of joint versus separate electorates, reservation of seats in legislatures, especially in the Muslim-majority provinces of Bengal and the Punjab, weightage to Muslims in provinces where they were in a minority, separation of Sind from the Bombay Presidency, and the introduction of reforms in the North West Frontier Provinces (NWFP). Resolution of the controversies centred around these demands was not easy, as became evident from the deliberations of the All-Parties National Convention (December 1928) and the Round Table Conferences in London. A new approach was thus called for to resolve the communal impasse, to draw Muslims into the Congress fold, and to reach over the heads of Muslim politicians to the rank-and-file Muslim voter. The lead was given by the Congress Working Committee (CWC) meeting, held at Wardha on 27–8 February 1937, to discuss the plan of Muslim mass contacts. Nehru took the initiative and, on 31 March 1937, urged provincial Congress committees:

> to make a special effort to enrole Muslim Congress members, so that our struggle for freedom may become even more broad-based than it is, and the Muslim masses should take the prominent part in it which is their due. Indeed when we look at the vital problem of independence and of the removal of poverty and unemployment, there is no difference between the Muslim masses and the Hindu or Sikh or Christian masses in the country. Differences

[4] Statement by Gandhi on 16 February 1930; see Mushirul Hasan (ed.), *Muslims and the Congress: Select Correspondence of Dr. M.A. Ansari, 1912–1935* (New Delhi, 1979), p. 101.

[5] Ibid., pp. 103–4.

only come to the surface when we think in terms of the handful of upper class people.[6]

The October 1937 session of Congress lent its approval to Nehru's plan and pointed out that its aim was to protect the religious, linguistic, and cultural rights of the minorities in order to ensure their participation in the political, economic, and cultural life of the nation.[7]

Organization of the Mass Contacts Campaign

The plan of Muslim mass contacts, pursued after the 1937 elections, in which Congress fared poorly in Muslim constituencies, was in some ways different from previous Congress mobilization campaigns. To begin with, it was based on a series of fresh assumptions that questioned the efficacy of negotiating with a handful of Muslim politicians for short-term political gains. 'We have too long thought in terms of pacts and compromises with communal leaders, and neglected the people behind them', observed Nehru. He called it a 'discredited policy' and hoped that Congress would not revert to it.[8] There was an equally unmistakable rejection of the earlier religiopolitical initiatives, such as Congress' support to the Khilafat cause, in favour of establishing direct contact with the Muslim masses. On the basis of an optimistic—some may say misleading—assessment of the 1937 elections, the Congress High Command felt that if the party could obtain support from a great majority of Hindus, it could also win over Muslims. Experience during the election campaign reinforced this optimism. Both Rajendra Prasad and Nehru were convinced that in many provinces there was much appreciation of Congress policies among Muslims.[9] Constrained by various factors, however, Congress was not able to realize their latent sympathy and take advantage of the 'new interest and awakening'.[10] The remedy, then, was to explain and project its programme, to impress on poor Muslim villagers that

[6] S. Gopal (ed.), *Selected Works of Jawaharlal Nehru* (hereafter cited *SWJN*), vol. 8 (New Delhi: Orient Longmans, 1976), p. 123. All references are drawn from this volume.

[7] Deepak Pandey, 'Congress–Muslim League Relations 1937–9: "The Parting of the Ways', *Modern Asian Studies*, 12 (1978), p. 643.

[8] *SWJN*, p. 128.

[9] For the statement of Rajendra Prasad, see *Bombay Chronicle*, 26 April 1937.

[10] *SWJN*, p. 123.

they would not lose under the Congress dispensation as their interests were identical with those of the Hindu poorer classes, and to convey the message that their real champions were Congress leaders, not the landlords and lawyers of the Muslim League. With a degree of persistence it could thus wean the masses away from the Muslim League and draw them into the nationalist fold.

On 31 March 1937, Nehru set out his ideas on 'The need for greater contacts with Muslims', directed Congress committees to concentrate on enrolling Muslims, and suggested the formation of committees to take in hand the work of increasing contacts with Muslim masses living in rural and urban areas.[11] The All-India Congress Committee (AICC) set up a cell to control and direct activities relating to Muslims, to propagate Congress' programme through newspaper articles and pamphlets, and to counteract anti-Congress propaganda. Kunwar Mohammad Ashraf, one of Nehru's most trusted lieutenants, was asked to run the cell. Impressed with Nehru's 'language of Marxism', Ashraf accepted the offer with the feeling that 'we were on the threshold of a fresh mass struggle' and the conviction that 'any honest and consistent anti-imperialist struggle led by the Congress would wean away the Muslim masses from the growing influence of Jinnah and the revived Muslim League'.[12]

The campaign was launched amid much fanfare. As secretary of the Political and Economic Information Department, the energetic Ashraf went on a countrywide tour, addressing innumerable meetings at which he referred to the mass contact programme as a 'decisive

[11] Ibid.

[12] Horst Kruger (ed.), *Kunwar Mohammad Ashraf: An Indian Scholar and Revolutionary 1903–1962* (Berlin: Academie-Verlag, 1966), pp. 112–13. It is rather surprising that there is no reference to Ashraf's involvement in the Mass Contact movement in M. Farooqi and N.L. Gupta, *Life and Works of Dr. K.M. Ashraf* (New Delhi, n.p., 1973). Ashraf's excitement was shared by his associates. His comrade, Sajjad Zaheer, a writer and one of the founders of the Progressive Writers' movement, recalled: 'As I belonged to the same Allahabad group of young Indians who had then arrived from Europe after finishing their education there, I wish to record here the feeling of hopefulness in and enthusiasm for . . . the success of our revolutionary mission with which we and a large number of young Indian intelligentsia were moved during that time.' See Sajjad Zaheer, 'Recent Muslim Politics in India and the Problem of National Unity,' in S.T. Lokhandwala (ed.), *India and Contemporary Islam* (Simla: Indian Institute of Advanced Study, 1971).

state' in Congress' history—'the state of revolutionary mass action'.[13] He exhorted Congressmen to form Ward and Mohalla committees that would take up the day-to-day struggle of the masses and advised them to organize peasants, industrial workers, and the unemployed on the basis of Congress' programme.[14]

Ashraf challenged the notion of a Muslim community with an exclusive and distinct political and social personality; the fundamental contradiction, according to him, was between the class interests of Muslim leaders and the political and economic demands of the Muslim masses; the 'religious outlook' was merely designed to obscure this fundamental division in Indian Muslim society.[15] Using Marxist phraseology with ease, Ashraf tried to dispel the notion that Indian Muslims could achieve freedom on their own and build up a strong and disciplined community. Political experience, in his opinion, demonstrated that a community could build its own strength through the national struggle and not by organizing itself on a communal basis. Politics was dictated essentially by class interests, and efforts to obscure class differentiation would lead to the suppression of the exploited elements.[16] The anti-imperialist struggle of the exploited and poor masses in India was 'essentially one and indivisible' and could not be carried out 'on the basis of separate political organizations working within a particular community.' Indian Muslims should join this struggle by participating in the agitational and organizational work of Congress—'the only joint organization of the Indian exploited masses which interprets and organizes this struggle'.[17]

Ashraf's strenuous efforts were backed by Nehru, who, with his usual flair and aplomb, set out to combat Muslim League propaganda, extended support to the launching of an Urdu periodical 'to give the Urdu-knowing public the ideological message of the Congress to fight all sectarian tendencies',[18] and rebutted Jinnah's charge that the Congress policy of mass contact was fraught with grave consequences.[19]

[13] AICC Papers, file no. 30/1937, Misc., p. 15, Nehru Memorial Museum and Library (NMML).

[14] AICC Papers, file no. 48/1937, p. 155; *Hindustan*, 10 October 1937, p. 5.

[15] AICC Papers, file no. 13/1937, p. 39.

[16] To Hassan Habib, editor of *Agra Citizen* (Agra), 15 July 1938, AICC Papers, file no. G-67/1938, pp. 17–21.

[17] Resolution proposed by Ashraf and Z.A. Ahmad at the 1938 Haripura Session of the Congress, AICC Papers, file no. G-103/1938.

[18] *Bombay Chronicle*, 10 July 1937; *SWJN*, p. 156.

[19] *SWJN*, April 25 and May 23 1937, pp. 125, 131–2.

To boost the campaign and provide it with the much needed legitimacy, Nehru turned to the Jhansi-Jalaun-Hamirpur by-election where Nisar Ahmad Khan Sherwani was pitted against his Muslim League rival, Rafiuddin Ahmad. Significance was attached to this election because Sherwani's victory, according to Nehru, would strengthen the Congress movement and give a 'tremendous fillip' to its crusade against communalism. 'I want to tell you', he wrote to Sherwani on 30 June 1937, 'that we regard your election campaign as a most important one and I hope that you and all Congressmen in Bundelkhand will realize this fact and do their utmost in it'.[20] Words were matched with action. Nehru placed Rafi Ahmad Kidwai in charge of the election campaign and mobilized friends and political comrades to take part in electioneering, urging them to 'work in earnest' and give 'all your great energy to this election'.[21] The energy, drive, and resourcefulness displayed by Nehru was truly remarkable.

Although Sherwani lost and the League rejoiced at its unexpected victory, Nehru was not disheartened. He referred to some positive gains that enhanced Congress' prestige and strength: the party contested a Muslim seat after many years; its candidate secured the majority of votes in Orai and Jhansi, which formed two of the three districts in the constituency; and the rural votes of peasants were almost entirely cast for Congress. For these reasons the Bundelkhand election was 'one of the most encouraging sign of times. It points to the inevitable growth of the Congress among the masses, both Hindu and Muslim'.[22] Gandhi shared Nehru's optimism, pointing out that the election was not a 'rout' but an 'honourable defeat' giving rise to the hope that 'if we plod away we can effectively take the Congress message to the Mussalmans'.[23]

The outcome of the election, some prophesied, would place the Mass Contacts programme in jeopardy. Such fears were unwarranted, however, as reports from some parts of the country indicated an unexpectedly favourable response, leading Nehru to announce that 'our efforts to increase our contact with the Muslim masses continue

[20] Ibid., June 30, 1937, p. 138. Also see letters to R.V. Dhulekar, June 30, 1937, and to Rafi Ahmad Kidwai, 1 July 1937, pp. 139, 146.

[21] To A. G. Kher and Manilal Pande, 30 June 1937, *SWJN*, pp. 140–1.

[22] To Rajendra Prasad, 21 July 1937, *SWJN*, p. 167; statement to the press, July 25, 1937, *SWJN*, p. 171; *Bombay Chronicle,* 27 July 1937.

[23] To Nehru, 30 July 1937, *The Collected Works of Mahatma Gandhi* (New Delhi: Government of India, 1967), LXV, p. 445.

to meet an encouraging response'.[24] What pleased Nehru and surprised many was the enthusiasm of newly mobilized groups such as the Ahrars,[25] the Khudai Khidmatgars, and the Socialists. They spearheaded the mass contact campaign in NWFP and the Punjab with the active backing of leaders who wielded considerable influence in certain areas and were known for their association with and involvement in nationalist politics. They included Khan Abdul Ghaffar Khan and his brother Khan Saheb, Saifuddin Kitchlew of Rowlatt satyagraha fame, the Socialist Mian Iftikharuddin, Mohammad Alam, Khalifa Fazal Din, and Babu Mohammad Din. Their presence was noted at a meeting in early May 1937 when mass contact committees were first formed in the Punjab.[26] A series of conferences held in the following month and addressed by Ashraf and Sajjad Zaheer had 'favourable impact on many Muslims'. Impressed by the success of one such gathering in Lahore, the Punjab Provincial Congress Committee (PCC) decided 'to hold a number of such meetings in the province to attract Muslims to the Congress.'[27] Such organized activity spelt danger to the Punjab Unionist Party and the Muslim League. They combined to launch a counter-offensive in order to keep their political base intact.[28] Their reaction reflected a recognition of the growing strength and popularity of the Mass Contacts programme in NWFP and the Punjab.

In the United Provinces (UP), the Mass Contacts programme appealed to Muslims in places such as Aligarh, Lucknow, Allahabad, Budaun, Pratapgarh, Ghazipur, and Shamli in Muzaffarnagar District, while in Jaunpur, for instance, 'the fresh wave is not being passed

[24] Circular to provincial Congress Committees, 10 July 1937, *SWJN*, p. 156. 'The Mussalmans of UP and Punjab,' reported the *Bombay Chronicle*, 3 June and 1 November 1937, 'are rallying round the Congress in large numbers much to the discomfiture of big landlords and the Muslim Leaguers'.

[25] S. Tufail Ahmad Manglori, *Ruh-i-Raushan Mustaqbil* (Budaun: n.p., 1946), p. 132; M. Rafique Afzal, *Political Parties in Pakistan: 1947–1958* (Islamabad: National Commission on Historical and Cultural Research, 1976), pp. 27–8; statement of Anwar Sabri, secretary of the UP Provincial Ahrar Committee, in *Leader*, 8 April 1937; resolution of the Provincial Ahrar Conference held in Lucknow, *Bombay Chronicle*, 19 April 1937. See also W.C. Smith, *Modern Islam in India: A Social Analysis* (New Delhi, n.p., reprinted in 1979), pp. 270–6.

[26] For details of this meeting held in a suburb of Lahore, see *Leader*, 6 and 12 June 1937.

[27] AICC Papers, file no. P-24(i)/1937, p. 8.

[28] *Bombay Chronicle*, 8 May 1937.

unobserved and we are sure that the Congress would open a way to us in approaching the masses.'[29] Equally noticeable was the favourable impression on groups such as the students of Aligarh Muslim University; the ulama of Deoband; the Shias of Lucknow, Jaunpur, and Amroha; and the Ansaris of Ghazipur and Mirzapur, who swelled the ranks of the All-India Momin Conference.[30] Here, too, the Muslim League sensed danger to its position, and Harry Haig, who succeeded Malcolm Hailey as governor of UP, noted that League leaders were 'alarmed at the Congress attempts on the Muslim masses' because they 'feel very strongly that if the community is to retain its individually, no efforts must be spared in resisting the attempts of the Congress to absorb them'.[31] The Raja of Mahmudabad read the danger signs in August 1937 and informed his political mentor, Muhammad Ali Jinnah, that Congress was exploring all avenues of approaching the Muslim masses, and would intensify its efforts in that direction; so 'it was essential that we have funds so that we may try to put up an organization analogous to the very efficient and aggressive organization of the Congress'.[32]

In other parts of the country the drive to enroll Muslims met with success. In neighbouring Delhi the groundwork for the prosecution of the Mass Contacts campaign was prepared by Congress Socialists such as Faridul Haq Ansari and Asaf Ali, and Muslim divines such as Maulvis Abdul Majid and Ahmad Saidboth associated with Congress from the time of the Rowlatt satyagraha. 'There has been a marked change in the attitude of Muslim masses', stated a Congress report,

29 Ahmad Khan president DDC to Ashraf, 24 July 1938 (in Urdu); Mohammad Aqil to Ashraf, April 30 1937 (in Urdu); and Hargovind Singh to Ashraf, 29 June 1937, respectively, in AICC Papers, file no. 42(B)/1937, Misc., p. 378, file no. 42(i)/1937, p. 557.

30 Aftab Ahmad Khan to Ashraf, 26 April 1937, AICC Papers, file no. 11/1937, Misc., p. 279; Fazalbhoy, editor of the University magazine, in *Bombay Chronicle*, 24 May 1937. The All-India Momin Conference was established in 1926 in order to focus on the separate and distinct interests of the weavers, variously known as Ansari and Momin. The conference, with its headquarters in Kanpur, claimed to have a membership of two lakhs with over 500 branches in UP alone. Abdul Qaiyum Ansari to Rajendra Prasad, October 9, 1939, Jawaharlal Nehru Papers (hereafter cited as Nehru papers), file no. 136, part 2, Nehru Memorial Museum and Library (NMML). For further details of the activities of the Momin Conference, see Manglori, *Ruh-i-Raushan Mustaqbil*, pp. 143–4.

31 Haig to Linlithgow, May 7 and 24, Haig Papers, Microfilm, NMML.

32 The Raja of Mahmudabad of M.A. Jinnah, 8 August 1937. Copies of these letters were made available to me by the courtesy of Mr Khalid S. Hasan.

'and primary membership among them has also increased'.[33] An 'Enrolment Week' observed in Bombay resulted in 500 Muslims joining Congress.[34] In Bihar the efforts were equally rewarding, especially in Patna, Champaran, and Purnea. Here Kisan Sabhas, the Students' Federation, the Muslim Independent party, and the *Jamiyat al-Momineen* were in the forefront of the Mass Contacts campaign.[35] Finally, the Mohalla and city Mass Contacts committees in Calcutta, Burdwan, and Comilla—all in Bengal—fared well. By May 1937 over 1,000 Muslims joined Congress in the suburbs of Calcutta.[36]

What was truly remarkable was that several organizations, representing a wide range of provincial, local, sectional, and religious interests, came around to supporting the Mass Contacts programme in an impressive show of solidarity with Congress. This was true of all-India organizations: the *Jamiyat al-Ulama*, dominated by the pro-Congress faction of Husain Ahmad Madani and Kifayatullah; the Shia Political Conference, founded in 1929 with a strong base among the small but influential Shias of Lucknow, Amroha, Bilgram, and Jaunpur; the All-India *Ahl-i-Hadis* League;[37] and regional parties and

[33] Annual Report of the Delhi PCC for 1937, AICC Papers, file no. P-25/1937, p. 60. *Leader*, 21 April 1937.

[34] Report for the month of September 1937, AICC Papers, file no. P-24(i)/1937, p. 13. Notice that, by December 1937, 3,894 Muslims joined Congress in Maharashtra. Report of the Maharashtra PCC, 8–31 December 1937, AICC Papers, file no. P-25/1937, p. 101. 'The Muslim Leaguers of our province,' reported Syed Abdullah Brelvi, editor of the *Bombay Chronicle*, 'are whipping themselves into furious activity. . . . Some local friends are even holding out threats of violence if we go on spreading our contacts with the masses'. To Ashraf, May 5 1937, AICC Papers, G-67/1937, p. 101.

[35] Wali Hasan to Ashraf, 20 June 1937; Syed Mahmud and Abdul Bari organized meetings, lectures, and conferences to mobilize support; so did Maulvi Nizamuddin, president of the Champaran branch of the Muslim Independent Party. *Bombay Chronicle*, 19 April and 18, 26 June 1936. Significant also was the support extended by the provincial *Jamiyat al-Momineen*. Hakim Wasi Ahmad to Rajendra Prasad, March 12 1937 (telegram), Valmiki Chaudhary (ed.), *Dr. Rajendra Prasad Correspondence and Select Documents* (New Delhi, n.p. 1984), vol. 1, p. 30.

[36] *Bombay Chronicle*, 18 May 1937. For an optimistic assessment of the work Calcutta Mass Contact Committee, see Manzoor Ahmad to Ashraf, July 13 1938 (in Urdu), AICC Papers, file no. 42/1937 (1), pp. 117–18.

[37] *Bombay Chronicle*, 25 November 1937. The Ahl-i-Hadis accepted the entire corpus of the Prophet Muhammad's hadis (traditions) and rejected the four juristic schools: Hanafi, Shafai, Maliki, and Hambali. For details, see Aziz Ahmad, *Islamic Modernism in India and Pakistan, 1857–1964* (London: Oxford Univer-

groups, such as the Khudai Khidmatgars in NWFP, the Ahrars in UP and the Punjab, and the Momin Conference in parts of UP and Bihar. Rallying the Shias, made possible by two important *fatawa* issued by their *Mujtahids* in Lucknow and Jaunpur, was the handiwork of a Shia, Wazir Hasan, who took advantage of estranged Shia–Sunni relations in UP to draw his community into the Congress movement.[38] Estranged from the Sunni-dominated Muslim League and irked by the violent outbursts over the *Madh-e-Sahaba* controversy in 1935–6, the Shias hoped to receive a better deal from the Congress ministry in UP.[39]

The Allahabad Conference, held on 15–16 May 1937, brought representatives of some of these groups on a common platform. Thus A.M. Khwaja as well as Wazir Hasan, who had chaired the Muslim League session in May 1936 and had since returned to the Congress fold, appeared alongside Muslim divines such as Maulanas Hifzur Rahman and Ahmad Said, and avowed socialists and communists such as Sajjad Zaheer, Mian Mohammad Iftikharuddin, Z.A. Ahmad, and Ashraf. There was much patriotic fervour, reminiscent of the early 1930s when conferences of the All-India Nationalist Muslim party, founded by M.A. Ansari, were held in different parts of the country. There was talk of extending 'unconditional support' to Congress, and speeches made on the theme of communal harmony and inter-communal unity elicited much interest. Reference was made to the unrepresentative character of the Muslim League, and its leadership—'these upper class gentlemen'—were castigated for their reactionary policies and their 'theories of inactivity and cowardice'.[40] This conference, masterminded by Ashraf and Azad, was a notable feat, the like of which was accomplished only once during the Khilafat movement; it was also a significant one in terms of being the first organized expression of Muslim support for Congress in the 1930s.

---

sity Press, 1967), pp. 113–22. The *Jamiyat al-ulama* was an association of religious leaders learned in Islamic law.

[38] *Leader*, 25 April and 9 June 1937.

[39] *Sarfraz* (Lucknow), 17 August 1937, AICC Papers, file no. 49/1937, Misc., p. 160.

[40] *Leader*, 18 May 1937; AICC Papers, file no. 12/1937, Misc., pp. 43–5. For Jinnah's criticism of the Allahabad Conference, see *Bombay Chronicle*, 20 April 1937.

Leadership and Representation

Lack of adequate evidence makes it difficult to place the protagonists of the Mass Contacts campaign in relation to their social, occupational, and political backgrounds. A rough survey, however, indicates that they were mostly urban based and drawn largely from the professional classes: lawyers, students, and teachers sharing socialist and Marxist ideas; journalists such as Syed Ali Ahmad, editor of a leading Patna-based weekly *Itehad*; Syed Abdullah Brelvi and Mohammad Nazir, editors of the *Bombay Chronicle* and *Mussawir*, respectively; Maulana Mujibur Rahman, founder and editor of the leading Calcutta newspaper *Mussalman*; Hayatullah Ansari, editor of the *Hindustan Weekly*, published first from Lucknow and later from Delhi; and Mohammad Ismail and Mohammad Jafri, editors of the Delhi papers *Daily Qaumi Akhbar* and *Millat*. Some sections of the mass contact leadership had been associated with Congress from the Khilafat days and were connected with the All-India Nationalist Muslim party and the Congress Muslim party, organizations founded in early 1929 to canvas support for the Nehru Report; others were drawn into the organization during the 1930–2 Civil Disobedience movement.

Among the most vociferous mass contact campaigners in UP were several young and brilliant lawyers, journalists, teachers, poets, and writers. Most of them were educated either in Aligarh or in British universities. Having been tutored in Marxism–Leninism, they shared a common commitment to the revolutionary transformation of Indian society through an alliance with radical elements in Congress. They brought to bear a Marxist perspective on communalism that was markedly different from both the religious-oriented approach of the Khilafatists and that of the Congress Muslims of Ansari's generation whose efforts to achieve Hindu–Muslim reconciliation found fruition merely in unity conferences, pacts, and short-term agreements. They rejected communal categories that they believed had been superimposed by the British to create fissures in the mass struggle and regarded any rapprochement with the self-styled leaders of the Muslim community as counter-productive. Congress, they argued, deserved support because it favoured abolition of the taluqdari system and liquidation of rural indebtedness and insisted on relief for the landless and the unemployed. The Muslim League, in contrast, was allied with the British government and was engaged in promoting the interests of the privileged classes; thus its real contradiction, according to Ashraf, 'lies in the fact that a few landlords and reactionaries want to exploit the backward Muslim masses for the redemption of their privileges and a fundamentally reactionary political outlook'.[41] In sum, then, the emphasis was not so much on 'mere honeyed phrases and appeals couched in eloquent and winsome phraseology to the communities to live in amity and grace', but rather on the unity and solidarity of the peasants and workers in their struggle against the British government and its collaborators.

Those Muslims who advocated this position were quite numerous and represented a powerful ideological strand among the Muslim intelligentsia, a fact that has gone unnoticed in most accounts of Indian nationalism. Prominent amongst them were K.M. Ashraf, a neo-Muslim from Alwar State who rose to political prominence in the 1930's as a member of the Congress Socialist Party (CSP) in charge of the minorities cell in the Congress; Z.A. Ahmad, an Aligarh graduate who joined the Economic Information Department of the AICC as secretary (1936–7) and was a member of the National Executive of the CSP from 1937 to 1940; Faridul Haq Ansari, cousin of M.A. Ansari, one of the founder members of the CSP and convener of the Mass Contact Committee in Delhi; Hayatullah Ansari of Firangi Mahal in Lucknow, a graduate of the Aligarh Muslim University and editor of the pro-Congress *Hindustan Weekly* from 1937 to 1942; Ansar Harvani, also an Aligarh graduate with the distinction of being both the founder and general secretary of the All-Indian Students' Federation (1936–9); Husain Zaheer, son of Wazir Hasan, educated in Lucknow, Oxford, and Heidelberg and an active supporter of the Mass Contacts campaign; and Husain's brother, Sajjad Zaheer, and young poets and writers such as Kaifi Azmi, Khwaja Ahmad Abbas, and Ali Sardar Jafri, who was expelled from Aligarh University for organizing a political strike in 1936. The adherence of such men gave the Mass Contacts campaign in UP a radical orientation and an ideological thrust that was lacking in earlier Congress efforts at popular mobilization.[42]

Equally vital was the part played by some leading ulama of Deoband and of the Jamiyat al-Ulama. The Jamiyat was founded in the wake of the Khilafat agitation in December 1919 and its alliance with Congress, although under strain in the aftermath of the Non-

[41] *Leader*, 15 April 1937; AICC Papers, file no. 31/1937, Misc., pp. 39, 207.

[42] Leaders of the CSP were strong supporters of a more general mass contacts strategy as analyzed by D.A. Low in chapter 7 in this volume.

Cooperation movement, remained largely intact. This was evident during the Civil Disobedience movement in 1930–2 when the Jamiyat favoured 'Muslims working shoulder to shoulder with their brethren in the fight for freedom' and its leaders such as Husain Ahmad Madani, Ahmad Said, Ataullah Shah Bukhari, Hifzur Rahman, and Moinuddin joined the ranks of satyagrahis with great enthusiasm. Their alliance with Congress continued uninterruptedly. In June 1937 a number of this group worked for the Congress candidate in the crucial Bundelkhand election and toured various parts of UP in connection with the Mass Contacts campaign.

In August 1937 Husain Ahmad Madani, president of the Jamiyat al-Ulama, appealed to his community to join Congress in the fight for freedom[43] and a year later propounded his theory of composite nationalism in *Mutahhidah qaumiyat awr Islam* (composite nationalism and Islam). In his letters to Mohammad Iqbal he argued that the word '*quam*' could be applied to any collective group regardless of whether its common characteristics were religion, common habitat, race, colour, or craft. It should be distinguished from *millat*, which refers to a collectivity with a *sharia* or *din*. Indian Muslims were fellow nationals with other communities and groups in India, although separate from them in religion. At present, he said, nations are made by homelands, as England, for instance, where members of different faiths constitute one nation. Madani argued that freedom from British rule was necessary for the welfare of Islam, so that Muslim religious duties could be properly performed. The Muslims were not strong enough to win this freedom for themselves, but needed the help of non-Muslim communities. He wanted independence for India so that Muslims could freely express their religious personality, enjoy a really Islamic system of education, and remove corruption from their social life by abolishing British-made laws.[44] On 3–6 March 1939, the Jamiyat called for cooperation with Congress 'according to Islamic principles and dictates of wisdom and foresight' and urged Indian Muslims to enlist as primary members of Congress and participate in its activities—'as it is the only constitutional way to reach the goal of

[43] *Bombay Chronicle*, 3 June and 16 August 1937; AICC Papers, file no. 30/1937, Misc., p. 585.

[44] The summary is based on Peter Hardy, *The Muslims of British India* (Cambridge: Cambridge University Press, 1972), pp. 227–8.

independence and achievement and protection of religious and national rights of Mussalmans'.[45]

Madani's sympathy for the Congress and the Jamiyat's advocacy of Indian nationalism represented a trend set by Maulana Mahmudul Hasan, principal of the *Dar al-Ulum* (Muslim theological seminary) at Deoband. In the mid-1930s, however, these views were vigorously challenged by Madani's two distinguished colleagues, Ashraf Ali Thanvi and Shabbir Ahmad Usmani, and by the theologian-politician, Maulana Abul Ala Mawdudi. In a series of articles in the monthly journal, *Tarjuman al-Quran*, Mawdudi first related the history of the Muslims in India, debunking Congress secularism, and showing the unsuitability of India for democratic rule. In the *Tahrik-i-Azadi-i-Hind awr Mussalman*, published in 1939, he arrived at the conclusion that the Muslims and the Congress movement had absolutely nothing in common, and registered an indictment of the Jamiyat for its acquiescence in the Mass Contacts campaign that was directed toward the 'total disintegration' of the Muslim community and was intended to subvert the faith of the Muslim masses and to convert them to Marxism.[46]

Mawdudi's frontal assault on the Mass Contact programme had the full backing of the Muslim League, but for different reasons. While Mawdudi and his ilk viewed the idea as a challenge to the traditional Muslim belief that Islam pervaded every sphere of human activity, and Congress advocated secular politics, Jinnah, who was averse to mass politics, viewed mass contact as a deliberate attempt to divide the Muslims and break the Muslim League by 'falsely representing that the Congress alone has got the monopoly to champion and fight for the freedom of India'.[47] The Muslim Leaguers saw in the Congress campaign a threat to their very existence and felt that, unless they organized like Congress and won over the Muslim masses, they might

[45] *Leader*, 8 March 1939.

[46] I.H. Qureshi, *Ulema in Politics: A Study Relating to the Political Activities of The Ulema in the South-Asian Subcontinent From 1556 to 1947* (Karachi: Ma'aref, 1974), pp. 335–8.

[47] *Bombay Chronicle*, 20 April 1937. The Pirpur Report (1938) also charged that the aim of mass contact was 'to destroy Muslim solidarity and create disruption in the community', and to 'lure' Muslims into the Congress fold by following a policy of 'divide and rule'. For Shaukat Ali's outburst, see *Bombay Chronicle*, 28 December 1937 and K.B. Sayeed, *Pakistan: The Formative Phase 1857–1948* (London: Oxford University Press, 1968), pp. 89–90.

find that Congress had walked away with their flock. For this reason the UP Muslim Parliamentary Board chalked out its own plan for mass contact and resolved to enroll 25 per cent of the adult Muslim population of the province as League members in just three months.[48] Following the directive, enthusiastic leaders such as the Raja of Mahmudabad did much propaganda work among the masses and insisted on its continuance. In September 1937 the Raja warned his comrades that the Muslim masses would not remain unsusceptible to Congress influence if 'we continue to neglect them' and suggested a plan of action to be worked out by men 'with determination and consciousness'.[49] Although Congress and the Muslim League had existed as separate organizations for a long time, never before was there such a rivalry between them for association with the Muslim masses.[50]

The importance of the ulama-League protest and the significance of their counter-offensive cannot be ignored or dismissed; nevertheless, it is crucial to take note of the ascendancy of the pro-Congress elements in the Jamiyat, forcing men such as Ashraf Ali Thanvi and Shabbir Usmani to resign from that body to fall in line with the Muslim League. Madani and Kifayatullah guided the affairs of the Jamiyat; others merely followed their lead. Also, the progress of the Mass Contacts campaign was not greatly hampered by the virulent propaganda of Jinnah and his newly found allies among the ulama. By mid-1938, as Table 1 indicates, a hundred thousand Muslims were enrolled as primary members of the Congress outside UP, Bengal, and the NWFP.[51] Of these, 25,000 were from Bihar, 15,000 from Madras, and 13,995 from the Punjab.

The Failure of Peasant Mobilization

The foregoing analysis strongly suggests that the widely held view, perpetuated by writers in Pakistan and uncritically accepted by historians of Indian nationalism, that the Muslim community rejected the Mass Contacts campaign unequivocally is mistaken. The evidence

48 *Bombay Chronicle*, 20 April 1937.

49 The Raja of Mahmudabad to Jinnah, 24 September 1937. Courtesy of Mr. Khalid S. Hasan.

50 Khaliquzzaman to Nehru, 29 June 1937; AICC Papers, file no. G-1/1937, p. 173.

51 AICC Papers, file no. G-22/1938.

TABLE 1

ENROLMENT OF MUSLIM PRIMARY MEMBERS BY 1938

Ajmer	477
Andhra	2,832
Assam	425
Bihar	25,000
Bombay	1,346
Delhi	1,114
Gujrat	1,600
Kerala	2,574
Maharashtra	3,894
Punjab	13,995
Sind	1,000
Tamilnadu	15,000

marshalled herein demonstrates that, despite vigorous opposition from the Muslim League and a section of the ulama, the Muslim Mass Contacts campaign launched by Congress enjoyed a fair measure of success in some parts of UP, Bihar, Bengal, and the Punjab. It failed, however, to have much of an impact in rural areas. This was not due to a resolute or determined Muslim opposition; it reflected the limited nature of Congress mobilization. Significantly, Muslim peasants and other underprivileged groups in the countryside, the very sections supposedly mobilized on a massive scale, were largely ignored, with efforts concentrated instead on enlisting urban-based ulama and the professional classes.[52]

What Nisar Ahmad, an advocate from Bahawalpur, observed on 31 March 1937, remained largely true of Congress' strategy in the years to come. Congress, he complained, had not reached the Muslim

[52] Some Muslims, such as Fahimuddin Noori, a regular contributor to the Delhi paper, *Alaman*, were opposed to the ulama being pressed into service. Their intervention in politics, he observed, would eventually prove 'harmful'. To Ashraf, 20 April 1937 (in Urdu); AICC Papers, file no. 41/1937, p. 173. For the role of *ulama*, especially in the Bundelkhand elections, see AICC Papers, file no. 30/1937, pp. 583–5.

masses—'the backbone of the community'—who, besides being familiar with the names of Gandhi and Mohammed Ali, were ignorant of 'everything else'.[53] Ashraf, too, conceded in mid-1938 that the Mass Contacts work in various provinces was 'totally unorganized' and that no '*substantial effort was made to come in direct contact with the Muslim masses in large numbers*' (emphasis added).[54] The pattern was thus similar to that from 1930 to 1932, when the Congress leaders decided to minimize Civil Disobedience propaganda in areas with a high proportion of Muslims in the population in order to avoid igniting communal passions.[55] They appear to have done the same in the mid-1930s, although for different reasons and with far more serious implications.

Another important conclusion that emerges from our analysis is not only strikingly different from standing accounts of Indian politics in the mid-1930s but is also inconsistent with the popular belief that by 1937–8 most Muslims were arrayed against the Congress and had rallied around the Muslim League banner. It is neither intended to suggest that Hindu–Muslim antagonism was not fairly widespread nor to deny Jinnah's success in capitalizing on the 'wrongs' done by the Congress ministries in UP and Bihar, but to argue that in 1937–8 neither did there exist a sharp communal political solidarity in the Muslim community. This is strikingly clear in Bengal, Punjab, and UP, where a common Muslim political identity had yet to crystallize, and the Muslim League was still struggling to acquire political legitimacy. The Krishak Praja party in Bengal and the Punjab Unionist party, organized essentially on cross-communal lines, maintained their ascendancy well until the mid-1940s, thwarting Jinnah's attempts to undermine their power and authority. Likewise, there was no clear sign of a complete polarization of communal forces in UP and little evidence of the so-called Muslim drift into the League. Hindu and Muslim landlords, although torn by personal feuds and jealousies,

[53] AICC Papers, file no. 41/1937, p. 27. Abul Hayat, one of Bengal's most consistent nationalists, regretted that the Congress leadership 'persistently neglected to pay heed to the needs and aspirations of the Muslim masses and always tried to come to a settlement with the top leaders of the Muslim League'. Abul Hayat, *Mussalmans of Bengal* (Calcutta: Robi Art Press, 1966), pp. 65–6.

[54] AICC Papers, file no. G-22/1938.

[55] Gyanendra Pandey, *The Ascendancy of the Congress in Uttar Pradesh 1926–1934: A Study in Imperfect Mobilization* (New Delhi: Oxford University Press, 1978), p. 149.

worked in close collaboration and acted in unison to protect their landed interests against the UP Tenancy Bill; in fact, the Hindu–Muslim landlord combination works reasonably well in the National Agriculturist party. Powerful landlords such as the Nawab of Chhatari, Nawab Jamshed Ali Khan of Bagpat, and Nawab Muhammad Yusuf of Jaunpur, although often swept by religious fervour, were more concerned to protect their class interests, represented by landlords' organizations, than their communal interests, represented by the Muslim League.

The Muslim divines, too, were not completely arrayed against the Congress. Although the ulama of the Barelvi and Firangi Mahal schools hitched their fortunes to the League bandwagon, most ulama of Deoband and of the Jamiyat al-Ulama joined forces with Congress. In April 1940 the Jamiyat sponsored an Azad Muslim Conference of nationalist Muslim parties such as the All-India Muslim Majlis, Khudai Khidmatgar, Shia Political Conference, Majlis i-Islam, Momin Conference, Krishak Praja party, and the Anjuman-i-Watan, which, in opposition to the Muslim League demand for a separate Muslim state, declared India as 'the common homeland of all its citizens irrespective of race and religion'. Representing at that time a substantial number of Indian Muslims, they assembled in Delhi to protest against the Pakistan idea and against the use made of the Muslims by the British government and others as an excuse for political inaction. Their views were summarized by Allah Bux Soomro, premier of Sind, and president of the conference, who said that to regard 'Muslims as a separate nation in India on the basis of their religion was un-Islamic'.[56]

The Muslim University at Aligarha—premier educational centre and the focus of intense intellectual and political activity since the days of Syed Ahmed Khan—mirrored some trends among the Muslim intelligentsia. It is a lesser known fact, obscured no doubt by Syed Ahmad Khan's opposition to Congress and Aligarh's participation in the Pakistan movement, that the university was in the forefront of the nationalist struggle in the 1920s and 1930s and remained a major centre of political activity. K.G. Saiyadain, who joined the institution in 1919 and was on the staff of the Teachers' Training College from 1926 to 1938, recalled his participation in the 'great Jubilee debate in 1926 when the students of the university endorsed with great acclaim

[56] For his role, see *Bombay Chronicle*, 18 and 26 June 1937.

a policy of united nationalism'. Campus politics in the 1930s remained unchanged, with men such as T.A.K. Sherwani, Choudhry Khaliquzzaman, Shuaib Qureshi, and A.M. Khwaja—all graduates of Aligarh and closely associated with Nehru and the Congress movement in UP—enjoying a greater following than leaders with communal proclivities. Most office-bearers of the influential Students' Union belonged to the radical alumni circles, anti-British and pro-Congress; the 1936 students' strike against the university's repression of nationalist activities as well as the opposition to a move initiated in the Students' Union in the same year to form an All-India Muslim Students' Federation, was organized in Aligarh; the widely circulated *Aligarh Magazine* retained its pro-Congress bias; and the theme of national unity and communal harmony—central to Mirza Samiullah Beg's (Nawab Mirza Yar Jung Bahadur) Convocation Address of December 1938—continued to evoke a ready response in Aligarh. The Mass Contacts campaign also struck a favourable chord in wider Aligarh circles. Its chief protagonists in UP, Bihar, and the NWFP were Khan Abdul Ghaffar Khan, A.M. Khwaja, Syed Mahmud, N.A.K. Sherwani, Zakir Husain, K.M. Ashraf, Ansar Harvani, Hayatullah Ansari, and Ali Sardar Jafri—all either educated at or closely connected with Aligarh.[57]

The political climate in the country in general, and in UP in particular, was thus no less conducive for the success of the Mass Contacts campaign than in 1930–1, when Congress launched the Civil Disobedience movement. True, there was now much evidence of mounting communal pressures and increased communal strife. It is also true that the 'highhandedness' of Congress Ministries in UP and Bihar was bitterly attacked; so was the singing of 'Bande Mataram', the hoisting of the tricolor flag, the introduction of Wardha and the Vidya Mandir schemes of education, which implied a Hindu orientation, the exclusion of Muslims from local bodies, the imposition of Hindi at the expense of Urdu, and the recurrence of communal riots. Yet, Congress was still able to count on the support of several powerful Muslim groups in the North-West Frontier provinces, UP, and Bihar, a fact that explains why the progress of Mass Contacts work caused panic in Muslim League circles and led Jinnah and his cohorts to launch a counter-offensive.

[57] The role of the Muslim intelligentsia is the subject of a separate study. See Mushirul Hasan, 'Nationalist and Separatist Trends in Aligarh, 1915–47', *Indian Economic and Social History Review*, 22 (1985), pp. 1–33.

THE COLLAPSE OF THE CAMPAIGN

Ashrafuddin Chowdhury, editor of the Comilla newspaper *Naya Bangla* and an associate of Subhas Chandra Bose, wanted to know whether the 'Congress Secretariat' would take up the mass contact work seriously and earnestly or whether it would remain 'a mere paper propaganda'.[58] He should have known better. Within two years of its launching, the Mass Contacts campaign ran into serious trouble not so much due to the Muslim League's opposition or the lack of Muslim support but because of Congress' own reluctance to pursue it with any vigour or sense of purpose. In the early summer of 1939 Mass Contact committees were scrapped, signifying the unhappy ending of a campaign that was started amid much hope and enthusiasm.

Why did this happen? Various explanations already exist. Some suggest that the programme, devoid of any social and economic content, offered 'too little too late';[59] others argue that it remained largely on paper, and secularist, and radical rhetoric in the end alarmed Muslim vested interests without winning over the Muslim masses.[60]

Part of the explanation must reckon with the fact that the idea was Nehru's brainchild, and he alone, along with some of his trusted comrades, pressed it relentlessly until it formed part of the Congress programme. Few Congress members shared his enthusiasm. Gandhi disapproved and preferred to proceed cautiously through constructive work among the Muslim masses by both Hindu and Muslim workers.[61] Reservations were also expressed by some of Nehru's Socialist allies, arguing that their concern was with the masses, not as Hindus or Muslims but as peasants and workers of all communities.[62] The idea of a separate Mass Contacts campaign for the Muslims, however, was consistent with the structure of Congress politics and its strategy of mobilization; in fact, it was a logical consequence of the approach

[58] To Ashraf, 16 April 1937, AICC Papers, file no.26/1937. Misc., p. 9.

[59] Gyanendra Pandey, *Ascendancy of Congress*, p. 151; Deepak Pandey, 'Congress–Muslim League Relations', pp. 643–9; Hardy, *Muslims of British India*, p. 227; Sayeed, *Pakistan*, pp. 89–90.

[60] Sumit Sarkar, *Modern India, 1885–1947* (New Delhi: Macmillan, 1983), p. 354; Bipan Chandra, *Communalism in Modern India* (New Delhi: Vikas, 1984), p. 300.

[61] *SWJN*, p. 225.

[62] B.P.L. Bedi, 'Communalism Enters Congress', *Congress Socialist*, 12 (June 1937).

followed from the time of the Lucknow Pact (1916) when the Congress leaders, in effect, recognized the distinct political identity of the Muslims.

The most bitter criticism of the Mass Contacts programme came from the Congress right wing. Their opposition was symptomatic of the ideological rift with the socialist Nehru and was based on the fear that the success of Mass Contacts would further bolster Nehru's image and provide him, as in the case of Gandhi during the Khilafat days, with a solid base among Muslims. They girded themselves to resist the campaign that threatened their political dominance and raised the chances of Nehru's Muslim, socialist, and communist allies dominating the Congress. G. B. Pant, Chief Minister of UP, thus argued that it was 'not necessary to lay emphasis on the Muslim mass contact' and advised Nehru that Congress should stick to its old policy and creed of representing the 'masses of India regardless of caste or creed'.[63] At the same time, he explained, he was busy securing the 'goodwill and cooperation' of the Muslims by appointing them to high government positions. 'Two of the six Hon'ble Ministers and three out of the twelve Parliamentary Secretaries', announced a government report, 'have been appointed from the Muslims'.[64] Likewise, J.B. Kripalani, general secretary of Congress, brusquely chided Riyazul Mustafa of Bulandshahr for having 'subscribed yourself as the secretary of the Muslim Mass Contacts Committee . . . as there are no such things in the Congress', and directed the UP Pradesh Congress Committee to ensure that 'such committees are disbanded'.[65] More discreet critics such as Morarji Desai pointed out that it was neither 'expedient' nor 'prudent' to implement the scheme in Gujarat on the false plea that there were no Muslim workers through whom the work could be done. 'If non-Muslims take up the work', he wrote, 'it will meet with no response and will perhaps give rise to a dangerous counter-propaganda'.[66]

[63] Nehru Papers, vol. 79, part I, pp. 65–6; V.N. Tiwary to Nehru, January 7, 1939, Nehru Papers, quoted in Deepak Pandey, 'Congress–Muslim League Relations', p. 649. For opposition of Mohanlal Gautam, see proceedings of the executive council of the UPPCC held at Allahabad on June 20 1937, recorded in UPPCC Papers (microfilm), reel no. 2, NMML.

[64] AICC Papers, file no. 1/1937, p. 41.

[65] 7 January 1939, AICC Papers, file no. P-20/1938, pp. 329, 341.

[66] To Ashraf, June 26 1937, AICC Papers, file no. 49/1937, p. 129. Ashraf's view, however, was that the 'average Mussalman hesitates to join the Congress

These were not exceptional or isolated instances. In several parts of UP, such as Agra, Bareilly, and Meerut, there were complaints of inactivity and 'idleness' on the part of Mass Contacts committees; in some cases their activities were hampered by shortage of funds and lack of any organized or coordinated line of action to fight the communal forces.[67] 'What is being done by the local Congress for mass contact?' asked an agitated secretary of the Young Muslim Party in Meerut. 'How many leaders have been called to Meerut for this object? How many Muslims have been enrolled here as Congress members? *So far I think the Congress diary is nearly blank*'.[68] The Bombay-based Socialist Yusuf Meharally was equally disappointed with the indifference of the Congress Committees, while a number of Calcutta Muslim leaders were dismayed by the Bengal PCC's reluctance to pursue the Mass Contacts campaign and enlist Muslim support.[69] They sought the intervention of Nehru, the leader whose integrated secular outlook inspired them most.

The drive to enlist Muslim support did not make much headway for another reason. Several leading Congressmen had unpleasant memories of the Khilafat and Non-Cooperation days when the Mahatma pandered to the religious sentiments of the Muslims and allowed them to dictate Congress policies. With Mass Contacts making rapid progress, they were now faced with the cheerless prospect of yet another Muslim 'influx'.[70] Fearful that with Nehru's backing and

---

not because he has any inherent dislike but because he is ignorant of what the Congress stands for'. To Morarji Desai, June 5 1937, p. 133.

[67] Manzer Siddiqi, editor of *Asia*, to Ashraf, 10 September 1938, AICC Papers, file no. 30/1937, Misc., p. 179; Damodar Swarup Seth to Ashraf, 20 August 1937, AICC Papers, file no. 42/1937 (2), p. 381; and Shamsul Huda, secretary, Barabazar Congress Committee, to Ashraf, AICC Papers, 48/1937, Misc., p. 73. A.K. Azad's pamphlet *Congress and Mussalmans* could not be distributed for lack of funds; AICC Papers, file no. 11/1937, p. 65.

[68] AICC Papers, file no. 47/1937, p. 62. (Emphasis added.)

[69] Yusuf Meharally, 'Non-Congress Ministries in the Melting Pot', *Congress Socialist*, 26 March 1938, p. 223; S.M. Ahmad to Ashraf, 19 August 1937 (in Urdu), AICC Papers, file no. 47/1937, p. 85.

[70] In anticipation of Congress' electoral victory in Bijnor and the expected Muslim entry into the party in large numbers, B.S. Moorie proposed to Bhai Parmanand and Raja Narendranath that all the Hindu Mahasabhites should join Congress to counteract the effect of such an influx. See *Bombay Chronicle*, 9 November 1937. Notice the comment of the Urdu daily *Hind*: 'Responsible Congressmen', wrote the Calcutta paper, 'have never countenanced the entry of

Gandhi's grudging support Muslims would wrest major concessions and begin to influence Congress policies, the Congress right wing, in alliance with the Hindu Mahasabha, fiercely attacked the Mass Contact programme and spared no efforts to thwart its success. Part of their strategy was to starve mass contact committees of funds, to fill them with their trusted lieutenants, and to ensure that Muslims were kept out of Provincial and District Congress Committees.[71] In Aligarh, for instance, Nehru got wind of the plan to exclude the only two Muslims who filed their nominations out of the fifty District Congress Committee (DCC) seats. He intervened to set matters right. In Budaun there was quite a furore when Idris Khan Lodi, associated with Congress for nearly two decades, was not allowed to contest a PCC seat. Lodi resigned in disgust, along with seventy-five other Muslims. In Mahoba and Hamirpur, there was a coalition among the Hindu members on the cry of danger to Hinduism to defeat a Muslim candidate from being elected to the Education Committee of the district board. 'The defeat of the Muslim candidate through Hindu communalism'. wrote Ramgopal Gupta, secretary of the district Congress Committee, 'has angered the Muslim public who cannot distinguish between a Mahasabhite Hindu and a Congressite Hindu'. Finally, in the vital Bundelkhand and Amritsar by-election the Congress right wing worked against two Congressmen of long standing—Nisar Ahmad Khan Sherwani and Saifuddin Kitchlew—and contributed to their defeat. Such belligerence could hardly inspire confidence among the Congress Muslims, who braved the fierce and bitter attacks of the League, resisting pressures to desert the Congress camp and becoming part of the communal front.[72]

Muslims in the Congress and they have in fact encouraged communalism'. Nehru to President, Bengal PCC, 10 April 1937, AICC Papers, file no. 49/1937, Misc., p. 251.

71 Manzar Rizvi of the Political and Economic Information Department brought this complaint to the notice of the Secretary, Nagpur PCC. Such reports also reached the AICC office from Jabalpur, Hamirpur, and Buland-shahar. For relevant information, see AICC Papers, file no. 30/1937, Misc., p. 63, 429; file no. 38/1938, p. 99. For Aligarh, see file nos P-20(2)/1938–39, p. 276; for Budaun see, Ashraf to K.D. Malaviya, January 12, 1939, AICC Papers, file no. 30/1937, Misc., p. 81, and Mahoba and Hamipur, 3 July 1937, AICC Papers, file no. 38/1938, p. 99.

72 Fida Ahmad Khan Sherwani attributed the defeat of his brother, Nisar, to the 'ruthless' neglect of Congress and reached the conclusion that 'a Mussalman has no place in the Congress'. To Nehru, 30 June 1937, AICC Papers, file no.

The success of the Mass Contacts campaign—as, indeed, of any such initiative—depended on the active backing of provincial and district Congress committees. This was not easily forthcoming for a variety of reasons. One of the reasons—one that constantly figured in the Muslim-owned Urdu press—was that these bodies were often controlled by men with anti-Muslim proclivities who had close links with the Hindu Mahasabha and other overtly communal organizations.[73] There was also the familiar charge of their involvement in communal conflicts. In Gorakhpur a *Holi* procession, with spears, swords, and sticks on display, was led by senior office-bearers of the DCC 'reacting very badly on the position of the Congress Muslims and on the prospect of Congress work in general'.[74] In Budaun and Bareilly, districts with large Muslim populations, local Congress leaders helped to exacerbate communal tensions, while in Dehradun an indignant Khushi Lal, chairman of the Municipal Board, warned Nehru of serious consequences if Congressmen promoted communal troubles, and 'try to impose a social boycott of all the Muslims for the sins, imaginary or real, of one or two'.[75] Lal was right. The presence of such elements in Congress made the task of drawing Muslims into the nationalist fold difficult and diminished chances of accomplishing Hindu–Muslim amity.

Congress' one and only attempt to isolate the communal elements

G-61/1937, pp. 197–199. See Kali Charan Nigam to Ashraf, 26 July 1937, AICC Papers, file no. 42(2)/1937, p. 391.

[73] Ashraf was posted with such news. The president of the Jessore Hindu Sabha, he was informed, was also a prominent member of the provincial, district, and town Congress committee. There were reports of an alliance between V.S. Savarkar, one of the founders of the Hindu Mahasabha, and the speaker of the Central Provinces Assembly. The links of many UP Congressmen, such as Madan Mohan Malaviya, with Hindu communal and revivalist causes is fairly well known. This was, incidentally, the strain of many editorial comments. See *Din Duniya Weekly* (Delhi), in Urdu, 11 February 1937; AICC Papers, file no. 41/1937, Misc., p. 107; Syed Hasan Baqai, editor of *Peshwa,* an Urdu monthly, to Ashraf, 5 August 1937, in Urdu, AICC Papers, file no. 47/1937, Misc. p. 123; *Hilal* (Bombay), AICC Papers, file no. 47/1937, Misc., p. 81. Abbas Husain, editor of *Akhbar Qaum wa Risala-i-Tamaddun,* to Nehru, 19 April 1937, AICC Papers, file no. 41/1937, Misc., p. 169. Also, references are to be found in Ashraf to Azad, 3 September 1938, AICC Papers, file no. 30/1937, Misc., p. 213, and M. Umar Khan to Ashraf, 8 May 1937, AICC Papers, file no. P-5/1948, pp. 77–81.

[74] To A.K. Azad, June 27 1938, AICC Papers, file no. 30/1937, Misc., p. 399.

[75] Ashraf to Lal Bahadur Shastri, April 5 1939, AICC Papers, file nos. 6(1)/1937, P-20(2)/1938–39, pp. 273–7 and p. 193.

was a dismal failure. On 11–16 December 1938, the CWC declared, probably at the initiative of Ashraf and his Socialist comrades,[76] the Hindu Mahasabha and the Muslim League as communal organizations and debarred *elected* members of Congress Committees from serving on similar committees in the Mahasabha and the League.[77] This decision, adopted somewhat belatedly, elicited much interest, and PCCs and DCCs all over the country wanted to know whether they could exclude the Hindu Mahasabhites from the Congress organization. 'In our belief,' wrote the secretary of the Bengal PCC, 'Congress organization will suffer very much in prestige and hold over the masses if Congress members be allowed to be members of the Hindu Mahasabha organizations'.[78] J.B. Kripalani, Congress' general secretary, ignored such views, however, and gave an interpretation that defeated the purpose of the CWS's resolution. He wrote to the secretary of the Bengal PCC:

> You must remember Article V(c) in the constitution refers not to primary members of any communal organization but to members of elected committees. There is therefore nothing in the Congress constitution, even if the working committee named some organizations as communal, in the sense contemplated by Article V(c) to prevent ordinary primary members of such organization from being office holders in the Congress organization.[79]

Inconsistent with the spirit of the CWC resolution, this interpretation gave a free hand to communal groups to move in and out of the Congress with ease and to meddle in its affairs brazenly. Congress' own position regarding communal organizations and the communal activities of its members remained dangerously vague.

[76] Ashraf to Mohanlal Saxena, September 3 1938, AICC Papers, file no. 30/1937, Misc., pp. 209–10.

[77] Resolution of the CWC, Wardha, 11–16 December 1938, AICC Papers, file no. P-1/1938. It has been erroneously pointed out by Bipan Chandra that in 1938 the Congress 'barred its doors' to the members of the communal organizations. Such factual inaccuracies, as, indeed, a number of methodological inconsistencies, are far too numerous to be recounted here. See Chandra, *Communalism in Modern India,* p. 149.

[78] Ashrafuddin Chowdhury to Kripalani, 16 August and 20 September 1938, AICC Papers, file no. P-5/1938.

[79] To Chowdhury, 6 October 1938, AICC Papers, file no. P-5/1938, p. 101. (Emphasis added.)

SUMMARY

The Mass Contacts campaign was Congress' last serious attempt to mobilize Muslims in a joint struggle against colonial rule. Although based on a set of assumptions that did not adequately take into account the presence of the 'third party' and the complexity of the communal problem, this campaign was conceived at a crucial historical juncture and was a significant move in the right direction. Pursued purposefully, it had the potential of weaning large sections of the Muslim community away from the Muslim League camp, a point so well made by some contemporary observers.[80] There can be no doubt that Nehru and other protagonists of Mass Contacts were confronted with numerous difficulties: the stout resistance of Jinnah, the lukewarm support of their own party comrades, and communal animosities manifest in Hindu–Muslim rioting and other forms of antagonism. These problems were not insurmountable, however, as would appear from Nehru's own assessment of the communal situation. The Muslim League, after all, was weak, divided, and disorganized, and its leader, Jinnah, did not yet command the allegiance of the more powerful groups in Punjab, UP, and Bengal. Congress, however, enjoyed a fair measure of support, a fact that places Jinnah's outburst against mass contact and the League's endeavors to arrest its progress, in perspective. Its inability to consolidate the gains of the year 1937 to 1938 was a sure case of letting an opportunity slip by. By letting the Mass Contacts campaign peter out, Congress allowed Jinnah, perhaps involuntarily, to take advantage of deteriorating communal relations and rally his community around the divisive symbol of a separate Muslim homeland; in fact, Ashraf suggested many years later that one reason why the League 'turned overnight into a full-fledged manager' was because Congress abandoned the struggle of mass contact for ministry-making.[81] This comment reflected a painful reality.

80 Dube Rai to Ashraf, 19 December 1937, AICC Papers, file no. 54/1937, Misc., p. 399; Faridul Haq Ansari, 'Communalism Clarified', *Congress Socialist*, 19 February 1938, pp. 122–3; Hayat, *Mussalmans of Bengal*, p. 65.

81 Kruger, *Kunwar Mohammad Ashraf*, pp. 413–14.

Chapter Eight

Jinnah and the Pakistan Demand

R.J. MOORE

ENIGMA

In an age sceptical of the historic role of great men there is universal agreement that Mahomed Ali Jinnah was central to the Muslim League's emergence after 1937 as the voice of a Muslim nation; to its articulation in March 1940 of the Pakistan demand for separate statehood for the Muslim majority provinces of north-western and eastern India; and to its achievement in August 1947 of the separate but truncated state of Pakistan by the Partition of India. Subcontinental judgements of Jinnah are bound to be *parti pris* and to exaggerate his individual importance. While Pakistanis generally see him as the Quaid-i-Azam, Great Leader, or father of their nation, Indians often regard him as the Lucifer who tempted his people into the unforgivable sin against their nationalist faith. Among distinguished foreign scholars, unbiased by national commitment, his stature is similarly elevated. Sir Penderel Moon has written:

> There is, I believe, no historical parallel for a single individual effecting such a political revolution; and his achievement is a striking refutation of the theory that in the making of history the individual is of little or no significance. It was Mr Jinnah who created Pakistan and undoubtedly made history.[1]

Professor Lawrence Ziring believes that Jinnah's 'personality . . . made Pakistan possible' and that 'it would not have emerged without him'.[2] Sir Cyril Philips has argued that without Jinnah's leadership

[1] Sir Penderel Moon, 'Mr Jinnah's Changing Attitude to the Idea of Pakistan', paper presented at Quaid-i-Azam Centenary Congress, Islamabad, 1976.

[2] L. Ziring, 'Jinnah: The Burden of Leadership', ibid.

regionalism would probably have competed seriously with Muslim nationalism as the aim of the Muslim majority provinces.[3]

Professor Nicholas Mansergh looks to Jinnah for 'the classic exposition of the two-nation theory' in his March 1940 address prefiguring the Pakistan resolution and revises sharply upwards the determining influence of the concept upon the interplay of men and events that culminated in the Partition of India.[4]

Yet the relation of Jinnah to the rise of the League and its demand and movement for Pakistan is still obscure. Eminent contemporaries were puzzled by the sources of his apparent power. For example, as last Viceroy, Lord Mountbatten thought the idea of Pakistan 'sheer madness' and wrote of Jinnah in bewilderment: 'I regard Jinnah as a psychopathic case; in fact until I had met him I would not have thought it possible that a man with such a complete lack of administrative knowledge or sense of responsibility could achieve or 'hold down so powerful a position'.[5] Mountbatten saw Jinnah as a leader whose 'megalomania' was so 'chronic' that he pursued his own power to the material detriment of his misguided followers.[6] British statesmen and officials and Congress leaders alike attached immense significance to vanity and pride in Jinnah's quest for Pakistan and their views continue to influence the historiography of the Partition.[7]

In a perceptive analysis Professor Khalid Bin Sayeed seeks the key to the relationship between Jinnah's personality and the Pakistan movement in the 'congruence' between the ambition of Jinnah, a domineering man whom reverses in life had made desperate, and the needs and characteristics of his people, 'a community . . . looking for

[3] C.H. Philips and M.D. Wainwright (eds), *The Partition of India: Policies and Perspectives, 1935–1947* (London, 1970), p. 29.

[4] N. Mansergh, *The Prelude to Partition: Concepts and Aims in Ireland and India*, The 1976 Commonwealth Lecture (Cambridge, 1978), pp. 26, 59.

[5] Viceroy's Personal Report no. 3, 17 April 1947, N. Mansergh and P. Moon (eds), *The Transfer of Power (TP)*, X (1981), Doc. 165.

[6] Mountbatten to Sir Stafford Cripps, 9 July 1947, CAB 127/139, Public Record Office (P.R.O.), London.

[7] E.g. Clement Attlee's draft memoirs, ATLE 1/13, Churchill Coll., Cambridge; Mountbatten on Nehru and Patel in letter to Cripps, 9 July 1947, Moon to J.McL. Short, 2 September 1946, CAB 127/150, P.R.O.; H.V. Hodson, *The Great Divide: Britain—India—Pakistan* (London, 1969), pp. 217–18; L. Collins and D. Lapierre, *Freedom at Midnight* (London, 1975), p. 101; S. Gopal, *Jawaharlal Nehru: A Biography*, I (London, 1975), p. 257; Tara Chand, *History of the Freedom Movement in India*, IV (Delhi, 1972), p. 574.

a great saviour . . . who was prepared to unite the community and bring earthly glory to Islam'.[8] Nevertheless, for Sayeed 'it continues to be an enigma how these people followed a leader who was so austere and so remote from them'.[9] The link, he speculates, was 'that this power-conscious man promised to them the political power which the Qur'an had promised to them and which their forbears had wielded in India'.

Historians have also emphasized the enigmatic nature of Jinnah's 'promise'—the vagueness of the Pakistan demand and the variety of constitutional forms that Jinnah seemed willing to accept in satisfaction of it.[10] Some have sought to resolve the paradox by construing the demand as a bargaining counter, whereby Jinnah sought to enhance the power of the League and himself within a united free India.[11] Others have argued that Jinnah was 'hoist with his own petard': he fell captive to his promise of separate statehood for six provinces and was left by the Partition with the truncated state that was alone consistent with the concept of a nation defined by the religious map of the subcontinent.[12]

The following analysis seeks to clarify the relation between Jinnah and the Pakistan movement during the decade preceding Partition, in terms of both his charisma and his constitutional strategy, but not, it should be stressed, in terms of party organization and political mobilization, on which much more work remains to be done.[13]

Sources of Charisma

Jinnah was born on Christmas day 1876 in a tenement house in

[8] K.B. Sayeed, 'The Personality of Jinnah and His Political Strategy', Philips and Wainwright (eds), *Partition of India*, pp. 276–93, esp. p. 282.

[9] Ibid., p. 293. Dr Ian Copland has recently observed that Jinnah 'remains an enigma' ('Islam and Political Mobilization in Kashmir, 1931–34', *Pacific Affairs*, 54.2 (1981), pp. 228–59).

[10] E.g. Tara Chand, *History of the Freedom Movement*, IV, pp. 321ff.

[11] See Moon, 'Jinnah's Changing Attitude', for an analysis of such arguments.

[12] E.g. S.R. Mehrotra, 'The Congress and the Partition of India', Philips and Wainwright, *Partition of India*, pp. 188–221, 216; A. Seal, 'Imperialism and Nationalism in India', J.A. Gallagher, G. Johnson and A. Seal (eds), *Locality, Province and Nation: Essays on Indian Politics, 1870–1940* (Cambridge, 1973), pp. 1–27, 24.

[13] For recent studies of mobilization, see Copland, 'Islam and Political Mobilization', esp. pp. 228–31, 257–9.

Karachi. He was to be the eldest of seven children of a hide merchant, whose modest means confined the family's living space to two rooms but somehow sufficed to despatch Jinnah at the age of sixteen direct from the Sind Madrasa to Lincoln's Inn. The exemplary pupil qualified for the Bar precociously young, but during his short four-year absence his mother and child-wife died and his father suffered financial ruin. He chose to make his way at the Bombay Bar. After three briefless and penurious years his powers of application, analysis, and advocacy brought him rapid success and wealth, the springboard to his political career. By the age of forty he had been prominent in the Indian National Congress, toured Europe with Gokhale, represented the Muslims of Bombay in the Imperial Legislative Council, and acted as principal negotiator of the Lucknow Pact for Congress–Muslim League unity. When Edwin Montagu visited India in 1917 he recorded meeting this 'young, perfectly mannered, impressive-looking . . . very clever man', who, 'armed to the teeth with dialectics' tied the Viceroy up in verbal knots.[14]

By the standards of his gilded youth the next twenty years of Jinnah's life were leaden. Poised to scale political heights he fell and suffered disappointment. Gandhi's Congress-Khilafat non-cooperation movement, which was inimical to his constitutionalist style, was partly responsible for this eclipse, but perhaps as important was the shift that the dyarchical provincial councils effected in Muslim politics. Given the realities of office and patronage the Punjab Unionist Party became the powerhouse of Muslim policy.[15] Confronted with Congress initiatives to inherit the central government of India, the All-India Muslim Conference, led from the Punjab by Mian Fazl-i-Husain, espoused schemes for entrenching the Muslims in quasi-sovereign provinces, yielding to a federal centre only such powers as they chose and given effective safeguards for Muslim interests. Jinnah remained a leader of the League and a member of the Central legislature but the action had moved elsewhere. In 1928 he was worsted by the forces of Hindu orthodoxy when he sought accommodation with Congress on an all-parties constitutional scheme. At the Round Table Conference he was suspected by the dominant Muslim delegates

[14] Cited in H. Bolitho, *Jinnah: Creator of Pakistan* (London, 1954), p. 70.

[15] A. Jalal and A. Seal, 'Alternative to Partition: Muslim Politics Between the Wars', C. Baker, G. Johnson and A. Seal (eds), *Power, Profit and Politics: Essays in Imperialism, Nationalism and Change in Twentieth Century India* (Cambridge, 1981), pp. 415–54; Moore, *The Crisis of Indian Unity, 1917–40* (Oxford, 1974).

as an unreliable conciliator, and he seemed to speak for no one but himself. For three or four years he turned his back on India and tried to settle in London, living in Hampstead and practising at the Privy Council Bar. When he returned to India in 1936 to set up the League's Parliamentary Board to contest the 1936 elections under the India Act of 1935s provisions for provincial autonomy, he was shunned by the Punjab Unionists. He remained hopeful of achieving an all-India Hindu–Muslim settlement under a Congress–League *rapprochement* until, after its electoral triumph, Congress made it apparent that its terms were the League's capitulation.[16]

Jinnah's personality and experience disposed him to feel bitterly the Congress denial of the Muslims' political identity. Lacking inherited status, from an early age his place in the world had rested wholly upon his own efforts. By observing a regimen of discipline and self-denial he had earned a place of dignity in Indian politics. The single-minded pursuit of professional and political success left him little opportunity to cultivate a private life that might mitigate the sense of public rejection. The exaggerated refinement of the English dress and personal style that he adopted seem more like carapaces than indulgences. The political reverses of middle-age were unrelieved by any of the usual pleasures of personal or domestic life. His marriage at the age of forty-two to the eighteen years old daughter of a Parsi friend had, after several unhappy years, finally collapsed in 1928. Her death soon afterwards left him bereaved and with a sense of guilt. For the rest of his life his sole companion was his loyal sister Fatima, who, from living with it daily, came to share his acute sense of persecution.[17]

Like Jinnah's personal standing the status that the Muslims had achieved by 1937 had been hard won. Latecomers to western education, official employment and party politics, they had, as collaborators of the British Raj, advanced rapidly in the twentieth century. In the United Provinces they had consolidated their tenure of land and won

[16] Z.H. Zaidi, 'Aspects of Muslim League Policy, 1937–47', Philips and Wainwright, *Partition of India*, pp. 245–75, esp. pp. 250–7. See also J.A. Gallagher, 'Congress in Decline: Bengal, 1930 to 1939', *Locality, Province and Nation,* pp. 269–325, esp. pp. 307–12.

[17] Lady Mountbatten wrote to her husband of Miss Jinnah in April 1947: 'Like Mr Jinnah, she has, of course, a persecution mania . . .' (*TP*, x, 207). M.L. Chagla, a useful witness, believed that she 'injected an extra dose of venom' into Jinnah's diatribes against the Hindus (*Roses in December* (Bombay, 1973), p. 119). For recollections of Jinnah see also the works of Kanji Dwarkadas.

weightage well beyond their numbers in councils and government service.[18] Since the first elections to the Montford councils they had succeeded to decades of Congress ascendancy in Bengal and won office in Punjab. The All-India Muslim Conference had defended separate electorates in both majority provinces and applied a strategy of 'provincial balance' to secure the separation of Sind from Bombay and its elevation, together with that of the North-West Frontier Province, to full provincial status. In 1936, the last year of his life, Fazl-i-Husain could reflect that the Muslim position was now 'adequately safe-guarded'.[19] The sense of achieved security owed much to checks that the India Act of 1935 seemed to place on the power of the Congress, for in its contemplated all-India federation a third of the seats were reserved to the Muslims and a third to nominees of the Indian princes. The emergence of Congress dominance in 1937 changed all that.

In March 1937, when Nehru remarked that the Congress and the Raj were the only two parties in India, Jinnah replied to the rebuff by claiming the Muslim League as a third, a rightful 'equal partner' of the Congress.[20] It was the Muslims of the Congress provinces who first apprehended the dangers of Hindu ascendancy under a Congress Raj and reacted with a sense of persecution.[21] Muslim grandees in the United Provinces grew anxious when Congress denied them a share in government and threatened their culture, property and prospects of public employment.[22] In Muslim minority provinces it seemed that under responsible government the Congress could withhold their participation in office permanently. In Muslim majority provinces Congress sought power through alignments with Muslim factions. Rajendra Prasad commented:

[18] L. Brennan, 'The Socio-Economic Background to Muslim Separatism in the United Provinces, 1900–1940', unpublished seminar paper, Flinders University, 1982.

[19] Azim Husain, *Fazl-i-Husain: a Political Biography* (Bombay, 1946), p. 265.

[20] Cited in Bolitho, *Jinnah*, pp. 113–14.

[21] See D. Pandey, 'Congress-Muslim League Relations, 1937–9: "The Parting of the Ways" ', *Modern Asian Studies,* 12 (1978), pp. 629–54.

[22] Brennan, 'Socio-Economic Background to Muslim Separatism', shows that in the UP 'for the first time since 1909 the Muslim élite seemed to have no leverage in the new institutions of government', 'many of the gains of the past thirty years seemed to be vanishing or at least under threat', and 'the foundations they had so carefully fought to build were shown to be straw'.

The attempt of our party in most [of these] provinces has constantly been to win over members of the government party and thus secure a majority for itself, so that it may form a ministry. In effect its action has been not so much to consider the criticised government measures on their merit and secure the adoption of its own programme by the government, but to try somehow or other to oust the party in power. The result . . . has been to create much bitterness against the Congress. . . .[23]

At the all-India level the Congress high command pursued its advantage by pressing the princes to fill their federal seats by election instead of nomination, which would open the prospect of sufficient Congress victories to destroy the statutory check upon its power.[24] Jinnah became convinced that parliamentary government would mean Congress 'totalitarianism' in India.[25] The only safeguard of equal rights to India's Muslims lay in their achievement of equality of power through their solidarity within the All-India Muslim League. Under his organization the League's membership grew from a few thousand to several hundred thousand in 1937–8.

Jinnah harped on the theme of equality. At the League's annual session at Lucknow in October 1937 he insisted that 'an honourable settlement can only be achieved between equals'.[26] He demanded of Nehru that Congress must recognize the League 'on a footing of perfect equality'.[27] He internalized the Muslims' sense of 'suffering and sacrifice' from the 'fire of persecution'. He expressed himself with personal conviction: 'I have got as much right to share in the government of this country as any Hindu'; and 'I must have [an] equal, real, and effective share in the power'.[28] The appeal was underpinned by an assertion that Islamic society was based on the equality of man.[29]

The essential link between Jinnah's leadership and the emergence of a Muslim national consciousness was that Jinnah personified the Muslims' sense of persecution by the Congress denial of their achieved status. The widespread assumption that vanity, pride, ambition and

23 Prasad to Patel, 11 October 1938, B.N. Pandey (ed.), *The Indian Nationalist Movement, 1885–1947: Select Documents* (London, 1979), pp. 127–8.

24 R.G. Coupland, *Indian Politics, 1936–42* (London, 1943), pp. 167–78.

25 Jinnah's presidential address to Muslim League at Patna, 26 December 1938, Jamil-ud-din Ahmad (ed.), *Speeches and Writings of Mr. Jinnah,* 2 vols (Lahore, 1960 edn), I, 67–81.

26 Ibid., p. 30.

27 Ibid., p. 139.

28 Ibid., pp. 36, 139, 184.

29 Ibid., p. 116.

megalomania were the dominant facets of his personality has masked it. In a similar way, the extension of impressions of his personality to generalizations about his political style has exaggerated the intellectual distance between the leader and his followers, obscuring the doctrinal cut and thrust from which emerged the constitutional strategy that would afford a refuge from persecution.

From Karachi to Lahore

Almost all who observed Jinnah described him as reserved, remote, aloof and, above all, lonely. His remoteness in later life was caused partly by his chronic bronchial infection, which had probably appeared in 1936,[30] and from July 1943 partly by the precautionary measures of up to three official bodyguards who were assigned to him after he was attacked by an assassin. But clearly he did not enjoy physical contact and kept the world at a distance. The famous monocle and frequent changes of clothing seem, like his aversion to shaking hands and travelling by train unless in a first class coupé, expressions of immaculacy. When Sir Stafford Cripps visited him in December 1939 he noted: 'Altogether he gave me the impression of an intensely lonely man in perpetual conflict with himself and with no one in whom he could confide or who could give him reliable advice, but he put his case with great ability and clarity.'[31] In January 1942 Sir Reginald Coupland visited him at his new house on Malabar Hill and was struck by the 'great forensic ability . . . admirable lucidity . . . and clear conclusions' of this 'very able advocate'.[32] His notes suggest Jinnah's clinical detachment and self-sufficiency, living and working in a mansion with 'beautiful rooms, lavishly furnished, and a most attractive curving marble terrace, with lawn beneath it sloping to a belt of trees with a gap in it through which the sea'. Jinnah plied him with League literature, 'largely reprints of his own speeches'. A few weeks later Coupland described Jinnah as 'virtually dictator' of the League,[33] a

[30] The earliest X-ray photograph in the Quaid-i-Azam archives at Islamabad (Q.A.P.) is dated Lahore, 26 October 1936.

[31] Cripps–Geoffrey Wilson diary of visit to India, 15 December 1939 (in possession of Mr Maurice Shock).

[32] Coupland's Indian diary, 1941–2 (C.D.), 17 January 1942, Rhodes House, Oxford.

[33] Ibid., 8 April 1942.

judgement that A.V. Alexander echoed at the time of the Cabinet Mission: 'Mr Jinnah, the so-called Man of Destiny of the Muslim League [is] a clever lawyer . . . and I should think in his own way pretty near to being a complete dictator'.[34] Mountbatten believed that 'the only adviser that Jinnah listens to is Jinnah'.[35]

Yet in the crucial eighteen months preceding the proclamation of the Pakistan demand at Lahore Jinnah's role in the formation and expression of constitutional thought and strategy was certainly not that of an isolated, lonely and self-sufficient leader.

In October 1938 Jinnah returned to a king's welcome in the city of his birth, Karachi, for a conference of the Sind branch of the All-India Muslim League.[36] He rode from the railway station in an open limousine at the head of a procession three miles long. Some 20,000 delegates were assembled, among them the provincial premiers Sir Sikander Hayat Khan (Punjab) and Sir Fazlul Haq (Bengal), the UP leaders Liaquat Ali Khan (Secretary of the League), the Raja of Mahmudabad and Chaudhry Khaliquzzaman, the old Khilafat leader Shaukat Ali, and prominent Sindhis. The main object of the Sindhis in organizing the conference was to bring to bear upon the province's faction-ridden Muslim establishment the unifying influence of the national body. The benefits of the separation from Bombay of this majority province had been squandered by the recourse of its Muslim premiers to Hindus for their survival. In July 1937 M.H. Gazdar (a future mayor of Karachi) had written to Jinnah in disgust at the state of Sind politics and proposed the creation of an independent Muslim state comprising the four north-western provinces.[37] The initiator and reception committee chairman of the conference was Sir Abdoola Haroon, a self-made merchant and industrialist prince of Karachi, campaigner for the separation of Sind, member of the Central Legislature (1926–42), founder of the Sind United Party on the model of the Punjab Unionists, and member of the League's Working Committee.[38] In his opening address he focused attention upon the need for

[34] A.V. Alexander's diary, 4 April 1946, Churchill College, Cambridge.

[35] Cited in Hodson, *The Great Divide*, p. 217.

[36] The following account of the Karachi conference draws heavily on A.K. Jones, 'Mr. Jinnah's Leadership and the Evolution of the Pakistan Idea: The Case of the Sind Provincial Muslim League Conference, 1938', paper presented at Quaid-i-Azam Centenary Conference, Islamabad 1976.

[37] Gazdar to Jinnah, 10 July 1937, cited in Ziring, 'Jinnah'.

[38] Alhaj Mian Ahmad Shafi, *Haji Sir Abdoola Haroon: A Biography* (Karachi, n.d.).

an all-India Hindu–Muslim settlement, failing which Muslims may need 'to seek their salvation in their own way in an independent federation of Muslim states', in the division of Hindu India and Muslim India 'under separate federations'.[39]

Haroon was moving further and faster towards a separatist objective than Jinnah, who emphasized the primary need to consolidate Muslims to resist Congress oppression. Fourteen months later Jinnah was still professing to be as much an Indian nationalist as Nehru, and in January 1940 he could still write of India as the 'common motherland' of Muslims and Hindus.[40] He was disquieted when Haroon incorporated the goal of an independent Muslim state in a resolution:

> The Sindh Provincial Muslim League Conference considers it absolutely essential in the interests of an abiding peace of the vast Indian continent and in the interests of unhampered cultural development, the economic and social betterment and political self-determination of the two nations, known as Hindus and Muslims, that India may be divided into federations, namely, the federation of Muslim States and the federation of non-Muslim States. This conference therefore recommends to the All India Muslim League to devise a scheme of constitution under which Muslim-majority-provinces Muslim Indian States and areas inhabited by a majority of Muslims may attain full independence in the form of a federation of their own. . . .[41]

Jinnah is reported to have entered a caveat: 'The Government is still in the hands of the British. Let us not forget it. You must see ahead and work for the ideal that you think will arise 25 years hence.'[42] Next day, with his tacit consent, Haroon's draft was passed thus modified:

> This conference considers it absolutely essential, in the interests of an abiding peace of the vast Indian continent and in the interests of unhampered cultural development, the economic and social betterment and political self-determination of the two nations, known as Hindus and Muslims, to recommend to the All India Muslim League to review and revise the entire conception

[39] Address of 9 October 1938, cited in Jones, 'Mr. Jinnah's Leadership'.

[40] See Jinnah's Osmania University speech, 28 September 1939, Ahmad, *Speeches and Writings of Mr. Jinnah*, vol. I, p. 87; Cripps–Wilson Diary, 15 December 1939; 'Two Nations in India', sent by Jinnah to *Time and Tide* on 19 January 1940 and published 9 March 1940.

[41] *Statesman*, 11 October 1938, cited in Jones, 'Mr. Jinnah's Leadership'.

[42] *Statesman*, 14 October 1938, cited in Mehrotra, 'The Congress and the Partition', p. 207.

of what should be the suitable constitution for India which will secure honourable and legitimate status to them.[43]

While the two-nations theory now became the League's creed it was clearly not synonymous with separatism. Even the mover of Haroon's original resolution, Shaikh Abdul Majid, expected that the Hindu and Muslim federations would be linked by a common centre for foreign affairs, defence and the settlement of disputes.[44] Clearly, too, Jinnah was drawn this far by the initiative of the Sindhis and the need to accommodate policy to it in the interests of solidarity.

Jinnah was unwell during the following weeks and made no speeches until 26 December at the League's annual session at Patna, when he spoke impromptu. He then observed the awakening of a 'national consciousness among the Muslims' comparable to that of the Hindus, but warned that a 'national self and national individuality' had yet to be developed.[45] The session authorized him to explore suitable constitutional alternatives to the 1935 Act,[46] and the following March the Working Committee set up a committee to examine those that had already appeared and others that might emerge.[47] Jinnah was to head the committee and eight others, including Haroon, Liaquat, Sikander, Nazimuddin (Bengal), and Aurangzeb Khan (NWFP) were empanelled. Next month Jinnah intimated that several schemes were before the committee, including one for dividing the country into Hindu and Muslim India. In fact the committee never met and the initiative remained in Haroon's hands.

During the interim between the Karachi and Patna conferences Haroon took a number of steps to advance the general cause of a separate federation of Muslim provinces and states. His resolve was strengthened by Congress activities in the states towards the end of the year.[48] He failed in an attempt to enlist the support of the Aga Khan.[49] However, the Council of the League now established a

[43] *Pioneer*, 15 October 1938, cited in S.S. Pirzada (ed.), *Foundations of Pakistan: All-India Muslim League Documents, 1906–47*, 2 vols (Karachi, 1970), vol. II, p. xix.

[44] Zaidi, 'Aspects of Muslim League Policy', p. 261.

[45] Pirzada, *Foundations of Pakistan*, vol. II, pp. 306–24.

[46] Ibid., p. 321.

[47] Ibid., pp. xx–xxi.

[48] Shafi, *Haji Sir Abdoola Haroon*, p. 139.

[49] Haroon's correspondence with Aga Khan in November–December 1938, in Shafi, ibid., pp. 137–42. For the Aga Khan's own notion of a 'United States of

Foreign and Inland Deputations subcommittee, and Haroon became its chairman. It was to send deputations abroad, to explain the views of Muslim India and counter Congress allegations that the Muslims were reactionary and unpatriotic, and from the Muslim majority to the minority provinces, to consolidate links between their organizations.[50] The committee performed some of the functions appropriate to offices for foreign affairs and propaganda. Haroon also involved it in planning when he asked Dr Syed Abdul Latif to meet it in Lahore in January 1939 to discuss his ideas for the recognition of the two nations by the redistribution of India into cultural zones.[51] Though Latif's approach was to accommodate the two nations within a 'common motherland' under a single federal authority, rather than to pursue the separate federations that he himself favoured, Haroon advanced Rs 2000 for the publication and foreign distribution of Latif's scheme in expanded booklet form.[52] The circulation of Latif's views in 1938–9, in pamphlets, the newspapers and the booklet, stimulated controversy over the constitutional future of Muslim India.

Much of the constitutional planning occurred in the Punjab, where there was already a significant legacy of separatist thought. As president of the League in 1930 the philosopher-poet of Lahore, Sir Muhammad Iqbal, had called for the amalgamation of the four north-western provinces, less some non-Muslim districts, into 'a Muslim India within India'.[53] As the religious units of India had never been inclined to sacrifice their individualities in a larger whole 'the unity of an Indian nation must be sought, not in negation, but in mutual harmony and co-operation'. The 'effective principle of co-operation' in India was the recognition of 'homelands' in which the Muslim might enjoy 'full and free development on the lines of his own culture and tradition'. In 1933 the Cambridge student Rahmat Ali, the Punjabi coiner of the name 'Pakistan', proposed the separation from India of a Muslim state embracing the four provinces and Kashmir, and soon

Southern Asia' see 'Scheme of His Highness Sir Aga Khan as modified by Sir Fazl-i-Husain, January 1936', ibid., pp. 118–21, and Jalal and Seal, 'Alternative to Partition', pp. 445–9.

[50] Shafi, *Haji Sir Abdoola Haroon*, 150–1.

[51] Haroon's introduction to Latif's *The Muslim Problem in India*, Bombay, July 1939, pp. v–viii.

[52] Ibid., *The Cultural Future of India*, Bombay 1938; *A Federation of Cultural Zones for India*, Secunderabad, 20 December 1938; *Statesman*, 30 March 1939.

[53] Pirzada, *Foundations of Pakistan*, vol. II, pp. 153–71.

afterwards launched the Pakistan National Movement.[54] During the year preceding his death in April 1938 Iqbal's opposition to a single Indian federation had hardened and he had urged Jinnah to demand one or more separate Muslim states, though he was silent as to their relations with the rest of India.[55]

In March 1939 the fact that the League Working Committee had Latif's scheme before it provoked one who signed himself 'Ahmad Bashir', secretary of the Pakistan Majlis, Lahore, to petition Jinnah, Liaquat, Haroon, Fazlul Haq and Sikander.[56] Latif's scheme would prejudice the political and economic integrity of Pakistan by casting the eastern tracts of the Punjabi and Kashmir into a Hindu–Sikh zone:

> As the scheme is likely to influence the natural boundaries of Pakistan I feel the interest of Pakistan and the Movement started towards the creation of an independent state in the north-west of India comprising the whole of the Punjab, Kashmir, the North Western Frontier Province, Sind and Baluchistan would materially suffer if the Cultural Zones Scheme is extended towards the North West of India. . . . The Pakistan mind is slowly believing in its physical whole and any attempt to disintegrate this natural geographical identity will certainly be detrimental to the cause of Muslim India.[57]

The references to the Pakistan Movement and the claim to the full four north-western provinces plus Kashmir suggest the influence of Rahmat Ali on the Pakistan Majlis of Lahore. However, the character that the Majlis subsequently manifested suggested the influence of Iqbal's ideas and there is good reason to believe that 'Ahmad Bashir' was the pen-name of Mian Bashir Ahmad, son of Justice Shah Din, a dear friend of Iqbal's and the subject of a eulogy by the poet when he died. The Majlis soon assumed the title 'Majlis-i-Kabir Pakistan, Lahore', suggestive of its reverence for the saintly poet who was also the prophet of Indian unity, and, in the spirit of Iqbal, argued: 'Nobody questions India's unity but how that unity can be achieved is a matter that deserves special attention of all the parties concerned. It is a matter . . . [that] must be given precedence to everything else.'[58] The recognition of 'separate homelands by dividing India into auto-

[54] Cited and discussed in Coupland, *Indian Politics,* pp. 199–201.

[55] Hafeez Malik (ed.), *Iqbal: Poet-Philosopher of Pakistan* (New York, 1971), appx, pp. 383–90.

[56] Ahmad Bashir to Jinnah etc., 22 March 1939, Q.A.P., file 96.

[57] Ibid. See also Ahmad Bashir letter to a newspaper, 7 April 1939, ibid.

[58] Ahmad Bashir to Jinnah, 21 October 1939, Q.A.P., file 96.

nomous homogeneous states' was 'the one and the only way to India's Unity'. The identification of 'Ahmad Bashir' as Mian Bashir Ahmad rests partly on convincing holographic evidence but also on the knowledge that Mian Bashir Ahmad, barrister of Lahore, was also a journalist (editor of the Urdu *Humayun*) and a poet, who wrote admiringly of Iqbal's political ideas and poetry and of Jinnah in prose and verse.[59] He was to be a member of the reception committee for the League's historic Lahore session in 1940 and a member of the Working Committee from 1942. This follower of Iqbal was to supply Jinnah with ringing passages for his inspiring Lahore presidential address.

In summer 1939 the alternatives open to the League were clarified by Sikander's formulation of a scheme for a loose all-India federation of zones including provinces and states,[60] and its rejection first by Bashir Ahmad[61] and then by scholars at Aligarh. The latter favoured the division of British India into 'three wholly independent and sovereign states'.[62] Two Aligarh authors, Professor Syed Zafarul Hasan and Dr M.A.H. Qadri, insisted that the Muslims of India, 'a nation by themselves', must not be 'enslaved into a single all-India federation with an overwhelming Hindu majority in the centre'. The three sovereign states of British India would be North-West India or Pakistan, Bengal, and Hindustan. The principalities within these states or exclusively on the frontier of one of them would be attached automatically, while those adjoining more than one state might choose their attachment. But Hyderabad must recover Berar and the Karnatic and

[59] Cf. the signatures on preceding letters and of '(Mian) Bashir Ahmad' on letter to Jinnah, 19 June 1946, Q.A.P., file 1092. For Bashir Ahmad, see Pirzada, *Foundations of Pakistan*, II, pp. 326, 462–3 (poems read at League's Lahore session, 22 March 1940, and Karachi session, 25 December 1943); Muhammad Daud Rahbar in Malik, *Iqbal*, p. 44. For his writings, see, e.g., ibid., bibliography; 'Quaid-e-Azam: Some Glimpses of His Greatness', Jamil-ud-din Ahmad (ed.), *Quaid-e-Azam as Seen by His Contemporaries* (Lahore, 1966), pp. 13–28.

[60] Sikander Hyat Khan, *Outlines of a Scheme of Indian Federation*, Lahore, 30 July 1939. See also Sikander's speech in *Punjab Legislative Assembly Debates*, 11 March 1941 (in V.P. Menon, *The Transfer of Power in India*, 1957, appx I, pp. 451–67). For another Punjabi scheme published in Lahore in summer 1939, see 'A Punjabi' [? Miyan Kifayat Ali] *Confederacy of India*, pub. by Sir Muhammad Shah Nawaz Khan of Mamdot.

[61] Ahmad Bashir, 'Sir Sikandar Hayat's Scheme' and 'Sir Sikandar's Federal Scheme', *Civil and Military Gazette*, 5 and 27 August 1939.

[62] Syed Zafarul Hasan and Muhammad Afzal Husain Qadri, *The Problem of Indian Muslims and its Solution*, Aligarh Muslim University Press, 14 August 1939.

become a fourth sovereign state, 'the southern wing of Muslim India'. Pakistan would include the four north-western provinces, Kashmir and other adjacent states. Bengal would embrace the existing province less the districts of Howrah, Midnapur and Darjeeling, but plus the districts of Purnea (in Bihar) and Syhlet (in Assam). Both Pakistan and Bengal would be Muslim states. Hindustan would comprise the rest of India but within it two new autonomous provinces—Delhi and Malabar—should be formed, with strong Muslim minorities. The three states would have separate treaties of alliance with Britain and should join together in a defensive and offensive alliance. The Hasan-Qadri scheme was commended warmly by eight Aligarh scholars who, at the same time, deplored Latif's proposals.[63] The scholars claimed to have discussed 'the Aligarh scheme' with its authors in principle and detail and were convinced that it went as far as possible to meet the just claims of the 'two nations'.

By September 1939, when Britain shelved the paper federation of the 1935 Act, Muslim constitutional thought was certainly turning against the federal principle, even as expressed in the zonal schemes of Latif and Sikander. A year after the adoption at Karachi of the two-nations theory its practical application was a live issue. On 18 October, when Lord Linlithgow spoke of India's destiny in terms of unity,[64] Bashir Ahmad protested to Jinnah at his blunt rejection of 'the national demand of the Muslims regarding the recognition of their separate national status'.[65] Next month the Aligarh group was provoked when Gandhi attacked the theory of separate Muslim nationhood.[66] On 15 November Professor Hasan, together with Dr Zaki Uddin and Dr Burhan Ahmad (two of the eight who commended the Aligarh scheme), and Ubaid Ullah Durrani, petitioned Jinnah at length

[63] Printed commendation by Amiruddin Kedwaii, Umar Uddin, Zafar Ahmad Siddiqi, Masud Makhdum, Dr Zaki Uddin, Dr Burhan Ahmad Faruqi, Jamil-ud-din Ahmad and Muddassir Ali Shamsee, n.d., but attached to similarly printed address by 'The Authors', d. September 1939, Q.A.P., file 96.

[64] Viceroy's statement, 18 October 1939, in M. Gwyer and A. Appadorai (eds), *Speeches and Documents on the Indian Constitution, 1921–47*, 1957, pp. 490–3.

[65] Ahmad Bashir to Jinnah, 21 October 1939. See also extract from his letter to Nehru, 6 December 1939, in S. Gopal (ed.), *Selected Works of Jawaharlal Nehru*, X (New Delhi, 1977), p. 420 n.

[66] Gandhi, 'Opinions Differ', *Harijan*, 11 November 1939, reported in *Statesman* (Delhi), 12 November 1939. Gandhi was replying to a private letter from 'M.A. of Aligarh' (see *Collected Works of Mahatma Gandhi*, LXX (1977), pp. 332–4).

upon the matter. They concluded: 'Neither the fear of British bayonets nor the prospects of a bloody civil war can discourage [the Muslims] in their will to achieve free Muslim states in those parts of India where they are in majority.'[67] Soon afterwards the several Muslim authors of constitutional plans met for ten days 'to evolve a consolidated scheme', which they sent to Jinnah confidentially.[68] This 'fresh plan on the basis that Moslems are a separate Nation' so constituted Muslim zones in the north and the east as to include seventy-two per cent of the total Muslim population of India. A Delhi province was added to the northern zone and all of Assam to the eastern. A third of the land mass of India was claimed.

On 1 February 1940 Haroon presided at New Delhi over a joint meeting of his Foreign Committee and the authors of schemes. It resolved to recommend that the Working Committee 'state its mind in unequivocal language with regard to the future of the Indian Moslem Nation'.[69] India's Muslims were a separate nation entitled to self-determination. In order to make that right effective 'the Moslems shall have separate National Home in the shape of an autonomous state'. The meeting's resolutions were sent to Liaquat (as League secretary) and to Jinnah on 2 February. Two days later the Working Committee adopted the nub of them[70] which was, of course, expressed in the Lahore resolution's call for independent Muslim states in the north-western and eastern zones of India.[71]

The Lahore expression of the two-nations theory as a demand for separate Muslim statehood was thus the culmination of eighteen months of controversy. The variety of its analogues goes far to explain the vagueness of the resolution over the delineation of the contiguous Muslim regions of north-western and eastern India and the contemplated relations between them. The notoriously obscure provision for 'territorial readjustments' was clearly a hold-all for additions to, as

[67] Typescript document, 4 pp., Q.A.P., file 96.

[68] 'Confidential Note for the President', n.d., ibid.

[69] Haroon to Hon. Sec. A.I.M.L., 2 February 1940, ibid.

[70] C. Khaliquzzaman, *Pathway to Pakistan* (Lahore, 1961), pp. 223–4. Khaliquzzaman grossly exaggerates his own role, though in March 1939 he had proposed to the Secretary of State a vague scheme for three or four separate federations of provinces and states under a small central co-ordinating body (ibid., 205–7; Marquess of Zetland, *'Essayez'*, 1956, pp. 248–9).

[71] A.I.M.L. session, 22–4 March 1940, Pirzada, *Foundations of Pakistan*, II, pp. 325–49.

well as reductions of, existing provinces.[72] Doubts about the desirable relations between the regions are revealed by the authorization of the Working Committee to frame a scheme providing 'for the assumption finally, by the respective regions, of all powers' such as 'defence, external affairs, communications, customs and such other matters as may be necessary'. Again, 'finally' suggests an antithesis to an interim period of co-ordination by a common authority, such, perhaps, as the resolution's seconder, Khaliquzzaman, favoured.[73] However, it is clear that by its separatist emphasis the resolution marked the firm rejection of Sikander's view that Muslim India's national destiny might be achieved within an all-India federation. He indeed acknowledged that his own preferred resolution was lost.[74] One possibility left open was that of an independent Bengal nation, the destiny most favoured by the resolution's proposer, Fazlul Haq.[75]

No more than the resolution itself was Jinnah's Lahore address the achievement of the Quaid unaided. The most remembered passages in his speech were drawn essentially unchanged from the representations of Bashir Ahmad and the Aligarh group. After roundly condemning the 1935 Act as unsuitable to India he followed Hasan and Qadri in quoting for criticism a London *Times* leader of 1 April 1937 that had consigned the difference between Hindus and Muslims to the realm of transient 'superstition', no real impediment to the emergence of a single nation. He then took his refutation of British views from Bashir Ahmad's condemnation of Linlithgow's statement of 18 October 1939:

Mian Bashir Ahmad	*Jinnah*
His Excellency the Viceroy thinks that this unity can be achieved with the working of the constitution as envisaged in Government of India Act, 1935. He	So according to the London Times the only difficulties are superstitions. These fundamental and deep rooted differences, spiritual, economic, cultural, social

[72] At the time Liaquat Ali Khan rightly said that the term 'territorial readjustments' connoted a Muslim claim to Aligarh and Delhi, an interpretation questioned by Pirzada in the light of later events (ibid., pp. xx–xxi).

[73] See above, n. 70, and below, p. 552.

[74] See his speech of 11 March 1941 (see n. 60).

[75] See Pirzada, *Foundations of Pakistan*, ii, pp. xxii–xxiii; Philips, *Partition of India*, p. 29.

Mian Bashir Ahmad	*Jinnah*
hopes that the passage of time will harmonise the inconsistent elements in India. May be he holds this view with sincerity, but it is in flagrant disregard to the past history of the sub-continent as well as to the Islamic conception of society. The nationalities which, notwithstanding thousand years of close contact, are as divergent as ever, can never be expected to transform into one nationality merely by being subject to the same constitution. What the *Unitary* Government of India has failed to bring about can not be achieved by the imposition of the *Federal* Government.	and political, have been euphemised as mere 'superstitions'. But surely, it is a flagrant disregard of the past history of the sub-continent of India as well as the fundamental Islamic conception of society *vis-a-vis* that of Hinduism to characterise them as mere 'superstitions'. Notwithstanding thousand years of close contact, nationalities which are as divergent today as ever, cannot at any time be expected to transform themselves into one nation merely by means of subjecting them to a democratic constitution and holding them forcibly together by unnatural and artificial methods of British Parliamentary Statutes. What the unitary government of India for 150 years had failed to achieve, cannot be realised by the imposition of a central federal government. It is inconceivable that the fiat or the writ of a government so constituted can ever command a willing and loyal obedience throughout the sub-continent by various nationalities except by means of armed force behind it.
It is, however, satisfying to note that His Excellency the Viceroy and the Secretary of State along with the House of Lords are fully alive to the fundamental differences between the peoples of the Indian continent. Yet unfortunately, they are unwilling to recognise their separate national status. It is more than truism to say that the Hindus and Muslims represent two distinct nationalities. Therefore, any attempt to dissolve their present differences which disregards this vital fact is doomed to precipitate. Hindu–Muslim problem is not an intercommunal issue and will never be solved on intercommunal lines. It is manifestly	The problem in India is not of an intercommunal but manifestly of an international character and it must be treated as such. So long as this basic and fundamental truth is not realised, any constitution that may be built will

Mian Bashir Ahmad

an international problem and therefore it must be treated as such. It will submit itself to a permanent solution on that basis alone. Any constitution be it in the form of Dominion Status or even 'Complete Independence', which disregards this basic truth, while destructive for the Muslims cannot but be harmful to the British and Hindus.

If the British Government is really serious and sincere in bringing about peace in the subcontinent, it should not only appreciate the difference but also allow the two nationalities separate homelands by dividing India into autonomous homogeneous states. These states shall not be antagonistic to each other, they on the other hand, will be friendly and sympathetic to one another; and by an international pact of mutual goodwill and assistance they can be just as united and harmonious as today are France and Great Britain. This is the one and the only way to India's Unity.

We are confident that it shall ensure eternal harmony, calm and friendliness between the Hindus and Muslims and materially accelerate the progress of the subcontinent.

If this method for the salvation of India's problems is not adopted the fate of the Muslims

Jinnah

result in disaster and will prove destructive and harmful not only to the Mussalmans, but also to the British and Hindus. If the British Government are really in earnest and sincere to secure peace and happiness of the people of this sub-continent, the only course open to us all is to allow the major nations separate homelands by dividing India into 'autonomous national states'. There is no reason why these States should be antagonistic to each other. On the other hand the rivalry and the natural desire and efforts on the part of the one to dominate the social order and establish political supremacy over the other in the government of the country, will disappear. It will lead more towards natural good-will by international pacts between them, and they can live in complete harmony with their neighbours. This will lead further to a friendly settlement all the more easily with regard to minorities by reciprocal arrangements and adjustments between the Muslim India and the Hindu India, which will far more adequately and effectively safeguard the rights and interests of Muslims and various other minorities.

Mian Bashir Ahmad

as a nation is sealed in India and no revolution of stars and no rotation of the earth would resuscitate them.

The Bashir Ahmad text was thus the source of Jinnah's 'quiet assertion' of the international status of the Indian problem that Mansergh has held to be 'the essence of his case'.[76] Jinnah notably dropped the emphasis (following Iqbal) upon present division as 'the only way to India's Unity' in future.[77] He continued by drawing upon the Aligarh petition of 15 November 1939 to fill out the rhetoric of his 'classic exposition of the two-nation theory'. Again, where the scholars' target was specifically Gandhi, Jinnah's is more generally the Hindus:

Aligarh scholars

It is extremely difficult to explain Mr Gandhi failing to appreciate and understand the real nature of Islam and Hinduism. Islam as well as Hinduism are not only religions in stricter sense of the word, but are in reality different and distinct social orders governing practically every individual and social aspect of their adherents. It should be clear beyond doubt that Hindus and Muslims cannot evolve a common na-

Jinnah

It is extremely difficult to appreciate why our Hindu friends fail to understand the real nature of Islam and Hinduism. They are not religions in the strict sense of the word, but are, in fact, different and distinct social orders and it is a dream that the Hindus and Muslims can ever evolve a common nationality, and this misconception of one Indian nation has gone far beyond the limits and is the cause of most of our troubles and

[76] Mansergh, *Prelude to Partition*, p. 27.

[77] Still, the Associated Press of India reported that as Jinnah spoke 'there were many in that huge gathering of over 100,000 people who remembered the late Mohammed Iqbal, the poet of Islam, the animator of the idea of Pakistan' (Pirzada, II, 327). Jinnah later wrote of Iqbal: 'His views were substantially in consonance with my own and had led me to the same conclusions as a result of careful examination and study of the constitutional problems facing India and found expression in due course in . . . the Lahore resolution. . . .' (Malik, *Iqbal*, 384–5).

Aligarh scholars

tionality. A few following arguments must convince Mr Gandhi on this issue.

1. That the Hindus and Muslims belong to two different cultures. They have totally different religious philosophies, social customs, laws and literature. They neither intermarry nor inter-dine together and, indeed, belong to two different civilizations which are in many aspects based on conflicting ideas and conceptions . . .
2. That the Hindus and Muslims drive [*sic*] their inspiration from different sources of history. They have different epics, different heroes and different episodes. Very often a hero of one is a foe of the other and likewise, their victories and defeats overlap. . . .

The above facts must convince every body that all those ties which hold people together as one social unit (Nation) are entirely wanting in the case of Hindus and Muslims of India. Nor there is any possibility of their ever being created here.

Mr Gandhi and other Congress leaders stress the significance of a common country and cite the examples of Egypt, Turkey and Persia. They only state a half truth in this argument.

Jinnah

will lead India to destruction if we fail to revise our notions in time. The Hindus and Muslims belong to two different religious philosophies, social customs, and literature. They neither intermarry, nor interdine together and indeed they belong to two different civilisations which are based mainly on conflicting ideas and conceptions. Their aspects on life and of life are different. It is quite clear that Hindus and Mussalmans drive [*sic*] their inspiration from different sources of history. They have different epics, their heroes are different, and they have different episodes. Very often the hero of one is a foe of the other and likewise their victories and defeats overlap. To yoke together two such nations under a single state, one as a numerical minority and the other as a majority, must lead to growing discontent and final destruction of any fabric that may be so built up for the government of such a state.

History has presented to us many examples such as the Union of Great Britain and Ireland, of Czechoslovakia and Poland. History has also shown to us many geographical tracts, much smaller than the sub-continent of India, which otherwise might have been called one country but which

Aligarh scholars	*Jinnah*
Egypt, Turkey and Persia are wholly Muslim countries and the Muslims there are naturally free to determine their own future. A discontent is bound to occur wherever two different people are yoked under a single state one as minority and the other as majority. A number of instances like those of Great Britain and Ireland, Czechoslovakia and Poland can exemplify the above. Further it is also too well known that many Geographical tracts which otherwise should have been called as one country, much smaller than the Indian sub-continent have been divided into as many states as are the nations inhabiting them. The Balkan Peninsula comprises of as many as eight sovereign states. The Iberian Peninsula is also likewise divided between the Portuguese and the Spaniards. Mr Gandhi stresses the historical unity of India even during the days of Muslim kings. We cannot accept his contention. No student of history can deny the fact that all along the last 12 hundred years India has always been divided into a Hindu India and a Muslim India. The extent of one or the other might have been varying from time to time, but the fact remains untarnished that Hindu and Muslim Indias have	have been divided into as many states as there are nations inhabiting them. Balkan Peninsula comprises as many as 7 or 8 sovereign states. Likewise, the Portuguese and the Spanish stand divided in the Iberian Peninsula. Whereas under the plea of unity of India and one nation, which does not exist, it is sought to pursue here the line of one Central Government when, we know that the history of the last 12 hundred years, has failed to achieve unity and has witnessed during the ages, India always divided into Hindu India and Muslim India. The present artificial unity of India dates back only to the British conquest and is maintained by the British bayonet, but the termination of the British regime, which is implicit in the recent declaration of His Majesty's Government, will be the herald of the entire break-up with worse disaster than has ever taken place during the last one thousand years under the Muslims.

Aligarh scholars

always been co-existing. The present unity of India dates back only to the British conquest. . . .

We want to assure Mr Gandhi that the ideal of having free sovereign Muslim states in India which now inspires a very large number of Muslims is not actuated by a spirit of hatred or revenge. It is initiated by an earnest desire of solving Hindu–Muslim problem on an equitable basis and epitomises the natural desire of Muslims of India to determine their future independently in the light of their own cultures and history.

Jinnah was carried to Karachi on the shoulders of his fellow Sindhis and soared to Lahore on the wings of poet- and philosopher-politicians of Lahore and scholars of Aligarh. The Great Leader who personified Muslim apprehensions synthesized plans to assuage them in acceptable formulations of Muslim nationalism (the two-nations theory) and separatism (the Pakistan demand).

THE MEANING OF 'TWO NATIONS'

In October 1939, when Lord Linlithgow called Jinnah into discussions with the Congress leaders about participation in government during the war, he was certainly recognizing him as the Muslim leader *par excellence.*[78] But in large measure Jinnah had earned the status by the solidarity that the league had then achieved. In May 1939 Sikander,

[78] For the discussions, see Gowher Rizvi, *Linlithgow in India: A Study of British Policy and the Political Impasse in India, 1936–43*, 1978, pp. 129ff.; K. Veerathappa, 'Britain and the Indian Problem (September 1939-May 1940)', *International Studies*, VII (1966), pp. 537–67; Moore, 'British Policy and the Indian Problem, 1936–40', Philips and Wainwright, *Partition of India*, pp. 79–94.

the senior Muslim premier, had observed publicly that Jinnah had answered for Muslims the question: 'Are we content to lose our identity and to be relegated to the position of political pariahs?'[79] Jinnah's mobilization of the League in reaction to Congress 'totalitarianism' under the 1935 Act had made it the voice of the putative nation. In December 1939 Liaquat estimated that it had over three million two-anna members. In the early wartime negotiations Jinnah could, pursuant to the two-nations theory, make acceptance of the League's status as sole Muslim spokesman the precondition of co-operation with government or Congress, thereby outflanking dissidents (be they even premiers) by appeals to the national will. It was another corollary of his theory that as one of the two nations Muslim India must be treated as the coequal of Hindu or Congress India. In consequence, the League called for the right to consultation prior to any British statement about India's constitutional future and to veto any scheme. By November, Rajendra Prasad (now Congress president) shrewdly perceived that Jinnah's insistence upon the League's equality with Congress would mean not only 'equality in the matter of negotiations' but also 'division of power in equal shares between the Congress and the League or between Hindus and Muslims, irrespective of population or any other consideration'.[80]

The meaning of the two-nations theory and its implications for Jinnah's leadership became manifest in League Working Committee resolutions in June 1940. In any wartime reconstruction of the central or provincial governments the League must receive half of the seats (more if the Congress was non-cooperating), Jinnah alone might negotiate with Viceroy or Congress, and without his consent no League member might serve on war committees.[81] The resolutions were a rebuff for Sikander, who, appalled at the grave implications for India of the allies' defeats in Europe, was negotiating with Congress leaders for a constitutional settlement.[82] In August a British statement, effectively according the Muslims a veto on any constitutional scheme,

[79] Cited in D. Pandey, 'Congress-Muslim League Relations', p. 647.

[80] Prasad to Nehru, 12 November 1939, B.N. Pandey, *Documents,* pp. 137–8.

[81] Resolutions of A.I.M.L. Working Committee, 15–17 June 1940, Q.A.P., file 95. See also Coupland, *Indian Politics*, p. 243.

[82] Sikander to Jinnah, 31 May 1940, Q.A.P., file 21; Coupland, *Indian Politics*, p. 241.

seemed to remove the danger of a Hindu raj.[83] Here was a major victory for the two-nations theory. Another was soon to follow.

Leading Muslim politicians, including the premiers, were now prepared to join war committees on a basis short of parity. By so doing they would, in effect, be compromising the cause of Muslim equality embodied in the two-nations theory. In summer 1941 Jinnah brought the theory to bear in order to force their resignations from the Viceroy's Defence Council. That this was not mere exercise of personal power but rather the execution of essential League policy is revealed by Liaquat's advice to Jinnah a month before the Working Committee met to consider the matter. Liaquat advised that Jinnah's condemnation of the collaborators had 'given expression to the feelings of a vast majority of Musalmans on the subject'.[84] The question now was 'whether the disciplinary action . . . should be taken by you or by the Working Committee and the Council' (an elected body of 465 members). Liaquat strongly advised the latter course:

> Let us put up an imposing show and I think the people will appreciate [it] if the Council is given an opportunity of expressing its views on the conduct of those who have let down the League. . . . Let it not be said that the decision is of only one individual or a few persons. Let the whole Council which is the most representative body of the League give its verdict and I have no doubt as to what the verdict will be. . . .

On 24 August the Working Committee demanded the collaborators' resignations from the Defence Council and expelled from the League those who resisted the verdict. The Council did not meet to ratify the action for two months but its attitude was not in doubt. Jinnah was, of course, aware of allegations that he was a dictator.[85] The two-nations theory enabled him plausibly to brand as 'traitors' Muslims who collaborated with the Raj on a basis short of parity. As national leader he saw it as his duty to identify their 'mistakes', leaving the Working Committee and the Council to determine their punishment.[86]

[83] Viceroy's statement of 8 August 1940, Gwyer and Appadorai, *Speeches and Documents*, pp. 504–5.

[84] Liaquat to Jinnah, 28 July 1941, Q.A.P., file 1092.

[85] Allegations of dictatorship remain prominent in Partition historiography (e.g. Collins and Lapierre, *Freedom at Midnight*, p. 103; Tara Chand, *History of the Freedom Movement*, IV, *passim*). Hodson wrote that Jinnah 'displayed his authority . . . imperiously in August 1941 (*The Great Divide*, 89).

[86] E.g., May 1944 speech, Ahmad, *Speeches and Writings of Mr. Jinnah*, II, pp. 47–50.

By applying the theory vigorously Jinnah engineered the nationalization of Muslim politics throughout the war. The theory's meaning was revealed most dramatically at Simla in June 1945, when Jinnah demanded not only Hindu–Muslim parity in the Viceroy's executive but also that all the Muslim members must be League nominees. The demand destroyed Lord Wavell's attempt to reconstruct his government on the basis of party representation.

Defining 'Pakistan'

In February 1941 Jinnah explained the meaning of 'Pakistan', for the term had not been used at Lahore:

> Some confusion prevails in the minds of some individuals in regard to the use of the word 'Pakistan'. This word has become synonymous with the Lahore resolution owing to the fact that it is a convenient and compendious method of describing [it]. . . . For this reason the British and Indian newspapers generally have adopted the word 'Pakistan' to describe the Moslem demand as embodied in the Lahore resolution. I really see no objection to it. . . .[87]

But the resolution was obscure on the demarcation of the Pakistan regions, their relation to each other, and any interim constitutional rearrangement prior to their 'finally' assuming such powers as defence, foreign affairs, communications and customs. While Jinnah demanded parity as the basis of participation in government, the vagueness of 'Pakistan' was such as to make impracticable its acceptance by the Raj a precondition of co-operation. He did, however, insist that no constitutional scheme that was inconsistent with its eventual achievement must be imposed. The 'Pakistan' demand meant that Muslim India's right to national self-determination must not be transgressed, not that separate statehood must be embodied in a constitutional settlement. Jinnah drew the distinction explicitly in his speeches.[88] The diversity of the schemes embodying 'Pakistan' that were extant in March 1940 helps to explain the obscurity of the Lahore resolution. Any precise scheme must surely divide the League. However, the resolution did provide for the Working Committee to prepare

[87] Press statement, *Statesman*, 19 February 1941.

[88] E.g., November 1940 and April 1941 speeches, Ahmad, *Speeches and Writings of Mr. Jinnah*, I, pp. 184–5, 259.

a particular scheme. Haroon's Foreign Committee seems to have continued to discharge the primary planning function.

In February 1941 a scheme recommended by the Haroon committee was leaked to the press.[89] Consistently with the direction pursued by the Aligarh scholars and the assemblage of authors during winter 1939–40, it delineated sovereign Muslim states: the four northwestern provinces plus a Delhi province; and Bengal (save Bankura and Midnapur districts) plus Assam. The principalities adjoining them might federate with them, and Hyderabad would become a separate sovereign state. For a transitional period the four powers listed at Lahore for assumption finally by the regions would be exercised by a coordinating central agency. Jinnah denied that the Working Committee had adopted the scheme and on 22 February it merely reaffirmed the Lahore resolution. The main effect of the leakage was to draw from Sikander a long, reasoned denunciation of 'Pakistan', if it meant separatism.[90]

In his presidential address to the League's session at Madras in April 1941 Jinnah emphasized the goal of 'completely Independent States in the North-Western and Eastern Zones of India, with full control of Defence, Foreign Affairs, Communications, Customs, Currency, Exchange etc.'.[91] The League would 'never agree' to an all-India constitution 'with one Government at the Centre'. As if to suggest that the two-nations theory did not restrict future development to the emergence of only two states he explained that in Hindu India there was a Dravidian nation. Dravidistan, to which the Muslims would stretch their 'hands of friendship'. In amplification of this trend in his thinking he told the Governor of Madras that he envisaged four regions—Dravidistan, Hindustan, Bengalistan, and the north-west Muslim provinces.[92] They would be separate self-governing dominions, each with its own governor-general controlling its foreign affairs and defence and responsible to the British Parliament through the secretary of state. Here was a scheme for subordinate dominions, with the princely states joining them and remaining apart under a Crown Representative. It bore some resemblance to Haroon's leaked scheme.

[89] *Statesman* (Delhi), 18 February 1941.
[90] Menon, *The Transfer of Power in India*, pp. 451–67.
[91] Pirzada, *Foundations of Pakistan*, II, pp. 359–71.
[92] Menon, *The Transfer of Power in India*, p. 105.

In February 1942 Khaliquzzaman explained a similar proposal to Coupland:

The Moslem demand is that Britain, after the war, should by Act of Parliament, establish the zonal system, before considering further Swaraj. British control would be still required at the Centre—apparently for an indefinite period—since Defence and Foreign Policy (which is practically all the Centre would deal with) should still be in British hands. The zones would have fiscal autonomy. If they couldn't agree on tariff policy, the British at the Centre would settle it. Pakistan, moreover, would require British aid and capital for its development before it would be able to stand alone.[93]

Khaliquzzaman seemed to be saying that in the event of a complete British withdrawal the Muslims would accept nothing short of sovereign Pakistan; but that they would welcome a protracted British presence—in effect, Indian unity under the Crown, with the sub-national zones standing as recognition of Muslim nationhood. Unlike Jinnah he was opposed to the cession of the non-Muslim districts of Punjab (Ambala division) and Bengal (Burdwan division).[94]

On the eve of Cripps's arrival in India Coupland analysed Jinnah's position on the Pakistan demand:

(i) While claiming Dominion status for Pakistan, Jinnah has more than once intimated that it need not be full Dominion status and that he would like Foreign Affairs and Defence to remain, at least for the time being, in British hands; and

(ii) he has never asked that H. M. G. should accept Pakistan, but only that it should not be ruled out of discussion nor the chances of its adoption prejudiced by the form of an interim constitutional system. Nevertheless, *Pakistanism might triumph as a counsel of despair.*[95]

The Cripps declaration proposed Dominion status for a Union of India, but though it did not accept Pakistan it did accord provinces the right to secede from the Union and become separate dominions.[96] Jinnah and the League saw it as recognizing the principle of Pakistan.[97] From the notes of Coupland, Cripps and the Intelligence Department there

[93] C.C., 2 February 1942.

[94] Ibid., 17 January and 2 February 1942. Coupland assumed these cessions in his own 'Agency Centre' scheme (*The Future of India*, 1943, p. 82).

[95] Memo. on Pakistan, 21 March 1942, C.D., pp. 269–70.

[96] Declaration as published, 30 March 1942, *T.P.* I, p. 456.

[97] Resolution of League Working Committee, 11 April 1942, ibid., p. 606.

can be no doubt that Jinnah and the League were disposed to accept the offer.[98]

On 28 March 1942 Jinnah 'stated [to Cripps] the League's acceptance of the Declaration'. On 7 April he intimated that 'he must hold back the League's acceptance till after the Congress has accepted'.[99] Coupland foresaw that if Congress rejected the offer the League would follow suit, 'so wording their rejection as to obtain some British and world support without losing face as Indian patriots'. On 9 April, when Congress seemed poised to accept, Jinnah was reported as saying 'that Pakistan could be shelved', given a satisfactory position in the Viceroy's executive and a suitable procedure for the secession of provinces.[100] When Congress rejected the declaration the League did likewise, deprecating H.M.G.'s objective of Union, the provision for a single constituent assembly in the first instance, and the eligibility of non-Muslims to participate in the Muslim provinces' decisions on secession.[101]

In February 1944 Jinnah stated that Britain 'should now frame a new constitution dividing India into two sovereign nations', Pakistan and Hindustan, with 'a transitional period for settlement and adjustment' during which British authority over defence and foreign affairs would remain.[102] The length of the period would depend upon the speed with which the two peoples and Britain adjusted to the new constitution. Though the statement clearly contemplated continued subordination to Britain it is too vague to be read as a shift from the notion of zonal dominions.[103] In September 1944 the Gandhi-Jinnah talks concentrated attention on the precise meaning of the Pakistan demand. The Bengal Provincial League now wanted 'a sovereign state in N.E. India that will be independent of the rest of India', though it was divided over the cession of the Burdwan districts, with some members arguing that their retention would win Hindu approval.[104]

98 See Moore, *Churchill, Cripps and India, 1939–45* (Oxford, 1979), p. 88 and n. 4; *T.P.* I, pp. 380, 392, 393. The Cripps Mission file (802) in the Q.A.P. is 'embargoed'.

99 C.D., pp. 185, 214.

100 C.D., pp. 221–2.

101 Working Committee resolution, 11 April 1942.

102 Ahmad, *Speeches and Writings of Mr. Jinnah*, I, pp. 582–6.

103 For further expressions of the idea, see ibid., I, pp. 383, 409, 477, 567–8.

104 See Richard Casey to Wavell, 11 September 1944, *T.P.* V, 13, 79; East Pakistan Renaissance Society, *Eastern Pakistan: Its Population, Delimitation and*

The talks themselves did little to clarify Jinnah's conception of Pakistan but he reiterated that for the regions in which the Muslims predominated it was they alone who must determine their future. Jinnah also spoke now of Pakistan as a single state.[105]

Throughout the war Jinnah contemplated the post-war emergency of one or two Pakistan 'dominions', coexisting with one or two Hindustan 'dominions' and the princely states, and with Britain retaining power over defence and foreign affairs. The separateness and equality of the Pakistan and Hindustan 'dominions' would be a recognition of the validity of the two-nations theory and of their right to eventual sovereign independence. The conception resembled that which some British Conservatives formed at the time of the Cripps mission and espoused until the eve of the transfer of power.[106]

Definition by Circumstance

With Labour's assumption of office in July 1945 it was soon apparent that there was not to be a gradual demission of power by stages but an early and complete withdrawal.[107] Jinnah now became adamant that there must be a single state of Pakistan and the League fought the elections of 1945-6 on that platform.[108] The announcement in February 1946 of the imminent despatch of a Cabinet Mission to settle the basis for independence and Jinnah's first meeting with the Mission on 4 April confirmed that Labour was in a hurry. Fortified by the League's electoral triumph, on 7 April Jinnah led a convention of 470 League members of the central and provincial legislatures to an unequivocal resolution in favour of 'a sovereign independent state comprising Bengal and Assam in the North-East zone and the Punjab, North-West Frontier Province, Sind and Baluchistan in the North-

Economics, Calcutta, September 1944. As early as 11 June 1940 Prof. A. Sadeque, Professor of Economics and Politics at Islamia College, Calcutta, sent to Jinnah a proposal for dividing India into Pakistan, Hindustan and 'Greater Bengal' (Q.A.P., file 106).

105 Pirzada, *Foundations of Pakistan*, II, p. xxx.

106 Moore, *Churchill, Cripps and India*, pp. 132–5. See below.

107 Moore, *Escape from Empire: The Attlee Government and the Indian Problem*, 1983, pp. 18–31.

108 E.g., interview of 8 November 1945. Ahmad, II, pp. 230–3.

West zone'.[109] Acceptance of this precise demand for Pakistan and its implementation without delay, by the creation of a Pakistan Constituent Assembly, was made the *sine qua non* for the League's participation in an Interim Government. The opening of the imperial endgame had precipitated an immediate and full-blooded definition of the Pakistan demand.

By 10 April Cripps had prepared a draft proposal for discussion with the Indian leaders and a few days later the mission confronted Jinnah with two alternative approaches that it advocated: either a truncated Pakistan, independent and fully sovereign but limited to the Muslim majority areas, and thus short of far more of the territories of Punjab, Bengal and Assam than the League had contemplated; or the grouping together of the whole of the six claimed provinces, beside a Hindustan group, within a Union exercising power over defence, foreign affairs and communications.[110] When Jinnah refused to choose either alternative Cripps prepared a draft that rejected a fully independent Pakistan. But it proposed a powerful subnational Pakistan, with its own flag, forces to maintain internal order, and enjoying parity with Hindustan in an all-India government. The League would draft its constitution and join with Congress on the basis of parity to draft the Union constitution.[111] The Mission was willing to concede its right to secede from the Union after fifteen years.[112] This remarkable scheme was the furthest that H.M.G. ever went towards accepting the full Pakistan demand.

It is scarcely surprising that Jinnah and the League were drawn into negotiations on the basis of this scheme, though some Leaguers speculated that Jinnah's departure from the Legislators' full-blooded resolution evidenced vacillation among 'weak-kneed' members of the Working Committee.[113] During the subsequent month of negotiations the Mission reduced the concessions to the demand in order to woo Congress, so that when its scheme was published on 16 May it was far less attractive to the League.[114] It split the six 'Pakistan' provinces into two groups, the formation of which was to depend upon the voluntary accession of each province to its assigned group. It aban-

[109] Pirzada, *Foundations of Pakistan*, II, pp. 512–13.
[110] *T.P.* VII, pp. 71, 82.
[111] Ibid., p. 126.
[112] Ibid., p. 82.
[113] See Ahmad to Jinnah, 29 May 1946, Q.A.P., file 1092.
[114] *T.P.*, VII, p. 303.

doned parity in the making of the Union constitution, enlarged the Union's power to include finance, and failed to provide for the secession of groups or provinces from the Union. Though some Leaguers feared that the Union's powers would enable Congress to abort the emergence of Pakistan,[115] the counsels that prevailed were that the Cabinet Mission's scheme met 'the substance of the demand for Pakistan'.[116] First, it provided that the provinces must enter constitution-making 'sections' that were co-terminous with the groups. Secondly, the section constitution-making procedure was to precede Union constitution-making. Thirdly, the Working Committee assumed, on the basis of discussions that Jinnah had had with the Viceroy, that the League would enjoy parity with Congress in an Interim Government, which seemed a tacit admission of Pakistan's right to separate nationhood.

Jinnah received written letters of advice from Aurangzeb Khan and Jamil-ud-din Ahmad that emphasized the advantages of accepting the Mission's scheme.[117] Ahmad, then Convenor of the League's Committee of Writers, expressed the 'prudent' strategy vigorously. The League should

> work the Plan up to the Group stage and then create a situation to force the hands of the Hindus and the British to concede Pakistan of our conception. . . . [We should] make known in most emphatic terms our objections to the Plan specially with regard to the Centre and declare that we will . . . not be bound to submit to a Union Centre which does not accord us a position of equality. We [should] give a chance to the Hindu majority to accommodate us at the Centre. . . . After we have made the constitutions of Groups B and C according to our wishes our position will be stronger than what it is now if we use our opporunities properly. We will have some foothold. When we reassemble in the Union Constituent Assembly we can create deadlocks on really important issues. . . . If the worst comes to the worst and the Hindu majority shows no willingness to compromise we can withdraw from the Assembly in a body, and refuse to honour its decisions. Ours will be a solid bloc as there won't be more than two or three non-League Muslims in the Assemb-

115 E.g., M.L. Qureshi (joint secretary of the League's Planning Committee) to Jinnah, 31 May 1946, Q.A.P., file 1092.

116 M.A.H. Ispahani, 'Factors Leading to the Partition of British India', Philips and Wainwright, *Partition of India,* pp. 330–59, 348–50.

117 Aurangzeb Khan to Jinnah, 19 May 1946, Q.A.P., file 12; Ahmad to Jinnah, 29 May 1946. See also typed lists of 'Advantages' and 'Disadvantages', n.d.; Liaquat to Jinnah, 21 May 1946; Prof. A.B.A. Haleem (Aligarh) to Jinnah, 23 May 1946; all in Q.A.P., file 12.

ly. . . . We will be on strong ground morally and politically because firstly we will have previously declared that we can never acquiesce in any Centre which reduces us to a subordinate position and secondly we will be in power in the Groups, and will be better able to resist the imposition of an unwanted Centre.

In the spirit of this advice the League resolved that:

. . . inasmuch as the basis and the foundation of Pakistan are inherent in the Mission's plan by virtue of the compulsory grouping of the six Muslim Provinces in Sections B and C, [it] is willing to co-operate with the constitution-making machinery proposed in the scheme outlined by the Mission, in the hope that it would ultimately result in the establishment of complete sovereign Pakistan. . . .[118]

Jinnah was authorized to negotiate for the entry of the League to the Interim Government. He wrote to Wavell to emphasize that his assurance of parity therein had been 'the turning point' in the League Council's acceptance.[119]

The League's strategy was destroyed by the Congress's refusal to contemplate parity in the Interim Government or the compulsory grouping of provinces for constitution-making, together with H.M.G.'s conviction that Congress goodwill was vital for a peaceful transfer of power.[120] In August 1946 Jinnah was driven to a course of 'direct action' by his mistrust of the Congress and H.M.G.'s infirmity.[121] Certainly, by December, when he and Nehru were called to London in a desperate attempt to secure agreement on sectional procedure, Jinnah had abandoned his mid-year hopes of realizing Pakistan through the Mission's scheme. He now reverted to the notion of a Pakistan dominion and rehearsed it not only with Attlee and the Cabinet Mission ministers[122] but also with British Opposition leaders.[123] Churchill, for whom a secret telegraphic address was established, assured him that the Pakistan areas could not be turned out of the Commonwealth as part of an Indian republic.[124] Indeed, in

[118] *T.P.* VII, p. 469.

[119] Jinnah to Wavell, 8 June 1946, ibid., p. 473.

[120] For elaboration see Moore, *Escape from Empire*, pp. 124–44.

[121] See, e.g., Jinnah's bitter complaint to Attlee and Churchill, 6 July 1946, *T.P.* VIII, p. 68.

[122] See, e.g., *T.P.* IX, p. 153.

[123] E.g., Churchill to Jinnah and Lord Simon to Jinnah, both 11 December 1946, Q.A.P., file 21.

[124] *T.P.* X, p. 229.

parliamentary debate Churchill affirmed that Muslim India and the princes should be accorded Commonwealth membership.[125] That winter Jinnah sought assurances that other Conservatives would support Pakistan's dominionhood. His inquiries converged with intrigues for separate princely dominions, to which he gave his blessing.[126]

Jinnah welcomed the prospects of a transfer of power on a provincial basis that Attlee's time-limit statement of 20 February 1947 foreshadowed.[127] In his first discussions with Mountbatten he sought a Pakistan dominion comprising the full six provinces,[128] but he did not oppose the option of separate sovereign provinces that the 'Dickie-bird' or Ismay plan ('Plan Balkan') offered. His objection to Plan Balkan was that it envisaged the severance from Punjab and Bengal of their non-Muslim areas. When he first saw the Plan he argued 'that power should be transferred to Provinces as they exist today. They can then group together or remain separate as they wish'.[129] When Mountbatten asked his views on H. S. Suhrawardy's proposal for 'keeping Bengal united at the price of its remaining outside Pakistan' he replied: 'I should be delighted. What is the use of Bengal without Calcutta; they had much better remain united and independent; I am sure that they would be on friendly terms with us.'[130]

Whereas in 1946 Jinnah had been prepared to find the Pakistan demand realized, at least temporarily, by the grouping of the six provinces within the Union of India, in 1947 he was willing to see it satisfied by the separate dominionhood of provinces. Now again he was frustrated by Congress, which was no less opposed to the instant loss to India of non-Muslim areas of provinces than it had been to their distant loss by secession from the Union. The outcome of negotia-

[125] *Commons Debates*, 12 December 1946, cols. 1362–70; 20 December 1946, cols. 2341–52. See also K. Dwarkadas, *Ten Years to Freedom* (Bombay 1968), pp. 195–6.

[126] See Sir W. Monckton to Lord Templewood, 15 January 1947 and reply, 16 January 1947, Templewood Coll., India Office Library, London.

[127] *T.P.* IX, p. 440; X, pp. 105, 165.

[128] Ibid.

[129] Ibid., p. 256. See also p. 276, annex. I.

[130] Ibid., p. 229. See also pp. 227–8, 264. cf. the common Pakistani belief that Jinnah saw Suhrawardy's scheme as a heresy (e.g. M.A.H. Ispahani, *Qaid-e-Azam as I Knew Him* (Karachi, 1967 edn), pp. 257–8). For relations between Jinnah and Suhrawardy over the scheme from February 1947, see Ziring, 'Jinnah'. A draft scheme for a 'Free State of Bengal', d. 4 June 1947, appears in Q.A.P., file 142.

tions in 1947, a dual transfer of power to a single truncated Pakistan dominion and a single Indian dominion (to one of which the states were obliged to accede), flowed from Congress policy and H.M.G.'s acquiescence in it.[131] Given the reversals that he suffered in the three-sided discussions from April 1946 to May 1947 it is scarcely surprising that Jinnah eschewed the prolongation of triangularity implied in proposals for Mountbatten to become governor-general of both dominions and the retention of a Joint Defence Council.[132] However, at the end of the Raj he still acknowledged Pakistan's need for British agency. The retention by Pakistan of British governors, chiefs of staff and civil and military officers was consistent with his expectation that the transfer of power would be a phased process.[133]

Man and Movement

At the age of sixty Jinnah made the cause of Muslim India his life. An extraordinary match of man and movement followed. Ambition, pride and vanity were less important to it than his refined sense of Muslim injury under Congress rule and his capacity to express the hurt and specify the cure. Like Gandhi he evoked national consciousness in opposition to felt wrongs.[134] While Gandhi had experienced India's emasculation by British imperialism Jinnah felt the impotence of Muslim India under Congress totalitarianism. Jinnah articulated not the Koran's promise of political power nor memories of the Mughals but the Muslim's sense of persecution at the sudden threat to all that he had achieved in the twentieth century. When the Congress governments resigned in November 1939 he rallied Muslims to celebrate

[131] Moore, 'Mountbatten, India and the Commonwealth', *Journal of Commonwealth and Comparative Politics*, XXIX, 1 (1981), pp. 5–43.

[132] See also A.K. Brohi, 'Reflections on the Quaid-i-Azam's Self-Selection as the First Governor-General of Pakistan', and S.M. Burke, 'Quaid-i-Azam's Decision to become Pakistan's First Governor-General', papers presented at Quaid-i Azam Centenary Conference, Islamabad 1976. Cf. Mountbatten's simple explanation in terms of Jinnah's vanity and megalomania, and Congress suspicions of Jinnah's fascist intentions (above, nn. 6–7).

[133] In May 1949 three of Pakistan's governors, the three chiefs of staff, and 470 military officers, were still British.

[134] For Gandhi see his *Autobiography: the Story of My Experiments with Truth* (Ahmedabad, 1927), and S.H. and L. Rudolph, *The Modernity of Tradition* (Chicago, 1967), II ('The Traditional Roots of Charisma: Gandhi').

their 'deliverance from tyranny, oppression and injustice'.[135] Jinnah's constitutional remedies were not of his own making. The Pakistan demand was no pet scheme of which he dreamed alone but an ideal to which he was converted by others, colleagues of long standing like Haroon, thinkers in the line of Iqbal, scholars of the Aligarh school. His very formulation of the two-nations theory drew upon their thoughts and words. His amplification of the theory into a demand for parity was a brilliant tactical manoeuvre, but its effectiveness rested on the willing support of the League, most notably when Linlithgow set up his Defence Council and Wavell attempted to reconstruct his executive. The tactic consolidated the League as the microcosm of the Muslim nation and Jinnah as its leader.

It is a paradox that the demand for separate Muslim statehood based on the existing Muslim provinces with territorial adjustments should finally have found recognition in a Pakistan truncated to a degree never envisaged by Jinnah and the League. It is inconceivable that they did not realize that the truncation was a logical corollary of the distribution of the peoples of the two nations. The arguments that they adduced to resist it could scarcely be accepted with justice by a departing Raj, whether they emphasized the need for hostages, or for matching minority populations for exchange in case of need, or for non-Muslim territories to make Pakistan viable economically. The incorporation of the full six provinces in Muslim zones could only have been secured by a British award, and it seems most likely that Jinnah envisaged such an award as a line of advance consistent with Britain's continuing presence in her own interests. In other words, he probably assumed a British withdrawal by stages, at the first of which the Pakistan zones would receive subordinate dominionhood, secured like the princely states by H.M.G.'s continuing control over defence and foreign affairs (as the 1935 Act had stipulated). His reference in October 1938 to a further twenty-five years of imperial rule, the Lahore resolution's emphasis upon all powers 'finally' passing to independent states, his wartime comments, his play for Pakistan dominionhood from December 1946, his reliance on British agency after August 1947, all support such a thesis. His acceptance of the Cabinet Mission's scheme might be seen similarly as evidence of a readiness to postpone full sovereign statehood, provided that the conditions of its eventual emergence were safeguarded, that is Muslim zones and

135 Appeal for 'Day of Deliverance', 2 December 1939, Ahmad, I, pp. 98–100.

parity in government. He was willing to associate the Muslim nation with central government on the basis of parity but he doubted that such a government could endure. He told Coupland as much:

Assume a 50:50 basis. . . . The central questions are just those on which Moslems and Hindus must disagree: e.g. (a) Defence: Hindu Ministers will at once want to Indianize in communal proportions. . . . (b) Tariff: Hindu Ministers will want high protection for industries, which are mainly in Hindu hands, to the detriment of the Moslems who are more confined to poor agriculturalists than the Hindus.[136]

Such caveats were urged upon Jinnah in May 1946, when he judged the disadvantages of a temporary union to be worth the prize of a safe passage through grouping to an eventual six-province fully sovereign Pakistan.[137]

Jinnah's planning was undermined by the Lahore Government's beliefs that Britain's post-war interests would be best served by immediate withdrawal, and that an orderly retreat and sound post-imperial relations with the subcontinent would alike be best achieved by enlisting Congress co-operation. His hopes of obtaining more than a truncated Pakistan depended upon an extended imperial presence of some sort. That they were no mere illusions is revealed by the sympathies of some leading British Conservatives and Liberals. As late as May 1947 Mountbatten's staff and the India Committee of Attlee's Cabinet espoused a scheme that permitted an independent India of many nations while the Chiefs of Staff advised that if Congress rejected Dominion status then Commonwealth membership might be accorded severally to West Pakistan, united Bengal, and even to a maritime state such as Travancore.[138]

Jinnah's readiness to accept, from time to time, quite different constitutional forms as consistent with the Pakistan demand flowed in part from the necessities of a dynamic situation, but in part, too, from the advice proffered by colleagues. In April 1946, 470 Muslim legislators voted for a single sovereign Pakistan of six full provinces; a few weeks later the Working Committee and the Council accepted a scheme for a Union of India; in April 1947 Jinnah endorsed Suhrawardy's plan for a 'Free State of Bengal'; two months later he accepted

[136] C.D., 17 January 1942.

[137] See, e.g., M.L. Qureshi to Jinnah, 31 May 1946, *loc. cit.*

[138] See my 'Mountbatten, India and the Commonwealth', 28–34; *T.P.* x, pp. 387, 416.

'moth-eaten' Pakistan. Yet the essence of the Pakistan demand—the right to a territorial asylum, to the self-determination of the Muslim nation in the north-western and eastern regions of India—was never compromised. Certainly, Jinnah planned that the regions should include virtually the whole of six provinces, whereas in the circumstances of 1947 he was left with a Pakistan defined by religious distribution district by district. Yet that outcome lends no support to speculation that the Pakistan demand was Jinnah's bargaining counter for power in a united India, or that the Partition hoisted him with his own petard.

Chapter Nine

Religious Leadership and the Pakistan Movement in the Punjab*

DAVID GILMARTIN

The emergence of the Muslim state of Pakistan in 1947 marked a watershed in the religious as well as the political development of Indian Muslims. But surprisingly little has been written on the nature of the religious support for Pakistan. Considerable attention has been focused on the ulama of Deoband, the great majority of whom opposed the creation of Pakistan, but this has done little to advance our understanding of the widespread religious backing for Pakistan in the mid-1940s, backing which made the Muslim League, as Peter Hardy puts it, 'a chiliastic movement rather than a pragmatic political party'.[1] In order to try to understand the sources of this backing, this paper will examine the nature of Muslim religious leadership before 1947 in the province Jinnah called 'the cornerstone of Pakistan'[2]—the Punjab. It will focus on the structure of religious leadership, particularly in the rural areas, and on the ways that that structure affected the relations of religious leaders with Muslim politics—first with the Unionist Party, which dominated the Punjab in the decades before partition, and finally with the Muslim League in the years leading to the creation of Pakistan.

**Modern Asian Studies*, 13, 3 (1979), pp. 485–517.

[1] Peter Hardy, *The Muslims of British India* (Cambridge: Cambridge University Press, 1972), p. 239.

[2] *The Tribune* (Lahore), 23 April 1943.

The Development of Muslim Religious Leadership

To find the roots of the structure of religious leadership in the Punjab, it is necessary to go back to the original conversion of the bulk of the population of western Punjab to Islam in the pre-Mughal era. Though little is known in detail about the conversion of the Punjab, it is usually credited to the work of Sufi mystics who established their *khanqahs* in western Punjab in the years following the establishment of the Delhi Sultanate and introduced the Sufi orders—the Chishti, the Suhrawardy, and the Qadri—into the Punjab.[3] These khanqahs served as local outposts of Islam which linked the diffuse, tribally organized population of the Punjab to the larger Islamic community. Subsequently it was these local centres—first the Sufi khanqahs and later the tombs of these Sufi saints—which provided the focus for Islamic organization in most of rural western Punjab, and it was to these centres that the population looked for religious leadership.

Religious leadership at these shrines was usually provided by a *sajjada nashin* (literally, 'he who sits on the prayer carpet'), who was normally a descendant of the original saint. The development of such hereditary religious leadership associated with Sufi shrines was a phenomenon, as Trimingham has observed in his study of the Sufi orders, found over much of the Islamic world as the influence of Sufism was increasingly routinized and popularized.[4] The hereditary religious authority of the sajjada nashin was largely based on the transmission of *baraka*, or religious charisma, from the original saint to his descendants and to his tomb. Because of this baraka, which linked the sajjada nashin to the original saint, the sajjada nashin was recognized as a religious intermediary who could provide access for the devotee to the favour of God. The effect of such hereditary leadership was to give stability to the Sufi shrines as local religious centres and to provide access to the religious benefits of the shrine to a wide circle of worshippers. 'The hospices with their associated tombs', Trimingham has written, 'became the foci of the religious aspirations of the ordinary man who sought the baraka of the saints'.[5]

[3] A general account of the conversion in Punjab is given in T.W. Arnold, *The Preaching of Islam* (Lahore: Sh. Muhammad Ashraf, 1963), pp. 285–7.

[4] J. Spencer Trimingham, *The Sufi Orders in Islam* (Oxford University Press, 1971), p. 173.

[5] Ibid., p. 27.

The exercise of this religious authority was associated with certain religious practices at the shrine. The links of the sajjada nashin to the original saint and the links of the original saint to God were dramatized every year in a ceremony marking the death anniversary of the saint, or *urs*. The urs, which literally means wedding, marked the union of the original saint with God, and the urs ceremonies themselves provided symbolic justification for the position of the sajjada nashin, who normally had to perform prescribed ceremonial duties which underscored his special links to the original saint as the inheritor of baraka,[6] and thus defined his effectiveness as religious intermediary. The role of the sajjada nashin as religious intermediary was commonly formalized by the tie of *pir* and *murid*, or master and disciple, between the sajjada nashin of a shrine and the worshipper. This did not bind the disciple to follow any rigid spiritual discipline; rather, it bound the disciple to accept the religious leadership of the pir, to whom he would usually make payments or offerings, and in return the pir provided access to baraka for the murid, which in immediate terms might include little more than the provision of magic amulets, but which would give the disciple some reasonable assumption that his prayers might be heard.[7] Religious learning or outward piety were not necessary attributes for a sajjada nashin. Though such attributes might increase his reputation and bring him new followers, his effectiveness as a religious leader rested on his descent from a saint, which, through the transmission of baraka, gave him access to the favour of God and thus the ability to act as a religious intermediary.[8]

The development of this form of hereditary religious leadership was of considerable significance, not only because it spread widely throughout the Punjab, but also because it facilitated a close relationship between religious and political authority. The transmission of baraka helped to stimulate the proliferation of shrines in the Punjab in the centuries following the conversion, particularly as the descen-

[6] Government of India, *Report of the Dargah Khwaja Saheb (Ajmer) Committee of Enquiry* (New Delhi: Government Press, 1949), pp. 28–9. The report discusses the development of the office of hereditary sajjada nashin and the duties the sajjada nashin was expected to perform.

[7] The role of a pir is discussed in Adrian C. Mayer, '*Pir* and *Murshid*: an Aspect of Religious Leadership in West Pakistan', *Middle Eastern Studies*, vol. 3, no. 2 (January 1967), pp. 160–1.

[8] Trimingham notes that the concept of *wilaya*, or saintship, had no necessary connection with moral distinctions, but rather was based on the ability to experience the favour of God. Trimingham, *Sufi Orders in Islam*, pp. 227–8.

dants and the *khalifas*, or deputies, of the original saints spread across much of the Punjab. Networks of shrines grew up which were loosely linked together within the Sufi orders; in many cases a large and well-known shrine became the centre of a network of much smaller shrines which were monuments to the disciples and descendants of the more well-known saint.[9] By the opening of the twentieth century, as one British officer noted, the districts of western Punjab along the Indus were 'dotted with shrines, tombs of the sainted dead . . . and to the shrines of the saints, thousands upon thousands of devotees resort, in the hopes of gaining something on the sacred soil. . . .'[10] Many such shrines had their own lines of sajjada nashins who served as pirs for large circles of these disciples, and the extent of their influence can be readily gauged from the report of one district gazetteer that 'practically every Muhammadan in the district has his pir'.[11]

Equally as important as the widespread geographical diffusion of this form of religious leadership in rural Punjab was the relationship of these religious leaders to political authority. The diffusion of shrines as local centres of religious authority produced a structure of religious leadership which mirrored the structure of political authority in much of western Punjab, where power was also diffused to a large extent among numerous petty tribal chiefs.[12] The sajjada nashins of the shrines were, in fact, in many cases closely associated with these local leaders.[13] More importantly, the relations of the sajjada nashins with

[9] The best example of such a network of related shrines is that of the Bokhari Syeds, the descendants of Syed Jalaluddin Bokhari of Uch, whose shrines are found in several districts of south-west Punjab. For a list of numerous surviving branches of the Bokhari Syeds in the twentieth century, see *Jhang District Gazetteer*, 1908, p. 58.

[10] Major Aubrey O'Brien, 'The Mohammadan Saints of the Western Punjab', *Journal of the Royal Anthropological Institute*, vol. XLI (1911), p. 511.

[11] *Multan District Gazetteer*, 1923–4, p. 120.

[12] The Ajmer Enquiry Committee suggested that the diffusion of shrines as centres of hereditary religious leadership 'presumably . . . received impetus from the feudal organization . . .' which was developing in India. *Report of the Dargah Khwaja Saheb (Ajmer) Committee of Enquiry*, p. 29.

[13] Though there is not very much evidence of this, such connections were apparently established from the time of the conversion when it was generally not by popular preaching, but by contacts between the Sufis and the local chiefs that much of the conversion was accomplished. This, at least, is the tradition of conversion of a number of the tribes. H.A. Rose, *A Glossary of the Tribes and Castes of the Punjab and North-West Frontier Province* (Patiala: Punjab Languages Dept., 1970), vol. II, p. 412; vol. III, pp. 417–18.

the Muslim state followed much the same pattern as the relations of these local chiefs with the state. The base of their religious authority in heredity rather than in piety made sajjada nashins, like tribal chiefs and other local leaders, readily susceptible to the common forms of state political control through the granting of honors, appointments and lands.[14] During Mughal times, the state established close ties with many of the important sajjada nashins; in one case at Multan the Mughals ever relied on a family of sajjada nashins to serve as their local Governors.[15] Such connections with the Muslim state added an important political dimension to the authority of many of the sajjada nashins, which increased their prestige and gave official recognition to their religious authority. By the end of the Mughal period, therefore, the religious influence of many of the sajjada nashins as custodians of the local outposts of Islam had become closely associated with their political influence as local outposts of the Muslim state.

Because of the pervasive development of such political connections during Mughal times, the decline of Mughal authority in Punjab had a substantial impact on the system of religious authority. Much has been written on the importance of the decline of the Mughal state for the religious development of Indian Muslims, but most of this has focused on the role of Shah Waliullah and his followers at Delhi in trying to reformulate Islam in order to compensate for the loss of state support for their religion. The decline of the Muslim state had a direct effect on the predominant system of religious leadership in the Punjab, however. As the links between the shrines and the Mughal state were snapped with the collapse of central Muslim political authority, many of the old sajjada nashins who had wielded local political authority under the Mughals were transformed into petty local chieftains, who were increasingly isolated from any connection with the larger Islamic community.[16] In response to this isolation, a movement developed in

[14] A detailed example of how such a relationship developed in the medieval Deccan sultanate of Bijapur is given in Richard Eaton, 'The Court and the Dargah in the Seventeenth Century Deccan', *The Indian Economic and Social History Review*, vol. 10, no. 1 (March 1973), pp. 50–4.

[15] The family is the Gilani Syeds, sajjada nashins of the shrine of Musa Pak Shaheed. Lepel Griffin and C.F. Massey, *Chiefs and Families of Note in the Punjab* (Lahore: Civil and Military Gazette Press, 1910), vol. II, p. 324.

[16] A good example of this is the sajjada nashin of the shrine of Baba Farid at Pakpattan. He asserted his independence of imperial control in the mid-eighteenth century and fought with other local chiefs. *Montgomery District Gazetteer*, 1933,

the eighteenth and nineteenth centuries to infuse new religious awareness into the existing forms of religious influence connected with the shrines to compensate for the collapse of the links between the local shrines and the state. This movement was embodied in a dramatic revival of the Chishti order which, perhaps because of its stronger traditions of independence from state authority, had gone into eclipse in Punjab during the years of Mughal dominance. The impulse for this revival came originally from Delhi, where the decline of the Mughals was most immediately felt, and was reflected in the work of Shah Kalimullah (1650–1729) and later Shah Fakhruddin (1717–-85) who sought to revitalize the Chishti order and impart to it a new spiritual intensity.[17] The Chishti revival in the Punjab can be traced most directly, however, from Shah Fakhruddin's most important disciple, Khwaja Nur Muhammad Maharvi, who established a khanqah near Bahawalpur in the mid-eighteenth century. Khwaja Nur Muhammad has been credited with having 'fostered the growth of the (Chishti) Silsilah to such an extent that other mystic fraternities seem to have been totally eclipsed'.[18] He attracted a widespread following among all classes of the population by emphasizing the mission of the Chishtis to revitalize Islam and by teaching the importance of personal adherence to the Shariat.[19] His influence was spread by a large number of khalifas who carried the mission of the Chishtis all across western Punjab. These khalifas themselves started khanqahs which later became the centres of shrines, and their khalifas in turn spread the revival still further.[20] The vitality of the Chishti revival continued well into the period of British rule in the Punjab and led eventually to a network of extremely influential Chishti shrines in rural west Punjab. These new Chishti shrines did not completely supplant the older shrines, many of which continued to exercise considerable influence, but the

p. 38. A similar pattern was followed by many of the Bokhari Syed sajjada nashins. *Jhang District Gazetteer*, 1908, pp. 58–60.

[17] Khaliq Ahmad Nizami, *Tarikh-e-Mashaikh-e-Chisti* (Karachi: Maktaba-e-Arifin, 1975), pp. 366–426, 460–529.

[18] M. Zameeruddin Siddiqi, 'The resurgence of the Chishti Silsilah in the Punjab During the Eighteenth Century', *Proceedings of the Indian History Congress*, 1970 (New Delhi: Indian History Congress, 1971), p. 408.

[19] Ibid., p. 409.

[20] In the major line of Chishti revival pirs who were spiritually descended from Khwaja Nur Muhammad, Khwaja Nur Muhammad himself had 30 khalifas, Shah Suleman of Taunsa had 63 khalifas, and Khwaja Shamsuddin Sialvi had 35. K.A. Nizami, *Tarikh-e-Mashaikh-e-Chisti*, pp. 555–6, 664–5, 706–8.

most important shrines of the Chishti revival—at Taunsa in Dera Ghazi Khan District, Sial Sharif in Shahpur District, Jalalpur in Jhelum District, and Golra in Rawalpindi District—became major new centres of religious authority.[21]

The importance of the Chishti revival in the development of Muslim religious leadership was that it brought a greater emphasis on the definition of Muslim identity according to the Shariat to the appeal of Muslim religious leaders in western Punjab, without at the same time challenging the forms of religious influence based on the shrines. Here it is most illuminating to contrast this revival with the religious reforms which grew out of the work of Shah Waliullah. Both Shah Waliullah and the Chishti revivalists were responding to the problems of providing religious leadership without the aid of a Muslim state, but whereas those who drew on the tradition of Shah Waliullah sought to do this by seeking ultimately to develop new forms of organization to produce an independent class of ulama which could set religious standards for the community, the Chishti revivalists sought to do it within the traditional forms of religious authority already popular in western Punjab. They continued to emphasize the khanqahs and shrines as local religious centres, and they relied on the traditional forms of influence, the piri–muridi tie and the urs. This continued organizational emphasis reflected the continued political structure of rural Punjab society, where power was diffused among a large number of rural, often tribally based leaders. The new Chishti pirs did not have the local political power of many of the older pirs who had politically served the Mughal state, but they were equally tied to local structures of rural authority, for their religious influence was often directed at the local political leaders upon whom they were frequently dependent for economic support.[22] In contrast to this, the reforms following on the work of Shah Waliullah were a product of the heartland of Muslim empire, where power had been concentrated in the central state and not diffused among numerous intermediaries to the same extent as in Punjab. In such circumstances, with the collapse of the Muslim state, Muslim religious leaders had been thrown to a greater degree on their

[21] Short biographies of the saints who founded these khanqahs are given by Nizami. There is a full biography of Pir Mehr Ali Shah of Golra; Maulana Faiz Ahmad Faiz, *Mehr-e-Munir* (Golra: Syed Ghulam Mohyuddin, 1973?).

[22] Siddiqi, 'The Resurgence of Chishti Silsilah', p. 409; Maulana Faiz Ahmad Faiz, *Mehr-e-Munir*, pp. 297–8.

own independent resources, and this may explain their greater concern with developing new forms of organization.

The contrast between these two traditions of religious leadership is of great importance in understanding the subsequent evolution of religious authority in the Punjab. The reformist tradition of Shah Waliullah produced eventually a recognizable class of ulama,[23] whose organization was increasingly defined in the late nineteenth century by the polemical defense of Islam from Hindu and Christian attacks and by the development of religious schools. In the Punjab, the most active of reformist religious leaders were the ulama of the Ahl-e-Hadis, whose tradition was drawn particularly from Shah Waliullah's emphasis on the study of the original Quran and *hadis* over the subsequent interpretations of the medieval schools of law.[24] In addition, ulama of Deoband, the premier religious school associated with the reformist movement, exerted an increasing influence in Punjab in the late nineteenth century, particularly in the cities and towns.[25] Though the Ahl-e-Hadis and the Deobandis differed in many important respects, they were alike in their rejection of the common forms of religious influence centred on the shrines. The Ahl-e-Hadis were the most categorical in their rejection of the forms of Islam based on the Sufi orders, but the leaders of Deoband, though usually initiated in the Sufi orders and familiar with Sufi practices, also rejected most of the organizational forms which had come to dominate popular religion in the Punjab. They did not approve, for example, of the centrality of the worship at tombs in religious organization, nor did they believe in the urs.[26]

In response to such attacks, another distinct perspective developed among those ulama who approved of the forms of popular Islam. This group of ulama, which generally crystallized under the name Ahl-e-Sunnat-o-Jamaat, defended the combination of religious awareness and popular leadership at the shrines which had characterized the

[23] W.C. Smith, 'The "Ulama" in Indian Politics', in C.H. Philips (ed.), *Politics and Society in India* (London: George Allen and Unwin, 1963), pp. 50–1.

[24] Barbara Metcalf, 'The Reformist Ulama: Muslim Religious Leadership in India, 1860–1900' (unpublished Ph.D. dissertation, University of California, Berkeley, 1974), pp. 304–9.

[25] Metcalf notes that the great bulk of early monetary contributions to the school at Deoband from the Punjab came from donors in the cities and towns; ibid., p. 194.

[26] Ibid., p. 261.

Chishti revival. Ironically, in defending the traditional forms of religious organization, these ulama also turned to the newer reformist organizational forms. This was evident in the founding in 1887 of the Dar-ul-ulum Naumania at Lahore, which served as a focus of Ahl-e-Sunnat-o-Jamaat influence,[27] and later in the founding in the 1920s of another religious school at Lahore, the Dar-ul-ulum Hizb-ul-Ahnaf, which tied the development of the Ahl-e-Sunnat-o-Jamaat perspective to a similar perspective being developed by Maulana Ahmad Raza Khan Barelvi in the United Provinces.[28] In spite of the founding of these urban religious schools, however, the distinctive significance of this group of ulama lay in its ties to the rural religious leaders associated with the shrines—ties which the predominantly urban based reformist ulama could not match. Several of the Chishti revivalists, such as Pir Mehr Ali Shah, sajjada nashin of Golra, took a close interest in the Dar-ul-ulum Naumania,[29] and other rural pirs in the revivalist tradition, most notably Pir Jamaat Ali Shah, an influential Naqshbandi sajjada nashin from Alipur Sayyedan in Sialkot District, had close connections with the Ahl-e-Sunnat-o-Jamaat ulama.[30] The significance of the Ahl-e-Sunnat-o-Jamaat perspective was, in fact, that it legitimized the traditional forms of religious leadership associated with the shrines according to the standards of religious education and debate developed by the reformers.

By the twentieth century, therefore, though the traditional forms of rural religious leadership associated with the shrines had been strongly challenged, the challenge had not gone unanswered. The structure of religious authority based on the shrines remained overwhelmingly dominant in rural Punjab, and the fundamental basis of religious leadership in the rural areas remained tied to the hereditary transmission of religious charisma. The focus of religious authority

[27] Hafiz Nazar Ahmad, *Jaiza-e-Madaris-e-Arabiya-e-Maghribi Pakistan*, II (Lahore: Muslim Academy, 1972), pp. 28–9; Iqbal Ahmad Faruqi, *Tazkira Ahl-e-Sunnat-o-Jamaat Lahore* (Lahore: Maktaba Nabviya, 1975), p. 263; *Naqoosh*, Lahore Number (February 1962), p. 538.

[28] Hafiz Nazar Ahmad, *Jaiza*, pp. 27–8; Faruqi, *Tazkira*, p. 321.

[29] Mohammad Din Kalim, *Lahore ke Auliya-e-Chisht* (Lahore: Maktaba Nabviya, 1967), pp. 143–4.

[30] Pir Jamaat Ali Shah was a Naqshbandi, but I have treated him as a revivalist since his religious concerns were very similar to those of the Chishti revival sajjada nashins. He made donations to both the Dar-ul-ulum Naumania and the Dar-ul-ulum Hizb-ul-Ahnaf. Haider Husain Shah, *Shah-e-Jamaat* (Lahore: Maktaba Shah-e-Jamaat, 1973), p. 116.

continued to be diffused among numerous shrines which were, in many ways, tied closely to the local political structures of rural society. But the currents of religious revival had produced a deep impact on the concerns of many of the sajjada nashins whose roots were in the Chishti revival. It was these revivalist leaders, who were a product of the era of religious ferment which had produced the reformist perspectives, and yet were, at the same time, closely linked as rural sajjada nashins to the local structures of Muslim power which had survived the Mughal collapse, who were to play a pivotal role in the developing relationship between religious leaders and Muslim politics.

Religious Leaders and the Unionist Party

The impact of the structural position of sajjada nashins on their political roles cannot be understood without describing briefly the structure of rural politics which grew out of the system of administration developed by the British in rural Punjab. In the nineteenth century the British had attempted to consolidate a system of rural administration which relied, particularly in west Punjab, on the local political influence of landed, often tribally based, intermediaries. In this the British were not departing from the established traditions of political control in west Punjab. But at the same time the British sought to bolster the position of these rural leaders by isolating the rural areas from the growing economic and political influences emanating from the cities which might have tended to undermine the position of these leaders. This policy found its fullest expression in the Alienation of Land Act of 1900 which, stated in general terms, barred the non-agricultural population from acquiring land in the rural areas.[31] From these roots a political tradition developed which emphasized both the unity of interests of the agricultural classes in opposition to the urban population and the continuing leadership of the agricultural classes by these landed intermediaries. It was this tradition which eventually produced the Unionist Party in the 1920s—a provincial party based on a pro-rural agriculturalist ideology and led by the landed leaders of rural society, which dominated Punjab politics for almost a quarter of a century before 1947.

[31] For a detailed account of the background to the development of the administrative tradition which produced the Land Alienation Act, see P.H.N. van den Dungen, *The Punjab Tradition* (London: George Allen and Unwin, 1972).

The political role of sajjada nashins in Punjab politics during this period must be seen in relation to the Unionist Party and to the British administrative policies which had helped to produce it. Many of the sajjada nashins, particularly those associated with the older pre-Mughal shrines, were very strongly tied into these same rural administrative structures which lay behind the development of the Unionists. The political role of many of these shrines in pre-British times has already been indicated; after the fall of the Mughals, many sajjada nashins established themselves as powerful local political figures. After the annexation of the Punjab the British soon discovered that in developing their own rural administration they could not ignore the political influence in the rural areas that many of these sajjada nashins had acquired. Many sajjada nashins were accordingly honoured by the British and given positions of local administrative authority. This was particularly true in southwest Punjab, where families of sajjada nashins were among the largest landholders in the area and were extremely influential in local affairs. In Montgomery district, for example, the British recognized the sajjada nashin of the shrine of Baba Farid Shakarganj at Pakpattan as one of the leading darbaris in the district.[32] In Jhang, Muzaffargarh and Multan districts sajjada nashins played leading roles as zaildars, honorary magistrates and district board members.[33]

In the twentieth century, as the British attempted to give political cohesion to a class of landed rural intermediaries who could be counted on to support their Government, they recognized the leading sajjada nashins as an important part of this class. The foundations for this recognition were provided at the time of the passage of the Alienation of Land Act of 1900 when in nearly all the western Punjab districts sajjada nashins were recognized as belonging to the agricultural classes receiving protection under the Act. The lands of these Muslim religious leaders, one British officer noted, required protection under the Act 'for political reasons' as much as those of any other group.[34]

[32] *Montgomery District Gazetteer*, 1933, pp. 108–9.

[33] *Jhang District Gazetteer*, 1908, pp. 58–60; *Muzaffargarh District Gazetteer*, 1929, pp. 75–7; *Multan District Gazetteer*, 1923–4, pp. 106–10.

[34] Under the Land Alienation Act sajjada nashins were not specifically recognized as agriculturalists, but Syeds and Qureshis, the 'tribes' to which most sajjada nashins belonged, were recognized as 'agricultural tribes' in most districts. The position of Muslim religious leaders as agriculturalist was, however, specifically discussed in the correspondence accompanying passage of the Act. Note by

Later, when the British consciously sought to define a class of 'landed gentry' by distributing canal colony land grants, many of the leading sajjada nashins were explicitly recognized as members of the 'landed gentry' class. The inclusion of these religious leaders among the 'landed gentry' was at first questioned by some; H. J. Maynard, for example, pointed out in the case of the Pir of Makhad of Attock district that 'it would be a straining of language to call the pir one of the hereditary landed gentry of the province'. But the Lieutenant-Governor, Sir Michael O'Dwyer, answered that whether truly 'landed gentry' or not, the influence of such religious heads could not be ignored. The Pir of Makhad, he pointed out, was 'regarded with veneration by many of the leading Frontier and western Punjab chiefs', and such influence had to be taken into account. The same could be said of other sajjada nashins whose hereditary religious influence might be put to political purposes. 'If a man has political influence and uses it well', O'Dwyer argued, 'the fact that he is connected with a religious institution and even to a certain extent derives his influence from that connection should not in my opinion stand in the way of obtaining a grant'. Subsequently many sajjada nashins were recognized as 'landed gentry', particularly in southwest Punjab, where in several districts religious families composed over a third of all those receiving 'landed gentry' grants.[35]

It was this recognition as landed rural leaders which provided the basis for the support of many of these sajjada nashins for the Unionist Party. The common political interests of sajjada nashins and the landed class which dominated western Punjab had been well established by the British by the time that Sir Fazli Husain began to try to organize a rural party in the Punjab Legislative Council in the early 1920s. Of the 27 members initially returned to the Council in 1920 for rural Muslim seats, five were from influential families of pirs,[36] and all of them seem to have been Fazli Husain's supporters. Fazli Husain made no special appeal to these sajjada nashins to join the Unionist Party when it was founded in 1923, but it was hardly necessary to approach

J. Wilson, Punjab Settlement Commissioner, 1 February 1901; Punjab Board of Revenue, file 442/1/00/4.

35 The case of the Pir of Makhad was debated in 1914. The case is in Punjab Board of Revenue, file 301/3/00/164A. Lists by district of those eventually receiving 'landed gentry' grants are in Punjab Board of Revenue, file 301/1176.

36 Great Britain, *Return Showing the Results of Elections in India*, Parliamentary Papers, vol. XXVI (1921), p. 18.

them as a special interest, for their interests, like those of other hereditary rural leaders, were largely defined by their roles as intermediaries in the rural administration and by their support of the Land Alienation Act. The religious concerns of most of these landed pirs seem to have been satisfied by the Unionist policy of seeking the advancement of Muslims through the reservation of places for Muslims in schools and in the Government services, and by the protection of the economic interests of the rural Muslims from the assault of the Hindu moneylender. For them it does not seem to have been important that the Party failed to define specifically Muslim interests according to a religious standard.[37]

Such a position, however, was not particularly calculated to win the support of those sajjada nashins who were a product of the eighteenth- and nineteenth-century religious revival in rural Punjab. The Chishti pirs in particular did not share the tradition of co-operation with the British administration, and their religious concerns extended well beyond the issue of the economic advance of the rural Muslims which dominated Unionist policy. As products of the religious revival, they were concerned with the religious identity of Muslims and with the spreading of a greater awareness of Islam. But significantly, despite these religious concerns, the revivalist sajjada nashins did not define politically a set of religious interests independent of the Unionist position. There are two reasons for this, both of which reflect the fact that the revival shrines, like the older shrines, were an integral part of the rural social and political milieu. First, the revivalist sajjada nashins, equally with the landed sajjada nashins, relied for the religious following, and usually for financial support as well, on the leaders of rural society, who were overwhelmingly Unionist supporters. A pir like Syed Mehr Ali Shah of Golra, for example, though he shunned association with the Government, nevertheless had intimate religious ties with many of the staunchest pro-Government and pro-Unionist Muslims,[38] and this prevented him from actively opposing the Unionist Party. Second, the political alternative for the revivalist sajjada nashins

[37] A good example of this attitude is provided by Pir Mohammad Husain, sajjada nashin of Shergarh, who was one of the leading spokesmen for the Unionist position in the Punjab Council during the 1920s. His view of the communal problem showed no sign of a distinctive religious perspective; 'the root cause of all the Hindu-Mohammadan disunion in the Province', he said, 'is the indebtedness of the masses. . . .' *Punjab Legislative Council Debates*, vol. VI, 1924, p. 229.

[38] Maulana Faiz Ahmad Faiz, *Mehr-e-Munir*, pp. 297–8.

was alliance with urban politicians who opposed the pro-rural Unionist policy, and though such an alliance would have provided a platform for religious criticism of the Unionists, it also would have put them in the same camp with the urban reformist ulama, whose attack covered the whole structure of rural religion. In such circumstances, the revivalist sajjada nashins, though often unhappy with the religious position of the Unionists, were unlikely to join in a concerted attack which threatened their own religious position in rural society.

The importance of the first of these considerations can be readily demonstrated by an example from one of the leading Chishti revival shrines. One of the most striking cases showing the importance of local ties in affecting the political outlook of the revivalist sajjada nashins is provided by the case of the shrine at Jalalpur in Jhelum district. In that case the sajjada nashins, Pir Fazl Shah, seems to have made a concerted effort to maintain the political independence of the shrine in order to press the religious concerns which lay behind the Chishti revival, but despite his efforts he was drawn into the local political factions which lay behind Unionist power. What cemented the ties of the Jalalpur shrine into local political rivalries were marriage connections with locally influential landed families. Pir Fazl Shah's mother was the daughter of one of the leading Rajput chiefs of the district, and his maternal uncle, Raja Ghazanfar Ali Khan, was an ambitious local politico who was later to become important in Punjab provincial politics.[39] During the 1920s Raja Ghazanfar Ali Khan worked 'hand in glove' with Nawab Mehr Shah, the younger brother of the sajjada nashins, in order to build a faction in Jhelum politics.[40] Despite such efforts to tie the shrine into local factional politics, however, Pir Fazl Shah made an effort to maintain the political independence of the shrine by organizing his religious followers in 1927 into an organization known as the Hizbullah, or 'party of God.' Annual meetings of the Hizbullah coincided with the yearly urs, and resolutions were passed on a number of religious and political subjects, thus providing the Pir with a platform for the political expression of an independent religious view.[41] But in spite of the opportunity this provided the Pir for independent religious rhetoric, the strength of his

[39] Dr Abdul Ghani, *Amir Hizbullah* (Jalalpur Sharif: Idara Hizbullah, 1965), pp. 520–4.

[40] Letter, W.R. Wilson (DC, Jhelum), to Calvert, 28 August 1926. Punjab Board of Revenue, file 301/3/C9/186 KW (19).

[41] Dr Abdul Ghani, *Amir Hizbullah*, pp. 337–87.

ties to the faction of his uncle and brother seriously undermined his independence when it came to political organizing. The Hizbullah organization carried significant political weight in Jhelum and western Gujrat Districts, but at election time in 1937 Fazl Shah threw its backing not behind an independent religious candidate, but behind his uncle, Raja Ghazanfar Ali Khan.[42] Ghazanfar Ali Khan, who had responded sympathetically to many of the Pir's earlier appeals from the Hizbullah platform, initially stayed aloof from the Unionist Party and ran on the ticket of the Muslim League, a primarily urban party at this time which provided him with an independent platform in Jhelum. Almost immediately after being elected, however, he accepted the offer of a Parliamentary Secretaryship from Sir Sikander Hyat Khan, the Unionist Premier, and he became a strong backer of the Unionist Party in the Assembly. The Pir's ability to maintain an independent religious critique of the Unionists was badly compromised, and this was indicated when the Unionists responded to criticism from the Pir by simply asking Raja Ghazanfar Ali Khan to keep the Pir in line.[43] The case of Pir Fazl Shah thus demonstrates the difficulty for the Chishti revivalists, despite their religious concerns, in escaping politically from the pressures of the rural social and political milieu of which they were a part.

The strength of the ties of these sajjada nashins into the rural political scene is even more clearly indicated when their position is contrasted with that of the reformist ulama of the towns. While rural sajjada nashins, even revivalist sajjada nashins like Pir Fazl Shah, maintained close ties with political leaders in rural Punjab, the political strength of the reformist ulama came from their very independence of such political ties. The thrust of their reforms, particularly the founding of the Dar-ul-ulum at Deoband, had been to provide an organizational structure for Islam in India which did not rely on traditional Muslim political power, either through the state or in the localities. For this reason, in their early development they had been largely apolitical,[44]

[42] Ibid., pp. 355–6.

[43] Note by Syed Afzal Ali Hasnie, Resident Secretary, Unionist Party to Sir Sikander, 2 February 1939, and draft letter to Raja Ghazanfar Ali Khan, n.d. Unionist Party Papers, file G-21. I would like to thank Mr Nazar Hyat Khan Tiwana of Chicago for permission to use these papers.

[44] Barbara Metcalf, 'The Madrasa at Deoband: A Model for Religious Education in Modern India,' in *Berkeley Working Papers on South and Southeast Asia*, vol. I (Berkeley: Centre for South and Southeast Asian Studies, 1977), p. 266.

but when they did enter politics after the First World War they did so with a new and independent political approach, which offered a religious critique of traditional Muslim politics. Unlike the rural sajjada nashins, therefore, many Deobandi ulama were prominent in the formation of the Jamiat-i-Ulama-i-Hind, the first independent organization of Muslim religious leaders in India, and through this organization many of the Deobandis began to play an active role in politics in opposition to the British administration and to the Muslim leaders whose power was tied to the administration.[45] This independent political role was demonstrated first during the Khilafat movement, when many of the most active reformist ulama supported the Congress non-cooperation programme.[46] Later it was many of these same men who formed the backbone of the Ahrar Party, which was founded in 1929 in opposition to the politics of the dominant rural Muslims in Punjab.[47] It was the Ahrar who offered the most coherent political challenge to the Unionists on religious grounds, and it was the Ahrar who should logically have provided the political focus for those dissatisfied with the religious leadership provided by the Unionist Party. But the Ahrar, having emerged to a large extent out of the religious concerns of the reformist perspective, were largely cut off from the politics and the religion of the rural areas. Though by no means exclusively a party of the reformist ulama, the Ahrar were, like the reformists, primarily urban in composition and represented socially the urban lower and middle class.[48] Their appeal represented not only a plea for heightened religious awareness, which did attract some of the rural revivalist sajjada nashins, but also an attack on the leaders of rural society, which alienated the support of these sajjada nashins. Despite a common concern with infusing Muslim politics with greater

[45] Peter Hardy, *The Muslims of British India*, pp. 189–95.

[46] Chairman of the Punjab Khilafat Committee was Maulana Abdul Qadir Qasuri of the Ahl-e-Hadis. Other prominent religious reformists in the movement included Maulana Daood Ghaznavi of the Ahl-e-Hadis and Maulana Habib-ur-Rahman Ludhianvi of the Deobandis. For a list of local Khilafat Committee members, see M. Shaukat Ali Khan, *Punjab Men Tehrik-e-Khilafat* (unpublished M.A. thesis, Punjab University, Lahore), pp. 134–8.

[47] W.C. Smith, *Modern Islam in India* (Lahore: Sh. Muhammad Ashraf, 1963), pp. 270–2. Smith gives the date of the founding of the Ahrar as 1930, but most other sources give the year as 1929.

[48] Y.B. Mathur, *Muslims and Changing India* (New Delhi: Trimurti Publications, 1972), p. 110.

religious awareness, therefore, the revivalist sajjada nashins and the reformist ulama were generally unable to unite politically.

To a certain extent the differences between the reformists and the rural revivalists can be traced to theological differences which were a product of the increasing definition of opposing religious perspectives during the late-nineteenth century. Theological controversies in fact flared with considerable frequency in the early-twentieth century, particularly between the Ahl-e-Hadis and their supporters and the pirs. One such controversy, for example, saw Pir Fazl Shah of Jalalpur defending the pirs and Sufis of the Punjab in 1917 against the attacks of Maulana Zafar Ali Khan.[49] Such differences in religious outlook were, however, even in the 1920s and 1930s not so strongly defined as to prevent in themselves co-operation among religious leaders of different perspectives on a common Muslim issue. Rather, theological controversies gave a cutting edge to the different political alliances of these groups based on their social position in the urban or rural areas. During the Khilafat movement, for example, there were several sajjada nashins who did support the movement to varying degrees, but they were generally unwilling to co-operate with the Congress and the Hindus in the more radical phase of the movement largely because in the Punjab, at least, the movement was as much anti-British and anti-rural party as it was pro-Khilafat.[50] The controversy which flared about the role of Pir Jamaat Ali Shah in the Khilafat movement indicated this clearly, for despite his having collected funds for the Khilafat Committee and having spoken in favour of the Khilafat cause, he was later criticized by the *Hamdard* of Maulana Muhammad Ali and the *Zamindar* of Maulana Zafar Ali Khan for having been pro-British, an attack which did not focus simply on Pir Jamaat Ali Shah, but on the Sufis in general.[51] Though Pir Jamaat Ali Shah strongly defended his record, such an attack can be seen in many ways as a general attack, not on his record, but on the social position of such

[49] Dr Abdul Ghani, *Amir Hizbullah*, pp. 224–5.

[50] Pir Fazl Shah, for example, helped to organize some sajjada nashins at the Pakpattan urs to send a pro-Khilafat telegram to the Viceroy, but he opposed boycott of schools, the police and the army as harmful to Muslims; ibid., pp. 255, 262. Of the major sajjada nashins in Punjab only the Pir of Sial seems to have actively supported the non-co-operation phase of the movement.

[51] Maulana Maulvi Mohammad Abul Majid Khan Qasuri, *Pir Syed Mohammad Jamaat Ali Shah . . . ke Mukhtasar Qaumi Karname* (Agra: Agra Akhbar Press, 1925), pp. 1–2. This pamphlet, which was written to defend Pir Jamaat Ali Shah, describes the controversy.

religious leaders and on their ties into the rural power structure which, whatever their religious sentiments, made them unlikely to support the full implications of the critique of Muslim politics offered by the religious reformists and urban Muslim leaders.

The same tension can be seen during the 1930s. The emergence of the Ahrar Party as a popular expression of religious awareness was heralded by the Kashmir agitation of 1931 and 1932. The leadership of this agitation was provided primarily by the same Muslims who had been most active in the Khilafat cause. Politically, as the British assessed it, the Ahrar movement represented 'in the main the urban Muslims, who are jealous of the ascendancy of wealthy land-owners in the Legislature and Executive'.[52] But as a religious agitation, and one which combined the assertion of the Muslim right to practice their religion in Kashmir with an assertion of Islamic orthodoxy in attacks on the role of Qadianis in the All-India Kashmir Committee, the Kashmir movement attracted support well beyond the social class of the Ahrar leaders who were directing it. As the agitation expanded in late 1931, even 'the Pirs,' the Chief Secretary wrote, 'have begun to take a hand and declare the efforts of the Ahrars to be activated by the right spirit of Islamic sympathy . . .'.[53] Pir Fazl Shah praised the spirit of the common Muslims during the Kashmir agitation as indicative of their willingness to sacrifice for Islam,[54] and Pir Jamaat Ali Shah donated 500 rupees to the cause.[55] But when it became necessary to define the political aims of the Kashmir movement, the differing perspectives of the groups became clear. The Ahrar leaders leaned toward the Congress as the centre of anti-British sentiment and the chief organizational alternative to the landowning class represented by the Unionists in the Punjab, and eventually they tried to turn the movement toward more openly pro-Congress and anti-Government aims.[56] As long as the movement had been religious in character and directed against the Hindu ruler of Kashmir, its support had been broad-based, but this pro-Congress move alienated much of the purely

[52] Punjab Fortnightly Report for the first half of November 1931. National Archives of India (NAI), Home Political, file 18/11/31.

[53] Ibid.

[54] Dr Abdul Ghani, *Amir Hizbullah*, p. 349.

[55] Akhtar Husain Shah, *Seerat-e-Amir-e-Millat* (Alipur Sayyedan: published by the author, 1974), pp. 403–4.

[56] Punjab Fortnightly Report for the second half of February 1932. NAI, Home Political, file 18/4/32.

religious sympathy the Ahrar had gained and prevented it from incorporating many of the rural religious leaders into the organization as a united religious front. Even though the Ahrar later tried to play down their connections with Congress, as far as the Kashmir agitation was concerned the damage had been done and the movement had lost much of its popular support.[57] The Ahrar remained, in fact, up until partition, essentially an urban movement.

The conflicting claims on the allegiance of the revivalist sajjada nashins in the political climate of the 1930s—claims of their own religious urges on one side and of their social position in the rural areas on the other—were nowhere more graphically dramatized than in the Shahidganj agitation of 1935 and 1936. The agitation over the Shahidganj Mosque in Lahore, which began after the Sikhs demolished the mosque in July 1935, produced the largest response from the sajjada nashins of Punjab of any religious cause before the movement for Pakistan. The sajjada nashins supported the agitation as a purely religious cause, which was on this occasion in no way compromised by the political leanings of the Ahrar, who were more concerned at the time about manoeuvring for the upcoming provincial elections. The initial leadership of the agitation in Lahore came instead from a group of urban agitators who were generally opposed to the pro-Congress attitude of the Ahrar, the Majlis Ittihad-i-Millat led by Maulana Zafar Ali Khan. After many of the leaders of this group were externed from Lahore, however, an attempt was made to give the sajjada nashins leadership in the agitation. At a special Shahidganj conference in Rawalpindi in September 1935, the Shahidganj agitators turned to Pir Jamaat Ali Shah to lead the agitation and appointed him Amir-e-Millat, or dictator of the agitation, at the same time inviting 'all Pirs and other religious leaders to openly identify themselves with the struggle . . .'.[58] This was an attempt, with the agitation otherwise stalled, to tap the thousands of religious followers of these pirs in the rural areas; the hope was, as one newspaper later put it, that 'simultaneously with the appointment of the Pir as the Amir his followers would enlist as volunteers'.[59] Some hoped that by naming Pir Jamaat

[57] Punjab Fortnightly Report for the first half of March 1932. NAI, Home Political, file 18/5/32.

[58] CID Report of the Rawalpindi Conference, 3 September 1935. NAI, Home Political, file 5/21/35.

[59] *Inquilab* (Lahore), 15 January 1936. Punjab Civil Secretariat, Press Branch, file 8331, vol. XI-A.

Ali Shah to head the agitation they might even be able to embarrass the Government by enlisting the thousands of followers of the Pir who were serving in the army.[60]

Assuming the leadership of such an agitation, however, put a rural sajjada nashin like Pir Jamaat Ali Shah in a very difficult position. Though other pirs, including Pir Fazl Shah of Jalalpur, Pir Qamaruddin of Sial Sharif, and Pir Ghulam Mohyuddin, the son of Pir Mehr Ali Shah of Golra, offered support for the agitation,[61] Pir Jamaat Ali Shah wavered in trying to chalk out a programme. At the Rawalpindi conference he had apparently joined in the general call for starting civil disobedience in order to regain the site of the mosque, but with his many connections to wealthy pro-Government Muslims he could not take too strong an anti-Government stand. As the Chief Secretary wrote immediately after the conference, 'Deeply as he may have appeared to have committed himself, there is some reason to think that he is not altogether comfortable about his position, and he may retreat from it. Influences are being brought to bear to this end'.[62] After conferring with other religious leaders, including many of the Barelvi ulama, he ultimately announced a plan to raise a million volunteers,[63] but in fact, other than organizing special days of mourning for the Shahidganj Mosque, little was done to organize the agitation, for Pir Jamaat Ali Shah himself was wary of the more radical demands of many of the urban agitators. By January 1936 the urban agitators of the Ittihad-i-Millat had become highly critical of the Pir's leadership. Two urban leaders issued a blistering attack on the Pir charging that 'the rich Muslims' were undermining the agitation and that the Pir was their tool,[64] while a Lahore daily charged that the Pir's statements seemed to reach the Government before they reached his own followers.[65] In order to try to salvage the agitation, Pir Jamaat

[60] CID Report of the Rawalpindi Conference, 3 September 1935. NAI, Home Political, file 5/21/35.

[61] Dr Abdul Ghani, *Amir Hizbullah*, p. 351.

[62] Appreciation of Shahidganj situation, F.H. Puckle, 6 September 1935. NAI, Home Political, file 5/21/35.

[63] Punjab Fortnightly Report for the first half of November 1935. NAI, Home Political, File 18/11/35.

[64] *Inquilab* (Lahore), 11 January 1936. Punjab Civil Secretariat, Press Branch, file 8331, vol. XI-A. The statement was made by Syed Habid and Mian Ferozuddin Ahmad.

[65] *Ihsan* (Lahore), 12 January 1936. Punjab Civil Secretariat, Press Branch, file 8331, vol. XI-A.

Ali Shah called a special Shahidganj conference at Amritsar in January 1936, but the results of the conference only seemed to confirm the criticism, for it fell largely under the control of some of his wealthy Unionist followers, including Mir Maqbul Mahmud, one of the Pir's murids and the brother-in-law of the Unionist leader, Sir Sikander Hyat Khan.[66] Apparently to save his own prestige, the Pir left immediately on Haj. The fate of Pir Jamaat Ali Shah in the Shahidganj agitation illustrates dramatically the conflicting pulls on the revivalist sajjada nashins and indicates why, despite their religious concerns, they failed to develop effectively a religious attack on the Government and the Unionist Party.

When the Unionists swept the elections of 1937, therefore, they did not have to face any general religious opposition to their position. The Ahrar Party, Maulana Zafar Ali Khan's Ittihad-i-Millat Party, and the Muslim League, which in Punjab at this time was primarily a small group of lawyers around Allama Iqbal, all contested the elections, but none showed significant strength in the rural areas. The Unionist programme, which was based on the economic advance of the rural classes and the support of the Alienation of Land Act, was a defense of the existing power structure in the rural areas. This programme had the strong support of most of the landed sajjada nashins on economic and political grounds. For the rural revivalists the Unionists offered no special religious appeal, but the tacit support of most was won either indirectly, through their personal ties to landed Unionist politicians in the localities, or else by reason of the lack of an acceptable religious alternative which did not threaten the structural and administrative bases of their position in rural society. The active religious support of such pirs for the Unionists was not required; their failure to join the religious opposition was enough to ensure Unionist success. As one of the local Unionist organizers analyzed the situation in 1936, 'The Ahrars have begun with an awfully vigorous propaganda. At least they presume to have captured the towns. Still we don't fear if they do not begin with the villages. Villagers, you know, follow these 'Pirs' blindly. . . . Take care of the 'Pirs'. Ask them only to keep silent on the matter of elections. We don't require their help but they should not oppose us . . .'.[67] In 1937, very few pirs opposed the Unionists,

[66] *Ihsan* (Lahore), 22 January 1936. Punjab Civil Secretariat, Press Branch, file 8331, vol. XI-A.

[67] Letter, Mohammad Bashir of Gurdaspur to Unionist Party headquarters, 9 May 1936. Unionist Party Papers, file D-17.

whose election victory reflected in many ways the triumph of the rural classes, both secular and religious, in the Punjab's political system.

Religious Leaders and the Muslim League

The relations between the Unionist Party and religious leaders in the 1920s and 1930s demonstrated that the political roles of religious leaders were determined primarily by their structural position in the rural or urban areas. The main division among the religious leaders in the Punjab, that between the sajjada nashins and the reformist ulama, assumed political significance because it paralleled the most important political cleavage in the Punjab, that between rural leaders and urban. The Unionists were able to gain at least the passive support of most of the sajjada nashins because the pro-rural Unionist ideology subsumed the concerns of many of these sajjada nashins as hereditary leaders whose position was tied closely to the structure of rural society. This did not mean that many of these sajjada nashins did not have strong religious concerns, but that as long as politics were channeled primarily by the urban–rural cleavage, these religious concerns could not easily find political expression.

The significant development in Punjab politics after 1937 which was to affect most deeply the political allegiances of religious leaders was the emergence of the Muslim League as a political party transcending the rural–urban distinction which had previously dominated Punjab politics. The key to this development was the League's emergence as an all-India party, which, unlike the Unionists or the urban parties of the Punjab, was concerned primarily with representing the interests of Indian Muslims at an all-India level *vis à vis* the Congress and the British. As leader of the League, Muhammad Ali Jinnah's all-India reputation allowed him to establish after 1937 a position of authority in Punjab Muslim politics independent of the provincial political parties which dominated Punjab affairs. But the establishment of such a position in Punjab politics was not accomplished immediately, nor was it an easy task for Jinnah. Jinnah's initial efforts to establish the League in the Punjab before the 1937 elections had brought him far closer to the urban parties than to the Unionists; it was the Ahrar, in fact, who were most sympathetic to his call for a united Muslim political party in 1936, while the Unionists, secure in their provincial strength, strongly rejected Jinnah's overtures for co-operation. But though Jinnah's interest in a new organization for Indian Muslims brought him closer to the urban Muslims, he was not an ideologue in the mould of the reformist ulama; he was interested in solid political strength and he was willing to compromise to develop it. Less than a year after the Unionist election victory of 1937, therefore, Jinnah forged a pact with the new Unionist Premier of the Punjab, Sir Sikander Hyat Khan, by which Jinnah essentially recognized the authority of the Unionists in Punjab politics in return for their joining the Muslim League and supporting it at the all-India level. This did not, in the short run, give Jinnah much additional authority in the Punjab itself, where the Unionist Party maintained its separate identity, but it established the League as a representative Muslim body, to which both the urban and the rural Muslim leaders of Punjab looked for the expression of Muslim political aspirations at the all-India level.[68]

The Sikander–Jinnah Pact was subsequently to arouse considerable controversy in the Punjab, for it did not end the conflicts between urban and rural Muslims. The effect of the Pact was instead to bring such conflicts to a large extent within the League itself. Though some of the urban Muslims, including the Ahrar, became increasingly hostile to the League after Jinnah's compromise with the Unionists, a large part of the urban Muslims supported the League after 1937, but they criticized sharply the role of the Unionists in the League and tried to block Unionist efforts to gain organizational control of the Punjab branch of the League after the Sikander-Jinnah Pact. Jinnah was bombarded in the years after 1937 with complaints from urban League supporters in Punjab that the Unionists were taking over the provincial Muslim League organization only to stifle its expansion.[69] In fact, there was considerable truth in this charge, for the Unionists, though

[68] Jinnah's and Sir Sikander's motives in forging the Pact at Lucknow in October 1937 remain the subject of considerable controversy. The best survey of the various factors involved is provided in Dr S.M. Ikram, *Modern Muslim India and the Birth of Pakistan* (Lahore: Sh. Muhammad Ashraf, 1970), pp. 237–51.

[69] An example of the kind of complaints against the Unionists to which Jinnah was subjected is provided by a letter from Malik Barkat Ali, leader of the urban faction in the Punjab League, to Jinnah in 1940. As a result of the Sikander-Jinnah Pact, Malik Barkat Ali wrote: 'the only persons who now form the so-called Muslim League are the Unionists, who owe allegiance first and last to Sir Sikander. Sir Sikander's only desire was to capture the organization of the League and then to keep it inert.' Letter, Malik Barkat Ali to Jinnah, 4 December 1940; file no. 215, Quaid-e-Azam Papers, Quaid-e-Azam Papers Cell, Pakistan Ministry of Education, Islamabad.

they supported Jinnah at the all-India level, were not seriously interested in an active Muslim political organization in Punjab, and they sought to dominate the League at the provincial level largely in order to keep it inert. Jinnah, however, though he realized the justice of this charge, was wary of taking action so long as the Unionists were politically dominant in rural Punjab. He put pressure on the Unionists whenever possible to adhere to League policy and to strengthen the League organization, but he could not intervene to stop their efforts to take control of the Punjab League without sacrificing his position of neutrality and openly identifying himself with urban Muslim opinion.[70] Though Jinnah was successful in keeping the League above the urban–rural conflict in the Punjab, therefore, it was, in the short run at least, largely at the expense of the development of an effective League organization in the province.

It was not until after the death of Sir Sikander in late 1942 that Jinnah saw an opportunity to free the League from its dependence on Unionist support in the Punjab without sacrificing the League's position of neutrality in the urban–rural political conflicts of the province. Sikander's death touched off considerable factional manoeuvring within the Unionist Party which led to the emergence of a group of young rurally-based leaders who opposed the new Unionist Premier, Malik Khizr Hyat Khan Tiwana, and rallied to the Muslim League standard.[71] With the support of this group, Jinnah began to put increasing pressure on the Unionist Premier to take steps to put life into the League organization and to give the unequivocal support of the Unionists to the concept of establishing Pakistan, which had formed the basis of the League's creed since 1940. When this pressure failed to force Malik Khizr Hyat to subordinate his own party interests in the Punjab to those of the League, Jinnah decided that, with a group of rural leaders now at his back, he could at last force a showdown with the Unionists. As a result, when Malik Khizr Hyat refused to

[70] Jinnah's attitude was exemplified when, as late as February 1943, he refused to give his sanction to an attempt by many of the urban Leaguers of Punjab to form a Muslim League Workers Board independent of the regular Unionist-dominated provincial League organization. *Eastern Times* (Lahore), 12 February 1943.

[71] Prominent in this group of young anti-Unionist and pro-League supporters were Mian Mumtaz Daultana, Nawab Iftikhar Husain Khan Mamdot, who was president of the provincial Muslim League, and Sardar Shaukat Hyat Khan, Sir Sikander's son, who was initially taken into the Ministry under Malik Khizr Hyat but who later split with the Unionists and was dismissed from the Ministry.

accede to League demands in 1944, Jinnah abrogated the Sikander–Jinnah Pact and Malik Khizr Hyat was expelled from the League. Jinnah apparently hoped that this would spark a large-scale shift of rural leaders from the Unionists to the Muslim League, but in the short run he may have miscalculated, for despite continued factional defections to the League, the Unionists continued to enjoy the support of the great bulk of rural Muslim Assembly members.[72] In the long run, however, Jinnah's policy paid off, for with the League firmly established as a symbol of Muslim political aspirations which was no longer associated exclusively with the urban Muslims, the League was able to force a showdown with the Unionists in the 1946 elections and to challenge them in the rural areas themselves.

The League's ability to appeal successfully for religious support in its attack on Unionist authority was in large measure the result of the independent position it had established. In his efforts to promote the League in 1936, Jinnah had initially developed fairly close contacts with the reformist ulama of the Jamiat-i-Ulama-i-Hind,[73] but since 1937, in trying to establish the neutrality of the League he had shunned contacts with religious leaders of any kind. At the time of the League's break with the Unionists in 1944, therefore, its contacts with religious leaders were very few. Paradoxically, however, it was precisely this long isolation from any organized group of religious leaders which was now to prove most important in facilitating the League's ability to gain religious support against the Unionists in the rural areas. Though Jinnah's isolation from religious leaders and his compromises with rural Muslim politicians had alienated his one-time allies among the reformist ulama, his policy had at the same time almost inadvertently opened up a new field of potential religious support from rural religious leaders. Appeals to rural sajjada nashins for support in opposition to the Unionists could now be made without associating the League with the religious attacks of the reformist ulama on the struc-

[72] The suggestion that Jinnah may have initially miscalculated comes from Imran Ali Khan, *Punjab Politics in the Decade Before Partition* (Lahore: South Asian Institute, University of the Punjab, 1975), pp. 42–3.

[73] Jinnah's relations with the Jamiat-i-Ulama-i-Hind at the time of the 1937 elections are indicated by the first point of the election programme of the Central Muslim League Parliamentary Board, which called for 'due weight' to be given in all religious matters 'to the opinions of Jamiat-ul-Ulema Hind and the Mujtahids'. Syed Rais Ahmad Jafri (ed.), *Rare Documents* (Lahore: Muhammad Ali Academy, 1967), p. 147.

ture of rural society—attacks which had alienated the rural sajjada nashins in the past. League leaders in the Punjab, who had been left with little solid political organization in the rural areas as a legacy of the Sikander–Jinnah Pact, were not slow to take advantage of this. In 1945 a number of Punjab League leaders began to appeal strongly for support on a religious basis, and among these, rural leaders took a prominent part. A good example is provided by Sir Sikander's son, Sardar Shaukat Hyat Khan, who played an important role in helping to escalate the League's religious propaganda in the rural areas. In June 1945 Shaukat was present at a Sargodha (Shahpur) District Muslim League conference at Sial Sharif, site of one of the major revival shrines, where he promised that as a Muslim League leader he would not deviate from the path of Islam.[74] Several months later Shaukat declared that Pakistan would have a 'government of the Quran',[75] and by January 1946 he was urging that as the Muslim League was fighting for Islam, 'every Muslim must take part in this jihad'.[76] By that time Shaukat's appeal was typical of that being made by many Leaguers, and rural religious leaders responded to such appeals by coming out strongly in favour of the League and Pakistan.

The most vital religious support for Pakistan came from the sajjada nashins of the revival shrines, who had long sought an outlet for expressing their religious concerns in the political arena. The logic of the support of these religious leaders for Pakistan, as they entered the Muslim League struggle in 1945, was not nearly so well developed as was, for example, the religious position of reformist ulama like Maulana Husain Ahmad Madani, who had long opposed the idea of Pakistan. But the basis of their position can be appreciated by briefly comparing their outlook with that of the Deobandi ulama. The Deobandi conception of the political role of Muslims in India had been, as Peter Hardy has observed, shaped deeply by the nature of their religious reforms. They emphasized religious education as the key to the united participation of Muslims in politics. Having answered the decline of the Muslim state by working to develop a Muslim community guided by a class of educated ulama which could regulate its own affairs, they were wary of the authority of Muslim politicians

[74] *Eastern Times* (Lahore), 6 June 1945.
[75] *Saadat* (Lyallpur), 14 January 1946. Reproduced in *Punjab Gazette*, pt III (September 13, 1946), pp. 867–8.
[76] *Nawai Waqt* (Lahore), 13 January 1946.

and of the idea of yielding power to a state controlled by such politicians. They had, as Peter Hardy says, developed a view of religious solidarity which was itself political and was based on the authority of the ulama, who interpreted the religious law and Muslim public opinion.[77] This view was threatened by the idea of a Pakistan in the hands of traditional Muslim politicians, such as those rural leaders who were increasingly coming to the support of the Muslim League. For the revivalist sajjada nashins, the idea of a Muslim community politically regulated by the ulama was a novel one. The thrust of their concern had always been to influence the political leaders and their followers to regulate their lives according to religious injunctions. This view had been dramatized in their religious relationships with local rural leaders, for example in Pir Mehr Ali Shah's insistence when accepting a leader like Sir Umar Hyat Khan Tiwana as a murid that he observe the injunctions of the Shariat.[78] The idea of a state in the hands of such leaders was for them perfectly natural, for in the establishment of such a state based on the Shariat, they could see the projection of their local religious work into a larger political arena.

This view explains in large part the attitude of these sajjada nashins toward Muhammad Ali Jinnah, which was in sharp contrast to that of the reformist ulama who generally distrusted Jinnah as a political man with little real awareness of Islam. The attitude of the revivalist sajjada nashins was well exemplified by that of Pir Jamaat Ali Shah. Jamaat Ali Shah had himself been Amir-e-Millat during the Shahidganj agitation, but he now congratulated Jinnah on having taken up this mantle for the Muslim community.[79] He is reported to have answered criticism of Jinnah at a Sunni religious conference at Benaras in February 1946 by saying: 'think of Jinnah Sahib whatever you like, but I say that Jinnah Sahib is "Wali Allah" '.[80] He is then said to have quoted Quran and hadis to prove it. Later, in another typical gesture, Pir Jamaat Ali Shah wrote to Jinnah advising him on the performance of the Haj and offering to accompany him. '. . . This proof of your

[77] Peter Hardy, *Partners in Freedomand True Muslims: The Political Thought of Some Muslim Scholars in British India, 1912–1947* (Scandinavian Institute of Asian Studies, 1971), pp. 40–1.

[78] Maulana Faiz Ahmad Faiz, *Mehr-e-Munir,* p. 297.

[79] *Nawai Waqt* (Lahore), 30 January 1946.

[80] Letter, Hamid Hasan Qadri to Jinnah, 22 July 1946. Punjab vol. II, Shams-ul-Hasan Collection, Karachi. I would like to thank Khalid S. Hasan for permission to use this collection.

fidelity to the strict principles of Islam will put your enemies to shame', he wrote, 'and they will never be able to raise their heads before you . . .'.[81] This kind of relationship with political leaders was nothing new for most of these pirs, and in contrast to the position of the reformist ulama of Deoband, it provided the political basis for their support of the Muslim League and Pakistan. The revival pirs had long been closely associated with the leaders of the Unionist Party at the local level, but they had at the same time, like the reformist ulama, been uneasy with the essentially secular basis for Unionist political organization in provincial politics. With the transfer of an important section of the rural Muslim leadership to the Muslim League in the political realignments after 1944, the revivalist pirs found in the Muslim League under Jinnah's leadership a political platform which allowed them to maintain their local political and religious connections and at the same time to express their religious concerns in politics at the provincial and national level.[82]

Ironically, however, the same structural considerations which disposed the revivalist sajjada nashins after 1944 toward the support of the Muslim League and Pakistan, also rendered them particularly difficult for the Muslim League to organize politically. As the Muslim League began to organize religious leaders behind its cause in 1945, it found that the only existing model for the political organization of religious leaders was the Jamiat-i-Ulama-i-Hind, which had grown out of the organizational reforms of the reformist ulama—reforms which had, in fact, sharply distinguished the reformists from the

[81] Letter, Jamaat Ali Shah to Jinnah, n.d. (July 1946?). Punjab vol. II, Shams-ul-Hasan Collection, Karachi.

[82] The importance of local religious ties between these pirs and their politically prominent followers should not, in explaining their support for Pakistan, be interpreted in too narrow a sense. By and large, it was not direct economic and political pressure from their followers so much as a more general concern for the shape of the new political system which pushed them toward support of the Muslim League. The Pir of Sial, for example, was one of the first revival pirs to actively enter the political field in support of the Muslim League, in spite of the fact that among his more wealthy murids were many of the Shahpur Tiwanas, who remained Unionists. Direct economic pressure from these local magnates is difficult to observe and seems in the emotionally charged religious atmosphere of 1945 and 1946 to have had little effect on the Pir's stance. One of the bigger Tiwana landlords, Nawab Allah Bakhsh, for example, continued to have a close religious relationship with the Pir of Sial in spite of their sharp political opposition, and before his death in 1948, the Nawab sought to dedicate 15 squares of his land in *waqf* as a family graveyard with the Pir of Sial as *mutawalli*.

sajjada nashins. Nevertheless, the leaders of the League, who had had little experience in the past in the organization of religious leaders, attempted to use the Jamiat as a model for a parallel organization of religious leaders. To create such a parallel organization they naturally turned first to ulama experienced in this form of organization, and this meant the minority of Deobandi ulama who showed sympathy to the League cause. Foremost among these was Maulana Shabbir Ahmad Usmani, who had once been an active member of the Jamiat-i-Ulama-i-Hind, and who now was called upon to head the new, pro-Pakistan Jamiat-i-Ulama-i-Islam. Ironically therefore, it was a group of Deobandis who led the new pro-Muslim League organization, but with the inauguration of the Punjab branch at Lahore in December 1945,[83] an attempt was made to expand the Jamiat-i-Ulama-i-Islam to include the rural religious leaders who comprised the bulk of the League's religious support. Maulana Ghulam Murshid, *khatib* of the Badshahi Masjid at Lahore, who organized the Punjab branch of the Jamiat-i-Ulama-i-Islam was well placed to do this, for though he had studied at Deoband and had been a student of Maulana Shabbir Ahmad Usmani, his family came out of the rural revivalist tradition in west Punjab.[84] Ghulam Murshid attempted to dramatize the representative character of the Jamiat-i-Ulama-i-Islam by organizing a big provincial session at Lahore in January 1946, at which he selected as chairmen of the different sittings of the conference ulama of different religious perspectives: Pir Jamaat Ali Shah at one sitting, Maulana Muhammad Ibrahim Sialkoti of the Ahl-e-Hadis at another, and Maulana Zafar Ahmad Thanvi of Deoband at yet another.[85] But for all the enthusiasm the conference generated, particularly by its resolve to defy a Government regulation prohibiting the use of undue spiritual influence in electioneering, the conference was limited generally to urban ulama and politicians. Few of the sajjada nashins other than Pir Jamaat Ali Shah appear to have participated. Though Maulana Shabbir Ahmad Usmani subsequently issued a poster calling for support of the League in the name of the 300 or so ulama and *mashaikh* who attended the

[83] *Inquilab* (Lahore), 16 December 1945.

[84] Ghulam Murshid's father was a *khalifa* of the Pir of Taunsa, and, in addition to Deoband, he studied at Ajmer. He was also principal for a time of the Dar-ul-ulum Naumania. Interview, Maulana Ghulam Murshid, Lahore, 31 December 1975.

[85] *Ihsan* (Lahore), 29 January 1946. Reproduced in *Punjab Gazette*, pt III (13 September 1946), p. 861.

conference,[86] the new Jamiat-i-Ulama-i-Islam was in fact ill-suited for the organization of the rural religious leaders who formed the backbone of the League's religious support, and whose influence remained diffuse and centred on the shrines.

The rural sajjada nashins who supported the League thus remained largely outside the Muslim League organization. But as the elections approached, this independence from the League organization proved to be a reflection of what was, in fact, their greatest political strength—their traditional ties into local rural politics which allowed them to exert influence in the local factional contests on which the election hinged. The significance of this can be readily appreciated from a preliminary election analysis published by the *Eastern Times*, a pro-League daily, in September 1945. The *Eastern Times* observed that, as in other elections, the outcome of the Unionist-Muslim League contest was likely to be decided by factional alignments in the rural areas. But the Muslim League, it noted, had gained a powerful weapon in countering the Government influence of the Unionists in such factional rivalries, for the League had 'not only a powerful slogan but also the support of practically all the important "pirs" in the province and "sajjada nashins" of the famous shrines of Tonsa, Golra, Alipur, Sialsharif, and Jalalpur'.[87] That the *Eastern Times* mentioned these five particular shrines was no accident, for these were probably the five most prestigious revival shrines in the Punjab. Though sajjada nashins of many of the older shrines played perhaps an even more active role in factional politics than the revivalists, as a group they were not able to match the role of the revivalists in using religion to undermine traditional Unionist factional strength in the countryside. In Multan District, for example, the family of the Gilani sajjada nashins of the pre-revival shrine of Musa Pak Shaheed provided the factional backbone of Muslim League support in the district, but its influence was countered by that of its traditional factional rival, the family of the sajjada nashins of the shrine of Bahawal Haq, which supported the Unionists.[88] Though the revivalist sajjada nashins were

[86] Poster, 'Ulama aur Mashaikh-e-Islam se Appeal', n.d. Mian Abdul Aziz Collection, Lahore. I would like to thank the family of the late Mian Abdul Aziz for permission to use this collection.

[87] *Eastern Times* (Lahore), 6 September 1945.

[88] Rivalry between these two families had been going on in the Multan Municipal Committee and in the District Board for decades. In 1945 and 1946, the competing Muslim League and Unionist parties in the district were often referred

not themselves factional leaders of the standing of these religious families, it was they who injected a religious fervour into the politics of Punjab which upset most the traditional factional alignments on which Unionist political strength had rested.

A good example of the influence of these sajjada nashins in local politics comes from Jhelum District, where the local faction associated with Raja Ghazanfar Ali Khan, the uncle of Pir Fazl Shah of Jalalpur, had shifted into the Muslim League at the time of the League-Unionist break in 1944. This faction was opposed in Jhelum by a strong Unionist group which continued to control the local boards even after Raja Ghazanfar Ali Khan's shift to the Muslim League. But during the second half of 1945, as the issue became an increasingly religious one and the pirs openly entered the contest, the Unionists found it impossible to hold this faction together. Not only did Pir Fazl Shah begin to campaign openly for the League, but other sajjada nashins also entered the field. 'The Muslim League has started very intense propaganda on religious lines', one Unionist worker wrote to his Party headquarters in December 1945. 'Pir M. Husain Shah, son of Pir Jamaat Ali Shah, is making a tour of the Jhelum Tehsil and issuing *Fatwas* that Muslim League is the only Islamic community and that all the rest are *Kafirs*'.[89] Two weeks later the Unionist organization in the district was desperate. 'I must bring to your notice', the district organizer wrote, 'that 80 per cent population of this district is "Pir-ridden". They are blind followers of Pirs. Pir Jamaat Ali Shah's son's personal contacts and Fatwas have created great obstacles in the way of our workers. . . . No amount of individual propaganda can convert the blind adherents of the Pirs'.[90] Under such pressure the Unionists watched almost helplessly as their factional support dissolved in Jhelum District. In the final election result the Unionists lost all three Assembly seats in the district, and the Muslim League carried over 75 per cent of the rural Muslim vote.

A similar story emerges in other districts as well. In Rawalpindi District, the influence of the family of Pir Fazl Shah was given a large

---

to as the Gilani party and the Qureshi party. See, for example, personal file of Abdus Sattar Shah, Unionist worker, Multan; Unionist Party Papers.

[89] Letter, Bashir Husain, Jhelum District Organizer, to Mian Sultan Ali Ranjha, Zamindara League (Unionist Party) Secretary, 13 December 1945. Unionist Party Papers, file D-44.

[90] Jhelum District Organization Monthly Report for December 1945, 2 January 1946. Unionist Party Papers, file D-44.

measure of credit by the Unionists for tipping the scales against them in Gujar Khan Tehsil,[91] while in Rawalpindi Tehsil the Unionist organizer felt in December 1945 that it was the Muslim League candidate's 'old machinations and election tricks, coupled with the out and out support of the Pir of Golra', which was responsible for the Muslim League's commanding position.[92] In Montgomery district Unionist leaders expected to carry the district until the very eve of the election, when the arrest of a local pir for openly violating the regulations against the use of undue spiritual influence caused a sensation in the district. Analyzing the subsequent defeat of all four Unionist candidates in the district, a local Unionist organizer remarked that the 'prosecution of Chan Pir was the chief cause of the general conflagration which had upset the jangli mind in all four tehsils'.[93] The influence of these pirs was certainly not the only factor in these elections, for in Montgomery district a reaction against the open exploitation of Government pressure by the district Unionist leader and the last minute defections of certain leading families to the Muslim League undermined the Unionist position in the final days before the election. But there is little doubt that the widespread support for Pakistan of the revivalist sajjada nashins in particular played a major role in the popular perception of the Muslim League campaign in the rural areas as a religious movement, which undermined traditional Unionist factional strength in the districts.

Perhaps the most ironic development in this connection was the almost desperate attempt by the Unionists, as the support of the sajjada nashins for the League escalated, to counter this religious element by turning for religious support to the ulama of the Ahrar and the pro-Congress Jamiat-i-Ulama-i-Hind, ulama who had long been their severest critics. The Unionists had made some organized attempts to win support among the sajjada nashins, but among the revivalists they had little success. As the religious nature of the campaign became more pronounced, they found that the only well-organized groups of religious leaders in opposition to the Muslim League were the reformist ulama who backed the Ahrar and the Jamiat-i-Ulama-i-Hind.

[91] Report of Mufti Murid Ahmad, Divisional Organizer, to headquarters, 3 February 1946. Unionist Party Papers, file E-105.

[92] Report of Rawalpindi Divisional Organizer, 19 December 1945. Unionist Party Papers, file F-29.

[93] Letter, Agha Barkat Ali Khan to headquarters, 8 January (February?) 1946. Unionist Party Papers, file D-59.

Unionist workers in the field in late 1945 and early 1946 were desperate for some sort of religious counter to the propaganda of the pirs and asked for religious support from wherever it was available. As the district organizer for Jhelum wrote in December 1945, political propaganda was of no use against religious appeals, and 'Fatwas in rebuttal are the only antidote, now'.[94] Either first-rate religious speakers like Syed Ataullah Shah Bokhari should be sent, he wrote, or else fatwas against the Muslim League should be obtained from Deoband or Bareilly and circulated in the district. The story was much the same in other districts. The last-minute telegram from Multan to Unionist headquarters—'Kindly send Maulvies . . .'—was typical.[95] And the Unionist leaders could only respond with those maulvis who were willing to attack the Muslim League. As the Unionist Secretary responded to the request from Shahpur District, 'I am sending a party of eight Maulvis who have come to me from Jamiat-i-Ulama-i-Hind, Delhi . . .'.[96] This alliance of the Unionists with their old enemies naturally seemed strange, and particularly so to the Muslim League, to whom it seemed to be pure opportunist politics. The pro-Muslim League daily, *Nawai Waqt*, made fun of this effort by the Unionists to get religious support, charging that they were so desperate that they were sending not trained maulvis, but Deoband undergraduates who were paid 30 or 40 rupees a month to do their propaganda, and were calling them Deobandi Fazal Ustads (or graduates).[97] In fact, the best of these religious men, like Syed Ataullah Shah Bokhari, were moving religious orators, but their use by the Unionists only pointed up dramatically the fact that the Muslim League had almost completely taken over the rural religious base on which the Unionist Party itself had once relied.

Summary and Conclusion

In this paper an attempt has been made to delineate the background

[94] Letter, Bashir Husain to Mian Sultan Ali Ranjha, 13 December 1945. Unionist Party Papers, file D-44.

[95] Telegram, Nur Mohammad to Mian Sultan Ali Ranjha, 18 January 1946. Unionist Party Papers, file D-51.

[96] Letter, Mian Sultan Ali Ranjha to Nawab Allah Bakhsh Tiwana, 16 January 1946. Unionist Party Papers, file D-45.

[97] *Nawai Waqt* (Lahore), January 23, 1946.

of the religious support for the Pakistan movement in the Punjab by looking in particular at the connections between the structure of religious leadership and the structure of Muslim politics in twentieth-century Punjab. Only the rough outlines of these connections have been provided, but nevertheless some important patterns have emerged. From the time of the conversion to Islam of much of the western Punjab at the hands of Sufi saints, religious leadership in the rural areas was focused on the hereditary sajjada nashins of the shrines of these saints. The position of these hereditary religious leaders was tied closely into the political organization of the rural areas, and this produced a considerable unity of political and economic interests between the religious and the secular leaders of rural society. Such common interests were strengthened by the British, who, in moulding a system of rural administration in the Punjab, recognized the sajjada nashins of these shrines as part of a single ruling class of hereditary rural leaders. When the Unionist Party emerged in the 1920s as a party of rural interests led by this class of rural leaders, sajjada nashins as a group were strongly disposed, therefore, to support it and to oppose the religious attacks on the Unionists which emanated from primarily urban reformist leaders.

As a result of a widespread revival of Sufi influence in western Punjab in the post-Mughal era, however, many of the sajjada nashins in twentieth-century Punjab had also developed very strong religious commitments to spreading a deeper awareness of Islam. This revival had spread initially through the Chishti order but was later widened by the development of the Ahl-e-Sunnat-o-Jamaat group of ulama who gave religious legitimacy to the continuing emphasis on the forms of religious influence centred on the shrines. The sajjada nashins who drew on this revival tradition were not satisfied with the secular basis of the political system developed by the Unionists, but due to their structural grounding as sajjada nashins in the rural political milieu, they did not generally give the Unionists active opposition. The Unionist Party was thus able, with tacit religious support in the rural areas, to build a strong system of political authority based on rural control, and this propelled the Party to its sweeping victory in the 1937 elections.

With the emergence of the Muslim League, however, which transcended the political question of rural interests versus urban, the revivalist sajjada nashins saw the opportunity to put rural politics on a more solid religious foundation. The concept of Pakistan was seen by them in traditional terms as the establishment of a religious state, ruled by the traditional leaders of rural society but firmly based on the Shariat. In the elections of 1946 the revivalist sajjada nashins provided the vanguard of religious support for Pakistan and played an important role in carrying the Muslim League to triumph over the Unionist Party. The victory was a sweeping religious mandate for Pakistan and marked the most important step on the road to Pakistan's formation.

The important role of the sajjada nashins in the Muslim League's election victory was also an important pointer to the nature of the Pakistan state which was to emerge. Structurally, the revivalist sajjada nashins were themselves deeply rooted in rural society and their support for the Muslim League in no way represented a repudiation of the class of landed leaders who had long wielded power in western Punjab under the Unionist banner. The victory for Pakistan represented only a call for a new religious definition of the old rural order, not for a new alignment of political power such as the reformist ulama had called for. The further definition of this system, however, remained to be developed in the new Muslim state.

Chapter Ten

The Growth of the Muslim League in the Punjab, 1937–46*

IAN A. TALBOT

> The hold which the idea of Pakistan rapidly gained over the imagination of the Muslim masses and the phenomenal growth of the Muslim League in popularity and power have puzzled many observers. In giving its allegiance to the Pakistan movement the Muslim community was not merely seeking to escape the domination of the Hindu. What filled the masses with the urge for action was the desire to recreate a truly Islamic society in which the justice, the democratic equality, the freedom from want and the devotion to social welfare that had characterized the earliest Muslim community should again prevail. It was the appeal of this idea which transformed the Muslim League from a body representing the upper classes of Muslims into a mass organization.
>
> Chaudhri Muhammad Ali, *The Emergence of Pakistan* (London 1967), pp. 40, 41

> The extent to which the Muslim League will be able to exploit the influences of families and clans in the service of its main election slogan in the individual constituencies will determine not only the future course of politics in this province, but also to a large extent the future of India.
>
> The Editor, *Eastern Times* (Lahore), 6 September 1945

On 15 August 1947 the British Raj in India drew to its close. The

* *Journal of Commonwealth and Comaparative Politics*, 13, 1 March 1982.

British, who had come to India as unifiers, divided and quit. The new nation state of Pakistan emerged to face an uncertain future. Even on Independence Day reports of communal massacres were received from the Punjab. They were the prelude to three months of communal violence, the terror which even to this day embitters relations between the two countries. How had the 'Great Divide' between Britain, India, and Pakistan come about? Why had partition arrived hand-in-hand with independence?

This question has frequently been asked during the past thirty years. The two explanations which still have the widest currency, however, are little more than elevations to the level of historiography of the polemic of the leading protagonists in the pre-independence struggle. Most Pakistani historians still explain Muslim separatism in terms of the two-nation theory which was the Muslim League's creed in the 1940s, while Indian historians claim that it was the result of the deliberate British policy of Divide and Rule, an argument which was first raised by Jawaharlal Nehru in the 1930s. 'Perhaps a dominant or decisive cause of Pakistan', K.B. Sayeed, one of the main exponents of the two-nation theory, has declared, 'is that there has never taken place a confluence of the two civilizations in India—the Hindu and the Muslim. They may have meandered towards each other here and there, but on the whole the two have flowed their separate courses—sometimes parallel and sometimes contrary to one another'.[1] A. Mehta and A. Patwardhan's work, *The Communal Triangle in India*,[2] is the classic exposition of the Divide and Rule theory. They, along with other Indian nationalist historians, point in particular to the British granting of separate electorates and communal representation in the legislatures as an intentional policy to create intercommunal political conflict and to prevent the growth of a national spirit. American and British scholars have recently advanced their own theories concerning the genesis of Pakistan. The American approach emphasizes the religious, cultural, and social changes brought about by the modernizing impact of British rule and asks how these encouraged separatism. British historians[3] have placed more emphasis on the role of govern-

[1] K.B. Sayeed, *Pakistan: The Formative Phase 1857–1948* (London, 1968), p. 12.

[2] A. Mehta and A. Patwardhan, *The Communal Triangle in India* (Allahabad, 1941).

[3] See for example D.J.H. Page, 'Prelude to Partition: All-India Moslem Politics, 1920–32' (unpublished D Phil thesis, Oxford University, 1974); and

ment and have examined the ways in which the administrative framework of the Raj encouraged Muslims to adopt a separatist platform in Indian politics.

Despite their different viewpoints all these theories have tended either to concentrate on the all-India struggle between the Muslim League and the Congress in the pre-partition period, or to turn their interest to the Muslim cultural heartland of the UP where the League gained its earliest foothold and where the demand for Pakistan was strongest. Little has been written about the Muslim majority areas, yet they held the key to the successful creation of Pakistan. Of all the major centres of Muslim population of the Punjab was the most important to the Pakistan scheme because of its strategic geographical position, its large Muslim majority, and its agricultural wealth. It formed the heartland of a future Pakistan state. Jinnah indeed called the Punjab the 'Cornerstone of Pakistan'. If the Punjabi Muslims had not supported the League's separatist demands Pakistan could never have come into existence. Yet little has been written about the League's development in the Punjab by historians of Muslim separatism.[4] No adequate explanation has yet been given for the League's spectacular advance during the decade which preceded partition. In the 1937 Punjab elections it had fared disastrously, putting forward a mere seven candidates for the eighty-six Muslim seats, only two of whom succeeded against the landlord Unionist Party. Less than a decade later, however, the League gained its revenge when it captured seventy-five of the Muslim seats in the 1946 provincial elections.

Penderal Moon, an ex-ICS man in the Punjab, simply attributes the League's rise to power to the alluring and irresistible appeal of the Pakistan cry to the Muslim masses.[5] Peter Hardy's suggestion that the Muslim League gained its electoral success in the Punjab by making an appeal over the heads of the professional politicians[6] raises more questions than it solves. For instance, how did the League by-pass the traditional holders of power within the province? And how can this explanation be reconciled with the fact that the majority of

F.C.R. Robinson, *Separatism among Indian Muslims: The Politics of the United Provinces' Muslims 1860–1923* (Cambridge, 1974).

[4] Virtually the only detailed account of the Muslim League's development in the Punjab is in S.M. Ikram, *Modern Muslim India and the Birth of Pakistan* (Lahore, 1977).

[5] P. Moon, *Divide and Quit* (London, 1961), p. 43.

[6] P. Hardy, *The Muslims of British India* (Cambridge, 1972), p. 238.

the League's candidates in 1946 were experienced politicians who had only very recently transferred their allegiance from its main rival, the Unionist Party? Pakistani historians have explained the League's success in the Punjab, as elsewhere in the subcontinent, solely in terms of the two-nation theory, but why was its electoral support weakest in those areas of the province where the Muslims formed an absolute majority of the population and where, according to the theory, their separate development and national identity and awareness ought to have been most clearly defined? Most recently of all, Paul Brass has developed a model for understanding Muslim separatism in north India.[7] He argues that the League grew there because there was both an elite which chose to manipulate separatist symbols in order to serve its own power interests and a socially mobilized community which responded to the sense of communal identification communicated to it. This argument, whether or not it works in the UP, which seems doubtful, fails to explain the League's success in the very different conditions of the Punjab.

The Muslim League's development in the Punjab also raises a number of wider questions concerning political mobilization in 'traditional' societies. These concern the relative importance of ideas and interests in moving peasant voters and the question whether levels of social mobilization are relevant to successful political mobilization in predominantly peasant societies. Was the League's success the result, as most existing theories of peasant political mobilization would have us believe,[8] of its ability to organize and appeal to a rapidly modernizing population whose political as well as social horizons had begun

[7] P. Brass, *Language, Religion and Politics in North India* (Cambridge, 1974), pp. 178ff.

[8] Most existing theories of peasant political activity contain the idea that social mobilization is a prerequisite for political mobilization. That is, it is only when peasants have greater access to the outside world as a result of increased education, improved communications, and extended contact with the national market that their political horizons also expand beyond the village. Lerner suggests that it is contact with a 'superior' culture which drives the peasants into external social and political activity. We have already referred to Brass's theory. Even Migdal, who maintains that the breakdown of peasant social structures rather than culture contact has led to increased peasant political activity, implies that social mobilization must precede large-scale peasant political mobilization. D. Lerner, *The Passing of Traditional Society* (Glencoe Illinois, 1958); J.S. Midgal, *Peasants, Politics and Revolution: Pressures towards Political Change in the Third World* (Princeton, 1974).

to expand beyond the mud walls of the villages, or because it had effectively utilized the 'traditional' social and religious networks to mobilize support? Did it generate support in the countryside merely by raising ideological religious appeals, or did it also concern itself with the peasants' immediate material interests?

This article sets out to answer at least some of the questions raised by the League's growth in the Punjab during the decade which preceded partition. It attempts to explain how League politics reached down and embraced the rural voters who held the key to the success of its demand for Pakistan.

Before examining the League's efforts from 1937 onwards to win support in the Punjab countryside, we shall first turn to the province's political system during the period of dyarchy which preceded this. Until the Montagu-Chelmsford Reforms were introduced in 1919, the Punjab had lagged behind other provinces in its constitutional development.[9] The Reforms extended the franchise and transferred control of certain 'nation-building' subjects of administration, such as local self-government and education, to Ministers responsible to the provincial Legislative Council. Until its creation political activity in the Punjab had been localized. Only occasionally, usually in the face of a common enemy, had the many small vertical political factions acted in a wider political framework than that of the locality. In West Punjab the local factions were led by the large landlords and the rural religious elite, the Sufi *pirs*, who had been drawn into politics despite the earlier opposition of such Sufi orders as the Chishtis to all political entanglements. In East Punjab, where there were far fewer large estates, leaders of the dominant kinship groups (*biraderis*) rather than landlords or pirs headed the local factions. Even after the creation of the Legislative Council, factionalism underpinned the Punjab's political activity. The Unionist Party functioned more as a grand coalition of the leading factions than as a modern political party. The landlords and pirs acted as brokers between the village communities and the provincial political system. At election time they mobilized their kinsmen, disciples, and tenants to vote for the Unionist Party in return for its promise of access to government patronage. The kinship group, the Sufi religious network, and the relationship between the landlord patron and his tenant clients formed the three traditional channels for mobilizing political support in the Punjab countryside. We shall ask for each what lay

[9] A. Husain, *Fazl-i-Husain: A Political Biography* (London, 1946), pp. 75ff.

behind the strength of their political influence and was this being weakened during the period of British Rule.

The kinship group (biraderi) was the most important unit in the Muslim social structure. Its membership hinged entirely on the tracing of descent through the paternal line. Children always belonged to their father's biraderi and most marriages took place within it. The ideal marriage was that of the cross-cousin type—marriage to a father's brother's daughter. Indeed, an individual's status was judged on his ability to give his daughters in marriage only to members of his own biraderi. Control of marriage was a major factor in maintaining biraderi cohesion, marriage transactions as a result being strictly regulated by a kinship group's ruling council (*panchayat*). The cohesion of the biraderis which gave them their political influence was the direct result of the coercive powers wielded by these 'ruling councils'. They took on a wide range of welfare and 'professional' functions and operated among kinship groups which continued to pursue traditional occupations on lines similar to the medieval guilds in Europe.[10] There was a tendency for the specialization of 'council' functions. One panchayat, for example, operated as the kinship groups' spokesman with government and ensured political solidarity, while another, usually composed of older members, concerned itself with adjudication in such 'internal' matters as inheritance disputes. Whether they were elected or hereditary, the 'ruling councils' wielded considerable coercive powers. The threat to expel a household from a biraderi could be likened in its severity in some respects to that of excommunication in the medieval church. It would leave the household defenceless in an often hostile world and would make future marriage transactions, which were so important, difficult or indeed impossible. Defiance and violation of a kinship group's norms was therefore a rare occurrence.

When the British devolved power to popularly elected bodies from the 1880s onwards, the kinship group became an important vote-bank. Its 'ruling council' traded its votes in return for patronage. Political solidarity was encouraged when kinship group members saw the benefits which accrued from this exchange system. Improvements in communications made possible greater kinship solidarity. The leading biraderis established a network of organizations throughout the province and during the 1920s and 1930s formed their own 'tribal' news-

[10] M.K.A. Siddiqui, 'Cast among the Muslims of Calcutta' in I. Ahmad (ed.), *Caste and Social Stratification among the Muslims* (Delhi, 1973), p. 148.

papers, the leading example of which was the *Jat Gazette*. These newspapers helped reinforce kinship solidarity and ensured that they spoke with one voice in politics.

Not all kinship groups, of course, achieved an ideal degree of cohesion and solidarity. The strongest biraderis within the Punjab always existed among the peasant proprietors. In the constant struggle to maintain their economic independence they needed the strength which kinship solidarity brought. Their kinship group organization was, as a result, tightly disciplined and took the form of successive tiers of 'ruling councils' which linked village 'councils' with regional and even provincial confederations of panchayats. Among landlords, however, personal and political rivalries often precluded kinship solidarity. The households of their kinsmen tended to be dispersed, which weakened their power. Biraderi solidarity was not as important to the large landlords as it was to the peasant proprietors. Their leadership of rural society rested not on the strength of their kinship ties but on their economic power. This made their tenants, the landless labourers, and the village menials dependent on them for survival. Within these groups vertical ties of economic dependency remained stronger than their loyalty to their fellow kinship group members. Landlords had taken over the role of the 'council' in settling disputes amongst them.

Among the voters of the east Punjab and Canal Colony districts in which strong groups of peasant proprietors existed, the kinship group played a vital role in mobilizing political support. The Unionist Party was careful in the 1937 elections to select as its candidates in these areas the council leaders of the dominant kinship groups. The League was unable to match it in this policy as it commanded little support among the rural population. Within the Lyallpur Canal Colony constituency, for example, the largest numbers of voters were members of the Arain biraderi; the Unionist Party therefore chose as its candidate Mian Nurullah, who was President of the provincial Arain Council. His ability to call on the kinship network for political support enabled him comfortably to win the seat. In a similar way the Unionist Party successfully selected the Secretary of the Punjab Rajput Council as its candidate for the Tarn Taran constituency in which the Rajput kinship group was dominant. In the eastern Rohtak district of the province the Unionist Party swept the board in both the rural Muslim and Hindu seats because it had captured the leading Jat biraderi's support.

In the western areas of the province where peasant owner-cultivators were far fewer in number,[11] the ties of economic dependency between a tenant and his landlord were more important than kinship loyalty in deciding voting. The landlords' power in the social structure of these areas rested on their ability to control such scarce resources as land, labour, credit, and in some areas water. It was reinforced still further by the facts that there was no strong village community to stand between the landlord and his individual tenants and that most landlords continued to live in their home districts despite the attractions of urban life. A landlord who lived on his estate was not only able to exercise his economic influence more closely but also to emphasize his social dominance through the adjudication of biraderi disputes[12] and the working of the *jajmani*[13] relationship. Punjabi landlords maintained close links with their estates in part because the region was unsettled, but in the main because social status was derived from the ownership of land.[14] Land was the major source of an individual's prestige (*izzat*).

Even though the Muslim landlords of west Punjab lived on their estates, the existence of a strong village community could still have diffused their power. In such areas of South East Asia as Java where cohesive village structures have existed, the vertical ties of dependence between a landlord and his clients have significantly been weakened. The village was able to form a key unit for peasant solidarity and defence and thus lessened the need for the peasants to turn to landlords in search of the guarantees of subsistence and security which lie at the heart of the patron–client relationship.[15] The 'villages' which were

[11] The proportion of the total cultivated area farmed by tenants rose from 43 per cent in the eastern Ambala district of the province to nearly 75 per cent in the western Multan district.

[12] Z. Bhatty, 'Status and Power in a Muslim Dominated Village of Uttar Pradesh' in Ahmad, *Caste and Social Stratification*, p. 96.

[13] Landlords gave the village menials a share of the crop in exchange for labour services. They were, for example, expected to attend and perform 'caste' services at the time of ceremonial occasions in the landlord's household. The jajmani relationship was not, however, a modern type of contract but was a permanent and hereditary social relationship.

[14] Punjabis still refer to their land today as their *patlaj*, a word which has a meaning similar to izzat, that of power, honour, and respect.

[15] J.C. Scott, 'The Erosion of Patron-Client Bonds and Social Change in Rural South East Asia', *Journal of Asian Studies*, 32 (1972), pp. 8ff and 28.

recorded in the British Land Revenue Records for such areas of west Punjab as Jhang and Shahpur were, however, merely administrative creations made for the sake of convenience and simplicity. The population of these areas continued to live as they had always done, scattered around wells, and did not form a homogeneous proprietory body.[16] Thus no communal barrier existed to protect the tenant from his landlord's power. The landlord was indeed the 'lord of the land'. The head of the Kot Gheba estate in the Attock District even kept his own retinue of mounted followers, all dressed in scarlet tunics, whom he had instructed in the use of 'sword and lance'.[17] He was complete lord and master of his land: 'his tenants feared him, admired him and even liked him, whilst they certainly always obeyed him'.[18] Throughout this part of the province 'the cardinal principle of the strong owner [was] that the tenant is a serf, without rights or privileges, but when this has once been admitted the tenant is not badly treated'.[19] The threat of eviction always hung over the tenants and ensured their loyalty to their landlord's faction.

British rule reinforced the economic importance of the large landlords and pirs. They were better able to take advantage of the commercialization of agriculture than were the poorer peasants.[20] The development of irrigation of south-west Punjab consolidated the power of such large tribal chieftains as the Tiwanas and the Daultanas and converted them into a powerful landowning class. The peasants' reliance on the landlords for credit and employment increased because of the agricultural revolution brought by the British, as it has indeed as a result of the recent Green Revolution in India and Pakistan.[21] Peasants needed credit more than ever before to pay the regular British Land Revenue taxes which were levied in cash rather than kind. Rising prices for essential commodities and foodstuffs and fluctuations in the value of cash-crop production also increased the demand for credit

16 *Jhang District Gazeteer* (Lahore, 1930), p. 133.

17 *Rawalpindi District Gazeteer* (Lahore, 1895), p. 139.

18 *Attock District Gazeteer* (Lahore, 1909), p. 229.

19 Ibid.

20 There was, for example, much less risk involved for them in switching to cash-crop production. Moreover, they possessed the surplus resources to invest in the new irrigation facilities provided by the British.

21 F.R. Frankel, *India's Green Revolution: Economic Gains and Political Costs* (Princeton, 1971), pp. 8ff. S. Ahmad, 'Peasant Classes in Pakistan' in K. Gough and P. Sharma (eds), *Imperialism and Revolution in South Asia* (New York, 1973), p. 217.

relief. Loss of access to uncleared land and common pasturage, together with rapid population growth which led to increased fragmentation of holdings, meant that the peasants needed extra sources of employment to survive. By 1939 it was estimated that 90 per cent of all landowners possessed uneconomic holdings and would thus need to turn to the landlords for employment.

The peasants' growing economic dependence on their landlord patrons increased their local political power. Few peasants dared risk eviction or loss of employment by being disloyal to their patron's faction. Moreover, the landlords' improved economic position enabled them if necessary to buy votes and bribe local election officials on a far wider scale than before. Another new source of landlord political power during British rule was the rural elite's close collaboration with a government determined to intervene in the countryside and set the pace of economic development. The landlords in Mughal and Sikh times had always needed the imprimatur of the State to reinforce their local authority and prestige but their ability to influence a central authority, which soon became the major source of credit, employment, and business activity within the province, gave them a source of strength which had not previously existed. British rule also provided the landlords with opportunities to operate on a wider economic and political scale than ever before. Their power became less localized as from the 1880s onwards they acquired land and property outside their home districts, mainly in the Canal Colonies but also in some of the towns. Province-wide marriage contacts developed between families as a common landlord interest began to emerge.[22] These assumed considerable political importance as they aided the development of the Unionist Party within the Punjab.

British policy had been geared to encouraging a loyalist landlord interest in politics from the 1840s onwards. Patronage in the form of grants of land in the Canal Colonies, appointments in the machinery of local government, and honorary ranks and titles were liberally distributed to the landlords and pirs in order to gain their support. The British in fact believed that every class in the Punjab had the potential to be transformed into loyal landholders. They even made grants of land in the Canal Colonies to college students, a policy which did not

[22] E. Hodges, 'The Faqir, the Industrialist and the Pirs: Debt, Status and Marriage among Four Punjabi Muslim Families' (unpublished paper presented to the seminar on Intermediate Political Linkages, Berkeley, March 1978), p. 7.

meet with particular success.[23] The British linked the interests of the Muslim landlords of West Punjab with those of the Sikh landlords of the central tract and the Muslim and Hindu peasant proprietors of the eastern regions of the province by the 1901 Alienation of Land Act. This measure halted the expropriation of the Punjab's farmers by the urban Hindu moneylenders—a process which had increasingly accompanied the commercialization of the province's agriculture. For the purpose of the Act, the population was divided into non-agriculturalist tribes. The former were forbidden to acquire land permanently in the countryside. The British went a stage further in encouraging the creation of an intercommunal agricultural class interest in 1919, when they granted agriculturalists a preferential right of recruitment to government service.[24] The 1919 Montagu-Chelmsford Reforms completed the institutionalization of the division between the province's rural and urban communities. Separate electorates were created for the towns and the countryside, only members of the statutory agricultural tribes being allowed to stand as candidates for the rural seats. The towns were allocated just four of the thirty-four Muslim elected seats in the Legislative Council.[25] The British in this way created the framework in which an intercommunal landlord party could successfully operate. The difficult task still remained of organizing the independent rural members into a political party. This was achieved in 1923 with the creation of the Punjab Unionist Party, thanks largely to the efforts of two men, Chaudhri Chhotu Ram and Mian Fazl-i-Husain. The Unionist Party's victory in the 1937 provincial election was thus the logical conclusion of over eighty years of British policy in the Punjab.

The list of successful unionist candidates contained most of the province's leading landlords and pirs. The latter had been particularly important in the Unionist Party's success as they controlled the most effective of all the traditional channels for mobilizing political support—the Sufi religious networks based on the shrine and the relationship between a pir and his disciple (the *piri-mureedi* relationship). They represented an authentic and living Muslim tradition which percolated down to the rural population which was excluded from the Urdu cultural world of the towns. The pirs' popular religious influence

[23] M. Gopal, *Sir Chhotu Ram: A Political Biography* (New Delhi, 1977), p. 19

[24] R.N. Nath, 'Punjab Agrarian Laws and their Economic and Constitutional Bearings', 65 *The Modern Review* (1939), p. 28.

[25] Husain, *Fazl-i-Husain*, p. 152.

sprang from the belief that they had inherited charisma (*baraka*) from their ancestors, the Sufi saints who from the eleventh century onwards had played a major role in the Punjab's conversion to Islam. The shrines (*dargarhs*) at which the pirs were centred acted as a link between the peasants and the wider Islamic world, serving, in Clifford Geertz's words as tiny 'theatre-states' in which was displayed a source of moral authority strikingly different from that of the surrounding areas.[26] Although the religious life centred on the shrine owed little to the classical Islam of the great tradition, it gave its rural adherents a strong sense of Muslim identity. Sufism was embedded in the life of the countryside. Although the smallest villages had their own mosque, peasant religious life was centred on the pir and the shrine rather than the *alim* and the mosque.

During the course of a year multitudes of people visited the shrines of leading pirs to seek spiritual or, more frequently, material blessing. A great trade in amulets was carried on. Over the years shrines became associated with particular miraculous powers. A shrine in the Shahpur district for example was famous for curing toothache! One in Hissar was particularly noted for its power of exorcism, while yet another was resorted to by sufferers from dog bites. Shrines became major centres of economic importance, both as employers and as consumers of local produce. Many of the larger shrines provided outdoor relief for their surrounding areas by opening dispensaries for the sick and soup kitchens (*langar-khanas*). Food was always distributed at shrines during the *Urs* celebrations, which were held on the anniversary of their saint's death when his soul was believed to have entered into union with God.

As the shrines' wealth increased, the outlook of their pirs and custodians (*sajjada-nashins*) became similar to that of other landowners. The shrines tended to support the *status quo* whether it was Muslim, Sikh, or, later, British. This was encouraged by the large amounts of land which governments from the time of the Delhi Sultanate down to the British to the pirs to ensure their loyalty. The requirement for becoming a shrine's custodian shifted from spiritual merit to political loyalty to the central authority.[27] Control of the

[26] The Sufi shrine's source of moral authority was external. Completely absent from its ritual functionings was the Indic principle of *karma*, of a self-regulating system of reward and retribution.

[27] R. Eaton, *Sufis of Bijapur 1300–1700: Social Roles of Sufism in Medieval India* (Princeton, 1978), pp. 217 and 241.

shrines enabled the state to deepen the roots of its authority in the countryside. For their part the pirs benefited from government patronage which came their way in the form of honours and land had their own considerable local authority enhanced by their collaboration with the government.

Over a period of time the leading shrines acquired large amounts of land as the state's grants of land were in addition to the considerable *waqf* endowments which they received from individuals. The descendants of Baba Farid, the Punjab's leading Sufi saint, possessed by the twentieth century a tenth of all the land in the Pakpattan *tehsil* in which the shrine was situated, some 43,000 acres in all.[28] Part of this land had come to them as state gifts during the period of Sikh rule.[29] The Shah Jiwana Bukhari Syed estate in Jhang was nearly 10,000 acres in extent,[30] while the pirs of Jahanian Shah owned nearly 7,000 acres.[31]

Hand in hand with the transformation of the Punjab's pirs into important landowners went a change in the piri-mureedi relationship which was to have important political consequences. An aspirant (*murid*) of a pir took an oath of obedience (*bayat*) to him. He thus entered into the pir-mureedi relationship with him. The pir thereafter acted as his disciple's spiritual guide and mediated between him and God; at the same time he was also the agent for bringing about his material desires through the exercise of his 'charisma'. The disciple in return was expected to be absolutely obedient to his pir. The relationship between a pir and his disciple was likened to that between the Prophet and his companions.[32] The relationship between a pir and his disciples was formalized and ongoing.[33] It created a focus of loyalty capable of transcending, although it could also reinforce, kinship ties. During Sufism's early period the immense political potential of the

[28] M.M.H. Nun, *Assessment Report of the Pakpattan Tehsil of the Montgomery District* (Lahore, 1921), p. 18. Punjab Proceedings P 11372 April 1922, part A, India Office Records (hereafter IOR).

[29] T.G. Singh, *Baba Sheikh Farid* (Delhi, 1974), p. 43.

[30] *Report on Administration of Estates Under the Charge of the Court of Wards for the Year ending 30 September 1921* (Lahore, 1922), statement no. I L 5 VI (3), Departmental Annual Reports, IOR.

[31] G.L. Chopra, *Chiefs and Families of Note in the Punjab*, vol. 2 (Lahore, 1940), p. 242.

[32] M. Milson (trans), *Kitab Adab al-Muridin of Abu al-Najib al-Suhrawardi. A Sufi Rule for Novices* (Cambridge Mass., 1978), p. 46.

[33] Pirs kept registers of their murids and frequently visited them to bestow their blessings in return for gifts.

piri-mureedi relationship was unfulfilled because it was not sufficiently widespread. The first Sufis in the Punjab initiated only a small number of disciples, who thereafter lived with them at their 'hospices' (*khanqahs*) and studied and undertook spiritual disciplines at their discretion. But by the twentieth century this had changed. Shrines had proliferated and the piri-mureedi relationship had lost its original elitism. Almost every Muslim in the Punjab had by this time his own pir. Indeed, to be without a pir was a cause for reproach. Pirs possessed large numbers of disciples. Pir Fazal Shah of Jalalpur in the Jhelum district alone claimed to have 200,000 murids. Despite its expansion the piri-mureedi relationship retained its former discipline and cohesion as its underpinning remained the absolute obedience enjoined upon a disciple to his pir. The improved communications brought by the British increased the pirs' contact with their disciples. They could visit them more easily during their customary tours and could even dispense their political 'advice' through the columns of the local newspapers. Because they could command support from members of rival kinship groups and because their networks of disciples spread over the length and breadth of the Punjab, pirs played a crucial role in vote gathering when the franchise was extended and politics became provincialized.

The importance which the Unionists attached to their cooperation in the 1937 elections comes out clearly in the words of Mohammed Bashir, the Unionist Party organizer for the Gurdaspur district: 'Villagers, you know, follow these "Pirs" blindly. . . . Take care of the "Pirs". Ask them only to keep silent on the matter of the elections. We don't require their help but [that] they should not oppose us.'[34] In fact a number of pirs played a leading role in the elections as candidates and propagandists for the Unionist Party. The pirs of Shergarh and Shah Jiwana were influential in mobilizing support for the Unionists in the Canal Colony districts. The rival Gilani and Qureshi pir families of Multan carved up the Multan and Shujabad constituencies between them. Fourteen of the leading pirs of the Punjab and its surrounding areas issued an election appeal on the Unionist Party's behalf.[35]

The only response which the Muslim League could make to the

[34] D. Gilmartin, 'Religious Leadership and the Pakistan Movement in the Punjab', *Modern Asian Studies*, 13 (1979), p. 504.

[35] W. Ahmad (ed.), *The Letters of Mian Fazl-i-Husain* (Lahore, 1976), pp. 592–4.

pirs' support for its main rival was to issue an appeal to the Punjabi Muslims exhorting them in the name of Islam to vote for candidates of the Muslim League Parliamentary Board.[36] The fact that it was issued in Urdu, the language of the educated townsman, rather than Punjabi revealed the limited extent of the League's appeal to the rural population at that time. The composition of the League's touring propaganda committee further highlighted the difficulties under which it laboured attempting to mobilize rural support. There was only one landlord amongst its fifteen members, no fewer than seven of whom were lawyers or urban politician from Lahore.[37] The Punjab League's influence in the countryside was so weak that it encountered great difficulty in finding candidates who were willing to oppose the Unionists. A derisory eight candidates finally fought under its banner.

The Unionist Party's victory in the 1937 elections created a major problem for the Muslim League. It had to undermine the Unionists' entrenched position if Jinnah's claim that it was the sole representative of Indian Muslims was not to sound embarrassingly hollow and his bargaining position in All-India politics be seriously weakened. This became even more imperative after the Lahore Resolution was passed in 1940, as the Punjab formed the heartland of a future Pakistan state. In order to challenge the Unionist Party's position the League had somehow to extend its influence from the towns into the villages. Its efforts to do so can be divided into three distinct phases. In the first, which began soon after the elections and was brought to an abrupt halt by the pact between Sikander the Unionist Premier and Jinnah in October 1937,[38] the League attempted to build a mass organizational base in the countryside. In the second, which lasted from 1937 until the collapse of the Jinnah-Khizr talks in April 1944, the League was effectively under Unionist control and had to rely on the efforts of the Punjab Muslim Students Federation and on urban religious leaders to popularize its demand for Pakistan amongst the rural voters. Towards the end of this period it also tried to win support by exploiting the existence of wartime discontent. The final phase, which really began

36 M.R. Afzal, *Malik Barkat Ali: His Life and Writings* (Lahore, 1969), p. 36.
37 *Civil and Military Gazette* (Lahore), 17 October 1936.
38 This pact, which was agreed at the October 1937 Lucknow Muslim League session, was surrounded by controversy from its inception. Whatever the interpretation of its signatories, its effect was to seal off the Punjab countryside from the Muslim League's influence as the control of the provincial League organization fell into Unionist hands.

in earnest only after the collapse of the Simla Conference in August 1945, saw an intensification of the process of exploiting the wartime economic dislocation. At the same time the League made a major effort to win over the support of the leading landlords and pirs. It was the success of this strategy which enabled the League to triumph in the 1946 Punjab elections. Before turning to this last and most vital period of the League's development in the province, we shall be briefly examine its earlier abortive efforts to expand into the countryside. The nature of its failure is instructive in understanding the process of present political mobilization in Muslim societies.

The belief that the peasants' commitment to Islam was stronger than their loyalty to their landlords or to their kinship group lay at the heart of the Punjab Muslim League's political strategy throughout the period 1937–45. The rural elite which remained loyal to the Unionist Party could, the League leaders believed, be by-passed by a direct appeal to the peasant masses. Why did this policy achieve such limited success? The answer lies in the fact that, firstly, the Punjab League's religious appeals were being made through the wrong channels and, secondly, that even when they were made through the right ones peasants are not readily moved by such appeals alone. They must be accompanied by efforts to solve their immediate social and economic problems in order to overcome their suspicion of outsiders. The League was able to achieve its breakthrough only when it had won over the support of the rural elite which controlled the traditional networks for mobilizing political support and when it had addressed itself to the peasants' wartime grievances. At first, however, it attempted to win support merely by unfurling the green flag of Islam.

Even before the Pakistan Resolution was passed in 1940, the Muslim League had resolved to use festivals such as Id 'to promote political unity and social solidarity amongst the Muslims of India'.[39] Mosques, because of their importance as centres of Muslim life, were similarly used to spread League propaganda. A grandiose proposal was once placed before the All-India Muslim League Working Committee to use 5,000 mosques in the Pakistan areas as League missionary sub-centres.[40] Propagandists were advised when they visited a village to join the prayers at the local mosque and gain its *imam's*

[39] Muslim League Council Meetings, vol. 253, pt. 2, p. 60. Freedom Movement Archives, Karachi University (hereafter FMA).

[40] Muslim League Working Committee Meetings 1943–7, vol. 142, p. 23, FMA.

permission to hold a meeting there. League meetings were held regularly in mosques, especially after the Friday prayers. Students who played an important part in League propaganda work not only in the Punjab but throughout India had in particular been trained to appeal to the voters along religious lines.[41] Students from the Punjab Muslim Students Federation were advised to follow the Prophet's example in all things during their visits to the villages. They were to join in the prayers at the mosque or lead them like 'Holy Warriors'. Their speeches were to be filled with emotional appeal and always to commence with a text from the Quran, invoking God's protection and praising His wisdom.[42] Because of its importance in north Indian society, poetry, particularly that of Iqbal, was to be declaimed at such meetings.[43]

When the Jinnah-Sikander Pact finally collapsed in April 1944, the Muslim League stepped up its plans to saturate the villages with propaganda. Provincial League leaders such as Mian Mumtaz Daultana continued, however, to ignore the need for winning over the rural elite's support. 'It is now becoming clear', wrote the League's General Secretary in July 1944, 'that in view of the determined government opposition our basic strength must come not from the landlords or the Zaildar-Lambardar class but from the masses of the Muslim people'.[44] During June and July large League conferences were held at Montgomery, Lyallpur, Sheikhupura, Sargodha, Jhang, Sialkot, and Rawalpindi.[45] For the first time ever primary League branches were established in such rural areas as Sargodha and Mianwali. In July alone it was reported that 7,000 members had been enrolled in these two areas.[46] Throughout most of the province, however, the League's

[41] The students who toured the Punjab during December 1945 from the Aligarh Muslim University had attended the League Worker's Training Camp to hear lectures on such topics as the Muslim League in the light of Islam, Islamic history, and the religious background to Pakistan.

[42] Translation of a pamphlet issued by the election board of the Punjab Muslim Students Federation, FMA.

[43] The Unionist Party employed *Mirasis* to work on its behalf during the elections. *Eastern Times* (Lahore), 30 December 1945.

[44] Report of the Punjab Provincial Muslim League's Work for June and July 1944 submitted to the All-India Muslim League Committee of Action 28 July 1944. Shamsul Hasan Collection, Punjab vol 1, General Correspondence.

[45] Ibid.

[46] Report of the Organizing Secretary, Rawalpindi Division, Muslim League, vol. 162, pt. 7, Punjab Muslim League 1943–4, pp. 74ff, FMA.

propaganda campaign made little impact on the mass of the rural population. 'League attempts to penetrate the villages', the Governor noted in July 1944, 'have been mainly confined to somewhat disjointed tours by peripatetic members of the Muslim Students Federation, the distribution propaganda pamphlets and approaches to village officials. These moves in spite of the Islamic appeal behind them have so far had little effect on the Muslim masses who are concerned with tribal and economic considerations [rather] than with party politics and do not appear to have affected the communal situation adversely'.[47] The Unionists continued to win district board and provincial assembly by-elections throughout 1944. In August, for example, they defeated the League in the Sialkot district board elections;[48] they also retained the Hoshiarpur and Kangra and Jhajjar Legislative Assembly seats. The Unionists' influence in the Dera Ghazi Khan district remained so great that the League was unable to field a rival candidate to Sardar Ghaus Mazari in the by-election which took place in its southern constituency in April 1945.[49] In many of the western districts of the Punjab it was faced with the same problem of having to resolve local factional rivalries which had impeded Mian Fazl-i-Husain's efforts to establish a popular base for the Unionist Party there a decade earlier. In the Gujjar Khan and Rawalpindi districts, factional rivalry was so acute that parallel Muslim Leagues competed against each other.[50] As late as May 1945 the League could still boast of a membership of only 1½ lakhs (150,000) in the Punjab.[51] Its efforts to use Islam as a mass mobilizer had made little impact because its religious appeals were mediated by outsiders who lacked personal influence in the villages and because they were based on sources of Muslim authority, the Quran, the alim, and the mosque, which were unimportant to the illiterate 'pir-ridden' villagers.

It became clear to the League's leaders that a different approach would have to be adopted if the Punjab was to be won over to support

[47] Punjab *Fortnightly Report* (hereafter FR) for the first half of July 1944. L/P&J/5/247. IOR.

[48] Punjab FR 23 August 1944 L/P&J/5/247. IOR.

[49] This by-election took place as a result of the death of Khan Bahadur Muhammad Hasan Khan Gurmani. The Muslim League was unable to find anyone to oppose Sardar Ghaus Bakhsh, a leading member of the Mazari Baloch tribe which maintained its wild, nomadic way of life even into the twentieth century.

[50] *Nawa-e-Waqt* (Lahore), 30 April 1945.

[51] *Eastern Times* (Lahore), 23 May 1945.

the Pakistan scheme. Although it contradicted the ideology of the two-nation theory, an appeal must be made to the 'tribal' loyalties of the Punjabi Muslims. The support of the traditional brokers, the landlords and pirs, was also needed. In addition an appeal would have to be made to the peasants' economic interests if they were to risk opposing the dominant Unionist Party. The League did not at first adopt all these new strategies. It was not until late in 1944 that it switched its attention from organizing local branches to winning over elite support. But it did make a start early that year in appealing to the rural population by exploiting the growing wartime discontent.

Whereas earlier in the war the countryside had escaped the worst effects of economic dislocation, by 1944 it suffered as much as the towns. Until 1944 high prices for wheat and other agricultural produce had compensated the province's farmers for inflation and shortages of consumer goods. But that autumn a substantial and sustained fall in agricultural prices set in.[52] Grain prices staged a recovery in the first few months of 1945, but as the year progressed the farmers became increasingly reluctant to market their goods. Political insecurity, the unfavourable prospects for the 1946 *rabi* crop, and the enticement of the black market all contributed to this. By December 1945, wheat, maize, and gram had virtually disappeared from the open market.[53] Many of the towns in the province, even in the Canal Colony areas, began to experience a wheat famine. The large landlords of the west Punjab still brought at least part of their grain to the market but virtually none came from the peasant proprietors of the east Punjab. The Unionist Government was forced to requisition grain from the villages there. This aroused great opposition: disturbances broke out as a result in the Ludhiana, Hoshiarpur, and Ferozepore districts right in the middle of the 1946 elections.[54]

Despite this favourable background, it is unlikely that the League would have adopted on a large scale the policy of exploiting wartime discontent if it had not been for the large number of communists who were entering its ranks at this time.[55] They were already skilled in this

[52] Punjab FR, 20 September 1944. L/P&J/5/247. IOR.

[53] Punjab Board of Economic Inquiry no. 90. *Annual Review of Economic Conditions in the Punjab 1945–6* (Lahore), pp. 6ff.

[54] Punjab FR, second half of February 1946. L/P&J/5/249. IOR.

[55] The extent of the communists' influence in the Punjab Muslim League was brought home in July 1944 when a leading communist, Daniel Latifi, became its Office Secretary.

type of propaganda, having used it successfully in the villages of the central Punjab during the winter of 1943.[56] The Punjab League attempted to crystallize peasant opposition to rationing and requisitioning of grain supplies which had been forced on the Unionist Party by the Central Food Department.[57] It also expressed their increasing dissatisfaction with the Unionist Party's failure to control inflation and to curb the profiteering activities of the Hindu and Sikh business community. Most important of all, however, the Muslim League linked the solution of the peasants' economic and social problems with the successful establishment of a Pakistan state. Members of the Punjab Muslim Students Federation were directed when they visited a village to 'find out its social problems and difficulties to tell them [the villagers] that the main cause of their problems was the Unionists [and] give them the solution—Pakistan'.[58] League propagandists took medical supplies, which had become increasingly difficult to obtain during the war with them to the villages.[59] They also distributed cloth there and endeavoured to obtain increased ration allowances for the peasants.[60] This policy was in marked contrast to that of the Unionist Party, which appeared increasingly out of touch with the needs of the rural population.

The strategy for exploiting wartime discontent became even more popular from the summer of 1945 onwards, when large numbers of demobilized soldiers began to return to the province only to face massive unemployment.[61] The League gained great popularity in the major recruiting areas of Rawalpindi and Jhelum by providing work for the ex-servicemen in its organization and by showing concern for

[56] Punjab FR, second half of October 1943 and first half of November 1943. L/P&J/5/246. IOR.

[57] The Jat minister, Chhotu Ram, was an outspoken critic of the requisitioning of foodgrains and the placing of a price ceiling on them. In October 1944 a deputation from the Punjab led by the Sikh Minister Baldev Singh unsuccessfully attempted to get the Central Food Department to lift its ban on the movement of grain between the Punjab and the UP.

[58] See note 42.

[59] *Eastern Times* (Lahore), 28 December 1945.

[60] Ibid., 28 August 1945.

[61] The speedy end of the war in Asia had taken the Unionist Government by surprise so that its plans to ease the problem of demobilization by resettling ex-servicemen on land in the Canal Colonies were not completed. Even by the end of 1946 less than 20 per cent of the demobilized soldiers registered with employment exchanges had been found work.Punjab FR, 14 December 1946. L/P&J/5/249. IOR.

their problems. It hammered home the message that, although the Unionists had given vast amounts of patronage to the 'recruit hunters' during the war, they were now offering to the returning soldiers 'A meagre bonus of Rs 5 per head [and] 50,000 acres of land for a million soldiers in the Punjab'.[62] Despite its late development in these traditionally 'loyalist' areas and the Unionist Party's considerable opposition, the League captured all six of the rural seats in the Rawalpindi and Jhelum districts in the 1946 elections. It also swept the board in the peasant proprietor areas of the east Punjab which had badly suffered from wartime dislocation. In the central and south-west Punjab, however, warweariness and anti-government feeling played a smaller part in the League's rise to power. Its success in these areas stemmed from its winning the support of the landlords and pirs who controlled the social networks through which votes were always gathered.

By the beginning of 1946 a third of the Unionist Party's landlord members had already deserted it and joined the League. In the two districts of Jhang and Sheikhupura all seven of the Muslim Legislative Assembly members had joined the League.[63] Although in other areas such as Amritsar and Gujarat the Unionist Party members remained steadfastly loyal, the League had nevertheless made a substantial inroad into its elite support. The landlords who had joined the League included among their number members of the Hayat, Noon, and Daultana families from which the Unionist Party had traditionally drawn its leadership. It had also lost the support of the pirs of Jalalpur, Jahanian Shah, Rajca, and Shah Jiwana who had represented it in the Legislature ever since 1923. The League had also captured the support of such other pirs as Pir Taunsa and Pir Golra, who had always provided the Unionist Party with valuable tacit support.

A multiplicity of social, economic, and religious reasons lay behind the decision of the landlords and pirs to quit the Unionist Party. They were set to the background of the break-up of the party's fragile factional unity following the death of its leader, Sikander Hayat Khan, in December 1942.[64] Also influential was the growing realization that

62 *Eastern Times* (Lahore), 29 September 1945.

63 Ibid., 13 September 1945.

64 Long-standing political rivalry existed between the Khattar group led by Sikander hayat Khan and the Noon-Tiwana group. There was considerable disappointment among the Khattars that one of their number did not succeed Sikander as Premier. Instead, the Premiership went to one of their rivals, Malik Khizr Hayat Khan Tiwana. Significantly, among the Muslim League 's first landlord converts

the British would soon be leaving India. As the war drew to a close, it seemed to many Punjabi Muslims that the Unionist Party's non-communal approach to politics and its loyalist stance had outlived its *raison d'etre*.[65] Although the first desertions from the Unionist Party occurred in April 1944 over the question of the All-India Muslim League's right to intervene in provincial politics, significantly it was the collapse of the Simla Conference in July 1945 which led to the decisive exodus from the Unionist Party of the leading landlords and pirs. The Punjabi landlords and pirs had become involved in politics for two main reasons—to safeguard their position in the localities and to increase their power and patronage. They sought to achieve this through membership of the Provincial Government and Assembly, through their control of the district boards and municipal committees and by securing appointments as *zaildars* (local government officials) and honorary magistrates. They supported the Unionist Party not out of loyalty but because it gave them access to patronage. The break-down of the Simla Conference because of Jinnah's demand that all Muslim nominees of the Interim Government must be Muslim Leaguers painfully brought home to the landlords that if they did not join the League they would be excluded in future from office and power.

Although it had earlier criticized the Unionist Party for using 'tribalism' and the peasants' superstitious reverence for pirs to win political support, the League did not quibble about adopting these same methods when it was in a position to do so. Indeed, it was so determined to field candidates who possessed traditional authority in the rural areas that it passed over many of its loyal workers in order to run 'covert' landlords and pirs on its ticket.[66] During the 1946 elections the League called on the personal influence in the villages of the landlords, the pirs, and the kinship group leaders of mobilize support.

As in 1937, the kinship group played an important part in mobilizing the votes of the peasant proprietors. This time Mian Nurullah used his influence among his fellow Arains in the Lyallpur district on the League's behalf. He devoted the biggest part of his electioneering

---

were such prominent members of the Khattar faction as Shaukhat Hayat (Sikander's son), Mir Naqbool Mahmood, and Mian Muntaz Daultana.

[65] *Eastern Times* (Lahore), 18 September 1945.

[66] A most blatant example of this policy was the League's selection of Sardar Barkat Hayat, Sikander's younger brother, as its candidate for the Punjab North Labour Seat instead of the President of the Rawalpindi Artisans Union who was at the same time Vice-President of the Rawalpindi Muslim League.

effort to the registering of voters rather than to popularizing the League's message. He knew that if he increased the number of voters from his kinship group he would almost certainly secure election.[67] Where strong kinship groups existed the League endeavoured to choose their leaders as its candidates.[68] The landlords who had joined the League used their influence over their tenants and their wealth to win votes for the League. The Sufi network remained, however, the most important channel for mobilizing rural political support.

In the period immediately preceding the provincial elections the Punjab League created a committee of men of religious influence known as the *Masheikh* committee in order to marshal Sufi support behind its cause. The pirs were not, however, easy to organize; few attended the Jamiat-ul-Ulema-e-Islam Conference which the Muslim League held at Lahore in January 1946, so most of its dealings with them had to take place at the local level. It approached individual pirs and asked them to issue '*fatwas*' in its support. These religious directives were disseminated by means of small leaflets and wall-posters as well as by publication in such papers as *Nawa-e-Waqt* and *Inqilab*. In them appeals to vote for the League were often couched solely in terms of the loyalty of a disciple to his pir and his Sufi order (*silsilah*). The following fatwa issued by Syed Fazal Ahmad Shah, Sajjada Nashin of the shrine of Hazrat Shah Nur Jamal, is a good illustration of this:

> An announcement from the Dargarh [shrine] of Hazrat Shah Jamal. I command all those people who are in my Silsilah to do everything possible to help the Muslim League and give their votes to it. All those people who do not act according to this message should consider themselves no longer members of my Silsilah.

Signed Fazal Ahmad Shah,
Sajjada Nashin Hazrat Shah Nur Jamal[69]

[67] Abdul Bari, President Lyallpur District Muslim League, to Jinnah, 23 January 1946. Shamsul Hasan Collection, Punjab, vol. 1.

[68] In many constituencies candidate selection was more important than the electioneering itself—a point taken up by the editor of *Civil and Military Gazette* (Lahore) on 4 September 1945: 'The parties have yet to choose their respective candidates and much thought and study will be needed for this important step in electioneering. The party which chooses a better set of candidates keeping in view the local alliances and clannish feelings will of course have a tremendous advantage.'

[69] *Nawa-e-Waqt* (Lahore), 19 January 1946.

Most of the leading Sufi shrines issued similar fatwas on the League's behalf. It achieved its greatest success in such areas as Jhang, Multan, Jhelum, and Karnal where it had obtained the support of the leading pirs. Khalid Saifullah, the editor of the pro-League *Eastern Times*, did not overstate the case when he wrote almost immediately after the 1946 elections:

What are the factors that have brought about the revolution in the Pakistani lands? What has made the great change possible? In my view the greatest praise must be lavished, as far as the Punjab is concerned on the Pirs . . . who when they saw the Pakistani nation in mortal danger emerged from their cells and enjoined upon their followers to resist evil and vote for the League and Pakistan.[70]

Historians have usually explained the Muslim League's growth in terms of the mass support for Pakistan. 'The bulk of the landed aristocracy remained loyal to the idea of a united India', Shahid Burki, for example, has recently declared, 'these provinces [Punjab, Sind, and the North Western Frontier] became Pakistan because a majority of their populations were Muslims and not because the politically powerful landed aristocracy gave Jinnah's movement overwhelming support.'[71] This study of the League's development in the key province of the Punjab has revealed, however, that the rural elite's support was crucial to its success. The landlords' and pirs' command of the rural population's votes was far more important in mobilizing support for the League than the popularity of its demand for Pakistan.

During the years 1937–44 the Punjab Muslim League frequently attempted to bypass the Unionist rural elite by appealing directly to the villagers but its efforts made little headway. Until large numbers of the Unionist Party's traditional supporters deserted it late in 1944 and in 1945, the League's prospects of winning power in the province were remote. By the eve of the crucial 1946 elections, however, it had the support of a large section of the rural elite. It was thus able to beat the Unionists at their own electioneering game. Pirs issued fatwas on the League's behalf, landlords used their economic influence and their leading positions in the kinship networks. The overwhelming support which the Muslim League received from the landlords and pirs enabled it to secure a resounding victory in the 'cornerstone' of Pakistan.

70 *Eastern Times* (Lahore), 15 March 1946.
71 S.J. Burki, *Pakistan under Bhutto 1971–7* (London, 1980), 14.

The Punjab Muslim League's success demonstrates how much more important 'traditional' social and religious networks may be in mobilizing political support than has been recognized by existing theories. There is no need to assume, as Paul Brass has done, that social mobilization is a necessary prerequisite for political mobilization in Muslim societies. In only six of the Punjab's twenty-nine districts did more than a fifth of the Muslims live in towns[72] and in only two districts could more than 2 per cent read English but the League was able to mobilize widespread support by relying on the Sufi and kinship networks. It was mainly through these but also through the linking of the Pakistan scheme to the solution of the villagers' wartime economic difficulties that League politics were able to reach down and embrace the rural voters who held the key to the successful creation of a new Muslim nation-state.

[72] Calculated from 1941 *Census, Punjab* (Lahore, 1941), pt. 1, Table XIII, p. 14.

Chapter Eleven

Bengal Politics and the Muslim Masses, 1920–47*

PARTHA CHATTERJEE

Let me explain at the outset that I shall, in this article, talk of two different worlds of politics—one, the organized world of governments, parties, legislatures, etc., and the other, the unorganized world of the politics of the peasant communities. The former world is familiar; the latter we know of only at those conjunctures when it comes into contact with the processes of organized politics. But the distinction is important in studying the role of the peasantry in the politics of colonial and post-colonial agrarian societies. I have elaborated elsewhere on the theoretical location of this distinction and its general implications for the historiography of modern India.[1] Let me simply point out here that the usual way of looking at the politics of the so-called 'developing' countries in the modern phase is to concentrate on those political processes which surround the formal machinery of the state, to see how far they penetrate into society, how increasingly large sections of the population are 'mobilized' into politics, how 'participation' increases, and perhaps how new processes are 'institutionalized'

* *Journal of Commonwealth and Comparative Politics* 13, 1, March 1982.

[1] I am grateful to Ujjwal Kanti Das and Madhumati Dutta for their help in the collection of data used in this article. For the theoretical and historiographical background, see Partha Chatterjee, 'Agrarian Relations and Communalism in Bengal, 1920–1935' in Ranajit Guha (ed.), *Subaltern Studies I: Writings on South Asian History and Society* (Delhi, 1982); 'Agrarian Relations and Politics in Bengal: Some Considerations on the Making of the Tenancy Act Amendment 1928', Occasional Paper no. 30, Centre for Studies in Social Sciences, Calcutta (September 1980).

as a result. The collective social activities of a very large part of the people of these countries are thereby relegated to the peripheries of the political system where their existence becomes noticeable only in those periodic spurts of agrarian unrest which seem to occur so suddenly, spontaneously, and locally, merely to subside once more into the normal passivity of age-old peasant life. These sudden outbursts are often designated as 'pre-political' and it is only when large peasant masses are brought into the fold of parties or elections or centrally organized agitational movements that the peasantry is recognized as having 'entered' politics.

It will be one of my contentions here that a study of the process of 'entry' of the peasant masses into organized politics of the modern kind requires an understanding of the relatively autonomous political authority which resides in the peasant communities. The important ideological element here is the notion of the formal state machinery as an authority external to the community. Perhaps this is more true in a country like India where, for most parts of the country, the formal state machinery has since early medieval times been organized more or less as a centralized imperial bureaucracy. The same perception regarding the state might not exist in places or periods where a formal state machinery is indistinguishable from local feudalism. Now, this perceptual distance of the state—the absence of organic links with the everyday world of peasant life—provides the analytical ground for explaining the sudden and unanticipated swings in popular opinion about the *sarkar* (government). It is also this perceptual distance which, when favourable structural conditions prevail in the organized world of conflict between sections of the ruling classes, creates room for the manipulative operation of popular politics and charismatic politicians.

Secondly, the specific constitution of state power, which in pre-capitalist formations can assume a wide range of forms varying from a centralized bureaucracy to virtually sovereign feudal lords, is important in analyzing ideologies or types of political movements among the peasantry. In the Indian case, for instance, the question of peasant movements against feudal or semi-feudal exploitation is much more problematical than actions against the bureaucratic state apparatus. The former is enmeshed in a host of relationships of mutual obligation, institutionalized in a wide variety of customary practices, and validated in specific ways in specific cultural contexts. There can rarely be a straight correspondence between the distinctly economic role of a feudal or semi-feudal landlord, especially in a period of structural change in the agrarian economy, and the perception of his role in the established social ideology of the community. But there are in each specific case recognized symbols of feudal authority: rituals and customs concerning, in most instances, feudal rights and property, their legitimation and display, and the superiority of physical force which is the final basis of feudal power, demonstrated in the right to punish any act of disobedience. Correspondingly, revolt against feudal authority involves acts of conscious violation of these symbols of authority—looting and destruction of property and desecration of objects of ritual significance.

Thirdly, a period when, with the extension of the sphere of 'representative' institutions, the arena of organized politics spreads to bring in sections of the peasant masses into a new kind of systematic political relationship with the state, the important thing to study is the nature of the *linkages* of peasant-communal politics with the structure of organized politics. It is here that the politics of 'mobilization' operates. Many of the more pervasive features of 'underdeveloped' politics, such as parochial loyalties of factionalism, are to be located in these linkages which politicians and parties from the organized world of politics seek to forge with the peasant communities. The question of linkages becomes particularly critical in situations where processes of economic differentiation within the peasantry are eroding the social base in which the ideological structures of peasant-communal politics are built.

This essay will use the analytical framework stated above in bare outline to present an argument about the course of development of Muslim politics in Bengal up to the partition of province in 1947. Many crucial points in this argument still rest on extremely inadequate data. However, the sketching of a theoretical argument of this kind may be of some help in locating the areas and directions of future research.

Congress and Khilafat

It was the Non-Cooperation-Khilafat movement of 1920 which brought for the first time an organized political movement to the Muslim peasantry of Bengal. The main impetus, or so at least it was reported in official circles, was provided by the *ulema* or religious preachers, 'mainly belonging to the Farazi sect', and the bulk of the agitators were 'itinerant *maulavis*' (Muslim preachers).[2] This movement also brought to the fore a new section of Muslim leaders, organizers of Khilafat and Non-Cooperation in different districts of Bengal, having strong connections with the religious and social leadership of the Muslim peasantry. Many of them were *maulanas* (Muslim scholars) themselves with considerable eminence as religious scholars —men like Abdullahel Baqi of Dinajpur, Maniruzzaman Islamabadi of Chittagong and Calcutta, Akram Khan of 24-Parganas, Shamsuddin Ahmed of Nadia, and Ashrafuddin Choudhury of Tippera.[3]

The depth and effectiveness of this Non-Cooperation–Khilafat propaganda can be judged from the fact that in the 1921 elections to the Council, when voting was declared to be *gunah* (sin), there was a very low Muslim turnout, particularly in Rajshahi, Dinajpur, and Rangpur, whereas in Chittagong and Noakhali illiterate grocers, carters, cobblers, and shopkeepers who had been put up as candidates in collective mockery of the entire edifice of constitutional reforms, won by huge majorities. In 1922, a conference of ulema at Comilla attended, it was said, by 10,000, pronounced non-cooperation to be 'obligatory' for all believers.[4]

The organizational form within which this new Muslim leadership

[2] In 1922, when the Government of India suggested that the Provinces think of utilizing the services of maulavis 'for propaganda on Muhammadan questions', the Government of Bengal promptly replied that it would be 'an expedient of doubtful value. The Khilafat agitation has been too prolonged and has gone too deep to make it worth trying to organize these men now for a counter-attack . . . .'

[3] Abdul Mansur Ahmed, himself an important member of this new Muslim leadership, has given a graphic account of his own social background and the kinds of cultural change that were occurring in Muslim rural life in eastern Bengal in this period. *Atmakatha* (Dacca, 1978). He came from a family which was Farazi and thus held in high esteem by others in the village. A great uncle had reportedly joined the *majahid* forces of Saiyad Ahmed Barelvi in the 1820s and fought the English. This great uncle, after he had returned many years later to his village in Mymensingh, became the leading spirit behind a movement to purify the ritual practices and social customs of the Muslim peasantry. The family held over a hundred *bighas* of land, but none of it was let out to tenants of sharecroppers, the cultivation being done mainly by hired labour. Abdul Mansur's grandfather could not read or write, but those in his father's generation could; Abul Mansur himself went to college in Dacca.

[4] See Rajat K. Ray, 'Masses in Politics: The Non-Cooperation Movement in Bengal, 1920–22'. *Indian Economic and Social History Review*, 11 (December 1974) pp. 343–410.

conducted the Non-Cooperation agitation in the districts was forged in the main by C.R. Das and his provincial Congress organization in Bengal. Besides recruiting for his Congress the support of the various revolutionary groups in Bengal, C.R. Das also attempted to reach beyond the small coterie of westernized aristocratic Muslim leaders of Calcutta to wider sections of the Muslim leadership in the districts. For this he also devised a programmatic form—a Hindu–Muslim pact—which, apart from allaying Muslim grievances about music before mosques and cow slaughter, provided that 55 per cent of government employees and 60 per cent of membership of local bodies in Muslim-majority districts would be reserved for Muslims. The pact achieved Das' immediate objective of rallying a broad-based Muslim support for Swarajist politics in the legislature and in the various elected local bodies. Many Muslims stood as Swarajist candidates in the elections of 1923 and the party scored major successes in the district boards of such heavily Muslim areas as Jessore, Dinajpur, and Mymensingh.[5]

There are now good reasons to suspect that this expression of mass organizational unity of the major nationalist forces in the C.R. Das period of Bengal politics was dependent on certain fortuitous, and quite temporary, conditions in the world of organized politics. Within a year after C.R. Das' death in 1925, the Hindu–Muslim pact was a dead letter, a series of communal riots had broken out in various districts, and most important Muslim leaders had left the Congress. Organizational unity lasted precisely as long as the groundswell of mass agitation could be sustained. And the concerns which prompted large masses of people to join in political actions in response to the efforts of party organizers were quite different from the formally articulated principles of 'nationalism'. To understand why mass political action in Muslim Bengal in the succeeding period contrasted so markedly in its organizational allegiance with the earlier phase, we need to study in much greater detail the ideological world of the peasantry in Bengal. But before we do this, we must first take note of certain salient features of Bengal's agrarian structure.

The Agrarian Structure and the Muslim Peasantry

As is well known, the legal form of land relations in most of Bengal

[5] *Report on the Administration of Bengal*, 1923–9, p. v.

had been shaped by the Permanent Settlement of 1793 and subsequent modifications made in 1859 and 1885. These legal provisions gave rise to two sets of rights over land—one, a right of proprietorship enjoyed, in the early-twentieth century, by some 150,000 zamindars (landlords) and nearly three million holders of intermediate tenures, and, two, a right of occupation held by those among the peasantry who had legally recognized rights of tenancy. It is also known[6] that the entire structure of *zamindari* and tenureholding property, subjected to a continuous process of fragmentation since the early nineteenth century, was by the 1920s on the edge of a crisis of massive proportions.

Secondly, with the emergence in the late nineteenth century of jute, and later of rice, as commercial crops, the dominant tendency in the sphere of agricultural wealth-making was in the direction of extensive rent exploitation (in most cases on the basis of rights of occupation rather than of proprietorship) and of usury coupled with the trade in rice and jute.

Thirdly, there was a strong tendency towards increased differentiation within the peasantry, with the emergence of a significant stratum of substantial peasantry at the top and the immiserization of a poor peasantry who lost their rights of occupation over the lands which they cultivated. There was, in fact, an increase in *de jure* and effective transfers of land from the small to the larger peasantry (or to tenureholders with large holdings in direct possession), with indebtedness as the usual mechanism for effecting such transfers. However, these did not, in most cases, lead to absolute eviction. Rather, the dispossessed peasant continued to cultivate the same plot of land, but with inferior rights and higher effective rents. This process manifested itself in particular in the increase in tenancies paying rent in the form of a share of the produce. There was also a strengthening, rather than a weakening, of various forms of 'unfree' labour, which reflected a declining bargaining position of the working peasantry, i.e. the small and landless peasants, *vis-a-vis* the landlords, whether proprietors, tenureholders, or superior *raiyats* (tenants).

However, and this is particularly important for our present discussion, the tendencies towards a differentiation within the peasantry were, in the early twentieth century, far more advanced in the south-

[6] See Partha Chatterjee, 'Agrarian Structure in Pre-Partition Bengal' in Barun De (ed.), *Perspectives in Social Sciences II* (Calcutta, forthcoming).

western and some of the northern districts of Bengal, and least advanced in the eastern districts. In the latter, the natural fertility of the soil, abundance of rain water, and the adoption of jute as a commercial crop gave the small peasantry a relatively viable economic status, and hence, until the late 1930s, a relatively undifferentiated social character. As it was, in sharp contrast to the distribution of land in the western and central districts, well over 70 per cent of the land was in the direct possession of cash-paying settled and occupancy raiyats in the districts of eastern Bengal (with the exception of Chittagong, Noakhali, and, to some extent, Bakarganj and Faridpur) (see Table 1). Besides, whatever direct evidence exists regarding the distribution of land-holdings by size shows quite unequivocally that the preponderance of a small peasantry holding less than two acres each was much stronger in the districts of eastern Bengal, especially Dacca, Faridpur, Bakarganj, Chittagong, Tippera, Noakhali, and Pabna, than elsewhere. This is also reflected in the fact that in 1921 or 1931 the proportion of agricultural labour to the total population was highest in the districts of southwestern and northern Bengal and lowest in east Bengal.[7]

TABLE 1

PROPORTION OF AGRICULTURAL LAND IN DIRECT POSSESSION OF PROPRIETORS, TENUREHOLDERS, RAIYATS, AND UNDER-RAIYATS (PERCENTAGE)

	Proprietors	*Tenure-holders*	*Settled and occupancy*	*Others*	*Under-raiyats*	*Muslims as % of total population*
Burdwan	5.02	20.54	38.37	33.19	2.88	18.53
Birbhum	5.09	14.80	56.01	21.44	2.66	26.50
Bankura	7.26	42.52	26.81	19.53	3.88	4.50
Midnapore	10.71	20.15	48.47	17.31	3.36	7.53
Hooghly	3.76	10.14	54.17	27.67	4.26	16.15
Howrah	4.51	8.36	55.94	27.61	3.58	21.13
24 Parganas	3.13	15.09	52.50	17.81	11.47	33.62
Nadia	4.37	13.09	46.01	27.35	9.18	61.74

[7] Ibid.

	Proprietors	*Tenure-holders*	*Settled and occupancy*	*Others*	*Under-raiyats*	*Muslims as % of total population*
Murshidabad	4.06	10.61	59.11	17.51	8.71	55.47
Jessore	2.51	9.69	52.47	7.80	27.43	61.88
Khulna	2.39	14.22	57.09	13.31	12.99	49.45
Dacca	8.79	5.84	77.69	6.54	1.14	66.81
Mymensingh	13.42	7.96	71.15	4.20	3.27	76.53
Faridpur	2.89	8.50	64.60	14.90	9.11	63.76
Bakarganj	9.23	26.42	55.80	4.88	3.67	71.59
Chittagong	22.55	50.73	21.61	1.82	3.29	73.73
Tippera	3.76	9.57	80.83	3.04	2.80	75.78
Noakhali	7.24	26.23	49.11	11.62	5.80	78.49
Rajshahi	7.40	5.14	72.18	6.26	9.02	75.72
Dinajpur	7.81	4.10	71.15	12.43	4.51	50.42
Jalpaiguri	8.08	31.62	38.58	12.91	8.81	23.91
Rangpur	6.81	4.78	77.17	4.30	6.93	70.78
Bogra	4.60	3.36	78.20	6.92	6.92	83.33
Pabna	7.42	6.97	73.23	8.40	3.98	76.89
Malda	8.60	7.04	73.32	8.75	2.29	54.23

SOURCE: Computed from *Survey and Settlement Reports* for each district. Last column from *Census of India*, 1931.

Now, it was also the districts of eastern and northern Bengal which were the predominantly Muslim areas of the province (see column 6 of Table 1). And it is a well-known feature of the social character of the peasantry of those districts that, whereas Muslims formed the overwhelming bulk of the peasantry, the landlords were mainly Hindu. However, this point, so widely regarded as being the most crucial in explaining Muslim politics in Bengal, requires some clarification.

If we take the strictly economic definition of the landlord as someone whose principal source of livelihood is rent from the land,[8]

[8] 'Zamindars and raiyats who do not cultivate but sublet their land come under

TABLE 2

RELIGIOUS COMPOSITION OF RENT-RECEIVERS, EXCLUDING DEPENDANTS (AS PERCENTAGE OF TOTAL RENT-RECEIVERS)

Division	*Muslim*	*Upper-caste Hindu**	*Others*
Rajshahi (excluding Darjeeling)	37.22	20.04	42.74
Dacca	33.44	38.50	18.06
Chittagong	49.13	30.74	20.13

* 'Upper-caste Hindu' means Brahman Baidya, or Kayastha. Of 'others' in the Rajshahi Division, the Rajbangshi were the largest single caste (8.51 per cent).

SOURCE: Computed from *Census of India, 1911,* vol. V pt. 2, pp. 222–3 and 379–81, table XV and appendix to table XVI (part II).

then Table 2 shows that the common perception about a predominantly upper-caste Hindu landlord class and a predominantly Muslim peasantry is quite incorrect at least for the Rajshahi and Chittagong divisions, i.e. for the northern and southeastern districts. We would, however, come closer to the commonly held impression if we make two qualifications to this finding. Firstly, there were a large number of upper-caste Hindu landlords excluded from these Census tables whose principal source of livelihood was income from professional or salaried occupations. But in the sphere of social relations they were still generally seen as part of the class of landlords. Secondly, if we take the tenancy categories of zamindar and intermediate tenureholder rather than the economic definition of a landlord, then the proportion of upper-caste Hindus among landlords would rise significantly in the Rajshahi and Chittagong divisions.

But even this would not entirely explain the significance of the Hindu–Muslim divide in the matter of mutual perceptions of landlord and peasantry in the predominantly Muslim districts of Bengal. What needs to be understood is the social character of the Muslim peasantry, the sense of a peasant community, and the significance of religion in

the category of rent-receivers, while zamindars and raiyats who cultivate their land and do not sublet are rent-payers.' *Census of India, 1911*, vol. V, part I, pp. 532–3.

sustaining an ideology of community solidarity, as well as the effects of differentiation within the peasantry. This is an area which has only recently become a subject of historical research, and much of what follows is based on very tentative results.

Of particular significance is the fact that, in certain districts of northern and central Bengal, there did exist in the early twentieth century a stratum of Muslim cultivators who were owners of very large holdings, who had let out large parts of their holdings to tenants, who were often officially designated as tenureholders, but who were socially and culturally part of the peasant community. In coastal Khulna, for instance, there were substantial cultivators (*abadkari praja*) who enjoyed many customary rights not common elsewhere among raiyats (tenants). Many were accepted as tenureholders under the Tenancy Act: 'No *nouveau riche* more ardently covets a rise in social status than the well-to-do Muhammadan cultivator of that district'.[9] The Noakhali Settlement Reports says of the Muslim cultivators of that district that many of them 'have risen to become middlemen, *howladars* and *talukdars*, and a few even zamindars [landlords], but they are all of the same stock', and many continued to cultivate even after acquiring superior rights.[10] In Tippera, too, it was reported that 'the majority of those who have raised themselves to the position of middlemen and subsist as rent-receivers and as *beparis*, small collecting agents in the jute and betel-nut trades, are of the same stock as the cultivators'.[11] In the northern district of Dinajpur, the Report says:

> Almost every village will reveal some large family of substantial cultivators. . . . As elsewhere in North Bengal, this jotedar class is socially supreme in the countryside. . . . Mostly holding 'jote' or raiyati right, they may have progressed in the world, and acquired superior proprietary rights in some estates, or for ease of collection, have taken a patni lease of a whole village from the landlords. Most union board presidents would be found to belong to the jotedar class with from 30 to 300 acres of land.[12]

On the other hand, in other parts of Bengal with large Muslim populations, for instance in the eastern districts of Dacca or Faridpur, there

[9] *Final Report on the Survey and Settlement Operations in Khulna*, p. 69.

[10] *Final Report on the Survey and Settlement Operations in Noakhali*, p. 27.

[11] *Final Report on the Survey and Settlement Operations in Tippera*, p. 21.

[12] *Final Report on the Survey and Settlement Operations in Dinajpur*, pp. 16–17. An account of the political career of one such Dinajpur politician is Aftabuddin Chaudhuri, *Atiter Katha* (Calcutta, 1973).

were few cases of cultivators operating in effect as intermediate rentiers.[13]

Peasant Ideology

Now, for the districts of the Dacca division, i.e. east Bengal proper, the picture is one of a relatively undifferentiated peasantry, predominantly Muslim (although there was a numerically significant scheduled caste population too), with a class of landlords very largely Hindu. For the Muslim-majority districts of Rajshahi and Chittagong divisions, i.e. north and southeast Bengal, the peasantry is not undifferentiated in economic terms, but those who were *jotedars* or substantial cultivators had, in fact, risen from the ranks of the rest of the peasantry, often participated in the cultivation of their lands, were socially part of the peasant community, and integrated to it within the same bonds of community solidarity.

But in all these areas the upper-caste Hindu zamindar or tenure-holder was clearly in a different social category. To this was added in the predominantly jute-growing districts of northern Bengal the presence of the *paschima* (usually Marwari) moneylender. Elsewhere, I have attempted[14] to analyze some of the connections between these structural features of society in the predominantly Muslim districts of east and north Bengal and the political ideology of peasantry. What emerges from this analysis is firstly, the role of the district towns, which always had larger Hindu concentrations than the neighbouring villages, as seats of both feudal and commercial exploitation of the peasantry; secondly, the role of religious festivals and processions as institutions of demonstration of feudal wealth and power; and, thirdly, the significance, in this context, of the innumerable disputes since the 1920s over 'music before mosques'. The other thing that is brought out is the organized strength, in a situation of political confrontation, of Hindu landlords, traders, and professionals in the towns and Muslim action in the countryside which often, as in Pabna in 1926, took on the characteristics of a peasant insurgency.

A study of the evidence of these 'riots' in the east and north Bengal countryside in the 1920s and 1930s also shows that the ideology which

[13] *Final Report on the Survey and Settlement Operations in Dacca*, pp. 41, 63; *Final Report on the Survey and Settlement Operations in Faridpur*, pp. 20,28.

[14] 'Agrarian Relations and Communalism in Bengal'.

shaped and gave meaning to the various collective acts of the peasantry was fundamentally *religious*. A very common feature of peasant violence against the symbols of feudal authority was the breaking of idols worshipped with great pomp and festivity in the landlords' houses. Some rioters said in court that they believed 'that to go out at night is thieving which is against the shariat [holy law], but it is a brave and laudable action to commit loot and plunder at any time'. A complaint from leading Hindu professionals of Kishoreganj alleged that 'the ruffians', although armed, 'entered the houses of Hindus and possessed themselves of holy Khargos reserved for sacrificing animals on special festivals. They held up several of these deadly weapons over the heads of the principal house-holders, until bonds, ornaments and cash were forthcoming in abundance'. Indeed, the very nature of peasant consciousness, the apparently consistent unification of an entire set of beliefs about nature and about men in the collective and active mind of a peasantry, is religious. Religion to such a community provides an ontology, an epistemology, as well as a practical code of ethics, including political ethics. When this community acts politically, the symbolic meaning of particular acts—their signification—must be found in religious terms. (It is hardly necessary to clarify that this is not something peculiar to a peasantry whose religion is Islam.)

Finally, the formally organized state is always perceived in peasant consciousness as something distant, an entity with which relations are bound by certain norms of reciprocity, where obedience is contingent upon fulfilment of the requirements of justice, but an entity which is not organic or integral to the familiar sphere of everyday social activity. It is capricious; benevolent at one moment, tyrannical at the next. In the Bakarganj disturbances in 1926–7, the Government was widely regarded as an enemy of Muslims in Bengal. In the Dacca riots of 1930 or in Kishoreganj in 1931, the British Government was thought to be on the side of the Muslims. In Dacca, people apparently believed that 'the Nawab Sahib of Dacca had become the lord of thirteen districts and it was ordered by him that no person would be arrested or convicted if Hindu houses were looted and burnt in those thirteen districts for seven days'. In Kishoreganj, looters were heard to have said that 'Government had given Swaraj to them for the space of fifteen days'. The District Magistrate in his tour through the riot-torn villages found one which was practically empty and was told that 'the villagers had all gone south to demand back their deeds from mahajans . . . everybody said this was the Government order promulgated about ten days previously'. A rioter wounded in a police shooting called out before he died, '*Ami British Governmenter praja, dohai British Government*' [I am a subject of the British Government, have mercy on me] and 'could not evidently understand why he had been shot'.

The Praja Movement

In a sense, what came to be known as the Praja movement began as part of the same process that had brought forward a new Muslim political leadership in Bengal at the time of the Khilafat movement. Given the social composition of the peasantry in east and north Bengal, anti-government movements among the masses inevitably began to voice the demands of an overwhelming part of the peasants in their status as *praja* or tenants. An English officer in Mymensingh summed this up by saying:

> What we are witnessing is the beginning of the break-up of the social and economic supremacy of the Hindu higher castes. The Muhammadans realize that where mere numbers count they must necessarily be a power . . . a particular grievance of which one often hears is the refusal of most Hindu landlords and their *amla* [agents] to allow even well-to-do Muhammadan tenants the courtesy of a seat.

One of the earliest dates usually cited in this connection is the Kamari-archar Praja Conference in Jamalpur, Mymensingh, in 1914 which was attended by many who were later to be among the foremost provincial leaders, such as Fazlul Huq, Akram Khan, Abul Kasem, Maniruzzaman Islamabadi, and Rajibuddin Tarafdar. The demands at this stage were limited to the abolition of the landlord's fee on transfers of land, the abolition of illegal exactions, reduction of rent, the tenant's right to trees, relief from indebtedness, and 'honourable treatment of Muslim tenants in the zamindar's *kutchery* [revenue office]'.[15] Such organized efforts continued through the 1920s, trying to combine sporadic local actions by peasants against landlords or their agents, or against moneylenders, into the more ordered forms of meetings,

[15] Jatindra Nath De, 'The History of the Krishak Praja Party of Bengal, 1929–47: A Study of Changes in Class and Inter-Community Relations in the Agrarian Sector of Bengal', (unpublished Ph.D dissertation, University of Delhi, 1977), p. 31.

processions, boycotts, strikes, and refusal to pay illegal ceases. By 1923 there were Praja Samitis in virtually every district in east and north Bengal. And a remarkable feature of this Praja leadership was its affiliation in terms of the major political groupings in provincial politics: in contrast to the westernized Calcutta-based Muslim leadership, these leaders were quite unequivocally members and supporters of the C.R. Das Congress.

This affiliation snapped completely in the space of three years following Das' death in 1925. There were widespread Hindu–Muslim riots in Bengal in 1926–7. The Calcutta-based professional and business elite, voicing the interests of the predominantly uppercaste Hindu *bhadralok* rentier classes now under considerable economic pressure, and using the organizational support of the revolutionary groups, assumed complete command over the provincial Congress organization, annulled the Hindu–Muslim pact, and virtually ousted from all important positions the new district leadership which had emerged in the course of the Non-Cooperation movement. Many Muslim leaders left the Congress at this point. The final blow was delivered in 1928 when an amendment was passed to the Bengal Tenancy Act. The entire Congress bloc in the legislature spoke and voted in support of the rights of landlords, while most Muslim members put up a futile fight in favour of the tenants.[16] Abul Mansur Ahmad quite clearly identifies this episode as the last straw on the camel's back: 'Neither in terms of the Muslim interest, nor of the praja interest, was it possible any longer to rely on the Congress.'[17]

From this time onwards organized politics among the Muslim masses of Bengal moved decisively away from the Congress. There was negligible Muslim participation in the Civil Disobedience movement (1930–2) in Bengal. On the other hand, the leadership of the Praja movement decided to form a provincial organization of their own. The All Bengal Praja Samiti was formed in 1929, and in 1931 it resolved to participate in all government institutions, legislatures, municipalities, and union boards. But this also created the need for an appropriate provincial leadership, one possessing the necessary skills to handle the intricate mechanisms of a foreign bureaucracy and having access to the right people in the right places. It is not surprising

[16] For a fuller discussion, see Chatterjee, 'Some Considerations on the Making of the Tenancy Act Amendment 1928'.

[17] Abul Mansur Ahmad, *Amar Dekha Rajnitir Panchas Bachhar* (Dacca, 1970), p. 61.

to find, as De shows,[18] that in the years 1930–4 the Praja Party was controlled at the top by a Calcutta leadership consisting of Sir Abdur Rahim, Khan Bahadur Abdul Momen, Sir Musharraf Hussain, and Akram Khan. Only in 1935 was this leadership challenged when, at the Mymensingh Conference, Fazlul Huq defeated Momen and became President of the Party. From this point the Krishak Praja Party (as it came to be called from 1936) became 'almost entirely an East Bengal party'.[19]

The other development which is important in understanding the course of the Praja movement is the impact of the depression of 1930–2 on the agrarian economy of east and north Bengal. The fragile support which had been provided to the small-peasant economy of the region by the cultivation of jute collapsed rather suddenly in those years. There is evidence to suggest that the agricultural credit which had been provided by moneylenders and traders to jute growers was no longer forthcoming; the highly centralized jute manufacturing interests in Calcutta also proceeded to tighten their control over the supply of raw jute. Credit now had to be sought from within the local agrarian economy. The data on land registrations shows a very clear and rapid rise in the transfer of land from small peasants in eastern Bengal in the 1930s, especially in Noakhali, Tippera, Dacca, Mymensingh, Bogra, and Pabna. One can, therefore, detect here the rise of a new class of substantial peasantry even in areas where it had not previously existed in any significant way. The small-peasant economy of east Bengal was thus set on a path of rapid decay; it was to receive its death blow in the Great Famine of 1943.[20]

On the political plane, an immediate effect of the depression was a sharp fall in the collection of rent, and hence in the collection of revenue. This was coupled in the west Bengal districts by the impact of the Civil Disobedience movement. In most parts of the province, however, the land revenue collection returned to normal from about 1933–4. But in Khulna, Faridpur, Bakarganj, Chittagong, Noakhali, Jalpaiguri, Rangpur, and Pabna, the revenue collections stayed well below 70 per cent of the total demand right through the 1930s (the normal collection being over 90 per cent).[21] This was ascribed in official circles to what was called the 'no rent' mentality. There is

[18] J.N. De, p. 88.
[19] Ibid., p. 92.
[20] For details see Chatterjee, 'Agrarian Structure in Pre-Partition Bengal'.
[21] Again, for details see ibid.

little evidence to suggest that this was a centrally organized movement. Certainly the central leadership of the Praja Party did not adopt any programme of this kind. Yet it is true that in many parts of east and north Bengal, peasants did not pay rent, or at least all of the rent customarily paid, and to the extent that there was any active agitation at the local level, the leadership was often provided by people who considered themselves part of the Praja movement.

THE HUQ MINISTRY AND THE PRAJA MOVEMENT

This is shown particularly by the predicament of Krishak Praja Party leaders after they went into a coalition ministry with the Muslim League in 1937. The papers of the revenue minister of that government contain numerous complaints from British officials that there was a widespread 'no rent' mentality caused by 'the sympathetic attitude of the present Government towards the raiyats . . . there are rumours that shortly Government will cancel arrears of rent and reduce the rate of rent'.[22] At the Revenue Conference of 1938, presided over by the Governor, several District Officers alleged that MLAs (legislators) affiliated to the ruling Party, besides communists and Congressmen, were agitating against the payment of rent,and the Governor said that 'District Magistrates wanted to know where they stood with regard to possible agrarian trouble, the extent to which they could use Section 144 and wanted a statement from Government that a deliberate "no rent" campaign would not be tolerated'. To this, Fazlul Huq, the Chief Minister, at first replied that 'the Praja Party was dominated by tenants though it would support the legal right of all'. He added that 'in some respects the authority of Government officers was being weakened but it was necessary to remember that the party system was in force and supporters had to be considered'. He said that 'if it could be proved that people were definitely able but were refusing to pay he would have no objection to the certificate procedure being introduced [for forcible recovery to rent]'. But the officers persisted in their demand for a clearer statement of the Government's position, and in the end Fazlul Huq agreed that 'strong action' was required and that he 'would

[22] Confidential note on discussion on 13–14 June 1938 on Revenue Department Memorandum 143T.-R. of 9 May 1938. B.P. Singh Roy Papers. Nehru Memorial Museum and Library.

speak to all MLAs and explain the reason for the introduction of such a procedure'.[23]

The last example also illustrates another crucial point, because what happened in the world of Muslim politics in Bengal in the period 1937–47 has a great deal to do with the structures and processes of the colonial state machinery. The year 1936 saw the peak of the Praja movement in Bengal, symbolized by the drama of the Patuakhali election in which Fazlul Huq defeated Khwaja Nazimuddin, a nephew of the Nawab of Dacca and a leading figure in the westernized aristocratic leadership of the provincial Muslim League.[24] Patuakhali also symbolized the context within which the Praja movement chose to function, for on the one hand there was mass agitation and populist rhetoric, on the other there were elections, ministries, bureaucratic procedures, and the compulsions of 'representative' politics. The Krishak Praja Party did not win an absolute majority in 1936–7 elections. They negotiated with the Congress about the prospects of a ministry, but this did not come to anything. Fazlul Huq then formed a coalition ministry with the Muslim League. the KPP's talks with Jinnah before the elections had broken down because the 'radicals' in the party had insisted that the abolition of the Permanent Settlement must form part of the programme. The first item on the KPP's own election manifesto had been 'the abolition of zamindari without compensation'.

Once the coalition ministry is formed, however, the story becomes one of a series of ignominious compromises. There was great dissatis-

[23] Minutes of the Revenue Conference, Darjeeling, 13–14 June 1938. B.P. Singh Roy Papers.

[24] As a matter of fact, there did not actually exist a formal provincial unit of the Muslim League in Bengal before 1936. There were two major provincial Muslim parties: the Krishak Praja Party and the United Muslim Party led by Nazimuddin, Nawab Habibullah of Dacca, Azizul Huque, etc. Only a few individuals such as A.R. Siddiqui, Khwaja Nooruddin, and M.A.H. Ispahani owed direct allegiance to the All India Muslim League. Immediately before the elections, after negotiations with Jinnah, the UMP agreed to contest the elections as the Muslim League. For the story of Jinnah's negotiations with UMP and KPP, see M.A.H. Ispahani, *Qaid-e-Azam Jinnah As I Knew Him* (Karachi, 1964), pp. 25–33. For details regarding the 1936–7 elections, see Humaira Momen, *Muslim Politics in Bengal: A Study of the Krishak Praja Party and the Elections of 1937* (Dacca, 1972). For the history of party politics and ministry making in the period 1937–47, see, besides Abul Mansur Ahmad, *Amar Dekha Rajnitir Panchas Bachhar*, and J.N. De, Shila Sen, *Muslim Politics in Bengal 1937–47* (New Delhi, 1976) and Kalipada Biswas, *Jukta Banglar Sesh Adhyay* (Calcutta, 1966).

faction among the 'radicals' in the KPP about the composition of the ministry which they described as 'subservient to British Imperialism and Bengal Landlordism'.[25] But this was the only kind of ministry Fazlul Huq could make. And the records on the working of the government departments in this period show quite unambiguously the very real power which the colonial bureaucracy continued to enjoy and exercise within the governmental process in order to protect established interests.[26] Besides, the British officers in Bengal clearly preferred Nazimuddin to Huq and used him as a foil against the Chief Minister and the KPP within the ministry.[27] The British commercial

[25] Nausher Ali, after he resigned from the ministry in June 1938, gave the following rundown on Huq's cabinet: Mr N.R. Sarkar, 'representative of the Bengal National Chamber of Commerce, capitalist, a gentleman too well-known in Bengal to require any comment'; Khwaja Nazimuddin and the Nawab of Dacca, 'scions of the Nawab family of Dacca . . . cannot express themselves in the language of the people of Bengal, perhaps have not passed a single day in any rural area in their life, having nothing in common with the masses of Bengal except perhaps the relationship of landlord and tenant'; Mr H.S. Suhrawardy, 'born and brought up in luxury in towns . . . Those who had the honour of working with him in public life know thoroughly well about his mentality and attitude towards the poor which was specially prominent during the passage of the Bengal Tenancy Bill in 1928'; Sir B.P. Singh Roy, 'a landlord and representative of the zamindars of the burdwan Division'; Maharaja Srishchandra Nandy of Cossimbazar, 'a well-known zamindar of Bengal'; Nawab Musharraf Husain, 'a zamindar, well-known tea magnate whose whole position is due to the labour of tea-garden coolies'. Nausher Ali to Fazlul Huq, 14 June 1938.

[26] Fazlul Huq circulated a note among his Cabinet colleagues in July 1938 in which he complained: 'I have been repeatedly suggesting that something should be done which will catch the imagination of the people and make the Ministry popular but all my suggestions have been turned down as either impracticable or difficult or harmful . . . I wish to emphasize the point that we are a thoroughly unpopular lot. I have heard it said by more than one responsible person that the public impression is that the present Cabinet is a "bankers" Cabinet'. Confidential note by Fazlul Huq, B.P. Singh Roy Papers.

[27] There is a great deal of documentary evidence on this. To cite one published source. H.J. Twynam, who was at one time Chief Secretary in Bengal, wrote the Viceroy in June 1942 recommending Nazimuddin's name for an official delegation of the Government of India to the USA: 'He gets on very well with Britishers, particularly enjoys a game of bridge, etc., and would probably get on equally well with Americans . . . I have little doubt that we shall see him as the Chief Minister in Bengal in due course, in which event I am confident that he will prove to be another Sir Sikander Hyat Khan'. Sir H. Twynam to the Marquess of Linlithgow, 24 June 1942, in Nicholas Mansergh (ed.), *The Transfer of Power 1942–7*, ii (London, 1971), 264–6.

interests worked through B.P. Singh Roy and N.R. Sarkar.[28] And landed interests were, in any case, well represented.

THE SWING TOWARDS THE MUSLIM LEAGUE

Fazlul Huq's coalition ministry could achieve little in terms of implementing the KPP's original programme. In three years' time Huq himself had to go into a coalition with the Hindu Mahasabha in order to save his ministry. In early 1943 Huq's second ministry fell and a Muslim League ministry was formed under Nazimuddin. These changing alignments among parties and leaders in the legislature and in the ministries, however, had little direct connection with mass movements or with the growth of party organizations among the masses. As I pointed out before, the Praja movement was not so much an organized party movement as a constellation, at a certain conjuncture in history, of largely local and spontaneous peasant agitations over a wide region; party leaders at provincial and district levels merely attempted to voice these demands. After 1937 the attempt by the 'radical' section of the KPP leadership to give legal and administrative shape to some of those demands proved a complete failure. At the same time rapid changes in the agrarian economy of eastern Bengal in the 1930s meant a quick decline in the former resilience of the small-peasant economy and the rise of a new class of substantial peasants. The extension of the franchise, the penetration of formal governmental institutions into rural areas, and the opening up of governmental appointments at local levels to a somewhat larger section of the rural population meant that there were more people now available to fill up the linkage positions between the structures of organized politics and the peasant communities in the villages. There was thus considerable extension of the arena of 'representative' politics as well as of the rhetoric of populism.

[28] For instance, a letter from Sarkar to Curtis-Millar, a prominent English businessman in Calcutta, suggests the existence of a 'group' including, besides the two of them, F.C. Brasher, Sir Victor Sassoon, and B.P. Singh Roy, and discusses government policy regarding elections to the Calcutta Corporation: 'I am writing this to you confidentially as I think that when we are working together politically I should not hide anything from you'. E.C. Benthall, another important Calcutta businessman, writes from England to B.P. Singh Roy, 'The facts you send me [regarding the present agrarian situation of Bengal] are most interesting and if opportunity offers I shall not fail to make discreet use of them in the right quarter'. B.P. Singh Roy Papers.

The failure of Huq's Krishak Praja Party thus led to a phenomenon that has since become very familiar in the electoral politics of the subcontinent: a sudden shift in 'popular' support—from the KPP to the Muslim League. In the elections of 1946 the Muslim League, now under the more energetic leadership of Suhrawardy, made a virtual sweep of the Muhammadan seats in the legislature. Now, in trying to understand the relevant processes here, there is very little by way of substantive research findings to go by. What appears from a surface reading of the available evidence suggests a continued climate of peasant agitation regarding zamindari oppression, translated in the Muslim-dominated areas into ideological terms that were pronouncedly anti-Hindu. Thus the grounds still existed for populist rhetoric as a means of gaining electoral support. At the same time the class of richer peasantry among Muslims had now obtained a clearer notion of their political objectives in terms of institutional power and patronage within and around the structures of government. It is also important to note in this connection the spread of formal education in English particularly among this section of east Bengal Muslims as a result of the establishment of a university in Dacca.[29] Whatever organized effort the Muslim League was able to mount in the Suhrawardy period consisted in large part of the spread of 'the Pakistan movement' among the Muslim literati and educated youth, particularly under the organizational leadership of Abul Hashim who became Secretary of the party in 1944.[30]

What, therefore, appears to have happened was a shift in party allegiance on the part of the *link* elements between the organized party leadership and the peasant masses. (It needs to be remembered here that the franchise was still restricted by property and other qualifications.) De states this rather straightforwardly: 'By 1943 the bulk of the Muslim *jotedar* base shifted to the Muslim League, leading to a mass exodus of members from the [Krishak Praja] Party . . . while a small but genuinely committed section joined the Communists; the

[29] This point has been well made in Mahmud Husain, 'Dacca University and the Pakistan Movement' in C.H. Philips and Mary Doreen Wainwright (eds), *The Partition of India: Policies and Perspectives, 1935–47* (London, 1970), pp. 369–73.

[30] See, in particular, Abdul Hashim, *In Retrospection* (Dacca, 1974). This autobiography shows in graphic detail the poor state of organization of the League in the Bengal countryside.

KPP virtually withered away'.[31] The organizational details of this shift have not yet been documented.

Was there an ideological change among the Muslim masses? We know in general that the sense of peasant community in its ideological dimensions has great resilience and persists in the social and political beliefs of peasant masses long after the material bases for its existence have been superseded. Was the widespread expression of the demand for Pakistan among the Muslim peasantry of east and north Bengal any different from, or anything more specific than, their desire to free themselves from zamindari domination, to establish a more just relationship with the state machinery? We cannot say for certain. There is a story by Atin Bandyopadhyaya about a village in Dacca. Felu Shekh is a small peasant who had once lost an arm when the Murapara Zamindars had sent in elephants to break up a meeting of recalcitrant tenants. A woman of the village had drowned while collecting crabs and reeds from the lake. The villagers are burying her. Felu has with him two printed notices which say, 'We shall fight and take Pakistan'. He places them gently over the body in the grave. Shamsuddin is the local leader of the Muslim League. 'Felu thought, "I have a broken arm. There's nothing I can do". Otherwise, he was so agitated that he felt he could rush off that very moment and bring back ten dead bodies and throw them at Shamu's feet and say, "Here, Mian, take these, I've brought them for you. Now divide up the country".'[32] From the years of Khilafat, through the Praja movement, to Pakistan is a long transition in terms of the history of organized politics in Bengal. Was there a change in the ideological world of the peasant communities? Only further research can give us more definite answers.

[31] J.N. De, p. 6.

[32] Atin Bandyopadhyay, 'Kimbadantir Surya', *Ekshan* (Autumn 1969), pp. 66–124.

Chapter Twelve

Divided Bengal: Problems of Nationalism and Identity in the 1947 Partition[1]

LEONARD A. GORDON

The birth of Bangladesh has stimulated Bengalis and many outsiders to reflect upon the past of Bengal, the partition of India, and the ethnic and national identity of Bengalis. The insiders in Bangladesh have fundamental problems of identity redefinition. They are concerned with what their primary identifications are, what their traditions are, and how they relate to West Bengal, to India, to Pakistan, and to the Muslim world. From the early euphoric days of Sheikh Mujib's return with his slogan of nationalism, secularism, and democracy, the nation has passed into more disturbing times in which such a formula does not suffice, and even arouses basic disagreements.

For outsiders, particularly historians and social scientists, that area offers a kaleidoscope through which to look at complex questions of nation formation, ethnic identity, political culture, and mobilization. The division of Pakistan has suggested anew that national and ethnic identities are not fixed essences. Men may make one choice in a period

[1] I want to thank my friends Anisuzzaman, Peter Bertocci, Ainslie T. Embree, Ronald B. Inden, Gail Minault, W.H. Morris-Jones, and members of Professor Embree's Indian History Seminar at Columbia University for destroying earlier versions of this paper. The research on which this paper is based was carried out under grants from the Columbia University Council for Research in the Social Sciences, American Council of Learned Societies, American Philosophical Society, and American Institute of India Studies, but none of the above is responsible for the content.

of crisis and other choices at another time. The very categories of 'Muslim', 'Hindu', 'Bengali', 'Indian', and 'Pakistani' must be considered. Recent literature on ethnicity presses all mappers of Bengali's past to look at processes and boundaries rather than static attributes of identity.[2] Analyses of the past which grouped men only as 'Hindus' or 'Muslims', 'Indian' or 'Pakistani', must yield to a multi-dimensional view of changing identifications with changing pressures upon the populations involved. Some Bengalis—meaning for the moment those living in the Bengal Presidency as it existed from 1912 to 1947, who spoke Bengali and participated in the economy of Bengal—who were pushed in a time of crisis to identify with one political community having a particular national design, demanded new choices in later circumstances.

The literature of the partition period—by participants and subsequent writers—glosses over certain difficulties. In most accounts the two-nation theory of Mr Jinnah and the long-term inevitability of the partition are assumed because two nations did emerge and a partition did take place in 1947. Many writers have been selective in a particular way: they have picked out the divisive elements and events and left out the ways in which patterns of co-operation and alliance existed up to August 1947. They have given men of the 1930s and 1940s almost no free choice. Their historicist approach has shown us men shaped by forces which were uncontrollable.[3] Some have traced the division of India back to medieval times, maintaining that Hindus and Muslims were never linked organically, but simply co-habited in the same territory. For example, Dr R.C. Majumdar in a book on nineteenth-century Bengal pictures eternal differences:

> A fundamental and basic difference between the two communities was apparent even to a casual observer. Religious and social ideas and institutions counted for more in men's lives in those days than anything else; and in these two respects the two differed as poles asunder. . . . The literary and intellectual tradition of the two communities ran on entirely different lines, and they were educated in different institutions, *Tols and Madrassas. . . . It is a strange phenomenon that although the Muslims and Hindus had lived together in*

[2] Fredrick Barth (ed.), *Ethnic Groups and Boundaries* (London, 1969), p. 24; also relevant for the theoretical and comparative issues raised are: Paul R. Brass, *Language, Religion and Politics in North India* (Delhi, 1975); and *The Politics of Separatism* (London, 1976).

[3] The most astute discussion of inevitability with which I am familiar is by Isaiah Berlin, 'Historical Inevitability' in *Four Essays on Liberty* (London, 1969).

Bengal for nearly six hundred years, the average people of each community knew so little of the other's traditions.[4]

Dr Majumdar goes on to mention that there were some shared beliefs and shared superstitions, but holds that 'In all vital matters affecting the culture, the Hindus and Muslims of Bengal, as elsewhere in India, lived in two water-tight compartments as it were'.[5] He says that there was little ill-feeling between the communities, but this was because they passed their lives separately.

Even in areas of the world where there have been sharp religious differences, and where serious riots and wars between ethnic groups have occurred, national division has not necessarily followed. Where religious divisions have closely coincided with economic and territorial cleavages, there has been a more likely possibility of partition.[6] All those interested in analyzing the partition of India, including those taking the separatist view like Dr Majumdar, must ask: how did political organizations in the period before the partition mobilize their followers and shape their identities so that for many in 1947 only religious affiliation was salient? And further, was 'Muslim', 'Hindu', or 'Sikh' a sign or a mask for some more fundamental differences as some writers have suggested.[7]

[4] R.C. Majumdar, *Glimpses of Bengal in the Nineteenth Century* (Calcutta, 1960), 5–6; in a similar vein see Amalendu De, *Roots of Separatism in Nineteenth Century Bengal* (Calcutta, 1974).

[5] Majumdar, p. 7. The differing versions of India's past and unity held by Dr Majumdar and those opposing his views have recently erupted into a controversy of some significance for India's present and future. Some advisers to the new Janata Government and Dr Majumdar have criticized certain government-sponsored and widely-used history textbooks as being too pro-Muslim and for trying to portray one Indian nation in the past and not two. Among the writers of the texts are Romila Thapar, Barun De, Amales Tripathi, and Bipan Chandra. See 'Tampering with Textbooks', *Times of India*, 28 August 1977, and 'Scholars Condemn Move against History Books', *Times of India,* 27 August 1977; also see the pamphlet by Romila Thapar, Harbans Mukhia, and Bipan Chandra, 'Communalism and the Writing of Indian History', (New Delhi, 1977, 2nd edn).

[6] More work should be done in comparing the different partitions carried out by the British during the present century. Some general works on the decolonization process are: Nicholas Mansergh, *The Commonwealth Experience* (London, 1969) and Rudolf von Albertini, *Decolonization* (New York, 1971). Partitionsfor example those of Ireland and Palestinehave not resolved the ethnic conflicts which contributed to them.

[7] T.N. Madan, 'The Dialectic of Ethnic and National Boundaries in the Evolution of Bangladesh', in S. Navlakha (ed.), *Studies in Asian Development* (New Delhi, 1974), pp. 168–9.

Those viewing the sequence of events during the twentieth century somewhat differently from Dr Majumdar have chosen a point, for example, communal riots in 1907 or in the 1920s or 1930s, and drawn straight lines to the division of 1947. The Muslim League and the Indian National Congress were functioning in 1907 and in 1936 and these were the two organizations commanding support in 1947 with whom Lord Mountbatten had to deal. So the organizational paths to the divide, some have argued, are clear.[8]

Mr Jinnah, Dr Majumdar, and others have argued that there always were two nations, but it cannot be assumed. Evidence of all sorts from local, regional, and national arenas must be offered to make the case. I believe it is important to look at patterns of Hindu–Muslim co-operation and alliances as well as the latent hostility, exploitation, and conflict. It may be that there were alternatives of relationship and identity available to men in the prepartition period, but that these relationship cutting across the Hindu–Muslim divide were not strong enough to resist pressures for communal division and for the mobilization of men on the basis of communal identity. But even these choices in the 1930s and 1940s were not fixed and irrevocable as we have lately learned. It is preferable to look at more fluid situations for the choosing and shaping of ethnic and political identities both before and after 1947 in an effort to avoid unnecessary historicism and grossly inaccurate history.

The Indian nationalist movement as it developed in Bengal during the last quarters of the nineteenth century was dominated by high-cast Hindus. These men recruited primarily from the Brahmin, Kayastha, and Vaidya castes played paramount roles in positions allotted to Indians in the British Raj, in the professions, and in the cultural life of Bengal. Men from the higher castes had flooded into Calcutta as it grew apace in the nineteenth century. They constituted a disproportionate percentage of Calcutta's population (compared to their percentage of the population of Bengal) which went along with their

[8] Richard D. Lambert, 'Hindu-Muslim Riots' (PhD thesis, University of Pennsylvania, 1951), p. 108; Dr Lambert points to the riots in the mid-1930s and says that from that point communal relations were 'irreparable'; John R. McLane, 'The 1905 Partition of Bengal and the New Communalism', in Alexander Lipski (ed.), *Bengal East and West* (Michigan, 1969), p. 39; Dr McLane points to the 1907 riots as crucial for the development of communal relations in Bengal.

preponderating participation in institutions of the British–Indian establishment. Faster to take to Western education and to see the paths to success in British India, they were also continuing to fill high status roles that caste forebears had carried out, albeit with different content, during earlier ages in Bengal.[9]

The nationalism propagated by the Indian National Congress (of which Bengalis served as presidents during 12 of its first 32 years) was a territorial creed. Within Indian territory were a variety of cultural groups who together formed the nation. Ideally, the Congress wanted Muslims, Sikhs, Christians, Parsees, as well as Hindus, to flock together under the Congress banner and work for increased participation by Indians in ruling their own country. The land might have specifically Hindu connotations for many Hindus as in Bankim Chandra Chatterjee's *Anandamath*, but the Motherland was to be a home, early Congressmen said, for the children of all communities.[10]

In fact, though, the Congress was a small elitist organization for its first thirty years that made no extensive or sustained efforts to recruit Muslims and low-caste Hindus, or to build a mass organization. In Bengal Proper (leaving aside Bihar, Orissa, Assam, and Chota Nagpur which constituted parts of the Lieutenant-Governorship of Bengal) the Muslims were a slight but growing majority. But the Muslims in Bengal (as classified by the census, for the moment) lagged behind the Hindus in education, the professions, and the government services. Most of the Muslims were lower-class cultivators in the eastern districts of Bengal Proper who were tenents in Hindu lands and borrowed money from Hindu money-lenders. The Hindus, though highly stratified themselves, included the dominant Indian minority functioning in collaboration with the British rulers. The Muslims were

[9] See Leonard A. Gordon, *Bengal: The Nationalist Movement, 1876–1940* (New York and London, 1974), prologue and part 1; J.H. Broomfield, *Elite Conflict in a Plural Society* (Berkley, 1968), Introduction; Anil Seal, *The Emergence of Indian Nationalism* (Cambridge, 1968), chs 2 and 3; S.R. Mehrotra, *The Emergence of the Indian National Congress* (Delhi, 1971); on the roles of high-caste Hindus in earlier times, see Edward C. Dimock and Ronald B. Inden, 'The City in Pre-British Bengal', in Richard L. Park (ed.), *Urban Bengal* (Michigan, 1969).

[10] Gordon, ch. 1; on Bankim Chandra see T.W. Clark, 'The Role of Bankimcandra in the Development of Nationalism', in C.H. Philips (ed.), *Historians of India, Pakistan and Ceylon* (London, 1962), 429–40; and Rachel R. Van Meter, 'Bankimcandra's View of the Role of Bengal in Indian Civilization', in David Kopf (ed.), *Bengal Regional Identity* (Michigan, 1969), pp. 61–70.

much slower to gain Western education in Bengal and even those few interested in regional and national politics often stayed clear of the Congress.[11]

There is difficulty in lumping together all the Muslims resident in Bengal as an ethnic category. Many of those in the small Muslim elite were Urdu-speaking Muslims who did not think of themselves as or call themselves 'Bengalis'. They usually did not speak Bengali and did not identify with the masses of Muslims in Bengal who were Bengali speakers. The models followed by the Urdu-speaking Muslims were the Arabic and North Indian aristocratic, cultural, and religious ones. Appeal was made to the Great Tradition of Islam and prestige was given to foreign birth, Arabic names, descent from the Prophet, Urdu speech, and membership in the Ashraf, or upperclass Muslim community in India.[12] Members of this group were descended from families who have lived in Bengal for generations or were recent arrivals, but in either case they identified themselves as Muslims rather then as Bengalis. They may well have not felt any Bengali identification at all; in fact, they looked down upon all those who spoke Bengali, to them the language of idolatry and of cowards.[13] They saw Bengali-speaking Muslims as closer to Hindus than to the world of Islam. The Urdu-Muslims in Bengal tended to be more urban than rural and tended to live in the western rather than the eastern districts of Bengal, though urban Urdu-Muslims lived in Dacca and the towns of eastern Bengal.[14]

Bengali-speaking Muslims often had an unsure identity and complicated feelings of inferiority to the Urdu-speakers and to the Bengali

[11] De, pp. 3ff; Gordon, pp. 8–9.

[12] Interview with Abu Sayyid Ayyub, Calcutta, 24 November 1972; Mustafa Nurul Islam, *Bengali Muslim Public Opinions as Reflected in the Bengali Press 1901–1930* (Dacca, 1973), pp. 218ff; Kenneth McPherson, *The Muslim Microcosm: Calcutta, 1918 to 1935* (Wiesbaden, 1974), 9ff; M.K.A. Siddiqui, 'Caste among the Muslims of Calcutta', in Surajit Sinha (ed.), *Cultural Profile of Calcutta* (Calcutta, 1972), pp. 34, 44, 47; W.C. Smith, *Modern Islam in India* (Lahore, 1963); P. Hardy, *The Muslims of British India* (Cambridge, 1972), pp. 116ff.

[13] Sufia Ahmed, *Muslim Community in Bengal 1884–1912* (Dacca, 1974), pp. 28ff, Islam, *Bengali Muslim Public Opinion*, pp. 218ff; for a discussion of non-identification with Bengal on the part of a Muslim who spent a good part of his life there, see Gordon, analysis of Ameer Ali, pp. 60ff.

[14] H. Beverley (ed.), Government of India, *Report on the Census of Bengal* (Calcutta, 1872); J.A. Bourdillon (ed.), *Report on the Census of Bengal* (Calcutta, 1881), I.

Hindus. A hint of their problem is given in the very terms used to refer to the population of Bengal by Bengalis: 'Bengalis' and 'Mussalmans'.[15] The Bengalis *par excellence* were the Hindus. Bengali Muslims who gave predominance to the Bengali identity element were in an unlabeled residual category. They were in such a category because they tended to be rural, illiterate, lower-class peasants upon whom the Urdu Muslims and Bengali Hindus looked down. As one prominent Bengali Hindu writer said in an interview shortly before his recent death, 'I would always go to a Muslim tailor or a Muslim bookbinder'.[16] For him and for many others the Bengali Muslim masses were peasants or craftsmen; they were the lowers to whom one did not pay much attention and from whom one did not except any exceptional achievement.

These Bengali Muslim masses spoke Bengali with some admixture of Urdu or Persian words, but Bengali nevertheless. They had a tradition of *dobhasi* literature specifically for Muslims; however, those literate in Bengali read the works of Hindu Bengalis as well. They were subjected to ridicule for speaking and writing a language which some of their co-religionists said was a Hindu language the mere use of which smacked of idolatry.[17] But as one of Bangladesh's leading literary historians, Anisuzzaman, wrote recently, they knew they were Bengalis and they were Muslims. Some tried to participate more fully in the Great Tradition of Islam by learning Urdu, but the great majority did not.[18]

To trace in brief compass the relations of Hindus and Muslims in twentieth-century Bengal politics, it is necessary to focus on long-term trends and crucial events. In the simplest terms, the trends are the further development of Indian nationalism, the rising political con-

[15] This is a common characterization in Bengal; a letter in the *Statesman* (Calcutta), 9 June 1973, mentions this set of categories and goes on to discuss the difficulties of what to call the Bengalis after the establishment of Bangladesh; a controversy has been going on for some time in Bangladesh as to whether its citizens should be called Bengalis or Bangladeshis; those who believe that the so-called 'Bihari' Muslims are equally citizens prefer the term Bangladeshi, which also differentiates them from the citizens of West Bengal.

[16] Interview with Buddhadeva Bose, Calcutta, 9 July 1973.

[17] Islam, p. 223; Ahmed, pp. 305ff.

[18] Anisuzzaman, 'Cultural Trends in Bangladesh: A Redefinition of Identity' (Seminar paper, Nuffield College Oxford, 17 February 1975); also Anisuzzaman, 'The World of the Bengali Muslim Writer in the Nineteenth Century (1870–1920)', (Seminar paper, University of Sussex, 9 May 1975).

sciousness of Muslims in Bengal and India, and the slow retreat of British imperialism. One vital period during which there was a confluence of the three trends was the years of the first partition of Bengal, 1905 to 1912. The decision to partition Bengal was prepared by permanent officials of the Raj and approved by the Viceroy, Lord Curzon. The first partition encouraged the idea of a Muslim-majority east Bengal and a Hindu-majority west Bengal, or the division of the province on the basis of community, though the British publicly insisted that the partition was made for administrative reasons only. This partition helped arouse Muslim political consciousness and extensive agitation led by Hindus against it. The division scared the economically-dominate Hindus majority of east Bengal, set off a brief flurry of communal riots in a few rural areas, precipitated a temporary revival of Dacca and aroused the demand for more attention to the long-neglected districts of eastern Bengal.[19]

A second action by the British Raj which contributed to communal cleavage was the legislative councils reforms of 1909 which included the provision for separate Muslim and General or Hindu electorates. This stipulation, favoured by the Viceroy, Lord Minto, and the Urdu-Muslims of north India had the long-run effect of encouraging political organization and electoral appeal on the basis of community affiliation with a given territorial constituency. However much this may have helped the less organized political group in the short run, it surely led to sharper communal division in the long run.[20]

A third development in which the British rulers played a con-

[19] Z.H. Zaidi, 'The Political Motive in the Partition of Bengal', *Journal of the Pakistan Historical Society* (April 1964); Pardaman Singh, 'Lord Minto and the Partition Agitation', 85 *Bengal Past and Present* (July-December 1966), pp. 141ff; Richard Cronin, 'British Administration of Eastern Bengal and Assam, 1905–12: The Bureaucracy and Nationalism in Partitioned Bengal' (PhD thesis, Syracuse University, 1974); Sumit Sarkar, *The Swadeshi Movement in Bengal 1903–1908* (New Delhi, 1973); also McLane.

[20] Mary, Countess of Minto, *India Minto and Morley 1905–1910* (London, 1934), pp. 109ff, gives Minto's view; other views of the reforms are given in Gordon, pp. 94–6. Under the 1909 reforms the Legislative Council of the Lieutenant-Governorship of Bengal had 26 elected members and 4 of these seats were reserved for members of the Muslim Community, the first such reservation in the council. The Lieutenant-Governorship of Eastern Bengal and Assam had 18 elected members and 4 of these were to be Muslims. The number was small, but it was a first step and was the result of vigorous lobbying by Muslim League leaders, *Parliamentary Paper*, vol. 67, no. 5, 1910; also see Broomfield, pp. 35–8.

troversial role was the founding of the Muslim League at a meeting of upper-class Muslims in Dacca during 1906. It does not seem important to argue about whether the British were at the Bengal and Indian Muslim community. Although the meeting was well held in Dacca, the main body of men were upper-caste Urdu-speakers from northern India. The Dacca host, the Nawab of Dacca, and his compatriots were devoted loyalists, supporters of the Raj, whose aim was the protection of the rights of Muslims. It claimed to speak for the Muslims of India and its London lobbyist, the Aga Khan, worked for the acceptance of communal electorates as a step in this direction.[21]

With the revocation of the Bengal partition in 1912 and the involvement of Britain in a war partly against Turkey, home base of the Muslim Caliphate, some Muslim leaguers swung towards alliance with the Congress and a number of staunch loyalists left the League. The 1916 Congress–League or Lucknow Pact marked the honeymoon period of Hindu–Muslim relations which lasted until the mid-1920s. The pact provided for a full-scale reform scheme to be considered by the Government of India. Among the points agreed to was an allotment of Muslim and non-Muslim seats in the provincial legislative councils. The pact allotted only 40 per cent of the Bengal seats to the Bengal Muslims, although they constituted slightly more than 50 per cent of the population.[22] Here, as in many future bargains between national political organizations, or between these organizations and the Raj, some regional voices were strong, some were weak. The Bengal Hindus in the Congress argued that in their region they were superior in talent, accomplishment, and political consciousness, so they merited a majority of the seats, though they constituted a minority of the population. All-India Muslim leaders and a few Bengal leaders accepted this pact, but in future years those who wanted support from the Muslim community in Bengal had to demand seats in the council proportional to their percentage of the population. During this honeymoon period the first important Bengal Muslim leader came into the limelight. He was A.K. Fazlul Huq, a talented, mercurial, lawyer who spoke English in court, but eloquent Bengali in his populist, political speeches. Huq went along with this pact, but like other Bengali Muslim

21 Aga Khan, *The Memoirs of Aga Khan, World Enough and Time* (London, 1954), pp. 76ff.

22 C.H. Philips, H.L. Singh, B.N. Pandey (eds), *The Evolution of India and Pakistan 1858 to 1947* (London, 1962), pp. 171–3.

leaders seeking support, soon recanted and advocated the larger demand.[23]

The rise of Huq is a sign of a larger social, economic, and cultural trend: the slow, but continuing development of a Bengali Muslim middle class and their entry into politics. In the 1920s some of the educated among the Bengali Muslims began to fight back against those, Hindu and Muslim, who derided them. Although one trend was to learn Urdu and assimilate to the great Tradition of Islam, another was to assert that Bengali was their language and that they would continue to use it and to write creatively it in.[24] Some wrote in a Bengali containing many Persian terms; others wrote, noted a famous Bengali Hindu writer, 'just like us'.[25] Several literary groups flourished at Dacca University and one poet emerged whom the entire Bengali literary world hailed as a master: Nazrul Islam. The Bengali Hindu writer (mentioned earlier) who looked down upon the Bengali Muslims was moved to write in his brief account of Bengali literature:

> His appearance synchronized with that great upheaval in Indian life known as the first non-cooperation movement. In those days when the whole of India experienced a sudden, a magical sense of release, we in Bengal found in Nazrul Islam a voice of the moment; of his poetry both assuaged and enhanced the thirst created by the new initiation. . . . Freedom from bondage was the keynote of the poems of his first phase, wild exuberant, delirious poems, intoxicated and intoxicating. Like Dwijendralal Roy and Satyendranath Datta before him, he wrote with equal ardour on Hindu and Muslim subjects, on the dark goddess Kali and on Kemal Pasha. His mind, nourished on the myths and legends of both, was at home as much in the Gangetic plains as in the Arabian desert. . . . Born a Muslim and married to a Hindu, he has been

[23] Gordon, p. 159; footnote 88 in that chapter gives references to many of the English and Bengali works on Huq.

[24] Islam, pp. 226ff; Ahmed, pp. 305ff; Kazi Abdul Wadud, *Creative Bengal* (Calcutta, 1950), *passim;* McPherson, *passim*; other valuable sources on the Muslims through these years are: Abul Hayat, *Mussalmans of Bengal* (Calcutta, 1966), pp. 74ff; Mahmud Husain, 'Dacca University and the Pakistan Movement', in C.H. Philips and Mary D. Wainwright (eds), *The Partition of India* (London, 1970), pp. 369–73; Humaira Momen, *Muslim Politics in Bengal* (Dacca, 1972); M.A.H. Ispahani, *Quaid-i-Azam Jinnah As I Knew Him* (Karachi, 1967, 2nd edn); Kamruddin Ahmad, *A Socio-Political History of Bengal and the Birth of Bangladesh* (Dacca, 1975, 4th edn); Shila Sen, *Muslim Politics in Bengal, 1937–47* (New Delhi, 1976; Abul Mansur Ahmad, *Amardekha Rajnitir Panchas Bachar* [*Fifty Years of Politics as I Saw It*] (Dacca, 1975, 3rd edn).

[25] Conversation with Bishnu Dey, Calcutta, 6 July 1973.

abused and doted on by Hindus and Muslims alike, himself partaking of the life of both. To meet him has been to love him. . . .[26]

Of course the radicalism and atheism of Nazrul Islam has not been shared by large numbers of Muslim Bengalis. But the reflected light of his genius shone upon them and his brightness attracted some Muslims and many of the literati and politically left, most of whom were Hindus.[27] As Nazrul could not easily be assimilated into the world of the Urdu Muslims, so other educated Muslim Bengalis found such a process impossible. One well-known critic wrote:

Iqbal has asked Mussalmans to achieve self-effacement by merging themselves in the wider Islamic brotherhood and State. The endeavour may not be chimerical for the Punjab Muslim because of his proximity to the Muslim world. But even for him the union may be geographical and not physical on account of the stubborn barriers of language. And for the Bengali Muslim the prospects are absurd like the endeavours of the Indian Christians to be the kith and kin of his European brother-in-faith.[28]

The differences in perspective between Urdu Muslims in Bengal and Bengali Muslims continued to be expressed in large and small ways through the pre-partition period. Another example, in politics, was in the vital matter of representation and electorates. Once Bengali Muslims saw that sheer numbers would count and that their numerical majority would give them political predominance, they were more willing to accept joint electorates. The Urdu Muslims, with more of an all-India perspective in which the Muslims were a considerable, but small minority, insisted upon separate electorates. Some Bengali Muslims worked in the Congress or were affiliated to the Congress and called themselves Nationalist Muslims.[29] Though their number

26 Buddhadeva Bose, *An Acre of Green Grass* (Calcutta, 1948), pp. 36–9.
27 Ibid., p. 39; Wadud, pp. 123–6.
28 Ibid., p. 125.
29 McPherson, 108ff; John Gallagher, 'Congress in Decline: Bengal 1930 to 1939', in John Gallagher, Gordon Johnson, and Anil Seal, *Locality Province and Nation: Essays on Indian Politics 1870–1940* (Cambridge, 1973); Ram Gopal, *Indian Muslims, A Political History* (Calcutta, 1959), pp. 241ff; N.N. Mitra (ed.), *The Indian Annual Register* (Calcutta, 1919–1947), gives reports of meetings of nationalist Muslims advocating joint electorates, 1931, 1932; some examples are Abul Hayat of Burdwan, Choudhury Ashrafuddin Ahmed of Comilla, Rezaul Karim, Syed Badruddoza of Murshidabad; and communists like Muzaffar Ahmed and Abdullah Rasul; KPP members close to the Congress and sometimes having joint membership were Abul Mansur Ahmad, Nausher Ali, Shamsuddin Ahmed,

was small, their continued activity indicates a larger potentiality: the possibility for a strong Hindu-Muslim alliance in Bengal to work against the British Raj.

In the great political awakening after the first World War, Mahatma Gandhi came to leadership in the nationalist movement and decided to include a specifically Muslim issue, the continuation of the Caliphate, as an aim of his national Non-cooperation campaign. The inclusion of this issue brought about unprecedented, though temporary, cooperation among Hindus and Muslims through India. Greater numbers participated in Indian politics than ever before.[30] In Bengal the nationalist leader was C.R. Das who saw the necessity of significant Muslim support for one aspiring to all-Bengal political leadership. Though the Muslims in the Bengal Legislative Council had only 40 per cent of the seats, their votes were essential to nationalists seeking a majority in a council still having phalanx of European and official members. Das was able to gain greater Muslim support for his Swaraj Party from 1923 to his death in 1925 than any Bengali Hindu leader was able to secure subsequently. Though even this support was shaky, he did arouse trust and confidence among some Muslims in Bengal at the risk of alienating some of the scared Hindus, who felt that any important concessions to the Muslims (which they thought Das had made in the Bengal Pact of 1923) spelled the imminent doom of the Hindus.[31]

After Das' death in 1925, the Swaraj Party was not effective again in securing Muslim support. Communal relations in Bengal began deteriorating as they were in other parts of India. Calcutta saw its first serious riots between Bengali Hindus and Muslims in which members of each community desecrated the religious shrines of the other. Arya

---

Humayun Kabir, Jehangir Kabir.

30 Judith M. Brown, *Gandhi's Rise to Power, Indian Politics 1915–1922* (Cambridge, 1972), pp. 190ff; Broomfield, pp. 146ff; P.C. Ghosh, *Mahatma Gandhi, As I Saw Him* (Delhi 1968), pp. 88ff; D.G, Tendulkar, *Mahatma* (New Delhi, 1960), I, pp. 280ff; Ravinder Kumar (ed.), *Essays on Gandhian Politics* (Oxford, 1971).

31 Broomfield, pp. 254ff. Under the Government of India Act of 1919 the reformed Bengal Legislative Council had 26 nominated members and 114 elected members. Of the 114 constituencies 39 were reserved for Muhammadan members, while 46 were general non-Muhammadan seats, generally thought of as the Hindu ones. Government of Bengal, *Report on the Working of the Reformed Constitution in Bengal, 1921–27* (Calcutta, 1929), pp. 136–41.

Samajists, Hindu Mahasabhites, and H.S. Suhrawardy (a past Caliphate supporter and ally of Das) helped fan the communal flames.[32]

There is no doubt that there was increasing communal identification and growing tension between communities in the years from the first Bengal partition in 1905 to the second in 1947. There were riots in East Bengal in 1907, in Calcutta in 1918 and 1926, in Dacca during 1930 and 1941, and smaller, less noted clashes at other times.[33] There seemed to be much tension in the two urban centres—Dacca and Calcutta—where the two communities were fairly evenly matched, and where each wanted to demonstrate its dominance. The riots had some cumulative effect, but no riot had the devastating political and psychological effect that the 1946 great Calcutta killing had. What does seem difficult to me is to demonstrate that any of these earlier riots led to partition or made it 'inevitable'. They were part of the increasing politicization of the period and manifestations of communal tension, but they did not prevent political alliance, or close personal friendships between members of the two major communities.

In the post-Swarajist period from the late 1920s, the Simon Commission and other bodies were re-examining the reforms of 1919 and pointing towards new constitutional advances. After a deadlock on communal representation, the British Prime Minister issued his Communal Award of 1932 which sent convulsions through the Hindu community of Bengal.[34] Again, as in the case of the first Bengal

32 See Government of India, Home Department, II/VII/1926, IIXXV/1926, 187/1926, and 209/1926.

33 Lambert, has the most complete account; other accounts of the Bengal riots include: McLane; Broomfield, 'The Forgotten Majority: The Bengal Muslims and September 1918', in D.A. Low (ed.), *Soundings in Modern South Asian History* (London, 1968), pp. 196–224; and, of course, there are Government reports on the riots including Government of India, Home Department, II/VII/1926 and II/XXV/1926, on the 1926 Calcutta riots; Government of Bengal, Political Department, *Report of the Dacca Enquiry Committee 1930*, on the 1930 Dacca riots; Government of India, Home Department, 5/7/42, which includes the Report of the Dacca Riots Enquiry Committee, 1942, on the 1941 Dacca riots; Lambert has an extensive and illuminating account of the 1946 riots, but the material collected by the Spens Commission to which he had access is not now available, or at least I have not been able to find it in archives in London, New Delhi, and Calcutta.

34 *Bengal Anti-Communal Award Movement, A Report* (Calcutta, 1939); Zetland Collection, India Office Library, London, file on the Communal Award, especially the numerous pamphlets by B.C. Chatterjee and the clippings from the Hindu press of the period; Gallagher, pp. 297–8.

partition, the British Government was acting in its own interest and now went against the better judgement of the governor of Bengal (Sir John Anderson) and the most famous of Bengali's past governors (the Earl of Ronaldshay), ignoring the possible disastrous communal effects in Bengal. Under the Award the Muslims (54 per cent of Bengal's population according to the 1931 census) were given 119 seats in an assembly of 250 members and the Hindus (43 per cent of the population) were given 80, of which 30 were later reserved for scheduled caste members under the Poona Pact. The India Office deliberately skewed these seat distributions from a fairer distribution on the basis of numbers alone in order to gain all-India Muslim support for the reform scheme.[35] In response to the Communal Award, Bengal Hindus started a long and bitter petition campaign and agitation against it, which, though justified, alienated them from the nationalist Muslims in Bengal and even from the central organization of the Indian National Congress.[36] A Congress Nationalist Party was formed which demolished the regular Congress candidates in the election for seats in the Central Legislative Assembly contested during 1934.[37]

Sarat Chandra Bose, earlier and in later years a champion of Hindu–Muslim alliance in Bengal, was elected unopposed from a Calcutta seat with both Nationalists and regular Congressmen claiming his support. The 1934 defeats resulted in the Bengal Congress, whose election board was headed by Sarat Bose in 1936, taking a stronger and more direct stand against the Communal Award than national Congress policy allowed. A controversy ensued with Jawaharlal Nehru accusing the Bengalis of thinking too much in communal terms and of converting the Bengal Congress into the Nationalist Party.[38] Sarat Bose responded vigorously, insisting that the Bengal Congressmen

[35] Ibid., pp. 296–8; 'Communal Decision' (Private Office Papers, L/PO/49, India Office Library); there are references to Zetland's (Earl of Ronaldshay) opposition in Zetland Collection, file on the Communal Award, and to Anderson's opposition in B.P. Singh Roy Papers, Nehru Memorial Library, New Delhi, letter from Sir John Anderson, 27 September 1934.

[36] AICC Papers, Nehru Memorial Library, New Delhi, file G249(i), 1936, Communal Award, general correspondence by Pandit Jawaharlal Nehru; Gallagher, p. 300.

[37] Dr B.C. Roy ran this election campaign for the Congress in Bengal; see his papers, Nehru Memorial Library, file on the Revival of the Swaraj Party, November 1933-May 1934, and file 1934, as general secretary of the Congress Parliamentary Board; 'Nationalist' in this context had Hindu communalist overtones.

[38] AICC Papers, file G24(i), 1936.

never lost sight of the main issue of gaining independence, but that they wanted an unequivocal position on the Communal Award. He wrote to Nehru on 9 October 1936: 'The fact is that the Nationalist Party in Bengal has become merged into the Congress and not that the Nationalist Party has swallowed the Congress in Bengal'.[39] However, one must conclude that the Congress in Bengal had become tainted with Hindu communalism and some of its membership shared the outlook of the Hindu Mahasabha.

In addition to the composite, territorial Indian nationalism propagated by the Indian national Congress, another ideology was spread starting in the 1920s (and perhaps even earlier) by the Hindu Mahasabha. According to the Mahasabha, Indian culture is Hindu culture, Indian nationalism must be Hindu nationalism. They stress the association of the Hindus with their sacred territory: Hindustan. In their view many Christians and Muslims were converts from Hinduism and must, if at all possible, be re-converted by *shuddhi* activities. The Mahasabha's leader V.D. Savarkar developed the concept of 'Hindutva' which '. . . embraces all the departments of thought and activity of the whole being of our Hindu race'.[40] Any one who wanted to live in the Hindu nation would have to accept Hindustan 'as his Fatherland as well as his Holy Land, that is, the cradle land of his religion'.[41] So Muslims, prima facie, would be excluded from first class citizenship in such a nation. They would be subjects or perhaps foreigners in the land in which they lived.

The Hindu Mahasabha was never strong as an organization in Bengal, but its leader, Shyama Prasad Mookerjee, became a prominent and articulate spokesman for this point of view during the 1930s and 1940s. He, more than any other Hindu leader in Bengal, spurred the fears of high-caste Hindus inside and outside the Bengal Congress. They would, he said, lose their predominance in the economic and educational systems, in the professions and government services, to the numerically superior Muslims.[42] The Mahasabha encouraged in-

[39] AICC Papers, file G24(i), 1936.

[40] Quoted in Donald Eugene Smith, *India as a Secular State* (Princeton, 1963, pp. 458–9; *Hindutva* was first published in 1923.

[41] Quoted in Smith, p. 458.

[42] There is no adequate biography of Shyama Prasad Mookerjee; one by a disciple, Balraj Madhok, *Dr Syama Prasad Mookerjee* (New Delhi, 1954); some of Mookerjee's statements are collected in his *Awake Hindustan!* (Calcutta, nd); the Proceedings of the Bengal Legislative Assembly, 1937–47, contain numerous

flexibility on a variety of issues touching Hindu-Muslim relations in Bengal: processions playing music outside mosques, tenancy legislation and educational reforms which would assist the predominantly Muslim rural masses, and limitations in the Muslim role in Calcutta Corporation and Calcutta University.[43]

The fears even included the prospective disintegration of Bengali culture. During an Anti-Communal Award movement meeting in 1936, a speech by the noted novelist Sarat Chandra Chatterjee was reported in the press:

> Looking at the question as a humble worshipper in the temple of Bengali literature, he would like to say that he had noticed with a feeling of anguish and pain that attempts were already being made aiming a blow at the Bengali language and literature. From his experience as a literature he could say that he had always found Bengali language to be rich enough to be a powerful instrument for the expression of any thought that had ever occurred to him. He could not therefore understand the meaning of the demands that were now being made in certain quarters to import certain percentages of words, some from Arabic and some from the Persian languages.
>
> His apprehension was that ten years would not elapse before the Bengali language would take a different shape altogether. The attack had already begun. And perhaps ten years hence Rabindranath would not be there in his field of activities; it might be that the speaker himself might not be also there and he shuddered to think what transformation the Bengali language and literature might undergo in course of these ten years if the dark forces that were already at work were not checked be times.[44]

It was fear of 'dark forces' that haunted the minds and threatened the dominance of nationalist Hindus in many areas of Bengali life.

Many Hindus in the Congress, nevertheless, remained more open in their definition of who was a Bengali and who was an Indian and more open to the gradual upgrading of the Muslims and their greater participation in public life. As greater democracy came to India, men such as Sarat and Subhas Bose saw that such increased participation was inevitable. They preferred to work with this long-term trend toward democratization and forge, if possible, bonds of political al-

---

of his speeches; some of his letters are to be found in Akhil Bharat Hindu Mahasabha Papers, Nehru Memorial Library, New Delhi.

[43] For example, see the speech by N.C. Chatterjee to the Barisal Hindu Conference, 9 September 1944; and other pamphlets of the Hindu Mahasabha in the organization's files in the Nehru Memorial Library.

[44] *Bengal Anti-Communal Award Movement*, pp. 31–2.

liance between Bengali Muslims and Hindus, between the Krishak Praja Party (led by Fazlul Huq) and the Congress, and even between the Muslim League and the Congress. These Hindus adhered to the composite, territorial nationalism of the Congress.[45] They included the poet Rabindranath Tagore who argued for communal alliance from 1907 until his death in 1941.[46]

When the 1932 Communal Award was announced, many Hindus were swept along in the protest against it including Tagore. But, as usual, he approached the issue with slightly different concerns. First, he felt that dividing voters on the basis of caste and community would further divide the Indian people. Second, he said, '. . . our Muslim brethren have suffered for long from inequality of advantages in various lines. With all my heart I should welcome its being gradually brought to a balance'.[47] He wanted the Hindus not only to be aware of an injustice to them, but to remember the long-term suppression of the Bengali Muslims, and also to note that the communal Award was an award of the British Prime Minister, not the Muslims. Further, Tagore said, '. . . I earnestly ask my Hindu brethren never to lose their temper and aggravate the injury into suicide'.[48] Tagore was one of the Hindu Bengalis who sought the path of mutual tolerance so that both communities inhabiting Bengal might flourish. He was appreciated by Muslims as well as Hindus in Bengal and his songs serve as national anthems today for Bangladesh as well as for India. There were bridge-builders as well as communalists on both sides of the communal divide through the 1930s and 1940s.

The final decade of British rule in India was marked by the implementation of provincial autonomy, the rising demand for Pakistan with many Muslims rallying behind this call, and the self-inflicted impotence of the Congress during the Second World War. The national Congress left a vacuum which gave the Muslim League time and room

[45] They included C.R. Das and Sarat and Subhas Bose, and quite a few other Congressmen and members of the left in Bengal; see Gordon, part 3, *passim*.

[46] Ibid., p. 93; there are numerous comments on Hindu-Muslim relations and calls for their unity in Tagore's essays; see, for example, Rabindranath Tagore, *Towards Universal Man* (Calcutta, 1961) and Tagore's collected essays in *Rabindra Racanabali* (Collected works of Rabindra, Calcutta, 1961), vols XII and XIII.

[47] *Bengal Anti-Communal Award Movement*, p. 16.

[48] Ibid., p. 17.

to develop its organization and to break the strength of regional Muslim leaders who were not eager to come under the discipline of Jinnah's League. The decade of increasing communal polarization culminated in the tumultuous events that signified the British exit and the partition of India into Muslim-majority and Hindu-majority nations.

In Bengal these national trends had their impact and shaped the future of the region, but at the same time there were efforts by Hindu and Muslim leaders to ally in provincial cabinets and finally, if possible, to preserve the unity of Bengal by making it an independent, sovereign nation. Although the alliance and unity attempt failed, it is important to analyze these endeavours to more fully understand both the partition and the emergence of Bangladesh a generation later.

The results of the 1937 elections (the first under the Government of India Act of 1935, which included the terms of the Communal Award), showed the Congress to be the largest single party with about 54 seats, and the 119 Muslims seats split evenly between the Muslim League, Huq's Krishak Praja Party, and independents. There were several possible ways in which a coalition government could be formed in the 250-seat Bengal Legislative Assembly. In the spring of 1937 it was national Congress polity to decline to form ministries and not even to consider forming coalition governments. Though Sarat Bose, leader of the Congress Assembly group, wanted to join with Huq and prevent Muslim League domination of the province, Bose obeyed party discipline and rejected the offer of the Governor, Sir John Anderson, to form a government. National Congress policy blocked an important opportunity for communal, rapprochement.[49]

Fazlul Huq was forced to join forces with the Muslim League in Bengal and form a cabinet dominated by the League. Huq went even further: he himself joined the League, splitting his own party; he made a number of irresponsible communalist charges against Congress ministries in 1939; and then he moved the Pakistan Resolution at the Lahore session of the League in 1940.[50] Huq did see the need for some

[49] Government of India Bengal Governor's Reports, 1937; Gopal, p. 246; a number of political leaders of the period mentioned this in interviews; Jehangir Kabir was most forceful in asserting that this was a turning point. The Congress also lost an opportunity for communal alliance in other provinces; the most famous lost opportunity was in UP. This failure had important implications. See Maulana Abul Kalam Azad, *India Wins Freedom* (New Delhi, 1959), pp. 160–2.

[50] A.K. Fazlul Huq, *Muslim Sufferings under Congress Rule* (Calcutta, 1939); Nehru challenged Huq to tour the countryside and investigate the charges one by

Hindu support of his government and the important post of Finance Minister was given to Nalini Ranjan Sarker, Hindu businessman, former Congressman, and confidant of Mahatma Gandhi.[51] A spokesman for the Hindu landlords of Bengal, Sir Bijoy Prasad Singh Roy, also entered the cabinet.[52] Two League leaders and future Chief ministers of Bengal played conspicuous roles: Khwaja Nazimuddin was Home Minister; H. S. Suhrawardy was Labour Minister, and also Finance Minister after Sarker resigned in December 1939.

Although provincial autonomy was another step to self-government, its implementation by a Muslim League-dominated government in a province with Bengal's demographic and economic structure encouraged the communalization of almost every issue. The Muslims, as mentioned, had a population majority, but still lagged in all spheres of public, professional, and economic life. they wanted to use their political position favouring Muslims, and the reservation of government positions of all kinds for Muslims. They did make headway, but also aroused a Hindu backlash that made communal co-operation tortuous.[53]

Though Huq was head of the Bengal ministry, he was a restless politician who was always looking for a better arrangement. From 1937 he wanted to escape the clutches of the Muslim League and the discipline of Jinnah as well as the control of Urdu-speaking Muslim businessmen whom he called 'these up-countrymen in Calcutta'.[54] The Bose group in the Bengal Congress (i.e., the dominant faction headed by Subhas and Sarat Bose) for its part continued to look for a change to join Huq and turn the Muslim League out of power.[55]

---

one, but Huq, though at first agreeing to do so, always put Nehru off; references to this are in Jawaharlal Nehru Papers, Correspondence with Fazlul Huq, Nehru Memorial Library, New Delhi.

[51] The career of Sarker is described in Gordon, pp. 252–3.

[52] Sir B.P. Singh Roy Papers, Nehru Memorial Library, New Delhi; Singh Roy was personally friendly with many Muslim leaders and zamindars, particularly with Khwaja Nazimuddin and H.S. Suhrawardy. This appointment made it difficult to help the poor cultivators.

[53] The wrangling over every issue is evident in the Proceedings of the Bengal Legislative Assembly, 1937 to 1941; official comments on this wrangling can be found in Government of India, Bengal Governor's Report's 1937–41.

[54] On strains between the regional and national Muslim leadership, see Gopal, pp. 272–9; Sharifuddin Pirzada (ed.), *Quaid-i-Azam Jinnah's Correspondence* (Karachi, 1966, pp. 55–67; Sen, *passim*.

[55] Gordon, pp. 297–90; Interviews with Surendra Mohan Ghose, New Delhi,

In 1938 Subhas Bose served as president of the Indian National Congress with Gandhi's blessing. When Bose sought a second term in 1939, the Gandhians turned on him, put up their own candidate, Sitaramayya, and resigned from the Working Committee. After Bose narrowly defeated Sitaramayya, a nasty intra-Congress struggle ensued which led to Bose's resignation as president. A few months later, in mid-1939, Subhas Bose was suspended from Congress leadership positions for three years for defying national policy.[56] Early the following year Sarat Bose was also suspended and the Bengal Congress was divided between the majority Bose group and the official bloc.[57] Though this schism in the Bengal Congress seriously weakened the Bengal vote in national Congress affairs, it also allowed the Boses more room to manoeuvre on the Bengal scene.

The outbreak of the Second World War in September 1939 brought changes in Indian domestic politics. The Congress ministries resigned in the Hindu-majority provinces with the Muslim League celebrating this step by holding 'deliverance day' meetings. Briefly, and perhaps unfairly stated, the Congress leaders moved from ineffectual individual *satyagraha* in 1940, to ill-planned revolt in August 1942, to three years of frustration in prison, 1942 to 1945.[58] In Bengal the Huq ministry continued but Nalini Sarkar, friend of Gandhi, enemy of the Boses, resigned over the war issue. This stimulated the Boses to continue private, though not secret, negotiations with Huq in an effort to form a new government to be headed by the Bose Congress group and Huq's followers in the League and Krishak Praja Party.[59]

1965, 1972; Mr Ghose was personally involved in these negotiations; interviews with Nirad C. Chaudhuri, Delhi, 1965; Mr Chaudhuri was Sarat Bose's private secretary during this period; interview with Santosh Kumar Basu, Calcutta, 28 November 1972; Mr Basu became a minister in the Progressive Coalition ministry formed in December 1941; there are also references in the Bengal Governor's Reports, 1937–41.

[56] Gordon, pp. 268–78.

[57] Many of the relevant documents are contained in *Working Committee and Bengal Congress* (Calcutta, 1940); this collection gives primarily the Boses' version; the other side can be found in B.C. Roy Papers, file on 'Congress Working Committee and AICC, May 1939 to February 1940', Nehru Memorial Library; and in AICC Papers, file P . . . 5, I, II, III, IV, BPCC.

[58] The feeling of frustration is expressed in Jawaharlal Nehru, *The Discovery of India* (London, 1956), chs I, IX, X; also see Michael Brecher, *Nehru, A Political Biography* (London, 1959), ch. XI; there are several accounts of the 1942 rebellion; a recent one is Francis G. Hutchins, *Spontaneous Revolution* (New Delhi, 1971).

[59] At one point Subhas Bose was exasperated at the failure of efforts to form

Subhas Bose escaped from India in January 1941 to join the Axis powers, but Sarat Bose, leader of the opposition in the Assembly, continued talks with Huq. The alliance with Huq and the reconstitution of the Bengal ministry, called the Progressive Coalition ministry, was finally accomplished in December 1941 after many meetings in Bose's Woodburn Park house.[60] But, viewing with horror the possibility that Sarat Bose would become Home Minister in such a government, the Government of India, in collaboration with the Government of Bengal, arrested Sarat Bose just before the new cabinet was formed. The charges included that Sarat Bose had held secret meetings with Japanese representatives in Calcutta and that he presented a danger to internal security.[61] For the Raj, law and order considerations were paramount in wartime. In a border province, shortly to be threatened by the rapid Japanese advance through South East Asia, Fazlul Huq was marginally acceptable (through watched carefully because he was believed to be politically unstable), but Sarat Bose, brother of an Axis collaborator, suspected of terrorist leanings, was impossible. Saratbabu was held, without trial, for the duration of the war. Lord Linlithgow, the Viceroy, wrote to Mr Amery, the Secretary of State for India, shortly after Sarat Bose's arrest:

> It is obvious that it was well to have got Sarat Bose away from here, for from what I gather the restriction on his interviews were of the lightest, and in fact one individual went so far as to suggest that it was almost the case that Cabinet meetings were held in his quarters in the jail! That is not satisfactory, and though I realize the difficulties of local officials in debiting interviews with the Chief Minister and company against Sarat Bose's quota, I see myself no reason why he should not have been subject to precisely the same degree of

---

a coalition and wrote to the Viceroy asking him to dissolve the Huq-League Ministry; the letter is reprinted in Subhas Chandra Bose, *Crossroads* (Calcutta, 1962), pp. 356–7; but after Subhas Bose left India in January 1941 his brother, Sarat, continued the efforts.

60 *Statesman*, December 1941, gives a day-to-day account of the formation of the Progressive Coalition; also see Mitra, *Indian Annual Register*, 1941, II, pp. 143–51; Reginald Coupland, *The Constitutional Problem in India* (London, 1945), part II, pp. 29–31; Government of India, Home Department, Political, file 232/1941, Ministerial Crisis in Bengal.

61 Government of India, Public and Judicial, file 7542/1945; Dr Sisir K. Bose, one of Sarat Bose's sons, informs me that Sarat Bose did secretly meet with a Japanese representative in Calcutta.

restrictions the prisoner of his class while his contacts with the Japanese were an additional reason for exercising the greatest care in his case.[62]

The new Ministry was formed, nevertheless, but Shyama Prasad Mookerjee, leader of the Hindu Mahasabha, became the most important Hindu member of the cabinet instead of Sarat Bose. This gravely weakened the Ministry because the Muslim members could not have much confidence in someone with his views. Mookerjee did not have Bose's commitment to Hindu–Muslim alliance and the former joined the Ministry to protect the rights of Hindus.

The second Huq ministry continued until April 1943, but was subjected to extraordinary pressures by the Raj, by the Muslim League (which had expelled Huq), and by having to deal with the Congress rebellion on August 1942, which, *inter alia*, involved the complete breakdown of government authority in parts of Midnapore district. The two Congress ministers from the Bose group remained in the Ministry until 1943, but Shyama Prasad resigned in late 1942, not because of any disagreement with Huq but because the Mahasabha leader claimed that British officials were abrogating the rights of the Hindus.[63] The Ministry was not notable for its achievements, but it was the last time that important representatives of the Hindu community in Bengal served together with prominent Muslims in a provincial cabinet.

Jinnah and his Muslim League supporters in Bengal campaigned against the Ministry and the British governor, Sir John Herbert, worked for the dissolution of it. Jinnah toured the province calling Huq a traitor to the Muslim community. Herbert wanted a more malleable chief minister and cabinet, particularly as the Japanese advanced through Burma and air raids threatened Calcutta. Herbert asked Huq to submit his resignation as the preliminary step, Huq later said, of forming an all-parties ministry. Herbert promptly accepted the resignation, even over the better judgement of the Government of

[62] Government of India, Public and Judicial, file 7542/1945, extract from private and personal letter from Lord Linlithgow to Mr Amery, 30 December 1941.

[63] One of Mookerjee's statements at this time is in Bengal Legislative Assembly Proceedings, Fifteenth Session, 1943, statement in the Assembly, 12 February 1943; other comments are to be found in Government of India, Home Department, Political, file 33/45/1942; Abul Mansur Ahmad, a Muslim leader of the period, in an interview in Dacca, June 1972, mentioned that the Muslims trusted Shyama Prasad much less than they did Sarat Bose.

India, rejected Huq's charges of trickery, and allowed Khwaja Nazimuddin, leader of the Muslim League in Bengal, to form a new ministry.[64] Several Hindus served in this ministry, but they were men with no following, who joined in hopes of personal glory.

With a League ministry in power and Congress leaders imprisoned or hopelessly outmanned, the Muslim League organization in Bengal was built up for the first time into something approaching a mass movement under the direction of its astute General Secretary, Abul Hashim, a Bengali Muslim leader from Burdwan district.[65] Through the years 1943 to 1946, Hashim and other League workers brought the Muslim student community and many Muslim intellectuals, based in Dacca and Calcutta, into the League for the first time. Muslim politicians who had been independents (Hashim himself had been an independent until 1943) or in the Krishak Praja Party shifted to the League. Hashim tirelessly toured the province finding men to organize the League in every district and even making contact with members of rival political parties, Fazlul Huq, the most popular Bengali Muslim leader of almost a generation, with Hashim's help, was pushed into temporary obscurity. Hashim followed Huq into the districts and occasionally disrupted his political meetings. Both Urdu-speaking and Bengali-speaking Muslims in Bengal flocked to the League in the few years before the partition as never before and never again after 1947.[66]

In the decade and a half before this great swing to the League, its programme had been gradually changing. In the late 1920s and 1930s League resolutions demanded 'safeguards' for the Muslim minority within India. But slowly in the 1930s and rapidly from 1940, the line changed: the Muslims in India were not a minority, but a nation, a nation called 'Pakistan' which insisted on equality with the Hindu nation. When the Pakistan resolution was put forth in 1940 Muslim League spokesmen from the Muslim minority areas saw that the

64 Huq's statements are in A.K. Fazlul Huq, *Bengal Today* (Calcutta, 1944); also see Mitra, *Indian Annual Register*, 1943, I, pp. 90–8; II, pp. 43–9, 126–33; a number of British ICS officers of the period mentioned that they believed that Herbert tricked Huq into submitting his resignation and that the government of India was none too happy about the way Herbert operated in this situation.

65 Interviews with Abul Hashim and Abul Mansur Ahmad, Dacca, 1972; it is clear from the election results of 1945–6; Abul Hashim, *In Retrospection* (Dacca, 1975); Sen, chs VI and VII; Abul Mansur Ahmad, chs 13–14.

66 Interviews with Abul Hashim and Abul Mansur Ahmad, Dacca, 1972; Hardy, pp. 235ff; Sen, pp. 182ff; Begum Shaista Ikramullah, *From Purdah to Parliament* (London, 1963), pp. 99ff.

establishment of a Muslim nation or nations in the north-west and north-east of India would still have them as a minority in the Hindu nation. But League leaders joined in a chorus proclaiming that the Muslim nation would protect the minority left behind. The most important concern was to get some territory completely free from potential Hindu domination. Muslims were asked to identify only as Muslims, no longer as Bengalis, Biharis, Punjabis, etc. The Muslim nation would be established in those territories where the Muslims were a majority, but the basis of nationality was membership in the religious community of Muslims, not residence.[67] To the Mahasabha the whole territory of Hindustan was sacred; to the Congress the whole territory of India was associated with their composite nationalism; but to the League, community counted first, specific territory was a secondary consideration. Yet if there had been no substantial area of India in which the Muslims were in a majority, the claim to independent nationhood would probably have been impossible.

In light of the political shifts during 1946 and 1947, it is necessary to look at the way in which the Pakistan idea was presented to Muslims in Bengal. In many cases it was surely a simple Muslims-versus-Hindus formula. Abul Hashim's version, in a widely circulated pamphlet, *Let Us Go to War* (1945), is more complicated since it implies a multi-nation rather than a two-nation theory. He said, in part:

> Free India was never one country. Free Indians were never one nation. In the past India was *Akhand* under the domination of Great Britain. Liberated India must necessarily be, as God has made it, a subcontinent having complete independence for every nation inhabiting it. However much weakness the Congress may have for the capitalists of Bombay and however much they may desire, by way of doing a good turn to them, to open opportunities for exploiting the whole of India under the cover of *Akhand Bharat*, Muslim India to a man will resist all attempts of the Congress to establish dictatorship in India of any coterie, group or organization. Pakistan means freedom for all, Muslims and Hindus alike. And the Muslims of India are determined to

[67] This gradual shift can be traced in G. Allana (ed), *Pakistan Movement: Historic Documents* (Karachi, 1968), 90ff; this is all further complicated by Jinnah's insistence that Pakistan was to be a secular state and not a theocratic one. (E.g. see his statement reported in the *Amrita Bazar Patrika*, 12 April 1946.) The question of Islamic or secular statehood is still a live issue in Pakistan and Bangladesh. It may be added that whatever Jinnah added to reassure the minorities of a future Pakistan, the Muslims in the majority areas were convinced that they would call the tune in this future Pakistan and the potential Hindu and Sikh minorities were not at all reassured by Jinnah's words.

achieve it if necessary, through a bloodbath. Thus, Congress ought to realize that when we Muslims talk of freedom and independence, we seriously mean it and Muslims of India are opposed to every kind of domination and exploitation—British or Indian. In Pakistan there will be just and equitable distribution of the rights and privileges of the state amongst all its citizens irrespective of caste, colour and creed. And it is not in the contemplation of the Muslims to reserve any advantage for themselves except their right to govern their own society according to the laws of the *Shariat.* It is untrue and mischievous to say that Pakistan means the domination of the Muslims and to say that Pakistan means opportunity for the Muslims to dominate and exploit others.[68]

For Hashim, who made it clear through his life that he considered himself a Bengali and a Muslim, India was multi-national and Bengal was one of the constituent nations. It happened that in the Bengal nation Muslims were a majority. But he did not want to create an exclusivist Muslim nation in Bengal. He wanted a socialist nation that for the moment would be joined to the Muslim nation in the northwest of India. In this Bengal nation all Bengalis would be welcome and the Muslims would be governed by the *shariat* as the Hindus would be governed in social and religious matters by their own laws. He tried to remind League leaders, even as he was building the League organization in Bengal, that the Pakistan Resolution read, in part:

. . . the areas in which the Muslims are numerically in a majority as in the Northwestern and eastern zones of India should be grouped to constitute 'Independent States' in which the constituent units shall be autonomous and sovereign.[69]

However Jinnah, Liaquat Ali Khan, and many of the Urdu-speaking Muslims in the League read the resolution, Hashim emphasized 'independent *states*', and Bengal was one of the states. Hashim's view of India differed from both the Congress and the League views.[70] The

[68] Hashim, p. 176.

[69] Allana, p. 227.

[70] Hashim, pp. 134ff; Hashim's view was closer to that of the Communist Party; see G.D. Adhikari, *Pakistan and National Unity* (Bombay, 1944) 3rd edn, for the Communist Party approach. Hashim insists in his account that he tried to resist the rewording of the Pakistan resolution from 'states' to 'state'. There are no minutes of Subjects Committee meetings of the Muslim League readily available nor were reports usually published in the press. From a scrutiny of published League documents and some press reports of the time, it appears that in 1946 the ambiguity in the wording of the 1940 resolution was eliminated at the time of the

Congress in its re-organization around 1920 had put its organization on the basis of linguistic regions; it always insisted, however, that these linguistic regions were not separate nations, but parts of one, multi-linguistic, multi-cultural regions was a nation and that some of the nation would be Muslim-majority nations. But he did not define nationality on the basis of religion as many in the League were doing in the 1940s. So we are left with the curious fact that the man whom many felt was more responsible for building the League organization had a different concept of nationality from the Muslim League.

At a meeting in Calcutta during 1945, concerned with giving some cultural meaning to 'Pakistan', another recent convert to the Muslim League, Abul Mansur Ahmad, writer and journalist, said that 'Pakistan' surely meant 'cultural autonomy'. He thought that religion and culture were different. By culture he seemed to mean Bengali culture and literature which he said was to some extent similar for Hindus and Muslims in Bengal, and to some extent dissimilar. He tried to demarcate what the culture of East Pakistan should be. It was to be Bengali culture freed from Hindu linguistic and religious shackles. it was to be Muslim, but distinctive from the culture of the West

Muslim League Legislators' Convention in Delhi, April 1946. From several sources it appears that Hashim did object to this change in a closed session of that Convention and was put in his place by Jinnah. Abul Mansur Ahmad, in an interview in Dacca, August 1977, told me that Hashim wanted two constituent assemblies for the Muslims (one for the east, one for the west), but that Jinnah squelched this idea and said this would make the Muslims appear ridiculous. Professor Abdul Rezzaque, of Dacca University, an expert on the history of the Muslims, also said in an interview, August 1977, that Hashim objected to the change in April 1946. Also see on this point, Sen, p. 207; Choudhry Khaliquzzaman, *Pathway to Pakistan* (Lahore, 1961), pp. 341–5, discusses whether or not Hashim made objections in 1946, but comes to no conclusion, except that he cannot remember the objections. It should be added that there was an effort by the Muslim League to eliminate the ambiguity in April 1941 when at a meeting of the All-India Muslim League in Madras the words in italics in the following phrase were added to the 1940 resolution: '. . . shall be grouped together to constitute independent states *which shall be one national homeland* in which the constituent units are autonomous and sovereign', *Bombay Chronicle*, 16 April 1941. There have been some suggestions that Hashim objected to this rewording in 1941, but I have not been able to find any concrete evidence to support this. In April 1946 Mr G.M. Syed, leader of the opposition in the Sind Assembly, objected to the change from 'states' to 'state' and said this would lead to the domination of the Punjab over the smaller units in the western wing of a future Pakistan. He said the Muslim League should be forced to go back to the voters to get ratification of this change. (*Amrita Bazar Patrika*, 13 April 1946.)

Pakistanis. So it was to be Bengali and Muslim, but divergent from the culture of other Bengalis and other Muslims.[71] This was yet another effort to define, however clumsily, the new nationality of the Muslims in Bengal, an effort that continues today.

At the same time the Muslims throughout India were giving their definitions of 'nation' and of 'Pakistan', the Hindus and other groups were also trying to come to grips with the demand for partition. The Congress, though it did not want the division of India, had begun to say: if it does have to come because of the adamant stand of the League then it must be done in such a way that the largest numbers of non-Muslims remain in India. What they brought up during the Cripps Mission in 1942 and held to during the post-war negotiations was that, if India was partitioned, then provinces would have to be partitioned as well. They might have to give Jinnah his Pakistan, but it would be minus the non-Muslim areas of the Punjab and Bengal adjacent to India.[72]

The position of the Hindu Mahasabha during the war period is stated by M. D. Biswas, writing to the Mahasabha President from the Bengal Provincial Hindu Mahasabha office, 6 October 1944:

> . . . I should like to take this opportunity of reiterating that no Hindu worth the name will support the vivisection of India. I may also assure you with all the emphasis at my command that not a single patriotic Hindu of Bengal will ever flinch from fighting the move of vivisection to the last drop of his blood.[73]

At about the same time the central Mahasabha office addressed letters to a number of Hindu religious leaders in India asking their attendance at a Akhand Hindustan Leaders conference:

> As a successor to the highest Hindu religious order you must be aware of the greatest threat to the integrity of Hindustan and consequent blow to the Hindu religion and culture in the so-called C.R. formula which envisages partition of India. The founder of the order to which His Highness belongs did believe

[71] His views are analyzed in Anisuzzaman, pp. 6–7; also see Abul Mansur Ahmad's collected essays, *End of a Betrayal and Restoration of Lahore Resolution* (Dacca, 1975), *passim*.

[72] A precise and intelligent analysis of the development of Congress policy is provided in S.R. Mehrotra, 'The Congress and the Partition of India', in Philips and Wainwright, pp. 188–221.

[73] Hindu Mahasabha Papers, Nehru Memorial Library, 1940–5, Working Committee file.

in the integrity of Hindustan. This is clear from the very fact that he established his *Maths* in four corners of the world. I humbly request your Holiness as a worthy successor of the highest Hindu religious [office] to give a lead in opposing this monstrous scheme.[74]

So the Mahasabha was more concerned that the Congress might accept some kind of partition than with the Pakistan proposal of the league itself. Hindus, they said, must stand together in the hour of need.

Shortly after the end of the Second World War the Government of India held the long-deferred elections for the provincial assemblies. The League's war-time mobilization efforts bore fruit: it swept almost all the Muslim seats in the Muslim-majority provinces giving its Pakistan demand some electoral backing for the first time. The Congress won almost all the general seats but contested few of the Muslim ones. In Bengal, Fazlul Huq and a sorry remnant of the Krishak Praja Party contested some Muslim seats with congress backing. Though Huq himself won, the party was finished, and the League won almost every other of the 119 Muslim seats. With this solid bloc of Muslim seats in the Bengal Assembly, the League could form a cabinet without any important Hindu support.[75] H. S. Suhrawardy later said that he had wanted to form a coalition with the Congress, but that its High Command had vetoed this suggestion.[76] Suhrawardy, as head of the League in Bengal, became the Chief Minister and formed a Muslim League cabinet, to which he later added a number of marginal Hindus

[74] Hindu Mahasabha Papers, 1940–5, Working Committee file.

[75] Mitra, *Indian Annual Register*, 1946, I, 'Chronicle of Events'; II, pp. 66–96; *Amrita Bazar Patrika* 1–14 April 1946, gives extensive reports on the election results and on the charges that the Muslim League, with the aid of the government, intimidated voters who wanted to vote for opposition Muslim candidates. All the precise figures are compiled in *Return Showing the Results of Elections to the Central Legislative Assembly and the Provincial Legislatures in 1945–46* (New Delhi, 1948).

[76] *Amrita Bazar Patrika*, 12–24 April 1946, presents a day-by-day account of these negotiations and prints the letters exchanged between Suhrawardy and K.S. Roy. Maulana Azad was also involved in the bargaining on behalf of the national Congress organization. Each side claimed that the other did not really want a coalition and acted in bad faith once the failure was announced. The Congress through K.S. Roy laid down five conditions which Suhrawardy went only part way to meet. Both sides appear to have been rather inflexible. Lord Wavell, Viceroy at the time, presents a different view from that of Suhrawardy and suggests that it was Jinnah, rather than the Congress high command, that prevented the formation of a Congress-League coalition government. See Lord Wavell, *Viceroy's Journal*, Penderel Moon (ed.) (London, 1973), p. 348.

who had no support in the Assembly. So Bengal, with the threat of partition hanging heavy, was back to Muslim League government. This government differed in personnel from the 1937–41 and 1943–5 ministries, but it again represented Muslim League domination and Congress–Hindu exclusion.

After almost four years' imprisonment, Sarat Bose was released in September 1945 when the Government of India was convinced that his younger brother Subhas Bose, leader of the Indian National Army, had died in a plane crash. The older Bose rejoined the Congress, ran its electoral campaigns in Bengal and the Punjab, and was himself elected to the Central Legislative Assembly, where he became leader of the Congress group. The Bose position had always been that India was one nation and that the Pakistan movement must be vigorously opposed. Sarat Bose had worked for Hindu–Muslim coalition before his internment, he redoubled his efforts in much more trying circumstances after the war.[77]

With the end of the war in Europe, the Viceroy, Lord Wavell, held a conference in Simla of Congress and League leaders that produced no positive results. In July 1945 Clement Attlee became British Prime Minister, heading a Labour Government, much more committed than Churchill's Conservatives to constitutional advance for India. In March 1946 a Cabinet Mission was sent to India to explore the possibilities for a Congress–League agreement. The Congress, with reservations, accepted provisions for an Interim Government, while the League concurred without reservations. Once the Congress interpretation was announced, the League backed away from the agreement.[78] While the Cabinet Mission was still in India, Sarat Bose said,

> I need hardly say that if any proposals are made in future for the dissection of the Punjab or of Bengal they will be strenuously resisted. There is absolutely no case for dissection either of the Punjab or of Bengal.
>
> Redistribution of Provincial boundaries on a linguistic basis is another matter and it will have to be considered on its merits at the proper time.[79]

[77] Sarat Bose's statements from this period are collected in Sarat Chandra Bose, *I Warned My Countrymen* (Calcutta, 1968); also see Nicholas Mansergh (ed.), VI *The Transfer of Power 1942–7* (London, 1976), pp. 47ff.

[78] Nicholas Mansergh, *Transfer of Power* (London, 1974), Wavell, pp. 137ff.

[79] Bose, *I Warned My Countrymen*, p. 154; in April 1946 when rumours began to spread that the Congress Working Committee might eventually agree to the partition of Bengal, Sarat Bose, then in Delhi, met Maulana Azad to voice his

So Sarat Bose adhered to the old Congress position: India is one although it is composed of many linguistic regions. The Cabinet Mission implicitly agreed that India was one by casting aside the demand for Pakistan and pressing for the formation of an Interim Government of Indian ministers from both Congress and League to see whether the parties could work together when given government responsibility.[80]

The Muslim League, however, felt that the Mission had shown bad faith in the negotiations and instead of joining the government at the centre, called for 'Direct Action Day' throughout India on 16 August 1946.[81] This 'Direct Action Day' led to one of the most terrible events in modern Indian history: the great Calcutta killing. This conflagration needed dry wood from which to start. It was to be found in the rising communal tension of the past decades, the political rivalry of the League and the Hindu-dominated organizations, and the struggle for control of Bengal's great capital city. Calcutta was the economic, administrative, cultural, and political hub from which spokes reached out in every direction to all of eastern India. If Calcutta was to be in Pakistan, as Jinnah had promised, then the Muslims wanted to show that they controlled it. If Calcutta was going to remain in India, then the Hindus wanted to demonstrate that it was their city. The Muslims were only about 20 per cent of Calcutta's population, but they controlled the state government. Both sides had been preparing for trouble, and riots over the INA trials in 1945 had shown how volatile the city was. Rioting, looting, and the massacre of members of each community by members of the other continued for several days until finally the army brought temporary peace. Between 5000 and 10,000 died and many thousands more were wounded and burnt out of their homes.[82] There had been riots before—in rural areas, in Dacca, and

---

objections and then arranged for meetings between prominent Bengal Congressmen and Azad to explain that partition was unacceptable to Bengalis. At one such meeting on 14 April 1946 Sarat Bose invited Azad along with Dr P.C. Ghose, Kiran Sanker Roy, Devendralal Khan, Sasanka Sanyal, and J.C. Gupta. A year later Sarat Bose could not gather such a group and was virtually alone in his objections to the partition on behalf of Bengali Hindus. Press report on 1946 meeting in *Amrita Bazar Patrika*, 16 April 1946.

[80] H.V. Hodson, *The Great Divide* (London, 1969), chs 11–12.

[81] Hardy, p. 249; Mitra, *Indian Annual Register*, 1946, II, 'Chronicle of Events', 29 July.

[82] Lambert, ch. VI; Francis Tuker, *While Memory Serves* (London, 1950), pp. 152ff.

in Calcutta, but never had there been bloodshed on this scale. And none of the earlier riots had the devastating political and psychological effect that the great Calcutta killing had.

During the past several years, I have interviewed about 70 participants in the events of the two decades before partition. Of many, I have asked: when did you think that there would be a partition and when did you come to believe that the British would leave India. Many of the individuals, Bengali politicians (Hindu and Muslim) and British ICS officers being the two most numerous categories of interviewees, said that they had thought in the 1930s that the end of the British era in India was fast approaching. But very few said that they had thought that there would be a partition of India before the middle 1940s. Many said that the clinching event was the great Calcutta killing. After that event, they said, Hindus and Muslims could not trust each other, would not live together. A number of Hindus, some in the ICS, and some in the nationalist movement, said they felt that this terrible bloodbath had been inspired by and was the responsibility of the Muslim League Government in Bengal at that time, and that after the August riots Hindus would never agree to live under a Muslim League Government, in free Pakistan, or in united independent Bengal, or in free federated India.[83]

The Spens Commission was set up to enquire into the causes of and responsibility for the riots. Though it gathered testimony, it never produced a report. Perhaps the government feared that the report itself might rekindle communal fires.[84] In the Bengal Legislative Assembly and in the nationalist press Congress leaders and the Hindu community blamed Chief Minister Suhrawardy, Nazimuddin, and the League Ministry for the riots.[85] Although the Muslim majority in the Assembly

[83] Some of the interviewees were: B.K. Acharya, ICS, M.O. Carter, ICS, R.C. Dutt, ICS, Ajoy K. Ghosh, ICS, Sir P.J. Griffiths, ICS, J.L. Llewellyn, ICS, Peter N. McWilliam, ICS, L.G. Pinnell, ICS, Annada Sankar Ray, ICS, and A.W. Mahmood who was in the Education Service; the political leaders included: Abul Mansur Ahmad, Santosh Kumar Basu, Tridib Chaudhuri, P.C. Ghosh, Surendra Mohan Ghosh, Samar Guha, Gopal Haldar, Abul Hashim, Jehangir Kabir, Hiren Mukherjee, Sasanka Sanyal, and P.C. Sen.

[84] Lambert used the Spens Commission materials; several of those interviewed by the Commission said that it broke off its work because of possible negative political consequences.

[85] Mitra; Bose, *I Warned My Countrymen*, pp. 155–7; Lambert, pp. 166–71; many Hindu politicians interviewed including Surendra Mohan Ghosh, who was

beat back no-confidence motions against Suhrawardy and the Ministry, much of the Hindu community grew more alienated from the Muslims and communal identification became ever more important as one's primary identity.

Sarat Bose, as one of those involved in the peace effort along with other Congress leaders, called for the resignation of the League Ministry and for the formation of an all-party ministry as the first step in solving the communal problem. Late in August he became a Minister in the Interim Government at the centre when the Congress took up the seals of office. But he did not have enough political muscle to bring about the coalition government in Bengal which Suhrawardy claimed was blocked by the antipathy of Sardar Patel, a key figure in the Congress party organization.[86]

When communal violence directed against a small, helpless Hindu minority began in the rural, East Bengal districts of Noakhali and Tipperah in October, Congress leaders including Gandhi went there to try to end the hostilities. They insisted that Suhrawardy's League Ministry was not doing enough to protect the Hindus.[87] Mahasabha leader Shyama Prasad Mookerjee, though still calling for Indian unity, said in a public statement that there was an organized campaign against the minority community.[88] Shortly after the communal rioting spread to Bihar where the Muslim minority was attacked by the Hindu majority. Jinnah, called, at this time, for an exchange of population as part of the Pakistan scheme, but Hindu politicians of all parties rejected this proposal as impossible.[89]

With the Interim Government in a stalemate between its League and Congress members, Viceroy Wavell flew to London with Nehru and Jinnah in early December to see if negotiations in that more bracing climate would be productive. They were not. So early the following year, the British Government decided to replace Wavell with Lord Mountbatten and set the date June 1948 for British with-

---

a Congress leader present in Calcutta at the time, blamed Suhrawardy and Nazimuddin.

[86] Mitra, p. 193; several of those interviewed, including Sasanka Sanyal and Surendra Mohan Ghosh, have testified to Patel's control of Congress politics and his desire to have more malleable men than Sarat Bose in control in Bengal.

[87] AICC Papers, Acharya Kriplani Report on Visit to Noakhali, 1946; Pyarelal, *Mahatma Gandhi, The Last Phase* (Ahmedabad, 1965), vol. I, book 1, pp. 277ff.

[88] Mitra, 27 October.

[89] Ibid, 26 November.

drawal.[90] While welcoming the announcement of the British Government, Shyama Prasad warned,

> Hindus will resist with their life blood any scheme of the perpetuation of slavery which will be inevitable if Bengal, as she is constituted and administered today, is allowed to become a separate independent unit cut off from the rest of India. Nothing can justify the transfer of nearly 35 millions of persons belonging to one community to the perpetual domination of an artificial majority which refuses to identify itself with the rising aspirations of the entire people.[91]

Mookerjee's statement signalled an important shift in Mahasabha polity; instead of calling unceasingly for Indian unity, for the indivisibility of the fatherland, believing the granting of the Pakistan demand likely, they were now willing to give up some territory in return for keeping the maximum number of Hindus in India. They now wanted the division of Bengal into a Hindu-majority West Bengal and a Muslim-majority East Bengal, whether or not Pakistan was established. Throughout the spring of 1947 Mookerjee became the single most vocal spokesman for the Bengali Hindus, and gradually, the majority of the Congress in Bengal, Bengal members of the Constituent Assembly, and members of the Congress Working Committee joined him in the demand for the partition of Bengal.[92] As the editors of the *Indian Annual Register* commented, one must understand the evil spirit of 1946 to understand why the partition was accepted in 1947.[93] The evil spirit of communal hatred allowed Shyama Prasad to mobilize the Hindu community for partition in 1947 and to bring the Mahasabha and Congress in Bengal together at this climatic moment.

The counter-movement to that of Shyama Prasad Mookerjee was slower to coalesce. Jinnah and the Muslim League obviously did not want to lose West Bengal and particularly Calcutta from their planned Pakistan. They had envisioned all of Bengal and all of the Punjab in their new Muslim-majority nation. But no Hindu leader could or would speak for the unity of Bengal on this basis. The only ground on which

[90] Hodson, pp. 189ff; Larry Collins and Dominique Lapierre, *Freedom at Midnight* (New York, 1975), pp. 13ff; on the shortcomings of the Collins-Lapierre version, see my review of their book in *The Journal of Asian Studies* (August 1976).

[91] Mitra, *Indian Annual Register*, 1947, I, 'Chronicle of Events', 22 February.

[92] Ibid.; AICC Papers, files CL-8, CL-14C, CL-14D, CL-21, Bengal Partition Papers, Nehru Memorial Library; Madhok, p. 20; Hashim, p. 137.

[93] Mitra, *Indian Annual Register*, 1946, I, p. 67.

some Hindu leaders would step forward was a plan for a united, independent Bengal.[94] Criticizing a Congress Working Committee resolution recommending division of the Punjab and Bengal passed in early March, Sarat Bose said on 15 March:

By accepting religion as the sole basis of the distribution of provinces, the Congress has cut itself away from its natural moorings and has almost undone the work it has been doing for the last 60 years. The resolution is the result of a defeatist mentality and [is] no solution of the communal problem.[95]

Although no longer a Congressman (having resigned at the end of 1946), Sarat Bose still adhered to the Congress idea of a composite nationalism and also hoped that the advance of socialism would form the eventual basis for communal harmony. Whether he thought Bengal could survive as a sovereign republic, or whether he thought this was the best way to keep Bengal together and eventually bring it back to India,[96] I do not know. But through these bitter spring months, he risked his political career and his life in trying to preserve the unity of Bengal. His most important ally was Abul Hashim, secretary of the Muslim League. Together they tried to persuade Suhrawardy, Jinnah, and Gandhi to work for a Bengal Republic.

Each of the protagonists directly or indirectly connected with the United Bengal movement had his own motivation. Hashim, based on the evidence of his entire career—he remained a Bengal unificationist until he died in 1974—was dedicated to a Bengal republic and never wanted to be in a Pakistan dominated by West Pakistani Muslims. And he did not want it to be part of India, though he remained in India for several years after the partition.[97] Sarat Bose was another ardent Bengal unificationist, but he was also for Indian unity, so he probably had his eye on eventual reunification with India. Kiron Shankar Roy went along with Sarat Bose for part of the route in this particular cause, for similar reasons. Gandhi wanted to prevent the division of

[94] Bose, pp. 181ff; Hashim, pp. 134ff; Pyarelal, *Mahatma Gandhi, The Last Phase* (Ahmedabad, 1958), II, pp. 176–90; *Statesman*, 27 April 1947, reported the formation of the All-Bengal Anti-Pakistan and Anti-Partition Committee by Sarat Bose. In a press statement at that time Fazlul Huq suggested that the British should remain rather than partition the country, *Statesman*, 26 April 1947.

[95] Mitra, *Indian Annual Register*, 1947, I, 'Chronicle of Events', 15 March.

[96] Sarat Bose's son, Mr Amiya Bose, suggested the latter interpretation of his actions in an interview, January 1976, Calcutta; Mr Bose was working closely with his father in Bengal politics at that time.

[97] Hashim, *passim*; interview with Abul Hashim, Dacca, June 1972.

India, and may have believed that by supporting United Bengal he might indirectly preserve one India. Gandhi encouraged Sarat Bose's efforts in the preliminary stages.[98] Jinnah seemed to support Bose, Hashim, and Suhrawardy because he may have thought that a united Bengal with a Muslim majority population would surely remain part of Pakistan.[99] Suhrawardy's motives are unclear, but he did hope to be the chief minister of whatever section of Bengal emerged with a Muslim majority or to be head of a Bengal Republic.[100]

After Mountbatten came to India on 24 March, he talked to political leaders of every political persuasion. He talked to Suhrawardy and Kiron Shankar Roy and asked them to go out and prove that there was widespread support for the United Bengal movement. He did this, not because he supported the United Bengal effort, but because he wanted to know if the movement had popular backing or was simply a paper plan of a few leaders.[101] In the tense communal atmosphere of 1947 the United Bengal leaders were not able to demonstrate that the Hindu public was against the division of Bengal. Even Hindus in East Bengal wrote to the central Congress office supporting the partition of Bengal though they would be left in a Muslim province or nation unless they migrated.[102] Shyama Prasad was successful in mobilizing the Hindu community for division; Sarat Bose and his allies could not resist the tide. Sardar Patel tried to persuade Saratbabu to come over to the Congress-Mahasabha point of view in a letter of 22 May,

> I am sorry to find that you have isolated yourself so completely from all-India politics and even in provincial politics you have not kept in touch with us. In these critical times, we cannot afford to be standoffish and must pool our resources and take a united stand. Vital matters which will leave their mark on generations to come have to be settled, and in such settlement it behoves all of us to contribute our best to the combined strength of the Congress.[103]

98 Pyarelal, II, p. 180.

99 Bose, pp. 193–4; Hashim, pp. 143ff.

100 Ibid., pp. 162–3; Abul Hashim claimed in an interview in Dacca, June 1972, that Suhrawardy worked for United Bengal, but then was in some way bribed or threatened by Jinnah and gave up the effort; though close associates for the crucial years of 1943 to 1946 these men ended up political enemies; after partition both remained in India for some time; for Suhrawardy's arguments for united Bengal see his lengthy press statement, *Statesman*, 28 April 1947.

101 Hodson, pp. 246–7; interview with Lord Mountbatten, London, 1 July 1975.

102 AICC Files, Bengal Partition Papers, CL-14C, CL-21.

103 *Sardar Patel's Correspondence 1945–50* (Ahmedabad, 1972), IV, p. 44.

Sarat Bose remained undaunted and tried to convert Patel to his view of Indian and Bengal unity. On 27 May, he wrote to Patel,

> Today the position is that communal frenzy is not the monopoly of the Muslim Leaguers; it has also overtaken large sections of Hindus, both Congressites and Mahasabhaites. The Congress stand regarding partition has been taken advantage of by the sections mentioned above to inflame communal passions further. It has also brought back the Hindu Mahasabha to life and considerably strengthened its position. . . . I consider it most unfortunate that the Congress Working Committee conceded Pakistan and supported partition. It is true that I have not been able to address public meetings yet for reasons of health; but having been in close touch with public opinion in West and East Bengal, I can say that it is not a fact that Bengali Hindus unanimously demand partition. As far as East Bengal is concerned, there is not the slightest doubt that the overwhelming majority of Hindus there are opposed to partition. As regards West Bengal, the agitation for partition has gained ground because the Congress came to the aid of the Hindu Mahasabha and also because communal passions have been roused among the Hindus on account of the happenings since August last. The demand for partition is more or less confined to the middle classes. When the full implications of partition are realized and when people here find that all they will get for Western Bengal province will be roughly one-third of the area of Bengal and only about half of the total Hindu population in Bengal, the agitation for partition will surely lose support. I entirely agree with you that we should take a united stand; but I shall say at the same time that the united stand should be for a united Bengal and a united India. Future generations will, I am afraid, condemn us for conceding division of India and supporting partition of Bengal and the Punjab.[104]

If one uses the evidence of the Congress files, then Patel was right and Sarat Bose was indeed isolated. But Sarat Bose was also right: the middle classes in West Bengal were the main propagators of the partition idea and the Mahasabha was calling the tune. And he was correct in suggesting that the partition would not solve the communal problem. For a number of reasons though Sarat Bose at this time did not hold big public meetings and attempt to mobilize wide support for his views. He is said to have been blacked out of the Congress press. He worked only on the top political level with a few Congress and League leaders.

A few other voices, with no support in the major communities, were raised against the division of Bengal. Mr J.N. Mandal, Scheduled Caste leader and Law Member of the Interim Government (nominated

[104] Ibid., IV, pp. 45–6.

by the Muslim League) said that the communal trouble was only a passing phase and would not be resolved by partition. 'It was', he said, 'not in the interests of the Hindus to divide, and the Scheduled Castes were definitely opposed to the idea'. He insisted that the Hindus of Eastern Bengal would lose all their property and be forced to migrate, so they should reconsider their support for partition.[105] But Mandal had little backing among the scheduled castes in Bengal, most of whose Assembly members were Congressmen.

Another voice against division of Bengal was the *Statesman*, which may be considered a spokesman for the European community in Bengal. In an editorial entitled 'Twilight of Bengal', on 24 April, the writer commented:

> Extremists have the upper hand. An evident exception nowadays is the chief minister, Mr H. S. Suhrawardy, whose reputation has risen since last year, and who is unpopular despite all his moderation, perhaps because of it. Politically-minded Hindus, though they could probably even now get seats in the Cabinet for the asking, have become so embittered that nothing less than division of the province will content them. during ten weeks or so, the movement for repartition of Bengal has grown from a cloud no bigger than a man's hand into a storm which blows over all the province and outside its borders, though the centre remains Calcutta. Fostered initially by the Hindu Mahasabha, which has not lost its influence with its seats in the Legislatures, it received strong impetus from the declaration of February 20 and the Congress Working Committee's resolution of March 8 on partition of the Punjab. It has now been taken over by the Provincial Congress Committee, which demands regional ministries. . . . What is needed in Calcutta is not Section 93, not hartals, but enlightened collaboration between leaders of all communities to restore peace . . . though politicians enlarge it, embitterment is real, and we see nothing to support the comforting notion that this is a passing phase. Instead, Bengal which once led the struggle for liberty and made its own union the token thereof, is plunging backwards, forging its own fetters of mutual suspicion and misery. Too few recognize the tragedy—to the extent, at any rate, of doing anything practical to arrest it.[106]

Sarat Bose and Abul Hashim went ahead with their efforts to avoid the tragedy in the best way they knew how, but their efforts were not practical. They even signed an agreement on 20 May which spelled out the terms for a United Bengal republic.[107] But the all-India figures

[105] *Statesman*, 22 April 1947.
[106] *Statesman*, 24 April 1967.
[107] Hashim, pp. 153–4.

who had flirted with the cause backed off one by one. Some Hindu leaders spread rumours that members of the Bengal Legislative Assembly were being bribed to back the unity of Bengal. Gandhi believed these rumours and disavowed any connection with the movement. Angry telegrams from Sarat Bose to Gandhi did not move the Mahatma.[108] Jinnah and Suhrawardy also moved away. Patel and Nehru succeeded in persuading Mountbatten that a united Bengal should *not* be one of the alternatives for which the Bengal Assembly would be allowed to vote. Mountbatten said in an interview, 'I did not want the Balkanization of India. If I let them vote for independent Bengal, then others would also want independence.'[109]

Under the guidelines laid down in the *Indian Policy Statement* of 3 June 1947 issued by His Majesty's Government, the Bengal Legislative Assembly met to decide on the partition of Bengal on 20 June. The rules of procedure specified that,

> The Provincial Legislative Assemblies of Bengal and the Punjab (excluding the European members) will therefore each be asked to meet in two parts, one representing the Muslim majority districts and the other the rest of the Province. . . . The members of the two parts of each Legislative Assembly sitting separately will be empowered to vote whether or not the Province should be partitioned. If a single majority of either part decided in favour of partition, division will take place and arrangements will be made accordingly.[110]

The members met jointly and then in West Bengal and East Bengal groups. At the joint session, 90 voted to join the existing constituent assembly (i.e., stay with India), while 126 voted to join the new constituent assembly (i.e., join Pakistan). The vote was almost wholly along communal lines with these exceptions: J.C. Gupta, a Congress leader was out of the country and did not vote; Fazlul Huq deliberately absented himself from the meeting and did not vote; Maulana Shamsul Huda, a Muslim member from Mymensingh, did not vote; Rup Narayan Roy, a scheduled caste member from Dinajpur did not vote; four scheduled caste members from East Bengal voted with the Muslims (Haran Chandra Barman, D.N. Barury, Bhola Nath Biswas, Gayanath Biswas); and two well-known Communists, Jyoti Basu, the present

[108] Ibid., p. 157; Pyarelal, II, p. 186; interview with Amiya Bose, Calcutta, January 1976.

[109] Interview, London, 1 July 1975.

[110] Philips, Singh and Pandey, pp. 398–9.

chief minister of West Bengal, and Ratanlal Brahmin, a labour leader from Darjeeling, did not vote.[111]

Then the members divided into two groups and the Maharajah of Burdwan presided over the meeting of members from the non-Muslim majority areas. They voted for partition 58 to 21. On this vote Jyoti Basu and Ratanlal Brahmin joined the other Hindu members and voted for partition. In the meeting of members from Muslim-majority areas, presided over by Nurul Amin, the delegates voted against partition (i.e., for joining the new constituent assembly which would include all of Bengal) by 106 to 35. Again four scheduled caste members voted with the Muslim majority and Fazlul Huq did not appear.[112] Thus the Congress-Mahasabha alliance successfully manoeuvred to keep West Bengal as a Hindu-majority province within a divided India. Given the limited choice before them, the Hindu Bengalis voted to split Bengal and remain part of a larger political entity, India. A united Bengal separate from Pakistan was not a choice and it is not clear that any would have voted for it. Even Sarat Bose's own brother, Satish Bose, and Kiran Sankar Roy voted for partition. Jinnah got his Pakistan, but it was one he called 'moth-eaten' because he lost East Punjab and West Bengal. A separate West Bengal ministry was sworn in with P.C. Ghosh as chief minister and Partition Councils and a Boundary Commission were established to carry out the practical work of division.[113]

When partition day came on 15 August 1947, Gandhi fasted and Sarat Bose remained at home with his family and a few close associates quietly lamenting the division of the Indian nation. Suhrawardy, squeezed out as chief minister of East Bengal by Nazimuddin, remained in Calcutta. Abul Hashim stayed in West Bengal until 1950 and functioned as the leader of the opposition in the West Bengal Assembly. Many Hindus in East Bengal decided to remain where they were and many Muslims in West Bengal decided to stay where they

[111] Mitra, *Indian Annual Register*, 1947, I, 5, 12; Hashim, p. 162; Bengal Legislative Assembly, *Proceedings*, 20 June 1947.

[112] Bengal Legislative Assembly, *Proceedings*, 20 June 1947.

[113] Government of India, Legislative Department (Reforms), 17 August 1947, *Report of the Bengal Boundary Commission: Partition Proceedings*, Bengal, vol. VI, contains the very different reports (and pleadings) of the Muslim and non-Muslim members; a similar report was prepared by Lord Radcliffe on the Punjab; Hugh Tinker has recently published an article on the Punjab situation, 'Pressure, Persuasion, Decision: Factors in the Partition of the Punjab, August 1947', 36 *Journal of Asian Studies* (1977), pp. 695–704; Hodson, ch. 18.

were. Quite a few have moved across the border since 1947, but there has never been the virtually complete transfer of population that took place in the Punjab. Some Muslims in India just could not conceive of another home than the one which they were familiar; others wanted to live in a state that was, at least theoretically, a secular one. At times of communal violence and during the Pakistan suppression of the Bengalis in 1971, there has been much shifting. Also during more peaceful times, some Muslims suffering from discrimination in India have decided to try Pakistan and some Hindus, constricted and fearful in East Bengal (later East Pakistan and Bangladesh since 1971), have packed up and gone to India.[114]

The marriage of the Urdu-Pakistan Muslims and the Bengali Muslims in East Bengal was never a happy one for significant differences always existed. The language controversy (Urdu versus Bengali) began shortly after independence, flared into violence in 1952, and helped lead to the United Front's smashing electoral victory over the Muslim League in 1954. Fazlul Huq came out of oblivion and temporarily allied with H.S. Suhrawardy, who had by then shifted to Pakistan.[115] Suhrawardy and others organized the Awami League, which remained a Muslim Bengali party regardless of its all-Pakistan pretensions. The electoral victory of the Awami League in 1970 and the military defeat of the Pakistan army in December 1971 marked the total triumph of the Muslim Bengalis, with Hindu allies, over the Urdu-Pakistan Muslims.[116]

114 Interviews with Abu Sayyid Ayyub, Calcutta, 24 November 1972; A.W. Mahmood, Calcutta, 23 July 1973; Jehangir Kabir, Calcutta, 20 July 1973; these men were among the Muslims who deliberately chose India because it was to be a secular state; there were serious riots in 1950 and 1964 and then the Bangladesh crisis of 1971; during the first two Hindus crossed into India and Muslims into Pakistan; during the third, both Hindus and Muslims supporting the Awami League crossed into India; among the materials on these crises are: *Recurrent Exodus of Minorities from East Pakistan and Disturbance in India*, a report to the Indian Commission of Jurists (New Delhi, 1965); Richard D. Lambert, 'Religion, Economics, and Violence in Bengal', 4 *The Middle East Journal* (1950), pp. 307–28; Rounaq Jahan, *Pakistan: Failure in National Integration* (New York, 1972), *passim*.

115 Ibid., pp. 45ff. Keith Callard, *Pakistan, A Political Study* (London, 1957), p. 30.

116 Jahan, epilogue, 'The Disintegration of Pakistan and the Birth of Bangladesh'; Kamruddin Ahmad, Abul Mansur Ahmad, pp. 671–816; Subrata Roy Chowdhury, *The Genesis o f Bangladesh* (Bombay, 1972).

Neither the partition of 1947 nor the establishment of Bangladesh has resolved communal and identity problems for Bengalis on both sides of the international border. The communal problem, which still exists, has not been eliminated, but has rather been internationalized as some predicted in 1947. The sanguine promises of Congress and Muslim League leaders that they would protect their communal brethren on the other side of the border have been shown to be hollow. Even threats of war have not been sufficient to protect the minorities. Only determination by the majority community and its government on each side of the border can bring peace. The India–Bangladesh and Hindu–Muslim enthusiasm of 1971 have evaporated and suspicion has grown again. A festering dispute over division of the Ganges waters is a forbidding sign of hostility into the present.[117]

Questions of identity also remain. Hindu Bengalis in West Bengal seem surest of their identities and their traditions. They are Hindus and Bengalis and Indians. Muslims in West Bengal, if they are Bengali speakers, are Bengalis, Indians, and Muslims. During periods of communal hostility, they have been accused of being foreigners or fifth-columnists, which must surely rankle with those who have made a courageous decision to remain in India. In Bangladesh the Muslims are now surer that they are Muslims and Bengalis, and they may see themselves as truer Bengalis than those in West Bengal. They are still sorting out their traditions in order to decide how they relate to Hindus and to Bengali literature written by Hindus. Some have at various times wanted to push Bengali in a Persian-Arabic-Urdu direction; others have advocated more Sanskritic Bengali.[118] The Hindus in Bangladesh, perhaps 7 million strong, must worry whether Bangladesh will become more and more a Muslim country where they are treated as outsiders. They may slowly move to India, but in doing so they would probably have to give up life-long homes and property as have most who have crossed the border since 1947.

All Bengalis, whether Hindu or Muslim, whether in Bangladesh

117 When I visited Bangladesh in June 1972, barely six months after what was still then called the war of liberation, suspicion against India was already high and it has continued to grow; at the same time Bangladesh has steadily moved toward normalization of relations with Pakistan and increasing trade with what was West Pakistan. On a recent visit in August 1977, feelings against India still seem hostile and are spurred on by the prominent journalist Enayatullah Khan in *Holiday* and *The Bangladesh Times*.

118 Anisuzzaman summarizes these trends.

or in India, have multiple identities. At different moments, especially 1947 and 1971, members of both communities have had to make choices about their primary identifications and their nationalities. Or, stated another way, they have had to order their multiple identity elements. But these were not fixed or necessarily final choices. Many who made one choice in 1947, lived to make a different one in 1971. The new choice, like the old one, was not inevitable until the very end, perhaps the night of 25 March 1971. Those who wanted Bangladesh could not go back to the range of choices of 1947, but made a choice within the possibilities of 1970–1. United Bengal was not an alternative in 1971 and the Indians in West Bengal, whatever their resentments against the central government, were not eager to leave the Indian union and set up a Bengali republic. The Bengali Muslims of 1946–7 chose to vote for Pakistan and a smaller national unit than united India; in 1970–1 they voted for autonomy and then fought for national independence of a still smaller unit over which neither Hindus nor Urdu-Muslims would have control.[119]

There are a number of interesting, if unanswerable, questions about Bengal and Bengalis during these past two generations. One is about the role of outside forces in shaping Bengalis in directions they might not have wanted to go. Outside forces—i.e., the political forces of the British Raj, the Indian National Congress and Muslim League organizations—were a factor in destroying every effort at communal co-operation in Bengal between 1937 and 1947. We cannot know whether the course of events would have been any different if Bengalis had had greater control over their own destiny, but we do know that these forces shaped Bengal's political development to a much greater extent than Bengal impinged on the bigger political system.

Another question has to do with the role of religion and cultural factors as contrasted with political and economic factors. The argument has been put forward that religion was 'employed as a "sign", or a "mask", as it were, to safeguard and promote political and economic interests'.[120] Thus religion is described as a more superficial aspect of the total society and culture than political or economic forces. It has been argued here that the various political organizations made use of religious ideologies—particularly the Muslim League and the Hindu Mahasabha. It is certainly true that the establishment first of

119 Madan, p. 178.
120 Ibid, p. 169.

Pakistan and then of Bangladesh has afforded Bengali Muslims, particularly middle class ones, greater economic and political opportunities. The Hindu middle class in West Bengal has also been better able to protect its political and economic interests than it might have been in a united Bengal. But the Hindu middle class in East Bengal has not been able to protect its interests and the Muslims remaining in West Bengal have often felt threatened. The partition has also given the Bengali Muslims in Bangladesh a more open field for cultural creativity and for practising their religion without outside interference. To the participants, religion *and* economic and political interests are important. It may be better to see religious and cultural factors and interests as operating together and at crucial times reinforcing each other. But if one dismisses religious and cultural factors, one has to explain support for partition among Hindus of East Bengal support for Pakistan among Muslims of West Bengal.

An outsider, viewing Bengali identities and societies still in flux, can hope that the aspect of mutual toleration in the Hindu and Muslim religions is stressed and that all in West Bengal and Bangladesh see that in the long run their interests will best be served by significant co-operation in economic, political, and cultural affairs.

Chapter Thirteen

The Illusion of Security: The Background to Muslim Separatism in the United Provinces*

LANCE BRENNAN

One of the most intriguing questions in the modern history of North India is why the Muslims of the United Provinces (now Uttar Pradesh, and referred to hereafter as UP, see Map 1) supported the demand for Pakistan when it was obvious that if they were successful they would have either to remain in a Hindu dominated India, or suffer the upheaval of migration. In recent years Paul Brass and Francis Robinson have debated the general question of Muslim separatism in UP, taking positions which Brass has described respectively as 'instrumentalist' and 'primordialist'. Brass argues that the Muslims were modernizing at a faster rate than Hindus, that they had a larger share of government jobs than their fourteen per cent of the population would warrant, and that Muslim politicians erected a myth of 'the backward Muslim' to protect this privilege and then selected communally divisive symbols to mobilize support for their own drive to power. In short, the 'instrumentalist' position argues the autonomy of the 'game of symbol selection' on the part of the politicians, and therefore of the significance of symbol response on the part of those who supported the Muslim League and its demand for Pakistan. Robinson, on the other hand, first disagrees that the backwardness of the Muslims was a myth, especially relative to the role they perceived

* Research for this paper was aided by the Australian Research Grants Committee and the Research Committee of Flinders University. Their support is gratefully acknowledged.

MAP 1. United Provinces administrative boundaries

SOURCE: Adapted from P.D. Reeves, B.D. Graham and J.M. Goodman, *A Handbook to Elections in Uttar Pradesh 1920–1951*, New Delhi, 1975.

they had played in UP society for many centuries, and secondly, he seeks to demonstrate that the religious and cultural assumptions of the Muslim political leaders shaped and directed their actions.[1]

This paper addresses only one aspect of this illuminating debate: the question of the condition of the Muslims of UP in the period 1900–40. To a large extent this discussion concerns only the Muslim elite, who held government jobs, owned land, sent their children to school, and participated in the political life of the province. It is, of course, the case that even the Muslim elite was not a coherent group, and that Muslim politics was concerned in part with conflicts between Muslims over such issues as the control of the Aligarh college, the leadership of the Muslim League, and the recitation of the Madhe Sahaba.[2] However, it is equally true that Muslim politicians in UP attended carefully to the economic, educational and political conditions of their community, especially of those sectors of the community from which they themselves were drawn: the landholders, professional men, and government servants. That is to say, Muslim politicians on the whole agreed that the socio-economic prospects of their fellow Muslims were an important element in UP politics. Much of the evidence adduced by Brass and Robinson in this aspect of their debate tends to be from the second half of the nineteenth century and the first twenty years of this century. As well as extending the period con-

[1] Brass and Robinson agree, however, on a number of points, viz. that the colonial government encouraged the Muslims to organize as Muslims; that Hindu revivalism was a limiting factor for both Hindu and Muslim elites; that pre-existing communal and educational institutions facilitated effective political mobilization when ethnic appeals were made; and that there were insufficient objective differences between Hindus and Muslims to bring about a separatist movement. Paul R. Brass, *Language, Religion and Politics in North India* (Cambridge, 1974), pp. 118–19; P.R. Brass, 'A Reply to Francis Robinson,' *Journal of Commonwealth and Comparative Politics*, vol. XV (1977), pp. 231–3; P.R. Brass, 'Elite Groups, Symbol Manipulation and Ethnic Identity among the Muslims of South Asia', in D. Taylor and M. Yapp (eds), *Political Identity in South Asia* (London, 1979), pp. 41–67; Francis Robinson, 'Nation Formation: the Brass Thesis and Muslim Separatism', *Journal of Commonwealth and Comparative Politics*, vol. XV (1977), pp. 215–30; F. Robinson, 'Islam and Muslim Separatism', in Taylor and Yapp (eds), *Political Identity*, pp. 79–107.

[2] See F. Robinson, *Separatism among Indian Muslims* (Cambridge, 1975), chs 5–7; the Madhe Sahaba problem arose when Sunnis, from about 1906, began to chant the praises of the first three Caliphs during the Muhurram procession. This innovation offended the Shias. Anti-Tabarra Association, *Exposition of the Madhe Sahaba Tabarra Question* (Lucknow, 1939).

sidered to 1940, this paper directs more attention to Muslim landholding, because it was the economic mainstay of the Muslim elite.

A discernible pattern emerges from tracing the fortunes of the UP Muslims during the period 1900–40. At the beginning of this century their position was under threat from a number of directions, but from them until 1937 they attacked their problems in the arenas of education, government employment, landholding, and politics to the point where they had almost stabilized their position in the province. In the ensuing two and a half years, however, the circumstances and trends of policy of Pandit Pant's Indian National Congress government threatened the bases of this stability, and produced among the Muslim elite a climate receptive to the appeals of the Muslim League and to a new end for Muslim separatism: Pakistan.

Muslim Problems in the First Decade of the Twentieth Century

At the turn of the century, the Muslim elite of the UP suffered a number of blows to their economic position. These were delivered by Sir Anthony MacDonnell, Lt. Governor 1896–1901 and a Roman Catholic Irishman who seems to have perceived in the landlords of UP, especially the Muslim elite, Indian analogues of the dominant landlords and Protestants of Ireland.[3] As well as the specific problems brought about by MacDonnell's policies relating to the official script and to recruitment, the Muslim elite was already in a weakened position in relation to education, government jobs and landholding.

TABLE 1

EDUCATION IN MODERN AND TRADITIONAL SCHOOLS 1881–1901
(PERCENTAGE OF STUDENTS ATTENDING)

	Hindu students		*Muslim students*	
	Govt. Schools	*Private Schools*	*Govt. Schools*	*Private Schools*
1881	82.3	17.7	56.3	43.7
1901	86.3	13.2	60.3	39.7

SOURCE: *Report of The Director of Public Instruction, NWP & Oudh*, 1880–1, and 1900–1, quoted in Robinson, *Separatism*, p. 39.

[3] I am grateful to Dr John Hill for this interpretation of MacDonnell's perception of UP society.

It is clear from Table 1 that Muslims at this time were lagging behind Hindus in terms of access to and participation in the modern education provided in government schools and leading to government jobs as distinct from the traditional education in the classical oriental languages and religions provided in private schools.[4]

Although in the total population a greater proportion of Muslims were literate than Hindus, in the towns male Hindus had a considerable advantage over male Muslims when it came to literacy and especially literacy in English. As these were the groups and skills employed in government service, the implications for Muslim elite employment in a modernizing society are obvious. MacDonnell's measure, permitting the use of Devanagari script in official court correspondence, and requiring that all new appointees should be able to read both Devanagari and Persian scripts, added a further dimension to the problems of the Muslim service families.[5] It was fortunate for them that in practice these policies were not imposed with the rigour MacDonnell would have wanted.

The attempt to remedy Muslim educational problems at university level by establishing the Muslim Anglo-Oriental College at Aligarh had fallen on a difficult period. Enrolments in the college fell from 595 in 1895 to 189 in July 1899; the accounts were in disorder; some patrons had suspended their grants; and the college was badly indebted.[6] The movement associated with lifting the college out of these problems became an important element in the revival of the Muslims in UP, but at the turn of the century the educational position of the UP Muslims was bleak.

Using the 1911 and 1921 census figures, Brass demonstrates that Muslims were well represented in government service and the liberal professions, outnumbered Hindus in the police, and that twenty-six per cent of them were landholders.[7] Employment in public service was particularly important in a bureaucratic state as Shafa'at Ahmad Khan, a spokesman for Muslim interests, explained in 1929:

[4] Robinson, *Separatism*, p. 39.

[5] Hamid Ali Khan, *The Vernacular Controversy* (Lucknow, 1900); evidence of Sheo Prasad, 4 April 1913, *Royal Commission on the Public Service in India 1913* [hereafter *P.S.C. 1913*], *P.P.*, 1914, vol. XXIII, p. 1083. F. Robinson, 'Municipal Government and Muslim Separatism', *Modern Asian Studies*, vol. 7 (1973), pp. 87–8.

[6] Gail Minault and David Lelyveld, 'The Campaign for a Muslim University 1898–1920', *Modern Asian Studies*, vol. 8 (1974), p. 146.

[7] Brass, *Language, Religion and Politics*, p. 156.

But administration in India is not merely a question of loaves and fishes. It is a question of power; of opportunity and of service. A Tahsildar or a Deputy-Collector wields an influence which is wholly disproportionate to the amount of pay he draws.[8]

The administrative services were divided, broadly, into three sections. The elite comprised the all-India cadres with the Indian Civil Service (ICS) at their peak. Below these men were the United Provinces Provincial Civil Service (UPPCS), with two branches, executive and judicial, accommodating deputy collectors and subordinate judges. These were followed by the Subordinate Services.

Details of communal representation in the administration of UP are incomplete but it is possible to make some comparisons over the period 1886–1939. The composition of the all-India cadres can be ascertained using the early *India Office Lists*, which also yield information about the upper levels of the UPPCS, but neglect those in the lowest salary ranges. There are, however, some sources which provide the latter, at least in part: the reports on the 1886 and 1913 Royal Commissions into the Public Service; the memorandum Shafa'at Ahmad Khan presented to the Simon Commission in 1928; an analysis made by Pandit Pant for the benefit of the Press Consultative Committee in January 1939.[9] The last two also contain details about the subordinate services, but reliance for earlier estimates has had to be placed upon the decennial census reports.

Taking the broad picture first, the census of 1911 indicates that out of the total of 123,022 persons engaged in the 'service of the state', 53.0 per cent were Hindus and 41.94 per cent were Muslims, and out of 85,623 police, 44.71 per cent were Hindus and 50.33 per cent were

[8] Shafa'at Ahmad Khan, Explanatory note, *Indian Statutory Commission*, vol. III, *Reports of the Committees appointed by the Provincial Legislative Councils to Co-Operate with the Indian Statutory Commission* [hereafter *Indian Statutory Commission, III, Provincial Reports*] (London, 1930), p. 376.

[9] *Royal Commission on the Public Services in India*, 1886 [hereafter *P.S.C. 1886*], *P.P.*, 1888, XLVIII, p. 55; *P.S.C. 1913*, *P.P.*, 1914, vol. XXIII, pp. 254, 305, and *P.P.*, 1916, vol. VII, p. 604; Shafa'at Ahmad Khan, *A Representation of the Muslims of United Provinces (India) to the Indian Statutory Commission* (Allahabad, 1928), appendix; Address by the Honourable Pandit Govind Ballabh Pant, Premier, United Provinces, to the members of the United Provinces Press Consultative Committee [hereafter Pant Address], file 1-R/39, col. 1, Rajendra Prasad Papers, Nehru Memorial Museum and Library [NML], New Delhi. The best source, the *UP Civil Lists*, was not, unfortunately, available to the author.

Muslims.[10] As Brass argues, Muslims clearly had a quite disproportionate share of overall government employment, and especially of employment in the lower levels of the subordinate services where numbers were concentrated. It seems likely that this resulted—at least in part—from the patronage of fellow Muslims, higher up the administrative ladder.[11]

The Muslim proportion of the provincial civil service was over double their proportion of the population. Figures supplied to the 1913 Royal Commission on the Public Services in India show that Muslims held 34.7 per cent of appointments in UP against 60 per cent held by Hindus. But it is clear that Muslims were not overly prominent in the judicial stream, providing only 19.6 per cent of subordinate judges, and 25.5 per cent of munsifs.[12] Moreover, this share was declining, since in 1886 Muslims had held 46 per cent of the total posts of subordinate judges and munsifs.[13] In the executive branch Muslims occupied 41.3 per cent of positions in 1913, against 48.6 per cent held by Hindus.[14] Within this broad figure, however, there was a distortion in that while in the four higher grades Muslims held 37.9 per cent of the positions and Hindus held 41.3 per cent, in the rank corresponding to a monthly salary of Rs 400 (and representing those recruited during Sir Anthony MacDonnell's Lt. Governorship) Muslims comprised 30.8 per cent of the grade and Hindus 61.5 per cent. Recruitment of Muslims picked up after macDonnell left to almost equal to that of Hindus.

In 1911, Indians had not penetrated to any great degree into the higher reaches of administration in UP. Of the seventeen Indian appointments at these levels ten were Hindus, six were Muslims, and one was Parsi. But more importantly, of the ten Hindus, six were there because they had passed the ICS entrance examination in England in open competition with British candidates, while only one of the Muslims had been able to do the same. Four of the other Muslims had been nominated to the Statutory Civil Service, and the other, a judge, had made his way by promotion from the lower courts.[15] That is,

10 *Census of India*, 1911, vol. XV, pt II, pp. 550–1, 558–9.

11 For a discussion of the importance of connection in the appointment of the clerical establishment, see Robinson, *Separatism*, pp. 40–5.

12 *P.SnC., 1913*, appendix VIII, *P.P.*, 1916, vol. VII, p. 604.

13 *P.SnC., 1886, P.P.*, vol. XLVIII, p. 55.

14 *P.SnC., 1913, P.P.*, 1914, vol. XXIII, p. 1083.

15 *India Office List*, 1911, pp. 22, 62–4. The last nomination to the Statutory

although they had a substantial proportion of the senior jobs held by Indians, this depended upon nomination rather than upon merit as measured by the entrance examination. Moreover, in the upper ranks of the Indian Educational Service and the Public Works Department, Muslims were far behind the Hindus.[16]

Within the police, Muslims were particularly prominent at this time, comprising 49.8 per cent of the officer cadre and 42.0 per cent of the general force.[17] But this is somewhat misleading because of the 78 superintendents and assistant superintendents 1st grade in 1911, there was only one Muslim. The remainder were British.[18] It is arguable that at this stage, though Muslims found the police force an important avenue of employment, they did not dominate its direction.

The general picture, then, is one where Muslims were numerous in the executive branch of the UPPCS, the middle ranks of the police, and among the subordinate services. But, they had suffered significant decline in the judicial service and, as MacDonnell had shown them, their position in the executive branch and the police was dependent on British favour. Moreover, any decline in the numbers of Muslims in the middle echelons of the system would place at risk the patronage necessary for recruitment into the lower orders of the bureaucracy.

Despite the great public sensitivity of the issue of government employment, many more Muslims relied upon landowning for their main source of income. Figures relating to landownership are difficult to ascertain,[19] but in the 1911 census 175,797 Muslims indicated that their main source of income was from 'rent of land': that is, three times as many as those who derived their main income from 'the services of the state'.[20] Evidence used in 1926 indicates that 342,909 Muslims paid Rs 12,450,348 or 17.4 per cent of the total land revenue demand.[21] But more than income was at stake. As Neale has indicated,

---

Civil Service had taken place in 1891.

16 *India Office List*, 1911, pp. 65–7.

17 *Report of the Administration of the Police of the U.P. for the Year ending 31 December 1910* (Allahabad, 1911), statement F.

18 *India Office List*, 1911, p. 61.

19 For an assessment of this problem, see Eric Stokes, 'The Structure of Landholding in Uttar Pradesh, 1860–1948', *Indian Economic and Social History Review*, vol. XII, 1975, *passim*.

20 *Census of India*, 1911, vol. XV, pt. 2, pp. 550–1.

21 *Proceedings of the UP Legislative Council* [hereafter *UPLC*], 23 February 1926, vol. XXVII, pp. 391–2. Muslims amounted to 15.09 per cent of landholders.

'Land is to rule', and landownership brought both local political influence and social honour.[22] Control of land was clearly an important determinant of the welfare and status of a community.

During the nineteenth century Muslim landowners had met with mixed fortunes. The British gained control over the province in a series of steps, commencing in 1793 with Banaras and finishing in 1856 with Oudh. In most of these annexations a Muslim power lost control of the land revenue—and hence of resources which could be distributed as patronage among the Muslim elite.[23] How the annexations affected the landholding rights of Muslim families is difficult to measure. In the case of Rohilkhand, however, it is possible to show that over the period 1774–1805 there had been a displacement of Muslim land control, at least partly as a result of British intervention in the region.[24] On the other hand, some Muslim *tahsildars* (revenue-collectors), like their Hindu colleagues, used their key position in the revenue system to good account to become owners of large estates.[25] But when the British moved in the 1840s against holders of revenue-free land grants (*muafi*), on the grounds that they did not hold valid titles to the privilege, it was mainly Muslims who were affected.[26] Similarly, after 1858, in regions where Muslims had predominated in the rebellion of 1857, they suffered heavily from the confiscation of their land. It was, however, not until the second series of 'regular' land revenue settlements were made in the period from 1868 to 1891 that there were reasonably accurate estimates of landholding by castes

---

The difference between the 1911 census figures and these arises mainly because the 1911 figures were for primary source of income.

[22] Walter C. Neale, 'Land is to Rule', in Robert E. Frykenberg (ed.), *Land Control and Social Structure* (Madison, 1969), p. 9; for the constraints on landowners in the management of their estates, see P.J. Musgrave, 'Landlords and Lords of the Land: Estate Management and Social Control in Uttar Pradesh 1860–1920', *Modern Asian Studies*, vol. 6 (1972), pp. 257–7.

[23] The exceptions were the northern Doab, Agra, Bundelkhand, Garhwal, and Jhansi. For the impact of the loss of patronage on one group of Muslims, see Reginald Heber, *Narrative of a Journey through the Upper Provinces of India* (London, John Murray, 1844), vol. 2, p. 234.

[24] L. Brennan, *Land Policy and Social Change in North India: Rohilkhand 1800–1911*. Research Monograph, no. 1, Centre for Southeast Asian Studies (University of Western Australia, 1978), p. 25.

[25] See, for example, the case of Kanpur, 1801–50, in Thomas R. Metcalf, *Land, Landlords and the British Raj* (Delhi, 1979), pp. 129–30.

[26] L. Brennan, 'Agrarian Policy and its Effects on Landholders in Rohilkhand, 1833 to 1870', *University Studies in History*, vol. V (1970), pp. 9–10, 15.

and communities. During the period until 1947 there were two further settlements for most of the 45 plains districts of the UP. The information about changes in Muslim landholding has been assembled from the reports of the settlements, from the figures gathered for the district gazetteers, and from the reply to a question asked in 1926 in the UP

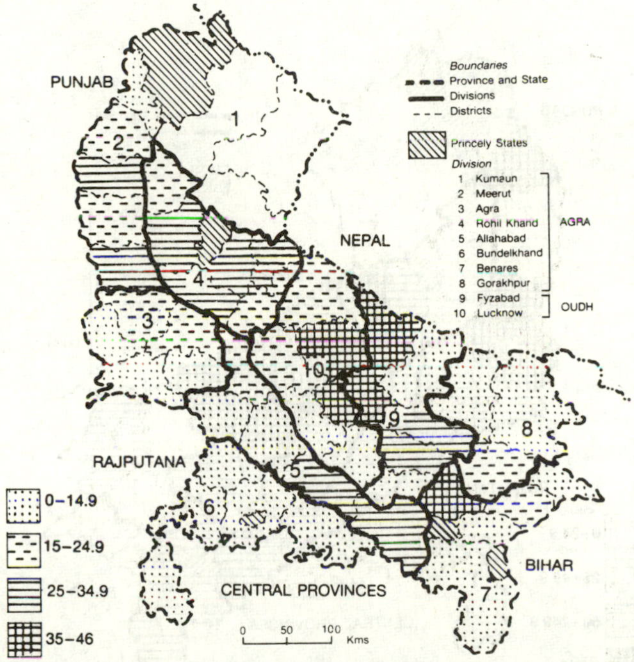

MAP 2. Percentage of rural land held by Muslims, c. 1892–1915

SOURCE: Settlement Reports and District Gazetteers.

Legislative Council on land revenue payments by district and community.[27] There are a number of problems about using such imperfect sources. The first is that there is a wide range of years for each set of settlements, viz. 1868–91, 1892–1915, 1916–44; the second is that in the early Oudh settlements only the Muslim percentage of 'villages'

[27] *UPLC*, 23 February 1926, vol. XXVII, pp. 391–2. The district gazetteers published in the first decade of this century contain Muslim landholding figures. Usually these were derived from the most recent settlement report, but occasionally a calculation was made especially for the gazetteer.

was calculated; and the third is that some districts, especially the poorer ones, were not resettled after 1916. The 1926 Council reply is useful in providing, for the first problem, figures for a single year, and for the third, the basis for estimates (however rough) of the Muslim share of landholding in districts without land settlements during the twenties and thirties.

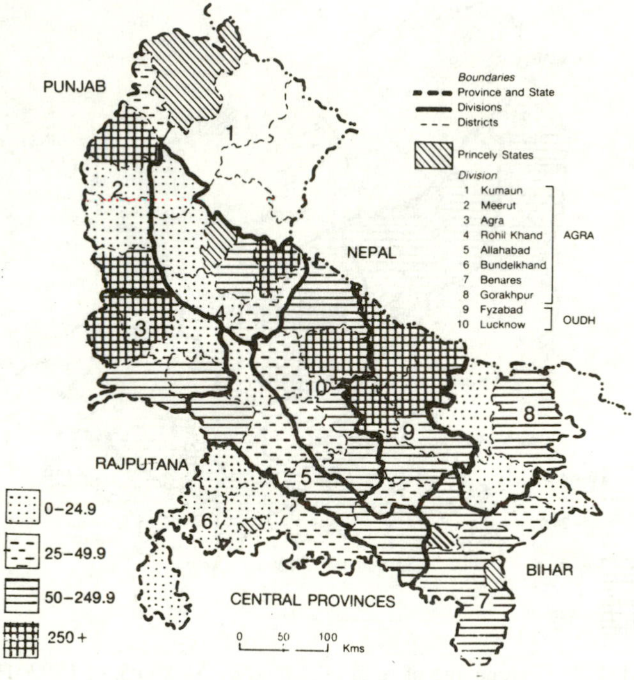

MAP 3. Average revenue payment by Muslims, 1926 (in rupees)
SOURCE: *UPLC*, 23 February 1926, vol. XXVII, pp. 391–2.

Map 2 demonstrates the condition of Muslim landholding at the beginning of this century. There were large variations in the extent of Muslim landownership, ranging from 45.5 per cent of the land in Barabanki to 1.0 per cent in Jhansi. It was concentrated in the Meerut, Rohilkhand and Lucknow divisions with another smaller concentration near Allahabad. Map 3 shows that there was also a considerable difference in the extent of landholding enjoyed by Muslims. Using figures disclosed in 1926 for the number of Muslim landholders and the land revenue paid by Muslims in each district, it is possible to calculate the average revenue paid by Muslims in each district. Apart from a few districts in the far west of the province, most of the districts with a high proportion of wealthy Muslim landlords lay in Oudh and eastern UP. The average revenue paid by western UP Muslim

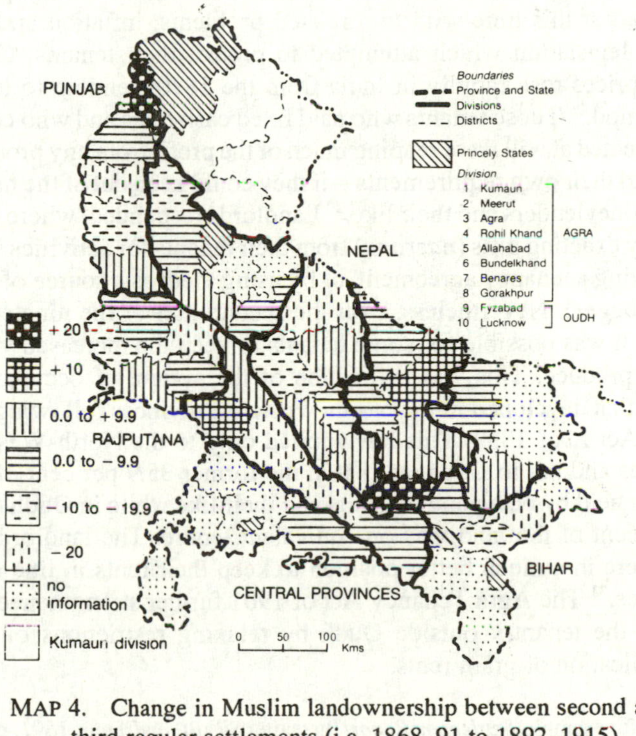

MAP 4. Change in Muslim landownership between second and third regular settlements (i.e. 1868–91 to 1892–1915)
SOURCE: Settlement Reports.

landlords was much lower. There had also been considerable variation in the changes in the area of Muslim landholding between the second and the third regular land settlements (1838–91 to 1892–1915). It is clear from Map 4 that they had a reduced share of the land in over two-thirds of the districts of the province. The scale of the reduction varied from 38 per cent in Sultanpur to 1 per cent in Barabanki. On the other hand, in Partapgarh they had improved their share of the land by 24 per cent. The general picture, however, is one of decline with an average reduction of about 3 per cent per district. The extent of the loss of land is more difficult to measure because it has not been possible to measure the expansion of cultivation in all districts and in some districts Hindu gains were due, at least partly, to the cultivation of new areas. This, however, still indicated the strengthening of the relative economic position of the Hindu community in the district.[28]

Muslim landlords, in common with their Hindu counterparts, contended at this time with two related problems: inflation and the tenancy legislation which attempted to protect their tenants. Commodity prices rose rapidly in India from the 1870s tending to leave rents behind.[29] Those tenants who paid fixed cash rents and who could not be ejected at will were reaping much of the profit from any produce surplus to their own requirements—if they could keep out of the hands of the moneylenders and their like.[30] Landlords responded, where they could, by exacting gifts (*nazrana*) from their tenants for activities such as renewing a tenancy agreement, or by using them as a source of free labour (*begar*). Nevertheless, over the second half of the nineteenth century, it was possible for some tenants to keep the increased value of their produce. This was a function of the system of occupancy-tenancy that developed in the North-Western Provinces following the Bengal Act X of 1859. This law applied only to the North-Western Provinces and not to Oudh, so that in the former 35.9 per cent of the land was held by occupancy tenants and their like while in Oudh only 5.6 per cent of the land was on equivalent tenure. The landlords of Oudh were in a much better position to keep their rents in line with price rises.[31] The Agra Tenancy Act of 1901 further strengthened the hand of the tenantry outside Oudh by relaxing restrictions on the communication of grain rents.

[28] See, for example, *Settlement Report* [hereafter *SR*] *Bulandshahr, 1891*, p. 16.

[29] K. L. Datta, *Report on the Enquiry into the Rise of Prices in India*, vol. I (Calcutta, 1915), pp. 30, 255–6; W.C. Neale, *Economic Change in Rural India* (New Haven, 1962), pp. 176–7; Toru Matsui, *Agricultural Prices in Northern India, 1861–1921* (Tokyo, 1977), vol. II, fig. 1–1.

[30] For an analysis of the complex relationship between zamindar, tenant, moneylender and commodity agent (eng. the *khandsari*), see Elizabeth Whitcombe, *Agrarian Conditions in Northern India*, vol. 1 (Berkeley, 1972), pp. 161–204.

[31] Neale, *Economic Change*, p. 100; *Report of the United Provinces Zamindari Abolition Committee* [hereafter *Z.A.C. Report*], vol. II (Allahabad, 1948), p. 921; Metcalf, *Land, Landlords and the British Raj*, pp. 222–5.

The pressures on both landlords and tenants provoked bitter antagonism between the classes and produced an enduring conflict over occupancy rights and commutation. One landlord wrote to a newspaper condemning ' . . . the system of granting occupancy-rights to tenants at all, the result of which is to make tenants, as soon as they acquire such rights, indifferent to the condition of their land, and they often sublet it on rates higher than they themselves pay to the *zamindar*'.[32]

Muslim landlords, who often relied for their living upon rents rather than upon the control of the debts of their tenants like the moneylending and sugar-manufacturing landlords, were particularly vulnerable to these pressures from the tenantry.

To these problems, which Muslim landlords shared with some of their Hindu counterparts, was added another which was to a large extent theirs alone. This was the automatic partition of deceased estates under the complex Muslim laws of inheritance. At times this resulted in estates being shared among a large range of relatives of the deceased.[33] As well as the possibility of a reduction of productive efficiency following an increase in the number of holdings, an appropriate adjustment in consumption levels was of ten resisted.[34] In those families where the sons had been unable to secure careers in public service or in commerce, the partition of the property produced considerable economic pressure. This was compounded in those cases where the young men led extravagant lives and had been led into debt even before inheriting their share of the property.[35] It is not surprising

32 *Nizam-ul-mulk* (Moradabad), 16 March 1900, in *Reports on the Vernacular Newspapers in the N.W.P. and Oudh* [hereafter *V.N.R.*], 1900, p. 125; for discussion of the economic and political significance of grain rents and their commutations, see Brennan, *Land Policy*, pp. 94–6, 118–19.

33 See Syed Ameer Ali, *Mahomedan Law*, vol. II, 3rd edn (Calcutta, 1908), pp. 61–75; and Kashi Prasad Saksena, *Muslim Law as administered in British India* (Allahabad, 1937), pp. 899–901.

34 Evidence of K.B. Saiyid Ain-ud-din (UPPCS), K.B. Saiyid Abu Muhammed (UPPCS) also argued that the inheritance laws broke small estates into small 'bits which are nor worth keeping'. On the other hand, Hindus were more likely to maintain estates under one management, *Report of the U.P. Provincial Banking Enquiry Committee*, vol. III (Allahabad, 1930), pp. 167–70.

35 *Naiyar-i-Azam* (Moradabad), 23 January 1888, *V.N.R.*, 1888, p. 77; 'Memorial to Lord Curzon from the Mahomedan subjects of the Queen-Empress of India, 1899', *Calcutta Law Journal*, vol. 2, 1905, p. 185n; C.M. King (Officiating Magistrate, Bareilly) to chief secretary to Govt., U.P., 1 June 1911, Govt.

then that the Muslim share of land was declining in many districts of the UP.

The problems facing the Muslim elite of UP in the first decade of the twentieth century were daunting. Economically they were shaky, in that of the three basic occupations on which they relied—executive positions in the PCS, the middle-ranking positions in the police force, and zamindari—the first two were vulnerable, and the latter (outside Oudh) was of declining value. They were not participating in modernizing education at the same rate as the Hindus, and their mother tongue, Urdu, was being attacked in its role as sole official vernacular language by Hindu enthusiasts. Moreover, there were pressures for the extension of political power to Indians—and as a minority they felt they would have little chance in a democratic system. The limited electoral system begun in 1893 had seen no Muslim elected to the UP Legislative Council.

The Muslim Response

By the early 1930s the UP Muslim elite had strengthened their position with respect to all the problems they had faced at the turn of the century. The manoeuvring which accomplished the political victories of separate electorates and weighting in the legislatures and municipal boards is well known,[36] but other responses, some of which were at the family level, are not well-documented. These struggles, especially those for political influence and for the protection of Muslim interests in the services, generated communal hostility, which was further fuelled by the *Shuddhi* and *Tabliq* movements, the bloodshed of the riots, and the propaganda activities of both Hindus and Muslims.[37] But despite this communal conflict, Muslim separatism at this time was concerned with maintaining or improving their position within a united India.

Muslim education made considerable headway. The Aligarh MAO College became a separate university in 1920, though it was

---

of India, Legislative Dept, A Proceedings, April 1913, no. 332, National Archives of India [N.A.I.], New Delhi.

[36] See Robinson, *Separatism*, pp. 133–74; Robinson, 'Municipal Government', *passim*.

[37] See Gyanendra Pandey, *The Ascendancy of the Congress in Uttar Pradesh, 1926–34* (Delhi, 1978), pp. 114–53.

not as independent of government control as some Muslim leaders wished.[38] But of even greater significance was the effort that had been put into providing a more modern education for the bulk of Muslim students, either in primary schools (known as 'mixed schools') operated by the district and municipal boards or in *makhtabs* and Islamia schools run by local Muslim communities with the aid of local grants. In the latter schools, religion was taught as well as secular subjects. As Table 2 indicates there had been a major improvement in the extent to which Muslims sent their children to government maintained and aided schools. Muslim politicians still claimed, however, that not enough was being done for Muslim children by Hindu dominated local boards, especially in the way of the appointment of Muslim teachers, the use of Urdu, and religious instruction in 'mixed schools'.[39]

TABLE 2

EDUCATION IN MODERN AND TRADITIONAL SCHOOLS 1901–35
(PERCENTAGE OF STUDENTS ATTENDING)

	Hindu students		*Muslim students*	
Year	*Govt./recognized Schools*	*Private Schools*	*Govt./recognized Schools*	*Private Schools*
1901	86.8	13.2	60.3	39.7
1921	96.2	3.8	83.5	16.5
1928/29	97.0	3.0	89.3	10.7
1934/35	97.5	2.5	89.8	10.2

SOURCE: Adapted from *Robinson*, Separatism, p. 39 and United Provinces of Agra and Qudh, Education *Dept., General Report on Public Instruction in the United Provinces of* Agra and Qudh, 1928/29 and 1934/35.

[38] Minault and Lelyveld, 'The Campaign for a Muslim University', pp. 187–9.

[39] Shafa'at Ahmad Khan, *What are the Rights of the Muslim Minority in India?* (Allahabad, 1928), pp. 70–1, 80–1; that Muslim literacy was improving faster than Hindu literacy (+40 per cent compared with +30.7 per cent between 1921 and 1931) also suggests the urgency of the drive for Muslim education, Brass, *Language, Religion and Politics*, p. 149; *makhtabs* and Islamia schools were expected to follow the government curriculum if they were to be 'recognized' and therefore eligible for grants from the local boards. Although the development of the Islamia schools was a marked step forward in Muslim education, it is clear that they suffered from a number of problems. This suggests that the Muslim children being educated in them may not have been receiving an education as

Muslims had achieved an almost fixed share in recruitment to the ICS because although most Muslim candidates could not score grades equivalent to their Hindu competitions, they were nominated up to a fixed proportion of the vacancies.[40] In the UPPCS similar arrange-

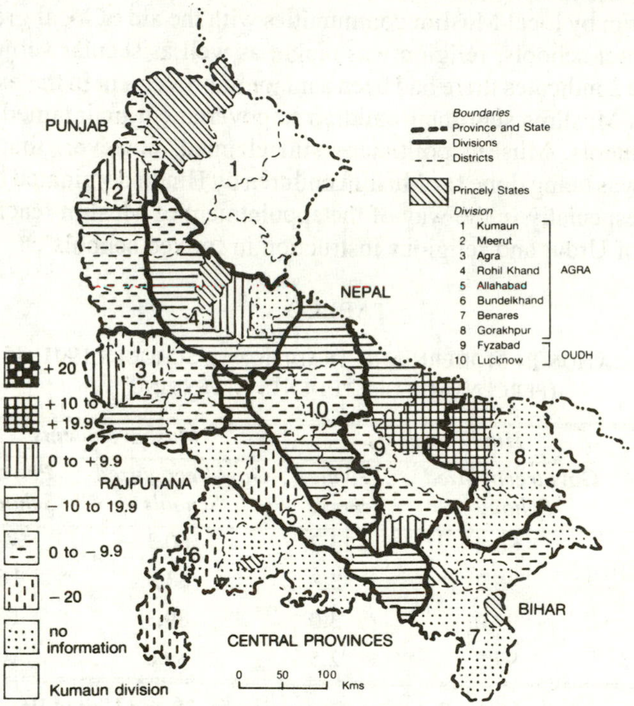

MAP 5. Change in Muslim landownership between second and third regular settlements (i.e. 1892–1915 to 1916–1947)

SOURCE: Settlement Reports, Rent Rate Reports, Assessment Reports.

---

good as those attending the schools run by local governments. See *Report of the Committee appointed to Inquire into and Report on the State of Primary Education of Boys of the Muslim Community and Educationally Backward Communities in the U.P.*, 1925–6 (Allahabad, 1940), esp. Appendix G, pp. 33–5. See also *UPLC*, 16 December 1925, vol. XXVI, p. 29.

[40] T. H. Beaglehole, 'From Rulers to Servants: the ICS and the British Demission of Power in India', *Modern Asian Studies*, vol. II (1977), pp. 238–9; David C. Potter, 'Manpower Shortage and the End of Colonialism: The Case of the Indian Civil Service', *Modern Asian Studies*, vol. 7 (1973), pp. 47–74.

ments were worked out from the early 1920s in most of the cadres, and though they still lagged in the judicial branch, they had a relatively favoured position in the executive branch.[41] Moreover, they had secured the agreement of the UP Committee cooperating with the Statutory Committee that Muslims should have a generous share in the services under a future constitution: the committee (which included Hindu members) agreed that,

> whilst realizing that it is impracticable for a definite communal proportion to be maintained in all services, we agree with our Muslim colleagues that, as far as possible, one-third of the appointments in the government services should be given to Muhammadans.[42]

The other main component of the UP Muslim elite's economic position was their control of land. It is difficult to chart the changes in their position from the first decade of the century to the 1940s because of the wide range of years over which measurements were taken and because some districts were not settled during the period, but Map 5 shows the changes in landholding in the plains districts between the third and fourth land revenue settlements, i.e. 1892–1915, 1916–47. It is clear that Muslims held a smaller share of the land at the close of the period and that when compared with the previous period (see Map 4) there were more districts in which they had not maintained their share of the land. But there were fewer districts (three as against seven) in which their share was reduced by 20 per cent or more, and of these only in Aligarh was there a particularly significant loss in terms of acres, representing about 5 per cent of the district.[43] This was

[41] For the system of communal proportions that developed in UP during the 1920s, see 'Note' by T. Sloan, 10 December 1928, in *Indian Statutory Commission, Selections from Memoranda and Oral Evidence by Non-Officials*, pt I (London, 1930), pp. 346–7. Muslims also held about half the positions of Deputy Superintendent Circle Inspector and Sub-Inspector in the police force. *UPCL*, 19 December 1925, vol. XXVI, p. 507.

[42] *Indian Statutory Commission, III, Provincial Reports*, p. 241.

[43] *Aligarh S.R. 1943*, p. 5; Bara Banki Muslims also lost considerably, but this is not apparent in the map because their holdings were so large, *Bara Banki S.R., 1930*, p. 2; the other districts with losses of 20 + per cent were Cawnpore and Dehra Dun. In the former this represented some 1.5 per cent and in the latter about 0.4 per cent of the total area. For Cawnpore, see Assessment Report [hereafter *A.R.*] *Tahsil Derapur, 1943*, pp. 2–3; *A.R. Tahsil Bilhaur, 1943*, p. 4; *Rent Rate Report* [hereafter *R.R.*] *Tahsil Cawnpore, 1942*, in *U.P. Gazette*, 25 July 1942, pt VIII, p. 1240. For Dehradun (the valley region), see *S.R. Tahsil Dehra, 1941*, p. 2.

reflected in the figure for the average decline of the Muslim share of total land per district dropping from 3 per cent to 1.8 per cent. There had also been a change in the location of the districts in which there had been a substantial reduction of the Muslim share of the land. In the west UP districts there was a lower rate of loss than previously, while in Oudh there was a strong shift against Muslim landholding, in that there were only two districts in which gains had been made, against ten where the Muslims' share had been reduced. These developments suggest that some measures were being taken to resist the slide into debt and loss of land, especially outside Oudh. The improved position of some Muslim families as a result of modernization of education and the guaranteed share in jobs in some government departments may have played a part in the process. The results of agrarian conflict during the Depression, when landlords expanded their sir land and ejected many occupancy tenants, may also have served to protect the interests of some Muslim landholders.[44] For those landlords enmeshed in debt, however, the Depression brought about particularly damaging circumstances, since it was not only more difficult to repay debts, but land values had declined from the levels of the late 1920s. The government, encouraged by the landlord dominated Legislative Council, stepped in with the UP Encumbered Estates Act of 1934, which in certain circumstances reduced the interest rate to be paid by debtors to 4.25 per cent largely protected the debtor's land and buildings, and when these had to be sold had them valued at pre-Depression prices.[45] These terms were particularly favourable to the landlords. The Depression, then, while it added to the difficulties of some landlords, provided others with an opportunity to eject their occupancy tenants, and even where landlords were forced toward bankruptcy, they were granted a measure of protection.

Muslims also protected their land by legal means. Some rich landlords (Hindus as well as Muslims) entailed their land under the

[44] For an insightful view of the situation during the Depression see Jawaharlal Nehru, On the Rent and Revenue Situation in UP, 18 April 1931, All India Congress Committee Papers [hereafter A.I.C.C. Papers), file 4/1931 (pt 1), NML; wholesale prices dropped more sharply than the rents of ordinary tenants. See Pandey, *Ascendancy of the Congress*, p. 160. Even allowing for a sharp reduction in collections there would have been no great shortfall in the absentee landlord's real income. See Neale, *Economic Change*, p. 238; and *ZAC*, I, p. 349.

[45] See Neale, *Economic Change*, p. 107. Other legislation further protected landlords by reducing interest rates and requiring moneylenders to keep records.

Agra Estates Act of 1920,[46] but the most favoured method of protection of estates from partition was the family trust—*waqf-al-ul-aulad.* Indeed, the story behind the use of family trusts illustrates some of the points I have been making about the response of Muslims to their perceived difficulties in the first decade of the twentieth century—and the place of religion in that perception.

In 1894 the Judicial Committee of the Privy Council ruled that family trusts were contrary to Muslim law. This provoked widespread Muslim concern. Their arguments were twofold: first, that the ruling was an unjustified attack of traditional Muslim practice by non-Muslims; and secondly, that by breaking down the trusts that existed—and this was especially the case in Bengal—many important Muslim families would be ruined. They argued that it was an essential element of Islamic law that a Muslim should be able to gain religious merit by dedicating property to God, thereby preventing its future alienation. The profits from the property could be assigned to the upkeep of the donor and/or his family, and on his death to his family and heirs to be administered by a trustee until the family line died out. The property would then revert to charity. In 1911, after a campaign lasting seventeen years the Muslims finally persuaded the British to allow Muhammad Ali Jinnah to introduce a private bill the first in the Governor General's Legislative Council. Following involvement by a wide range of Muslims from most sects and interests, the bill was enacted in 1913, legitimizing waqf-al-ul-aulad, an institution Muslims believed already to be legitimate. The process by which this act was forced on the Government of India demonstrated the close interaction of religious percepts with social and economic behaviour within the Muslim community. The sense of being able to behave as a Muslim was equally important as being able to protect an economic position.[47]

Waqf-al-ul-aulad was a tool to use to retain land (and other property) in a family. How far did the Muslim landowners of UP use it? There is evidence from official sources, as well as from interviews,

[46] By 1925 some eight major estates had been settled under the Agra Estates Act of 1920. Six of these were Hindu and two were Muslim, *UPCL*, 19 August 1925, vol. XV, p. 12.

[47] See, for example, Mahomed Yusoof (pleader, High Court, Calcutta), to Viceroy, 7 June 1906, Govt of India, Home (Judicial) Dept. A Proceedings, July 1907, no. 82, NAI; and note by Aziz Mirza (Hon. Secty, All India Muslim League) 7 March 1911, file 33, Muslim League Papers, Archives of the Freedom Movement, University of Karachi.

that Muslim landlords in UP used waqf to protect their families.[48] Establishing the extent of the land protected over the province is somewhat more difficult.

There are two sources of information on the extent of the use of waqf-al-ul-aulad but neither is wholly satisfactory. These are the last set of settlement reports and the statistics gathered for the Zamindari Abolition Committee in October 1947. These measure slightly dif-

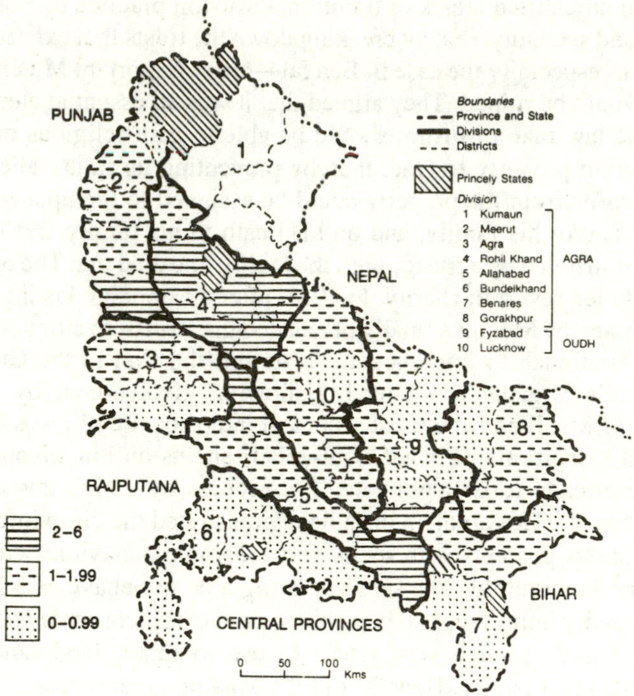

MAP 6. Percentage of land revenue paid by Muslim waqf-al-ul-aulad property, c. 1944.

SOURCE: *ZAC*, II, pp. 48–9 and 83–4.

[48] *Govt Resolution on the Revenue Administration of the U.P.* [hereafter *UPRA*], *1929–30* (Allahabad, 1931), pp. 8–9, 17; K.W. Knox, Settlement Commissioner, *UPLC*, 11 July 1930, vol. XLVIII, p. 178; *S.R. Etah, 1944*, p. 2; *A.R. Kaimgunj, Farrukhabad district*, p. 8; interview with Dr Moin ul Haq (Secretary of the Pakistan Historical Society), Karachi, 28 January 1979.

ferent aspects of the question: the settlement reports measure the acreage involved, while the Zamindari Abolition Committee figures measure land revenue payments. Moreover, the settlement reports are incomplete in their reporting of waqf-al-ul-aulad. Eight districts were not settled after 1913, and therefore there was no possibility that any figures on waqf relating to these districts would be taken. It also seems likely that not until the early 1920s were settlement officers encouraged to indicate the extent of dedicated land. Therefore, five districts were settled before figures began to appear. In the remaining settlement reports, another difficulty occasionally appears when the land designated as dedicated land includes both Muslim and Hindu public and private trusts. In these circumstances the text sometimes suggests the extent of waqf-al-ul-aulad, but some figures remain as estimates based on the proportion of Muslim landholding in the district and any information available elsewhere about gifts to temples and schools. The figures on private trusts in the statistics volume of the *Report of the Zamindari Abolition Committee* cover the entire province, but do not distinguish between Muslim and Hindu trusts. There is also the added complication that it is not possible to distinguish between the private and public components of the trusts which included both private and public (i.e. charitable) beneficiaries—a common practice amongst Muslims. Both sets of data have been used to construct Map 6. Where the settlement report specifies Muslim waqf-al-ul-aulad, and where it stemmed from a settlement in the 1940s, the figure given has been used after a comparison with the Zamindari Abolition Committee figures. Where, there is no settlement report, as in half of the cases, an approximation based on the Zamindari Abolition Committee figures has been made. Where there is evidence that the Muslim community was the main user of private trusts, as in Allahabad division,[49] it has been assumed that two-thirds of the private trusts were waqf-al-ul-aulad. Where there is no evidence of this kind, it has been assumed that half of the private trusts were in Muslim hands. The figures resulting from these calculations probably underestimate the extent of private Muslim trusts since mixed trusts have been excluded, and it is clear from the Zamindari Abolition Committee questions on waqf and trusts, and the discussion of the issue in the report, that waqf-al-ul-aulad was the main question under review.[50]

[49] *UPRA, 1929–30*, pp. 8–9, 17.
[50] *ZAC*, vol. I, pp. 416–17; *ZAC*, vol. II, pp. 48–9, 83–4.

Moreover, here is much greater evidence of the use of trusts by Muslims than by Hindus.[51]

But given the problems of using the figures, what can be said about the incidence of waqf-al-ul-aulad? First, as might be expected, it appears to have been a practice that grew over time. That is, there was a higher rate of waqf noted in the reports of districts settled in the late 1930s, than in the 1920s. In the 1920s settlements the average was about 4 per cent of the total Muslim landholding in a district; in the settlements of the 1939–44 period it had grown to about 12 per

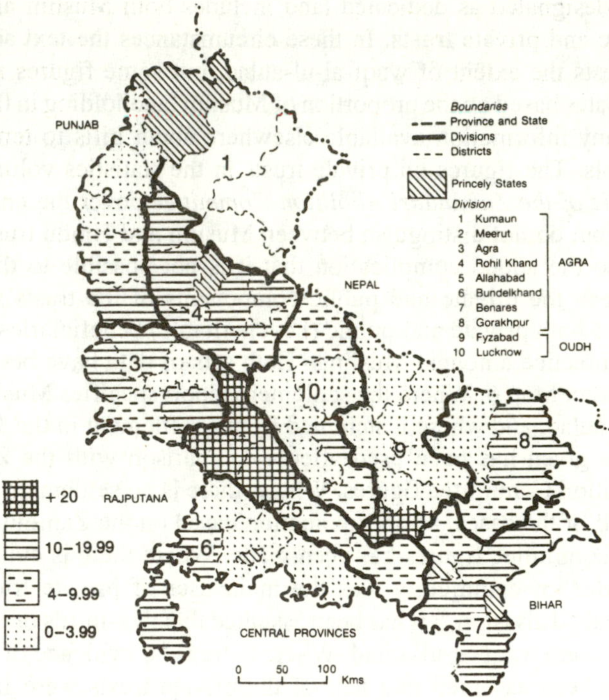

MAP 7. Land held waqf-al-ul-aulad as a percentage of Muslim land c. 1944.

SOURCE: *ZAC*, II, pp. 83–4; *UPLC*, 23 February 1926, vol. XXVII, pp. 391–2; Settlement Reports, Rent Rate Reports, Assessment Reports.

[51] When Hindu trusts are mentioned in reports they usually refer to trusts of temples and charitable institutions. For example, see *Mainpuri S.R., 1944*, p. 2.

cent. This suggests that more people were concerned to protect their family property and saw private trusts as an appropriate method.

The geographical distribution of Muslim private trust property is illustrated in Map 6 which shows the estimated proportion of land revenue paid by waqf-al-ul-aulad property. It is clear from the map that Muslim private trust property was concentrated in the Rohilkhand and Aligarh divisions, with other centres around the two major administrative cities of the province, Lucknow and Allahabad.

In Map 7 an attempt has been made to indicate in which districts waqf-al-ul-aulad was most favoured by Muslim landlords. This has been done by expressing the land revenue paid by waqf-al-ul-aulad land as a percentage of Muslim land-revenue payments.[52] It is clear, first, that the pattern descerned in Map 6 is repeated, with many of the districts in Rohilkhand and Aligarh divisions having between ten and twenty per cent of Muslim land under waqf-al-ul-aulad. The second point that is obvious is that there were very low rates of private trusts in Oudh. This can be explained by the fact that the taluqdars of Oudh, who owned much of Oudh, were already protected by the possibility of entailed primogeniture under the Oudh Estates Act of 1869 and the Oudh Settled Estates Act of 1900,[53] as well as by the Court of Wards (which rescued large estates from mismanagement), and later by the UP Encumbered Estates Act of 1934. That is, Muslim taluqdars (like their Hindu class-fellows) did not need to use the waqf-al-ul-aulad mechanism to hold their estates together. The third aspect is that in eastern UP, where Muslims had only a modest share of land ownership, there was a greater use of waqf-al-ul-aulad than in Oudh: in four districts between ten and twenty per cent of Muslim land was protected by private trusts.[54]

[52] The percentage is calculated by dividing the figure estimated for waaf-au-ul-aulad in 1947 by the Muslim share of the land revenue given in 1926. This may slightly decrease the percentage because in most districts Muslims would have lost land in the intervening years.

[53] In 1899 a NWP zamindar and MLC, Nawab Faiyaz Ali Khan, congratulated the Oudh taluqdars on their good fortune in securing 'the preservation of old and hereditary estates', and hoped that 'the precedent thus set in their case . . . may . . . mean that the days of our own salvation from the ruinous effects of alienation and even division of our own estates are not far off, *UPLC*, 2 April 1899, vol. I, p. 35.

[54] Bundelkhand had a low incidence of private trusts, reflecting the success of the legislation protecting landholders in that region. See Neale, *Economic Change*, pp. 89–90.

What then does this tell us about the use of waqf? It seems likely that the smaller zamindars in western UP were the most likely to use what was a cheap way of protecting their land from future partition and extravagance, and this is supported by the comments of Dr Moin ul Haq, from Moradabad, who indicated that it was the smaller Muslim landlords of Moradabad who 'jumped at the chance to protect their property'.[55] It seems likely that a similar set of circumstances produced the use of private trusts among Muslims in eastern UP. How far it was successful in its protective role is difficult to determine because of the short time over which the trusts operated. The most that can be said is that it might have been responsible in part for the slowing down of the rate of decline in Muslim landholding: it was certainly a psychological prop for men concerned about the future of their families.

The UP Muslim elite had more than stabilized their political position: they had won some notable victories. They gained separate Muslim electorates in the Legislative Council in 1909, and then in the Lucknow Pact of 1916 secured an initial agreement by the Congress to separate electorates and to 30 per cent of the seats of any reformed Council. In subsequent reforms they retained these gains at the provincial level, and also achieved separate electorates and weightage in the local boards. And between 1920 and 1937, a Muslim was always selected by the governor as a member responsible for one of the transferred departments in the UP government. These achievements were further buttressed by their belief, following the enactment of the Government of India Act of 1935, that they were guaranteed Muslims would be included in any elected ministry, and that the governor would effectively protect their interests.[56]

[55] Interview, Dr Moin ul Haq, Karachi, 28 January 1979.

[56] For the political history of the period up to the Khilafat movement, see Robinson, *Separatism, passim*, and 'Municipal Government', pp. 89–121. For the basis for Muslim views of their position under the 1935 Govt of India Act, see the 'Instrument of Instructions to the Governor of Madras issued under the Government of India Act, 1935, 8 March 1937', in Sir Maurice Gwyer and A. Appadorai, *Speeches and Documents on the Indian Constitution, 1921–47*, vol. I (Bombay, 1957), p. 379. The 'Instructions' to the Governor of the UP followed a similar wording in enjoining the Governor to appoint to his ministry 'in consultation with the person who in his judgement is most likely to command a stable majority in the Legislature, those persons (including so far as practicable members of important minority communities) who will best be in a position collectively to command the confidence of the Legislature'. Subsequent paragraphs contained instructions about safeguarding the legitimate interests of minorities, including

The Muslim elites' position in UP in the mid-1930s appeared to be fundamentally sound. They had guaranteed shares of recruitment to civil service jobs; the education of their children was becoming more attuned to the times; though still possessing a declining share of the rural land in the provinces, the rate of decline had eased and there were three or four mechanisms to protect what they retained; they had a large and separate share of the seats in the local bodies as well as in the provincial and central legislatures and they believed they would have a share of the cabinet posts in the new government arising out of the 1935 Reforms. Some of these developments, especially those relating to entailment of property and educational choice, were family decisions and produced few ripples in UP society. The cost of buttressing their position in other directions—especially over jobs and political concessions—was a contribution to bickering in the legislature and violence on the streets.

CONGRESS RAJ, 1937–9

The first indication to the Muslim elite that for the first time since 1920 they would not play a significant role in the government of the UP, came after the elections in 1937. The loose coalition, painstakingly formed of groups within Muslim politics, which had fought the election as the Muslim League, was denied the role it had expected in the new ministry. Although they had not captured as large a proportion of the Muslim constituencies as the Congress had of the general constituencies, they had won twenty-seven seats in the Legislative Assembly, and as such were in the largest Muslim group. Whether the UP Muslim League leaders had been promised a role in a coalition government prior to the election remains unclear. But despite the sparring between Nehru and Jinnah at the national level, there had been co-operation between the UP League and the Congress during the election,[57] conversations occurred about the ministry both before and after the Congress had decided to 'accept office',[58] and the League

an injunction to be guided by previously 'accepted policy' in relation to the due proportion of appointments in the services.

[57] Nehru to Rajendra Prasad, 21 July 1937, R. Prasad file, Nehru Papers, NML.

[58] Nehru to Pant, 30 March 1937, file E/1/36, AICC papers; Pant to Nehru, 2 April 1937, Pant file, Nehru Papers.

had not opposed Rafi Ahmad Kidwai, the leading Congress Muslim, in a by-election in late April 1937.[59] The UP League leaders were, however, offered a role in the ministry only if they were prepared to disband as a political party and in effect join the Congress. They believed this would destroy the fragile unity of the Muslims, weaken them as a political force, and therefore prevent them from protecting those elements of the constitution, such as separate electorates, over which many of the nationalist Muslims among them had broken from the Congress in the late 1920s.[60]

The disappointment of the UP League leaders' hopes of sharing in a coalition was compounded in May 1937 when the *Jamiat-ul-ulema-i-Hind*, the foremost organization of ulema in India, renounced the League and announced its support for the Congress. Shortly afterwards, Hafiz Muhammad Ibrahim, an MLA from Bijnor district, closely associated with the Jamiat-ul-ulema-i-Hind, resigned from the League and joined the Congress. Disappointment turned to anger when Ibrahim became one of the two Muslim ministers in Pandit Pant's Congress government. It appeared to the League leaders that the appointment of Ibrahim to the ministry was the price for the defection of the influential *ulema*.[61]

The other issue that concerned Muslims was the question of the governor's powers. While the Congress leaders wanted to diminish

[59] The League's first choice as candidate had asked for more than the party could afford in the way of electoral expenses, but there seems to have been no last minute efforts to procure a replacement for a seat which had been won by a League candidate in the general election. Choudhury Khaliquzzaman, *Pathway to Pakistan* (Lahore, 1961), pp. 154–8.

[60] S.N.A. Jafri (Deputy Director, Dept. Public Information, Govt of India), Note regarding the Muslim parties in India, 7 December 1934, in Govt of India, Home Depot., Political Branch, file 150/34, NAI; Mushirul Hasan, *Nationalism and Communal Politics in India, 1916–28* (New Delhi, 1979), pp. 287–301; Khaliquzzaman, *Pathway*, p. 98. It is difficult to agree with Mehrotra's view that the Congress had not asked a high price for the inclusion of Muslim League members in the ministry. The two points he identifies as the main conditions, the cessation of League activities in the legislature as a separate group, and the dissolution of the League's Parliamentary Board, would have prevented the relationship between the parties from being that of a 'coalition'. The League could not have existed as an effective political force in the UP under these conditions. S.R. Mehrotra, 'The Congress and the Partition of India', in C.H. Philips and M.D. Wainwright (eds), *The Partition of India* (London, 1970), pp. 198–9.

[61] Khaliquzzaman, *Pathway*, pp. 157–8; Pant to Nehru, 20 July 1937, Pant file, Nehru papers.

the governor's role the League leaders demanded that the Congress should give reassurances to the minority groups in the provinces in which Congress was moving towards government.[62] The Muslim elite was to argue over the next two and a half years that the British governors were unable to protect the minorities from Congress—or rather Hindu—domination.

The scene at the opening of the first Legislative Assembly session under the new constitution abounded in symbols that indicated that the political system was no longer to be dominated by an anglicized version of the 'husk culture' of UP. A newspaper described the scene in the following terms:

> All the galleries in the House were filled to overflowing and they had to accommodate nearly six times as many as could find seats. The Premier, who clad in white *dhoti* and *kurta* and other Congress Ministers were loudly cheered as they entered the House and there were deafening shouts of '*Inquilab Zindabad*', and other favourite Congress slogans from the galleries in flagrant violation of the well-known rule that there should be no demonstrations in the galleries. . . . Some Congressmen who were non-members found their way into the House and seated themselves alongside the members. . . . All Congress members were clad in *khadi* and put on Gandhi caps. Mr Shanti Swarup (Hardoi) had a large Congress flag planted by his side. . . . Professor Ram Saran (Moradabad), another Congressite, was seen spinning all the time in the House.[63]

To the eyes of the Hindu reporter the change in the dominant symbols was manifest: what must it have seemed to the Muslim elite?

Adjustments to the new political circumstances also had to be made at the district level. Indeed, in some districts attempts were made to organize 'parallel administrations' during September and October 1937.[64] Pant, on learning of this, had circulars sent to the District Congress Committees (DCCs) and district officers. Damodar Swarup Seth, the secretary of the UP Provincial Congress Committee (UPPCC), instructed the DCCs that the administration now represented a Congress government and called for harmony between the local Congress workers and the district administration.[65] C.W. Gwynne, the chief

62 Mehrotra, 'Congress and Partition', p. 197.

63 *Leader*, 31 July 1937, p. 9. For a discussion of the 'husk' culture see D. A. Low (ed.), *Soundings in Modern South Asian History* (Canberra, 1968), pp. 5–11.

64 Sir Harry Haig (Gov. U.P.) to Lord Linlithgow (Viceroy), 16 and 23 October 1937, in Haig Papers, MSS Eur F 115/12, India Office Records, London.

65 *Leader*, 13 December 1937, p. 6.

secretary, gave complementary orders to the district officers.[66] Some Muslims saw this as a threat to the impartiality of the administration, and it became a centrepiece of the charges levied against the Pant government in the *Pirpur Report*.[67] All Damodar Swarup Seth's injunctions, however, did not stop Congressmen from trying to use their party membership to bring down public servants, especially those at the lower levels of the bureaucracy and police force.[68]

The gains which Muslims had made at the local level were also threatened by the new government. In March 1938 a joint committee was set up to examine the structure of the existing law and machinery relating to local self-government. Although the report of this committee does not seem to have been published until after the Second World War, the trend of change was obvious at the time. The question of separate electorates was the key issue dividing Hindus and Muslims on the committee. The majority report wished 'to root out' separate electorates,[69] but a note of dissent from one Muslim MLA, warned that the 'decision of this question by a majority vote without [the] willing consent of the Musalmans will lead the province in[to] a controversy outside [the] legislature whose consequences may be very undesirable indeed'.[70]

The position of the UP Muslim elite was politically weaker than it was at any stage since 1907. They no longer felt they had ministerial representation or British protection, they were concerned at the growing pressures on the bureaucracy, and there were signs that their protected position in local government was to be attacked. Each of these developments had implications for their ability to hold on to the gains they had made in other areas since the early years of the century. In these circumstances, even if the Congress government had been more than generous to Muslim interests in terms of public service

[66] C. W. Gwynne, Circular to all district magistrates, 10 November 1937, Haig Papers, MSS Eur F 115/12.

[67] The *Report of the Inquiry Committee appointed by the Council of the All-India Muslim League to Inquire into Muslim Grievances in Congress Provinces*, 1938, pp. 73–4.

[68] See *Hindustan Times*, 24 September 1938, p. 10.

[69] *Report of the Local Self-Government Committee*, pt II (Allahabad, 1948), p. 4.

[70] Ibid., p. 42. The Muslim members also objected to the chairmen of local boards being elected separately from the other members (and therefore not subject to no-confidence motions), the loss of local control over primary education, and the diminution of the role of Urdu in local administration.

jobs, educational policy, and land policy, it is likely that the Muslim politicians would have turned to agitational politics. As it was, Pant and his government had also to answer to the wider objectives of the nationalist movement and to their own, basically Hindu, constituency. At best they could hold the balance even.

Wild claims were made by some Muslims about government recruitment, such as the assertion that 'Pant had decided to give employment only to those who had participated in the 1930 civil disobedience movement', thereby excluding Muslims,[71] and there was general Muslim uneasiness about the question of communal proportions in the services. What happened in this sphere in the first Congress ministry? Apart from some rural development jobs the ministry did not control recruitment, which in April 1937 had been placed in the hands of the UP Public Service Commission. But the ministry could make alterations to recruitment formulae. For example, in November 1938 the government announced that ten places would be open for competition in the executive branch of the UPPCS, with six places going to Hindus, three to Muslims, and one to a member of a scheduled caste which, apart from the latter, were roughly the proportions of the previous period. But one other addition was made: 'One in each class [Hindu and Muslim] will go to a candidate belonging to the tenant class standing highest in order of merit . . .'.[72] The Muslim elite would thus have only two successful candidates. In the previous year four of the eleven successful applicants were Muslims. The change was slight, but it pointed to the new directions being taken in recruitment policy.

How far did having a Congress government in Lucknow affect the totality of Muslim public employment? The figures indicate that the changes were small (as would be expected, given the slow impact of recruitment on total numbers), amounting in most categories to a percentage point or two from 1928 to 1939. But there are some interesting points that emerge. The first is that, generally, it is in the higher ranks that any Muslim decline occurs over the period from 1928. This will be explored in more detail below, but over this time the percentage of Muslims declined in the executive branch of the

[71] *Statesman*, 19 October 1938, p. 5. The Pant ministry had, in fact, attracted the ire of the UP Congress organization when in its first appointment, of the Advocate-General, a non-Congressman was selected. He appeared at the opening of the legislature, however, with a Congress flag in his lapel.

[72] *Hindustan Times*, 13 November 1938, p. 4.

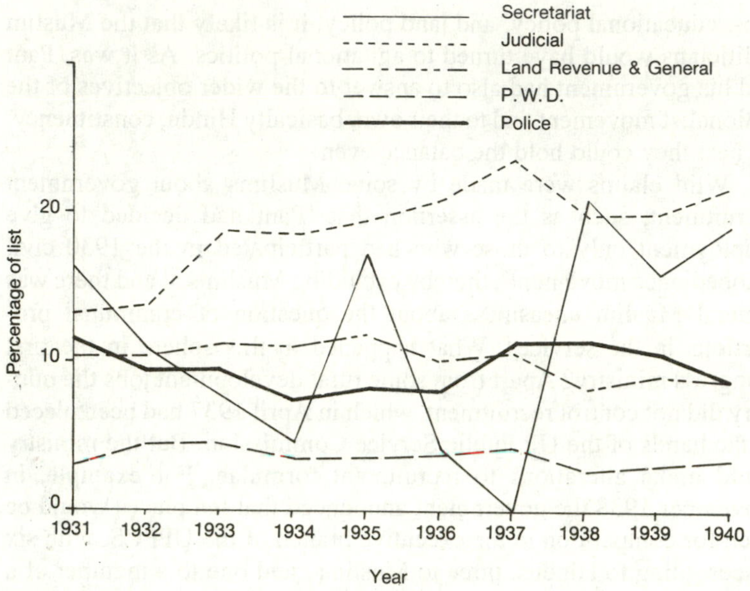

FIGURE 1. Percentage of senior Muslim officers in major Public Service departments in UP, 1931–40

UPPCS and amongst Deputy Superintendents and Inspectors of Police. Muslims also lost ground among the Head Constables, though they still provided almost two-thirds of their number. On the other hand there was an increase of Muslims in the ranks of Sub-Inspectors and Kanungos.[73]

Using the *India Office Civil Lists*, it is possible to make firmer comments on the communal composition of the ICS cadre and the

[73] Shafa'at Ahmad Khan, *Representation*, Appendix, pp. 60–77; Pant Address, Appendix 1; *UPLC*, 21 August 1939, vol. 6, pp. 64–5. The increase of Muslims in the lower ranks of police officers may have been due to deliberate recruitment during the civil disobedience movement Govt. of India, *India in 1931–32* (Calcutta, 1933), p. 181; Anandswarup Gupta, *The Police in British India, 1861–1947* (New Delhi, 1979), pp. 468–9. The officers included in the calculations on which these graphs are based, were those listed in the UP cadres of the ICS, PCS, Indian Police, and Indian Service of Engineers. For the last three services, the lists comprise only senior officers in receipt of monthly salaries of Rs 1000 and over. Officers who appeared were included if they remained on the UP list. The Secretariat list includes officers on special duty.

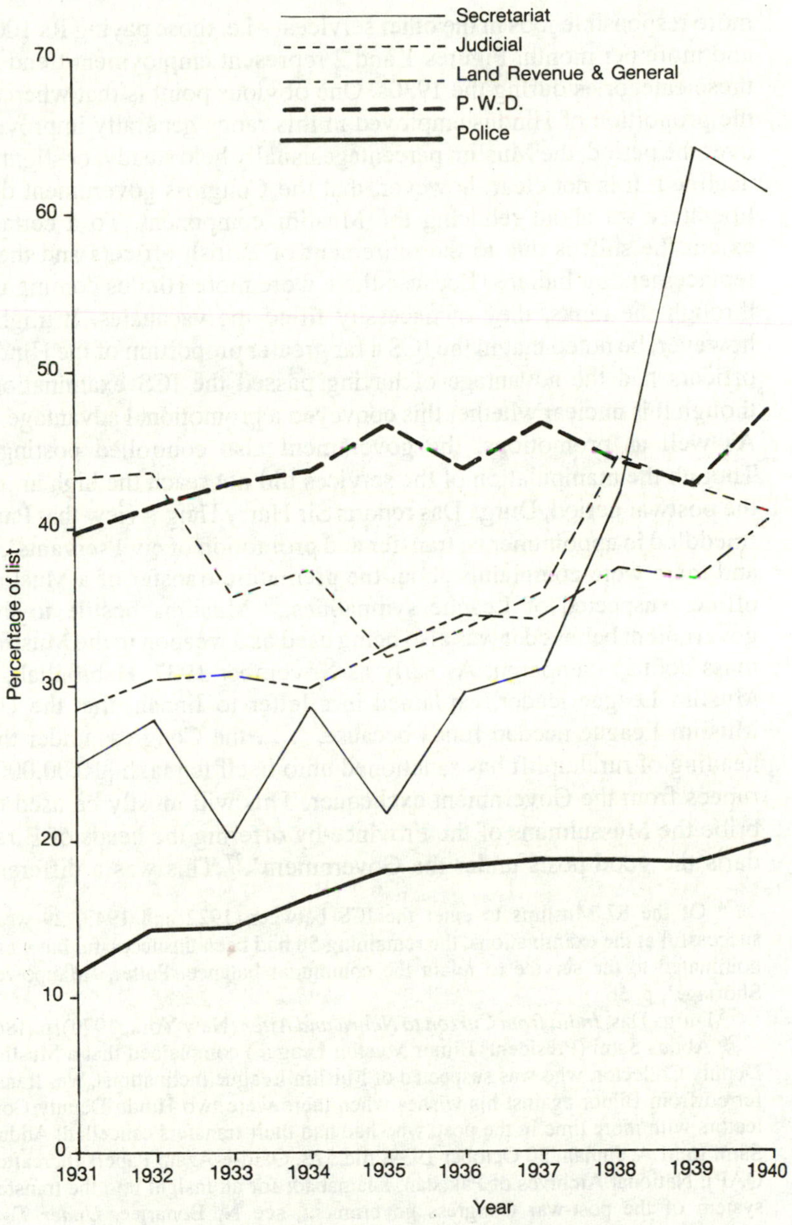

FIGURE 2. **Percentage of senior Hindu officers in major Public Service departments in UP, 1931–40.**

more responsible jobs in the other services—i.e. those paying Rs 1000 and more per month. Figures 1 and 2 represent employment trend in these categories during the 1930s. One obvious point is that whereas the proportion of Hindus employed in this range generally improved over the period, the Muslim percentage usually held steady, or slightly declined. It is not clear, however, that the Congress government deliberately set about reducing the Muslim component. To a certain extent the shift is due to the retirement of British officers and their replacement by Indians. Because there were more Hindus coming up through the ranks, they of necessity filled the vacancies. It might, however, be noted that in the ICS a far greater proportion of the Hindu officers had the advantage of having passed the ICS examination, though it is unclear whether this conveyed a promotional advantage.[74] As well as promotions, the government also controlled postings. Though the manipulation of the services did not reach the high art of the postwar period, Durga Das reports Sir Harry Haig's view that Pant 'meddled in appointments, transfer and promotion of civil servants',[75] and there were complaints about the premature transfer of a Muslim officer suspected of League sympathies.[76] Muslims hostile to the government believed it was also being used as a weapon in the Muslim mass contact campaign. As early as November 1937, Habibullah, a Muslim League leader, explained in a letter to Jinnah, that the UP Muslim League needed funds because, '. . . the Congress under the heading of rural uplift has sanctioned unto itself ten lakh [10,00,000] rupees from the Government exchequer. This will mostly be used to bribe the Mussulmans of the Province by offering the heads of Biradaris the good posts under the Government'.[77] This was a different

[74] Of the 87 Muslims to enter the ICS between 1922 and 1943, 29 were successful at the examinations, the remaining 58 had been unsuccessful but were nominated to the service to retain the communal balance. Potter, 'Manpower Shortage', p. 56.

[75] Durga Das, *India from Curzon to Nehru and After* (New York, 1970), p. 186.

[76] Abdus Sami (President, Bijnor Muslim League) complained that a Muslim Deputy Collector, who was suspected of Muslim League inclinations, was transferred from Bijnor against his wishes when there were two Hindu Deputy Collectors with more time in the post, who had had their transfers cancelled. Abdus Sami to M.A. Jinnah, 30 October 1939, file 578, Qaid-e-Azam Papers [hereafter QAP], National Archives of Pakistan, Islamabad; for an insight into the transfer system of the post-war Congress government, see N. Bonarjee, *Under Two Masters* (Calcutta, 1970), p. 233. Bonarjee was Chief Secretary at the time.

[77] Habibullah to Jinnah, 24 November 1937, file 270, QAP; cf. *Pioneer*, 22 August 1938, p. 1, and 28 August 1938, p. 8.

type of complaint: not that Hindus were getting jobs which should have gone to Muslims, but that Muslims were being 'bought' by Congress.

The general picture, then, of public employment for Muslims during the first Congress ministry was rather mixed. Though they retained a larger share of jobs than their proportion of population 'entitled' them to, they were losing some of the gains of the previous twenty or so years, and they were not progressing into the more influential positions and higher ranks of the services at the same rate as their Hindu colleagues. Moreover, there were signs that political considerations were being taken into account in the question of transfers, and in the appointment of some of the subsidiary services. But even so, what may have been more worrying was the growing pressure for less Muslims in the public services: as Pant himself put it,

> I think it is not wise on the part of Muslims to lay undue stress on the question of communal proportion in services. Their attitude in this matter is already creating a reaction among the Hindus. We are now receiving representations to the effect that there is no reason why the Hindus should have less than what they are entitled to on a population basis. . . . It may even recoil on them [i.e., the Muslims] and make it difficult for people to deal with these questions as generously as they would like to.[78]

It was the last sentence which held the nub of the new situation. The Muslims were no longer dealing with the British on these questions of communal proportions in the services, but with the Congress, a political organization dependent on Hindu support. It had become politically unwise to press too hard on this question if the objective was the maintenance of the Muslim position.

The educational policies being developed by the Congress government also alarmed the Muslim elite. The initial cause for concern was the promotion of the Wardha scheme of Basic Education, which urged a common education in Hindustani with a considerable practical content in the curriculum. Although Muslim educators were involved in drawing up the scheme, Muslims attacked it as anti-Muslim. To a certain extent this was related to the conflict over the nature of Hindustani.[79] But it was also related to the lack of religious teaching in the Basic Schools, to co-education, and to the general association of

78 Pant Address.

79 *Statesman*, 24 October 1938, p. 14.

the scheme with what was known of Gandhi's educational ideas.[80] The full implications of the educational changes were spelled out in the report of the Acharya Narendra Dev Committee on Primary and Secondary Education in the UP which was presented in February 1939. As well as endorsing the scheme of Basic Education in the primary schools, the report also called for large changes in the secondary system. Although it recommended that Hindustani should be the medium of instruction in all schools and colleges, it recommended that 'provision be made for the teaching of Hindustani with Urdu script for the benefit of Muslim boys and girls.'[81] The implication was clear: Hindustani would normally be written in *devanagari*. As well as these important linguistic recommendations, the committee made two other proposals that hit at the Muslim education system. The first was that control of primary and secondary education should be 'vested in a central authority' under the final authority of the Minister of Education. This would considerably decrease Muslim influence on education in towns in which they were a majority and controlled the municipal boards. The other set of recommendations was aimed at providing one set of educational institutions for all communities by converting the Islamia schools into Basic schools, and bringing of efficiency equivalent to the State schools, and teaching the syllabus prescribed for the Basic schools.[82]

These recommendations undermined the separate character of Muslim education in the UP and especially attacked Urdu and the Islamia schools and *makhtabs*, the institutions the Muslims developed over the previous twenty years to improve their secular education without sacrificing the religious education they valued so highly. The first Pant ministry was unable to implement the committee's proposals because of the intervention of the Second World War and the subsequent resignation of the Congress government. But the determination of the Congress to carry through these changes was obvious and the Muslim educational system had, at best, gained a short-term reprieve.[83]

[80] *Statesman*, 5 October 1938, p. 4.

[81] Report of the first Acharya Narendra Dev Committee of 1939 [hereinafter Dev Committee, 1939], ch. XVI, pt V, no. 59g, in *Report of the Secondary Education Reorganisation Committee, Uttar Pradesh, 1953* [hereinafter *Sec. Ed. Report, 1953*] (Lucknow, 1953), Appendix I, p. 6A.

[82] Dev Committee, 1939, ch. XIV, pt V, nos 59b, d, e, 60, and pt IX, no. 73–4, in *Sec. Ed. Report, 1953*, Appendix I, pp. 6A, 9A.

[83] On their return to power in 1946, the Congress rapidly reorganized education

Zamindari, the remaining element of the Muslim elite position, was also threatened by the Congress electoral victory. It was clear even before the 1937 election campaign that the Congress were concerned to improve the conditions of the tenant—especially *vis-a-vis* the larger landlords.[84] This general aim was reiterated in the streets outside the Legislative Assembly prior to its opening when both Pant and Nehru promised to assist the kisans. But the nature of the changes remained unclear and there was conflict about agrarian policy in the party. Congress election policy did not embrace the abolition of zamindari, but Nehru's words to the cultivators on this occasion demonstrated the way he, at least, was thinking: 'As a result of your strength we have achieved the present power and if the present programme does not succeed to bring your succour, other steps will be taken.'[85]

The main thrust of Congress policy was developed through the new tenancy legislation introduced into the Assembly in late 1937. As Ajit Prasad Jain, Parliamentary Secretary in the Revenue Department, put it, '[in the legislation] the smaller landlord has been shown considerable concessions against the big landlord and the rights as also the security of the tenants is being increased.'[86] They attacked the larger landlord's position by limiting the amount of land which could be classified as *sir*, thereby restricting his ability to profit from letting this land at uncontrolled rents. The Statutory tenant under the previous legislation became a Hereditary tenant, whose rights passed to his heirs instead of ceasing five years after his death. The tenant was also further protected against ejectment, from distraint for the recovery of rent, and from *begar* and all ceases except those sanctioned by the government.[87]

Although it is clear that there was no deliberate communal intent in the legislation, Muslim landlords argued that it was 'destructive of the culture of the minority community, sustained by the patronage of

---

in the UP on even more rigorous lines. Hindu became compulsory, *Sec. Ed. Report, 1953*, Appendix III, pp. 23a–24a.

84 For an outline of a questionnaire the UPPCC sent to local committees on agrarian questions, see *Pioneer*, 30 May 1936, pp. 1, 16: It raised the possibility of zamindari abolition and its political impact on the Congress.

85 *Leader*, 31 July 1937, p. 9. Even before the opening of the legislature, Congress legislators had passed resolutions, in party meetings, pressing for a committee to investigate landlord-tenant relations. *Leader*, 29 July 1937, p. 10.

86 *Pioneer*, 6 November 1937, p. 8.

87 The clearest statement of the implications of the tenancy legislation of 1939 can be found in Neale, *Economic Change*, pp. 107–20.

the Muslim landed aristocracy'.[88] Dealing with the bill, however, posed political problems for the Muslim League leadership because they claimed to represent Muslims of all social classes. They therefore attempted to protect the landed interest without marching arm-in-arm with the landlords[89] by directing their attacks on the bill in ways which could build support among both Muslim landlords and tenants, and especially by emphasizing advantages which the new legislation gave to the moneylenders. Zahir-ud-din Faruqui, for example, argued that the League was not behind the other communities regarding the question of the abolition of capitalism, but 'there was no reason why the landlords were singled out, when other capitalists were left alone'.[90] But as the bill was debated clause by clause, it became obvious that the League was putting up a defence of the landlord's position.[91] And yet the Act was not such a great threat to the interests of the bulk of the Muslim landlords. The sections limiting distraint and ejectment did reduce the power of all landlords, but only a few large landlords were affected by the restrictions on sir.[92] The pressures building up within the Congress were much more threatening. Acharya Narendra Dev, the Congress Socialist leader, made these threats clear in March 1939, when he said

> If we want to revive the village, we have to democratise it, to rid it of its exploiters of various kinds—people who fatten on others' labour. The village must be cleaned and cleared of these obstructions in the path of progress. Landlordism, therefore, must go. There must be no equivocation in this matter.[93]

[88] Durga Das, *Curzon to Nehru*, p. 187.

[89] When the Nawab of Chhatari, the leading Muslim landlord-politician, offered to bring the Muslim landlord MLAs and MLCs into the League parliamentary party in mid-1937, Khaliquzzaman prevailed against the move. At this time he clearly wished to leave the way open for a subsequent coalition government with the Congress. Chhatari to Jinnah, 12 August 1937, file 242, QAP; see also Khaliquzzaman's comment at the opening of the legislature 'that the Congress programme of works would meet with the approval of everyone in the House, though there might be differences here and there', *Leader*, 2 August 1937, p. 9.

[90] *Hindustan Times*, 12 November 1938, p. 7. Rafi Ahmad Kidwai exposed the League's tactics of obfuscating their land policies in a brilliant speech reported in the *Leader*, 12 November 1938, p. 12.

[91] See, for example, the conflicts over improvements and subletting of groves, *Leader*, 9 December 1938, p. 10.

[92] Sir Harry Haig, 'The United Provinces and the new constitution,' *The Asiatic Review*, vol. 36, 1940, p. 430.

[93] Presidential address to the Annual Conference of the All India Kisan Sabha,

It was clear that the attempt to remove the zamindars had not been abandoned, and there were some landlords who realized it.[94]

That the tenancy legislation had not been more far-reaching had been the result of the ability of the smaller landlords among the Congress legislators to exert pressure on the ministry, not of the efforts of the landlords and Muslim League whose achievement was mainly to delay its implementation.[95] The landlords could not even use their numbers in the Legislative Council to block the measure. As Tomlinson points out, Rafi Ahmad Kidwai, the revenue minister, was able to scare some of the zamindars and manipulate the moneylending interests in the Council to get the bill passed. The price for *bania* support appears to have been a UP Debt Redemption (Amendment) Bill favourable to their interests.[96]

The auguries of the opening of the UP legislature under the new constitution in 1937 had proved to be correct. The dominance of the *khadi* clad congressmen had ushered in a new political system. Despite the attempts of the Congress government to be generous to Muslims,[97] some of the old certainties were gone: viz., the British dominated provincial government seeking to balance Muslim and Hindu interests; the Muslim ministers of the dyarchy period; the conservative influence of the zamindar members of the old Legislative Council. Now, for the first time since 1909, the Muslim elite seemed to have no leverage in the new institutions of government. This was reflected in the way the Congress could push its legislation, slowly but inexorably, through the legislature: legislation which altered the agrarian system and debt laws, and promised to change the hard-fought gains in education and

---

Gaya, in Acharya Narendra Dev, *Socialism and the National Revolution* (Bombay, 1946), pp. 52–3.

[94] See for example K.B. Haji Maulvi Muhammad Nisarullah's speech in *UPLC*, 16 September 1939, vol. VI, p. 930.

[95] Damodar Swarup Seth to Nehru, 18 April 1938, file P/20/38, AICC Papers.

[96] B.R. Tomlinson, *The Indian National Congress and the Raj, 1929–42* (London, 1977), p. 97.

[97] In early 1939 the UP Government Publicity Department published an Urdu pamphlet which claimed to show that the Congress government had been more than generous to the Muslims in respect of jobs in the services, in imposing no new restrictions on Muslim religious observations (while it had for Hindus), and in releasing from prosecution Muslims who had attacked Ministers. This raised a considerable furore among Hindus without, it seems, impressing the Muslim elite. These concessions, even if accurately reported, remained the largesses of Congress patronage. See *Leader*, 21 April 1939, p. 4.

local government. Following the Gwynne circular, district administration was suspected of being dominated by local Congressmen,[98] and the proportion of Hindus in the higher cadres of the services was growing. Many of the gains of the past thirty years seemed to be vanishing or at least under threat, and there was little that the Muslim elite had been able to do about it.

By mid-1939 the Muslim elite of the UP had lost their illusions: the foundations they had fought so hard to build were shown to be straw. It was from this time that they began to embrace a new separatism, encouraged by the Muslim League leaders' appeals to their sense of brotherhood and to their secular and religious fears. Previously they had aimed at striking a set of bargains with the Hindus in the province—now their objective was complete separation from the Hindus.

What I tried to show here is that in the period 1900–37, alongside the struggle waged by Muslim politicians for constitutional and employment safeguards, there were corresponding attempts by Muslims to cope with the threat of economic degradation through adjustments to educational choices and in the management of family property. As elements of both these aspects of the Muslim elite response called for recognition by the government of special rights, they demonstrated Muslim separatism and inspired communal conflict. But although the separatism of this early period shared a great deal with the separatism of 1939–47, in that it comprised a mixture of religious/communal sentiment and a sense of disadvantage, there was one basic difference: by 1939 there was no way in which the Muslim elite could recapture the gains they had fought so hard to achieve in the years following MacDonnell's departure. With this in mind, the endorsement of the 'two nations' theory by the Muslim elite of the UP becomes more understandable, not just as an attempt to preserve a privileged position, nor simply as a response to the manipulation of communal symbols by League politicians, but as deeply felt reaction to the sudden collapse of a position rebuilt over 30 years. Perhaps it was a sense of frustration and helplessness which drove them into accepting the demand for Pakistan, which when successful, would eventually see many of them forsake their homeland, and leave those Muslims who remained without political leadership from within their own community.

[98] Haig, 'UP and the new constitution', p. 427.

Chapter Fourteen

'Communalism' in Princely India: The Case of Hyderabad, 1930–40

IAN COPLAND

> The time has come when the communal holocaust must be confined to the Indian States, the time has come when both the Hindu and Muslim newspapers must be prevented from blowing communalism into British India. There was a time when our politicians like Gokhale rightly used to take pride in Indian States being free from communalism, which was a vice in British India . . . But the table appears to have been turned.
>
> C.S. Ranga Iyer, 1934

Measured by its most visible symbol—riots—Hindu–Muslim 'communalism' rose dramatically in India during the early twentieth century.[1] However, to judge from contemporary sources, the baneful impact of communalism was less pronounced in princely India than in British India. According to Sir Conrad Corfield, doyen of twentieth-century British political officers, 'communal disturbances were practically unknown in the States'.[2] More tellingly, perhaps, 'the comparative absence of communal strife' in the princely states impressed both Sir John Simon's Parliamentary Commission of 1927

[1] See the tabular statements for the period 1923–8 in the *Report of the Indian Statutory Commission* (London, 1930), vol. IV, pp. 108–20, and vol. VI, pp. 586–99.

[2] Sir C. Corfield, *The Princely India I Knew: From Reading to Mountbatten* (Madras, 1975), p. 48. See also Sir Michael O'Dwyer, *India as I Knew It, 1885–1925* (London, 1925), p. 141; and Sir Arthur Lothian, *Kingdoms of Yesterday* (London, 1951), p. 184.

and Oxford's Sir Reginald Coupland, who visited India on behalf of the Warden and Fellows of Nuffield College in 1942.[3]

How does this verdict stand up when tested against the evidence? Hyderabad, second largest and most populous of the states, provides a useful benchmark.

At first sight, Hyderabad seems the perfect exemplar of Corfield's thesis. The State had the reputation of being a place where 'good relations and toleration [prevailed] . . . between the two major communities', where Hindus and Muslims settled their differences in a 'spirit . . . of give and take' rather than in the streets.[4] And by and large this reputation would appear to have been well deserved. During the first three and a half decades of the twentieth century, Hyderabad experienced only three serious communal disturbances—at Gulbarga in August 1924, at Goarta in August 1929 and at Aland in January 1933. If one compares this record with the statistical picture for British India in the 1920s assembled by the Statutory Commission, the contrast is striking.

However, that is about as far as the contrast can be sustained. Between 1937 and 1940 Hyderabad's much vaunted communal accord was irreparably shattered by a series of bloody riots (Table 1) and political demonstrations culminating in a nine-month campaign of civil disobedience by over 8000 Hindus against the Darbar. To be fair, the *satyagraha* of 1938–9 was not expressly anti-Islamic; but its massive scale, and the fact that it was fought to secure 'freedom of religion', made it anathema to the State's Muslim minority. Determined to protect their patrimony, the Muslims organized counter-demonstrations and exacted indiscriminate reprisals. On 28 November 1938, 2000 armed Muslims processed through the capital shouting 'Nizam Zindabad' and 'Hindu Sabha and State Congress Satyagraha murdabad'; on 5 March 1939 a bus carrying *satyagrahis* to Hyderabad

[3] Statutory Commission *Report*, vol. 1, p. 29; and R. Coupland, *Indian Politics, 1936–1942* (London, 1943), p. 178. The quotation comes from the Statutory Commission.

[4] 'Review of the Hyderabad Agitation' complied by the Intelligence Bureau, Home Dept Govt of India, May 1939, Home Political file 43/3/39 (hereafter, Home Pol.), National Archives of India (hereafter, NAI), p. 1; and note by Sir Theodore Tasker, Revenue and Police Member, Nizam's Executive Council, dated June 1939, India Office Records (IOR), India Office Library (IOL), London, R/1/29/1921.

TABLE 1

MAJOR COMMUNAL DISTURBANCES IN HYDERABAD 1937–40

Date	*Place(s)*	*Participants*	*Casualties*	*Damage*
Dec. 1937	Ganjoti	n.a.	2 +	n.a.
March 1938	Chakur, Gulbarga	n.a.	3 +	n.a.
April 1938	Dhulpet	c. 10,000	c. 200	*six mohullas* extensively damaged
June 1938	Udgir	20 arrests	1 +	n.a.
March 1939	Hyderabad	50 +	5 +	n.a.
March 1940	Bidar	n.a.	3 +	100 shops destroyed
Sept. 1940	Vijatpur	n.a.	15	n.a.
Sept. 1940	Nander	n.a.	17	n.a.

was 'set upon by irate bystanders'; on 22 April a batch of 102 protesters under police escort was ambushed by a party of Muslims in Tuljapur; the same day, Muslim *goondas* attacked Hindus celebrating 'Hyderabad Day' at Sultanshahi.[5]

For all that the Hyderabad authorities tried to make light of these incidents, it was apparent to all concerned that the communal situation had undergone a sea-change. In his report on the Dhulpet riot of April 1938, British Resident D.G. Mackenzie observed that relations between Hindus and Muslims in Hyderabad had 'received a shock from which it will not be easy to recover'.[6] By 1940 it was evident that they would never recover. Hindus and Muslims would henceforth take divergent paths, the one leading to integration with democratic India, the other to a quixotic bid for independence. What on earth had happened to the old 'spirit . . . of give and take'?

As one would expect, the upheavals of 1937–40 in Hyderabad caused considerable soul-searching in official circles. They also drew comment in the press and from British Indian politicians. Consequently

[5] 'Review of Hyderabad Agitation', pp. 13–14.

[6] Resident's fortnightly report for the first half April 1938, IOR, R/1/29/ 1669.

there is no lack of informed speculation about the causes of the imbroglio. Hard evidence, though, is less plentiful. The British Residency records in the India Office Library contain little more than head counts and narratives of events, while the Darbari files to be found in the Andhra Pradesh Archives are tantalizingly patchy in this area; for instance, I was unable to trace the internal report on the Dhulpet riot to which Prime Minister Sir Akbar Hydari alludes in his covering letter to the Viceroy.[7] Hence, the discussion in this essay will focus on the one aspect of Hyderabad's communal history in this period which is relatively well-documented—the satyagraha of 1938–9.

Most nationalist writers ascribe the movement of 1938–9 to popular resentment against the 'irresponsible, autocratic and medieval' rule of the Nizam.[8] That it was a mainly Hindu movement is explained away by the assertion that Hindus bore the brunt of the Nizam's oppression: 'Hyderabad is a State', declared one vernacular newspaper, 'in which being a Hindu itself is an offence'.[9]

Ironically, this interpretation rests upon a view of the Hyderabad Darbar first expounded by the British. In November 1925 the newly-appointed Resident, Sir William Barton, undertook a secret enquiry into the Nizam's affairs; his report stunned the British Authorities for it demonstrated that the Darbar's administration had 'broken down', that 'gross misrule' prevailed, and that the people had 'almost reached the limit of their endurance'. It would 'hardly [have been] possible', commented the Secretary of State Lord Birkenhead, 'to frame a blacker indictment against any ruler'.[10] In the wake of Barton's exposé a reluctant Nizam was forced to appoint several British officers to key administrative posts. One of them, Revenue Member of Council Richard Chevenix-Trench, recalled later: 'What we found [in 1927] was the negation of decent government . . . erected into a system.'[11]

Many of the faults detected by Barton persisted into the 1930s. Chief of these was the ruler himself, Nizam Mir Osman Ali, who had presided over the State since 1911, remained firmly in the saddle and continued to act in ways which alternately infuriated and revolted his

[7] Sir A. Hydari to Priv. Sec. Viceroy, 19 April 1938, IOR R/1/29/1719.

[8] R. Tirtha, *Memoirs of Hyderabad Freedom Struggle* (Bombay, 1967), p. 67.

[9] *Dig Vijay* (Sholapur), no. 43, 27 April 1939, Sita Ram Papers, file 32, pt 3, NAI.

[10] Birkenhead to Lord Irwin, 22 April 1926, Irwin Collection, Sec. of State's Letters, vol. I, IOL.

[11] Trench to Sir T. Tasker, 29 August 1949, Tasker Coll. vol. 17, IOL.

advisers: pathologically shy of strangers, the Nizam watched over his favourite daughter with a zeal that came 'perilously close to insanity';[12] for amusement, he took nude photographs of his European guests with cameras concealed in the palace bathrooms, visited graveyards at night, and watched operations in the City hospital; though one of the richest men in the world, his greed for money was so insatiable that in the 1930s he fell into the habit of attending the wedding receptions of rich nobles in the hope of soliciting presents (*nazars*) from the guests; surrounded by wealth, he corresponded with his ministers on scraps of toilet paper and drove around in a 20-year-old car, draped in a dirty threadbare blanket. Sir Theodore Tasker, who knew him as well as anyone, thought him 'a case for an alienist'.[13]

More importantly, Hyderabad in the 1930s remained the feudal preserve it had always been. Fifteen per cent of the State belonged exclusively to the Nizam and was utilized by him for his private benefit. Another 27 per cent comprised hereditary, tax-free *jagirs* owned by a handful of aristocrats and titled officials. Additionally, the royal family received Rs 100 lakhs a year from the treasury for living expenses. By contrast, expenditure on public welfare was miserly: in 1938–9 Hyderabad spent less than 16 per cent of its budget on education, health and development as against 21 per cent in the Central Provinces, 25 per cent in Bombay and 30 per cent in Madras, its nearest neighbours.[14]

Continuity also prevailed in the constitutional sphere. By the 1930s government by royal fiat had given way to government by ministers and council; but the council was a sham. It could not initiate or reject legislation, and its 20 members included only six non-officials, two nominated by the Prime Minister and four chosen by 'jagirdars' and 'pleaders of the High Court', a combined electorate of less than 2000 voters. Denied constitutional expression through the council, public opinion was stifled in other ways too. Books and news-

[12] 'Handing over note' by Sir Terence Keyes, Resident at Hyderabad, dated April 1933, Keyes Coll. vol. 31, IOL.

[13] Note by Tasker, 23 April 1972, Tasker Coll. See also Tasker's diary entry for 29 July 1939, in which he describes the Nizam's rapacious behaviour at 'X's' wedding. Tasker Coll.

[14] 'A Peep into Hyderabad', reprinted in *The Tribune* (Lahore), 5 June 1939. Hyderabad's literary rate—4.9 per cent—was half that of the surrounding provinces. 'Conditions In Hyderabad, 1939', Jawaharlal Nehru Coll., subject file 102/2 Nehru Memorial Museum and Library (hereafter, NMML), New Delhi.

papers were heavily censored and freedom of assembly was circumscribed by a royal *firman* which required organizers of public meetings to seek prior permission from the police.

Last but not least, there are good grounds for thinking that the Nizam's rule affected Hindus more adversely than Muslims. In 1931 Hindus comprised over 84 per cent of Hyderabad subjects while Muslims made up just 20 per cent; yet Muslims dominated the government and enjoyed a disproportionate share of its bounty. For example, they held three out of four gazetted appointments in the public service (Table 2), occupied one in three places in State-run schools and colleges (Table 3), and consumed about 94 per cent of the Ecclesiastical Department's budget for religious charities.[15]

TABLE 2

GAZETTED APPOINTMENTS IN HYDERABAD 1931

Department	*Hindus*	*Muslims*	*Total*
Secretariat	16	54	70
Finance	15	26	41
Revenue	20	196	216
Judicial	12	136	148
Police & Jail	13	40	53
Education	53	183	236
Medical	45	41	86
Public Works	34	62	96
Other	40	126	166
Totals	248	864	1,112

[15] During the 1930s the Ecclesiastical Dept spent an annual average of Rs 300,000 on Islamic charities, Rs 15,000 on Christian charities and Rs 3000 on Hindu charities. Other large sums were expended on Islamic institutions abroad. Between 1926 and 1932 Rs 10,000,000 was given to Aligarh University, Rs 500,000 to the London mosque, Rs 100,000 to the Jama Masjid in Delhi, Rs 100,000 to a mosque in Palestine; Rs 100,000 to a proposed Muslim military school, Rs 80,000 to a Muslim association in Turkey, and Rs 232,000 to the travelling expenses of Muslims going to Mecca. Gen. Sec. Hindu Mahasabha, to Pol. Sec. Govt. of India, 24 December 1936, Mahasabha Papers, file R-7 of 1936–7, NMML; *The Tribune*, 7 June 1939; and B.S. Moonje to B.N. De, 13 Feb. 1938, Moonje Papers, Subject file 47, NMML.

TABLE 3

EDUCATION IN HYDERABAD, 1935–6

Level	*Hindus*	*Muslims*	*Total*
Primary	183,370	83,100	266,470
Middle	20,895	18,898	39,793
High	14,356	14,384	28,740
Totals	218,621	116,382	335,003

In fact, the Hindus were doubly penalized because it was their money which mainly underwrote the Darbar's largesse. Taking into account the communal distribution of tax-free jagir holdings and taxable *khalsa* lands, Resident Keyes in 1933 estimated that 'from 95 to 97 per cent' of the State's land revenue was contributed by the Hindu community.[16] If so, they were greatly over-taxed.

However, the most controversial aspect of the Darbar's administration was not its fiscal policy but its religious policy. The building and repair of places of worship was subject to the jurisdiction of the State Ecclesiastical Department whose predominantly Muslim staff had a legal right to disallow projects in areas 'where the population of the followers of Islam' was 'considerable';[17] not surprisingly, Hindu applications tended to get 'pigeon-holed for long periods'.[18] Music, an intrinsic part of Hindu ritual, was prohibited within 'forty steps' of any mosque. On Muslim holy days, for example during the months of Ramadan and Mohurrum, Hindus were encouraged to worship indoors and all public ceremonies involving music were banned. The Hindus complained that these regulations infringed their right to freedom of worship, and several nominally independent observers, including the French Roman Catholic Bishop of Nagpur, who toured Hyderabad in June 1939, came out in support of their stand.[19]

Nevertheless I find it difficult to accept that the situation in Hyderabad was one of systematic 'Islamic' oppression. For one thing,

[16] Keyes' handing over note, About 80 per cent of the state's *khalsa* lands, which were subject to tax, belonged to Hindus. There was no income tax.

[17] *Firman* of 1908, quoted in *The Tribune*, 7 June 1939.

[18] The Bishop of Nagpur, quoted in Lord Zetland to Lord Linlithgow, 4/5 July 1939, IOR, L/P8S/13/621.

[19] Ibid.; also Sir F. Wylie, Gov. of C.P., to Viceroy, 23 July 1939, IOR, R/1/29/1921.

this notion assumes that the local Hindu and Muslim communities were solid monolithic blocs, when in fact they were both deeply divided by caste and sect: on the Hindu side there was acute rivalry between Brahmins and non-Brahmins and between partisans of Telegu and Marathi, the two main vernaculars spoken in the Nizam's dominion; on the Muslim side there was endemic conflict between Sunnis and Shi'as and between native Hyderabadis and immigrants from British India, colloquially known as *mulkis* and *ghair-mulkis*. Politically these dichotomies were at least as important as the religious one. Indeed the pivotal issue in Hyderabad politics down to the 1930s was probably the mulki–non-mulki schism, which, though it had cultural overtones, was primarily a dispute about jobs.[20]

The communal interpretation also fails on economic grounds. Despite their relatively meagre foothold in the bureaucracy, the Hindus do not deserve to be classified as a deprived proletariat. They dominated the agricultural sector, comprising 86.2 per cent of 'cultivators of all kinds' according to the 1931 census; they monopolized wholesale and retail trade and banking; and they were well represented in the learned professions of law, medicine and accountancy. Indeed, the Hindus' commercial hegemony was so complete that the Darbar's Director of Public Information was able to justify the introduction of a policy of positive discrimination towards Muslims in the public service as a kind of welfare measure:

> The Hindus have the greater part of the trade and industry and consequently most of the private wealth of the State; most of the men of influence in the districts—village patels etc.—are Hindus; therefore there are few ways of livelihood left open to the Muslims except Government service. . . . Yet even in Government service there are over 300 Hindu gazetted officers.[21]

Conversely, Hyderabad's Muslims did not form an homogeneous ruling class. While a few thousand Muslim officials and jagir-holders

[20] As the Nizam's Subjects League, formed in 1935 to protect mulki interests, put it: 'services in Hyderabad are manned mostly by Northern Indians and these gentlemen have formed a sort of caucus and a clique with a view to keep[ing] out the others from the administration. Secondly, they suffer from an unbearable superiority complex which is most galling and irritating to the Mulkies.' Syed Abid Hasan, *Whither Hyderabad?* (A *Brief Study of Some of the Outstanding Problems of the Premier Indian State*) (Madras, 1935), p. 44.

[21] Marmeduke Pickthall to L.F. Rushbrook-Williams, 23 January 1932, Andhra Pradesh Archives (hereafter, AP), Hyderabad, R/1/47/10/105. In fact, 96,670 out of 99,184 village officers were Hindus!

lived in ostentatious luxury, tens of thousands of their co-religionists languished at the bottom end of the social spectrum in menial occupations such as domestic service, agricultural labouring, soldiering, and the peddling trade. As a contemporary put it: 'The fact . . . is that every second beggar you meet in the streets is a Muslim. . . . Can rulers also be beggars, criminals, defaulters and paupers? How absurd! . . . Let us rid our minds of the idea that we are members of the ruling class, because we are not.'[22]

Thirdly, and most importantly, the Hindu case does insufficient justice to the Darbar's religious policy. It is true that the latter imposed curbs on the public display of religious fervour but these were seen by the Darbar as a necessary evil to 'prevent strife between [the] . . . communities' and consequent damage to persons and property: 'the long established policy', declared Prime Minister Hydari, 'is full religious tolerance for all subject to the minimum amount of regulation necessary to prevent disturbance of the public tranquility'.[23] Moreover the regulations appear to have been enforced, in the main, even-handedly. Notwithstanding the alleged bias of the Ecclesiastical Department, 150 new Hindu temples were built and 825 existing ones repaired between 1930 and 1938.[24] On the other hand, Muslims, who were subject to the same rules as regards religious buildings and processions as the Hindus, sometimes had their applications turned down by the Ecclesiastical bureaucrats. For example, in May 1938 Muslim leader Bahadur Yar Jung was refused permission to hold a rally in honour of the Prophet's birthday; yet a few months later evangelist Swami Narinderji was allowed to lead a Dasserah procession through the streets of Hyderabad City—an event which, incidentally, helped to create a favourable atmosphere for the subsequent satyagraha.[25] Indeed, some elements of the government's religious policy posed a direct affront to Muslim sensibilities: Christmas and other non-Muslim festivals were honoured with public holidays; gov-

22 'An Appeal to Hyderabad Muslims by One of Them', quoted in Hasan, *Whither Hyderabad*, p. 180.

23 Pol. Member, Hyderabad Exec. Council, to Sec. Int. Aryan League, 11 September 1934, Mahasabha papers, file P-7 of 1936–7; and Hydari to Gandhi, n.d., IOR, R/1/29/192.

24 *Times of India* (Bombay), 7 June 1939.

25 Karen Leonard, 'The Mulki-Non Mulki Conflict', in R. Jeffrey, (ed.), *People, Princes and Paramount Power: Society and Politics in the Indian Princely States* (Delhi, 1978), pp. 91–2.

ernment servants were forbidden to lend their support to 'any movement for conversion to Islam or any other religion';[26] and there was a total ban on cow slaughter, which made it difficult for Muslims to celebrate the festival of Bakr-'Id in appropriate style. Press censorship, too, seems to have been enforced impartially. Between 1935 and 1938 several Hindu newspapers were prosecuted for inflaming communalism but so, too, were *al-Azam* and *Rahbar-i-Deccani*, both leading Muslim papers.[27]

The Darbar's bi-partisanship in matters of religion was personified, strange to say, by the head of State. Generally painted as an arch-communalist, Nizam Osman Ali tried hard to deal fairly with his Hindu subjects. He often attended Hindu festivals, and on several occasions stepped in to defend Hindu officials accused of impropriety, in one instance overturning a Council decision to retire four officers who had stood up for a Hindu sub-inspector of police accused of insulting the Prophet![28] Osman Ali's personal beliefs were also quite eclectic. Though nominally a Hanafi Sunni, he was strongly attracted to Sufi ideas and regularly worked 'himself into a considerable state of Shia enthusiasm during the Mohurrum [festival]'.[29] Needless to say, all this made him extremely unpopular with orthodox Muslims and in 1936 the British Resident predicted 'a fanatical attempt on the life of the Nizam's person or . . . a pogrom of Shiahs in the alleys of Hyderabad City' if he persisted in his obsession.[30]

If any one religious group did fare badly at the hands of the Hyderabad Darbar during the 1930s it was possibly the Arya Samaj. The Samaj's newspapers were proscribed more frequently than those belonging to other denominations, its officials were shadowed by the police, and Arya preachers were 'sometimes prosecuted for holding meetings under trees while their applications for building places of worship were pending'.[31] However, in some ways the Aryas are the exception which proves the rule. For one thing, there were not many of them, only a few thousand compared to 10 million Hindus. For another, the Arya Samaj's beliefs and practices differed in several

[26] Hydari to Raja Narendranath, 15 May 1939, AP, R/1/47/10/886.
[27] Hydari to Resident, 23 April 1938, IOR, R/1/29/1725.
[28] 'Conf'dl. note' by Resident, dated October 1933, IOR, R/1/29/1853.
[29] Resident to Priv. Sec. Viceroy, 10 January 1938, IOR, R/1/29/1668.
[30] 'Secret note' by Resident, dated March 1936, IOR, R/1/24/1853.
[31] Minutes of meeting, Pol. Dept. Govt. of India, 27 July 1939, IOR, R/1/29/1922.

crucial respects from those of mainstream Hinduism and the Darbar felt these justified treating the Aryas more severely—a point we shall return to later. Finally, the Samaj does not seem to have suffered too much from the persecution allegedly meted out to it: according to figures published in the *Times of India* in 1939 the Aryas were three and five times better served by way of places of worship than Muslims and Hindus respectively.[32]

On the evidence presented above, Hyderabad in the 1930s was clearly not an 'Islamic state' in the sense that the term is now generally understood. Nor does it seem to have been particularly repressive by contemporary standards. The Nizam may have been eccentric and capricious but by the 1930s he could no longer act independently of his executive council which was made up largely of distinguished Muslim politicians and ex-ICS officers from British India; there was a separate judiciary pledged to uphold the rule of law, a civil service recruited mainly by competitive examination, and a sophisticated revenue administration whose 'general standard of probity and . . . efficiency' was said by British observers to compare favourably with that in the provinces.[33] All things considered, there seems no reason to disagree with the Shankaracharya of Jyotimath, Badrinath, who concluded after investigating the Hindus and Aryas' complaints first hand in June 1939 that 'there has been a little exaggeration'.[34]

However, if this reading is correct it raises a tricky problem of interpretation. If the Hindu and Arya Samajist subjects of the Nizam were not genuinely oppressed, why did over 8000 of them feel compelled to wage civil disobedience against the Darbar in 1938–9 in order to ventilate their grievances?

The enigma of 1938–9 becomes even more puzzling when considered in the context of the Hyderabad political tradition. Down to 1938 the State was politically quiescent; there were no mass-based parties and criticism of the government in the press and on the public platform was muted in tone. At the fourth Hyderabad Political Conference held at Akola in 1931, President-elect Ramachandra Naik eulogized:

our Ruler, whose extraordinary ability and capacity for hard work and whose

[32] There was one temple for every 82 Aryas, one mosque for every 265 Muslims and one temple for every 382 Hindus. *Times of India,* 7 June 1939.

[33] Note by R.M. Crofton, dated 20 October 1938, IOR, R/1/29/1853.

[34] *Bombay Chronicle*, 7 July 1939.

simple habits are recognised by everyone, and are the pride of his people, and whose reign has been made glorious by the construction of various public buildings and huge reservoirs . . . and who has given liberal grants for many other subjects of public utility.[35]

This patriotic theme was echoed by the founders of the State's first real political party, the Hyderabad State Congress. In its public statement of September 1938 inviting Hyderabadis to join the new organization, the Provisional Committee of the Congress stressed their 'sincere loyalty to the Asaf Jahi throne' and promised to 'always strive to enhance the prestige and power of the King who is the embodiment of the glory and power of this State'.[36]

There is little here to suggest that Hyderabadis in the 1930s were seething with discontent against their ruler. How does one explain a movement that apparently materialized out of nothing?

Part of the problem would disappear if it could be shown that the 1938–9 satyagraha was actually less popular than it appears on the surface. The Darbar, not surprisingly, favoured this view. In April 1938 Prime Minister Hydari observed to the Resident that:

The actual number of demonstrators who have come forward on their own initiative from within the State has been extremely small and of these the men of any status have been nil. It can be said with certainty that if the influx from outside could be stopped, there would be practically no Arya Samaj or Mahasabha *satyagraha in Hyderabad.*[37]

Later, Hydari assayed that 'over 80 per cent' of the satyagrahis were foreigners.[38]

The Darbar's figure is certainly too high. Its own police records, summarized in Table 4, indicate that no more than 72 per cent of the five and a half thousand demonstrators arrested between February and May 1939 hailed unambiguously from British India, and though it is probable that a majority of the large number of 'unclassified' prisoners

[35] N. Ramesan (ed.), *The Freedom Struggle in Hyderabad* [*FSH*], vol. IV (Hyderabad, 1966), p. 77. As Akola was outside the Nizam's dominions, the statement quoted may be taken as a genuine expression of feeling, since there was no immediate threat of police reprisals against the participants.

[36] Statement of 5 September 1938, ibid., p. 137.

[37] Hydari to Resident, 3 April 1939, IOR, R/1/29/1920.

[38] Hydari to Resident, 19 June 1939, IOR, R/1/29/1929.

who refused to disclose their addresses were British subjects also, some could have been locals fearful of official persecution. On the other hand, lumping the two categories together does not convert the Hyderabadis into a majority; and it is hard to see how the disclaimers issued in this regard by the movement's leaders can be reconciled with their admission that, as of July 1939, 5,700 satyagrahis had been recruited from as far afield as Rajasthan and Punjab.[39] On balance, a figure of 70 per cent 'outsiders' looks reasonable.

TABLE 4

ARRESTS FOR CIVIL DISOBEDIENCE IN HYDERABAD, FEBRUARY–MAY 1939

Period	*British Indians*	*Hyderabadis*	*Unclassified*	*Total*
1–14 February	110	–	41	151
15–28 February	–	–	156	156
1–14 March	152	23	–	175
15–31 March	521	–	105	626
1–14 April	421	284	223	928
15–30 April	1,379	190	81	1,650
1–14 May	693	60	216	969
5–31 May	701	–	211	912
Total	3,977	557	1,033	5,567

It is also correct to say that the satyagraha received a cool reception from the vast majority of the Nizam's subjects. During the first few weeks of the campaign there was 'a conspicuous display of enthusiasm on the part of the public' with crowds of up to 1,000 watching the daily drama of civil disobedience in the capital. But by early November 'public sympathy for the Satyagraha movement [had begun to] . . . wane'[40] and by mid-1939 the ritual had become so commonplace that even the arrival of *jathas*, [bands] several hundred strong, failed to arouse more than 'bored interest' among 'a few idle

[39] V.D. Savarkar, Presdt Hindu Mahasabha, to M.S. Aney, 2 July 1939, Aney Papers, subject file 7, NMML.

[40] Rahmat Yar Jung, Commissioner of Police, Hyderabad, to Ali Yavar Jung, 5 November 1938, AP, R/1/47/10/936.

onlookers'.[41] Against that, quite a few local Hindus, including at least one prominent Arya Samajist, Baji Krishen Rao, and the largest Hindu landowner in the State, Maharaja Sir Kishen Pershad, spoke out against the agitation, while several Hindu politicians who had been at the forefront of demands for reform in mid-1938 refused to get involved with what one sneeringly dubbed an enterprise of 'irresponsible and misguided youths'.[42]

Equally relevant to our problem is the question of motivation. What prompted so many non-Hyderabadis, who were presumably not directly inconvenienced by the Darbar's religious policy, to travel so far to take part in the civil disobedience campaign? According to the satyagrahis' campaign newspaper, *Dig Vijay*, the prime factor was personal commitment:

> Our dictators, [leaders] who are the pick of their province, and these trustworthy workers of the Arya Samaj have kept up the traditions of the movement untarnished. Each succeeding Dictator . . . on assuming charge of the duties of the office, puts himself heart and soul into the movement, works hard day and night, tours to distant places, addresses mass meetings and looks after the various parts of the intricate machinery. His short term of office is strenuous and full of responsibility.
>
> In the history of satyagraha there have seldom been seen such hardened and well-disciplined volunteers who have rendered so creditable a record of self sacrifice and devotion to duty.[43]

The Hyderabad Government, however, had no doubt that the mainspring was self-interest. To quote Hydari again:

> What with the hirelings employed, with the type of Satyagrahis taking liquor in order to commit Satyagraha, with the innumerable lies told by those who shouted most here about 'truth', and with the opportunist use made by the forces of agitation by vested interests against recent agrarian legislation which limits usury, and is designed to relieve rural indebtedness and which prevents the peasant's land from falling into the hands of the Sowcars [moneylenders], the whole thing has left a bitter taste in one's mouth.[44]

Both portraits are crude and overdrawn, but both contain a kernel of truth.

[41] Hydari to Resident, 19 June 1939, IOR, R/1/29/1921.

[42] Note by Hydari on a conversation with Madpati Hanumanth Rao, *Vakil*, 2 August 1938, AP, R/1/47/10/718.

[43] *Dig Vijay*, 27 April 1939, Sita Ram Papers.

[44] Hydari to Gandhi, 5 January 1939, IOR, R/1/29/1803.

On the Darbar's side, it must be said that many satyagrahis appear to have joined for casual or at least non-ideological reasons. Hydari may have been exaggerating when he declared that the civil disobedience campaign was in 'some aspects . . . a picnic',[45] but there is no doubt that many people took part in the campaign out of curiosity, in a spirit of adventure, or because they saw it as an opportunity to prove their manliness. Indeed, some satyagrahis brought before the courts were visibly miffed when they received light prison sentences which apparently did not accord with their notions of martyrdom. Conversely, a number of participants were drawn in by peer group pressure. Something like one-sixth of all those arrested subsequently apologized to the Hyderabad authorities for their conduct and police reports indicate that several wept as they did so; probably most of this group would never have crossed the border but for their fear of ridicule.[46]

The proposition that some of the satyagrahis may have had a shallow commitment to their cause is further borne out by the rather meagre information I have been able to obtain, mainly from police records, about the social profile of the demonstrators. As one might expect, the majority were fairly young. Of the 105 satyagrahis arrested between October and November 1938 for which age data are available, 15 were under 20 years, and 62 under 24 years, while some jathas which arrived during 1939 from Maharashtra included boys as young as 12 and 13.[47] Socially disadvantaged groups were also prominent. The demonstrators arrested in the early phase of the campaign were typically students, artisans, petty traders, and vagrants, and to judge from those who provided the police with details of their incomes, the majority must have been struggling to survive.[48] Last but not least, a

[45] Hydari to Resident, 19 June 1939, AP, R/1/47/10/718.

[46] 'Review of Hyderabad Agitation', p. 7; *Dig Vijay*, no. 54, 10 May 1939, Sita Ram Papers: police reports in AP, R/1/47/10/936; and Hydari to Resident, 19 June 1939, AP, R/1/47/10/718. According to British sources 115 apologies had been received in one jail alone by May 1939; nationalist sources also admit that 'some' prisoners apologised.

[47] Police files in AP, R/1/47/10/936; and Resident's fort, report for 1st half February 1939, IOR, R/1/29/2018.

[48] The occupations of those arrested in October-November 1938 are given as: students (20), retail traders (19), beggars and unemployed (14), vakils and pleaders (11), teachers and private tutors (9), 'privately employed' (6), goldsmiths (5), tailors (5), motor mechanics and drivers (5), life-insurance agents (3), cooks (2), electricians (2), carpenters (2), clerk (1), waiter (1), *hakim* (1), and temple official

substantial number of satyagrahis appear to have come from broken homes or to have suffered personal disappointments. For instance, Sri Hari Govind, aged 19, had lost both his parents; G. Mohan Reddy, 22, had been turned out of the house by his father; Shanker Rao and Digamber Rao, both 21, had failed the matriculation exam; the father of Krishna Rao, 20, was serving a life-sentence for murder; and Lakshman Rao, 22, was in his father's bad books for 'having given up education'. Poor, rootless, in some cases psychologically distressed, these young men represented a natural constituency of discontent waiting to be harnessed.[49]

Another relevant consideration, which helps to explain why the satyagraha attracted so many outsiders, is the fact that their travel was subsidized. The leader of the jatha which arrived from Poona on 4 February 1939 confessed that his group had been given Rs 40 by the editor of the *Mahratta* newspaper to go to Hyderabad; another jatha claimed that they had been funded to the tune of Rs 50 per head by a Mr Gokhale of Bombay. Altogether, the Hindu Mahasabha spent over Rs 70,000 financing the civil disobedience campaign and most of this apparently went on providing rail fares at an average cost of Rs 15 a head. The Arya Samaj's outlay was even larger—over three lakhs, according to one British estimate—and most of this seems likewise to have been expended on fares.[50]

It must be conceded, too, that self-interest played a part in the movement. Some satyagrahis plainly enlisted in the hope of bettering their lot. Shaik Chandulal Nabi Sahib and Shaik Mohiuddin Saheb, whose presence was touted by the Hyderabad State Congress as evidence that its movement was supported by Muslims, rather spoilt the effect by confessing afterwards that they had tagged along 'on the promise that they would get good posts'.[51] Later, the Mahasabha hinted that the agitation might be called off if Hindus were appointed

(1). Daily earnings of the 23 who provided details ranged from one to two rupees. Data from police dossiers in AP, R/1/47/10/936.

49 Ibid., Karen Leonard makes a similar point in her study of the Kayasthas of Hyderabad, remarking that the 'Kayasths in the more militant political and religious movements tended to have marginal economic and social status'. Karen I. Leonard, *Social History of an Indian Caste: The Kayasths of Hyderabad* (Berkeley, 1978), p. 222.

50 Resident's fort. report for 1st half Feb. 1939, IOR, R/1/29/2018; V.D. Savarkar to M.S. Aney, 2 July 1939, Aney Papers, subject file 7; and Viceroy to Sec. of State, 26 July 1939, IOR, R/1/29/1922.

51 *FSH*, IV, p. 157.

to government jobs 'in sufficient numbers'.[52] Others appear to have participated in order to further their political ambitions. For example, the sixth 'Dictator', Mahashe Krishen, refused to abide by the ruling of the Sholapur 'War Council' that jathas should not exceed 25 persons and insisted on leading 1000 volunteers across the border. Rumour had it that Krishen was out to obtain the greatest amount of publicity for himself and for his newspaper, the *Pratap*.[53] Similar considerations may have prompted the involvement of the Democratic Swaraj Party leaders who joined the movement in May 1939 when shrewd judges were saying it would soon be over. According to the British their object was 'to secure the crown of martyrs by suffering incarceration in the [Hyderabad] State jails for a few days'.[54] Finally, vested interests opposed to the Darbar's agrarian programme may also have had a finger in the pie. The nine new agrarian measures added to the Hyderabad statute book during 1938[55] collectively threatened the profitability of moneylending, an occupation dominated by immigrant Hindus and Aryas, and the setting up of a 'sowcar's committee' in Hyderabad City during the summer of 1938 shows that at least some moneylenders intended to fight the legislation. Could they have become involved in clandestine activity as well? The Darbar believed so. 'I think we shall soon find', surmised a senior official, '. . . that the City Sowcar's Committee is at the back of the Satyagraha movement'.[56] Unfortunately, hard evidence for this thesis is lacking; however, the fact that three local leaders of the movement[57] worked for a Lahore-based insurance company owned by an Arya Samajist banking family lends it some plausibility.

On the other hand, there is something to be said for the high-minded view advanced by the *Dig Vijay*. The fact that many of the satyagrahis came from British India and that some accepted money to take part does not prove that they were 'hired trouble-makers' with no interest in the welfare of the Hyderabad Hindus. On the contrary,

[52] Press statement by Sanatan Dharma Sabha in *Hindustan Times* (New Delhi), 22 June 1939.

[53] Report by Central Intelligence Officer, Lahore, n.d. IOR, R/1/29/1921.

[54] 'Review of Hyderabad Agitation', p. 10.

[55] They included a Land Alienation Restriction Act (modelled on the famous Punjab Act of 1901), a Moneylender's Regulation, a Land Mortgage Act, and a Bank Act.

[56] S.N. Bheruaba to Ali Yavar Jung, 3 November 1938, AP, R/1/47/10/718.

[57] Viz, Ramkishen Doot, Baswant Rao, and Srinivas Rao Havaldar.

most of the demonstrators interviewed by the police appear to have had a very keen sense of what they were about.

Moreover, the lurid stories that filtered back from Hyderabad would have made any casual volunteer think twice before joining a jatha. Congressman Jamnalal Bajaj examined five ex-prisoners in December 1938 and saw enough bruises and injuries 'to be convinced beyond all doubt' that they had been 'subjected to unwarranted, physical violence'.[58] Other returnees claimed to have been starved, flogged, chained up and 'baked in the burning sun at noon'.[59] There were even reports of deaths. On 3 May the *Dig Vijay* carried a moving story about the demise of a satyagraha prisoner in Chanchalguda Central Jail:

> Vishnuji s[on] o[f] Bhagwant Tandurkar died in a jail on 2nd May. There was a deep wound on the back of his head. A large quantity of blood had gone out of it. Blood had come out of his nose, too. It was evident that he had been beaten in jail. The wound at the back of his head had also been caused by a lathi-blow. Marks of [a] lathi-blow were also visible on his arm and below the head.[60]

By June the Arya Samaj was insisting that at least 10 prisoners had died in custody.[61] Prospective recruits who read this propaganda or saw the stark photographs of bruised bodies that accompanied it would have been left in no doubt that satyagraha was a serious business involving real risk to life and limb.

Nevertheless, conditions in the Hyderabad jails were nothing like as grim as the Arya Samaj's broadsheets suggested. The death of so many prisoners looks bad, but it is not statistically remarkable. People can die of things other than lathi blows, and the mortality figures are quite consistent with those recorded in British Indian jails during the 1930s as being attributable to natural causes.[62] Moreover, the satyagraha army that poured into Hyderabad in 1939 was not an ordinary

[58] Bajaj to Hydari, 3 December 1938, Bajaj Papers, NMML.

[59] *Dig Vijay*, no. 54, 10 May 1939, Sita Ram Papers.

[60] Ibid., no. 48, 3 May 1939.

[61] M. Sudharkar, Sec. Int. Aryan League, Delhi, to Col. Wedgwood-Benn, M.P. (teleg.), 21 June 1939, IOR, R/1/29/1921. Later estimates went as high as 23.

[62] The British Indian mortality rate from 'natural causes' was 10 per 1000 prisoners a year. Reckoning that Hyderabad's 8000 satyagraha prisoners stayed an average of two months, the statistical expectation would be a loss of 12 or 13 prisoners, which is very close to the number who actually died. Note by Sir Theodore Tasker dated 15 July 1939, Home (Pol.) 43/3/39.

sample. It included, as of mid July, 350 boys under 15 years of age and 132 men over 60. Indeed, the presence of children and old people was so conspicuous that the Hyderabad authorities began to suspect that they had been specially recruited for propaganda purposes:

I am convinced [wrote S. T. Hollins, the Nizam's Director General of Police] that the Arya Samaj deliberately sends sick and infirm persons to court arrest in the hope that they would die a natural death in our jails and so give the Arya Samaj an opportunity of accusing us of causing their death by ill treatment.[63]

Of course none of this rules out the possibility of foul play. But if torture did occur, the jail authorities made little attempt to hide the evidence. The bodies of all Aryas who died in custody were handed over to the Samaj for cremation, and in each case the Samaj's representatives signed receipts attesting that the bodies were 'in good condition'. Nor is the evidence of the Arya Samaj's photographs entirely reliable. As Police Minister Theodore Tasker remarked caustically, 'The faking of photographs and the injuries of dead bodies are easy expedients'.[64] As for the prisoners at large, it appears that conditions varied from jail to jail. When Hollins toured the State's penal institutions in April 1939 he found that overcrowding had caused minor problems at Gulbarga and at the temporary jail built in Hyderabad City to mop up some of the overflow; nevertheless he came away satisfied with the way the majority of prisons were being run, and cited the new 'camp jail' at Gulbarga as an example:

We have rented a bungalow that is pleasantly situated on an eminence outside Gulbarga Town, and some of the leaders such as Narayanswami, Lala Kashal Chand, and Murani Lal . . . live in this bungalow. They are very happy there as they have servants to wait on them and they are supplied with books, papers, periodicals, writing material etc.[65]

Besides, many satyagrahis never went to jail. The hundreds who agreed to apologize were held overnight or for a couple of days at most, then put on trains back to their place of origin, those in need being provided with fare-money by the Darkar. Generally, these short-

63 Note dated 14 July 1939, ibid.

64 Note by Tasker, 15 July 1939, Home (Pol.).

65 Note by Hollins, dated 14 July 1939, ibid. Hydari told Gandhi that the diet given to the prisoners included ghee, mutton and cereals, and that newspapers were supplied to them. *FSH*, IV, p. 160.

term detainees found little to complain about. When a 515-strong jatha led by fifth 'Dictator' Ved Vrat Vanprasthi arrived from Pusad (CP) on 5 May, it created a logistic problem for the Hyderabad police which resulted in the satyagrahis remaining unfed for 24 hours. Next day, however, an 'open air kitchen' equipped with utensils, foodstuffs and cooks was brought in 'specially' from the district headquarters of Nander over 40 miles away, and the prisoners were soon messing comfortably at the government's expense. Ever on the lookout for police brutality, the *Dig Vijay* conceded that only one volunteer had been roughly handled, adding that the constable responsible had been 'reprimanded' by his superiors for his 'improper behaviour'.[66] Would this group have taken back harsh memories of their stay? Somehow I doubt it.

Let us recall our findings so far. We have established that most of the people involved in the agitation of 1938–9 were outsiders trucked and railed in from British India; that many of these came for a variety of personal reasons extraneous to the religious situation inside the State; and that the movement's domestic following was mainly drawn from the ranks of the urban proletariat of Hyderabad City, a class conditioned to violence and vulnerable to manipulation by community leaders. Yet this still leaves the hard core of the movement to be accounted for. What drove the Hindu and Arya leaders to take the desperate step of waging civil disobedience against the Hyderabad government when, as indicated above, the plight of their co-religionists was not really desperate? The argument that follows stresses two factors, both ultimately deriving from British India: politicization and proselytization.

During the 1930s political events in British India enhanced the prospect of constitutional change in the princely states. In 1935 the Government of India Act bestowed a substantial measure of responsible government on the provinces, and two years later, the first general elections held under the expanded franchise provisions of the new constitution resulted in an unexpected triumph for the Indian National Congress, the nationalists being returned with absolute majorities in six out of eleven provinces, including Bombay, Central Provinces and Madras. For a time the Congress vacillated about the morality of taking

[66] *Dig Vijay*, no. 53, 9 May 1939, and no. 54, 10 May 1939, Sita Ram Papers.

office but in September 1937 it put its reservations aside and grasped the reins of power. A worried Theodore Tasker noted: 'the rise of Congress to power in the three Provinces which enclose Hyderabad has inevitably quickened all the forces opposed to the existing order in the State.'[67]

Another threat to the status quo loomed as a result of the Government of India Act's provision for a future all-India federation of provinces and states. While the final shape of the proposed compact had still to be resolved, it was assumed that the states would be subject to federal laws enforced by upright federal officials whose presence would serve to curb civil rights abuses by princely regimes. Similarly, while the 1935 Act did not require the states to select their representatives in the federal legislature by popular vote, it was generally supposed that the experience of participating in a democratic forum would inexorably drag the governments of the states in the same direction.

Partly to avoid this contingency and partly to appease his overlords in the Raj, who had come round to the view that some constitutional change in the states was needed to hold the line against the Congress, the Nizam in September 1937 appointed a five-member Committee under the Chairmanship of Professor D.B. Aravamudu Aiyengar to prepare a scheme of reforms. However, the strategy backfired. Despite its limited terms of reference, the advent of the Aiyengar Committee raised hopes that the Darbar was bent on a new course, while the Committee's decision to invite submissions from the public encouraged people to start organizations to lobby their point of view. One of these—the Hyderabad Peoples' Convention—opened a new chapter in Hyderabad politics when it solemnly called for 'the attainment of responsible government by the people . . . under the aegis of the Asaf Jahi dynasty'.[68] At the same time the appointment of the Aiyengar Committee helped to sharpen the boundaries of communal conflict. While the Hindu middle class praised the Darbar for its farsightedness, the Muslim elite forecast violent repercussions if the Committee's report led to the setting up of a democratic system.[69]

67 Note dated Dec. 1937, IOR, R/1/29/1853.

68 Note by C.C. Herbert, dated 16 November 1938, IOR, R/1/29/1803.

69 Note by Director, Intelligence Bureau, Govt of India, dated 10 June 1939, Home (Pol.), 42/2/39; and extracts of anonymous letters received by the Nizam threatening retaliation in IOR, Pol. (Intl.) Colls 11/57 (3).

Even the Hyderabad Peoples' Convention, which included a number of Muslims, failed to agree about the degree of democratic reform that was needed, and the Convention eventually broke up when four out of five Muslims on the Working Committee refused to endorse its final submission, leaving the militants to regroup in July 1938 under the banner of the Hyderabad State Congress.

By styling itself in this manner the local democratic front acknowledged its debt to the Indian National Congress of Gandhi and Nehru. Publicly, the two bodies maintained the fiction that they were separate and autonomous, but no one, least of all the Hyderabad authorities, were taken in by this charade. Frequent comings and goings between Wardha and Hyderabad were monitored by the Darbar's agents in the Central Provinces and it soon became apparent that the local body was receiving advice, encouragement and possibly financial help from the Congress Working Committee, the key middleman in this operation being Kanak Chander Daika, an official of the All-India Spinners' Association based in Bidar.[70] Later, on the strength of a damning report from Padmaja Naidu,[71] Congress attempted to distance itself from the Hyderabad satyagraha and in December 1938 persuaded its protégé to withdraw altogether from the campaign. However, this policy reversal by the Congress merely underscored the extent of its influence in Hyderabad. As Gandhi wrote immodestly in *Harijan*, 'the State Congress people have been acting under my advice'.[72]

Congress's patronage of the democratic movement in Hyderabad was predicated on the assumption that all-India federation was coming and that the States were crucial to its chances of capturing power at the federal centre.[73] In this respect its interests overlapped with those of the Hindu Mahasabha which had done badly in the elections of

[70] A.H. Ansari to Mehdi Yar Jung 16 and 26 October 1938, AP, R/1/47/10/718, and 'Review of Hyderabad Agitation', p. 2.

[71] Long extracts from this report are quoted in Lucién Benichou, 'From Autocracy to Integration: Political Development in Hyderabad State, 1938–1948', Ph.D. thesis, Univ. of W.A., 1985, pp. 102–4. Naidu accused the HSC of being unrepresentative, timid and communal.

[72] *Harijan*, 18 February 1939, p. 167.

[73] This point is argued at some length in my article 'Congress "Paternalism": The High Command and the Princely States, 1920–1940', in *South Asia* (forthcoming). For the Darbar's views on Congress strategy see note in H. Rahman, dated 27 March 1938, AP, R/1/47/10/914; and Hydari to Resident, 23 November 1938, IOR, R/1/29/1803.

1937 and which saw in the largely Hindu-populated states[74] a potential reservoir of votes; like the Congress, the Mahasabha had eyes on Hyderabad's generous allocation of 19 seats in the federal legislature, which were certain to be filled by Muslims if the Nizam was allowed to have his way. Additionally, the Mahasabha was moved to support the popular movement in Hyderabad as a means of getting back at the Muslim Ahrar Party for its encouragement of peasant unrest in the Hindu-ruled states of Kashmir and Alwar in 1931 and 1933, and as a way of carrying its message into the south, where the Hindu community was divided, 'weak and disorganized'.[75]

Another group which took an active interest in Hyderabad's affairs during 1938–9 was the All-India State People's Conference (AISPC), an umbrella organization of princely subjects based in Bombay. Like the Mahasabha the AISPC was weak in the south and saw the budding confrontation in Hyderabad as an opportunity to extend its influence into an 'unfathomed part' of the Subcontinent.[76] It was also mindful of Hyderabad's strategic importance as the premier Indian state and the enormous impetus a victory over the Nizam would give to the popular movement elsewhere: 'If we could succeed there,' mused B.V. Shikhare of Miraj, 'we should have success all through'.[77] Thus, the AISPC encouraged its Hyderabad friends to take a tough line with the Darbar and to settle for nothing less than full responsible government. Later, when the Hyderabad State Congress was outlawed under a euphemistically titled Public Safety Ordinance, AISPC workers were among the first to rally to its aid.

The fourth national party which contributed to the politicizing of Hyderabad was the All-India Muslim League. Bitterly opposed to the form of federation embodied in the Government of India Act for the same reason that the Mahasabha was in favour of it, the League believed that its best hope of survival lay in the creation of a separate 'Muslim federation' of provinces and states. In 1938 the Sind Provincial Muslim League Conference called on the government.

[74] The Hindu population of the States in 1921 was 53.5 million, the Muslim population 9.5 million. Statutory Commission *Report*, vol. 1, p. 26.

[75] M. Krishna Rao, Sec. Madras Arya Samaj, to Sec. Mahasabha, 18 November 1937, Mahasabha Papers, file M-3 of 1935–7. As of 1937 the Mahasabha had not a single branch south of the Krishna.

[76] See, for example, H.M. Joshi to Balwantrai Mehta, Sec. AISPC, 28 May 1938, AISPC Papers, file 44 of 1937–41, NMML.

[77] Shikhare to Mehta, 17 June 1938, ibid.

> to devise a scheme of Constitution[al reform] under which Muslim majority provinces, Muslim Native States, and areas inhabited by a majority of Muslims may attain full independence in the form of a federation of their own, with permission to any other Muslim State beyond the frontier to join the Federation.[78]

Subsequently League President M.A. Jinnah made it clear that his concept of 'Muslim Native States' included states *ruled* by Muslims. This definition conveniently opened the door to the entry of Hyderabad, and in 1939 Jinnah took advantage of an invitation to the Nizam's birthday celebrations to do some lobbying along these lines.[79]

Of these four organizations two—the League and the Mahasabha—were overtly communalist parties. A third, the AISPC, though committed in principle to secularism, was effectively a Hindu party controlled by men whose outlook had been conditioned by the Maharashtrian revivalist movement of the late nineteenth century, with its cults of Ganesh and Shivaji.[80] With such patrons it is no wonder that the Hyderabad political movement eventually polarized along communal lines.

The movement of individuals between British India and Hyderabad constituted a further mechanism of politicization. In 1930 about 50 young men left Hyderabad to join Gandhi's civil disobedience campaign[81] and over the next decade hundreds more of the Nizam's subjects went abroad to attend annual sessions of the Congress, the Mahasabha and the League.[82] Another, much larger group of middle class Hindus left the State during the 1930s to further their education, while thousands of Muslims from North India flocked south in search of jobs in the State's expanding public service. In the process, the Hyderabad intelligentsia became less parochial and more receptive to all-India concerns and values. In 1936 the British Resident noted that 'the Mulki movements had greatly hardened, while men from outside in recent years have sometimes been communal in outlook'.[83] Typical

[78] Quoted in B.S. Moonje to [illegible], 10 December 1938, M.S. Aney Papers, subject file 7.

[79] Resident to Pol. Adviser, 2 October 1939, IOR, R/1/29/1860.

[80] On the AISPC's anti-Muslim bias see N.C. Kelkar's presidential speech to the Party's fourth annual session, 22 July 1933, IOR, Pol. (Intl.) Colls 11/9; and B.V. Shikhare to B. Mehta, 17 June 1938, AISPC Papers, part I file 44 of 1937–41.

[81] Resident to Pol. Sec., 20 June 1931, IOR, R/1/29/760.

[82] Five hundred Hyderabadis are said to have attended the Haripura session of the Congress in February 1938, *FSH*, IV, p. 182.

[83] Note dated March 1936, IOR, R/1/29/1853.

of the latter was Nawab Mehdi Yar Jung who came to the Council from the Education Department of the United Provinces. In 1931, following a bloody Hindu–Muslim riot at Cawnpore, Mehdi Yar Jung took Resident Keyes and aside and

told me . . . that every Muhammadan ought to arm and that the Muhammadans of the Punjab ought to threaten to kill two Hindus for every Muhammadan killed in Cawnpore. He professes to believe that all the Hindus intend to exterminate and enslave all the Muhammadans as soon as they get Swaraj.[84]

Nevertheless, the importance of these professional contacts with British India should not be over-emphasized. Lacking branches and having few primary members inside the State, British Indian political parties cannot have had much impact on the thinking of the people who provided most of the perpetrators of communal violence—the urban proletariat. What caused this class to become politicized? The key factor in their case seems to have been religious evangelism, in particular the fierce competition for converts that developed between the Arya Samaj and the Ittihad-ul-Muslimeen.

The Arya Samaj had started life as a religious reform movement and to the extent that it continued to espouse 'Vedic *dharma*' in opposition to the 'Sanatan *dharma*' of orthodox Hinduism its natural enemies were Hindus, not Muslims. However, in the last decade of the nineteenth century it began sponsoring the reclamation of low-caste Hindus who had been converted to Islam. This reconversion process, which the Aryas called *shuddhi* or 'purification', drew them into direct conflict with Muslims who previously had had to compete only with the foreign-based Christian missionary movement.[85] Small and geographically isolated from the heartland of Arya power in the Punjab, the Hyderabad Samaj was initially cautious about poaching Muslim converts; but this moderate policy was abandoned in the 1930s. Under new leaders Mahatma Narayan Swami and Pandit Narinderji, the local body embarked on a vigorous expansion and recruit-

[84] Resident's fort. report for 1st half April 1931, Pol. (Intl.) Colls 4/6.

[85] On the history and doctrines of the Samaj see Richard G. Fox, 'Urban Class and Communal Consciousness in Colonial Punjab: The Genesis of India's Intermediate Regime', in *Modern Asian Studies*, vol. 18 (1984), pp. 459–89; Kenneth W. Jones, *Arya Dharm: Hindu Consciousness in 19th-Century Punjab* (Berkeley, 1976); J.T.F. Jordens, *Dayananda Sarasvati: His Life and Times* (Delhi, 1978), and *Swami Shraddhananda: His Life and Causes* (Delhi, 1981); and G.R. Thursby, *Hindu–Muslim Relations in British India* (Leiden, 1975), ch. II and ch. IV, pp. 136–72.

ing programme which resulted in the opening of over 100 additional branches and the acquisition of a number of schools, orphanages and newspapers.[86] With these considerable new resources behind it, the Samaj stepped up the tempo of its proselytizing, concentrating especially on untouchables who had been recently converted to Islam. By the middle of the decade shuddhi ceremonies had become commonplace in Bidar and Udgir Districts and were beginning to make their appearance in other parts of the country.[87]

The equivalent of the Arya Samaj on the Islamic side was the Ittihad-ul-Muslimeen or Society for the Unity of Muslims. Founded in 1926 by a retired Darbari official, the Ittihad was at first little more than a scholarly forum for the State's mulki elite; but as the 1930s wore on it became progressively more political, more popular, and more chauvinistic. The key factor—or more accurately figure—in this transformation was a young jagirdar named Nawab Bahadur Yar Jung. Energetic, handsome, able to sway huge crowds with impassioned oratory,[88] Bahadur Yar Jung was a truly charismatic leader, and in the early 1930s he applied his extraordinary talents to the task of shoring up the Muslim position in Hyderabad by means of a large infusion of Hindu converts. His model was the *tabligh* ('education') movement founded in North India in 1924. Tabligh societies were set up under Ittihad auspices throughout the State and several hundred missionaries hired to carry the Koranic message into the countryside.[89] By the end of the decade perhaps 20,000 untouchables had been converted to Islam as a result of Bahadur Yar Jung's activities.[90]

[86] By the late 1930s the Samaj had altogether about 150 State branches, 18 in Hyderabad City. See Leonard, *Social History*, p. 222; Hydari to Resident, 23 April 1938, IOR, R/1/29/1725; and Resdt to Pol. Sec. 12 July, 1939, IOR, R/1/29/1921.

[87] On the activities of Arya preachers Bansilal and Shamlal in Bidar and Udgir, sec *FSH,* IV, pp. 88–9.

[88] His mellifluous Urdu is alleged, on one occasion, to have moved the Nizam to tears. Benichou, 'From Autocracy to Integration', pp. 138–9. He was ennobled with the title of Nawab in 1930 partly in recognition of his contribution to the Urdu language.

[89] The most remarkable tabligh preacher of the 1930s, Siddiqi Dindar, achieved great success among the Lingayats by posing as an *avatar* of their caste-deity Channa Basweshar. *Mahratta* (Poona), 8 July 1938; *FSH*, IV, p. 88; and Resident's fort. report for 1st half July 1937, IOR, R/1/29/1311.

[90] Resident's fort, report for 1st half September 1936; *Mahratta*, 8 July 1938; and C.M. Elliot, 'Decline of a Patrimonial Regime: The Telengana Rebellion in India, 1946–51' in *Journal of Asian Studies*, vol. XXIV (1974–5), p. 37n.

The other important agent in the politicizing of Hyderabad's Muslim proletariat was the Khaksar party started in British India in the early 1930s by Allama Mashriqi. Loosely modelled on Hitler's brown-shirts, the Khaksars favoured a totalitarian-style regimen of parades, uniforms, marches, and physical training, and while Mashriqi himself spoke of 'discarding communalism' and claimed to be interested only in fostering a spirit of mutual co-operation among Muslims, Hindus inevitably saw his organization as a Muslim militia. Introduced into Hyderabad in 1936, the Khaksar movement spread with such 'accelerated speed' that by 1938 it was able to mount two-thousand strong counter-demonstrations against the State Congress.[91]

As the competition for converts between the Ittihad and the Samaj heated up, the tone of their religious propaganda became increasingly shrill. One Arya preacher accused his opponents of being liquor-swilling charlatans; while another declared that converts to Islam were traitors whose womenfolk deserved to be 'molested by Goondas'. In reply the Urdu paper *Rahbar-i-Deccani* called for an all-out war against the 'latrine of idol worship' and promised that it would take steps to ensure that 'all the teachings of the Vedas and the Manusmriti' were 'made to disappear' from Hyderabad. Not to be outdone, Muslim missionary Siddiqi Dindar urged his co-religionists to 'kill . . . heretics' who disparaged Islam.[92] The pernicious effect of this propaganda on the minds of the Hindu and Muslim masses was amplified by alarmist rumours. It was said that Siddiqi intended to 'proceed to Afghanistan to collect a huge gang of pathans' to terrorize Hindus and 'eradicate the famous holy shrines of Humpi and Venkataraman'; that the Khaksars proposed to 'convert Hindustan into Pakistan'; and that Hindu prisoners were being forcibly converted to Islam in the Nizam's jails:[93] 'fantastic stories', noted Tasker glumly, 'have been poured into credulous ears'.[94]

91 Rahmat Yar Jung to Mirza Ali Yar Jung, 10 August 1936, AP, R/1/47/10/903.

92 Arya speeches 15 April and 5 July 1938, quoted in 'The Arya Samaj in Hyderabad', 1939, Sita Ram Papers; *Rahbar-i-Deccani*, 20 April and 4 June 1938, quoted in 'Nizam Defence Examined', Sita Ram Papers file 32; and speech by Siddiqi, 1931, ibid.

93 Memorial from Chandulal, Sec., Arya Samaj, Hyderabad to Viceroy, June 1935, Mahasabha Papers, file p-3 of 1933–4; *Dig Vijay*, no. 51, 7 May 1939, Sita Ram Papers; and 'Nizam Defence Examined' p. 32.

94 Note dated June 1939, IOR, R/1/29/1921.

Perhaps the most potent of these myths grew out of an incident which occurred in the town of Ganjoti, Osmanabad district. One evening in December 1937 a group of Hindu weavers heading home after work were waylaid by a gang of Muslims, and in the ensuing scuffle one of the weavers named Dasmayya sustained fatal injuries. So far as can be ascertained Dasmayya was not even an Arya Samajist, let alone an Arya preacher; yet in a short space of time he had been transmogrified by the Arya Samaj into the fearless missionary, 'Ved Prakash':

> One day the oppressors . . . caught Ved Prakash and after throwing him down, and placing a knife on his throat, said to him, 'If you want to live accept Islam'. What a strange ultimatum, what an anxious moment, what an awful scene! . . . On one side was life and love and relatives and worldly happiness and on the other was the knife of his oppressor on the throat and the terror of death . . . [But] Dharam came out victorious. The blood of the brave infused Ved Prakash with passion, bravery and fearlessness, and Ved Prakash smiled and said, 'I am prepared to die but I cannot leave my Vaidic Dharam'. No sooner were these words uttered than the knife cut through the throat of Ved Prakash. Blood began to flow and the soul fled away leaving this message for young Aryas: 'If one calamity comes after another let it come . . . truth has taught me this lesson, [that] if life goes for the sake of religion let it go.[95]

In the emotion-charged atmosphere of 1938 few Hindu readers of this harrowing tale paused to question its authenticity. Soon, outraged letters and telegrams protesting 'Ved's' murder were pouring into the Darbar and the British Residency from all over India.[96] Many of these concerned citizens would swell the ranks of the Arya Samaj's jathas in 1939.

With Hindu and Muslim militants itching for action and the rest of the population fully expecting to be set upon any moment by goondas from the other side, it was only a matter of time before conflict occurred. Oddly, given their numerical inferiority, Muslims seem to have been the initial aggressors; in addition to the aforementioned incident at Ganjoti, Hindus were attacked at Hamnabad-Manik Nagar in 1936 and at Chakur and Gulbarga in March 1938, and Aryas at Nilanga in 1935 and at Udgir in June 1938. Once aroused, though, the Hindus gave as good as they got. All the three people killed at

95 The *Ved Sandesh*, quoted in 'The Arya Samaj in Hyderabad', pp. 39–40.
96 Resident's fort. report for 2nd half of March 1938, IOR, R/1/29/1669.

Gulbarga were Muslims—two of them, coincidentally, relatives of Bahadur Yar Jung—and so were most of the casualties of the Dhulpet riot of April 1938. Indeed, the Darbari committee which looked into the Dhulpet disturbances found no evidence whatever of Muslim provocation but plenty of Hindu premeditation; for example, reports that Hindus armed with *lathis* and brickbats had been seen congregating in the bazaar before-hand, and the fact that the procession of Hazrat Syed Jalaluddin which provided the occasion for the riot had been held for many years previously without incident.[97]

Each of these incidents left a legacy of grief-stricken friends and kin with a score to settle, and so a cycle of communal violence was set in motion. Significantly, Hyderabad City remains to this day one of the most riot-prone towns in the subcontinent.[98]

In the short term, however, the main consequence of the riots was a hardening in the posture of the Arya Samaj. Having for years nursed a grudge against the Darbar and its mulki henchmen, the Samaj saw the deepening unrest as a golden opportunity to pressure the Hyderabad authorities into doing something about its religious grievances. In February 1938 the *Arya Vir* newspaper advised its readers to 'rise up and shake Hyderabad to the very foundation'; in March, Arya preacher Baldeo called on his followers to 'secure the throne of Nizam within 6 months'. 'This is the hour of trial', added the *Jhanda* of Bombay.[99]

Not wanting to get involved in a quixotic attempt to overthrow the Hyderabad State by force, the more moderate leaders of the Arya Samaj in Delhi tried to find a diplomatic solution to the crisis. In April 1938 the Working Committee of the International Aryan League addressed a letter to the Darbar demanding an 'early settlement' of Hindu grievances in the areas of worship, schools, preaching, censorship, festivals, conversion of prisoners, and access to the public ser-

97 Resident to Viceroy's Priv. Sec. 18 April 1938, and Hydari to Viceroy's Priv. Sec., 19 April 1938, IOR, R/1/29/1719.

98 Gopal Krishna in his study of communal violence in India during the 1960s rated Hyderabad as a town given to 'persistent violence', with serious out-breaks in eight out of ten years: 'Communal Violence in India: A Study of Communal Disturbance in Delhi', *Economic and Political Weekly*, vol. XX, no. 2 (January 1985), p. 66. The most recent communal outbreak in the City was in August 1984 when 'at least' 15 people died. See Armarth K. Menon, 'The Communal Canker', *India Today*, vol. IX, no. 16, August 16–31, 1984, pp. 24–5.

99 *Arya Vir*, 7 February 1938; speech of 29 March 1938; and *Jhanda,* 27 July 1938, quoted in 'The Arya Samaj in Hyderabad'.

vice. But the Hyderabad Government refused to concede that any serious problems existed.[100]

This left the Aryan leadership with only one recourse. In June, Aryan League President, G.S. Gupta announced that the Samaj would commence non-violent satyagraha in Hyderabad before the end of the year. The 'hour of trial' had arrived.

The most striking thing about communalism in Hyderabad during the 1930s is the extent to which it derived directly from British India. Communal attitudes were inculcated by press reportage of riots and controversies in provinces; they came in as part of the cultural baggage of immigrant public servants and returned students; and they were fostered, sometimes unwittingly, but often for quite cynical reasons, by British Indian organizations eager to gain a foothold in the State. Among the latter, the most influential by far was the Arya Samaj—a society with its headquarters in Delhi and its roots in the Punjab. Although the bulk of the Samaj's membership was locally-born, many of its leaders were Punjabi immigrants and it was dependent on the parent body for missionaries, literature and funds. Thus its behaviour was coloured by the recent political history of North India in which the Samaj had played a leading and stormy role. Conversely, the leaders of the International Aryan League in Delhi saw their involvement in Hyderabad and the developing confrontation with the Darbar as part of a continuing offensive, a southward extension, as it were, of their long-running war against Islam. If not obvious before, the British Indian connection became manifest in 1938–9 when the Samaj, in concert with the Hindu Mahasabha, sent thousands of jathadars into Hyderabad in support of its campaign for civil rights. Despite claims to the contrary by its leaders, the satyagraha of 1938–9 was staffed, financed and directed mainly from outside the state; and such success as it eventually achieved was due more to British fears of communal repercussions in the provinces, than to the agitation itself, which left most Hyderabadis unmoved.[101]

[100] In June Aryan League President Gupta went to Hyderabad and attempted to negotiate a settlement with Hydari. He failed. A year later after months of struggle, the two men would finally resolve their differences. For the terms of this compact, see 'The Achievement of Satyagraha in Hyderabad State' (1939), Sita Ram Papers, file 36.

[101] On this see 'Review of Hyderabad Agitation', pp. 16–17; and circular letter from Viceroy to Gov's [April 1939], IOR, R/1/29/1920.

A few comparisons may help to drive home the point. Hyderabad, though perhaps the most dramatic case, was by no means the only princely state which succumbed to communal violence during the 1930s. Kashmir, Junagadh, Alwar, Bharatpur, Jind, Kapurthala, Bahawalpur, Malerkotla, Ramdurg, Jaipur and Travancore all experienced communal disturbances of unprecedented magnitude; and in nearly every case a 'foreign hand' was involved; the Ahrar Party and the Ahmadiyya Sect in Kashmir, the Ahrars and the Mahasabha in Alwar and Kapurthala, the Khaksars in Jaipur, and the Congress and the ISPC in Ramdurg and Travancore.[102] Recalling these events in 1940, Baroda's Dewan V.T. Krishnamachari drew the obvious moral: 'the greatest danger to avoid', he told Jamnalal Bajaj, 'is introducing into the State[s] the communal animosities that have gathered around political organizations in British India'.[103]

This brings us back to the issue raised at the beginning of the paper. If the growth of communalism in the states owed much to the intervention of outside agencies, it would indicate that there was something about princely India that discouraged or inhibited communal conflict. What could it be?

The theory favoured by British officialdom was that the princely states were theocracies in which expressions of religious unorthodoxy were forbidden. In its dispatch to the Secretary of State on the Prabhas Patan riots of 1893, the Government of India noted that:

> The ordinary course of things in a Native State is that one or . . . other religion is dominant in the administration, and that the party professing the creed

[102] On Kashmir see my article, 'Islam and Political Mobilisation in Kashmir, 1931–34', in *Pacific Affairs*, vol. 54, no. 2 (1981), 228–59; on Alwar see NAI, Home (Pol.) file 112/1/34, appendix II to notes; on Jind, Resident's fort. report for 1st half August 1934, IOR, R/1/29/1251; on Kapurthala, memorial dated 9 January 1934 from the Central Hindu Sabha, B.S. Moonje Papers, NMML; on Jaipur, memorial by Khaksar Movement, Lahore, February 1939, and press statement by J. Nehru, 4 March 1939, All India Congress Committee, file 29 of 1939, NMML; on Ramdurg and Travancore, my article 'Congress Paternalism'. Some irony attends the mention of Congress in this context for of all the major political parties it was the most strident in its condemnation of communalism. Yet it would be wrong to conclude that Congress was *non*-communal. Parties in India are known at grass roots level not so much by their ideology as by the company they keep, by who their supporters are. Since Congressites in the 1930s were predominantly (and in some regions almost exclusively) caste Hindus, it acquired, not altogether unfairly, a reputation as the vehicle of this community.

[103] Krishnamachari to Bajaj, 3 May 1940, Bajaj Papers.

which is not that of the ruling power has to submit to the loss of the priviieges which it would enjoy if it were in the ascendant or free to carry out its rights as it pleased.[104]

However, this was not 'the ordinary course of things' in Hyderabad. The Darbar of Nizam Osman Ali was authoritarian and rapacious, but it was not an Islamic theocracy: Hindus and other non-Muslims were free to worship as they pleased at home and in the grounds of their temples and to the extent that there were formal restrictions on public worship Muslims, too, were penalized. What is more, my impression is that most of the other big states followed similar policies. Like the Nizam, many of the Hindu princes were eclectic in their personal behaviour: some—such as Jodhpur—patronized Muslim festivals; others—Bikaner was one—surrounded themselves with Muslim advisers. In fact, no less than seven major Hindu-ruled states in the mid-thirties had Muslim prime ministers.[105] The relevant model here is not Oriental fanaticism but—ironically—British Indian neutrality.

Hence, if the princely states were less prone to communalism than the provinces it was not because their darbars deliberately favoured one side over the other; evidently, some other factors must have been operating. What characteristics, apart from their traditional polity, distinguished the states from the provinces? Two immediately spring to mind: their smaller industrial base, and their lower level of politicization.

If the subcontinent generally was economically 'underdeveloped' in the early twentieth century the princely states were still more so.[106]

[104] Govt of India to Sec. of State public dispatch of 27 December 1893, Pol. Dept Int'l A. December 1894, 113–55, NAI.

[105] On Bikaner see Beneshaim Wahie to B.S. Moonje, 28 May 1933, Moonje Papers, subject file 33. Wahie attributed the woes of Hindus in Bikaner and other Rajput states to 'princes who . . . seem to gain more pleasure in the company of non-Hindus'. The seven states were Mysore, Tavancore, Patiala, Kapurthala, Datia, Jhalawar and Gwalior. Interestingly, Christopher Bayly has recently argued in somewhat similar vein about the 18th and early 19th centuries. Bayly contends that the regional struggles for power that attended the decline of the Mughal Empire fostered 'the emergence of an all-India military culture' whose religious expression at the courtly level was primarily syncretic. If Bayly is right, the *darbari* syncretism of the 1930s could be an inherited characteristic, for what were the 'princely states' but the surviving lineal descendants of these 18th century warrior kingdoms? See 'The Pre-history of Communalism? Religious Conflict in India 1700–1860', in *Modern Asian Studies*, 19 (1985), p. 183.

[106] On this general issue see John Hurd, 'The Economic Consequences of

Even Hyderabad, the 'premier' state, was overwhelmingly agricultural: 90 per cent of the population lived in villages; just under four per cent of the workforce was employed in secondary industry; and the only considerable factories were textile mills with a combined labour force of 7000 in 1937—one per cent of the Indian total.[107] In this largely pre-capitalist economy, there was little or no class formation, still less anything that could be called class consciousness. Political development is rather more difficult to measure than economic growth but here again there is little doubt that the states lagged behind the provinces. In British India political parties had been active for nearly a century and Congress alone possessed a membership of several million; there was representative government; and by 1935 nearly half the adult male population had the vote. Compare this with Hyderabad. In the Nizam State government was irresponsible; there were no effective political parties until the 1930s; and in October 1938 the HSC had fewer than 1500 members.

Could the relative 'backwardness' of the states have insulated them from communal conflict? Quite possibly. Studies of communalism in Brtish India have repeatedly demonstrated that there is a connection between economic development, political mobilization and religious tension, and several theories have been put forward to account for this. The Marxists, for instance, see communalism as a surrogate for class conflict; they argue that the close concordance in many parts of India between class and community caused the proletariat to express their 'rational' material grievances in outbursts of religious fanaticism. Other historians hold that communalism was encouraged by British imperial policies, such as the concession of separate electorates to religious minorities. Others again prefer to emphasize the effect of British constitutional reforms; according to the latter argument, the extension of the franchise made it necessary for aspiring leaders to tout for votes among the masses with the result that politics became increasingly suffused with inflammatory religious rhetoric.

Again, the case of Hyderabad is instructive. Communal tension in the Nizam State began to grow precisely at that moment when,

---

Indirect Rule in India', in *The Indian Economic and Social History Review*, vol. XII (1975), 169–82.

107 Figures adapted from *Census of India*, various volumes, 1931 . . . 1941, and *The Hyderabad Problem*, p. 28.

following Congress's victory in the 1937 elections and the appointment of the Aiyengar Committee, the political elite started to build parties and canvass mass support. And when the mounting tension spilled over into large-scale violence at Dhulpet in April 1938, the ranks of rioters were swelled by recruits from the city's proletariat, conspicuous among them workers from the Azamjahi Textile Mills.[108] Mere coincidence? Contemporaries did not think so. Lamenting the failure of the informal Hindu–Muslim 'Unity Committee' established after the Dhulpet riots to agree on a formula for restoring communal harmony, a darbari official wrote that they 'had very nearly reached amicable decisions when the appointment of the Iyengar [*sic*] Committee and the starting of a Hyderabad Peoples' Convention sounded the death-knell of this peace move . . . [this is what happens when] controversial questions [are] . . . decided by votes instead of being settled by mutual compromise'.[109]

Not all the princely states, of course, were alike in their socio-economic makeup. Many were far more 'backward' than Hyderabad, while a few, such as Mysore and Baroda, were quite industrialized and progressive. Yet the variety of conditions that prevailed inside princely India does not disprove the contention that communalism went hand in hand with modernization. What it does suggest is that our generic categories are too broad and simplistic. Instead of looking at the 'states' and 'provinces' as collectivities, we should try to establish which regions of the subcontinent—which states and districts, which cities and villages—had a history of communal violence and whether this propensity had anything to do with their socio-economic profile. So far this has not been attempted for the colonial period. Analyses of communalism in British India have been preoccupied with the question of when, not where, and although several recent writers have remarked, in passing, on the uneven nature of its geographical spread within the provinces, none has given serious attention to the problem of transmission.[110] Gopal Krishna has made a beginning

[108] *The Hyderabad Problem*, p. 56.

[109] Memo unsigned, n.d. [apparently written October 1938] AP, R/1/47/10/868. The official's chronology is astray, however, since the Aiyengar Committee was appointed in 1937, well before Dhulpet.

[110] Both Sugata Bose, 'The Roots of "Communal" Violence in Rural Bengal: A Study of the Kishorganj riots, 1930', in *Modern Asian Studies*, vol. 16 (1982), p. 464, and Dipesh Chakrabarty, 'Communal Riots and Labour: Bengal's Jute Mill-Hands in the 1890s', in *Past and Present*, vol. 91 (1981), pp. 141–2, claim

by piecing together the data for independent India in the 1960s.[111] When someone comes up with a similarly comprehensive picture for colonial India, we will be able to approach the study of communalism with more confidence.

that communal violence came to Bengal firstly through the activities of 'up-country', mainly Bihari, workers.

111 Krishna, 'Communal Violence in India', pp. 61–74.

Chapter Fifteen

Toba Tek Singh

SAADAT HASAN MANTO [Translated by KHALID HASAN]

A couple of years after the Partition of the country, it occurred to the respective governments of India and Pakistan that inmates of lunatic asylums, like prisoners, should also be exchanged. Muslim lunatics in India should be transferred to Pakistan and Hindu and Sikh lunatics in Pakistani asylums should be sent to India.

Whether this was a reasonable or an unreasonable idea is difficult to say. One thing, however, is clear. It took many conferences of important officials from the two sides to come to this decision. Final details, like the date of actual exchange, were carefully worked out. Muslim lunatics whose families were still residing in India were to be left undisturbed, the rest moved to the border for the exchange. The situation in Pakistan was slightly different, since almost the entire population of Hindus and Sikhs had already migrated to India. The question of keeping non-Muslim lunatics in Pakistan did not, therefore, arise.

While it is not known what the reaction in India was, when the news reached the Lahore lunatic asylum, it immediately became the subject of heated discussion. One Muslim lunatic, a regular reader of the fire-eating daily newspaper *Zamindar*, when asked what Pakistan was, replied after deep reflection: 'The name of a place in India where cut-throat razors are manufactured.'

This profound observation was received with visible satisfaction.

A Sikh lunatic asked another Sikh: 'Sardarji, why are we being sent to India? We don't even know the language they speak in that country.'

The man smiled: 'I know the language of the *Hindostoras*. These devils always strut about as if they were the lords of the earth.'

One day a Muslim lunatic, while taking his bath, raised the slogan '*Pakistan Zindabad*' with such enthusiasm that he lost his footing and was later found lying on the floor unconscious.

Not all inmates were mad. Some were perfectly normal, except that they were murderers. To spare them the hangman's noose, their families had managed to get them committed after bribing officials down the line. They probably had a vague idea why India was being divided and what Pakistan was, but, as for the present situation, they were equally clueless.

Newspapers were of no help either, and the asylum guards were ignorant, if not illiterate. Nor was there anything to be learnt by eavesdropping on their conversations. Some said there was this man by the name Mohamed Ali Jinnah, or the Quaid-e-Azam, who had set up a separate country for Muslims, called Pakistan.

As to where Pakistan was located, the inmates knew nothing. That was why both the mad and the partially mad were unable to decide whether they were now in India or in Pakistan. If they were in India, where on earth was Pakistan? And if they were in Pakistan, then how come that until only the other day it was India?

One inmate had got so badly caught up in this India–Pakistan-Pakistan–India rigmarole that one day, while sweeping the floor, he dropped everything, climbed the nearest tree and installed himself on a branch, from which vantage point he spoke for two hours on the delicate problem of India and Pakistan. The guards asked him to get down; instead he went a branch higher, and when threatened with punishment, declared: 'I wish to live neither in India nor in Pakistan. I wish to live in this tree.'

When he was finally persuaded to come down, he began embracing his Sikh and Hindu friends, tears running down his cheeks, fully convinced that they were about to leave him and go to India.

A Muslim radio engineer, who had an M.Sc. degree, and never mixed with anyone, given as he was to taking long walks by himself all day, was so affected by the current debate that one day he took all his clothes off, gave the bundle to one of the attendants and ran into the garden stark naked.

A Muslim lunatic from Chaniot, who used to be one of the most devoted workers of the All India Muslim League, and obsessed with bathing himself fifteen or sixteen times a day, had suddenly stopped doing that and announced—his name was Mohamed Ali—that he was Quaid-e-Azam Mohamed Ali Jinnah. This had led a Sikh inmate to declare himself Master Tara Singh, the leader of the Sikhs. Apprehending serious communal trouble, the authorities declared them dangerous, and shut them up in separate cells.

There was a young Hindu lawyer from Lahore who had gone off his head after an unhappy love affair. When told that Amritsar was to become a part of India, he went into a depression because his beloved lived in Amritsar, something he had not forgotten even in his madness. That day he abused every major and minor Hindu and Muslim leader who had cut India into two, turning his beloved into an Indian and him into a Pakistani.

When news of the exchange reached the asylum, his friends offered him congratulations, because he was now to be sent to India, the country of his beloved. However, he declared that he had no intention of leaving Lahore, because his practice would not flourish in Amritsar.

There were two Anglo-Indian lunatics in the European ward. When told that the British had decided to go home after granting independence to India, they went into a state of deep shock and were seen conferring with each other in whispers the entire afternoon. They were worried about their changed status after independence. Would there be a European ward or would it be abolished? Would breakfast continue to be served or would they have to subsist on bloody Indian chapati?

There was another inmate, a Sikh, who had been confined for the last fifteen years. Whenever he spoke, it was the same mysterious gibberish: '*Uper the gur gur the annexe the bay dhayana the mung the dal of the laltain.*' Guards said he had not slept a wink in fifteen years. Occasionally, he could be observed leaning against a wall, but the rest of the time, he was always to be found standing. Because of this, his legs were permanently swollen, something that did not appear to bother him. Recently, he had started to listen carefully to discussions about the forthcoming exchange of Indian and Pakistani lunatics. When asked his opinion, he observed solemnly: '*Uper the gur gur the annexe the bay dhayana the mung the dal of the Government of Pakistan.*'

Of late, however, the Government of Pakistan had been replaced by the Government of Toba Tek Singh, a small town in the Punjab which was his home. He had also begun enquiring where Toba Tek Singh was to go. However, nobody was quite sure whether it was in India or Pakistan.

Those who had tried to solve this mystery had become utterly confused when told that Sialkot, which used to be in India, was now in Pakistan. It was anybody's guess what was going to happen to Lahore, which was currently in Pakistan, but could slide into India any moment. It was also possible that the entire subcontinent of India might become Pakistan. And who could say if both India and Pakistan might not entirely vanish from the map of the world one day?

The old man's hair was almost gone and what little was left had become a part of the beard, giving him a strange, even frightening, appearance. However, he was a harmless fellow and had never been known to get into fights. Older attendants at the asylum said that he was a fairly prosperous landlord from Toba Tek Singh, who had quite suddenly gone mad. His family had brought him in, bound and fettered. That was fifteen years ago.

Once a month, he used to have visitors, but since the start of communal troubles in the Punjab, they had stopped coming. His real name was Bishan Singh, but everybody called him Toba Tek Singh. He lived in a kind of limbo, having no idea what day of the week it was, or month, or how many years had passed since his confinement. However, he had developed a sixth sense about the day of the visit, when he used to bathe himself, soap his body, oil and comb his hair and put on clean clothes. He never said a word during these meetings, except occasional outbursts of '*Uper the gur gur the annexe the bay dhayana the mung the dal of the laltain.*'

When he was first confined, he had left an infant daughter behind, now a pretty young girl of fifteen. She would come occasionally, and sit in front of him with tears rolling down her cheeks. In the strange world that he inhabited, hers was just another face.

Since the start of this India–Pakistan caboodle, he had got into the habit of asking fellow inmates where exactly Toba Tek Singh was, without receiving a satisfactory answer, because nobody knew. The visits had also suddenly stopped. He was increasingly restless, but, more than that, curious. The sixth sense, which used to alert him to the day of the visit, had also atrophied.

He missed his family, the gifts they used to bring and the concern with which they used to speak to him. He was sure they would have told him whether Toba Tek Singh was in India or Pakistan. He also had a feeling that they came from Toba Tek Singh, where he used to have his home.

One of the inmates had declared himself God. Bishan Singh asked him one day if Toba Tek Singh was in India or Pakistan. The man chuckled: 'Neither in India nor in Pakistan, because, so far, we have issued no orders in this respect.'

Bishan Singh begged 'God' to issue the necessary orders, so that his problem could be solved, but he was disappointed, as 'God' appeared to be preoccupied with more pressing matters. Finally, he told him angrily: '*Uper the gur gur the annexe the mung the dal of Guruji da Khalsa and Guruji ki fateh . . . jo boley so nihal sat sri akal.*'

What he wanted to say was: 'You don't answer my prayers because you are a Muslim God. Had you been a Sikh God, you would have been more of a sport.'

A few days before the exchange was to take place, one of Bishan Singh's Muslim friends from Toba Tek Singh came to see him—the first time in fifteen years. Bishan Singh looked at him once and turned away, until a guard said to him: 'This is your old friend Fazal Din. He has come all the way to meet you.'

Bishan Singh looked at Fazal Din and began to mumble something. Fazal Din placed his hand on his friend's shoulder and said: 'I have been meaning to come for some time to bring you news. All your family is well and has gone to India safely. I did what I could to help. Your daughter Roop Kaur . . .'—he hesitated—'She is safe too . . . in India.'

Bishan Singh kept quiet. Fazal Din continued: 'Your family wanted me to make sure you were well. Soon you will be moving to India. What can I say, except that you should remember me to bhai Balbir Singh, bhai Vadhawa Singh and bahain Amrit Kaur. Tell bhai Bibir Singh that Fazal Din is well by the grace of God. The two brown buffaloes he left behind are well too. Both of them gave birth to calves, but, unfortunately, one of them died after six days. Say I think of them often and to write to me if there is anything I can do.'

Then he added: 'Here, I brought you some rice crispies from home.'

Bishan Singh took the gift and handed it to one of the guards. 'Where is Toba Tek Singh?' he asked.

'Where? Why, it is where it has always been.'

'In India or in Pakistan?'

'In India . . . no, in Pakistan.'

Without saying another word, Bishan Singh walked away, mur-

muring: '*Uper the gur gur the annexe the be dhyana the mung the dal of the Pakistan and Hindustan dur fittey moun.*'

Meanwhile, exchange arrangements were rapidly getting finalized. Lists of lunatics from the two sides had been exchanged between the governments, and the date of transfer fixed.

On a cold winter evening, buses full of Hindu and Sikh lunatics, accompanied by armed police and officials, began moving out of the Lahore asylum towards Wagha, the dividing line between India and Pakistan. Senior officials from the two sides in charge of exchange arrangements met, signed documents and the transfer got under way.

It was quite a job getting the men out of the buses and handing them over to officials. Some just refused to leave. Those who were persuaded to do so began to run pell-mell in every direction. Some were stark naked. All efforts to get them to cover themselves had failed because they couldn't be kept from tearing off their garments. Some were shouting abuse or singing. Others were weeping bitterly. Many fights broke out.

In short, complete confusion prevailed. Female lunatics were also being exchanged and they were even noisier. It was bitterly cold.

Most of the inmates appeared to be dead set against the entire operation. They simply could not understand why they were being forcibly removed, thrown into buses and driven to this strange place. There were slogans of '*Pakistan Zindabad*' and '*Pakistan Murdabad*', followed by fights.

When Bishan Singh was brought out and asked to give his name so that it could be recorded in a register, he asked the official behind the desk: 'Where is Toba Tek Singh? In India or Pakistan?'

'Pakistan,' he answered with a vulgar laugh.

Bishan Singh tried to run, but was overpowered by the Pakistani guards who tried to push him across the dividing line towards India. However, he wouldn't move. 'This is Toba Tek Singh,' he announced. '*Uper the gur gur the annexe the be dhyana mung the dal of Toba Tek Singh and Pakistan.*'

Many efforts were made to explain to him that Toba Tek Singh had already been moved to India, or would be moved immediately, but it had no effect on Bishan Singh. The guards even tried force, but soon gave up.

There he stood in no man's land on his swollen legs like a colossus.

Since he was a harmless old man, no further attempt was made to push him into India. He was allowed to stand where he wanted, while the exchange continued. The night wore on.

Just before sunrise, Bishan Singh, the man who had stood on his legs for fifteen years, screamed and as officials from the two sides rushed towards him, he collapsed to the ground.

There, behind barbed wire, on one side, lay India and behind more barbed wire, on the other side, lay Pakistan. In between, on a bit of earth which had no name, lay Toba Tek Singh.

Chapter Sixteen

The Partition of India in Retrospect

MOHAMMAD MUJEEB*

I remember a discussion with Dr Iqbal, whom the Jamia Millia had invited to preside over a meeting to be addressed by an eminent Turkish guest, early in 1935. The discussion was frank and informal, and the subject was the destiny of the Indian Muslims. Iqbal had, about five years earlier, expressed the view that Muslims must have territory of their own, a homeland, where they could make the obligatory experiment of living according to the shari'ah. This view was diametrically opposed to the principle on which the Jamia was founded, that Muslims must live and work with non-Muslims for the realization of common ideals of citizenship and culture. The discussion was long and interesting, and entirely free from that bitterness which later marred every exchange of views between nationalist and pro-Muslim League Muslims. To the best of my recollection, Iqbal could find no reasonable ground for rejecting the principle being followed by the Jamia Millia; he only maintained his own point of view, and it also became clear that the Muslims he had in mind were Punjab Muslims who, according to him, were still too weak to stand on their own feet and felt the need of political power to support them socially and economically.

The two points of view presented in the discussion with Iqbal still exist. The territory where Muslims could live in accordance with the shari'ah is now Pakistan, and the Jamia Millia is still where it was, working for the same ends. In November 1946, it had succeeded in bringing together the most eminent leaders of the Congress and the Muslim League on the same platform, and obtained from both an

* A former Vice-Chancellor, Jamia Millia, Delhi.

acknowledgement of the value of religious, cultural and political aims to which it was committed.

This is by way of introduction to the first point I wish to consider, namely whether a partition of the country was necessary to enable the Muslims to live in accordance the ideals of Islam.

It would be embarrassing to look back to the period of Muslim rule in India. The aspiration to live according to the spiritual ideals of Islam was confined to a small number of individuals; political power was in the hands of a minority, which believed necessarily in expediency rather than moral principle. To illustrate the organic unity of religious and political activity the Muslim has to go back to the days of the Prophet and the first two successors, and to find some ground for rejecting the validity of all that happened subsequently down to his own time. But no historical justification is necessary for the quickening of the religious spirit, and there were several revivalist movements. They were, however, basically theological. The Wahhabis and the Faraizis showed some tendency towards political action, but their leadership had little or no understanding of political ideas or methods. Their sectarian character asserted itself more and more, with the result that they became a disintegrating rather than a unifying influence. The Barelvi School, with its bitter condemnation of the Wahhabis, the Ahl-i-Hadith, with their insistence on recourse to the traditions as the source of guidance and their rejection of the four schools of jurisprudence, the Ahl-i-Qur'an, with their rejection of all other sources of guidance except the Qur'an, were all purely theological in principle and became sectarian in practice. They reduced the teachings of Islam to a set of opinions and the practice of Islam to a search for the most reliable authority on what were essentially matters of detail. Sir Syed Ahmad Khan had a larger view of life than any of the purely religious leaders, and one must be grateful to him for having given commonsense its rightful place in religious thought. Dr Iqbal was a great poet and thinker, but he did not lead what is traditionally regarded as a religious life and did not aspire to religious leadership. Maulana Azad's real contribution to a re-construction of the Islamic ideal of an active political life inspired by the highest spiritual and moral values lies unobserved in a few paragraphs of his *Tarjum al-Quran*.

The most recent among the religious movements are the Jama'at-i-Islami and the Tablighi Jama'at. In the literature of the Jama'at-i-Islami we find categorical assertions of the superiority of the shari'ah of Islam over all other principles and forms of social and political organization, but its real appeal derives from a rhetorical denunciation of western civilization. The Jama'at-i-Islami has also evolved a concept of the Islamic state, of which any Muslim anywhere can be a citizen, and which will be the best governed because only Muslims of acknowledged piety and integrity will be entitled to hold office and to be elected to its consultative bodies. The Tablighi Jama'at, founded by the late Maulana Ilyas, aims at making those who know something about the beliefs and practices of Islam teach those who know little or nothing about them. It is the only movement that is not theological and aggressive. It has brought all classes of people together in a common realization that they are members of a community, and this membership can have meaning and value if the beliefs and practices on which their community life is based are understood and observed by all.

Since we are trying to analyse the reasons which led to the partition, the material question in this context is whether any expressions of religiosity among Muslims encountered opposition from the non-Muslims or were hampered by the fact of the Muslims being a minority. The answer is that all opposition which Muslim religious movements have had to face has come from the Muslims themselves. Disputes arising from Hindu objections to cow-sacrifice and Muslim objections to music before mosques have generally been engineered by mischief-makers and their effects have been local and temporary. On the other hand, Sufis and their graves have been venerated by Hindus. I remember that shortly after the orgy of violence in Bihar I visited the grave of a Sufi on the banks of the Ganges. The Muslims living in the *dargah* had fled and the place looked desolate. But soon a group of Hindu women appeared. They performed circumambulations and prostrations, as if nothing had happened that affected their sentiments of veneration for the tomb of a Muslim saint.

But even if there was full freedom for the realization of the spiritual and ethical ideals of Islam, Muslims could still aspire to the creation of an Islamic state as something ideally necessary, and demand territory where this state could be established. My own belief is that the concept of an Islamic state should be present in the mind of every Muslim and should serve as a guide and a corrective in his political conduct. I do not remember that this belief was shared by the prominent men and women of Uttar Pradesh in the Muslim League camp. They were just not the type of persons who would undertake the intellectual task of analyzing the concept of an Islamic state. Their allegiance to it was rhetorical; they did not care to be intelligent or serious. The usual answer given to me when I put questions about the political structure of the Islamic state was that this was a matter to be thought about when we had Pakistan. But draft constitutions of the Islamic state were also drawn up. One such constitution was sent to me for scrutiny. I found that the person or persons who had drawn it up had no knowledge of even the elements of political science and the working of governments. This was inevitable. Those who were thinking of creating an Islamic state did not realize that they were creating in a vacuum something which grows out of established political and social ideas and habits, that it must be the culmination of efforts directed to a particular end and not the starting-point of a religious and political adventure.

The absence of habits, tendencies, institutions that could serve as a foundation for the ethics if not the political structure of the Islamic state was a serious shortcoming. It could have been somewhat compensated by a revival of faith. I observed nothing of this kind among the people I knew. Prominent men in the Muslim League of Uttar Pradesh took to praying at least in public when the inconsistency of representing Islam and neglecting even the elementary obligations was made a point of attack by critics, but prayer and fasting are social forms the mere observance of which is no indication of religious zeal. If religious sentiment had been genuine, charitable institutions, orphanages, schools and colleges financed by Muslims would have benefited. To the best of my knowledge none of them obtained any financial support or, if the League was too poor to afford this, even moral support from the Muslim League. On the contrary, the theological seminary of Deoband was disowned for political reasons, and the Jamia Millia was regarded with suspicion or disfavour because it associated itself with basic education and persisted in professing admiration and reverence for Mahatma Gandhi (who, as we know, was the one man who saved the Muslims jettisoned by the Muslim League). If, in November 1946, M.A. Jinnah agreed to attend the silver jubilee function of the Jamia Millia, it was due more to the tact and persuasive power of Dr Zakir Husain than to any change in the attitude of the League.

So much for the religious aspect of the demand for Pakistan. Could we reasonably consider this demand, and the two-nation theory on which it was based, the symptom of an awakened and vigorous political consciousness? Specifically, was there an awareness of needs of

Muslims which could be fulfilled only through common political action by Muslims? Were there any positive and general aims that could be regarded as the logical consequence of particular aims already realized?

I shall discuss this question with reference only to Uttar Pradesh and Delhi, because, as already indicated, I happen to have personal knowledge of the Muslim League leadership of these areas.

There were needs that could be regarded as the particular needs of the Muslim population of these areas. The number of Muslim cultivators was nowhere large or concentrated except in Mewat, to the west of Delhi. The Tablighi Jama'at of Maulana Ilyas did considerable work of education and reform among the Mewatis or Meos, who were known to be a hardy and lawless people. The political leadership did nothing constructive, but entered the field in the years immediately before the partition to exploit the newly awakened religious consciousness of the Meos and create conflicts with their neighbours which could only lead to their ruin. In the rural areas of Uttar Pradesh there were large numbers of small landlords whom spendthrift habits had reduced to poverty. They needed to be rehabilitated through co-operative enterprises of banking, seed procurement, irrigation, etc. These small landlords were also in need of education in disciplined living, which could be imparted best by a body like the Muslim League, which had both a religious and a political character. Instead, the frustration and despair of this class was exploited for political ends which could not possibly bring its members any benefit and which, on the contrary, placed their lives and properties in danger because of the passions roused by the propaganda of the League.

In the cities, the artisan classes stood in great need of education and organization. The Muslim community would not have had to regard itself as economically backward in the twentieth century if its leadership had spent in educating its artisans half the effort it wasted in persuading Muslims of the upper classes to take to English education. Muslim craftsmanship enjoyed great prestige. It had lost considerable ground because of the competition with machine-made goods, but also recovered somewhat when Europeans set the fashion of preferring hand-made to mass-produced goods. Muslim weavers, embroiderers, tin, silver and gold smiths, workers in ceramics, shoemakers, to name only the prominent categories, lived and worked within a horizon limited by their lack of education and were severely handicapped by spendthrift habits which kept them on the verge of penury. They were also undependable. But while the educator turned his eyes elsewhere, the preacher never went beyond the occasional sermons he was invited to deliver. The outlook and the habits of the craftsman did not change, and in spite of natural gifts he remained far behind his time and, therefore, economically insecure.

In Uttar Pradesh and Delhi—the situation was different in other parts of the country—the more prosperous merchants dealt mainly in imported goods, and their business depended upon a liberal import policy. But though the risk was obvious, hardly anything was done to establish industries that would support trade. In industry the Muslims would naturally have had to face keen competition, but there was no other way out. There would not, however, have been discrimination against Muslims by Hindu consumers. For a few years, under the influence of the idea that the Muslim consumer should support the Muslim trader, I made it a point to buy what I needed in Muslim shops in Old Delhi. There were good and bad salesmen among the Muslims; the shops of the good salesmen were always crowded, and Muslim customers were an insignificant part of the crowd. But when I tried to propagate my idea in my family circle, I met with a rebuff. The ladies of the family, who did most of the spending, had a very poor opinion of the merchandise offered by Muslim shops and they did not care for the manners of the shopkeepers either.

This is, I believe, sufficient indication that the needs which found political expression were not the needs of the community as a whole but those of a class, which consisted of big and small landlords, and the lawyers, doctors, government servants who belonged to the families of these landlords. Businessmen, unless they belonged to the class, could not be full members; the ulama did not belong to the class. The existence of this class would, of course, be overlooked or even denied when the principle of the equality of all Muslims was under discussion, and it was disintegrated enough to create the illusion that it did not exist. But if I were asked to give the one all-important reason for the upsurge of sentiment which ultimately led to the partition of the country, I would say that it was the reaction of this class to the realities of democracy.[1]

[1] *'Class' among Indian Muslims of Uttar Pradesh.*

Below are given two extracts which are self-explanatory. The first is from a speech of Sir Syed Ahmad Khan delivered at a public meeting in Lucknow, after the third session of the Indian National Congress held in Madras in 1887. He severely criticized the solutions of the first Congress about representation in the

I belong to this class myself. I remember my own reactions when I visited the Uttar Pradesh assembly. It was, I believe, the inaugural session. There were crowds of people in the visitors' galleries and the hall, but hardly a face that was known to me. I was simple-minded enough to ask a man standing next to me where the Chief Minister was, and I got in reply a reproachful look and the remark, 'Can't you see he is sitting there'? I felt extremely uncomfortable. I could not spot anyone dressed like me, the language spoken around me was not the Urdu which I thought was the language of Lucknow, the cultural metropolis of Uttar Pradesh, and there seemed to be no one within sight worth talking to. I left the assembly building with a feeling of mingled panic and disgust. But I was in the fortunate position of not having to go there again; I was a teacher, I kept away from politics and had the leisure to educate myself. What of the sixty-six Muslim members of this assembly, of whom twenty-nine belonged to the

---

Councils by election. And the other is from a book, 'The Heavenly Ornaments', which served as a religious and social guide.

(1) 'You will see that it is one of the necessary conditions of sitting at the same table with the Viceroy, that the person concerned should have a high social status in the country. Will the members of noble families in our country like it that a person of lower class or lower status, even if he has taken the BA or MA degree and possesses the necessary ability, should govern them and dispose of their wealth, property and honour? Never. Not one of them will like it. The seat of the Counsellor of the Government is a place of honour. Government cannot give it to anybody except a man of high social status. Neither can the Viceroy address him as "My Colleague", or "My Honourable Colleague", nor can he be invited to royal levees which are attended by dukes, earls and other men of high rank. So Government can never be blamed if it nominates men of noble families.'

'Just think of what happens as a result of competitive examinations in England. You know that there everybody, high or low, whether he is the son of a duke, an earl, a gentleman or a tailor's son, has an equal right to appear for the examination. European officers who take their examination in England and come over here are so remote from us that we have no idea whether they are sons of Lords or Dukes or of tailors and if we are governed by a person of low birth we do not know it. But that is not the case in India. In India, the people of higher social classes would not like a man of low birth, whose origin is known to them, to have authority over their life and property.'

(2) 'Shaikhs, Sayyids, Ansaris, Alawis are equals; the Mughals and Pathans are all one race (*qaum*), and cannot compare with Shaikhs and Sayyids. Weavers, barbers, washermen are not the equals of tailors. There is also a grading on the basis of whether the father or grandfather was converted to Islam.' Thanawi, Maulana Ashraf Ali: *Bihishti Zewar*, part IV, pp. 9–10. Nur Muhammadi edition, Karachi. Date of publication not given.

Muslim League? They could not follow my example and walk out of the building.[2]

Before the elections in United Provinces under the Act of 1935, the Congress and the Muslim League had formed a kind of alliance against those who were pro-British or not dependable as nationalists, who belonged to no party and hoped to win the election and make a political career on the basis of personal influence. The Muslim League was not very successful, and secured only twenty-nine out of sixty-six seats. The Congress victory was overwhelming, and a ministry could be formed without the assistance of any other party or the independents. The attitude of the Congress leadership to the informal arrangement made with the Muslim League leaders gradually changed and as the negotiations over the appointment of Muslim ministers proceeded, it became more and more obvious that the Congress would dictate the terms of any agreement that was arrived at. I was at home in Lucknow when the draft of the agreement proposed by Maulana Azad on behalf of the Congress was sent to Choudhry Khaliquzzaman. My immediate reaction on reading it was that the Muslim League was being asked to abolish itself. This was an attack not on the persons who wanted to become ministers but on the whole class that had painfully organized itself and was still feeling very shaky. Jawaharlal Nehru made matters still worse by writing to the Muslim League president that there were only two forces in India at that time—British imperialism and Indian nationalism. 'The Muslim League represents a group of Muslims, no doubt highly estimable persons, but functioning in the higher regions of the upper middle classes and having no common contact with the Muslim masses and few with the Muslim

[2] The 66 Muslim members of the first Legislative Assembly belonged to the following categories:

Nawabs, rajas, zamindars	21 (including two women)
Khan Bahadurs (persons who had been awarded the second lowest title of honour because they had given some proof of 'loyalty')	12
Advocates (also from zamindar families)	23
No precise category	10
	66

lower middle class.'[3] This, as I have already indicated, was my own view of the situation, and knowing Khaliquzzaman and other leaders of the Muslim League as I did, I would have dropped the words 'highly estimable'.

But it was very poor statesmanship that transformed a difference of opinion over a ministerial post or two into a national struggle in which a class felt that it was fighting for its life. It would not have shattered Nehru's prestige if, because of him, the Muslims had got one ministerial post more than they were entitled to; and if Khaliquzzaman had been made a minister the League in Uttar Pradesh would most probably have dissolved of itself. Khaliquzzaman was a very charming person and an eloquent speaker, but he was not a full member of the class because he lacked the requisite property qualification. There would have been resentment against his appointment among those who regarded him as an outsider, and he would either have had to resign or to work against the class which it was his ambition to represent and lead. Nehru and Azad together cleared the way for his becoming the valiant knight of an insulted and injured community.

The conflict between the Muslim League and the Congress might have been on a different level and far less bitter if the Congress governments had not reflected the upsurge of the masses. Most of the new leaders were not known to the Muslims. They were, therefore, not persons but just Hindus, and Nehru, who belonged in every way to the class, had gone and identified himself with them. He had even denied the existence of the culture of which the class was so proud. Nehru's ideas did not impress the class; it was not interested in anything intellectual, except as a matter of occasional conversation, and invariably preferred epigrams to truth. It was not impressed by what Congressmen called their sacrifices, because it regarded suffering as something not required by its code, especially suffering for a cause. The British had obtained dominion over India because of their superior force, and that was generations ago. The Congress had achieved the right to govern not through an exhibition of superior intelligence or power, but through non-violence which, again, did not impress the class because it was something foreign to its traditions. The class, therefore, felt no scruples about saying anything so long as

[3] Ram Gopal, *The Indian Muslims*, p. 251.

it hurt the Hindus whom the Congress had seated in the high places, or the Hindus in general.

But we must also remember that this class was provided with sufficient excuses for saying ugly things. There was something unbearably upstartish in the conduct of the Congress underlings, who were inclined to talk as if they were both the government and the country. All standards of refinement were reduced to the status of laws without sanctions. Urdu lost its legal position almost overnight, and a language which had no musical values and a large number of words which it seemed incredible the tongue of man had ever spoken was installed in its place. Further, while on the one hand the will of the majority seemed to be an argument which swept everything before it, an attempt was made by the Congress, through a programme of mass contact, to drive a wedge between the class and the Muslim masses. The land reforms that formed an essential part of Congress policy, though intended in fact to benefit the farmer, threatened to deprive the class of its only means of sustenance. It was inevitable that the class should retaliate as vigorously and as viciously as it could.

Those who had witnessed the religious fervour of the Muslims in the early days of the khilafat movement should not have underrated the effects of the appeal to Islam which the class was bound to make. Once the Indian Muslim hears—and rumour is a more powerful incitement than reasoned statement of fact—of any actual or intended act derogatory to Islam, he gets agitated. He has no inclination to verify the truth of any statement made; his mind is submerged in indignation, and his indignation suggests to him that the more aggravating the news, the truer it must be. He has also a predilection for the spectacular. When some Muslim critics of the scheme of basic national education came across the recommendation in the syllabus of basic education that movements to the rhythm of music or elementary dance movements should form part of the physical culture activities in the school, they picked upon it as an indication that in the new schools Muslim girls would be forced to learn dancing. No deductions made from this could be too wild, and basic education stood condemned not only as an attack on Muslim culture but on all ideas of decency. About the same time as the publication of the report on basic education, the chief minister of the Central Provinces (now Madhya Pradesh) introduced a system of schools to be financed or endowed with land by the population that derived benefit from them. These schools were to be called Vidya Mandirs or temples (lit. houses) of knowledge. This scheme of the chief minister had no relationship with national policy or the policy of the Congress governments, but was widely criticized by the Muslims as an attempt to turn schools into temples. These were the major 'atrocities' to which others were added, and the fuse was lighted for the explosion which ultimately split up the common country into India and Pakistan.

The principle on which the country was divided is known as the two-nation theory. This was the final form of the sentiments and taboos which had always kept the Hindus and Muslims apart from each other. Because of the passion with which the theory was advocated by the Muslim League after 1940, it seems to be a creation of Muslim fanaticism, and to show the distance and impossibility of communication between the Muslim classes and the Hindu masses. But India had been declared to consist of two nations by V.D. Savarkar in his presidential address at the annual session of the Hindu Mahasabha in 1937, three years before the Muslim League did so, and again in December 1939, three months before the Muslim League's Pakistan resolution.

It was not enough, however, to collect and magnify instances of Congress atrocities and Hindu fanaticism. The Muslim League was accused with different motives by its supporters as well as its opponents of 'doing' nothing. Since it had no plans for such development as would strengthen the Muslims economically, and since organization of itself as a disciplined party was almost impossible because of the type of people who were its members, the Muslim League had to think of doing something spectacular. It found a very suitable occasion when the Congress ministries resigned in protest against the viceroy's declaration of war against Germany without any reference to them. The Muslim League utilized this opportunity to celebrate deliverance from Hindu *raj*. A religious as well as political colour was given to this celebration and every Muslim who felt aggrieved or irritated or, what was more important, every Muslim who was on the look-out for some form of collective amusement was stimulated to exercise his ingenuity in commemorating the occasion. There was general satisfaction among Muslims over what they had 'done' to express their sentiments, and the next step was to express these very sentiments in oratorical and actual violence.

It is not the purpose of this paper to relate the course of events. In conclusion, it needs only to be said that once the sentiments of the Muslim masses had become involved in the demand for partition, it was not necessary for the Muslim League leadership to define its aims, or to declare what it proposed to do if the demand for Pakistan was conceded. It was certainly beyond the intellectual and moral capacity of the class in United Provinces which rejected the rule of the majority community to plan any alternative. When the catastrophe came, even its own members were left to shift for themselves. Some fled in panic, some crossed over deliberately and, like my own family, unnecessarily; some stayed behind because it was not possible for them to leave, or because they did not want to leave. If today we argue backwards from the partition of India as the solution of the Hindu–Muslim problem, it would appear that either there was no problem at all, or that it required an entirely different approach, if there was to be any solution.

Chapter Seventeen

Some Memories

RAJA OF MAHMUDABAD*

> All we have gained then by our unbelief
> Is a life of doubt diversified by faith,
> For one of faith diversified by doubt:
> We called the chess-board white—we call it black.
>
> *Bishop Blougram's Apology* by Robert Browning

My involvement with the movements for national independence in India was a deeply personal involvement and a lifelong one. It is therefore perhaps apt to start on a personal note. My estate of Mahmudabad, one of the large holdings in north India, had been handed down to me by my forefathers. My father, the late Maharaja Muhammad Ali Muhammad Khan, throughout his life actively participated in various political and cultural movements in the country. One of his major interests had been the advancement and improvement of Indian education. This was reflected both in his long and close association with the movement for the elevation of the Aligarh College to the status of a national Muslim university, and in his material and moral support of the Hindu University at Benares. In politics, his view of nationalism was similarly wide and this made him acceptable to both the mainstreams of Indian nationalism. He was one of the important leaders of the Muslim League in his time and twice presided over its sessions. At the same time he took an active interest and participated in the deliberations of the Indian National Congress.

I would not merely be fulfilling a filial duty in saying that my

* Closely associated with Jinnah and the Muslim League from 1936: youngest member of the All-India Muslim League Working Committee

father was known for his high sense of charity, his public spiritedness, his loyalty to his friends and his deep love of freedom. Among his friends he counted several well-known British, Hindu and Muslim names. Sir Harcourt Butler was more of a brother than a dignitary-friend. My father always addressed him as 'Bhai Sahib'—an eloquent phrase which includes in itself sentiments of mutual love, respect and trust. From among the Hindus, in fact from among all other Indians with the exception of Muhammad Ali Jinnah, Motilal Nehru was more a member of our family than a friendly visitor. I distinctly remember that in our house in Lucknow a room was reserved for him and no other guests were allowed to stay there. From the day I learnt to speak, I addressed him as uncle and received from him a rare degree of affection and love which not many people are capable of giving. Here I should like to recall one episode which illustrates the qualities of Motilal Nehru and his status in our family. But first a short digression is in order.

From my childhood I had shown somewhat Tolstoyan inclinations of detesting the class to which I belonged and what it stood for. This may perhaps have been due to the love I bore for my mother, who came from a learned and respectable family, but one of moderate means. Her family had produced notable scholars and reformers such as 'Allama Ghulam Hussain Kintoori, Maulana Hamid Husain—author of 'Abaqatal Anwar', and Justice Maulana Karamat Husain—founder of the first Muslim girls' college in the United Provinces. Her marriage to my father had been the result of my grandmother's great desire of marrying someone from a Syed family. The early realization that this matrimonial alliance in no way affected the modest and even tenor of my mother's own family brought home to me the fact that principles need not be the monopoly of the learned rich: grace and dignity after all are taught by the heart and not by the dancing instructor. My maternal uncles continued to live as they used to, unmoved and uninfluenced by their new connection with the aristocracy; even my mother, now a maharani, with an income which must have seemed immense to her, did not give up the simple values ingrained in her by her parents. It was not surprising, therefore, that I did not feel at ease in the feudal society into which I had been born.

Coming back to the earlier reference to Motilal Nehru: partly under my mother's influence and partly because right from my childhood my eyes saw 'khaddar' clad nationalists in our house, I could never bring myself to wearing the expensive and flamboyant clothes prescribed by the traditions of our family and class. Instead I began putting on the homespun, which of course, was intensely distasteful to my father who, it is interesting to note, never raised an eyebrow at seeing practically all his nationalist friends in similar apparel. One day, when Motilal was staying with us, I put on a new coarse 'khaddar' dress and was rather pleased with myself when, all of a sudden my father walked in, looked at me with disapproval and pointed towards my clothes. Stunned by his reaction I stood there with my head hanging down and at a loss to think of an answer. At this moment, uncle Motilal appeared and looking at my terrified expression and at my father's angry face, and divining the situation, said, 'Baita, if you want to wear "khaddar", you should wear it as I do.' By this he meant that I should use the fine quality stuff which he wore. Now it was my father's turn to find himself in a predicament, for soon a gift of several bails of fine spun 'khaddar' arrived from Motilal and my father could raise no further objections to my wearing it. If I were to sum up my impressions of Motilal, I would say that here was a man who would not be out of place in the seat of authority. He had the manner and the polish of a man both born to authority and the right to exercise it.

Motilal Nehru was not the only person who had left a deep impact on my youthful years. Mrs Sarojini Naidu and Rajkumari Amrit Kaur were like sisters to my father and I always called them by the Urdu equivalent of the English, 'aunt'—phupi. Another frequent visitor and a friend of the family was Dr Ansari.

Brought up in this atmosphere and amid such people, the first serious words which reached my ear were not very complimentary to the British. From my childhood I heard my Indian tutors and nurse-maids telling stories about the mutiny and of British repression and Indian suffering. The gentleman who taught me to read the Quran related to me what he had heard from his father who had fought the British during the mutiny in Muftiganj in Lucknow. My conversations with him did not endear the British to me. In fact at this time, a general anti-British feeling simmered under the surface amongst all of us, particularly among those who had witnessed or heard about the terrible deeds of 1857. One extreme instance of this is the way in which a disease was wished to the British instead of the person who suffered from it. The phrase in general use which I first heard from my eighty-year-old nurse when I complained of headache was: 'Baita dard tum-hain kyun ho, angrez bandon ke ho' (My son, why should you have pain, may God give it to the British).

Some of my personal experiences added to such hearsay. During Sir John Simon's tour of India in 1927, my father was a vehement opponent of the Simon commission and had helped the Lucknow Congress party in its demonstrations and protests against Simon's visit to Lucknow. When Simon was being entertained at a tea party by the taluqdars of Oudh, kites were flown from various points in the city and were then cut in such a way that they dropped at the place of the feast. They carried on them the words 'Simon go back'. The administration was furious and part of the brunt of their anger was borne by us. Long before the party was due to start a party of policemen arrived, surrounded our house and searched it so thoroughly that even my room was not spared. This left a very bad impression on my mind although later apologies were made to my father by the deputy commissioner of Lucknow and the home member.

Next year something happened which shocked me personally to an even greater extent. The all-parties conference was meeting in Lucknow and nearly all the leaders were staying in our house. I was then attending La Martiniére College, and one morning in the history class our teacher, who was an Anglo-Indian, interrupted the usual lecture and referred to the conference and called its leaders 'swines'. Without a moment's thought I stood up in my seat and said, 'My father is also a nationalist'. Then, throwing my book at him I walked out of the room. I might add that the principal, who himself was an Englishman, but a different kind of a person, saved me from rustication. A few days later I was to learn that the history teacher was asked to leave. A great majority of my classmates were Anglo-Indians and did not conceal their contempt for us Indians either. We were called, 'Niggers and Blackies'. We could then not do much, but I definitely remember that our reaction to this was: all right a day will come when we shall have our revenge.

I was also deeply pained by the attitude of some of our class towards the British administrators. Sometimes I saw the scions of distinguished families having to take off their shoes before entering the deputy commissioner's office. Both my head and my heart revolted at this show of cringing sycophancy. My reaction to all this can perhaps be best expressed by recalling that about this time I began collecting photographs of the nationalist leaders and treasured them as my most valuable possessions. When I heard of the Kakori incident I applauded the men responsible for it. Bhagat Singh was another 'terrorist' who then appealed to me and his photograph occupied a prominent place in my room.

Ever since my younger days the conduct of Britain's relations with her empire has been a fascinating source of study for me—in particular British conduct and institutions in India. The air of patronage introduced by the new system of administration created an hierarchy of its own and replaced the prevailing currents of court intrigue and sycophancy which marked the decaying Indian society. I, and many of my countrymen, were impressed as well as puzzled by the frank and open discussion of the actions and policies of British administrators by those who watched over British interests on the one hand and the system of patronage on the other. In my opinion, the greatest single factor which impressed many Indians with its sense of fair play and justice, its high sense of responsibility and its seriousness of purpose, was the impeachment of Warren Hastings. British good intentions were proved, and above all it reflected the inherent strength of British democracy and the principle that those who exercise power are accountable for the way in which they exercise it. However, we found a marked contrast between the principle of patronage created and encouraged by the British in India and the principle of responsibility to parliament which was respected and practised in Britain. For some reason the Englishman, born and bred in an open society, was content to establish and sustain a closed society in India. Improvement came with painful slowness: in small halting instalments.

The system of patronage built into the British Indian administrative machine often went too far and even survived the coming of the 'great' reforms of 1935, as the following illustrates. In 1936, soon after I had joined the Muslim League, I was summoned to lunch with his excellency, the governor of the United Provinces. In those days to enter Government House was an honour coveted by all but given to few. But to me the atmosphere of solemn formalities was nothing new. My initiation into the complex system of official protocol had been made complete during my father's life by his close personal relations with the higher reaches of the administration. I was the only guest and therefore serious conversation began right away.

My host informed me that he knew that I had joined the Muslim League and asked me if I was fully aware of the possible consequences of my action. I pleaded ignorance but pointed out that participation in public life was a perfectly normal thing to do. My host assumed an added air of authority and adjusted himself more firmly in his chair.

For the first time in my life I realized that an invitation to a meal is not necessarily an act of hospitality. He again asked me if I knew that my estate was a gift from the British sovereign, adding after I had nodded in assent, that I held it at his pleasure. He continued that he was willing to give me time to reconsider my position and to dissociate myself from one whom he called 'the arch enemy of the British Raj'. After a few minutes of conversation I realized that this 'arch enemy' was none other than M.A. Jinnah. On my asking what I was expected to do, he ordered that I should join the National Agriculturist party and made it clear that the British government had no intention of letting the activities of Jinnah and his party continue and that I would have to watch my steps in future. But I told him in reply that I was already committed to Jinnah having given him my word that I would stand by him and that it was impossible for me to break my promise. Later we ate in silence broken only by the formal phrases. I came home half-dazed by the governor's strange behaviour and felt disgust for a system which hindered a person's choice of parties.

M.A. Jinnah had had very close relations with the Mahmudabad family since his youth. My father signed his marriage contract on Jinnah's behalf; while Maulana Muhammad Hasan Najafi signed for Mrs Jinnah. The ring which Jinnah gave to his wife on the wedding day was my father's gift. The Jinnahs spent their honeymoon at Nainital in our house.

My first meeting with Jinnah took place in 1923 when I went to Delhi with my father and met him at the Maiden's hotel. I was then only nine but two memories still cling to my mind: I was introduced to Jinnah by my father as 'Your uncle Jinnah' and I was impressed by Mrs Jinnah's beauty. She gave me Rs. 500 to buy toys which at that time was a great deal of money.

Our second meeting took place in 1925 or 1926 at Butler Palace in Lucknow. I had just returned from school when my father took me to meet him and we sat talking on the terrace. He was dressed in a Chinese silk suit with a rather high collar to his shirt. He called me to his side and asked me about my studies. Then came the question, 'What are you, a Muslim first or an Indian first?' Although I hardly understood the implications of the question at that age, I replied 'I am a Muslim first and then an Indian.' To this he said in a loud voice, 'My boy, no, you are an Indian first and then a Muslim.' I stood there with downcast eyes and tears welled up. I thought I had made him cross. Jinnah patted me and was probably going to say something when my father asked me to go and play as they were going to have a serious conversation.

The venue of our next meeting was London where in 1933 I met him at his Hampstead house and had lunch with him. I was accompanied by my cousin and brother-in-law, a younger brother of the Raja of Pirpur. Most of the conversation related to family and property matters as Jinnah was one of the trustees of the Mahmudabad estate. But I remember my brother-in-law asking him when he was finally coming back to India, and Jinnah replying 'Probably before long.' He looked happy and relaxed, and showed me round his house and it was here that I met Dina, his daughter, for the first time. After a few days, at a dinner at the Berkeley Hotel I told him that he must come back to India. To which again he replied, 'I will be coming very soon.'

In March, April 1936, I was asked by Jinnah to come to Delhi to see him. I stayed at the Maiden's hotel for a week and met him once or twice. On one of these occasions Jinnah asked me to accompany him to the home of a friend who was also a friend of my father. We walked over to the Western Court where Deep Narayan Singh, a nationalist leader, had a suite. I was introduced to him and they started talking about politics. Jinnah then asked me about my plans and whether I was prepared to join him in politics. I told him that I intended joining the Shantiniketan and that Sir Rabindranath Tagore had already agreed to take me in. Then came the moment which changed the later course of my life. Deep Narayan interrupted me and said, 'No, you should enter politics and stand by the side of your uncle. That would be the best form of education for you. By joining him you will be putting yourself in the hands of a great Indian patriot and nationalist.' Before we parted company I had decided that I would be prepared to stand by him.

From this date onwards my association with Jinnah became close indeed, except for a short period to which I will come later. I made it a practice to go and stay with him in Bombay or Delhi for about three months every year. All that I had was at the disposal of the League. When I joined I hardly realized that before long the League and the Congress would be poles apart. For I still thought that the two organizations were like two parts of the same army fighting a common enemy on two fronts. With all my nationalistic tendencies and my association with the Congress and other progressive political workers and leaders some of whom I personally knew and admired, I might have joined the Congress. But my enthusiasm cooled down when to my great disappointment I found that instead of trying to understand the League policies, Jawaharlal Nehru showed nothing but contempt for the Muslim League and its leader to whom I had given undivided loyalty. The more Nehru spoke contemptuously and violently about the League and Jinnah, the more I disliked the Congress. This feeling was shared by a large number of the Muslims I knew who, but for this, would have shown less antipathy to the Congress. There was a general feeling that Nehru and Jinnah were talking at each other and that there was not much substance to this personal political dialogue.

The results of the general election startled the Muslims into an awareness that the Muslim League's failure to attract more Muslim voters was manifestly the result of Muslim political disunity. When they saw the solid Congress successes in several provinces they realized that in order to win a similar success, at least in the Muslim majority provinces, two things were essential: a closing of their ranks and a re-organization of the Muslim League. It was widely felt that the time had come to develop the League into a broad-based mass organization which could effectively safeguard Muslim rights and interests. We in the United Provinces felt that the next session of the League should be held at Lucknow and accordingly invited the League to do so. For us it was a happy coincidence that the League was holding its session in the same town where in 1916 another session had met under Jinnah. Another coincidence was that the chairman of the reception committee of the 1916 session had been my father, and now in 1937 this honour fell on me. Little did we realize then that the closing words of my welcome address—'we are here not to follow history but create it'—were to prove true.

The closing of the ranks became immediately obvious in the number of the Muslim leaders who assembled at the Lucknow session. Several provincial leaders, who had fought the last elections at the head of small independent groups and won some seats in almost every province, now joined the Muslim League, thus bringing it much strength. The chief ministers of Assam, Bengal, and the Punjab attended and offered their loyalty and co-operation. Apart from a few 'Nationalist Muslims', there were hardly any Muslim leaders of note who remained outside the League.

In terms of organization and structure a new chapter opened in the history of the League after October 1937. Branches of the League were opened even in the remotest village; paid workers were employed; speakers were trained; the recruitment campaign was accelerated, funds were collected; and membership fee was brought down from four to two annas a year. An uncommonly large number of leaders of different levels toured the whole country to carry the message to the common man. This message was simple enough to appeal even to those people who could not or did not understand the implications of joining a political party. The appeal was for unity, for once unity came other things could then be expected to follow.

The Congress was in office for over two years. The general impression prevalent amongst the Muslims was not at all favourable to the Congress régime. Irrespective of whether all the instances quoted by the League were true or not, the general feeling among the Muslims of all classes was that Hindu *raj* had arrived. I shall here refer to only one aspect. Whereas there is always a spirit of self-righteousness inherent in any majority community, anywhere in the world, in assimilating and absorbing minority communities, the apprehensions created by the Wardha scheme of education in Muslim minds has generally been underestimated. Certain features of the scheme, for example the emphasis on manual work, were basically sound, but these were overshadowed by its general spirit of indoctrination. We know that a system of education can be used to inculcate in the minds of youth certain doctrines and ideas which may run counter to their cultural traditions and values. Any scheme based on the ideology of one political party or one leader is viewed by the minorities and other groups as an attempt to unduly influence the thoughts of every one in the mould of the ruling party. ('An-nasu 'Ala Deeni Muloo-kihim', 'The mass of the people generally followed the path of their rulers.') In a country such as India, where the Hindus, Muslims, Sikhs, Christians had to live together, it was absolutely essential to have a system of education which allowed complete freedom of thought, expression and discussions, so that the teacher, whether of one denomination or another, could seek the truth and teach it. This was impossible under the Wardha scheme, for it was meant to proclaim the political creed of one party as the truth. There was no room in it for any other ideals and it was bound to emphasize the superiority of one political philosophy or conviction over others, thus encouraging intolerance instead of understanding.

What added to Muslim anxiety was the uncertain future of Urdu under the scheme. The scheme made Hindustani a compulsory subject, but it soon became evident that Hindustani, at least to Gandhi's mind, was something quite different from Urdu. It must be remembered that for the Muslims, Urdu was not merely a medium of communication or thinking, but a vital part of their culture. By imposing Hindustani, the Wardha scheme was in fact asking the Muslims to give up a language which had been one of the common bonds between the Hindus and the Muslims in favour of one yet to be created.

Instead of understanding the Muslim mind, the Congress tried to solve the problem by recruiting more and more Muslims to its fold. There may be nothing wrong in a political party trying to enrol members from various communities, but in fact the Muslim mass contact campaign brought a bad name to the Congress ministries. The campaign was run by Congress workers while the Congress was in office, which conveyed to the Muslim mind that this enrolment was being carried out, not by the Congress party, but by the provincial governments. Like those of the Congress, many of the League workers were also mercenaries, but unlike the Congress workers they did not carry the stigma of belonging to the ruling party. This actually turned out to be one of the factors responsible for the failure of the campaign and added to Hindu–Muslim bitterness.

Perhaps the Congress did not realize that office brings its own disadvantages. The party in power is more exposed to criticism of every kind by those who are in opposition, without always being able to justify its policies. In this respect the League worked from a point of vantage, and Jinnah, supreme tactician that he was, fully used this advantage.

As pointed out earlier, it was at the Lucknow session that steps had been taken to convert the League into a mass organization. The results were astounding and membership jumped from a little more than half a million in 1937 to over a million in 1941. But in mass nationalist movements figures of membership are no index to a party's following. It is absurd to say that in 1941 only a million Muslims supported the League, for we all know that by this date the League had succeeded in winning the sympathy of an overwhelming majority of the Muslims. A major factor in this growth was the new ideal which the League had put before the people in 1940. The idea of a separate Muslim state in India stirred the imagination of the Muslims as nothing else had done before.

But the League had to pay a price for this swift success. In the new momentum which the League now gained, several elements aligned themselves with it. Their influence was not entirely wholesome. Some of these were conservative in opinion and hindered the activities of the progressive element, thus making the League out as less radical than it actually was. Several members of the landed and moneyed classes also came in and lent support to the conservative thinking in the party. Then there were those who seemed more anxious to gain power and influence than to put in long constructive effort.

A different kind of infiltration took place with the coming of the conservative religious element for whom time had not moved since the Khilafat days. They had no conception of running a modern political movement on sophisticated lines. Their thinking was limited to the contemplation of an Islamic state, and they interpreted to the masses the League ideals in terms to which they were accustomed. There was yet another smaller group of some university teachers, which stood for greater emphasis on Islam in League politics. During 1941–5, I myself came under its influence and was one of the founder members of the Islamic Jamaat. We advocated that Pakistan should be an Islamic state. I must confess that I was very enthusiastic about it and in my speeches I constantly propagated my ideas.

My advocacy of an Islamic state brought me into conflict with Jinnah. He thoroughly disapproved of my ideas and dissuaded me from expressing them publicly from the League platform lest the people might be led to believe that Jinnah shared my view and that he was asking me to convey such ideas to the public. As I was convinced that I was right and did not want to compromise Jinnah's position, I decided to cut myself away and for nearly two years kept my distance from him, apart from seeing him during the working committee meetings and on other formal occasions. It was not easy to take this decision as my associations with Jinnah had been very close in the past. Now that I look back I realize how wrong I had been.

It is perhaps not fully realized that the Muslim League between 1937–47 was the first purely political movement of the Indian Muslims. Not only were Sir Syed Ahmad Khan's effort concentrated on the educational and cultural improvement of the Muslims, but he went further and actually discouraged them from active political participation. The first Muslim mass movement was that of the Khilafat and it was predominantly religious in character though the politicians ran it. It was only after the re-birth of the League in 1937 that the Muslim masses awoke to political consciousness. Three factors helped to develop and sharpen this consciousness. One was the Congress attitude of indifference and, at times, hostility. Another was the leadership which, under Jinnah, broke new ground and fashioned new political strategy. Still another was the part played by religious appeal in the heightening of this consciousness. The leadership at the top was generally secular-minded and trained in modern political methods, but on the lower levels and especially among the field workers propaganda on religious lines was the general practice.

Long life and maturity are as important to a nationalist political movement as they are to a human being. In less than ten years the revived Muslim League had to reorganize itself; to spread the message among the masses; to provide an ultimate objective, to fight for this objective and to achieve it. The speed at which things moved in India during these ten years made the achievement of the goal more important, almost imperative, than the purification of the organization itself. And the Congress, with its long life and experience, also found it impossible to divest itself of the communal-minded elements within its fold. Consequences for India were grave. Despite the best intentions of the leaders on both sides certain uncontrollable forces were let loose which thrived on religious frenzy. And for a time goodwill and amity disappeared from India. I can well recall the general sense of gloom and despondency that pervaded the two newly-created nation states; instead of the joy and expectancy which should have been ours after these years of struggle there were only premonitions of impending conflicts and a promise of future struggle.

But that is another story: a story which the sons of the sons of those who fought for freedom may live to write another day. For the present this is all that I have to say.

> However, in the years to come,
> 'If you're still living, never say never.
> What is certain isn't certain.
> Things will not stay as they are . . . and
> Never becomes Before The Day Is Out.'
>
> *In Praise of Dialectics*, Bertolt Brecht

Annotated Bibliography

This brief guide to further reading is not comprehensive. Some of the works cited in the footnotes of the previous papers have been mentioned again here, and the reader is advised to make use of those references as a further source of bibliographical information. A useful survey of writings on the transfer of power (1945–7) is by A.K. Majumdar in B.R. Nanda (ed.), *Essays in Modern Indian History* (Delhi, 1980).

Documentary Histories

There is no worthwhile documentary history of India's Partition. The volumes edited by A.C. Banerjee (1961 and 1965, in 2 vols), C.H. Philips (1962) and Maurice Gwyer & A. Appadorai (1957, in 2 vols), need to be updated in the light of fresh materials made available in the libraries and archives of India, Pakistan, and the United Kingdom. The British official documents on the transfer of power, jointly edited by Nicholas Mansergh and E.W.R. Lumby, are designed to assist in the understanding of official policy during the years 1942–7, to which are attached illuminating excurses on many aspects of the Indian nationalist struggle. It is a highly commendable effort. The Indian Council of Historical Research project—'Towards Freedom'—is nearing completion. This may shed new light on the movement towards Independence and Partition.

The Collected Works of Mahatma Gandhi and the *Selected Works of Jawaharlal Nehru* lay bare the communal controversies and provide rich information on the reactions of the Mahatma and of Jawaharal Nehru to the Muslim League's ideological assault on their visions of a united India. The papers of Rajendra Prasad and Vallabhbhai Patel (*Sardar Patel Correspondence 1945–50*, edited by Durga Das, 12 vols, Ahmedabad, 1971–4) are invaluable source-materials.

The All-India Muslim League records, housed in the Karachi University Library, have not been published. The only documentary record is edited by Sharifuddin Pirzada, in two volumes. There are miscellaneous collections of Mohammad Ali Jinnah's speeches and writings, which are being edited by Dr S.Z.H. Zaidi of the School of Oriental and African Studies in London. Dr Zaidi has already put together the Jinnah-Isphahani correspondence.

P. Rozeena, *Jamiyat al-ulama-i Hind: Dastaveez Markazi Ijlaas, 1919–1945* in 2 vols (Islamabad, 1980) has compiled the documents of the Jamiyat-al ulama, an organization close to the Congress and opposed to the 'two-nation' theory. There is no printed documentary record of other organizations, such as the all-India Majlis-i Ahrar, the RSS and the all-India Hindu Mahasabha, though their annual deliberations are recorded in the *Indian Annual Register*, edited by N.N. Mitra.

General Histories and Surveys

The Partition of India: Policies and Perspectives, edited by C.H. Philips and M.D. Wainwright, delineates the diversity of approaches and interpretations of the contributors. Peter Hardy singled out Mohammad Mujeeb's essay, included in this volume, as an attractively rueful account of the reactions to the Congress victory of 1937 in the United Provinces, by a Muslim 'who is himself a bearer of Mughal culture'. The Raja of Mahmudabad's contribution in the same volume is a poignant account of a man who plotted a nationalistic course in his public life but was caught up in the communal cross-fire in the 1940s.

A volume of seminar papers, *Myth and Reality: The Struggle for Freedom in India, 1945–47*, edited by A.K. Gupta (Delhi, 1987) suggests further lines of enquiry. Some contributors analyse the reaction of noted Hindi, Bengali, and Punjabi writers and poets to the trauma of the Partition. This is also the theme of M.U. Menon's study 'Partition Literature: A Study of Intizar Husain', *Modern Asian Studies* (hereafter *MAS*), vol. 14, no. 3, 1980. For a collection of short stories on the Partition, see Ramesh Mathur and Mahendra Kulasrestha (eds.), *Writings on India's Partition* (Delhi, 1976).

Students will find much that is valuable and instructive in Peter Hardy's *The Muslims of British India* (Cambridge, 1972). Readers seeking a broad introduction to the nature of Muslim separatism should turn to the debate between Francis Robinson and Paul Brass published in the *Journal of Commonwealth and Comparative Studies* (November

1977), and to the review article by P.G. Robb, 'Muslim Identity and separatism in India: the significance of M.A. Ansari', *Bulletin of the School of Oriental and African Studies*, vol. LIV, part I, 1991. And the comparative study *Partition in Ireland, India and Pakistan: Theory and Practice* (London, 1984), by T.G. Fraser.

In *Communalism in Modern India* (Delhi, 1984) Bipan Chandra argues that communalism was not based on real conflict but on a distorted reflection of real conflict, and that it was not a conceptualization of social reality but its 'false consciousness'.

Other works which serve as a background to the evolution of 'Muslim nationhood' are those by W.C. Smith, Aziz Ahmad, Mohammad Mujeeb, I.H. Qureshi, Khalid bin Sayeed, Hafeez Malik, Syed Raza Wasti, K.K. Aziz and Bipan Chandra. Apart from Smith, Mujeeb, and Bipan Chandra, the authors provide a post-facto justification of the 'two-nation' theory. The official history of the 'Freedom Movement in Pakistan' is a shoddy piece of scholarship. Many other works are superficial, some are inaccurate and not a few are polemical.

The accounts of Shiva Rao, Durga Das, Khushwant Singh, J.N. Sahni, M.S.M. Sharma and K. Rama Rao make interesting reading. Shiva Rao and Durga Das in particular were well-informed because of their close association with leading nationalists.

The adoption of the Lahore Resolution in March 1940 led to a number of publications on the prospect of Partition and its implications for the subcontinent. B.R. Ambedkar wrote *Pakistan or the Partition of India* (Bombay, 1946). The Congress perspective was provided by Beni Prasad, *The Hindu–Muslim Questions* (Allahabad, 1941); Humayun Kabir, *Muslim Politics, 1906–1942* (Calcutta, 1942); Rajendra Prasad, *India Divided* (Bombay, 1946) and Syed Tufail Ahmad Manglori, *Mussalmanon ka Raushan Mustaqbil* (Delhi, 1945). The Congress socialists also wrote on the subject: Asoka Mehta and Achyut Patwardhan, *The Communal Triangle in India* (Allahabad, 1942); Shaukatullah Ansari, *Pakistan—The Problem of India* (Lahore, 1945). After a distinguished record of service to the nation, Patwardhan died in early August 1992. For a damning critique of the Congress 'surrender' over the Pakistan issue, published after independence, see Rammanohar Lohia, *Guiltymen of India's Partition* (Hyderabad, 1970).

The Muslim League viewpoint in the 1940s was expressed in F.K.K. Durrani, *The Meaning of Pakistan* (Lahore, 1944); Mohammad Noman, *Muslim India—Rise and Growth of the All-India Muslim*

(Allahabad, 1942); Qazi Mohammed Isa, *It Shall Never Happen Again* (Delhi, 1946). Militant Hindu nationalism, on the other hand, was expressed in the works of Savarkar and Shyama Prasad Mookerjee, and more recently in H.V. Seshadari's *The Tragic Story of Partition* (Banglore, 1982).

British scholars, civil servants, and journalists, who reflected on India's Partition include Hugh Tinker, Penderel Moon, E.W.R. Lumby, Nicholas Mansergh, H.V. Hodson, Ian Stephens and Leonard Mosley. *The Last Days of the British Raj* (London, 1961) by Mosley, and Penderel Moon's *Divide and Quit*, describe the communal holocausts on the eve of Partition, as well as after it.

Memoirs, Autobiographies and Political Biographies

One outcome of India's independence was a sudden surge in the publication of memoirs, often self-indulgent, by persons who were connected with the government or the administration, or associated with political bodies and movements at various levels and, in that capacity, involved in the negotiations leading to Independence and Partition. Prominent amongst them are the memoirs and autobiographies of: Rajendra Prasad, *Autobiography* (Asia Publishing House, 1957); Abul Kalam Azad, *India Wins Freedom* (The Complete Version: Delhi, 1988); K.M. Munshi, *The End of an Era* (Bombay, 1957) and *Indian Constitutional Documents, vol. 1: Pilgrimage to Freedom, 1902–1950* (Bombay, 1967). N.B. Khare, who was communally oriented and was ideologically close to Munshi, summed up his experiences in *Political Memoirs or Autobiography* (Nagpur, 1959). In sharp contrast, Kanji Dwarkadas, an old comrade of Jinnah, offers a liberal perspective in *Ten Years to Freedom, 1938–1947* (Bombay, 1968). So does another liberal lawyer-politician, Chimanlal Setalvad, in *Recollections and Reflections* (Bombay, 1946).

For the version of those who monitored Gandhi's activities and followed developments in the 1940s, see G.D. Birla, *In the Shadow of the Mahatma: A Personal Memoir* (Bombay, 1953); Shriman Narayan, *Memoirs: Windows on Gandhi and Nehru* (Bombay, 1971); N.K. Bose, *My Days with Gandhi* (Calcutta, 1953); Sudhir Ghosh, *Gandhi's Emissary* (London, 1967).

Nirad C. Chauduri follows events in Bengal and Delhi in his characteristically magisterial style in *The Autobiography of an Un-*

known Indian (London, 1951) and his *Thy Hand Great Anarch! India 1921–52* (London, 1987). Both his works reflect his pronounced anti-Muslim proclivities. For a balanced and sensitive account in the same genre, see G.D. Khosla, *Memory's Gay Chariot: An Autobiographical Narrative* (Delhi, 1985), and his *Stern Reckoning: A Survey of the Events Leading Up To and Following the Partition of India* (Delhi, 1989 edn.).

The Transfer of Power in India (London, 1957) and *The Story of the Integration of the Indian States* (New York, 1956), both by V.P. Menon, are essential readings.

Lesser-known but highly readable autobiographical accounts include: K.A. Abbas, *I am not an Island: An Experiment in Autobiography* (Delhi, 1977); M.C. Chagla, *Roses in December: An Autobiography* (Bombay, 1974); M.R.A. Baig, *In Different Saddles* (Bombay, 1967). Chagla and Baig were at one time closely associated with Jinnah.

Important memoirs, autobiographies and reminiscences of persons connected with Muslim organization include: Choudhry Khaliguzzaman, *Path way to Pakistan* (Lahore, 1961); *The memoirs of Aga Khan: World Enough and Time* (London, 1954); M.A.H. Isphahani, *Quaid-e-Azam As I Knew Him* (Karachi, 1966 edn.); Firoz Khan Noon, *From Memory* (Lahore, 1966); Chaudhri Muhammad Ali, *The Emergence of Pakistan* (New York, 1967); Z.A. Suleri, *My Leader* (Lahore, 1982); Syed Shamsul Hasan, *Plain Mr Jinnah* (Karachi, 1976); Wali Khan, *Facts are Facts: The Untold Story of India's Partition* (Delhi, 1987).

Well-known memoirs by British civil servants are: Francis I.S. Tucker, *While Memory Serves* (London, 1950); Alan Campbell-Johnson, *Mission with Mountbatten* (London, 1951); Conrad Corfield, *The Princely India I Knew: From Reading to Mountbatten* (Madras, 1975); *The Memoirs of Lord Ismay* (London, 1960), and Wavell's Indian diary, *Wavell: The Viceroy's Journal*, edited by Penderel Moon.

There is considerable literature on Gandhi and Nehru. Likewise, there are biographies of Jinnah, of which many are of indifferent quality. Stanley Wolpert's *Jinnah of Pakistan* (Delhi, 1984 edn) is extensively researched and readable.

Jawaharlal Nehru found the description 'Nationalist Muslim' rather vague, but insisted on applying it to 'well-known persons who have been in the Congress and suffered for the cause of India's freedom repeatedly'. Not much is known about such Muslims. A detailed study on Dr M.A. Ansari is attempted in Mushirul Hasan's *A Nationalist Conscience: M.A. Ansari, the Congress and the Raj* (Delhi, 1987). Works on Khan Abdul Ghaffar Khan, Rafi Ahmad Kidwai, Hasrat Mohani, Saifuddin Kitchlew and Yusuf Meharally are sketchy and analytically poor. Maulana Abul Kalam Azad alone is a subject of several lively and sympathetic biographies. The standard works on him include I.H. Douglas, *Abul Kalam Azad: An Intellectual and Religious Biography*, edited by Gail Minault and C.W. Troll (Delhi, 1988); V.N. Datta, *Maulana Azad* (Delhi, 1990); Mushirul Hasan (ed.), *Islam and Indian Nationalism: Reflections on Abul Kalam Azad* (Delhi, 1992). Other recent publications in Urdu and English are listed in Mushirul Hasan, *Islam and Indian Nationalism*.

Finally, for biographies of notable British actors see, R. Wingate, *Lord Ismay: A biography* (London, 1970); John Glendoven, *The Viceroy at Bay: Lord Linlithgow in India, 1936–1943* (London, 1971); Gowher Rizvi, *Linlithgow and India: A Study of British Policy and the Political Impasse in India, 1936–1943* (London, 1978); V. Brittain, *Pethick Lawrence* (London, 1963); Philip Ziegler, *Mountbatten: The Official Biography* (London, 1971).

Works on Partition and Related Themes

R.J. Moore, Anita Inder Singh, Ayesha Jalal, Farzana Shaikh and Paul Brass have added new dimensions to and enriched the discussion on Partition. There are other writings as well which detail aspects of Congress-League relations, trace the evolution of the demand for Pakistan and assign blame to various individuals and parties for the subcontinent's nightmare in the period 1946–8. For example, M.N. Das, *Partition and Independence of India: Inside Story of the Mountbatten Days* (Delhi, 1982); H.M. Seervai, *Partition of India: Legend and Reality* (Bombay, 1989); Deepak Pandey, 'Congress–Muslim League Relations 1937–9: The Parting of the Ways', *MAS*. 12, 4, 1978; certain illuminating essays in the two collections edited by D.A. Low, *Congress and the Raj; Facets of the Indian Struggle 1917–47* (London, 1977) and *The Indian National Congress: Centenary Hindsights* (Delhi, 1988), and a third edited by Richard Sisson and Stanley Wolpert, *Congress and Indian Nationalism: The Pre-Independence Phase* (California, 1988).

In the wake of the historical literature produced at Cambridge in the 1970s, there was a welcome interest in exploring the rise of Indian nationalism in the provinces and the localities. The communal question, however, was generally viewed in an all-India perspective and the focus remained on the national arena and on national organizations, such as the Indian National Congress and the all-India Muslim League. Francis Robinson and Paul Brass were the first to shift the focus of analysis from the nation to the provinces of British India. This tradition has continued in British and American universities, though less so at centres of historical research in India and Pakistan.

I have already discussed the writings of David Gilmartin, Ian Talbot and Prem Choudhry on Punjab. Sarah F.D. Ansari has recently published an incisive study entitled *Sufi Saints and State Power: The Pirs of Sind, 1843–1947* (Cambridge, 1972). This is surely the first major work which examines the relationship between Muslim religious leaders and the colonial state in a region that was distant from the main centres of British India.

Most Muslims in the subcontinent lived in Bengal. Not only was this province the scene of overtly 'communal' movements, it also generated a lot of Hindu–Muslim writing. As a result, there is considerable scholarly literature on the communal tangle including the writings of Broomfield, Sumit Sarkar, Rajat Kanta Ray, Kenneth Mcpherson, Tanika Sarkar, Sugata Bose, Partha Chatterjee and Amalendu De. Their works cover the years of the swadeshi movement until the early 1930s. Surprisingly, very little has been written on the decade thereafter. The reasons need to be explored. Recently, Suranjan Das has made a comprehensive and convincing analysis of the structure of communal riots in Bengal.

The United Provinces is generally regarded as the heartland of 'Muslim separatism' and the storm-centre of the movement towards Partition. Yet secondary literature on such themes is pathetically inadequate. For the province as a whole. Paul Brass alone offers a comprehensive analysis. We await the publication of Mukul Kesavan's M.Lit. thesis written at the University of Cambridge. For the role of Deoband in the Pakistan movement we are still dependent on the book by Z.H. Faruqi, *The Deoband School and the Demand for Pakistan* (Delhi, 1967). We know very little about the role of the Barelwis, though a thesis on the subject has been submitted at the Columbia University by Usha Sanyal. For the role of the Aligarh Muslim University, described by Jinnah as the 'arsenal of Muslim India', see Mushirul Hasan, 'Nationalist and Separatist Trends in

Aligarh, 1920–1947', in A.K. Gupta (ed.), *Myth and Reality: The struggle for Freedom in India 1945–47* (Delhi, 1987), and Zoya Hasan, *Dominance and Mobilization: Rural Politics in Uttar Pradesh* (Delhi, 1989). Harold Gould's miscellaneous essays on Fyzabad are now available in a single volume*Politics and Caste*, vol. 3 (Delhi, 1990).

It is time for a historian of UP to announce:

Laga raha hoon mazameen-i nau ke phir ambaar
Khabar karo mere khirman ke khosha-cheeno ko